ARCHITECTURAL
DESIGN GRAPHICS

ARCHITECTURAL DESIGN GRAPHICS

Marco Ciriello

McGRAW-HILL

New York   Chicago   San Francisco   Lisbon   London
Madrid   Mexico City   Milan   New Delhi   San Juan
Seoul   Singapore   Sydney   Toronto

Catalog-in-Publication Data is on file with the Library of Congress.

McGraw-Hill

A Division of The McGraw·Hill Companies

Copyright © 2002 by The McGraw-Hill Companies, Inc. All rights reserved.
Printed in the United States of America. Except as permitted under the United
States Copyright Act of 1976, no part of this publication may be reproduced or
distributed in any form or by any means, or stored in a data base or retrieval system,
without the prior written permission of the publisher.

1 2 3 4 5 6 7 8 9 0 DOC/DOC 8 7 6 5 4 3 2

ISBN 0-07-135524-3

The sponsoring editor for this book was Cary Sullivan
and the production supervisor was Pamela Pelton. It
was set in Times Roman by Lone Wolf Enterprises, Ltd.

Printed and bound by R. R. Donnelley & Sons Company.

McGraw-Hill books are available at special quantity discounts to use as premiums
and sales promotions, or for use in corporate training programs. For more
information, please write to the Director of Special Sales, McGraw-Hill,
Professional Publishing, Two Penn Plaza, New York, NY 10121-2298. Or contact
your local bookstore.

CONTENTS

ACKNOWLEDGMENTS

I wish to acknowledge my great debt to my friend Tatiana Charter for her review and suggestions on the form of the written text. I also want to acknowledge Ms. Lori Brown of McIlhargey/Brown & Associates Ltd. and Mr. Eugene Radvenis of E.V. Radvenis Inc. for giving permission to publish some of their work, which greatly enriched the content of this book.

I wish to express my gratitude to Roger Woodson, president of Lone Wolf Enterprises Ltd., and Rick Sutherland and Barbara Karg of the Lone Wolf management team. Their invaluable organizational efforts made the development of this book a pleasurable experience.

ABOUT THE AUTHOR

Marco Ciriello holds a degree in Architecture from the University of Rome. He is the principal of Ecodesign in Vancouver, British Columbia. His professional activity has been prolific and diverse; he has designed numerous and different types of buildings and has conducted urban studies. His keen interest in sustainable development and sustainable habitat dates back to his university studies, and it continues to be an important aspect of his professional career.

Ciriello's research in the field of aesthetics led him to express himself not only in architecture, but also as a painter and art show curator. His work has been displayed in several group shows as well as one man shows. His paintings are in private and public collections.

Ciriello taught at the Emily Carr College of Art and Design in Vancouver and lectured at Pearson College in Victoria, B.C., Douglas College in Vancouver, and at the University of Rome, Department of Architecture, where he also lead research in the psychology of architecture. Ciriello is the author of *Architectura Sapiens* (1997) and many articles on a wide variety of subjects.

CHAPTER 1
THE DRAWING SET

An architectural project is a process that involves an act of graphic, oral, and written communication translated into the realization of an object. In this process, the role of an architect can be condensed into the tasks shown in Figures 1.1 and 1.2.

The chapters that follow will analyze each of the above tasks in detail. Since the main medium of communication in this process is graphic expression, an understanding of what makes graphic communication effective is fundamental. It is from these basic principles that this book begins.

Any graphic element that is part of a project can acquire a different function and role in the process. Any element, from the smallest item to the most complex system, can become administratively, technically, and legally important.

These rules, as outlined in Figure 1.2, will allow the creation of simple, clear, and effective communication. If these rules are applied at the very beginning of the project, even to the most basic elements, such as the title block or the choice of paper size, one can derive several guidelines that can be used in every project (see Figure 1.3).

PAPER SIZE

Choosing the right paper size for the drawings is dependent on: **a.** the type of project; **b.** the size of the building or the complex; **c.** the organization of the drawing set; **d.** the type of construction contract; **e.** the phasing of the project.

Basic Role of the Architect

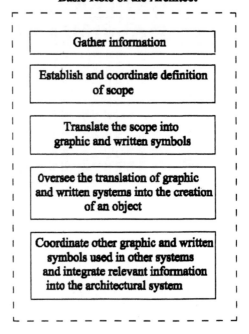

FIGURE 1.1 The role of the architect.

Rules of Effective Communication

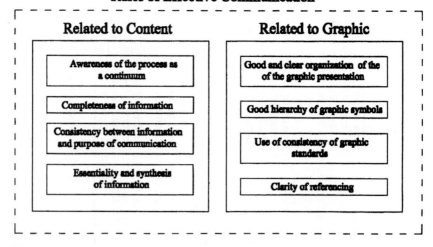

FIGURE 1.2 Rules of effective communication related to content and graphics.

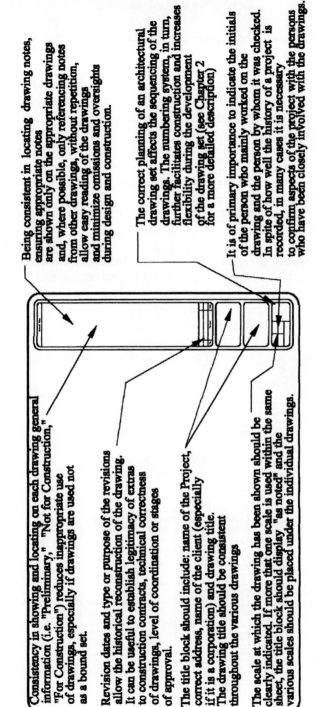

Being consistent in locating drawing notes, ensuring appropriate notes are shown only on the appropriate drawings and, where possible, only referencing notes from other drawings, without repetition, allow easy reading of the drawings and minimize omissions and oversights during design and construction.

The correct planning of an architectural drawing set affects the sequencing of the drawings. The numbering system, in turn, further facilitates construction and increases flexibility during the development of the drawing set (see Chapter 2 for a more detailed description)

It is of primary importance to indicate the initials of the person who mainly worked on the drawing and the person by whom it was checked. In spite of how well the history of a project is recorded, in many cases it is necessary to confirm aspects of the project with the persons who have been closely involved with the drawings.

Consistency in showing and locating on each drawing general information (i.e. "Preliminary," "Not for Construction," "For Construction") reduces inappropriate use of drawings, especially if drawings are used not as a bound set.

Revision dates and type or purpose of the revisions allow the historical reconstruction of the drawing. It can be useful to establish legitimacy of extras to construction contracts, technical correctness of drawings, level of coordination or stages of approval.

The title block should include: name of the Project, correct address, name of the client (especially if it is a corporation) and drawing title. The drawing title should be consistent throughout the various drawings

The scale at which the drawing has been shown should be clearly indicated. If more that one scale is used within the same sheet, the title block should display "as noted" and the various scales should be placed under the individual drawings.

FIGURE 1.3   Vital information included in architectural drawings.

1.3

The use of standard size of paper is recommended for the following reasons: **a.** waste is reduced since printers tend to use the same standards; **b.** any reproduction maintains the same layout and border proportions; **c.** Reductions and enlargements of the drawings are facilitated since the different sizes of paper have the same L/W ratio. There are two primary types of standards: The ISO and the ANSI/ASME Standards. The ISO are used in all industrialized countries except the USA and Canada.

In USA and Canadian office applications, the following paper formats are widely used today: letter 8½ x 11, legal 8½ x14 , executive 7½ x10 and ledger/tabloid 11 x 17. There is also an American National Standard ANSI/ASME Y 14 that is still used for technical drawings paper size: **a.** 8½ x 11 **b.** 11 x 17 ; **c.** 17 x 22 ; **d.** 22 x 34; **e.** 34 x 44 . The new American National Standard ANSI/ASME Y14.1m 1995 now specifies the ISO A1—A4 formats for technical drawings (see Figure 1.4).

The new A series follows the following rules: **a.** the height divided by the width of all formats is the square root of two (1.4142); **b.** format 0 has an area of one square meter (10.764 Sq. Ft.); **c.** format A1 is A0 cut into two equal pieces, i.e. A1 is as high as A0 is wide and A1 is half as wide as A0 is high; **d.** all smaller A series formats are defined in the same way by cutting the next largest format in the series parallel to its shorter side into two equal pieces; **e.** the standardized height and width of the paper format is a rounded numbers of millimeters; **f.** the format of the new standard can be generalized through the following formula as shown in Figure 1.5.

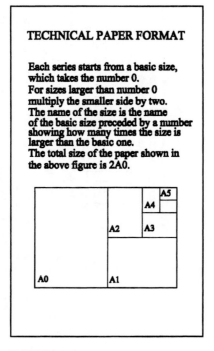

FIGURE 1.4   A technical paper format.

Standard Paper Sizes for Technical Drawings

The new American National Standard ANSI/ASME Y14.1m 1995 now specifies the ISO A0-A4 formats for technical drawings.

Type	Format (mm)	Format (inches)
A0	841x1189	33 1/8 "x 46 7/8"
A1	594x841	23 3/8 "x 33 1/8"
A2	420x594	16 1/2 "x 23 3/8"
A3	297x420	11 3/4 "x 16 1/2"
A4	210x297	8 1/4 "x 11 3/4"

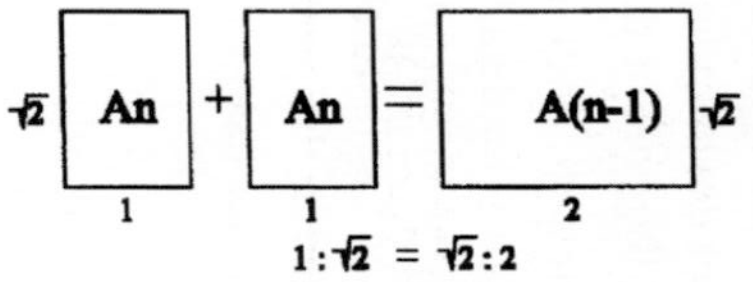

$$\sqrt{2}\ \boxed{A_n} + \boxed{A_n} = \boxed{A_{(n-1)}}\ \sqrt{2}$$

$$1 : \sqrt{2} = \sqrt{2} : 2$$

Ratio between ISO paper sizes		
71%	sqrt(0.5)	An -> A(n+1)
141%	sqrt(2)	An -> A(n-1)

Additional standards still used in the USA and Canada (ANSI/ASME Y 14.1)

Type	Format (mm)	Format (inches)	Type	Format (mm)	Format (inches)	Type	Format (mm)	Format (inches)
A	216x279	8 1/2 "x 11"	C	432x559	11 "x 22"	E	864x1118	34 "x 44"
B	279x432	11 "x 17"	D	559x864	22 "x 34"			

FIGURE 1.5 Standard paper sizes for technical drawings.

The A0 format offers certain advantages over the A1 size: **a.** provides more drawing surface which, in case of large projects, might be required to convey the necessary information on one sheet; **b.** allows more flexibility in the organization of the set; **c.** reduces the number of sheets required to complete the set.

On the other hand the A0 format is difficult to manage on site and for the consultants. This last consideration outweighs the previous ones. Ultimately, A0 format should be used only when it is recognized that it is absolutely necessary.

We have stated that the project is a *process*. Its development is subdivided in different stages to which the rules of effective communication should apply.

EFFECTIVE COMMUNICATION

The type of client (a private individual, a developer, or an institution) or the type of construction contract determines the direct involvement of the client (or the client's representative) in the first stages of the design, and even throughout the process (including in the development of the construction documents, the tender and contract negotiation as well as in the contract administration). A private individual inexperienced in construction matters who wishes to have his house custom designed will rely on the architect to decide technical matters more than an experienced developer or project manager. With these last two types of clients the discussions on possible choices will occur at a different level of involvement as shown in Figure 1.6. The indicated subdivision in stages is important because:

1. From the administrative point of view: **a.** it is referenced in the client/architect contract through the description of the project and its intent. The early stages allow the rapid identification of any discrepancy from the scope indicated in the contract and the actual scope of work that is delineated more clearly with the further development of the project; **b.** it identifies clear stages of approval on the part of the client.

2. From the design point of view: **a.** it allows verifying the scope and related parameters from the general to the detail in a continuous process. It is a methodology that, if applied with effective monitoring, should provide opportunities for revisions and adjustments that should not change dramatically the conclusions reached in the previous stage (see Figure 1.7); **b.** it also relates to specific activities associated with the project (i.e. marketing, financing, budgeting)

It becomes even clearer why the rules of effective communication are important. If we analyze the ones related to the *content* and we associate them with the process indicated in Figure 1.8 and Figure 1.9, a series of observations can be derived (the rules related to the *graphic* part of the communication will be discussed in more detail in Chapter 3):

1. Viewing the process as a continuum allows us: **a.** to build consistently on the previous stage; **b.** to rely on previous results; **c.** to maintain an

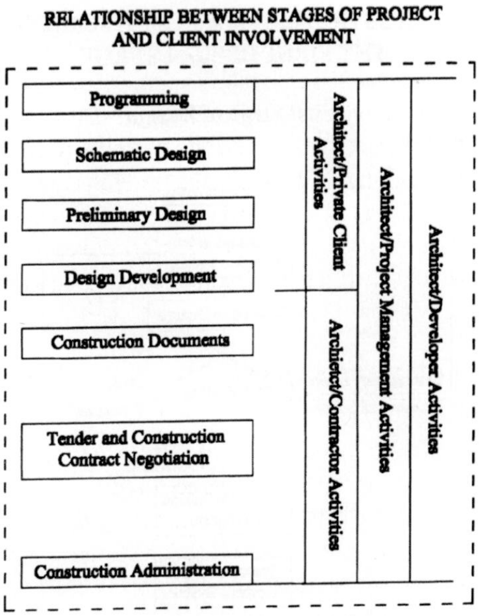

**RELATIONSHIP BETWEEN STAGES OF PROJECT
AND CLIENT INVOLVEMENT**

FIGURE 1.6 Stages of project and client development.

overview of the objectives; **d.** to minimize contradictions and maximize consistency.

2. Completeness of information: **a.** allows the client to assess the outcome of a particular stage; **b.** allows the design team to evaluate effectively what has been achieved; **c.** minimizes extensive revisions of the results of previous project stages.

3. Consistency between information and purpose of communication: **a.** allows us to focus specifically on the achievement of a particular stage; **b.** creates open-ended conclusions which should increase the number of options considered for the further definition of variables.

4. Essentiality and synthesis of information: **a.** eliminate distractions and potential conflicts; **b.** reduce the time of the analysis; **c.** highlight the fundamental variables.

The results that derive from the above observations are indicated in Figure 1.9.

Each stage of the project has a related drawing set specifically developed for that stage. The size, the type, and the stage of the project (with a range that spans from the single family unit to a multimillion-dollar development) determine the required information and the extent of the analysis to be performed. There are basic questions that must be posed: the answers to these questions are fundamental to the definition of the project at its various stages. These answers are reference points that should be kept constantly in mind in order to achieve the best results (see Figure 1.10).

PROCESS OF VERIFICATION THROUGH THE FIRST DESIGN STAGE

First Stage of Design

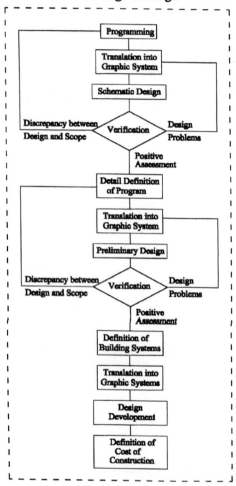

FIGURE 1.7   The verification process through the first design stage.

RELATIONSHIP BETWEEN ARCHITECT AND CLIENT/ DEVELOPER ACTIVITIES THROUGH THE PROJECT

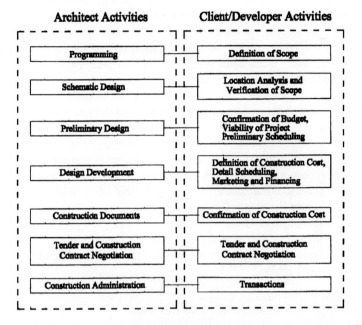

FIGURE 1.8   The architect and client/developer relationship throughout project activities.

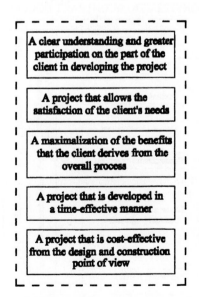

FIGURE 1.9   The architect and client/ developer relationship throughout project activities, with results deriving from clear communication

SPECIFICATIONS AND PROJECT MANUAL

From the design development forward, the set of drawings alone is no longer sufficient to provide the members of the project team with all the elements needed to answer the fundamental questions. A form of more elaborate description of the components has to be developed and added to the architectural package. Initially very schematic, and in many cases in the form of a list, the specifications gradually appear to complement the drawings. During the development of the construction documents, this description will turn into a complete *project manual*. The understanding of the project manual structure and the various types of specifications, as well as their function is very important since these documents are complementary to the drawings.

The role of the specifications in a project is to convey the type of technical and prescriptive information that is better expressed in a descriptive form, rather than through graphic communication (although very often some graphics are included in the specifications). In taking this role, the specifications allow the drawings to be simplified and to maintain their main function, which is primarily to address form, shape, dimension, and location (see Figure 1.11). The difference between *specifications* and a *project manual* resides in the complexity and completeness of the document.

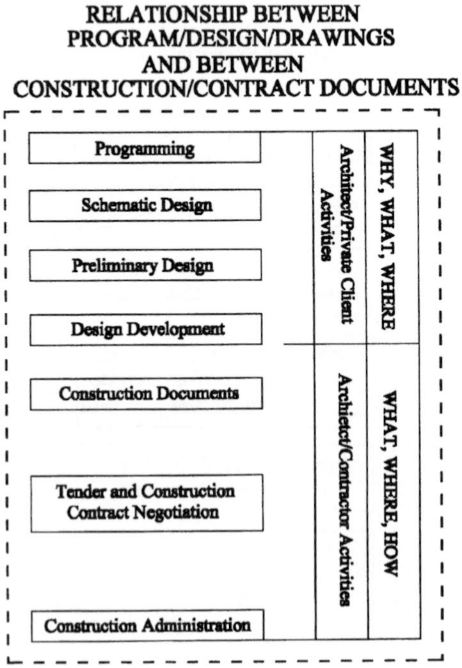

**RELATIONSHIP BETWEEN
PROGRAM/DESIGN/DRAWINGS
AND BETWEEN
CONSTRUCTION/CONTRACT DOCUMENTS**

FIGURE 1.10　The relationship between the program/design drawings and between the construction and contract drawings.

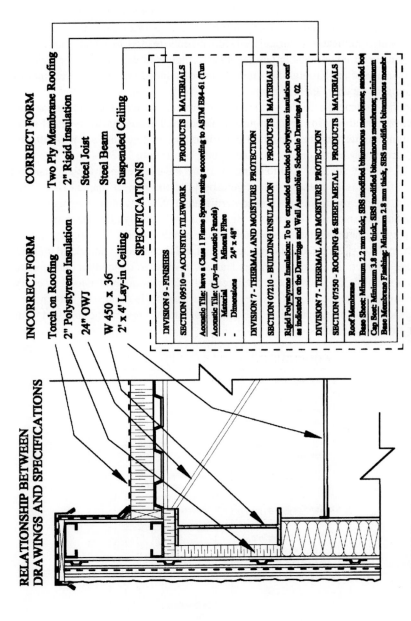

FIGURE 1.11 The relationship between drawings and specifications.

PROJECT MANUAL

A project manual in part stems from and includes the technical aspect of the specification, but in addition, contains procedural and legal requirements (i.e. bidding documents, applicable contract form, documents related to equal employment opportunity or labor wage requirements. See Figure 1.12)

Because of the variety of documents to be included and the precise expertise required to develop these documents, the architect is only one member of the team that contributes to the writing of the project manual, The architect should place particular care in coordinating, circulating and obtaining comments from all the appropriate persons, including the client and/or the client's representatives (i.e. attorneys, insurance agents, consultants. See Figure 1.13).

AIA and Canadian Architectural Institute have developed typical standard forms for many of the administrative aspects of the project manual (i.e. agreements, bonds, bid forms, insurance certificates). The advantages of using such forms are: **a.** they are known to most of the people involved in the construction industry; **b.** there is no confusion about their contents or previous interpretations of their parts; **c.** contractors know their intent and therefore do not add to the price of the contract contingencies for unclear documents; **d.** the contract administration is simplified because the procedures and processes are understood by everyone involved in the project. Since a project manual is expressly written for a specific project, the appropriate individuals should still review the standard forms and provide comments.

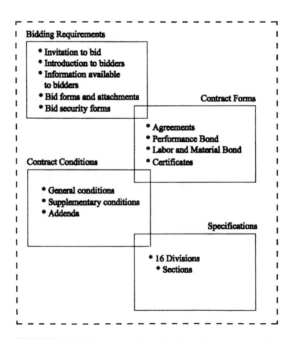

FIGURE 1.12   The organization of a typical project manual.

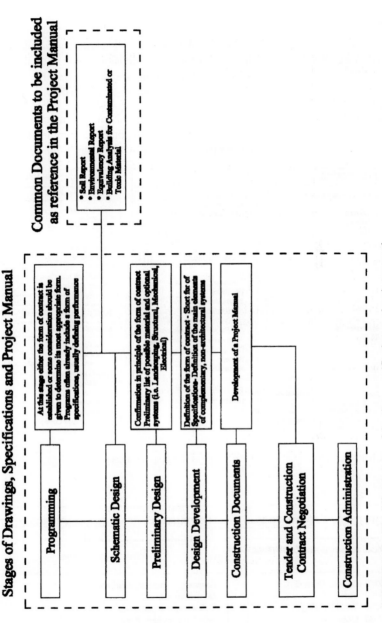

FIGURE 1.13 The different stages of drawings, specifications, and project manual.

1.13

Organizing the Specifications

One of the most common manuals used to organize the specifications is the *Masterformat—Master List of Section Titles and Numbers*. It is produced jointly by the Construction Specifications Institute (USA) and the Construction Specifications Canada (see Figure 1.14). The system uses a subdivision base on 16 divisions, which in turn, are organized in sections. The sections are identified with a five-digit code, as shown on Figure 1.15. There are different kinds of specifications as well as different methods to develop them as indicated in Figures 1.16, 1.17 and 1.18.

TYPICAL SPECIFICATIONS ORGANIZATION

16 DIVISIONS	SECTIONS	Subdivided in three parts		PART 2	Products
1. General Requirements	Part 1 General			Subdivided in Articles	
2. Site Work	Part 2 Products			- Manufacturers	
3. Concrete	Part 3 Execution			- Materials	
4. Masonry				- Manufactured Units	
5. Metals				- Equipment	
6. Wood and Plastic	**PART 1**	General		- Components	
7. Thermal and Moisture Protection	Subdivided in Articles			- Accessories	
8. Doors and Windows				- Mixes	
9. Finishes	- Summary			- Fabrication	
10. Specialties	- References			- Source Quality Control	
11. Equipment	- Definitions				
12. Furnishings	- System Description				
13. Special Construction	* Submittals			**PART 3**	Execution
14. Conveying Systems	* Quality Assurance			Subdivided in Articles	
15. Mechanical	* Project / Site Conditions			- Examination	
16. Electrical	* Sequencing and Scheduling			- Preparation	
	- Delivery, Storage and Handling			- Erection, Installation, Application	
	- Warranty			- Field Quality Control	
NOTE: The Articles included in each	- Maintenance			- Adjusting	
Section cover a broad spectrum				- Cleaning	
of the items to be included in the	* If not sufficiently covered in			- Demonstration	
Specifications. It is not intended for	Division 1 "General Requirements"			- Protection	
every Article to appear in every				- Source Quality Control	
Sections. Only the ones pertinent to					
a Section should be included in that					
part of the Specifications					

FIGURE 1.14 The organization of a typical specifications document.

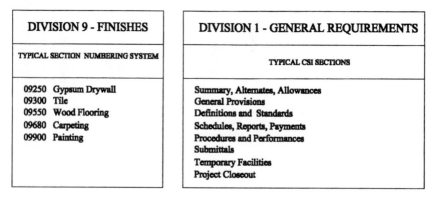

DIVISION 9 - FINISHES	DIVISION 1 - GENERAL REQUIREMENTS
TYPICAL SECTION NUMBERING SYSTEM	TYPICAL CSI SECTIONS
09250 Gypsum Drywall 09300 Tile 09550 Wood Flooring 09680 Carpeting 09900 Painting	Summary, Alternates, Allowances General Provisions Definitions and Standards Schedules, Reports, Payments Procedures and Performances Submittals Temporary Facilities Project Closeout

FIGURE 1.15 Samples of five-digit codes and general requirements in the specifications.

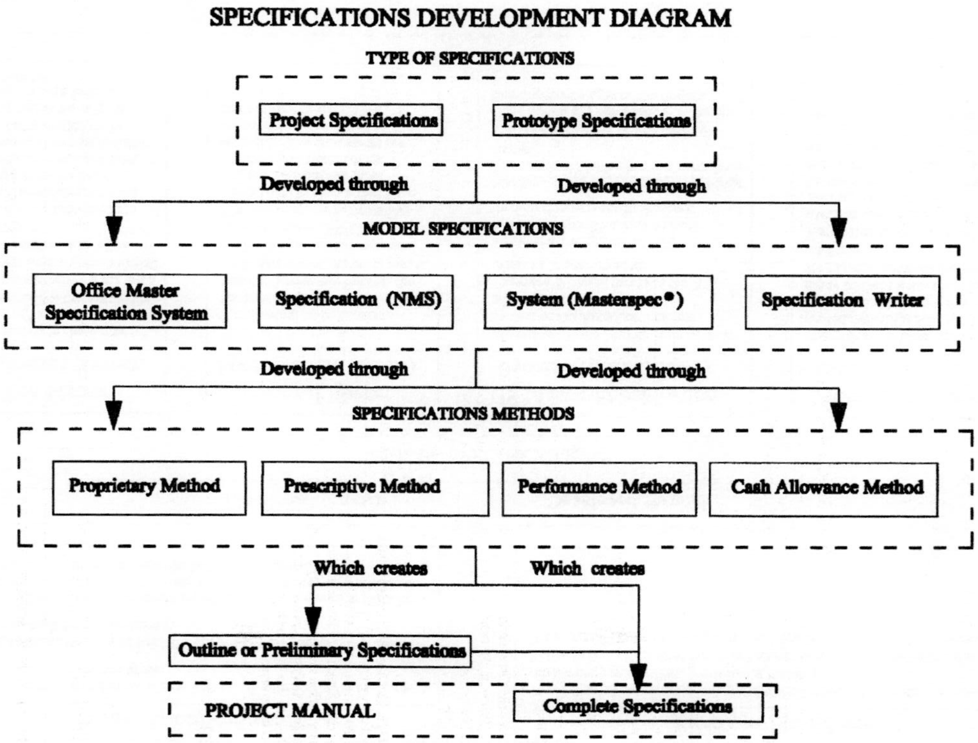

SPECIFICATIONS DEVELOPMENT DIAGRAM

TYPE OF SPECIFICATIONS

Project Specifications	Prototype Specifications

Developed through

MODEL SPECIFICATIONS

Office Master Specification System	Specification (NMS)	System (Masterspec®)	Specification Writer

Developed through

Developed through

SPECIFICATIONS METHODS

Proprietary Method	Prescriptive Method	Performance Method	Cash Allowance Method

Which creates

Which creates

Which creates

PROJECT MANUAL

Outline or Preliminary Specifications	Complete Specifications

FIGURE 1.16 Diagram of the development of specifications.

1.15

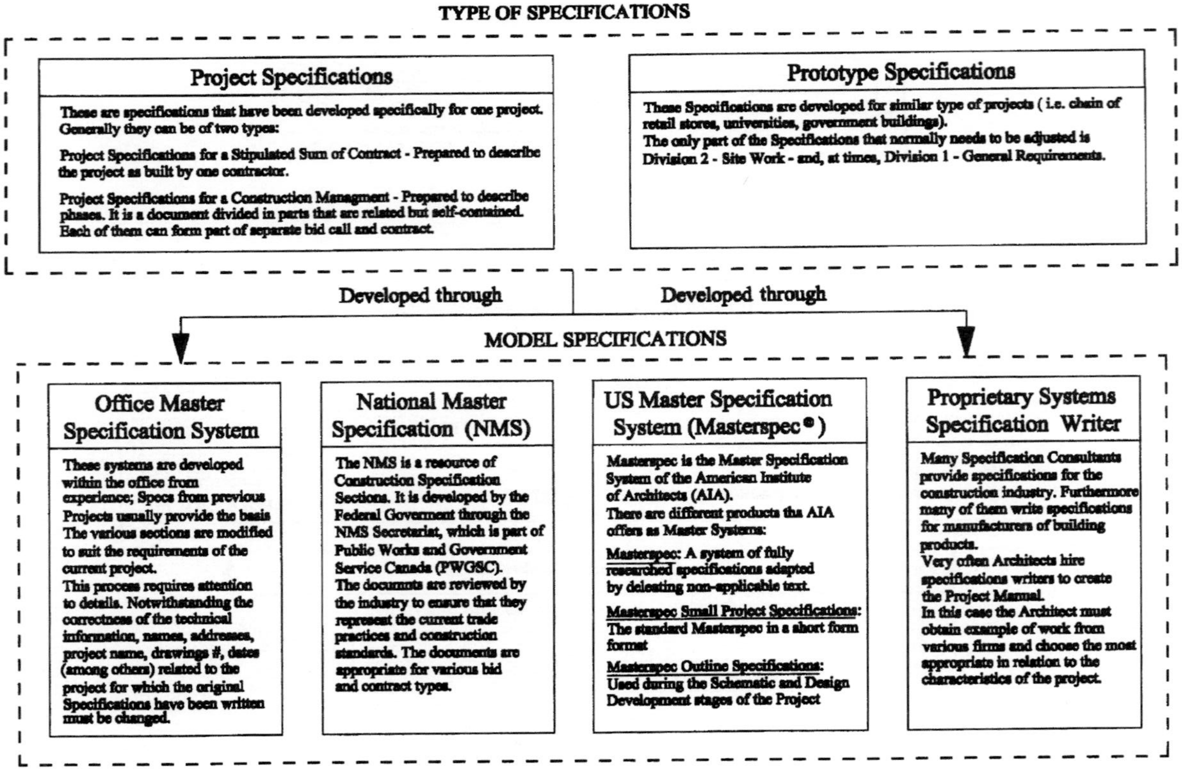

TYPE OF SPECIFICATIONS

Project Specifications

These are specifications that have been developed specifically for one project. Generally they can be of two types:

Project Specifications for a Stipulated Sum of Contract - Prepared to describe the project as built by one contractor.

Project Specifications for a Construction Management - Prepared to describe phases. It is a document divided in parts that are related but self-contained. Each of them can form part of separate bid call and contract.

Prototype Specifications

These Specifications are developed for similar type of projects (i.e. chain of retail stores, universities, government buildings).
The only part of the Specifications that normally needs to be adjusted is Division 2 - Site Work - and, at times, Division 1 - General Requirements.

Developed through

Developed through

MODEL SPECIFICATIONS

Developed through

Office Master Specification System

These systems are developed within the office from experience; Specs from previous Projects usually provide the basis. The various sections are modified to suit the requirements of the current project.
This process requires attention to details. Notwithstanding the correctness of the technical information, names, addresses, project names, drawings #, (since among others) related to the project for which the original Specifications have been written must be changed.

National Master Specification (NMS)

The NMS is a resource of Construction Specification Sections. It is developed by the Federal Government through the NMS Secretariat, which is part of Public Works and Government Service Canada (PWGSC). The documents are reviewed by the industry to ensure that they represent the current trade practices and construction standards. The documents are appropriate for various bid and contract types.

US Master Specification System (Masterspec®)

Masterspec is the Master Specification System of the American Institute of Architects (AIA).
There are different products the AIA offers as Master Systems:

Masterspec: A system of fully researched specifications adopted by delineating non-applicable text.

Masterspec Small Project Specifications: The standard Masterspec in a short form format

Masterspec Outline Specifications: Used during the Schematic and Design Development stages of the Project

Proprietary Systems Specification Writer

Many Specification Consultants provide specifications for the construction industry. Furthermore many of them write specifications for manufacturers of building products.
Very often Architects hire specifications writers to create the Project Manual.
In this case the Architect must obtain example of work from various firms and choose the most appropriate in relation to the characteristics of the project.

FIGURE 1.17 Project, prototype, and model specifications.

1.16

SPECIFICATIONS METHODS

Proprietary Method	Descriptive Method	Performance Method	Cash Allowance Method
This type of specifications calls for specific materials, products systems and equipment using their trade names and model numbers. Within the claims made by the manufacturer in his literature, the particular suitability of the product for the specified use should be investigated by the Architect. There are two types of Proprietary Specifications: "Sole Source": this type does not allow substitutions. For example, in an expansion, doors of the same type as the existing doors are installed in the new part to match the existing type. "Equal": this type allows for substitutions by naming several products as "equal". Division One generally well defines the procedure through which the Contractor asks for approval of an alternate material	Through this method the Architect describes in detail all the materials, components, methods of assembly, chemical and physical properties. No brand name is used to identify the components. This type of specifications requires an extensive knowledge and the Architect, as long as the specifications are followed by the contractor, assumes complete responsibility for the performance of the specified object or assembly. Descriptive Specifications can be considered as the "Sole Source" type since they do not allow for alternate. Unless an Architect is absolutely sure of the end and result, this type of specifications should be avoided.	In this case the desired end result becomes the focus of the specifications. The precise description of the components is not indicated. The process used for the construction and the products are specified through extensive use of references. This type of Specification can be challenging, but rewarding. On one hand, the conditions under which the system must operate have to be absolutely clear to the Architect. Furthermore aspects like aesthetics can be difficult to specify. On the other hand, performance Specification can eliminate the contractor in finding a particular component or an inventive solution for a specific building. This method requiring that minimum standards be exceeded.	Sometimes the decision can on some items is delayed to meet budget objectives. When details, materials, finishing, components have not yet been decided, Cash Allowance Specifications are used. A sum of money specified by the Architect is set aside to be used to construct the project's components that are the subject of the Section in which the Cash Allowance Method is used. Although not all the elements are defined, this type of Specifications should indicate the installation process, a specific sum of money and methods of measuring cost to be applied against the allowance amount. If the costs exceed considerably the amount specified, the contractor is normally entitled to change additional fees.

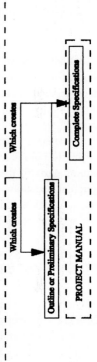

FIGURE 1.18 Proprietary, descriptive, performance, and cash allowance specifications models.

Regardless of which model or method is used, reference standards are an important part of the specifications: they provide the parameters through which the work can be impartially evaluated and clear understandings of the quality of work that is expected. Standards are established by organizations like governmental agencies, trade manuals and associations, and test agencies. ASTM and UL are very familiar names.

When including such reference it is imperative to verify: **a.** the correct number; **b.** the latest revision date; **c.** the compatibility of the latest revision with the products, material and procedures specified

The following steps can function as a guideline for the preparation of the specifications: **a.** review the scope of the specifications related to the stage and the characteristics of the project; **b.** review the latest drawing set and schedules; **c.** review consultants' drawings, reports, and requirements of authorities and codes; **d.** review all the minutes of meetings; **e.** decide on the type of construction contract to be suggested or review established agreement; **f.** decide on the method of specifications to be used; **g.** obtain the most appropriate and most updated master specification model; **h.** create an index of divisions and sections for the complete project; **i.** circulate index and standard forms to consultants, client or client's representative for comments; **j.** make a list of issues, questions to be answered, information to be obtained; **k.** review index and standard forms according to comments; **l.** draft the sections coordinating each section with the remaining parts of the document and with the drawings and related documents; **m.** circulate sections to consultants, client or client's representative for comments; **n.** check standards manuals for latest edition and possible revisions; **o.** review sections according to comments; **p.** proof-read; **q.** print final copy.

SURVEY SYSTEM

For obvious reasons, another fundamental element and starting point of a design process is the property on which the project will be built. A *property* is a more complex and artificial concept than the word *land* implies. The term *property* includes conventions that are superimposed on the natural characteristics of the terrain. These conventions can effect and limit the choices that an architect has. To represent these conventions, graphic and written systems called *surveys* have been developed. Being familiar with these systems allows the architect to operate professionally in order to maximize the potential of the property. In the United States the land distribution can be subdivided in two classes:

1. The 13 original states plus, Hawaii, Kentucky, Maine, Tennessee, Texas, Vermont, and West Virginia are known as state-land states because the state made the land grants. Especially in the southern states, where a survey reference system was not set up, legal descriptions usually are based on a survey system called *metes and bounds*. It is a system that, to describe the lot, uses location and description of the local flora and physical characteris-

tics of the land like trees, rocks, streams, and adjacent lots owned by other landowners, and in more recent days, man-made landmarks.

2. In the remaining thirty states, or public-domain states, the federal government made the land grants. These states use a subdivision of the land called U.S Public Land System (USPLS) based on the Federal Township and Range System, which are identified through surveyed references called meridians, baselines, townships, and ranges. In this social organization land was generally owned through either: Federal Land Grants (purchased or homesteaded) or Military Bounty Lands.

Metes and Bounds Surveys

In a metes and bounds method, the following information describes the boundary of a property (see Figures 1.19 and 1.20):

1. A commencing point, which clarifies the location of the land related to a well-known and recoverable landmark. In rural or early surveys such landmarks would have been descriptions naming natural features like trees, creeks intersected or encountered in laying out the boundaries of the property. In urban areas such landmarks could be an intersection of the right-of-way boundaries of streets.

2. A point-of-beginning. The function of this statement is to prepare the reader from the description of the parcel that will follow. This is not necessarily the exact beginning of the property.

3. The indication of the physical objects (monuments) that mark the location of ends of each line.

4. A direction for each line.

5. A distance between each corner (metes).

6. The area of the land.

7. Reference to a plat or map survey as basis of the land description.

8. Names of adjacent property owners (i.e. "with Tolly's line").

In urban areas, the point of reference chosen might refer to man-made landmarks like: "Commencing at the large iron post found at the intersection of the boundary line between the Fraser Estate and Grant Estate and the northernmost rights-of-way line of Bridgeport Highway, thence, in an easterly direction along said nethermost right-of-way line of Bridgeport Highway. South 75 degrees 30 minutes 15 seconds East, a distance of 386,76 feet to the point-of-beginning, thence, in a northerly direction parallel with the boundary line between the Fraser Estate and the Grant Estate, North 31 degrees 01 minutes 32 seconds East, a distance of 500 feet" (see Figure 1.21)

METES AND BOUND SURVEY SYSTEM IN RURAL AREAS

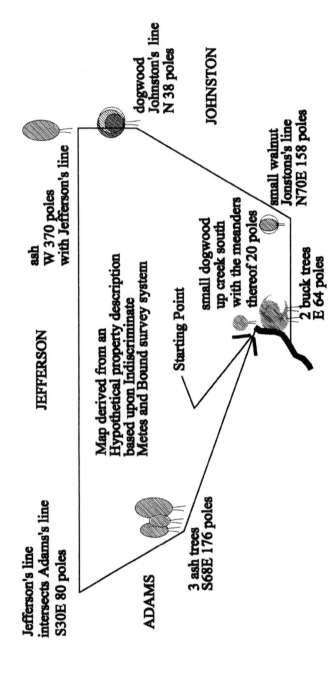

FIGURE 1.19   The metes and bounds survey system in rural areas.

Jefferson's line
intersects Adams's line
S30E 80 poles

ash
W 370 poles
with Jefferson's line

dogwood
Johnston's line
N 38 poles

JEFFERSON

JOHNSTON

small walnut
Jonstom's line
N70E 158 poles

Map derived from an
Hypothetical property description
based upon Indiscriminate
Metes and Bound survey system

Starting Point

small dogwood
up creek south
with the meanders
thereof 20 poles

2 buck trees
E 64 poles

ADAMS

3 ash trees
S68E 176 poles

1.20

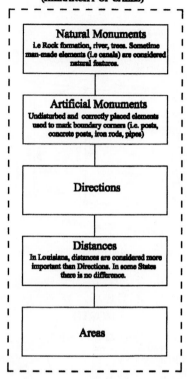

FIGURE 1.20 The hierarchy of calls in a metes and bounds description.

One of two directional systems, or *headings*, could be present on the plan:

1. Standard Compass Degree System (used in most areas) where the typical value is expressed specifying first a compass point (north, south, east or west), then the degrees, and finally another compass point (i.e. S40E). Figure 1.22 exemplifies various headings at ten degree intervals. Surveyors still use this system today

2. Compass Point System: used only in some parts of the United States, is based on the 32 points of compass, as shown in Figure 1.23. For example in the definition "North by East one quarter point North" the term "by" is represented with a small "x."

Various types of units are recorded in plats or maps, which in a recent well-reported survey plat, should be compared with the modern measure of the survey foot.

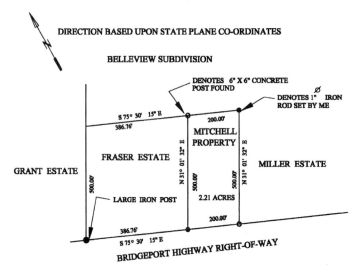

FIGURE 1.21   The metes and bounds system in urban areas.

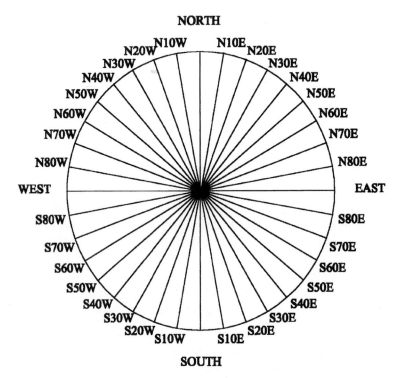

FIGURE 1.22   The standard compass degree system.

COMPASS POINT SYSTEM

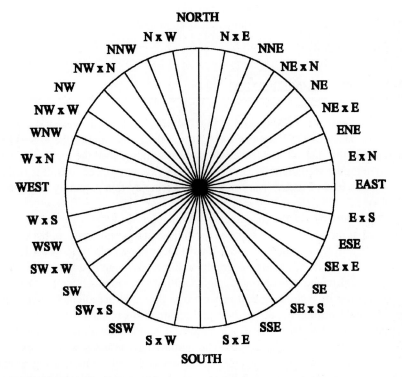

FIGURE 1.23   The compass point system.

1 rod = 1 pole = 1 perch = 16 ft. 6 in.

1 Gunter's chain = 66 ft. = 100 links (lk) = 4 rods

1 mile = 5280 ft. = 80 Gunter's chains (ch)

1 nautical mile = 6076.10 ft.

1 fathom = 6 ft.

1 hectare = 10.000 m2 = 2.471 acres

1 acre = 4 roods = 160 perches

1 acre = 43.560 ft. 2 = 10 sq. chains

In property titles, the word *meander* often indicates land that borders a river or a stream. In this case there are three possibilities: **a.** the surveyor did not conduct any survey of the stream recording only that the stream bounded the property; **b.** the surveyor surveyed the stream and described that specific boundary usually without recording intervening points (i.e. "S35W 45 rods, S47W 70 rods, S15W 112 rods to a birch on the bank"); **c.** the surveyor reduced the meandering to a straight line.

The word *corner* was used to describe any point on the survey. When a point is described as *a corner* it should not necessarily be interpreted as the vertex of an angle. To identify a 30 or 40 acre parcel described in deeds, the U.S. Geological Survey's 1:24,000 topographic maps can be generally used as base.

PUBLIC DOMAIN SYSTEM

The Land Ordinance of May 20, 1785 and of May 18, 1796, as well as the Northwest Ordinance of 1787, are the documents at the foundation of the U.S. survey system and the sales of land. The first document introduced the rectangular survey system; the second modified the numbering system for sections. It is still the system that is used today. The original numbering system is mainly still current in Ohio.

The following are the fundamental elements of the Public Domain System: **a.** principal meridian—a reference to locate east and west ranges; **b.** base line—a reference to locate north or south townships; **c.** township lines—east to west lines that define the township geographical limits; **d.** range lines—north to south lines that define the township geographical limits; **e.** range—reference assigned to a township by measuring east or west of a principal meridian; **f.** township—area created by arranging 36 sections in a square of 6 x 6; each side of the square measures six miles. The sections are numbered beginning with the one located at the northeast corner of the square. The numbering continues west to six, then south by one and east by six again. This is repeated until the numbering reaches 36; **g.** section—the basic unit of the system. A square tract of line that measures one mile by one mile; it contains 640 acres. (See Figures 1.24 through 1.26.)

Each section is further subdivided into ½, ¼, and ¹⁄₁₆. This indicates a rigid mathematical relationship of the parts always being half of the next largest portion of land (see Figures 1.27 and 1.28)

The identification of the location starts by specifying if a township is north or south of a specific baseline as well as east or west of a certain principal meridian. This means that the identification T2N, R1E of the second principal meridian means the second township north of the base line in the first range east of the second principal meridian.

The description of a land parcel usually follows an order that first lists the smallest part of the system and continues with the next largest size. SW1/4 of NE1/4 of Section 1, T2S, R1E 1st PM indicates the southwest quarter of the northeast quarter of Section 1 in Township two south, range one east of the first principal meridian. The USPLS system is based on a theoretical model that originally has been applied in very difficult circumstances and sometime with possible shortcuts made by the contractors that were employed by the government. This situation produced results that deviated from the geometries that were theoretically prescribed by the system.

MERIDIANS AND BASE LINES SURVEY REFERENCE SYSTEM

Denotes areas that use Metes and Bound Survey System

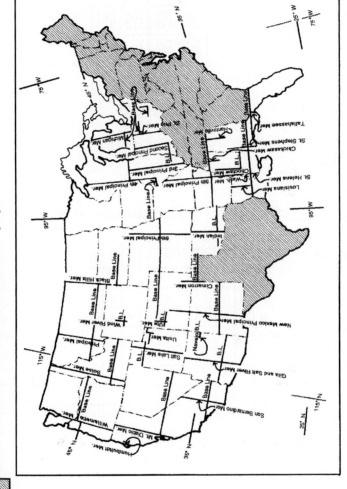

FIGURE 1.24 The meridians and base lines survey reference system.

TOWNSHIP AND BASE LINES SYSTEM

Third Principal Meridian
Range Line
Base Line
Initial Point
Township Line
T2N R2W
T2N R1W
T2N R1E
T2N R2E
T1N R2W
T1N R1W
T1N R1E
T1N R2E
T1S R2W
T1S R1W
T1S R1E
T1S R2E
T2S R2W
T2S R1W
T2S R1E
T2S R2E

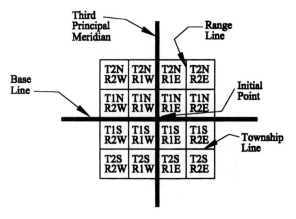

FIGURE 1.25 Township and base lines system.

TYPICAL TOWNSHIP AND SECTION ORGANIZATION

26 25 30 29 28 27 26 25 30 29
35 36 31 32 33 34 35 36 31 32
2 1 6 5 4 3 2 1 6 5
11 12 7 8 9 10 11 12 7 8
14 13 18 17 16 15 14 13 18 17
23 24 19 20 21 22 23 24 19 20
26 25 30 29 28 27 26 25 30 29
35 36 31 32 33 34 35 36 31 32
2 1 6 5 4 3 2 1 6 5
11 12 7 8 9 10 11 12 7 8
Township Boundary

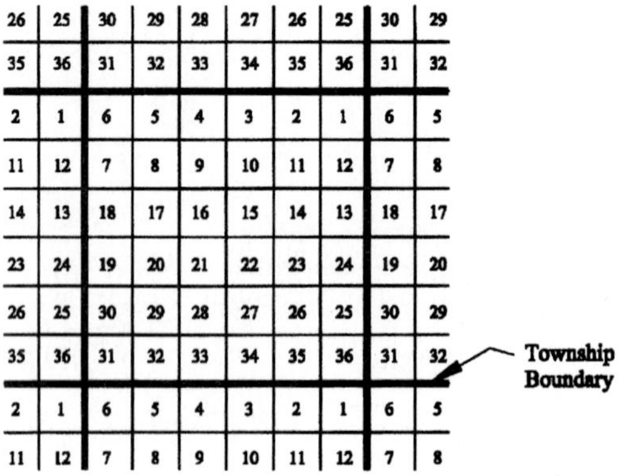

FIGURE 1.26 The typical township and section organizations.

However, the USPLS system is not invalidated by these discrepancies since the rule that dictates the development of the parcels relies on the location of the actual corners and the subdivision in half of their actual distance (see Figure 2.29 and 1.30).

Declination

Both systems used to identify a parcel of land rely on determining angles to which property lines are orientated. To determine such angles, a surveyor uses a

TYPICAL SECTION SUBDIVISION

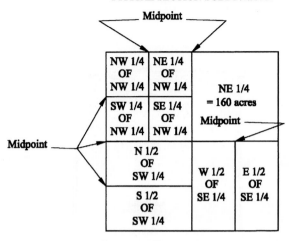

FIGURE 1.27 A subdivision of a typical section.

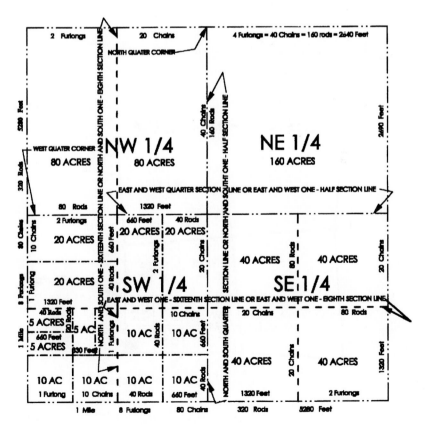

FIGURE 1.28 Types of measurement units in a typical section.

POSSIBLE DISCREPANCY BETWEEN POSTED
SECTIONS AND TYPICAL RECORDED SECTIONS

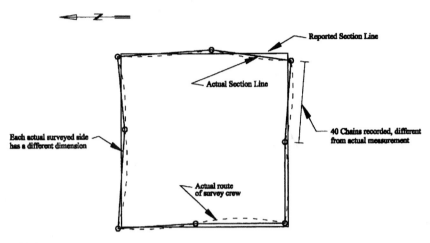

FIGURE 1.29   The possible discrepancy between posted sections and typical recorded section.

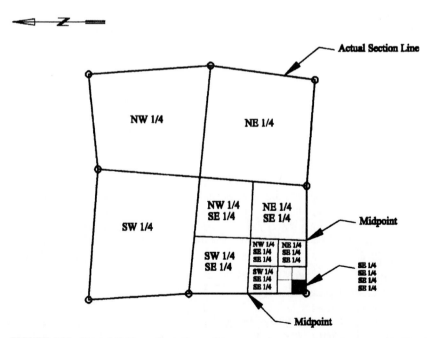

FIGURE 1.30   The subdivision of irregular sections.

compass that points to the magnetic north. Magnetic north changes, and is differently located in relation to the true north by an amount that is dependent on the year in which an observation is made. The amount of difference between true north and magnetic north is called *declination*.

PLATTED SUBDIVISION OR URBAN SYSTEMS

The metes and bound system and the USPLS are mainly suited to survey large tracts of land. In the USPLS the subdivision of land is specified up to ⅟₁₆ of a section. A system that successfully has allowed recording smaller parcels of land is the *platted subdivision*.

A platted subdivision usually requires the confirmation and recording of the corners of the property to be subdivided, which refers to a more general system (USPLS or Metes and Bounds) and surrounding properties or right-of-ways. Then a system of subdivision internal to the property has to be devised and recorded.

In principle the concept of the platted subdivision has the following advantages: **a.** in urban situations the creation of the block simplifies the description of a particular lot; **b.** the plat can be a useful tool in any sale; **c.** the geometry of the property is very clearly described on paper; **d.** deeds can refer to lot and block as well as describe the parcel using a metes and bound description, which can refer to street right-of-way corners and also to adjoining lots; **e.** the platted subdivision does not depend upon monumentation or possession to create boundaries to the property.

Survey Plan Evaluation

It is always advisable to commission a new survey plan before a property is altered or improved. The accuracy of the survey is fundamental in developing a project. Even if a survey had been performed and a plat had been produced previously, they were not necessarily done for the same purpose for which the property must now be surveyed.

It has to be considered that surveyors will record what is visibly present on the parcel of land, or elements that the user requests to be shown on the map. It is therefore important that the user, in this case the architect (who is not necessarily the client), discusses the purpose of the survey plan with the surveyor before the survey is performed. Furthermore the client's lawyer should conduct a complete title search to discover the state of the property from the legal, financial, and logistic (i.e. servitudes registered on the property) point of view. As indicated, the surveyor will not automatically conduct a title search. In the case of right-of-way, easements and other servitudes, the surveyor will indicate them on his plan only if there is evidence on-site that might suggest that such servitudes exist. For complete information to be shown on a survey the architect should ask the surveyor to comply with the Minimum Standard Detail Requirements for ALTA (American Land Title Association)/ACSM (American Congress On Surveying & Mapping).

Such standards refer to four types of surveys: A, B, C, and D (see Figure 1.31). Common errors in deed descriptions are illustrated in Figure 1.32. The following are information that generally should be shown on the survey to be used for a project:

1. Minimum size of paper 8½ x 11.
2. North arrow and bearing base.
3. Legal description.
4. Date of the survey.
5. Name and address of the surveyor.
6. Signature and seal of the land surveyor.
7. Legend of all symbols and abbreviations used.
8. Flood zone designation (if applicable).
9. Easements and servitudes (burdening and/or benefiting the property) record of which have been given to the surveyor (i.e. roads, right-of-ways, water courses, drains, telephone, telegraph or electric lines, water sewer, oil or gas pipelines) whether on, across, or adjoining the property if they appear to affect the surveyed property.
10. Land area.
11. Contours.
12. All existing buildings with main floor elevations, number of storys indicated and located by measurement perpendicular to the boundary lines of the property. If no buildings are erected, the plat should indicate "no buildings."
13. The character and location of all walls, building, fences within two feet of either side of the boundary lines.
14. Projections, encroachments and structural appurtenances (i.e. fire escapes, bay windows, doors and windows that open out, flue pipes, stoops, eaves, cornices, areaways, steps, trims etc.).
15. Evidence of use by other than the occupants. Encroachment of driveways or alleys on adjoining properties should be shown.
16. All improvements (in addition to buildings such as signs, parking areas or structures, swimming pools, retaining walls, pavements, etc.)
17. Parking areas and, if striped, the striping and the number of parking spaces.
18. Indication of access to a public way such as curb cuts, marked driveways.
19. Adjoining properties.
20. Point of beginning and remote point of beginning, if different.
21. Monuments clearly differentiated between found and placed at all major corners of the boundary of the property. Monuments found beyond the surveyed premises on which establishment of the corners of the surveyed premises are dependent.
22. Dimensions of all sides of the property. Differences between record dimensions and measured dimensions should be indicated on the plan. Record and measured distances from the nearest street right-of-way in urban or

SURVEY CLASSIFICATION

AMERICAN LAND TITLE ASSOCIATION and AMERICAN CONGRESS ON SURVEYING & MAPPING				
Condition	Class of survey			
	A	B	C	A
	Urban	Suburban	Rural	Mountain or Marsh
Accuracy of bearing in relation to source (max. allowable)	+/- 15 sec.	+/- 20 sec.	+/- 30 sec.	+/- 40 sec.
Linear distances accurate to (max. allowable)	+/- 0.05 ft. per 1000 ft.	+/- 0.1 ft. per 1000 ft.	+/- 0.15 ft. per 1000 ft.	+/- 0.2 ft. per 1000 ft.
Calculation of area - accurate and carried to nearest ____ decimal place of acre to 1 acre to 10 acres to 100 acres to 1000 acres	 .0001 .001 .01 .1	 .0001 .001 .01 .1	 .001 .01 .1 .2	 .001 .01 .1 .2

FIGURE 1.31 A survey classification using classes developed by the American Land Title Association and the American Congress on Surveying and Mapping.

suburban areas as well as recovered lot corners and evidence of lot corners should be noted.

23. Set-backs or building restriction lines which have been platted and recorded in subdivision plats or which appear in a record document which has been delivered to the surveyor. Name and widths of streets and rights-of-way, as well as the distance from the nearest street intersection, should be given. Rights-of-way of streets abutting the premises registered but not open should be also indicated.

24. Private roads, driveways and alleys.

25. Radii.

26. Bearings of all sides or angles at each corner. All bearings should read clockwise where possible. Difference between record bearings and measured bearings should be noted on the survey.

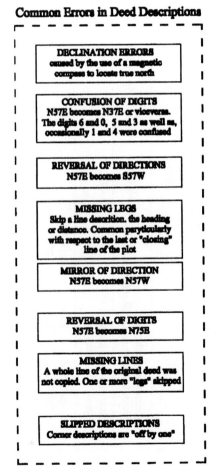

FIGURE 1.32 Common errors in deed descriptions.

27. Name of the client and purpose of the survey.
28. Certification.
29. Limiting notes or phrases.
30. Scale and graphic scale.
31. Trees, major vegetation, rivers and creeks, lakes, ponds, springs, ravines, top of banks, and any other natural feature bordering or on the property.
32. Location of all utilities serving the property, including without limitation:
    a. All railroad tracks and sidings.
    b. All manholes, catch basins, valve vaults or other indications of other subterranean uses.
    c. All wires and cables (including their function) crossing the surveyed premises, all poles on or within ten feet of the surveyed premises, and the dimension of all cross-wires or overhangs effecting the surveyed premises.
    d. All installations by utilities companies on the surveyed premises.
33. Observable evidence of cemeteries.
34. Significant observations not otherwise disclosed.

CHAPTER 2
PLANNING AN ARCHITECTURAL SET

OVERVIEW

The purpose of this chapter is to provide a conceptual system that will allow the planning and organization of an efficient architectural drawing set. The method adopted is based on the establishment of project categories through the use of variables (i.e. *size* of the project). These variables are then identified through parameters (in the case of the variables associated with *size of the project* the parameters are: small, medium, and large).

Characteristics are then assigned to each of the newly created sub-categories. The system is designed to achieve a level of flexibility that facilitates combinations of these characteristics. The result is a model designed to maximize the variety of project types that can be identified and categorized.

The sub-categories proposed represent only precise reference points. Each of their characteristics can be extrapolated and combined with others assigned to different sub-categories to create intermediate cases closely resembling the characteristics of any given project.

In order to achieve an effective result, an element of judgment will be required to choose the appropriate graphic representation to represent a particular characteristic. For this reason, the relationship among the parts that create the graphic representation and the type of information that it carries is explored and clarified. This knowledge is fundamental in order to correlate the characteristics properly with the required type of drawings.

GENERAL CONSIDERATIONS

A good and clear organization of a set of drawings is as important as the information that it contains. Each drawing must fulfill one of two fundamental functions; either the drawing provides the information, or it states in which part of the system such information is provided. The planning of an architectural set, therefore has to be considered very carefully. The choice of the type of organization is based upon: **a.** stage of the project; **b.** the type of project.

Stages of a Project

As noted earlier, the reference points are the following stages: **a.** programming; **b.** schematic design; **c.** preliminary design; **d.** design development; **e.** construction drawings.

CATEGORIES AND STAGES OF PROJECTS

In a very general way, two fundamental variables can be used to categorize projects: size and complexity. (It should be noted that the term complexity does not refer to technical aspects. It defines the required degree of articulation of the graphic material required for effective communication). These variables have an important direct influence on the decision as to which is the most appropriate organization of the drawing set to be adopted for a particular project.

Both size and complexity can be further subdivided into subcategories:

1. Size: subdivided into
    a. Small—a project can be identified as small when it has the following characteristics (Figures 2.1, 2.2):
        (1) Comprised of only one element or one prototype to be built.
        (2) Each floor plan(s), elevation(s) and section(s) can be completely drawn on a sheet of A1 format at a scale that does not require further enlargements or elaborations in order to comply with "the rules of good communication."
    b. Medium—a medium project can be considered as such when (Figure 2.3):
        (1) It is composed of one building to be built or one prototype to be used.
        (2) Each floor plan, elevation(s) and section(s) can be completely drawn on a sheet of A0 format at a scale that does not require further subdivisions in order to comply with "the rules of good communication." Only enlargements of limited areas of the main building (i.e. washrooms, kitchen, lobbies and the like) might be necessary for clarification.
    c. Large—a project can be categorized as large when (Figures 2.4, 2.5):

(1) It is comprised of one or multiple buildings.

(2) Plans, elevation(s) and section(s) cannot be completely drawn on a sheet of A0 format. Further subdivision of the images is necessary in order to represent the drawings at a scale that allows the graphics to comply with "the rules of good communication" and to facilitate the use of the drawings for the purpose for which they were conceived and issued.

2. Complexity

   a. Simple—a project can be considered simple when:

      (1) The element or elements fulfill one ordinary main function, with secondary functions limited and strictly auxiliary, in space and scope, to the main function (i.e. washrooms, kitchens, lobbies etc.).

      (2) Building the project requires only:

         (a) Standard components.

         (b) Standards techniques well known in general and within the various industries.

         (c) Materials, assemblies, components, techniques and finish products are well documented and well supported by published literature that establishes clear and well-known references.

         (d) Components and materials can be simply and completely described on the general floor plans and general elevations.

         (e) Assemblies can be shown clearly and completely in sections and limited details.

         (f) Specifications can be included on the drawings.

         (g) Consultants' scope of work is limited.

         (h) Contract administration is very limited and only one field review for each of the divisions included in the scope of work plus one final review.

         (i) The value of the work does not require the issuance of a complete project manual except for a standard construction contract.

Figures 2.6 and 2.7 illustrate a project that can be defined as large/simple for the majority of the characteristics listed except for:

      (j) The consultant's scope of work.

      (k) Contract administration is not limited.

      (l) The specifications are part of a project manual.

   b. Complex— projects can be considered complex when (see Figures 2.8 through 2.14):

      (1) The element or elements fulfill either one or multiple functions.

      (2) Construction requires:

         (a) Standard and/or custom components.

         (b) Standard and/or unique techniques.

(c) Materials, assemblies, components, techniques and finished product which are either well documented and well supported by published literature showing clear and well-known references or which are used in a particular way, created and conceived specifically for the project components. Such materials cannot be described simply and completely on the floor plans and elevations.

(d) General sections to be used as reference only for assemblies shown on detail sections and details.

(e) Specifications separate from the drawings.

(f) A comprehensive consultants' scope of work.

(g) Comprehensive contract administration.

(h) The value of the work requires the issuance of a complete project manual.

The combinations of these variables create the following project categories:

1. Small and simple (i.e. a garage, a small addition).
2. Small and complex (i.e. an economical custom-designed house).
3. Medium and simple (i.e. a multi-family building, a commercial building).
4. Medium and complex (i.e. a mansion, a multi-family buildings, an office building).
5. Large and simple (i.e. a warehouse complex).
6. Large and complex (i.e. a multi-functional complex, a shopping center).

Although this definition of projects is rather broad, it provides a conceptual framework necessary to begin rationalizing a methodology which, in its applications, has infinite variations and particular cases.

There are other factors that affect the extent to which a set of drawings should be developed (i.e. type of client, type of contract, type of tender call). The influence of these variables, although important, does not fundamentally change the category to which the project should be allocated (see Figures 2.15, 2.16). It affects only the project allocation. In other words, if a project were considered *medium complex*, the secondary factors might shift the project into another category, for example towards the *medium simple*. Thus it might be possible to reduce the scope of work, just because the type of client and the relationship with the contractor, as well as the type of construction contract, do not require the development of the set as in other circumstances (see Chapter 11 for the relationship between contract documents, type of project delivery, and construction contracts). In such cases, care should be taken in stating the limitations of the information in order to minimize the professional liability.

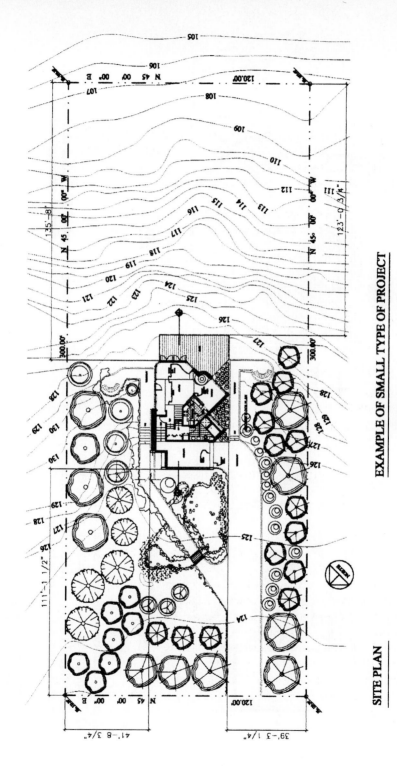

SITE PLAN

EXAMPLE OF SMALL TYPE OF PROJECT

FIGURE 2.1 Example of small type of project.

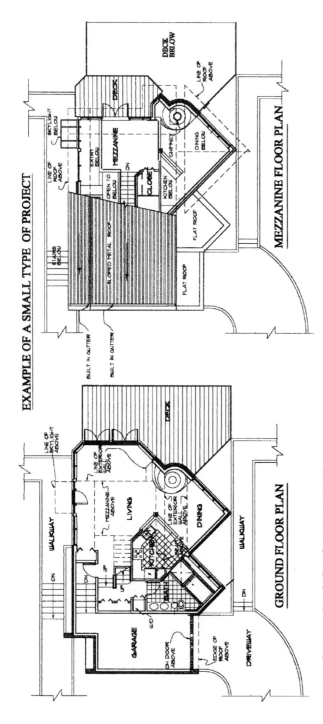

EXAMPLE OF A SMALL TYPE OF PROJECT

GROUND FLOOR PLAN

MEZZANINE FLOOR PLAN

A project can be defined as "Small" if:

a) Comprised of only one element or one prototype to be built.

b) Each floor Plan(s), Elevation(s) and Section(s) can be completely drawn on a sheet of A1 format at a scale that does not require further enlargements or elaborations to comply with "the rules of good communication".

FIGURE 2.2   Example of small type of project.

2.6

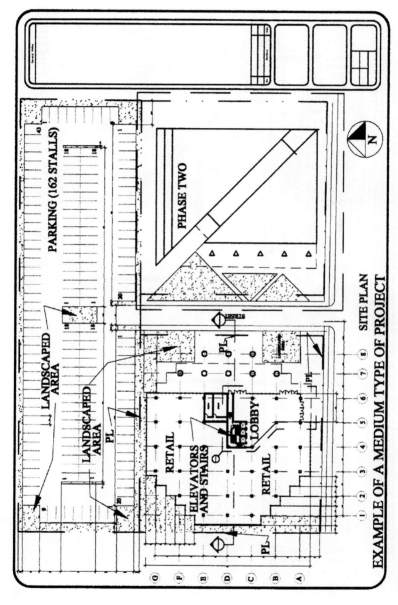

FIGURE 2.3 Example of a medium type of project.

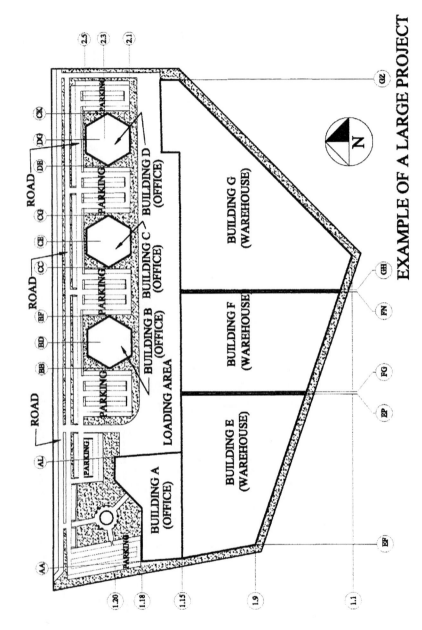

FIGURE 2.4 Example of a large type of project.

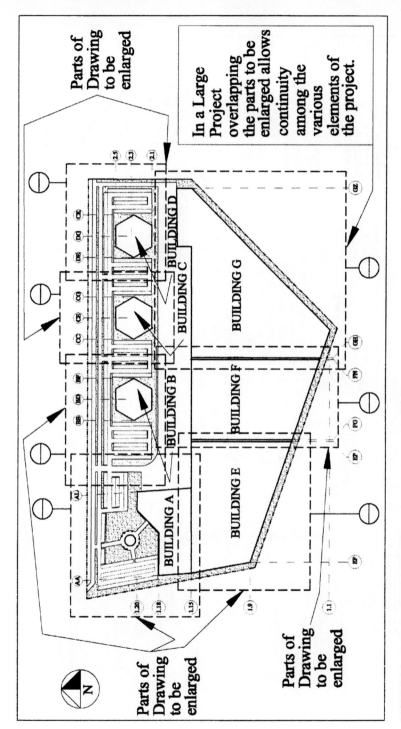

FIGURE 2.5 Example of compartmentalization of a large type of project.

2.9

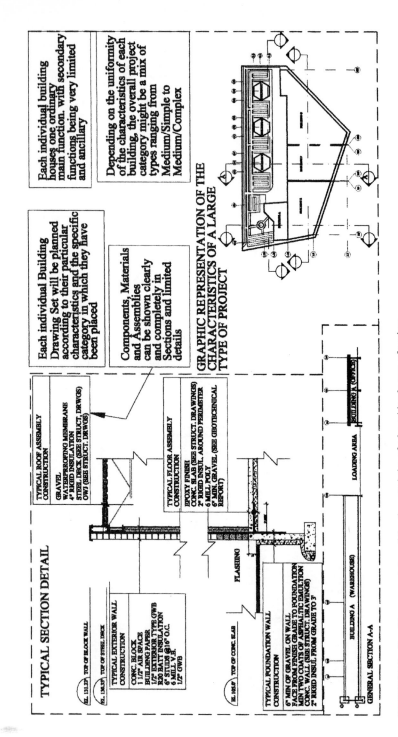

FIGURE 2.6 Graphic representation of the characteristics of a large/simple type of project.

TYPICAL SECTION DETAIL

TYPICAL ROOF ASSEMBLY CONSTRUCTION

GRAVEL
WATERPROOFING MEMBRANE
4" RIGID INSULATION
STEEL DECK (SEE STRUCT. DRWGS)
OW/ (SEE STRUCT. DRWGS)

TYPICAL FLOOR ASSEMBLY CONSTRUCTION

EPOXY FINISH
CONC. SLAB (SEE STRUCT. DRAWINGS)
2" RIGID INSUL. AROUND PERIMETER
6 MILL POLY
6" MIN. GRAVEL (SEE GEOTECHNICAL REPORT)

TYPICAL EXTERIOR WALL CONSTRUCTION

CONC. BLOCK
1 1/2" AIR SPACE
BUILDING PAPER
1/2" EXTERIOR TYPE GWB
R20 BATT INSULATION
6" STUD @16" O.C.
6 MILL V.B.
1/2" GWB

TYPICAL FOUNDATION WALL CONSTRUCTION

6" MIN OF GRAVEL ON WALL
FACE FROM FINISH GRADE TO FOUNDATION
MIN TWO COATS OF ASPHALTIC EMULSION
CONC. WALL (SEE STRUCT. DRAWINGS)
2" RIGID INSUL FROM GRADE TO 3'

EL. 131.5' TOP OF BLOCK WALL
EL. 124.33' TOP OF STEEL DECK
EL. 105.0' TOP OF CONC. SLAB

FLASHING

BUILDING A (OFFICE)

LOADING AREA

BUILDING A (WAREHOUSE)

GENERAL SECTION A-A

Each individual building houses one ordinary main function, with secondary functions being very limited and ancillary

Depending on the uniformity of the characteristics of each building, the overall project category might be a mix of types ranging from Medium/Simple to Medium/Complex

Each individual Building Drawing Set will be planned according to their particular characteristics and the specific category in which they have been placed

Components, Materials and Assemblies can be shown clearly and completely in Sections and limited details

GRAPHIC REPRESENTATION OF THE CHARACTERISTICS OF A LARGE TYPE OF PROJECT

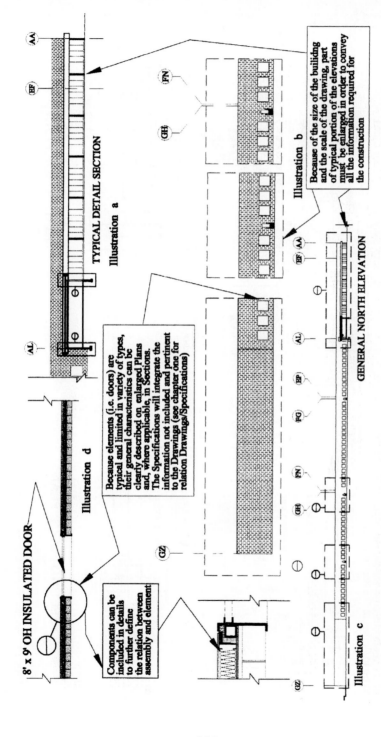

FIGURE 2.7 Graphic representation of the characteristics of a large/simple type of project.

TYPICAL DETAIL SECTION

Illustration a

Illustration b

Because of the size of the building and the scale of the drawing, part of typical portion of the elevations must be enlarged in order to convey all the information required for the construction

Illustration d

Because elements (i.e. doors) are typical and limited in variety of types, their general characteristics can be clearly described on enlarged Plans and, where applicable, in Sections. The Specifications will integrate the information not included and pertinent to the Drawings (see chapter one for relation Drawings/Specifications)

8' x 9' OH INSULATED DOOR

Components can be included in details to further define the relation between assembly and element

GENERAL NORTH ELEVATION

Illustration c

2.11

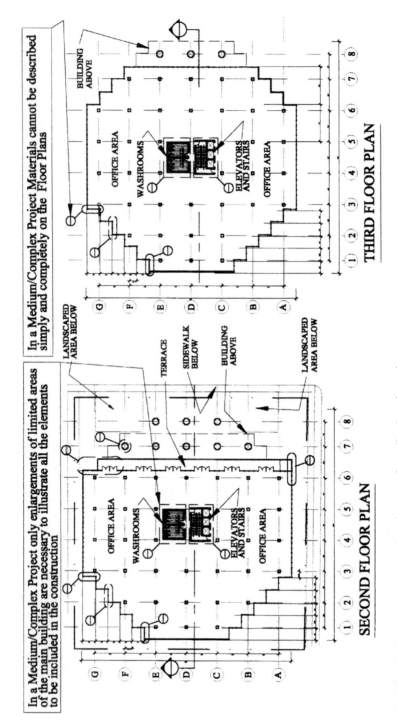

FIGURE 2.8 Graphic representational requirements of a medium/complex project.

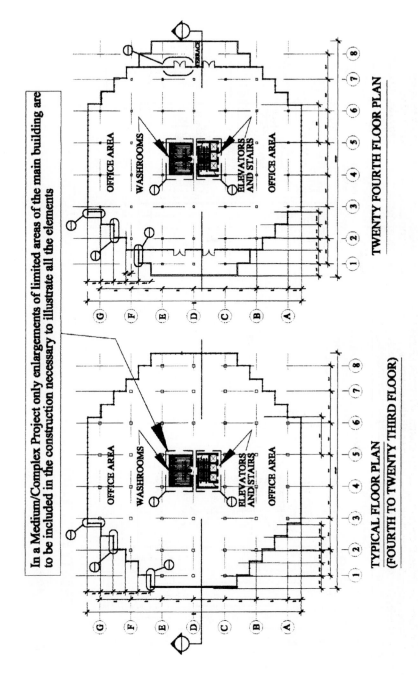

In a Medium/Complex Project only enlargements of limited areas of the main building are to be included in the construction necessary to illustrate all the elements

OFFICE AREA

WASHROOMS

ELEVATORS AND STAIRS

OFFICE AREA

TWENTY FOURTH FLOOR PLAN

OFFICE AREA

WASHROOMS

ELEVATORS AND STAIRS

OFFICE AREA

TYPICAL FLOOR PLAN
(FOURTH TO TWENTY THIRD FLOOR)

FIGURE 2.9 Graphic representational requirements of a medium/complex project.

2.13

In a Complex Project, depending on the design, Materials, Assembly Components, Techniques and Finish Products are either well-documented and well-supported by published literature, or they are used in a particular way, created and conceived specifically for the Project Component. In the latter case a more comprehensive set of details must be provided in order to clarify the intent of the design and the technical requirements.

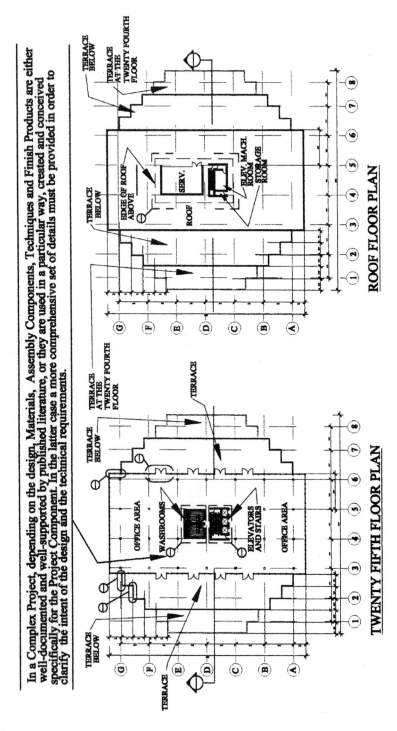

ROOF FLOOR PLAN

TWENTY FIFTH FLOOR PLAN

FIGURE 2.10 Graphic representational requirements of a medium/complex project.

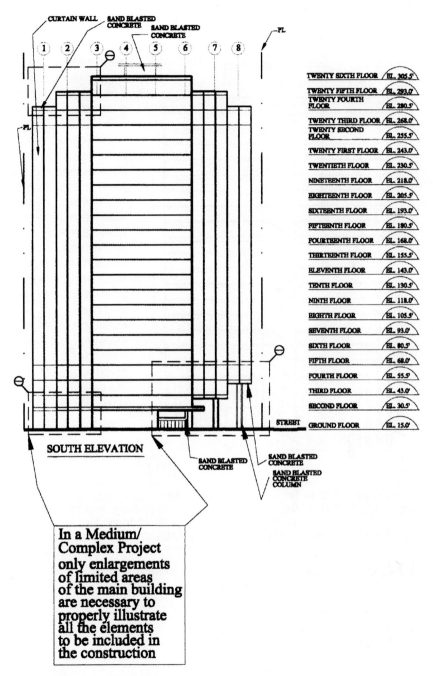

FIGURE 2.11 Graphic representational requirements of a medium/complex project.

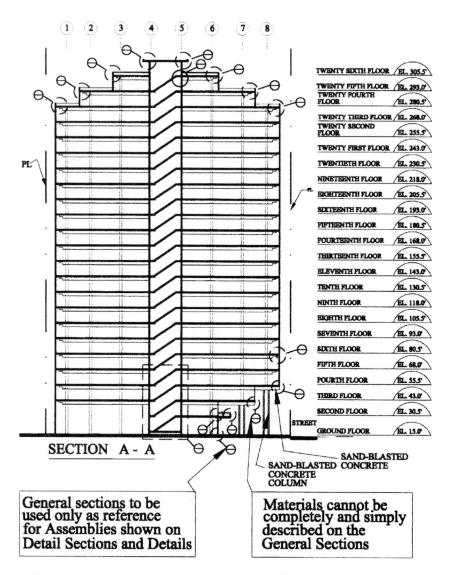

FIGURE 2.12 Graphic representational requirements of a medium/complex project.

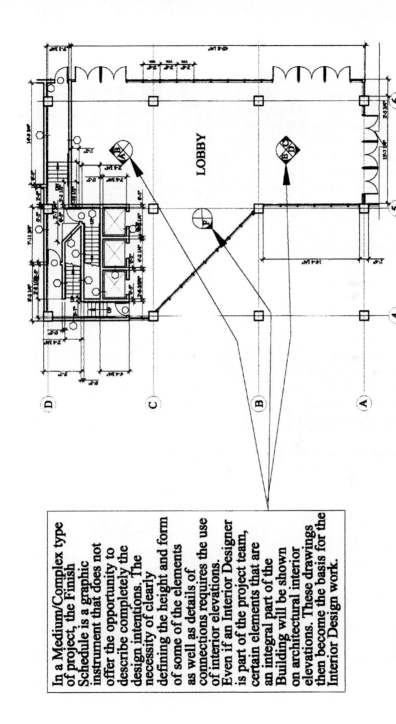

In a Medium/Complex type of project, the Finish Schedule is a graphic instrument that does not offer the opportunity to describe completely the design intentions. The necessity of clearly defining the height and form of some of the elements as well as details of connections requires the use of interior elevations. Even if an Interior Designer is part of the project team, certain elements that are an integral part of the Building will be shown on architectural interior elevations. These drawings then become the basis for the Interior Design work.

LOBBY

FIGURE 2.13   Graphic representational requirements of a medium/complex project.

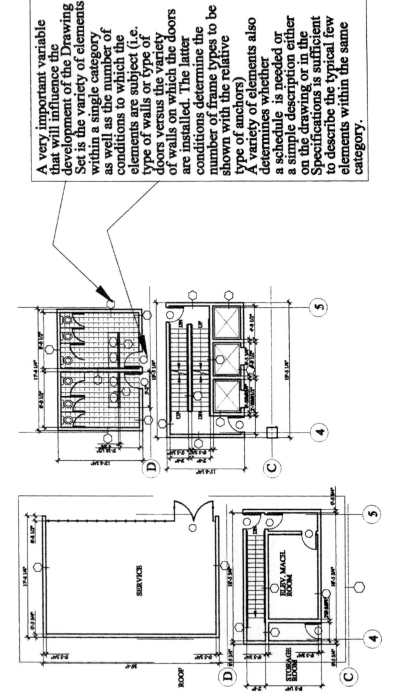

A very important variable that will influence the development of the Drawing Set is the variety of elements within a single category as well as the number of conditions to which the elements are subject (i.e. type of walls or type of doors versus the variety of walls on which the doors are installed. The latter conditions determine the number of frame types to be shown with the relative type of anchors)

A variety of elements also determines whether a schedule is needed or a simple description either on the drawing or in the Specifications is sufficient to describe the typical few elements within the same category.

FIGURE 2.14 Graphic representational requirements of a medium/complex project.

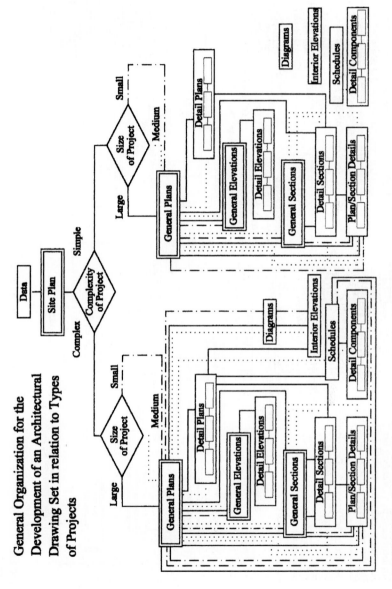

General Organization for the Development of an Architectural Drawing Set in relation to Types of Projects

FIGURE 2.15   General organization for the development of an architectural drawings set in relation to type of projects.

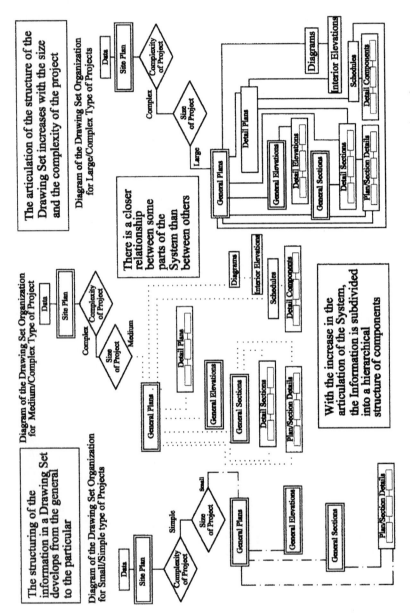

FIGURE 2.16 Diagrams of architectural drawing sets of the organization for small/simple, medium/complex and large/complex type of projects.

From the diagram shown on Figure 2.1 one can derive the following conclusions and basic rules to be applied when an architectural set is planned: **a**. the structuring of the information develops from the general to the particular; **b**. the articulation of this structure increases with the size and the complexity of the project; **c**. with the increase in the articulation of the system, the information is subdivided into a hierarchical organization of components (this becomes necessary when the information cannot be communicated simply and clearly and/or the complexity of the multi-layering of data is not appropriate for the scale or the purpose of the drawing); **d**. there is a more direct relationship among some parts of the system than others. This characteristic can guide the referencing of the information and the sequencing as well as the numbering of the drawings. Figure 2.17 illustrates the relationships between the parts of the drawing set.

Because of this dynamic, the previously described questions related to the scope of the drawings—*where*, *what*, and *how*—have different references in different phases of the project.

At the schematic and preliminary design stage, because of the exploratory character of the information, the *where* question is answered by the urban analysis, site analysis, and site plans. Since the building is still seen in its totality, the floor plans, elevations, sections and perspectives answer the *what* questions. The elements related to the *how* question are connected to the program, the budget, the analysis of systems and to the construction method. This is part of the verification mechanism shown in Figure 1.7 in Chapter 1.

At the design development stage, the program and, in general, the form and functions of the elements of the project have been defined. Attention is now shifted almost completely towards the object(s) to be built. The relationship between the questions *where*, *what*, and *how,* can be elaborated in a more hierarchical form and primarily by the elements of the building (see Figures 2.18, 2.19).

The relationship between the parts and a logical development through which a user can easily familiarize himself with the project form the basis for the sequencing of the drawings. As we saw from Figures 2.15, 2.16 and 2.17, some drawings are common to all type of projects. Irrespective of size of the work, the architectural drawing set will include: **a**. project data; **b**. site or key plan; **c**. plan(s); **d**. elevation(s); **e**. section(s).

Without these drawings it is rarely possible to convey the information needed to perform the work while still adhering to the stipulated price and maintaining mutual understanding and agreement on the final result.

In addition to the above drawings a complete set could include: **a**. detail plans; **b**. detail elevations; **c**. detail sections; **d**. plan details and section details; **e**. interior elevations; **f**. reflected ceiling plans; **g**. schedules (see Chapter 11 for a detailed description of these types of drawings).

The sequence described above could be one of many that can be recommended for the organizing of the set. The drawings indicated with an asterisk could be called *floaters*, since they can occupy different positions in the set. The schedules, for example, could be placed in front, just after the project data sheet.

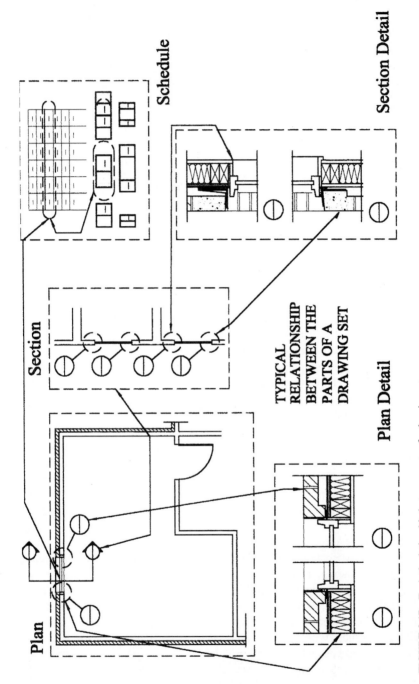

Schedule

Section Detail

Section

**TYPICAL
RELATIONSHIP
BETWEEN THE
PARTS OF A
DRAWING SET**

Plan Detail

Plan

FIGURE 2.17 Typical relationship between parts of a drawing set.

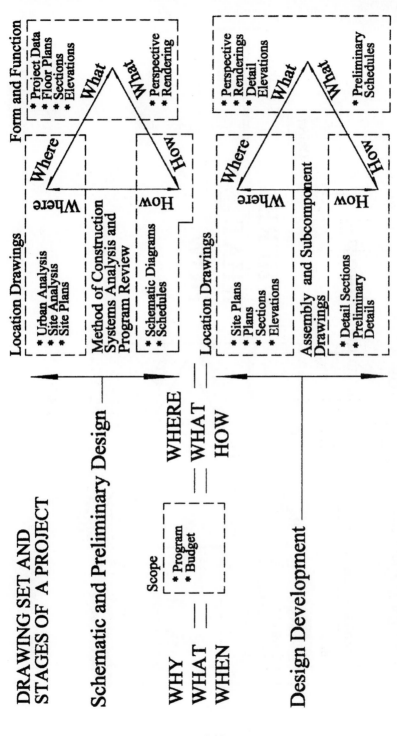

FIGURE 2.18 Drawing set and stages of project.

2.23

DRAWING SET AND STAGES OF A PROJECT

Construction Drawings

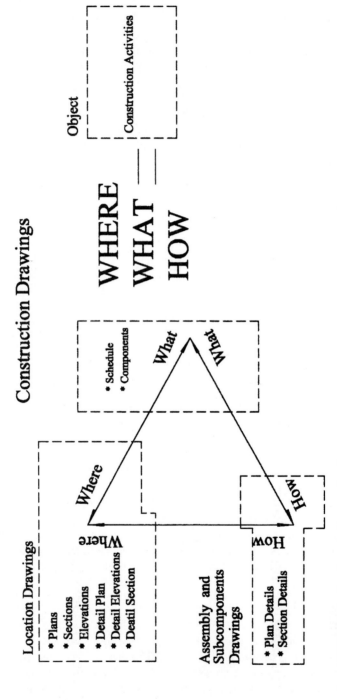

FIGURE 2.19 Drawing set and stages of project.

It would be appropriate since many of the schedules are developed between the design development stage and the early phases of the construction drawing stage. The schedules are also of primary importance in defining the project standards and confirming budgets as well as being fundamental in pricing.

The reflected ceiling plans may be placed just after the detail sections in order to better understand the plan details and the section details. On the other hand, if these drawings are included in the detail plans, they might clarify the detail sections. Much will depend on the complexity of the design and of the drawings.

Finally, the interior elevations may be associated with the schedules since much information conveyed by the schedules affects the interior elevations (i.e. finish schedule, door schedule). This means that only some schedules can be placed at the beginning of the set.

Based on the foregoing observations, the order chosen in any given case may vary. However the logic that dictates the method adopted for numbering the drawings remains fundamentally unaffected.

The above principles are very important because the scope of the work is largely dependent upon the characteristics of the project which, in turn, are reflected in the fee. Since the production of the drawings usually represents the major task within the scope of work, locating a project in the wrong category could have the following consequences:

1. Over- or underestimating the value of the work to be produced. As a result, in the latter case the amount contemplated in the fee might not be sufficient to complete the work; in the former an architect might price himself or herself out of the market because the fee may be considered too expensive.

2. Missing key detail(s) or drawing(s), which could result in:
    a. No consequences if the detail can be produced on time when the contractor requests it and does not affect the cost of construction.
    b. Delay in the construction schedule if the detail cannot be produced on time or requires ordering of additional material. This may result in a loss for the client and a potential increase in cost of construction either because of the need for additional material or because of the lengthening of the construction period (or both).
    c. Potential disruption of the construction schedule, possible increase in construction cost, risk of causing a disservice to the client, loss of credibility if the detail reveals a discrepancy in the drawings.

Very often a project may initially appear simpler than it proves to be during its development. Therefore, a careful analysis should be conducted before the planning of the drawing set is started. It is helpful if the architect follows fundamental steps such as: **a.** keep an accurate record of all the discussions, findings and analysis; **b.** collect all the information pertinent to the project from the client and authorities; **c.** become familiar with the site in terms of surroundings, constraints, topography, possible geology; **d.** establish the type of consultants required for the project; **e.** establish a preliminary contact with the consultant and discuss the project; **f.** establish the scope of work for the consultants; **g.** list the tasks included in the architectural scope of work related to the requirements of the client; **h.** divide the architectural tasks as they relate to the stages of the project; **i.** extrapolate tasks that relate to drawings and create a drawing list for the different stages of the project.

Numbering the Drawings

There is no absolute accepted standard universally utilized for sequencing the drawings. There are systems like the CI/SfB (a classification system for building information), through which one might attempt to integrate drawings, specifications and material/components take-off as much as possible. However, these methods are very specialized and, because of their high level of articulation, they are still regarded as over-designed and too complex for the average office.

There are various less-articulated methods that can be employed to achieve an efficient result in organizing and numbering a drawing set. They are dependent on the amount of documentation that is required for a particular project, on the characteristics and on the circumstances surrounding the project. Two such methods can be called *sequential* and *serialized* as illustrated in Figures 2.20 and 2.21.

The first system simply organizes the drawings in a sequential order. The second sets up numeral series for the different types of drawings and then orders and numbers the drawings within a particular series.

The sequential method is appropriate for the organization of a project that can be completely conceived at the beginning or for stages of projects that do not require a high articulation of the information within the same type of drawings (i.e. plans, sections, elevations etc.). In order for this method to be effective, the project must be characterized by very stable conditions. However, conditions in a project are not totally under the control of the architect (e.g. market conditions, financial conditions, political changes). For these reasons the sequential method can be applied efficiently only to small/simple and some medium/simple projects. Many times, either because of the initial planning on the part of the professional, or because the conditions are changed, it is necessary to insert drawings within the sequential order and the sequential method is of necessity transformed into a hybrid (sequential/serial). Then, letters like a, b, c are introduced after a drawing number to avoid the re-numbering of the set. Depending on how advanced the development of the project is, reorganizing a set of drawings can be very time consuming and can result in inconsistencies, errors and omissions (i.e. having to coordinate anew all the referencing symbols).

The method that organizes drawings using series of numbers allows: **a.** the flexibility that is necessary in complex and large projects; **b.** consistent referencing since the series can be standardized; **c.** improvement production since the design team is familiar with the numbering system right at the beginning of the project and a complete standard list of drawings can be used as point of reference in the planning of the drawing package; **d.** the construction team to familiarize

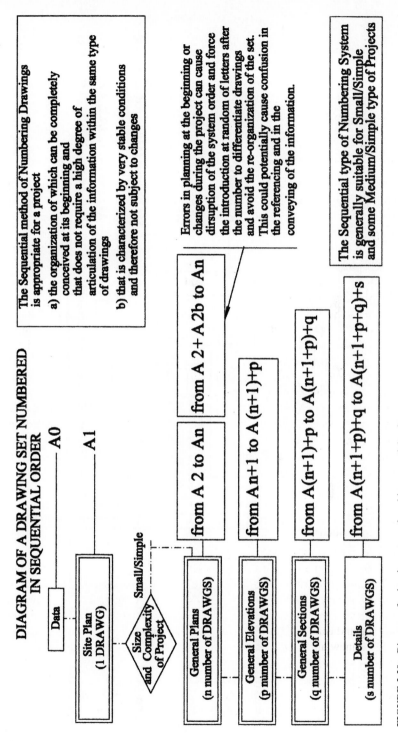

DIAGRAM OF A DRAWING SET NUMBERED IN SEQUENTIAL ORDER

The Sequential method of Numbering Drawings is appropriate for a project

a) the organization of which can be completely conceived at its beginning and that does not require a high degree of articulation of the information within the same type of drawings

b) that is characterized by very stable conditions and therefore not subject to changes

Errors in planning at the beginning or changes during the project can cause disruption of the system order and force the introduction at random of letters after the number to differentiate drawings and avoid the re-organization of the set. This could potentially cause confusion in the referencing and in the conveying of the information.

The Sequential type of Numbering System is generally suitable for Small/Simple and some Medium/Simple type of Projects

Data

Site Plan
(1 DRAWG) — A1

— A0

Size and Complexity of Project — Small/Simple

General Plans
(n number of DRAWGS) — from A 2 to An — from A 2 + A2b to An

General Elevations
(p number of DRAWGS) — from An+1 to A (n+1)+p

General Sections
(q number of DRAWGS) — from A(n+1)+p to A(n+1+p)+q

Details
(s number of DRAWGS) — from A(n+1+p)+q to A(n+1+p+q)+s

FIGURE 2.20 Diagram of a drawing set numbered in sequential order.

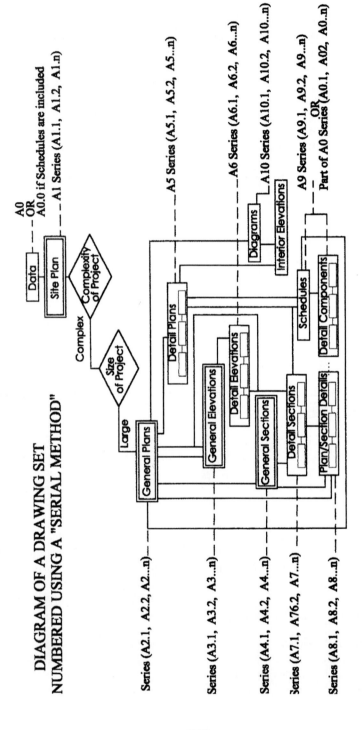

DIAGRAM OF A DRAWING SET
NUMBERED USING A "SERIAL METHOD"

FIGURE 2.21   Diagram of a drawing set numbered using a serial method.

2.28

themselves with the project very quickly and to remember the location of the drawings better; **e.** the design and construction team to focus quickly and effectively on more fundamental aspects of the work.

The standardization of the numbering of drawings is very important in repetitive projects based on a prototype. In fact, the advantages listed in favor of the standardization might lead an office to adopt such a method and apply it to every project. Standardization means that the list of the series of drawings does not change. The list of drawings functions as a key to indicate which series are used and which ones are not used.

On the other hand, if the total number of sheets required for each series is in the order of two and only the details at the end of the project might require more sheets, it is possible that the use of the serial system is not justified.

The proposed categories of projects and their characteristics in conjunction with the method of organization and numbering illustrated above can now be expanded. These principles have the potential of been used as basic guidelines that can be further elaborated and tailored to each type of project. The characteristics of each category can be individually extrapolated and woven in combinations that would alter the organization of a particular prototype. However the result will still be within the proposed framework. The fundamental questions of *where*, *what*, and *how* are always at the root of the structuring of the information.

An Intermediate Project

Figures 2.1 and 2.2 show a construction that has been defined as small. Upon superficial analysis, it may appear to be also a *simple* project. In that case, the drawing set would be conceived according to the diagram shown on Figure 2.22. At a closer look, however, its characteristics are not so straightforward.

In Figure 2.22, this project of a simple small cottage (basically one large room with one car garage, a kitchen, one bathroom and a mezzanine with a terrace), where every component is standard except for the glazing, a few elements in the bathroom, and exterior railings, demands the introduction of a certain type of drawing (i.e. the window and door schedules). This type of drawing departs from the organization of a drawing set required to complete a project which, at a first glance, could be considered small/simple. This is because the information regarding these items must be displayed using the same methodology that is used in complex projects. Such a requirement places this project in an intermediate category between small/complex and medium/complex. In addition, the following elements led to the decision to adopt the graphic representation shown:

1. An interior designer had been engaged. Her work had not been completed at the time of tender. However, outline specifications for the finishes had been included in the contract documents as well as a description of the location of the items. General interior elevations, therefore, had been devel-

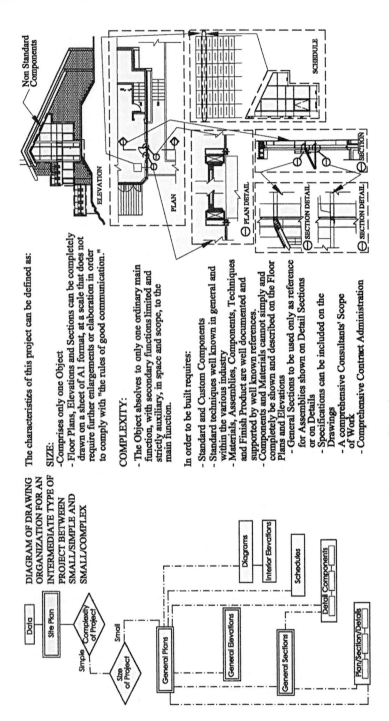

DIAGRAM OF DRAWING ORGANIZATION FOR AN INTERMEDIATE TYPE OF PROJECT BETWEEN SMALL/SIMPLE AND SMALL/COMPLEX

The characteristics of this project can be defined as:

SIZE:
- Comprises only one Object
- Floor Plans, Elevations and Sections can be completely drawn on a sheet of A1 format, at a scale that does not require further enlargements or elaboration in order to comply with "the rules of good communication."

COMPLEXITY:

- The Object absolves to only one ordinary main function, with secondary functions limited and strictly auxiliary, in space and scope, to the main function.

In order to be built requires:

- Standard and Custom Components
- Standard techniques well known in general and within the various industry
- Materials, Assemblies, Components, Techniques and Finish Product are well documented and supported by well known references.
- Components and Materials cannot simply and completely be shown and described on the Floor Plans and Elevations
  - General Sections to be used only as reference for Assemblies shown on Detail Sections or on Details
  - Specifications can be included on the Drawings
  - A comprehensive Consultants' Scope of Work
  - Comprehensive Contract Administration

FIGURE 2.22   Relationship between the parts of an intermediate project.

2.30

oped to define a general scope of work and determine a cash allowance for finishes and millwork. The diagrams and the interior elevations were used in lieu of the finish schedule.

2. Interior elevations were developed to allow planning for display of the art collection owned by the client.

3. Engineered shop drawings were requested in the appropriate sections of the specifications for interior and exterior railings, glazing, and skylights.

4. A structural engineer, a mechanical engineer (due to the specific temperature range to be maintained for the art work), an electrical/lighting specialist engineer and a landscape architect had been engaged as consultants.

5. The manufacturer (a metal artist and a fireplace specialist) who had been hired directly by the owner to provide the fireplace hood and chimney, had produced detailed engineered drawings for the complete fireplace, following the general guidelines of the elevations. The architect had coordinated his work with the project structural engineer and the interior designer.

The diagram of the drawing organization, shows the schedules, the detail components, diagrams and interior elevations as part of the drawing package. The remaining drawing organization conforms to the description of small/simple projects.

This system offers the following advantages: **a**. the development of the interior elevation provides an opportunity to study the project more comprehensively from the aesthetic and technical point of view. In this way, the cross coordination necessary to minimize errors and omissions becomes productive rather than passive, as may occur when only plans, elevations, sections and details are coordinated; **b**. gives the requirements of the work of the various consultants and specialists, improves performance in terms of system design and checking during construction, may reduce construction costs by avoiding the over designing of systems, and reduces the architect's liability. These benefits help to offset the added overhead created by using different offices as well as the coordination time and related expenses required by the architect. Figures 2.23–2.42 illustrate a variety of data sheets, site plans, foundation plans, floor plans, elevation formats, section formats, and detail sheets for a sampling of project types.

AN ALTERNATE FORM OF REPRESENTATION: A BOUND BOOKLET OF ARCHITECTURAL DETAILS

In the present context, the term *complex* has been used to describe the degree of articulation of the graphic information. There is one additional variable that affects the architectural set: the amount of information related to the variety of elements and conditions. If the content of each part is substantial (i.e. plan and section details and/or schedules and/or detail plans), then the format of their representation must be considered. To carry or handle a set of drawings comprised of many sheets can be impractical. In such cases, an alternate and more efficient system is the creation of a bound booklet of detail and related information.

The size of each sheet may be either 8½ x 11 or 11 x 17. The use of both formats at the same time should be discouraged for the following reasons: **a.** the smaller sheet can be easily missed when bound between larger sheets with resulting confusion and inefficiency; **b.** at the initial stage of booklet planning the architect may decide to place smaller sheets at the beginning of the booklet followed by the larger format. However, sheets with additional information are often added as the booklet develops, in which case after a certain stage of the contract documents or during construction, the architect may use larger sheets; **c.** the uniformity of the format adds to the general perception of a well-organized system. Similarly, in the case of larger sizes of sheets (i.e. A1 or A), the above principles support the consistent use of a standard and uniform format of drawing paper throughout a given project.

The choice between one or the other of the two sizes brings both advantages and disadvantages. The 8½ x 11 format is: **a.** easily transmitted through fax in its entirety, without appreciable distortions or change in size. The scale of the drawings is therefore accurate; **b.** easier to carry and reproduce. On the other hand, the 11 x 17 format: **a.** offers a larger drawing area; **b.** allows larger title blocks, making information like revisions and scale more readable; **c.** makes it less likely that stamps like "Preliminary" or "Not For Construction" will cover part of the drawing; **d.** renders the booklet easier to spot in a busy environment like a construction site or a construction office. Overall the 11 x 17 format is more suited for this type of information.

In the final analysis, the booklet must be coordinated with organizational system of the drawings. The sheets, being part of an assembly that can be initially planned with only a degree of approximation, carry their own numbering system which should be subdivided into series. The first sheets show the list of drawings. The series, since a booklet is used normally in larger projects, can refer to parts of the project and carry letters that might remind the reader of a particular component (like "T" for tower followed by the number that references the floor and, ultimately, the number of the detail.)

If the booklet is not clearly organized, it can be a very confusing tool, time-consuming and frustrating for the users, contributing to mistakes, omissions and unsatisfactory results. It is to be kept in mind that most of the information carried in the booklet refers to particular aspects of the project. Each unit or part of specific information must be presented so that: **a.** it can be identified as quickly and as easily as possible; **b.** it can be related to the context of the general project as quickly and easily as possible; **c.** once it has been coordinated with the rest of the project, the graphic and the text contains all the data necessary to minimize the use of information not shown on that particular sheet.

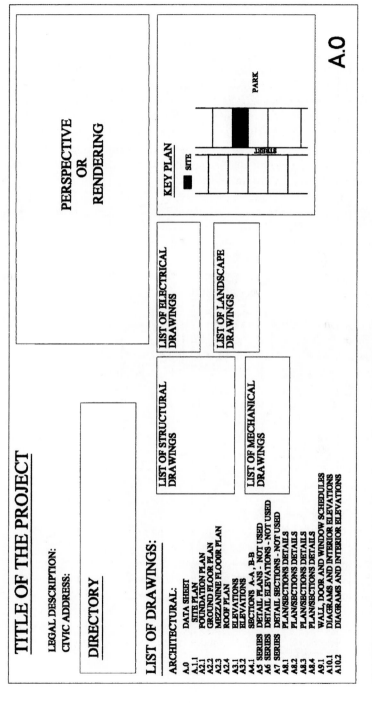

FIGURE 2.23 Typical data sheet format for an intermediate project between small/simple and small/complex.

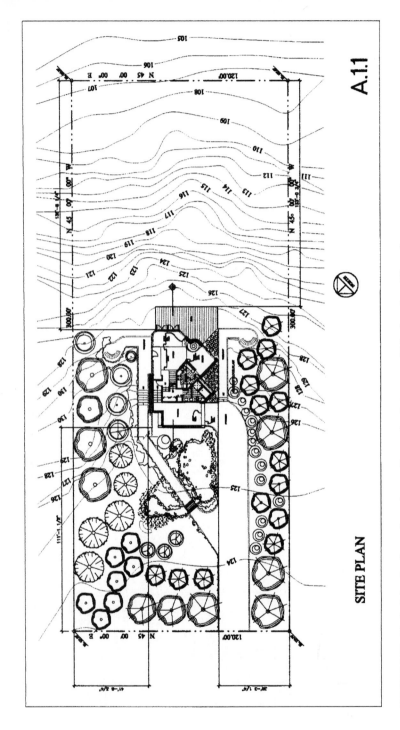

FIGURE 2.24 Typical site plan format for an intermediate project between small/simple and small/complex.

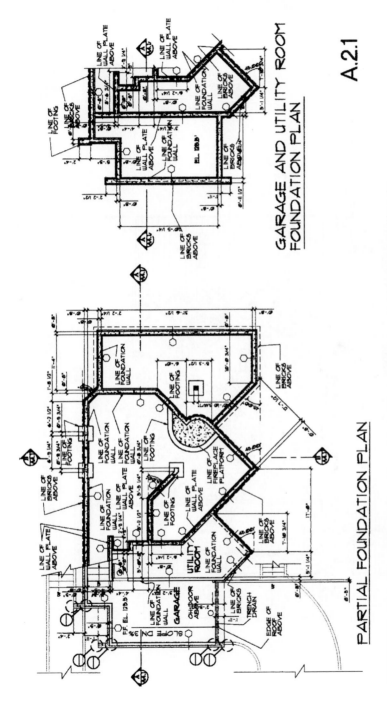

GARAGE AND UTILITY ROOM
FOUNDATION PLAN

A.2.1

PARTIAL FOUNDATION PLAN

FIGURE 2.25 Typical foundation plan format for an intermediate project between small/simple and small/complex.

2.35

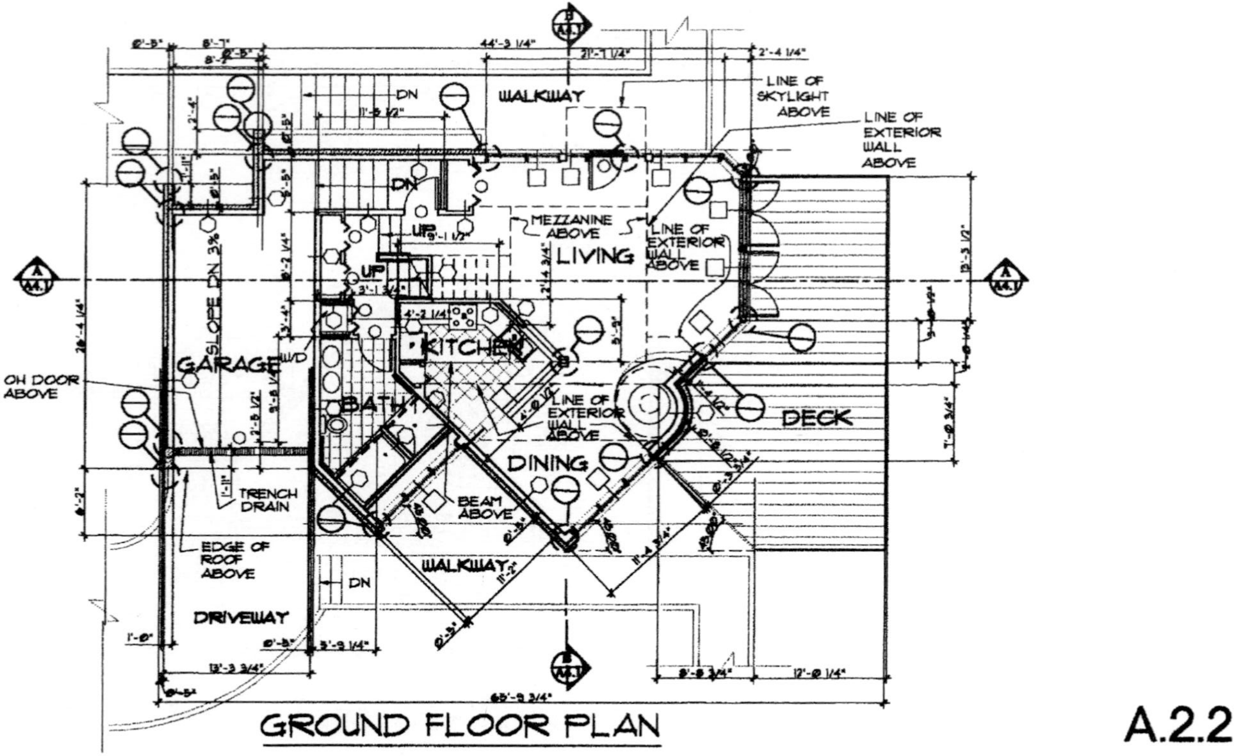

GROUND FLOOR PLAN

FIGURE 2.26 Typical ground floor plan format for an intermediate project between small/simple and small/complex.

2.36

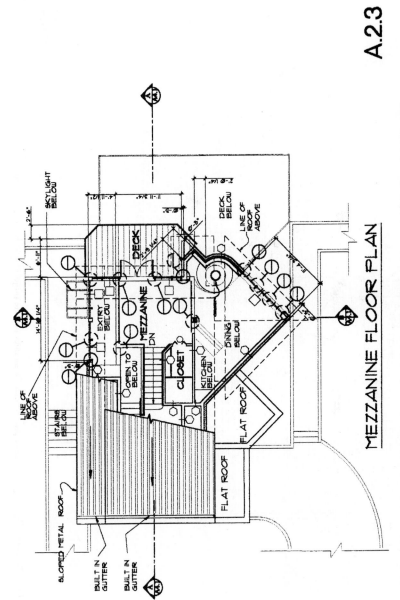

A.2.3

MEZZANINE FLOOR PLAN

FIGURE 2.27 Typical upper floor plan format for an intermediate project between small/simple and small/complex.

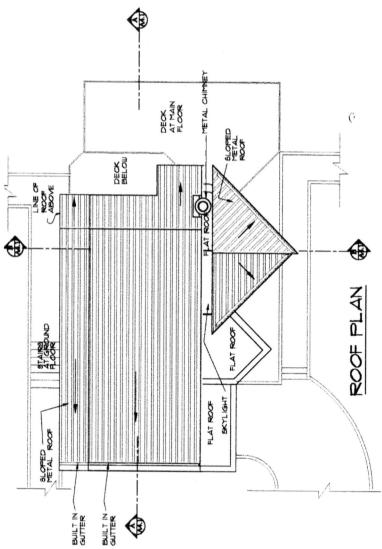

FIGURE 2.28 Typical roof plan format for an intermediate project between small/simple and small/complex.

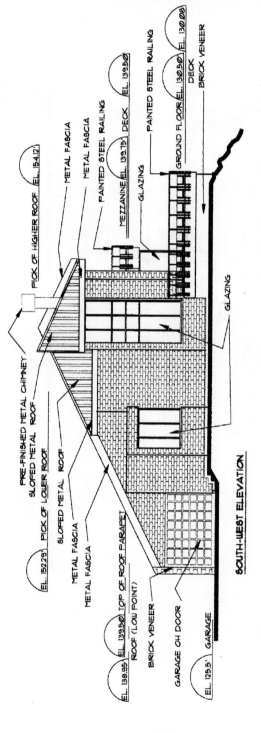

PART OF A.3.1

FIGURE 2.29 Typical elevation format for an intermediate project between small/simple and small/complex.

2.39

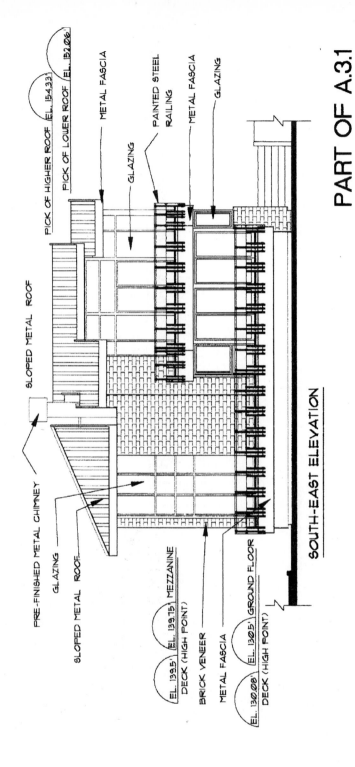

PART OF A.3.1

PICK OF HIGHER ROOF EL. 154.33'
PICK OF LOWER ROOF EL. 152.06'

METAL FASCIA

GLAZING

PAINTED STEEL
RAILING

METAL FASCIA

GLAZING

SLOPED METAL ROOF

PRE-FINISHED METAL CHIMNEY

GLAZING

SLOPED METAL ROOF

EL. 139.5' EL. 139.75' MEZZANINE
DECK (HIGH POINT)

BRICK VENEER

METAL FASCIA

EL. 130.05' GROUND FLOOR
EL. 130.08 DECK (HIGH POINT)

SOUTH-EAST ELEVATION

FIGURE 2.30 Typical elevation format for an intermediate project between small/simple and small/complex.

2.40

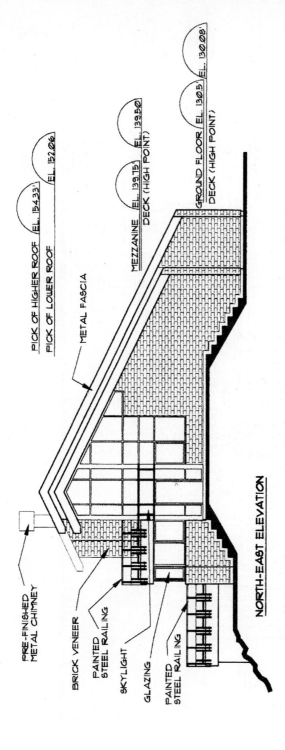

PART OF A.3.2

FIGURE 2.31 Typical elevation format for an intermediate project between small/simple and small/complex.

PRE-FINISHED
METAL CHIMNEY

BRICK VENEER

PAINTED
STEEL RAILING

SKYLIGHT

GLAZING

PAINTED
STEEL RAILING

NORTH-EAST ELEVATION

PICK OF HIGHER ROOF EL. 154.33'

PICK OF LOWER ROOF EL. 152.06'

METAL FASCIA

MEZZANINE EL. 139.75' EL. 139.50
DECK (HIGH POINT)

GROUND FLOOR EL. 130.5' EL. 130.08'
DECK (HIGH POINT)

2.41

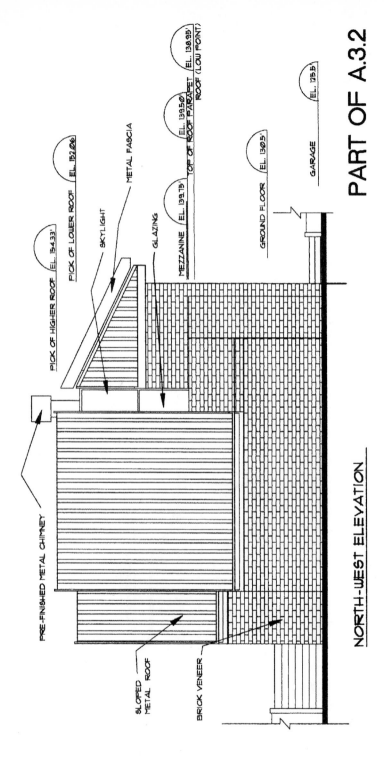

PICK OF HIGHER ROOF (EL. 154.33')

PICK OF LOWER ROOF (EL. 152.06')

METAL FASCIA

SKYLIGHT

GLAZING

MEZZANINE (EL. 139.75')

TOP OF ROOF PARAPET (EL. 139.50)

ROOF (LOW POINT) (EL. 138.95')

GROUND FLOOR (EL. 130.5')

GARAGE (EL. 125.5')

PRE-FINISHED METAL CHIMNEY

SLOPED METAL ROOF

BRICK VENEER

NORTH-WEST ELEVATION

FIGURE 2.32 Typical elevation format for an intermediate project between small/simple and small/complex.

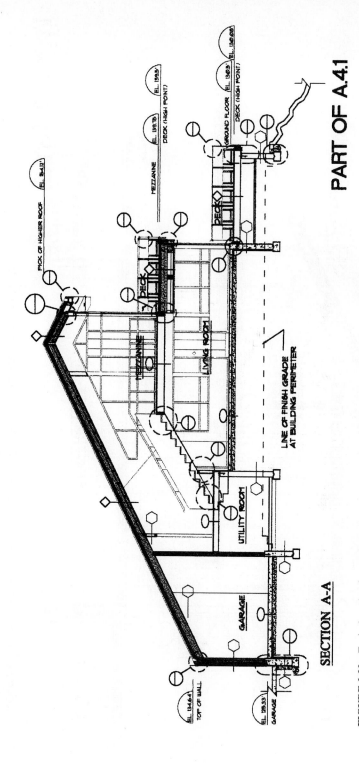

FIGURE 2.33 Typical section format for an intermediate project between small/simple and small/complex.

2.43

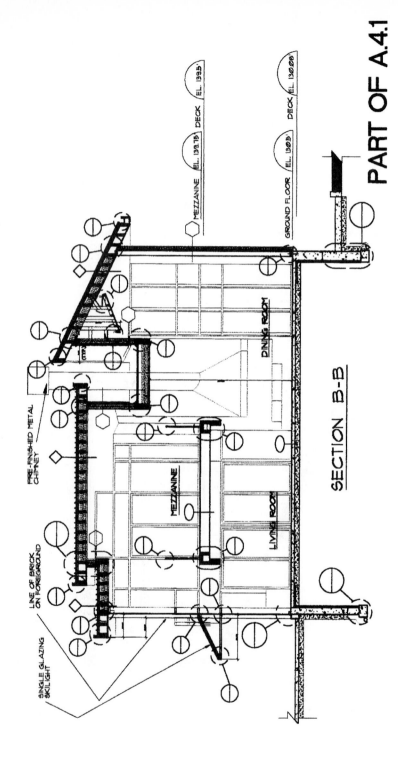

FIGURE 2.34 Typical section format for an intermediate project between small/simple and small/complex.

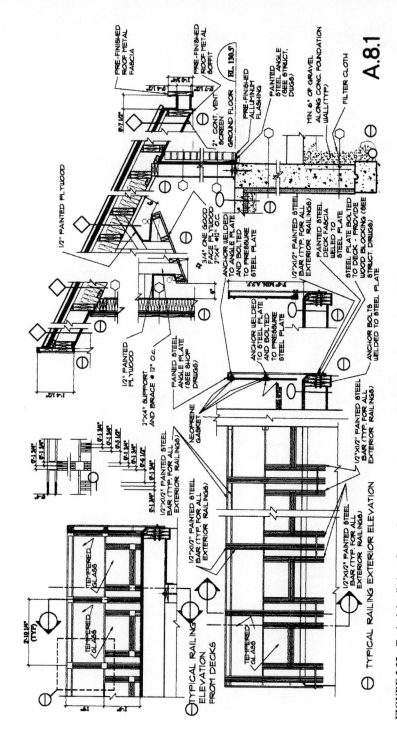

PRE-FINISHED ROOF METAL FASCIA

PRE-FINISHED ROOF METAL SOFFIT

2" CONT. VENT SCREEN

EL. 130.5

PRE-FINISHED ALUMINUM FLASHING

GROUND FLOOR

PAINTED STEEL ANGLE (SEE STRUCT. DWGS)

MIN. 6" OF GRAVEL ALONG CONC. FOUNDATION WALL (TYP)

FILTER CLOTH

A.8.1

1/2" PAINTED PLYWOOD

3/4" ONE GOOD FACE PLATE PLYWOOD 2"X4" @12" O.C.

1/2" PAINTED PLYWOOD

2"X4" SUPPORT AND BRACE @ 12" O.C.

PAINED STEEL ANGLE PLATE (SEE SHOP DWGS)

ANCHOR WELDED TO ANGLE PLATE AND BOLTED TO PRESSURE STEEL PLATE

ANCHOR WELDED TO STEEL PLATE AND BOLTED TO PRESSURE STEEL PLATE

1/2"X1/2" PAINTED STEEL BAR (TYP. FOR ALL EXTERIOR RAILINGS)

PAINTED STEEL DECK FASCIA WELDED TO STEEL PLATE

STEEL PLATE BOLTED TO DECK - PROVIDE WOOD BLOCKING (SEE STRUCT. DWGS)

ANCHOR BOLTS WELDED TO STEEL PLATE

NEOPRENE GASKET

1/2"X1/2" PAINTED STEEL BAR (TYP. FOR ALL EXTERIOR RAILINGS)

1/2"X1/2" PAINTED STEEL BAR (TYP. FOR ALL EXTERIOR RAILINGS)

TYPICAL RAILING EXTERIOR ELEVATION

1/2"X1/2" PAINTED STEEL BAR (TYP. FOR ALL EXTERIOR RAILINGS)

1/2"X1/2" PAINTED STEEL BAR (TYP. FOR ALL EXTERIOR RAILINGS)

TEMPERED GLASS

TYPICAL RAILING ELEVATION FROM DECKS

TEMPERED GLASS

TEMPERED GLASS

FIGURE 2.35 Typical detail sheet format for an intermediate project between small/simple and small/complex.

2.45

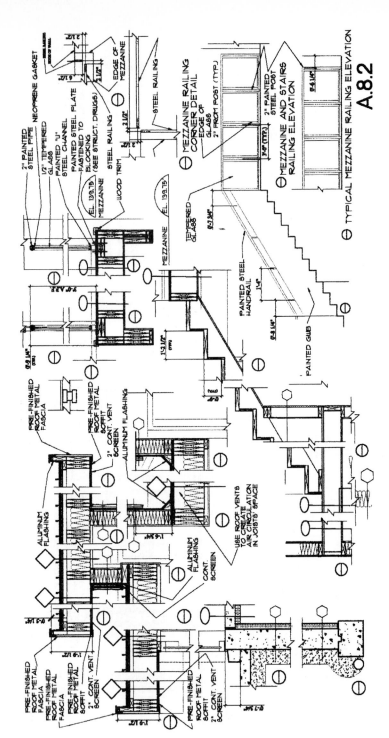

FIGURE 2.36 Typical detail sheet format for an intermediate project between small/simple and small/complex.

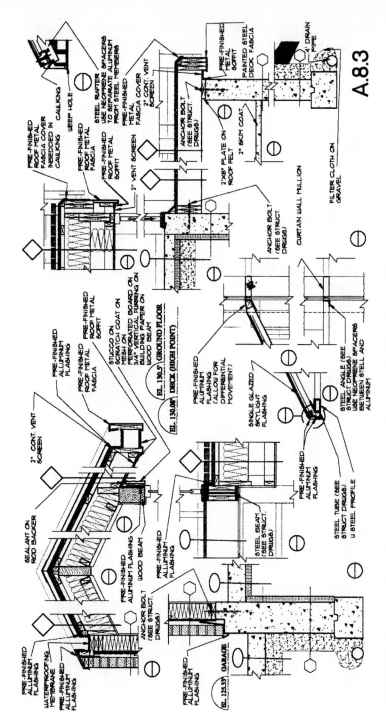

FIGURE 2.37 Typical detail sheet format for an intermediate project between small/simple and small/complex.

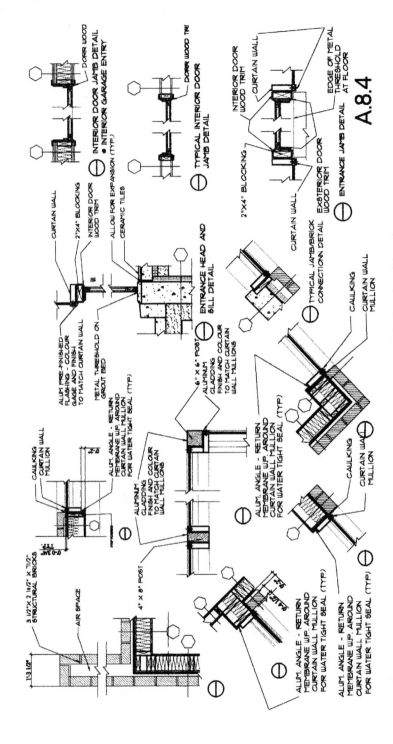

FIGURE 2.38 Typical detail sheet format for an intermediate project between small/simple and small/complex.

2.48

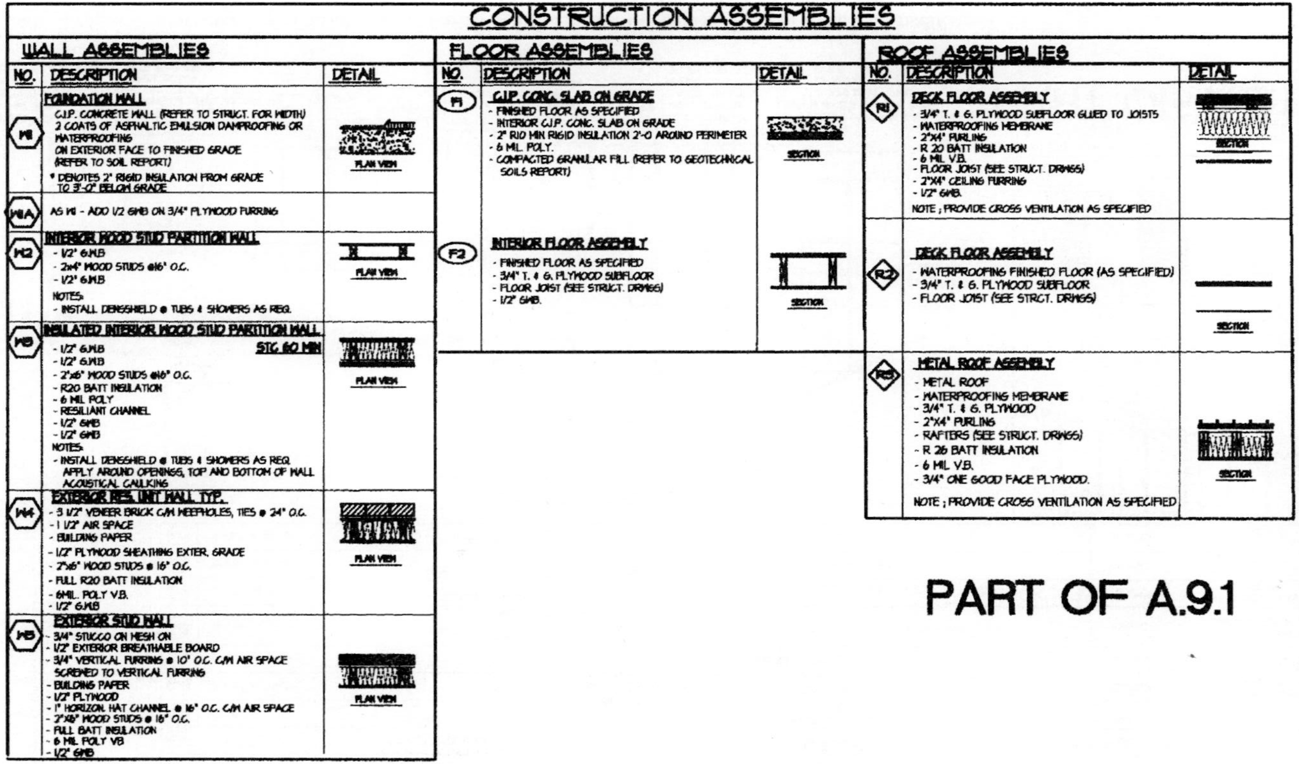

CONSTRUCTION ASSEMBLIES

WALL ASSEMBLIES

NO.	DESCRIPTION	DETAIL
W1	**FOUNDATION WALL** - C.I.P. CONCRETE WALL (REFER TO STRUCT. FOR WIDTH) - 2 COATS OF ASPHALTIC EMULSION DAMPROOFING OR WATERPROOFING - ON EXTERIOR FACE TO FINISHED GRADE - REFER TO SOIL REPORT * DENOTES 2" RIGID INSULATION FROM GRADE TO 3'-0" BELOW GRADE	PLAN VIEW
W1A	ADD 1/2 GWB ON 3/4" PLYWOOD FURRING	PLAN VIEW
W2	**INTERIOR WOOD STUD PARTITION WALL** - 1/2 GWB - 2x4 WOOD STUDS @16" O.C. - 1/2 GWB NOTE: - INSTALL DENSSHIELD @ TUBS & SHOWERS AS REQ.	PLAN VIEW
W3	**INSULATED INTERIOR WOOD STUD PARTITION WALL** **STC 50 MIN** - 1/2 GWB - 1/2 GWB - 2"x6" WOOD STUDS @16" O.C. - R20 BATT INSULATION - 6 MIL POLY - RESILIENT CHANNEL - 1/2 GWB - 1/2 GWB NOTES: - INSTALL DENSSHIELD @ TUBS & SHOWERS AS REQ - INSTALL VAPOUR BARRIER APPLY AROUND OPENINGS, TOP AND BOTTOM OF WALL - ACOUSTICAL CAULKING	PLAN VIEW
W4	**EXTERIOR BRICK VEN. WALL TYP.** - 3 1/2" VENEER BRICK C/W WEEPHOLES, TIES @ 24" O.C. - 1/2" AIR SPACE - BUILDING PAPER - 1/2" PLYWOOD SHEATHING EXTER. GRADE - 2"x6" WOOD STUDS @ 16" O.C. - FILL R20 BATT INSULATION - 6 MIL POLY V.B. - 1/2 GWB	PLAN VIEW
W5	**EXTERIOR STUD WALL** - 3/4" STUCCO ON MESH ON - 1/2" EXTERIOR BREATHABLE BOARD - 3/4" VERTICAL FURRING @ 10" O.C. C/W AIR SPACE - SCREWED TO VERTICAL FURRING - BUILDING PAPER - 1/2" PLYWOOD - 1" HORIZON. HAT CHANNEL @ 16" O.C. C/W AIR SPACE - 2"x6" WOOD STUDS @ 16" O.C. - FILL BATT INSULATION - 6 MIL POLY VB - 1/2 GWB	PLAN VIEW

FLOOR ASSEMBLIES

NO.	DESCRIPTION	DETAIL
F1	**C.I.P. CONC. SLAB ON GRADE** - FINISHED FLOOR AS SPECIFIED - INTERIOR C.I.P. CONC. SLAB ON GRADE - 2" RIGID INSULATION 2'-0 AROUND PERIMETER - 6 MIL POLY. - COMPACTED GRANULAR FILL (REFER TO GEOTECHNICAL SOILS REPORT)	SECTION
F2	**INTERIOR FLOOR ASSEMBLY** - FINISHED FLOOR AS SPECIFIED - 3/4" T. & G. PLYWOOD SUBFLOOR - FLOOR JOIST (SEE STRUCT. DRWGS) - 1/2 GWB	SECTION

ROOF ASSEMBLIES

NO.	DESCRIPTION	DETAIL
R1	**DECK FLOOR ASSEMBLY** - 3/4" T. & G. PLYWOOD SUBFLOOR GLUED TO JOISTS - WATERPROOFING MEMBRANE - 3/4" FURRING - R 20 BATT INSULATION - 6 MIL V.B. - FLOOR JOIST (SEE STRUCT. DRWGS) - 2"x4" CEILING FURRING - 1/2 GWB. NOTE: PROVIDE CROSS VENTILATION AS SPECIFIED	SECTION
R2	**DECK FLOOR ASSEMBLY** - WATERPROOFING FINISHED FLOOR (AS SPECIFIED) - 3/4" T. & G. PLYWOOD SUBFLOOR - FLOOR JOIST (SEE STRUCT. DRWGS)	SECTION
R3	**METAL ROOF ASSEMBLY** - METAL ROOF - WATERPROOFING MEMBRANE - 3/4" T. & G. PLYWOOD - 2"x4" PURLINS - RAFTERS (SEE STRUCT. DRWGS) - R 28 BATT INSULATION - 6 MIL V.B. - 3/4" ONE GOOD FACE PLYWOOD. NOTE : PROVIDE CROSS VENTILATION AS SPECIFIED	SECTION

PART OF A.9.1

FIGURE 2.39 Typical wall type schedule format for an intermediate project between small/simple and small/complex.

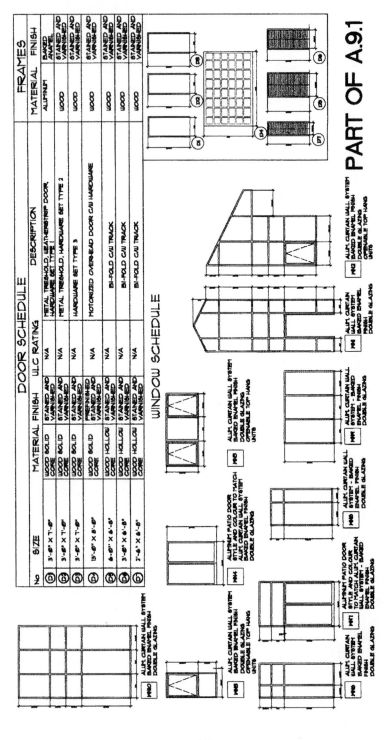

FIGURE 2.40 Typical window and door schedule format for an intermediate project between small/simple and small/complex.

2.50

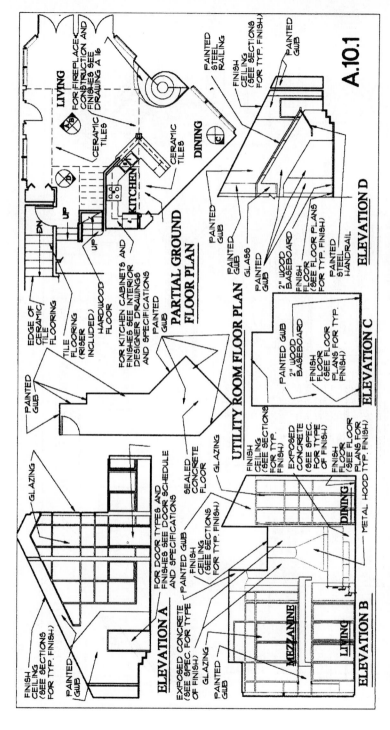

FIGURE 2.41 Typical interior elevation format for an intermediate project between small/simple and small/complex.

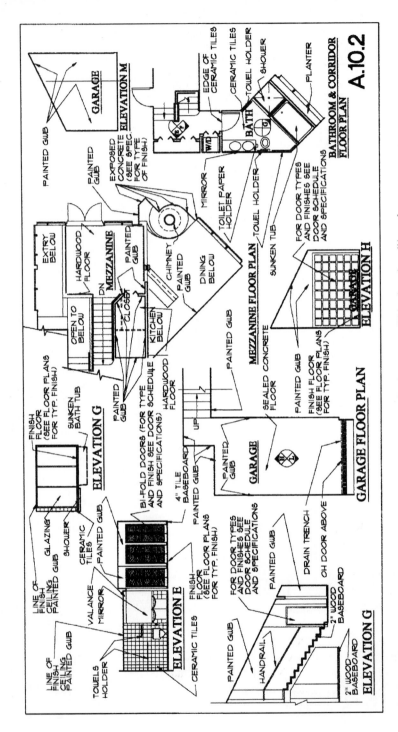

FIGURE 2.42 Typical interior elevation format for an intermediate project between small/simple and small/complex.

CHAPTER 3
DEFINITION OF SCOPE

The training of architects as generalists allows them to function as coordinators and problem solvers. This multi-faceted training is applied daily in many domains. The involvement of the architect in a project may be very broad or it may be limited to particular tasks. It may involve direct participation in every aspect of a project (i.e., from the very initial programming, site search, and financial analysis to the project closing.) On the other hand the architect may only produce the initial sketches, which will be further developed by another professional. That is why it is very important to define the scope of work right at the initial stage of a project. It is clear that the beginning of the relationship with the client is one of the most important elements in developing the scope of work. The fundamental tools for clarifying what is expected from an architect at the very beginning of a project are:

1. The ability to *listen* increases objectivity and minimizes assumptions.

2. A general knowledge of the characteristics of a particular type of project. This allows the architect to understand the general requirements and to ask the right questions.

3. A knowledge of the client's business operation. In the context of establishing the scope of work, this type of information is acquired not so much in order to impress or to conduct a financial check, as to understand what is expected from the professional. it allows the professional to become familiar with the specifics of the client's operation and consider their implications on the project. On the other hand, if a client has already some expertise relevant to the project, the architect will probably not include the work related to such activity in the architect's scope of work. The client's financial status might also affect the scope of work and, therefore, the fee at some level.

4. Consistency in continuously clarifying every aspect of the relationship and of the project. It is very important to avoid making assumptions. At the risk of stating the obvious, it is better to ask one more question than to draw the wrong conclusion. Misunderstandings often ruin a good relationship that could otherwise have been very successful.

Before meeting or finalizing the business relationship with a client, an architect should take the time to research similar projects as well as to investigate the client's modus operandi, understand his or her values, and clarify ultimate goals. In some cases, the architect's clear understanding of the project and the expertise involved might indicate to the client that considerably less might be required than what she or he believed to be the case at the beginning of the project.

DEFINING A PROGRAM

For the above reasons, it is apparent that the scope of work has a broad spectrum. Even before starting the design the architect could be engaged for one or more of the following tasks: feasibility studies, site analysis and selection, functional programs, master plans, re-zoning, arranging for proposal calls, building surveys, audits and measured drawings, financial and business plans, historical evaluation and/or due diligence reports. All of these tasks can be characterized as pre-design stage. This is only an instrumental definition, since as part of a unified process, the preliminary analysis is already part of the design.

At the foundation of the development of each item listed lies the definition of a program. The program can be considered as a series of activities that identify both the overall and the detail objectives of a project, in a form that can be smoothly translated into a design (see Figure 3.1). In order to accomplish this task, through subsequent stages which become more and more detailed, the program is developed using conceptual tools as objective as possible in their approach.

Usually a program includes the following information: **a.** description of the project and its context; **b.** statement of the goals and objectives of the program; **c.** general description of the methodology used to reach the findings and the historic data; **d.** list of requirements and characteristics, which includes: space requirements for each activity and description of activities, amenities, parking, circulation and orientation, regulatory requirements, community goals and concerns, ecological and environmental issues; **e.** relationship among the functions and/or operational diagrams; **f.** background information; **g.** representation of spaces through diagrams; **h.** general scheduling of the project documentation and completion date; **i.** budget; **j.** construction project delivery method.

Depending on the type, size and complexity of the project, one or more of the items listed might not be relevant for inclusion in the program. Conversely, in specialized projects some programs are very specific. They may include information like prototype layouts, typical specifications, special equipment, requirements for systems, and furniture schedules.

PROGRAM CONCEPTUAL STAGES

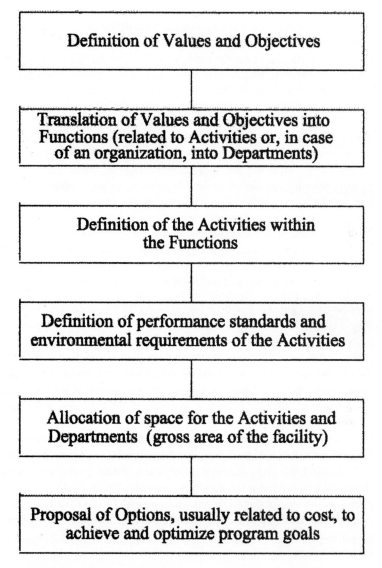

FIGURE 3.1 Program conceptual stages.

The tasks related to the approval process and by-laws will require an especially attentive review with the authorities to establish the process and a comprehensive list of: **a.** zoning requirements; **b.** applicable codes; **c.** urban guidelines; **d.** design guidelines; **e.** approval process; **f.** authorities and departments to be involved in the approval process.

At the core of the issues are the fundamental values that affect the concept of the project. The extent to which these values have to be analyzed depends on the scale of the project and on its function. For example, urban-scale interventions and institutional complexes are affected more directly by social values than single buildings and private developments. (See Figure 3.2.)

The magnitude of the project and the type of variables involved affect the amount of attention that must be given to programs describing larger issues than those immediately affecting the project. For example, these issues might be related to economics, education or health policies. In these cases, the specific program for the project must be integrated with the consideration of long and medium range programs involving the broader issues. (See Figure 3.3.)

The steps indicated in Figure 3.1 can be transmitted through a process represented by a grid where aspects of the system to be analyzed are combined with the stages of the analysis (Figure 3.4). To achieve a thorough understanding of the nature of these issues, several tools and techniques can be employed:

1. User participation. There are various reasons for this approach: **a.** the insight gained from/through of the daily involvement is very valuable to assess issues, relationships, systems and deficiencies; **b.** user involvement will increase the sense of belonging and the user satisfaction at the end of the process; **c.** participation in the design process will improve the efficiency in the use of the facilities; **d.** greater acceptance of compromises is experienced because the users will be aware of the trade-offs and the reason for the adopted solutions.

2. Definition of a rational process. In order to achieve it: **a.** the premises must be correct; **b.** the attitude of the consultant must be as objective as possible; **c.** the method, the process, and the evaluation system used to collect facts should be designed as scientifically as possible. This means that, given the premises, the results should be reached through objective methods and the process used to arrive at these conclusions can be repeated for verification.

3. Establishment of an orderly system using a sequential method characterized by increasing definition of the aspects and issues. This facilitates: **a.** focusing on the objectives. This goal is achieved through a linear process developed at each stage by considering general solutions for broader issues. The linear process pinpoints these solutions and tailors them to the particular aspects of each issue; **b.** avoiding distraction by premature details not important for the evaluation at a particular stage.

4. Use of a clear communication system, written and graphic. This system should be articulated in order to communicate at different levels and to be

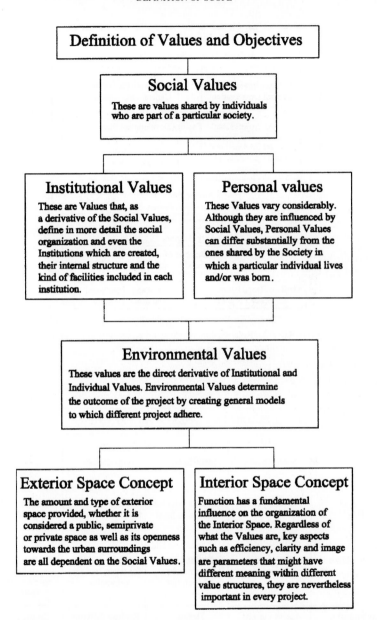

FIGURE 3.2   Fundamental values affecting the concept of the project.

able to clarify concepts for a broader spectrum of users. The positive
effects of this principle are: **a.** a more effective and complete feedback
from the users; **b.** clear results that better convey the message to designer
and guarantee the continuity between program and further development of
the project.

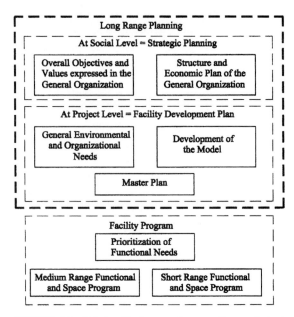

FIGURE 3.3 Relationship between long, medium and short range planning.

TYPICAL STAGES AND TASKS OF PROGRAMMING				
	Investigation Stage	Identification Stage	Exploration Stage	Resolution Stage
Level of Use	Past and present	Generate optimum utilization level	Explore options to create optimum utilization level	Identify best option
Type of Use	List present Uses	Define basic requirements of operation	Explore options for organizational principles	Define most appropriate operational system
Relationship between Uses	Assess current relationship	Define performance standards	Explore different relationship and systems	Define best organizational system
Use of	List existing Spaces	Identify Environmental requirements	Explore alternate space organization	Identify best use of space

FIGURE 3.4 Typical stages and tasks of programming.

The following activities help in achieving these goals: **a.** visit similar facilities; **b.** interview users; **c.** identify fundamental parameters and define a rating system to classify existing facilities and or similar facilities; **d.** review accredited literature related to the issues at hand; **e.** design questionnaires, matrixes, graphic materials to: collect data, communicate objectives, analyze results, and communicate results.

There are various methods through which a program can be developed. The following three, or combinations of them, are often used: **a.** *Traditional Planning Process:* with this method there is a very limited input on the part of the staff. The administrative services maintain the liaison between the consultants and the staff. The design is provided either by the consultants or by the facility authorities; **b.** *Joint Planning Process:* this method is based on the collaboration between the members of the joint planning group, constituted by consultants and representatives of the staff. The most important factor is that the delegates of the various departments, elected by their peers, have total control of the process. They have final approval on any decision. The consultants are used as advisors to the delegates. The delegates produce layouts with the assistance of the consultants; **c.** *Directed Planning Process:* in this case interviews are conducted by specialists (consultants) and the consultants produce layouts which are reviewed by the managers for approval and sign-off.

The range of the tasks in a program can be very diversified. In order to be properly developed, some subjects might need the expertise of specialists (consultants.) This is why, once the general scope of work is identified (i.e., master planning, historical review, etc.), the next step for the architect is to identify the type of consultants required to complete the work.

CRITICAL APPROACH TO PROGRAMMING

A program can be viewed either as a specific process that reinforces the general current concept of a systemic prototype or as a critical stance that questions the status quo. The latter approach looks critically at the very essence of a traditional solution to a particular issue, the organization of a particular system, or even the system itself. If a critical approach is adopted, the analysis broadens to consider all the elements involved in creating a certain concept. In the case of a school, for example, a critical program might review the very essence of the meaning of culture and how spiritual and mental development should be encouraged. This might result in a system that puts more emphasis on the development of the capacity to integrate information rather than the memorizing of facts. In turn, the physical characteristics of an environment, which would support such a philosophy, are those that would promote diversified experiences as well as helping to integrate them. It is an environment that is conducive to continuity instead of separation and specialization. It is an environment that is flexible in responding to change in needs and situations. As described in Figure 3.5, the components needed to generate a complete system and which should be considered in a critical approach are:

1. *Supporting component* (i.e., Ideology = Models = Industries or Institutions = Ideological Patterns)

2. *Prototypical component* (Models = Facilities = Physical Patterns)

3. *Responsive component* (Models = Users = Psychological and Behavioral Patterns)

A critical approach is stimulated by observations that could originate in personal interests resulting in specific studies or observations made during the creation of a program.

Once dysfunctional characteristics are identified, the following observations facilitate the rationalization of the characteristics of the various components and the definition of a program for an alternate system: **a.** the clues to the organization of the system are given by the patterns that are created in it and by it. These patterns and their interaction should be identified and very clearly graphically represented; **b.** the initial observations that triggered the critical approach might be only the tip of the iceberg. Once the analysis described in item **a** is advanced, further investigation on the effects of the system on the responsive component should be conducted; **c.** in order to create an alternate to a system, new goals and values have to be identified. These are based on the findings of the activities described in items **a** and **b**; **d.** in any task of a programmatic process there is the necessity of a point of reference that would allow the professional to relate findings or proposals to solutions that optimally express goals and values. A new prototypical component, therefore, should be created; **e.** in order to propose a viable change that would allow the new value and goals to be applied, a realistic approach should be constantly maintained. It is necessary, therefore, to identify which area and aspects of the present system can be immediately modified and where modifications should occur in a more leisurely fashion.

GRAPHIC ANALYTICAL REPRESENTATION

A *graphic analytical representation* is a translation into a graphic system of concepts, parameters or findings that are part of an analysis conducted on a particular subject(s) or object(s). It is very effective especially where multiple factors have to be considered simultaneously. This is one of the major differences between graphic language and spoken language. The latter tends to follow a linear sequential pattern. Other advantages of the use of a graphic medium are: **a.** the possibility of observing the image and commenting upon it at the same time; **b.** because of the immediate communication and the simultaneous consideration of multiple levels of the message, a graphic image facilitates the discovery of alternate solutions; **c.** the capability of representing abstract concepts. (See Figures 3.6 and 3.7.)

These aspects can be very helpful if particular rules are followed. Some graphic systems, because of their flexibility, are characterized by an intrinsic ambiguity, especially if the subject that they deal with is conceptual. The following points sug-

BASIC COMPONENTS IN AN ANALYTICAL PROGRAMMATIC PROCESS

Supporting Component

This category includes systems that, because of their characteristics, generate the need for the Prototype. Depending on the nature of the system under analysis, this component could be made of specific Industries that need certain type of infrastructure to operate. An accepted method can certainly be considered a Supportive Component that determines a particular sequence of events translated in a Prototype (i.e. Teaching Method that translate into Typical Schools or Typical Schools Components)

Prototypical Component

Once the needs of the Supporting Component are identified, its characteristics leads to the creation of the Prototype. The Supportive Component, in order to generate a Prototypical Component that is constituted by a Facility, must identify a Model that is in turn translated into Patterns. These Patterns are the cause of a certain behavioural response (psychological and physical) of the Responsive Component. The patterns are not the original reason of a status quo, but they are the clue that could lead to the reasons

Responsive Component

This Component is constituted by the individuals that access a certain Prototypical Component: the users. Depending on the goals of the Supportive Component, the effects on the Responsive Component could vary considerably. In the case of commercial sectors, for example, if the Supportive Component focuses only on profit, the consequences for the Responsive Component could potentially be negative at different levels (i.e physical and/or psychological)

FIGURE 3.5   Basic components in an analytical programmatic process.

ALTERNATE GROUPING OF DIFFERENT ELEMENTS

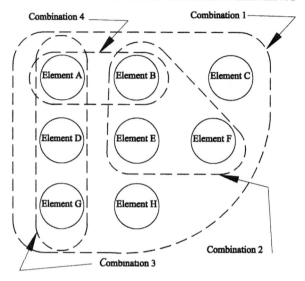

The combinations expressed in the diagram can be considered simultaneously. A characteristic which supports, reinforces and makes the analytical process more effective.

FIGURE 3.6   Alternate grouping of different elements.

VARIATIONS ON A BASIC LAYOUT

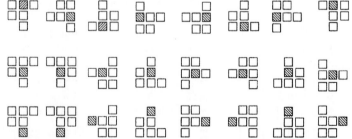

The elements and combinations shown use a vocabulary that can be associated with different concepts: from a plan, where each square represents a space, to relationships among tasks in a particular sequence. In this diagram only two variables are introduced: the position of the hatched square and the orientation of the overall system.

Because of the symbolic characteristics of the elements, the observer is able to concentrate on the variation of the variable proposed. Other aspects such as the shape of the space or the duration of certain activities, are of secondary importance at this point (unless these aspects are intended to be part of the meaning of the symbols.

FIGURE 3.7   Variations on a basic layout.

gest an interpretive framework, which tends to mitigate this ambiguity, thus improving comprehension of the message:

1. Verify if an individual who is not familiar with the concept can understand the meaning of the graphics without any explanation. If the message is not clear, modify the graphics by adding a layer of definitions (i.e., a legend for the symbols, a general explanation pointing to the graphic elements, a statement that summarizes the issues and the manner in which the graphics represents them, as shown in Figure 3.8).

2. In case of abstract concepts (like different types of relationships, hierarchical importance of activities), use symbols or connections between symbols that can be psychologically associated with that concept. Figure 3.9 shows some possible symbols.

3. In the case of concrete elements (i.e., a space) use generic symbols to identify the elements (i.e., circles, ellipses or squares).

4. Once a functional grammatical or interpretative system for the meaning of the symbols is established, it is important to be consistent and use it throughout the various representations.

Figures 3.10 through 3.13 show four very commonly employed graphic tools: **a.** matrix; **b.** bubble diagram; **c.** area diagram; **d.** network and flow charts.

There are various graphic tools that can be used to express concepts (like relationships), characteristics (like orientation), sequences (like activities) or systems (like organization of departments). Their characteristics make each of them more suitable to express particular concepts than others.

The following graphic material, schedules and diagrams are commonly used in programs and pre-design analysis: **a.** *Programmatic Elemental Summary Sheet*: this is a way to condense the information on each component. It can contain data on the present status and on the requirements and characteristics of the particular component. It should be specific, detailed and articulated. However it should be also designed to maintain the format typical of a summary (see Figure 3.14); **b.** *Statistical Diagrams*: historical data and projected trends allow prediction of future needs; **c.** *Interview Questionnaire*: this is a tool that facilitates in-depth acquisition of information about the system which is then analyzed through the experience of the users (see Figure 3.15); **d.** *Adjacency, Visual and Acoustical Privacy Matrix*: in any environment it is of fundamental importance to articulate the spaces in such way that communication, circulation and resources are optimized (see Figure 3.16); **e.** *Summary of Space Requirements and Alternates*: in order to understand the gross area of the building required by the system, it is necessary to assess the typical area required for each department and explore alternates. This is a matrix indicating on one hand the type of spaces and on the other the areas required and the optional variations; **f.** *Functional Performance Standards Diagram*: this diagram represents the ideal characteristics and articulation of the environment, which are the result of the requirements of the system.

The symbols shown on the diagram can acquire different meaning which are dependent on the context in which the symbols are placed and their correspondence with the concepts.

The circles, for example, can identify either an activity, a space or both. This ambiguity is very effective in delivering the message simultaneously at different level as long as it does not create confusion.

An arrow could indicate a traffic flow or could emphasize a sequence. The meaning of each symbol, therefore, must be very specific. One graphic tool used to assign clear meaning to symbols is the legend.

In creating a diagram of a system leading to the definition of an environment to accommodate that system, the following stages should be followed:
a) First the list of items should be determined
b) Second, the description of the requirements and of the characteristics of each item should be compiled
c) Third the relationships should be identified
d) The physical characteristics of the environment should be established.

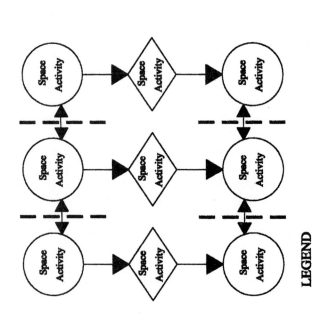

LEGEND

➤ Denotes Flow

– – – Denotes Security

◯ Space and/or Activity

FIGURE 3.8 Levels of definition of a graphic diagram.

3.12

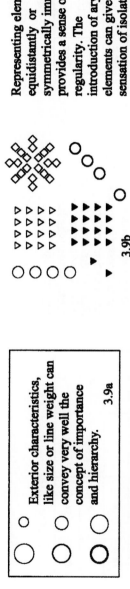

Exterior characteristics, like size or line weight can convey very well the concept of importance and hierarchy. 3.9a

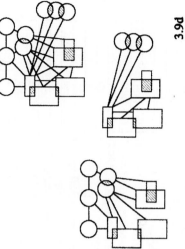

Representing elements equidistantly or symmetrically immediately provides a sense of regularity. The introduction of arythmic elements can give a sensation of isolation, a sense of importance, of time or of space.

3.9b

3.9d

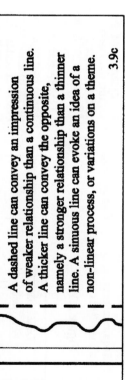

A dashed line can convey an impression of weaker relationship than a continuous line. A thicker line can convey the opposite, namely a stronger relationship than a thinner line. A sinuous line can evoke an idea of a non-linear process, or variations on a theme.

3.9c

The use of multiple characteristics of the elements or lines provides very sophisticated and effective graphic communication. However it is important not to load the graphics with overlapping concepts. If the graphics are too complex, they become counter-productive and instead of facilitating communication, might impede it. In this case, it is better to present the concepts in two different diagrams and then integrate them.

FIGURE 3.9   Relationship between symbols and psychological concepts.

3.13

Requirement

Figure 3.10b

Figure 3.10d

RELATIONSHIP MATRIX

The type of Matrix shown in Figure 3.10a is used to indicate a single list of items (i.e. type of spaces) related to requirements (i.e. level of lighting) or requirements between items (i.e. proximity). In Figure 3.10b a second type of matrix is represented. In this second case it is necessary to define the meaning of the third variable within the matrix by giving a "title" to the matrix (i.e. requirements for "Proximity of Space")

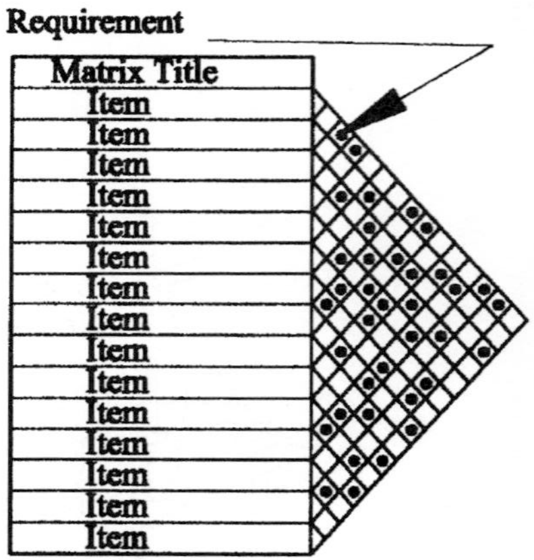

COMPARISON MATRIX

These two types of Matrixes are used either to illustrate a comparison between certain items by listing their characteristics (i.e. options in cars) or performance (i.e. speed acceleration) referring them to the Items (Figure 3.10c), or to represent rating among the Items Figure 3.10d

Requirement to be specify if the headings of the Matrix are both Items

Figure 3.10a

Figure 3.10c

FIGURE 3.10   Type of matrixes.

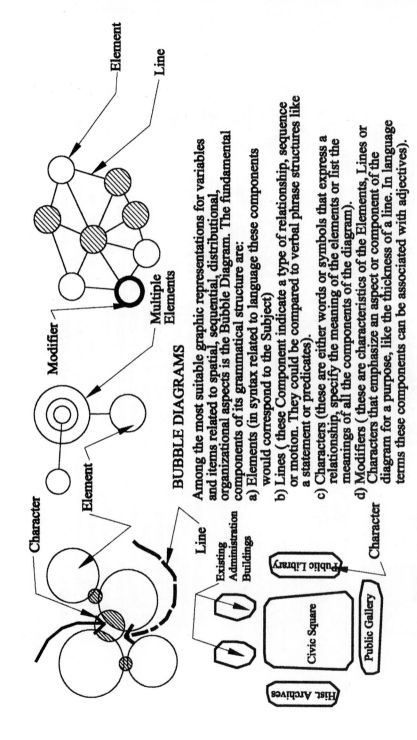

BUBBLE DIAGRAMS

Among the most suitable graphic representations for variables and items related to spatial, sequential, distributional, organizational aspects is the Bubble Diagram. The fundamental components of its grammatical structure are:

a) Elements (in syntax related to language these components would correspond to the Subject)

b) Lines (these Component indicate a type of relationship, sequence or motion. They could be compared to verbal phrase structures like a statement or predicates).

c) Characters (these are either words or symbols that express a relationship, specify the meaning of the elements or list the meanings of all the components of the diagram).

d) Modifiers (these are characteristics of the Elements, Lines or Characters that emphasize an aspect or component of the diagram for a purpose, like the thickness of a line. In language terms these components can be associated with adjectives).

FIGURE 3.11 Type of bubble diagrams.

TYPES OF AREA DIAGRAMS

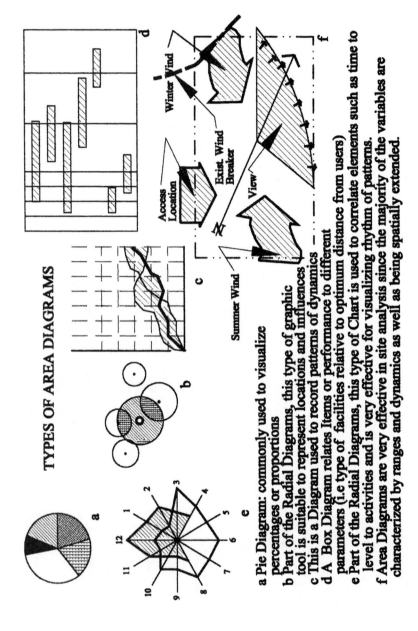

a Pie Diagram: commonly used to visualize
   percentages or proportions
b Part of the Radial Diagrams, this type of graphic
   tool is suitable to represent locations and influences
c This is a Diagram used to record patterns of dynamics
d A Box Diagram relates Items or performance to different
   parameters (i.e type of facilities relative to optimum distance from users)
e Part of the Radial Diagrams, this type of Chart is used to correlate elements such as time to
   level to activities and is very effective in site analysis since the majority of the variables are
   characterized by ranges and dynamics as well as being spatially extended.
f Area Diagrams are very effective in site analysis since the majority of the variables are
   characterized by ranges and dynamics as well as being spatially extended.

FIGURE 3.12   Types of area diagrams.

TYPES OF FLOW CHART DIAGRAMS

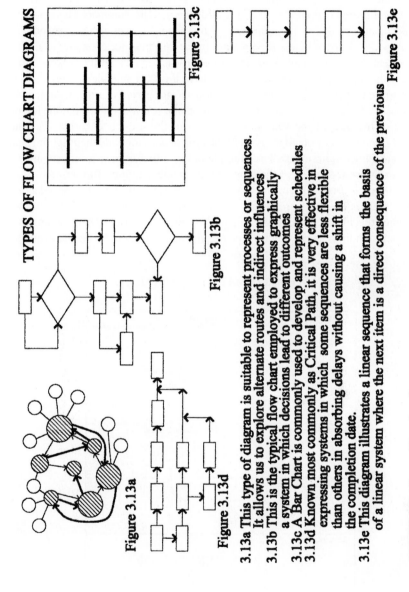

Figure 3.13a

Figure 3.13b

Figure 3.13c

Figure 3.13d

Figure 3.13e

3.13a This type of diagram is suitable to represent processes or sequences. It allows us to explore alternate routes and indirect influences

3.13b This is the typical flow chart employed to express graphically a system in which decisions lead to different outcomes

3.13c A Bar Chart is commonly used to develop and represent schedules

3.13d Known most commonly as Critical Path, it is very effective in expressing systems in which some sequences are less flexible than others in absorbing delays without causing a shift in the completion date.

3.13e This diagram illustrates a linear sequence that forms the basis of a linear system where the next item is a direct consequence of the previous

FIGURE 3.13   Types of flow chart diagrams.

3.17

It becomes the model for the future development of the project (see Figure 3.17); **g.** *Activity Summary Chart and Occupancy Analysis:* this chart and analysis can be expressed by a matrix. It summarizes various parameters which are of basic importance for design considerations (see Figure 3.18); **h.** *Orientation Matrix and Orientation Grid Diagram:* as result of the activity summary charts and of the occupancy analysis, the orientation of the various spaces can be defined (see Figure 3.19). A space that is used mainly in the morning, for example, would be best orientated east or south/east. In case of restriction or conflict of some kind, a space that is used daily should generally have the most suitable orientation versus a space that is used occasionally or for a shorter period of time. Establishing the space orientation is obviously not an automatic result derived from the hours, period of the day, of the year and frequency of the uses. It is based, also and indeed foremost, on a detail analysis of the type of activities and their lighting and environmental requirements. For example, a room that is used for art requires a north exposure regardless of the schedule. Dynamic activities, furthermore, have different exposure requirements than contemplative activities; **i.** *Site Selection Issues*: these issues can be represented in a matrix where one side lists the site and the other the ideal characteristics of the location like orientation, topography, view, surroundings, accessibility, type of suitable facilities to be ideally available in the area.

PROGRAMMATIC ELEMENTAL SUMMARY SHEET

Occupants	Environmental, Behavioral Psychological and Design Objectives
Type of Use	Authorities Requirements
Security Level	Materials and Finishes
Environmental Characteristics	Furnishings
Adjacencies	**SKETCH OR DIAGRAM OR PHOTO OF MODEL**
Special Requirements and Equipment	

FIGURE 3.14   Programmatic elemental summary sheet.

TYPICAL INFORMATION SHEET
FOR AN OFFICE PROGRAM

General information like Company, date (when the form was distributed and when it was returned), Name of the Department Head, Present Location, Building, Floor(s), Name of Person Interviewed, Title of the Person Interviewed, Telephone Number of the Person Interviewed (Information required)	
Description of the general function of the Department	Special activities that require particular environment
Indication if the Department is located in one place or is spread over more than one location Locations to be indicated	If a secretarial pool, private secretaries or a word processing centre is used.
Requirement of the department to be placed in one location or indication of which section can be accommodated on another floor or building	If a central reception area is appropriate for the system requirement
Requirements of proximity with other Departments or other Functions.	What type of common rooms are required within the Department (i.e. conference rooms, lunch room)
Type of records to be kept within the Department. Type of storage. Rate of record growth or annual transfer to a central location.	Important changes predicted in the organizational structure of the Department.
Present and predicted future configuration of the equipment	Any problem in the present general organization of the Department
Type of special equipment New purchased equipment	Number of people presently working in the Department. Type of ranking, category.

FIGURE 3.15 Typical information sheet for an office program.

ADJACENCY, VISUAL, ACOUSTICAL AND PRIVACY MATRIX

				1	2	3	4	5	10	11	12	13	14	21	22
▼ Continuous Contact ◆ Weekly Contact															
● Daily Contact ▽ Visual Contact Daily Contact ○ Privacy															
○	Room	1	(activity name)			◆					▼				
	Room	2	(activity name)				●						▼		●
	Room	3	(activity name)	◆				●		◆	◆		◆	●	
○	Room	4	(activity name)		●										
	Room	5	(activity name)			●				▽		●			
○	Room	10	(activity name)									◆			
	Room	11	(activity name)			◆		▽					◆		
	Room	12	(activity name)	▼		◆						●			
	Room	13	(activity name)					●	◆		●		▽		
	Room	14	(activity name)		▼	◆							▽		▽
○	Room	21	(activity name)			●				◆					
	Room	22	(activity name)		●								▽		

FIGURE 3.16   Adjacency, visual, acoustical and privacy matrix.

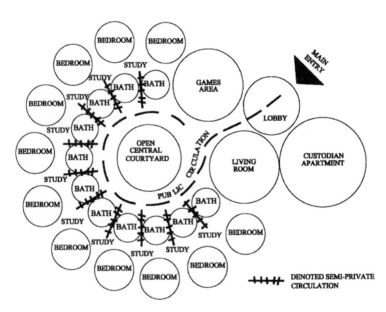

FIGURE 3.17   Functional performance diagram of a student dormitory.

ACTIVITY SUMMARY CHART AND OCCUPANCY ANALYSIS

DPT	ROOM OR TYPE OF SPACE	HOURS/DAY	DAY/WEEK	WEEK/MONTH	MONTH/YEAR	PUBLIC	SEMI/PRIVATE	PRIVATE	SHARED	100-120 SQ.FT.	120-200 SQ.FT.	200-300 SQ.FT.	300-500 SQ.FT.	500-1000 SQ.FT.	OVER 1000 SQ.FT.	REMARKS
DPT	ROOM OR TYPE OF SPACE	8	5	4	12		●						●			
	ROOM OR TYPE OF SPACE	8	5	4	12	●					●					
	ROOM OR TYPE OF SPACE	8	5	4	12			●				●				
	ROOM OR TYPE OF SPACE	3	5	4	12				●						●	FROM 8:00 A.M. TO 11:00 A.M.
	ROOM OR TYPE OF SPACE	8	7	3	12		●					●				
	ROOM OR TYPE OF SPACE	8	2	4	12		●	●				●	●			
	ROOM OR TYPE OF SPACE	5	3	4	12			●		●						FROM 8:00 A.M. TO 2:00 P.M.
DPT	ROOM OR TYPE OF SPACE	8	1	4	5	●									●	REMARKS
	ROOM OR TYPE OF SPACE	4	5	4	12		●							●		FROM 12:00 P.M. TO 4:00 P.M.
	ROOM OR TYPE OF SPACE	7	3	4	3		●						●			FROM 9:00 P.M. TO 4:00 P.M.
	ROOM OR TYPE OF SPACE	3	5	1	12		●					●	●			FROM 1:00 P.M. TO 4:00 P.M.
	ROOM OR TYPE OF SPACE	8	7	3	12			●				●				
	ROOM OR TYPE OF SPACE	8	2	4	7				●					●		
	ROOM OR TYPE OF SPACE	5	3	4	12	●							●			FROM 11:00 A.M. TO 4:00 P.M.

FIGURE 3.18 Activity summary chart and occupancy analysis.

		MORNING	AFTERNOON	EVENING	DAILY	BIWEEKLY	WEEKLY
DEPARTMENT	ROOM OR TYPE OF SPACE				●		
	ROOM OR TYPE OF SPACE		●	●		●	
	ROOM OR TYPE OF SPACE	●	●	●	●		
	ROOM OR TYPE OF SPACE	●	●		●		●
	ROOM OR TYPE OF SPACE	●		●			●
	ROOM OR TYPE OF SPACE	●	●	●			●
	ROOM OR TYPE OF SPACE	●			●		
DEPARTMENT	ROOM OR TYPE OF SPACE		●	●	●		
	ROOM OR TYPE OF SPACE	●	●			●	
	ROOM OR TYPE OF SPACE	●	●	●	●		
	ROOM OR TYPE OF SPACE			●		●	
	ROOM OR TYPE OF SPACE		●	●		●	
	ROOM OR TYPE OF SPACE	●	●	●		●	
	ROOM OR TYPE OF SPACE	●	●		●		
DEPARTMENT	ROOM OR TYPE OF SPACE		●	●		●	
	ROOM OR TYPE OF SPACE	●				●	
	ROOM OR TYPE OF SPACE	●	●				●
	ROOM OR TYPE OF SPACE	●	●	●	●		
	ROOM OR TYPE OF SPACE	●	●	●	●		
	ROOM OR TYPE OF SPACE	●	●			●	

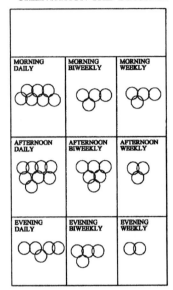

ORIENTATION MATRIX AND ORIENTATION GRID DIAGRAM

FIGURE 3.19 Orientation matrix and orientation diagram.

SCHEMATIC DESIGN

After the definition of a project program and the pre-design tasks that have been considered as part of the scope of work, the next phase of a project is the schematic design. This is the phase in which the conclusions and requirements expressed in the program are transformed into physical characteristics and alternate solutions are tested. This is also the stage in which the design project team is assembled or confirmed. If the team of consultants has been engaged only for the programmatic stage, the architect, in conjunction with the client, issues proposal calls for consultants' professional services extending to the total project scope of work. The following is a list of documents to be issued and information to be requested from the consultants (usually three per discipline):

1. From the architect to the consultants: **a.** a general description of the project; **b.** a copy of the program; **c.** general scope of work related to the stages of the project; **d.** structure of the fee related to the stages of the design and construction; **e.** relevant information and documentation like survey, soil report, environmental issues if they are not included in the program; **f.** list of information to be included in the fee proposal (see the following list).

2. From the consultants to the architect: **a.** description of the firm, its general philosophy, its qualifications and the equipment used or constantly avail-

able to the firm; **b.** experience in similar projects; **c.** list of personnel to be assigned to the project, their role and qualifications; **d.** fee structured in accordance with the instructions received from the architect; **e.** general conditions; **f.** hourly rates; **g.** proof of liability insurance and type of policy.

The involvement of the appropriate consultants and their early assessment of the solutions explored is recommended because their input can point out aspects that add to the value of the overall analysis and increase the financial and technical efficiency of the project. At this stage the consultants' input which can be useful to the architect are: **a.** general considerations on the benefits of using one building system versus another; **b.** the advantages from the building systems standpoint of a particular orientation and positioning of the building; **c.** list of alternate technologies and their physical characteristics; **d.** physical parameters that affect efficiency between net and gross areas, overall height, floor to floor as well as floor to ceiling required dimensions; **e.** site equipment, required distances from property lines and preferred locations; **f.** impact of off-site equipment or installations; **g.** servitudes to be created to implement a certain solution (i.e., R.O.W.); **h.** impact on surroundings and environment.

It is not unusual for a client to require a preliminary assessment of different sites before the most appropriate parcel of land or a building is purchased. In this case, it is reasonable to include the site analysis and the schematic design in the programmatic scope of work as part of the feasibility study. (In many projects, the feasibility study is a stage that is considered separate from the program; in others, this scope of work is carried out by the programmer). On the other hand, if the site has already been acquired, its characteristics can become part of the various analyses carried out during the design stage. The restrictions determined by the geometrical configuration, the topography, geology, surroundings, orientation and accessibility can therefore be considered as well as the limitations imposed by zoning by-laws or building code requirements. In this situation, the methodology for the site analysis illustrated in the following pages belongs in this section.

SITE ANALYSIS

Depending on the type and size of the project, the objectives of the program and the characteristics of the surrounding environment, not all the parameters included in the analysis shown in Figures 3.20, 3.21, 3.22, 3.23 are applicable for the same project. For commercial projects, for example, aspects that might affect the generated income such as accessibility, exposure, view, geometric characteristics and ratio between the dimensions, zoning restrictions and by-law requirements, environmental aspects and symbolic characteristics are among the most important factors to be considered. Factors that affect the cost of construction such as geology, topography, surrounding buildings, accessibility during construction, existing structures to be demolished, easements and rights-of-way are very important in every type of project. Cultural aspects come into play especially when structures built for common use and the social implications are considered. The variables, therefore, have been broken down into categories to assist in choosing the most appropriate one or ones for a particular project program.

SCHEMATIC DRAWINGS

The developing of a program is traditionally considered a non-standard service. Whether or not the architect is involved in its development, the client is responsible for providing the following information, without which the schematic design stage of a project cannot start: **a.** list of activities, their scheduling, space requirements and relationships; **b.** requirements for flexibility and expansion; **c.** list of special equipment, systems to be included, their characteristics and requirements; **d.** construction budget, time frame and schedule; **e.** legal and physical surveys; **f.** soil and environmental analyses; **g.** professional reports of consultants related to the issues that affect the project.

Tasks from **a** to **d**, as we have seen, can be completed with the direct involvement of the architect which helps the client in clarifying and systematizing goals. In tasks **e** and **f** the architect fulfills a coordinating function. In task **g** the architect can advise the client on the type of professionals needed to deal with to issues brought forward by the client or discovered by the architect. Furthermore, it is advisable that the architect coordinate the consultants' work. Without this information, a schematic design cannot start.

If the information is available and the site analysis is completed, an architect is in a position to produce the graphic documentation that would allow the formulation of the adequate conclusions. It is important to consider that such findings must also lead to the next stage. This means that the architect has to maintain a global view of the project. He or she should always anticipate the issues related to key aspects that might belong to the next stage but might directly affect the conclusions reached at the current stage of the project. In other words the architect must always be at the so called head of the game. Many failures and much loss of confidence on the part of the client occur because of lack of control in the relationship between stages of the project and development of issues lying at the core of the project.

GRAPHIC MATERIAL

If a program is well-constructed at the schematic design stage, the architect should be able to concentrate on:

1. The efficient and appropriate use of the site in relation to: **a.** zoning, and urban design requirements; **b.** building, health and safety codes compliance; **c.** balance between site area/building area ratio and appropriate site coverage; **d.** accesses, parking location, traffic and circulation.

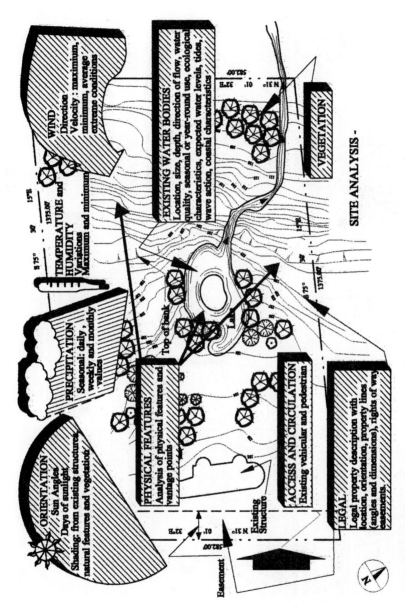

FIGURE 3.20 Site analysis.

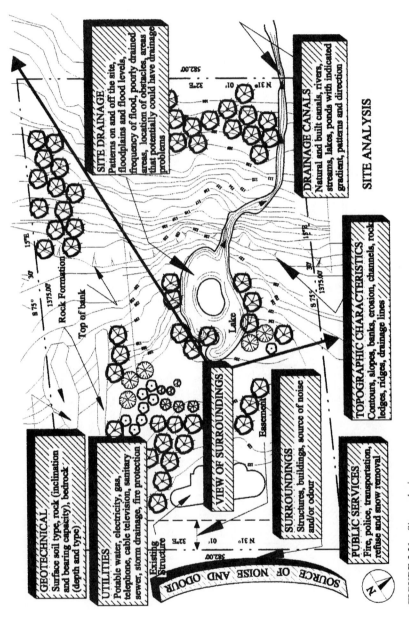

FIGURE 3.21 Site analysis.

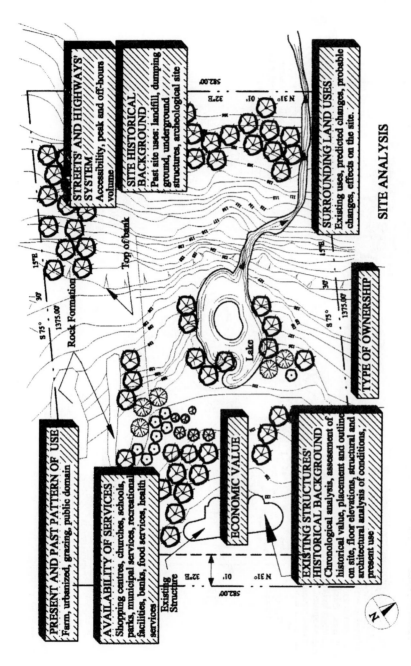

FIGURE 3.22 Site analysis.

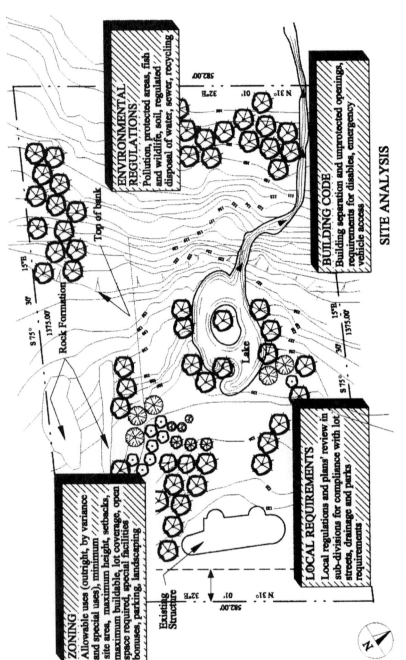

ZONING
Allowable uses (outright, by variance and special uses), minimum site area, maximum height, setbacks, maximum buildable, lot coverage, open space required, special facilities bonuses, parking, landscaping

ENVIRONMENTAL REGULATIONS
Pollution, protected areas, fish and wildlife, soil, regulated disposal of water, sewer, recycling

BUILDING CODE
Building separation and unprotected openings, requirements for disabled, emergency vehicle access

LOCAL REQUIREMENTS
Local regulations and plans' review in sub-divisions for compliance with lot, streets, drainage and parks requirements

Rock Formation

Top of bank

Existing Structure

Lake

SITE ANALYSIS

FIGURE 3.23 Site analysis.

2. The relation between the geometrical and formal characteristics of the project and the surroundings (the character of the project, at this point, to be discussed only in general terms as a potential formal solution).

3. The efficient and qualitative use of the parts of the project in relation to orientation, area, distribution, circulation views and any other programmatic variable.

4. The quality and suitability of materials and colors (to be discussed in a general way, as options).

5. The coordination of the consultants involved and the integration of their findings into the project.

6. Budget and preliminary cost of construction.

In order to verify and at the same time explain the relationship between the program and the schematic designs proposed, it is important to create graphic material that illustrates this relationship. The benefits of creating these presentations extend beyond the explanation to third parties of the choices made. It allows a clarification among the members of the design team as well, and it permits the identification of possible unresolved issues. In the latter case it is better to bring such aspects forward to the client's attention for appropriate action. This might mean going back to the programmatic phase to provide the answers needed in order to proceed with the project (see diagram in Figure 1.7 in Chapter 1).

It is fundamental to keep in mind that, in order to minimize decisions made at random, a logical and consequential process should be followed and represented. The schematic design drawings set should display the following information (some items indicated in the description of the various architectural drawing sets do not apply to smaller projects):

1. An urban analysis and an environmental impact analysis showing the main features related to the project. The extent of the analysis or its necessity is dependent on the type of project and the influence that the surrounding have on it and vice versa. For a private house, for example, the immediate surroundings are a good indication of the extent of the impact. An expanded analysis can give indications of the appropriate character and issues such as noise sources. A general overview of the neighborhood provides background for considerations on the type of services readily available and the social milieu (see Figure 3.24).

   For a commercial development like a shopping center or an entertainment center, the analysis of competing developments and the size of the "catch area" as well as traffic, road system and public transportation analysis should be included. In addition, the urban texture and configuration could give an indication about other factors such as need for common amenities or common space within the development to mitigate a lack of such facilities at the neighborhood level. Figure 3.25 provides basic principles of urban analysis that allows a comparison of the urban structure under review with the characteristics illustrated and assessment of the former. A hierarchical list of vehicular and pedestrian thoroughfares is provided in Figure 3.26.

The relationship between public, semi-public, semi-private and private spaces is discussed in Figure 3.27; schematic examples of the interaction among these spaces are given in Figure 3.28 as well as in Figure 3.29.

Efficiency in traffic distribution is based especially on road and public transportation systems that provide: **a.** primary high and medium speed connectors for long-range travel on these routes: number of intersections is minimized in order to improve efficiency and reduce risk. Usually traffic running along these routes has the right-of-way; **b.** secondary medium speed thoroughfares for medium-range travel: this type of connector is the distributor, which provides access to the local traffic. The number of the intersections is increased but stop signals for local traffic allow an efficient flow of vehicles; **c.** local low speed connectors for short-range travel: this type of connector is used normally for one of two blocks when you are very close to the destination; **d.** pedestrian and bicycle systems that are as autonomous and self-sufficient as possible: modern planning recognizes the importance of providing opportunities and a system of routes that allow people either to walk or to use non-polluting and energy-saving means of transportation. The use of planning based on neighborhood vocabulary tends to follows this approach; **e.** convenient and ample parking.

2. An accurate survey.

3. Preliminary soil analysis.

4. Graphic representation of the zoning by-law and other by-law restrictions. (The zoning information, except for height restrictions, if not complex or articulated, can be included as part of the site analysis.)

5. Graphic analysis of the site and clear representation of its main features including easements, rights-of-way or any other type of servitude. (See *Site Analysis* in this chapter.)

6. Options for the position on the site of the proposed building (or buildings) and proposed services (including parking) with a detail graphic description of the advantages and disadvantages of each solution. Fundamental data as well as format and design principles related to this item are provided from Figures 3.30 through 3.39.

7. Shadow Diagrams (see Figures 3.40 through 3.44 for techniques and data related to the development of shadow diagrams).

8. On a complex project a circulation pattern diagram should be included.

9. Schematic sections of the building (or buildings) and of the site (in urban areas, surrounding buildings should be included in the section) to show massing, relation to surroundings and shadow diagrams.

10. Very schematic axonometry is helpful to illustrate aspects of the project.

11. Project data related to program requirements should be provided.

12. A report that includes: **a.** the index; **b.** the list of drawings; **c.** the executive summary; **d.** key aspects of the program (in an executive summary form);

e. zoning, code and environmental requirements; **f.** the status of the project; **g.** a description of the various solutions considered specifying: the general characteristics, the conceptual basis, the building systems, advantages and disadvantages; **h.** the cost analysis; **i.** outstanding issues; **j.** conclusions and recommendations.

Sketches can illustrate very well the social and environmental characteristics in which a project is designed. The advantages of expressing such concepts graphically have been already illustrated. Perhaps it can be added that using the same type of language (in this case graphic) for the analysis and the proposed design, adds consistency to the quality of the presentation and allows the observer to easely relate the premises to the solutions.

FIGURE 3.24 Graphic representation of social and environmental characteristics. *(Courtesy McIlhargey/Brown Associates)*

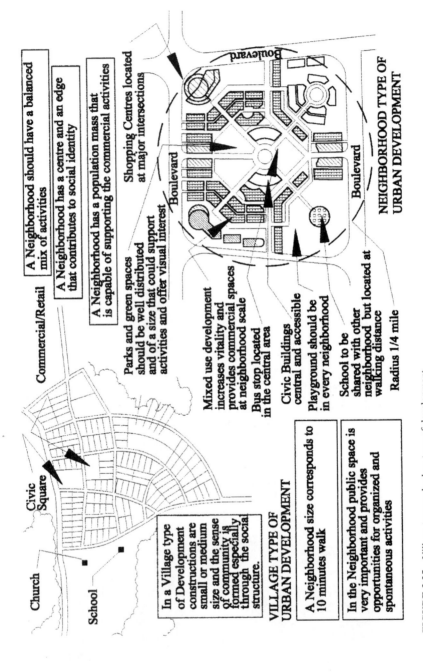

Church

School

Civic Square

Commercial/Retail

A Neighborhood should have a balanced mix of activities

A Neighborhood has a centre and an edge that contributes to social identity

A Neighborhood has a population mass that is capable of supporting the commercial activities

Shopping Centres located at major intersections

Parks and green spaces should be well distributed and of a size that could support activities and offer visual interest

Mixed use development increases vitality and provides commercial spaces at neighborhood scale

Bus stop located in the central area

Civic Buildings central and accessible

Playground should be in every neighborhood

School to be shared with other neighborhood but located at walking distance

Radius 1/4 mile

Boulevard

Boulevard

Boulevard

NEIGHBORHOOD TYPE OF URBAN DEVELOPMENT

In a Village type of Development constructions are small or medium size and the sense of community is formed especially through the social structure.

VILLAGE TYPE OF URBAN DEVELOPMENT

A Neighborhood size corresponds to 10 minutes walk

In the Neighborhood public space is very important and provides opportunities for organized and spontaneous activities

FIGURE 3.25   Village type and urban type of development.

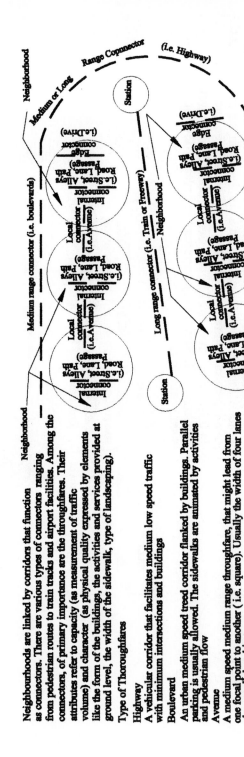

Neighbourhoods are linked by corridors that function as connectors. There are various types of connectors ranging from pedestrian routes to train tracks and airport facilities. Among the connectors, of primary importance are the throughfares. Their attributes refer to capacity (as measurement of traffic volume) and character (as physical quality expressed by elements like the form of the buildings, the activities and services provided at ground level, the width of the sidewalk, type of landscaping).

Type of Thoroughfares

Highway
A vehicular corridor that facilitates medium low speed traffic with minimum intersections and buildings

Boulevard
An urban medium speed treed corridor flanked by buildings. Parallel parking is usually allowed. The sidewalks are animated by activities and pedestrian flow

Avenue
A medium speed medium range throughfare, that might lead from one focal point to another (i.e. square). Usually the width of four lanes plus parallel parking.

Drive
It is a boundary between a natural setting and the urban development. With the increasing urbanization of areas it might maintain its name but not its function.

Street
A low speed local connector, it allows vehicular movement in medium high density areas. Pedestrian activities are less intense and more localized.

Road
A usually two lane plus parallel parking local low speed connector flanked by small constructions (i.e. houses), set well back, and continuous landscaping.

Alley
Service roads (i. e garbage collection),that run at the back of buildings. Sidewalks are not constructed. Usually provide entrances to underground or surface parking.

Lane
Small thoroughfares that run at the back of houses. They accommodate utilities.

Passage
A narrow pedestrial connector tha provides, for example, access between the main thoroughfare and a lane or parking. Shops could add to the character.

Path
Narrow or pedestrian route in natural setting or between buildings. Parallel parking is usually allowed. The sidewalks are animated by activities and pedestrian flow

FIGURE 3.26   Hierarchy of vehicular and pedestrian thoroughfares.

3.33

RELATIONSHIP BETWEEN PRIVATE, SEMI-PRIVATE, SEMI-PUBLIC AND PUBLIC SPACES

The traditional organization of an artificial environment can be broken down to two main elements associated with the goals and the means to achieve the goals: in architectural terms, one category is represented by the spaces which accommodate functions and the other by connectors (or ways) to reach them. The most successful designs, whether at the urban or at the single project scale, consider the connector as goal as well. A space is qualified by its purpose, the opportunity that it offers to develop, perform or suggest an activity and its aesthetical qualities. This principle is applied to the totality without subdivision or differentiation between means and goals. It is important, therefore that a continuity in the development of all three characteristics of the space is considered and applied. In this context the use of Public, Semi-Public, Semi-Private and Private Spaces is very important in order to develop such continuity.

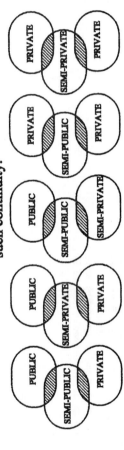

FIGURE 3.27 Relationship between private, semi-private, semi-public and public spaces.

3.34

EXAMPLES OF RELATIONSHIP BETWEEN PRIVATE, SEMI-PRIVATE, SEMI-PUBLIC AND PUBLIC SPACES

With the increase in density, especially in the central metropolitan areas, the space dedicated to the transition between type of spaces (i.e. Semi-Private and Semi-Public) has become very valuable. This created a considerable pressure on Architects who are asked to minimize such features labled as "amenities". However the proper hierarchical organization of the various types of spaces is one of the main factors to achieve a livable habitat. Figure 3.28a shows a type of Semi-Private Space that is functionally minimized. The stairs are placed on public property, which would require a permit from the city, and the landing is sufficient to allow persons to stand and open the door. In residential type of uses this arangement can be adequate. In case of commercial uses, as Semi-Public space its size needs to be increased. Figure 3.28b could be seen as a Semi-Public Space that is used for seating outside a cafe or restaurant. In this case the edge can provide a semi-transparent separation that enhances privacy but does not cut off the activities from the Public Space.

Figure 3.28c is a variation of the type of space shown in Figure 3.28b. Figure 3.28d shows a type of Semi-Private Space that could be associated with residential medium density uses (townhouses type) with a front porch. The change in elevation increases privacy.

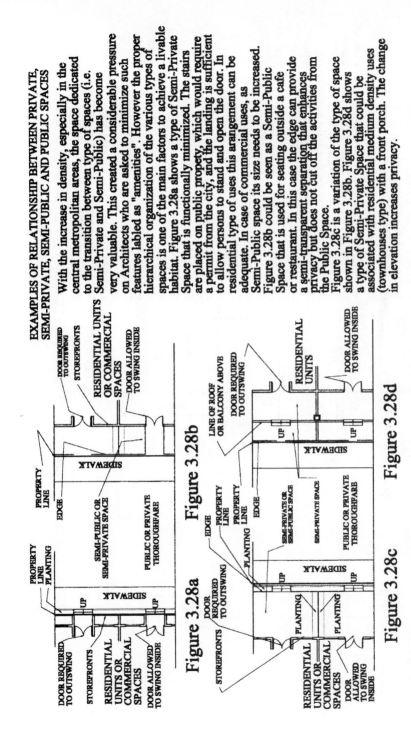

FIGURE 3.28   Examples of relationship between private, semi-private, semi-public and public spaces.

Figure 3.29a provides an example of the relationship Public/Semi-Public/Semi-Private Space. The functional aspect of the Portico is to protect the pedestrian from the elements; the activities that effect this space are those carried out in the Semi/Private space and beyond the colonnade, in the other Public Space (i.e. a square or a pedestrian thoroughfare). If both activities are varied and act as catalysts, the environment becomes vibrant. For this reason it is important for the width of the portico to be generous.

Figure 3.29b shows the traditional relationship between a Public and a Semi-Public Space, where there is no transition. Depending on the type of activity conducted in the Semi-Public Space, this type of relationship (i.e. walking and buying in a store) carries similarities in the type of activities for which a lack of transition is not strongly felt.It remains that a variety of functions increases vitality and opportunities for meaningful experiences. The type of spaces, therefore, should support the occurrences of both organized and spontaneous activities.

Figure 3.29c and 3.29d introduce spaces that expand the possibilities by offering a variety of type of areas in which activities can be accommodated or permanent features can be installed providing a centre of attraction.

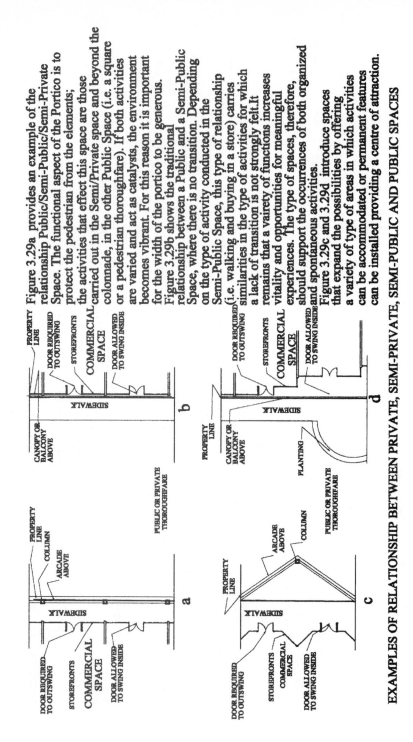

EXAMPLES OF RELATIONSHIP BETWEEN PRIVATE, SEMI-PRIVATE, SEMI-PUBLIC AND PUBLIC SPACES

FIGURE 3.29 Examples of relationship between private, semi-private, semi-public and public spaces.

3.36

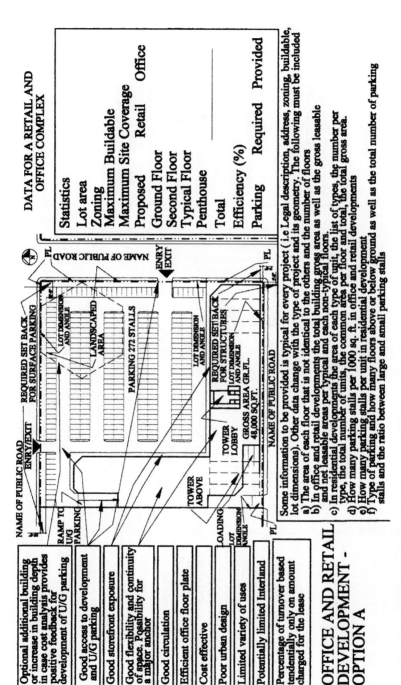

FIGURE 3.30   Office and retail development layout—Option A.

3.37

OFFICE AND RETAIL DEVELOPMENT - OPTION B

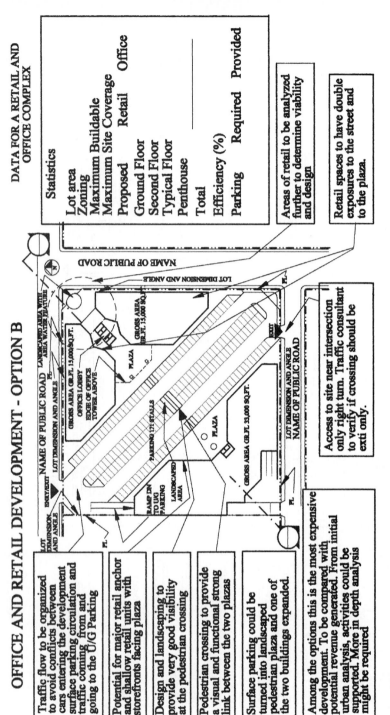

DATA FOR A RETAIL AND OFFICE COMPLEX

Statistics

Lot area
Zoning
Maximum Buildable
Maximum Site Coverage
Proposed   Retail   Office
   Ground Floor
   Second Floor
   Typical Floor
   Penthouse

Total
Efficiency (%)
Parking   Required   Provided

Areas of retail to be analyzed further to determine viability and design

Retail spaces to have double exposures to the street and to the plaza.

NAME OF PUBLIC ROAD

LOT DIMENSION AND ANGLE

LOT DIMENSION AND ANGLE   NAME OF PUBLIC ROAD

LANDSCAPED AREA WITH AREA WATER FEATURE

PL

GROSS AREA GR.FT. 15,000 SQ.FT.

OFFICE LOBBY

EDGE OF OFFICE TOWER ABOVE

PLAZA

PARKING 171 STALLS

PLAZA

LANDSCAPED AREA

RAMP DN TO UG PARKING

GROSS AREA GR.FT. 33,000 SQ.FT.

PL

LOT DIMENSION AND ANGLE

ENTRY/EXIT   NAME OF PUBLIC ROAD

LOT DIMENSION AND ANGLE

EXIT

Access to site near intersection only right turn. Traffic consultant to verify if crossing should be exit only.

Traffic flow to be organized to avoid conflicts between cars entering the development surface parking circulation and traffic coming from and going to the U/G Parking

Potential for major retail anchor and shallow retail units with storefronts facing plaza

Design and landscaping to provide very good visibility at the pedestrian crossing

Pedestrian crossing to provide a visual and functional strong link between the two plazas

Surface parking could be turned into landscaped pedestrian plaza and one of the two buildings expanded.

Among the options this is the most expensive development. To be compared with potential revenue generated. From initial urban analysis, activities could be supported. More in depth analysis might be required

FIGURE 3.31   Office and retail development layout—Option B.

OFFICE RETAIL DEVELOPMENT - OPTION C

DATA FOR A RETAIL AND OFFICE COMPLEX

Statistics

Lot area
Zoning
Maximum Buildable
Maximum Site Coverage
Proposed   Retail   Office
Ground Floor
Second Floor
Typical Floor
Penthouse

Total
Efficiency (%)
Parking   Required

Very efficient location of parking in relation to retail spaces

Urban typology with very poor standards of exterior space quality

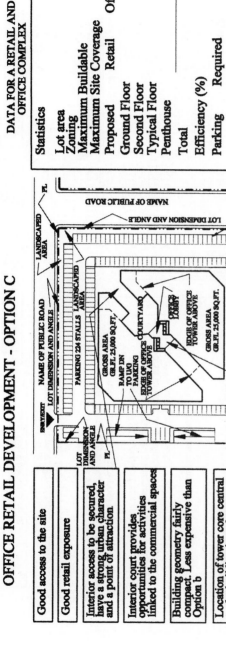

NAME OF PUBLIC ROAD
LOT DIMENSION AND ANGLE
LANDSCAPED AREA
PARKING 224 STALLS LANDSCAPED AREA
GROSS AREA GR.FT. 25,000 SQ.FT.
RAMP DN TO U/G PARKING
EDGE OF OFFICE TOWER ABOVE
EDGE OF OFFICE TOWER ABOVE
COURTYARD
GROSS AREA GR.FT. 25,000 SQ.FT.
LOT DIMENSION AND ANGLE NAME OF PUBLIC ROAD
REQUIRED SET BACK FOR SURFACE PARKING (TYP.)
ENT/EXIT
LOT DIMENSION AND ANGLE
PL.

Good access to the site

Good retail exposure

Interior access to be secured, have a strong urban character and a point of attraction.

Interior court provides opportunities for activities linked to the commercial spaces

Building geometry fairly compact. Less expensive than Option b

Location of tower core central to the building in order to minimize circulation

Limited variation of spaces that would support a variety of activities

Good vehicular circulation

FIGURE 3.32   Office and retail development layout—Option C.

TYPICAL PARKING LAYOUT

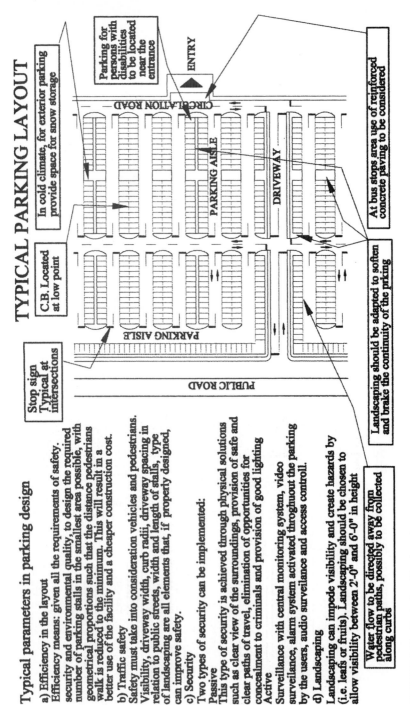

Typical parameters in parking design

a) Efficiency in the layout

Efficiency means: given all the requirements of safety. security and environmental quality, to design the required number of parking stalls in the smallest area possible, with geometrical proportions such that the distance pedestrians walk is reduced to the minimum. This will result in a better use of the facility and a cheaper construction cost.

b) Traffic safety

Safety must take into consideration vehicles and pedestrians. Visibility, driveway width, curb radii, driveway spacing in relation to public streets, width and length of stalls, type of landscaping are all elements that, if properly designed, can improve safety.

c) Security

Two types of security can be implemented:

Passive

This type of security is achieved through physical solutions such as clear view of the surroundings, provision of safe and clear paths of travel, elimination of opportunities for concealment to criminals and provision of good lighting

Active

Surveillance with central monitoring system, video surveillance, alarm system activated throughout the parking by the users, audio surveillance and access controll.

d) Landscaping

Landscaping can impede visibility and create hazards by (i.e. leafs or fruits). Landscaping should be chosen to allow visibility between 2'-0" and 6'-0" in height

Labels within the figure:

- In cold climate, for exterior parking provide space for snow storage
- Parking for persons with disabilities to be located near the entrance
- ENTRY
- C.B. Located at low point
- CIRCULATION ROAD
- PARKING AISLE
- DRIVEWAY
- PUBLIC ROAD
- Stop sign Typical at intersections
- At bus stops area use of reinforced concrete paving to be considered
- Landscaping should be adapted to soften and brake the continuity of the prking
- Water flow to be directed away from pedestrian paths, possibly to be collected along curbs

FIGURE 3.33   Typical parking layout.

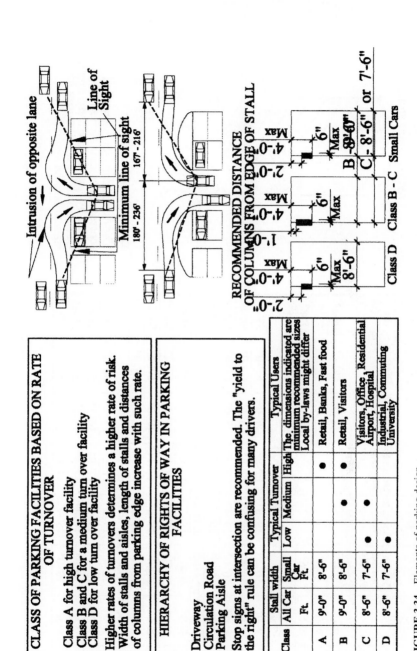

CLASS OF PARKING FACILITIES BASED ON RATE OF TURNOVER

Class A for high turnover facility
Class B and C for a medium turn over facility
Class D for low turn over facility

Higher rates of turnovers determines a higher rate of risk. Width of stalls and aisles, length of stalls and distances of columns from parking edge increase with such rate.

HIERARCHY OF RIGHTS OF WAY IN PARKING FACILITIES

Driveway
Circulation Road
Parking Aisle

Stop signs at intersection are recommended. The "yield to the right" rule can be confusing for many drivers.

| Class | Stall width | | Typical Turnover | | | | Typical Users |
	All Car Ft.	Small Car Ft.	Low	Medium	High		The dimensions indicated are minimum recommended sizes Local by-laws might differ
A	9'-0"	8'-6"			●		Retail, Banks, Fast food
B	9'-0"	8'-6"			●		Retail, Visitors
C	8'-6"	7'-6"		●			Visitors, Office, Residential Airport, Hospital
D	8'-6"	7'-6"	●				Industrial, Commuting University

FIGURE 3.34 Elements of parking design.

3.41

RECOMMENDED ALL CAR PARKING LAYOUT DIMENSIONS

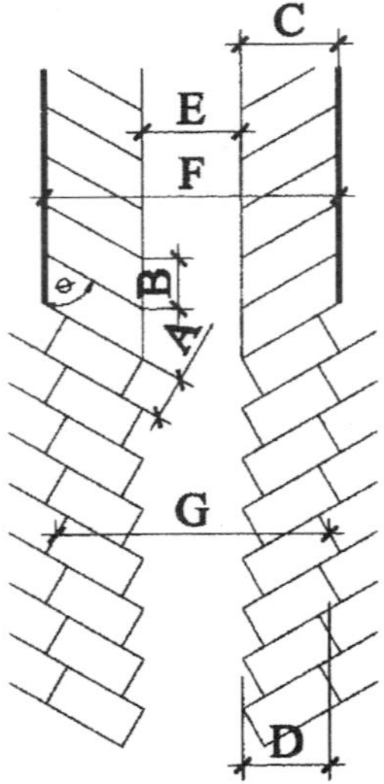

DIMENSIONAL REFERENCE

The dimensions recommended represent the minimum standards. Local by-law requirements might vary. Check with local authorities for the standards to be applied.

Class	A Basic Stall	B Stall Width Parallel to Aisle	C Stall Depth to Wall	D Stall Depth to Interlock	E Aisle Width	F Wall to Wall	G Interlock to Interlock
Two-Way Aisle with 90 Degree Parking							
A	9'-0"	9'-0"	17'-4"	17'-4"	24'-0"	58'-8"	58'-8"
B	9'-0"	9'-0"			23'-0"	57'-8"	57'-8"
C	8'-6"	8'-6"			23'-0"	57'-8"	57'-8"
D	8'-6"	8'-6"			22'-0"	56'-8"	56'-8"
Two-Way Aisle with 60 Degree Parking							
A	9'-0"	10'-4"	19'-6"	17'-8"	24'-0"	63'-0"	59'-4"
B	9'-0"	10'-4"	19'-6"	17'-8"	23'-0"	62'-0"	58'-4"
C	8'-6"	10'-0"	19'-4"	17'-6"	23'-0"	61'-8"	58'-0"
D	8'-6"	10'-0"	19'-4"	17'-6"	22'-0"	60'-8"	57'-0"
One-Way Aisle with 75 Degree Parking							
A	9'-0"	9'-4"	19'-1"	18'-0"	20'-0"	58'-2"	56'-0"
B	9'-0"	9'-4"	19'-1"	18'-0"	19'-0"	57'-2"	56'-0"
C	8'-6"	8'-10"	19'-0"	17'-11"	19'-0"	57'-0"	54'-10"
D	8'-6"	8'-10"	19'-0"	17'-11"	18'-0"	56'-0"	53'-10"
One-Way Aisle with 60 Degree Parking							
A	9'-0"	10'-4"	19'-6"	17'-8"	17'-1"	56'-2"	52'-5"
B	9'-0"	10'-4"	19'-6"	17'-8"	16'-1"	55'-2"	51'-5"
C	8'-6"	10'-0"	19'-4"	17'-6"	16'-1"	54'-9"	51'-1"
D	8'-6"	10'-0"	19'-4"	17'-6"	15'-1"	53'-9"	50'-1"

FIGURE 3.35 Aisle and parking stall recommended dimensions.

RECOMMENDED ALL CAR PARKING LAYOUT DIMENSIONS

Class	A. Basic Stall	B. Stall Width Parallel to Aisle	C. Stall Depth to Wall	D. Stall Depth to Interlock	E. Aisle Width	F. Wall to Wall	G. Interlock to Interlock
One-Way Aisle with 45 Degree Parking							
A	9'-0"	12'-8"	18'-8"	15'-6"	14'-1"	51'-5"	45'-1"
B	9'-0"	12'-8"	18'-8"	15'-6"	13'-1"	50'-5"	44'-1"
C	8'-6"	12'-1"	18'-4"	15'-4"	13'-1"	49'-9"	43'-9"
D	8'-6"	12'-1"	18'-4"	15'-4"	12'-1"	48'-9"	42'-9"
One-Way Aisle with 30 Degree Parking							
A	9'-0"	18'-0"	16'-6"	12'-7"	14'-1"	47'-1"	39'-3"
B	9'-0"	18'-0"	16'-6"	12'-7"	13'-1"	46'-1"	38'-3"
C	8'-6"	17'-1"	16'-1"	12'-5"	13'-1"	45'-3"	38'-1"
D	8'-6"	17'-1"	16'-1"	12'-5"	12'-1"	44'-3"	37'-1"

RADIUS AND GRADE

Radii to the outside edge of the inside travel lane for spiral ramps connecting the level of parking is 29'-6". It is recommended not to exceed eight turns.

Recommended Maximum Slopes

5% for sloped floors
10% for straight ramps
8% for spiral ramps

Ramps that are exposed to the weather and having a gradient of more than 10% should be heated.

PEDESTRIAN MOVEMENTS

Entrance to Building

Pedestrian movement parallel to Aisles

Entrance to Building

Entrance to Building

Entrance to Building

When pedestrian movement is perpendicular to Aisles, walkways should be introduced to provide pedestrian with safe and clear routes

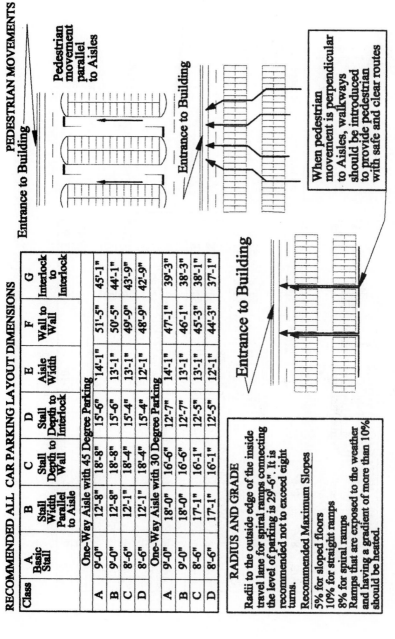

FIGURE 3.36   Recommended aisle and parking stall dimensions—safety measures for pedestrian traffic in a parking design.

RECOMMENDED SMALL CAR PARKING LAYOUT DIMENSIONS

Class	A Basic Stall	B Stall Width Parallel to Aisle	C Stall Depth to Wall	D Stall Depth to Interlock	E Aisle Width	F Wall to Wall	G Interlock to Interlock
Two-Way Aisle with 90 Degree Parking							
A/B	8'-6"	8'-6"	15'-1"	15'-1"	21'-8"	51'-10"	51'-10"
C/D	7'-6"	7'-6"	15'-1"	15'-3"			
Two-Way Aisle with 60 Degree Parking							
A/B	8'-6"	9'-10"	17'-4"	15'-6"	21'-0"	55'-8"	52'-0"
C/D	7'-6"	8'-9"	16'-10"	15'-3"		54'-8"	51'-6"
One-Way Aisle with 75 Degree Parking							
A/B	8'-6"	8'-10"	16'-9"	15'-9"	17'-1"	50'-7"	48'-7"
C/D	7'-6"	7'-10"	16'-6"	15'-7"		50'-1"	48'-3"
One-Way Aisle with 60 Degree Parking							
A/B	8'-6"	9'-10"	17'-4"	15'-6"	15'-1"	49'-9"	46'-1"
C/D	7'-6"	8'-9"	16'-10"	15'-3"		48'-9"	45'-7"
One-Way Aisle with 45 Degree Parking							
A/B	8'-6"	12'-1"	16'-8"	14'-11	12'-1"	45'-5"	41'-11"
C/D	7'-6"	10'-8"	16'-0"	14'-5"		44'-1"	40'-11"
One-Way Aisle with 30 Degree Parking							
A/B	8'-6"	17'-1"	14'-11"	11'-3"	12'-1"	41'-11"	34'-4"
C/D	7'-6"	15'-1"	14'-1"	10'-10"		40'-3"	33'-9"

OVERHANG REQUIREMENT

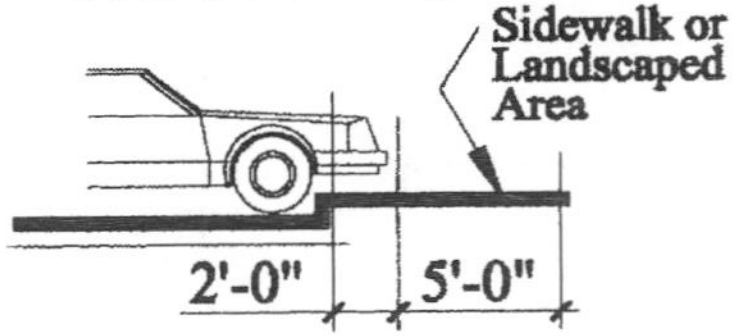

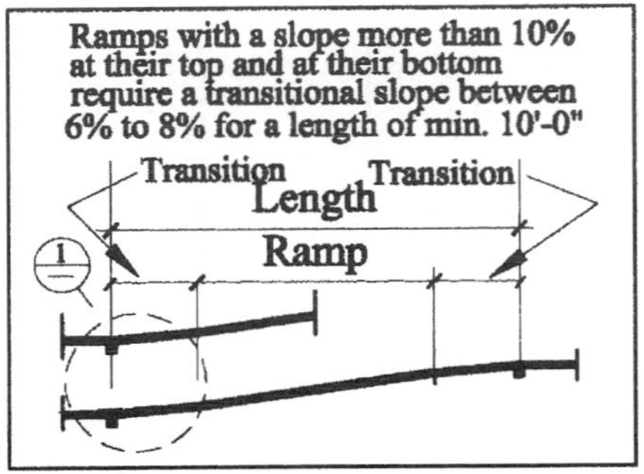

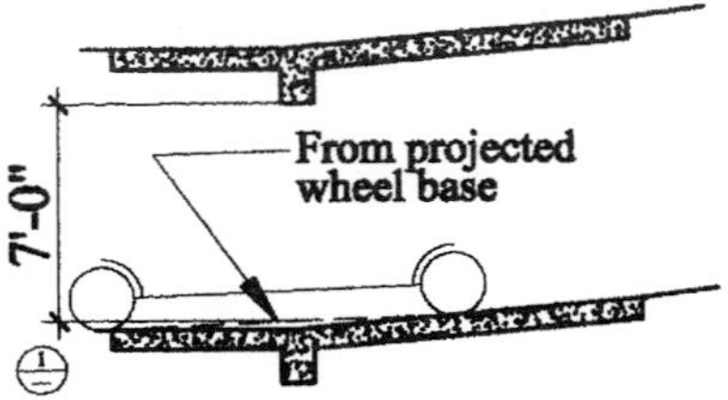

Sidewalk or Landscaped Area

5'-0"

2'-0"

Ramps with a slope more than 10% at their top and at their bottom require a transitional slope between 6% to 8% for a length of min. 10'-0"

Transition   Transition
Length
Ramp

From projected wheel base

7'-0"

FIGURE 3.37   Recommended aisle and parking stall dimension—elements in parking and ramp design.

LIGHTING LEVEL FOR PARKING STRUCTURES

	Horizontal Illumination (Lux)	
	NPA (1)	IES (2)
Vehicle Entrance	440	550
Vehicle Exit	220	-
Stairwells, exit lobbies	220	110/165/220 (3)
Parking areas		
General areas	66	55
Minimum at bumper walls	22	14
Ramps and Corners	-	11
Roof and Surface	22	26

(1) NPA - National Parking Association
(2) IES - Illuminating Engineering Society of North America
(3) Average lux for low/medium/high activity areas

TRUCK AND TRAILER AVERAGE DIMENSIONS

	Double Semitrailer	Conventional Semitrailer	Straight Body Truck
Length (A)	70'-0"	55'-0"	17'-0" to 40'-0'
Width (B)	8'0"	8'-0"	8'-0"
Height (C)	13-6'	13-6'	13-6'
Floor Height (D)	4'-0" to 4'-6"	4'-0" to 4'-6"	3'-0" to 4'-0"
Track (E)	6-6'	6'-6"	5'-10"
Rear Axis (F)	3'-0" to 4'-0"	4'-0" to 12'-0"	2'-3" to 12'-0"

Individual States prescribe maximum height, length and weight of trucks and trailers which may differ from the average dimensions. Check with authorities.

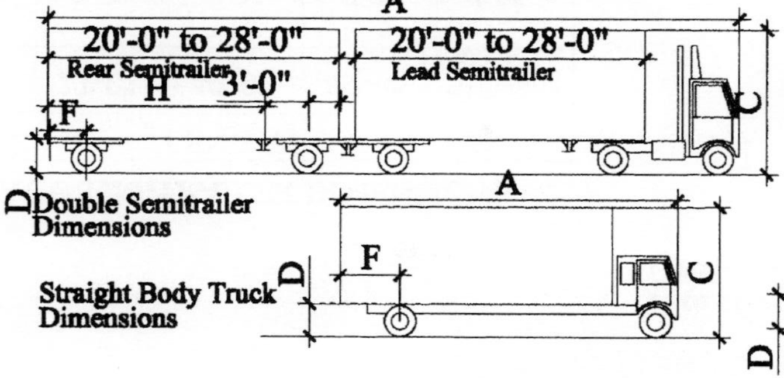

Semitrailer Dimensions

Double Semitrailer Dimensions

Straight Body Truck Dimensions

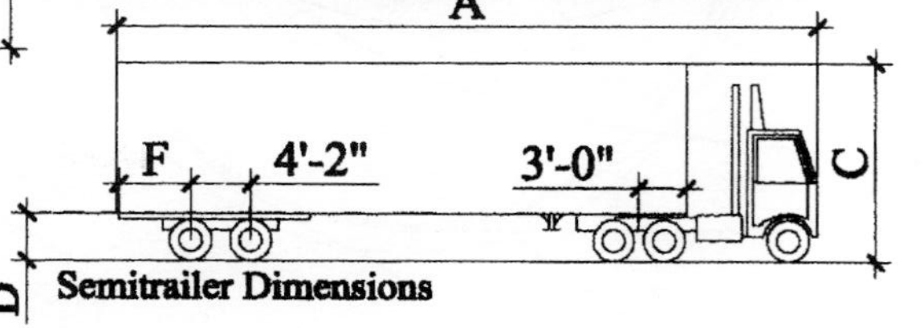

FIGURE 3.38   Lighting level for parking structures and truck/trailer average dimensions.

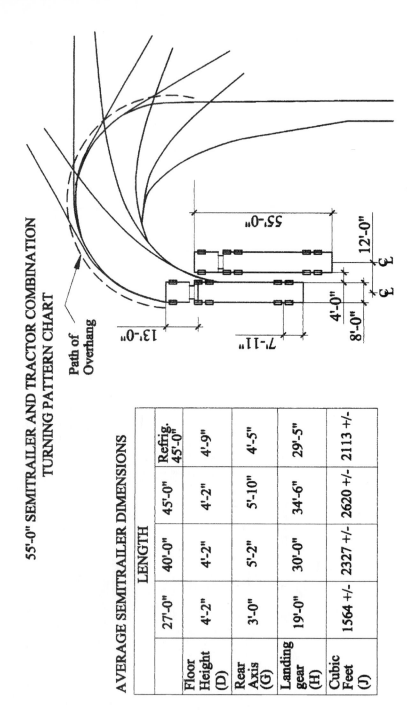

FIGURE 3.39 Fifty-five semi-trailer and tractor combination turning pattern charts—average semi-trailer dimensions.

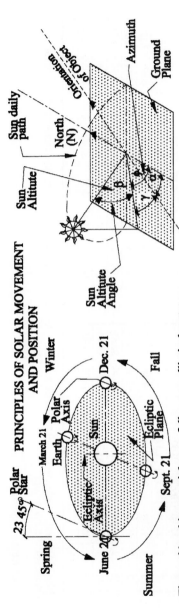

PRINCIPLES OF SOLAR MOVEMENT AND POSITION

The earth's orbit around the sun follows an elliptical pattern. The earth's axis is inclined by 23.45° in relation to the perpendicular to the plane of its elliptical orbit. This is one of the characteristics that determine the changing of the seasons and variations in the length of the day and the night. The angle, called declination, varies during the year. The following are its values at the 21st day of each month (they do not change appreciatively from year to year): Jan 19.9, Feb. -10.6, Mar. 0.0, April+ 11.9, May +20.3, June +23.5 July + 20.5, Aug. +12.1, Sept. 0.0, Oct - 10.7, Nov. -19.9, Dec. -23.5

DETERMINATION OF SOLAR POSITION

The following are the two mathematical formulas to be used to determine the sun's position any time and at any latitude:

(Solar Altitude) $\quad \sin \beta = \cos L \cos \delta \cos H + \sin L \sin \delta$

(Azimuth) $\quad \cos \phi = \dfrac{\sin \beta \sin L - \sin \delta}{\cos \beta \cos L}$

β = Solar altitude above horizon

L = Latitude of the place (negative for south hemisphere)

δ = Declination of the Sun (negative for south declination

H = Hour angle of the sun = 0.25 x (number of minutes from local solar noon). H = 0 at noon. Hour = 15°

φ = Solar Azimuth, which is the angle created by the South earth axis and the projection on the horizontal plane of the line between the earth and the sun.

FIGURE 3.40 Principles of solar movement and position.

3.47

SUN ALTITUDE AND AZIMUTH VALUES

26° N Latitude

Hours		June 21st		Mar./Sept. 21st		December 21st	
		ALT	AZM	ALT	AZM	ALT	AZM
AM							
6	6	10.05	111.30	0.00	90.00		
7	5	22.82	105.97	13.45	83.30	2.23	62.48
8	4	35.93	101.15	26.71	75.80	13.76	54.88
9	3	49.24	96.45	39.46	66.33	24.12	46.30
10	2	62.69	91.17	51.11	52.79	32.66	33.01
11	1	76.25'	82.21	60.25	31.43	38.46	17.65
12		87.45	0.00	64.00	0.00	40.55	0.00
	PM						

30° N Latitude

Hours		June 21st		Mar./Sept. 21st		December 21st	
		ALT	AZM	ALT	AZM	ALT	AZM
AM							
6	6	11.48	110.59	0.00	90.00		
7	5	23.87	104.30	12.95	82.37	0.38	62.40
8	4	36.60	98.26	25.66	73.90	11.44	54.15
9	3	49.53	91.79	37.76	63.43	21.27	44.12
10	2	62.50	83.46	48.59	49.11	29.28	31.73
11	1	75.11	67.48	56.77	28.19	34.64	16.77
12		83.45	0.00	60.00	0.00	36.55	0.00
	PM						

34° N Latitude

Hours		June 21st		Mar./Sept. 21st		December 21st	
		ALT	AZM	ALT	AZM	ALT	AZM
AM							
6	6	12.86	109.78	0.00	90.00		
7	5	24.80	102.54	13.39	81.48		
8	4	37.07	95.28	24.49	72.11	9.08	53.67
9	3	49.49	87.10	35.89	60.79	18.38	43.12
10	2	61.79	76.00	45.89	45.92	25.86	30.65
11	1	73.17	55.10	53.21	25.60	30.81	16.05
12		79.45	0.00	56.00	0.00	32.55	0.00
	PM						

38° N Latitude

Hours		June 21st		Mar./Sept. 21st		December 21st	
		ALT	AZM	ALT	AZM	ALT	AZM
AM							
6	6	14.18	108.87	0.00	90.00		
7	5	25.60	100.70	11.77	80.63		
8	4	37.33	92.25	23.20	70.43	6.69	53.12
9	3	49.13	82.47	33.86	58.38	15.44	42.30
10	2	60.58	69.06	43.03	43.16	22.40	29.74
11	1	70.61	45.67	49.67	23.52	26.96	15.45
12		75.45	0.00	52.00	0.00	28.55	0.00
	PM						

Note: Azimuth angles to be calculate from South towards East for the AM hours and from South towards West for the PM hours.

FIGURE 3.41   Sun altitude and azimuth values.

SUN ALTITUDE AND AZIMUTH VALUES

42° N Latitude

Hours	June 21st		Mar./Sept. 21st		December 21st	
AM	ALT	AM	ALT	AM	ALT	AM
6	15.44	107.87	0.00	90.00		
7	26.28	98.78	11.09	79.84		
8	37.38	89.19	21.81	68.88	4.28	52.82
9	48.45	77.96	31.70	56.21	12.46	41.63
10	58.95	62.79	40.06	40.79	18.91	29.00
11	67.64	38.62	45.88	21.82	23.09	14.96
12	71.45	0.00	48.00	0.00	24.55	0.00
PM						

46° N Latitude

Hours	June 21st		Mar./Sept. 21st		December 21st	
AM	ALT	AM	ALT	AM	ALT	AM
6	16.63	106.77	0.00	90.00		
7	26.82	96.80	10.36	79.09		
8	37.22	86.15	20.32	67.45	1.86	52.65
9	47.47	73.66	29.42	54.27	9.46	41.12
10	56.95	57.25	36.98	38.75	15.41	28.41
11	64.40	33.33	42.14	20.43	19.23	14.56
12	67.45	0.00	44.00	0.00	20.55	0.00
PM						

SHORT METHOD TO DETERMINE SHADOW DIAGRAMS (42° Latitude - June 21st at 2 PM)

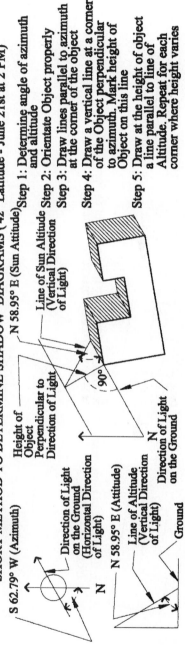

Step 1: Determine angle of azimuth and altitude

Step 2: Orientate Object properly

Step 3: Draw lines parallel to azimuth at the corner of the object

Step 4: Draw a vertical line at a corner of the Object perpendicular to azimuth. Mark height of Object on this line

Step 5: Draw at the height of object a line parallel to line of Altitude. Repeat for each corner where height varies

N 58.95° E (Sun Attitude)

Line of Sun Altitude (Vertical Direction of Light)

Height of Object Perpendicular to Direction of Light

S 62.79° W (Azimuth)

Direction of Light on the Ground (Horizontal Direction of Light)

N

N 58.95° E (Attitude)

Line of Altitude (Vertical Direction of Light)

N

Direction of Light on the Ground

Ground

FIGURE 3.42 Sun altitude and azimuth values—short method to determine shadow diagrams.

DETAILED METHOD TO DETERMINE SHADOW DIAGRAMS (June 21st at 2 PM)

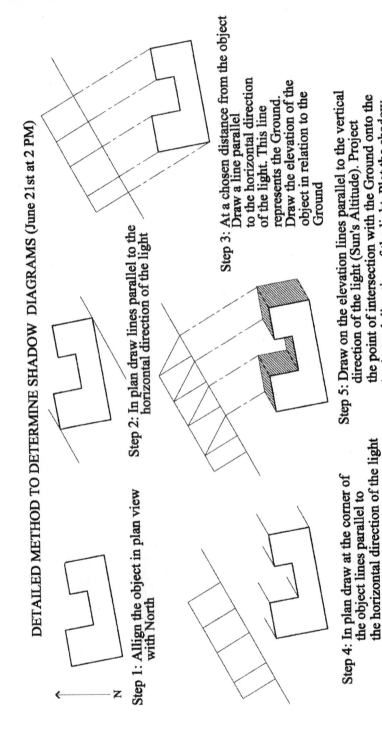

Step 1: Allign the object in plan view with North

Step 2: In plan draw lines parallel to the horizontal direction of the light

Step 3: At a chosen distance from the object Draw a line parallel to the horizontal direction of the light. This line represents the Ground. Draw the elevation of the object in relation to the Ground

Step 4: In plan draw at the corner of the object lines parallel to the horizontal direction of the light

Step 5: Draw on the elevation lines parallel to the vertical direction of the light (Sun's Altitude). Project the point of intersection with the Ground onto the horizontal direction of the light. Plot the shadow.

FIGURE 3.43   Detailed method to determine shadow diagrams.

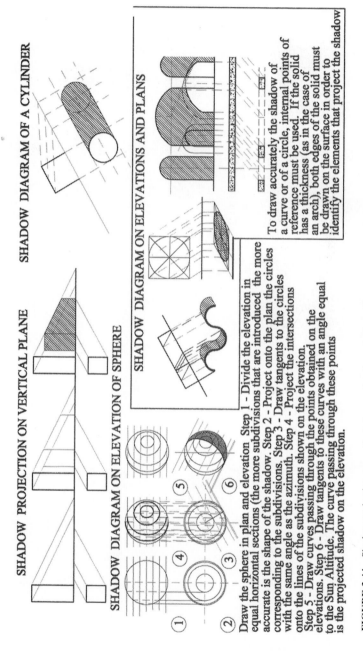

SHADOW PROJECTION ON VERTICAL PLANE   SHADOW DIAGRAM OF A CYLINDER

SHADOW DIAGRAM ON ELEVATION OF SPHERE

SHADOW DIAGRAM ON ELEVATIONS AND PLANS

Draw the sphere in plan and elevation. Step 1 - Divide the elevation in equal horizontal sections (the more subdivisions that are introduced the more accurate is the shape of the shadow. Step 2 - Project onto the plan the circles corresponding to the subdivisions. Step 3 - Draw tangents to the circles with the same angle as the azimuth. Step 4 - Project the intersections onto the lines of the subdivisions shown on the elevation. Step 5 - Draw curves passing through the points obtained on the elevations. Step 6 - Draw tangents to these curves with an angle equal to the Sun Altitude. The curve passing through these points is the projected shadow on the elevation.

To draw accurately the shadow of a curve or of a circle, internal points of reference must be used. If the solid has a thickness (as in the case of an arch), both edges of the solid must be drawn on the surface in order to identify the elements that project the shadow

FIGURE 3.44 Shadow projection on vertical plane and various shadow diagrams.

CHAPTER 4
PRELIMINARY DESIGN

Before we proceed in describing this stage, it should be clarified that the subdivision between schematic design and preliminary design is used normally in larger projects or in projects (like shopping centers) where: **a.** the interaction between various elements of the project (like parking underground and/or on surface, location of the building, distribution and size of major anchors) can be approached in very different ways. Therefore certain solutions have to be tested at the schematic level and in a diagrammatic form before a more detailed study of the project can be conducted; **b.** the financial viability of the project requires marketing strategies to secure certain key elements before the project can proceed; **c.** the project requires multi-level approval.

In general, the decision to adopt a subdivision in two phases is based on an effort to avoid producing work that is founded on faulty premises and to obtain preliminary intermediate approval from the client and/of authorities. If such verification cannot be obtained, the activities could lead not only to wasted efforts but could risk frustration among the team and on the part of the client, loss of confidence inside and outside the office, throwing the project off schedule (with time to be recuperated and a further loss in the quality of future work), and an overall disservice to the client(s).

In many other cases where the project is not complex, the client is a single entity, and the variables of the project are defined and point to clear solutions, the differentiation between schematic design and preliminary design or between preliminary design and design development can be eliminated and combined in one step called either schematic design (in the first case) or design development (in the second case). The combination adopted will depend on the complexity and number of variables to be discussed at the schematic design stage (i.e., options for the position of the building, conflicting aspects and prioritization of variables) or at the design development stage (i.e., possible options for the internal distribution, various appropriate aesthetical characters).

In the schematic stage the team has reached some general conclusions. Issues like the characteristics of the site, environment and/or urban surroundings, options for the positioning of the building, the possible locations and general configuration of elements like parking and or amenities, zoning restrictions, accesses, possible building systems, and general aesthetical philosophy have been identified. It is important to realize that these solutions are not yet firmly set. The project is still in a fluid stage. In order to narrow down the most suitable options without being distracted by unnecessary details, considerations have mostly related to the general characteristic of the development. However, approval from the owner on the solution and concept to be used as a starting point to develop this phase has been already obtained at the end of the schematic design phase (otherwise the preliminary design stage cannot start). At this stage, more specific studies are conducted based on this solution and concept. Aspects like the general character of the building(s), materials, and more specific considerations for the building systems have still to be approached. If the preliminary work has been carried out on solid bases and with the proper methodology, the solutions reached in this stage will corroborate the previous findings.

The character and materials of the building are a very important focus of this stage. In addition, aspects like the relationship between floor elevations and exterior grading, the general proposed slope of the exterior finished surfaces, the general design of the hard and soft landscaping, and the schematic interior distribution and circulation patterns are studied. This stage can be also defined as a pre-design development phase. This means that in the preliminary phase all the most important aspects of the project are studied and option(s) are illustrated for the most representative part of the development. If these solutions are in accordance with the program and the subsequent discussions (apart from possible partial revisions), in the design development phase they can be extended and adapted to all the conditions of the project.

In principle, options for the aesthetical philosophy that will guide the project have been either included in the program or they have been discussed with the client and the consultants in the schematic design stage. Thus the architect has already obtained some indication of the preferences and/or technical limitations and advantages of certain ideas. Based on these considerations, specific views, parts of the building(s), urban elements and main features are explored and represented.

By the definition given to this phase, the architect needs to consider aspects that will be developed more specifically in the next phase. Elements and issues that will be explored in more detail in the design development stage must be already considered at this stage: **a.** aesthetical solutions for the most representative parts of the building and preliminary studies of technical details related to these parts; **b.** a consideration of and allowances for the thicknesses of walls, slabs and floor assemblies, particularly regarding dimensions that are critical because of some programmatic requirement, code related issues, computation of gross areas, general functions, or aesthetical aspects; **c.** range of spacing of structural columns related to the different characters and/or material to be used for the development; **d.** impact of the different aesthetic solutions on the type and size of the electrical and mechanical system and equipment (i.e., sizes of service rooms, and mechanical and electrical equipment to be installed inside and outside the building(s)).

PRELIMINARY GRAPHIC MATERIAL AND PRESENTATION DRAWINGS

The styles of the graphic material used to create a presentation and illustrate the project at this stage can be very different but, nevertheless, all can be effective. One characteristic that is common to all of them is their highly artistic and explicit graphic quality. Sometime these drawings are very descriptive (for example, sketches of exterior detail or rendered sections used to illustrate complex solutions), or less detailed if their purpose is to convey only the general intent of whatever aspect of the project is described in them. For the above reasons, in most cases, the drawings at this stage fall into two categories: **a.** more schematic technical drawings: this material indicates the overall site and buildings in a diagrammatic form, although more detailed than what has been presented at the schematic design stage; **b.** presentation drawings, combined with the more schematic material, are used for particular purposes (like marketing) or to highlight either specific areas and aspects of the project or a general intent (in which case drawings that are part of the schematic and more technical category might be substituted.). This is applicable, for example, when the natural and landscape features are predominant and they are rendered in detail on the site plan). A preliminary design architectural set comprised of:

1. Site Plan. (see Figure 4.1). This drawing, depending on the type and scale of project, should include, with various degrees of detail: **a.** an accurate parking layout (on surface and/or underground, if required); **b.** hard and soft surfaces, paving, sidewalks and features within and outside the site; **c.** dimensioned access points; **d.** location of all buildings; **e.** general dimensions and setbacks from property lines; **f.** orientation; **g.** access points to buildings; **h.** vertical vehicular and pedestrian circulation; **i.** main existing features, including street lighting, possible existing buildings to be demolished, electrical lines, transformers, hydrants, telephone structures, trees; **j.** immediate surroundings; **k.** project data related to the requirements indicated in the program. The drawing should highlight variances from the program.

   In many cases it is useful to incorporate the ground floor plan into the site plan (see Figure 4.3). This type of drawings allows us to study and discuss very clearly the relationship between inside and outside, accesses, exposure, views, orientation, materials (especially floor treatment).

Another type of presentation that is very effective and useful in the analysis of the project is the reintroduction of the site plan which indicates the shadows projected by the proposed buildings, the site elements, the landscaping as well as the surrounding buildings (see Figures 4.3 through 4.6).

2. Floor plans (see Figure 4.7). They should show: **a.** general floor elevations; **b.** general dimensions; **c.** internal schematic layout; **d.** glazing; **e.** Doors; **f.** typical furniture layout (if critical because it is a main element of the program. At this stage the layout is developed only for major and/or prototypical components of the project.)

3. Elevation(s) (see Figures 4.8 and 4.9). The following elements and data should be indicated on this type of drawings: **a.** main materials; **b.** height of building (or buildings) and elevation of each floor; **c.** maximum allowable heights; **d.** property lines.

4. Section(s). The following elements should also be included: **a.** existing finished grade elevations; **b.** proposed finish grade elevations; **c.** finish floor elevations; **d.** heights floor to floor; **e.** height of roof and roof parapet; **f.** maximum allowable height.

5. Shadow analysis of shadows cast by the surroundings as well as by the proposed buildings (see Figure 4.10).

6. Massing of the building related to surroundings (see Figures 4.11, 4.12, 4.13, and 4.14).

7. Axonometry or schematic perspective of the most prominent views of the building and from the building related to the surroundings. These drawings will show the formal character of the building or buildings (see Figures 4.15 and 4.16).

8. Diagrammatic landscaping and use of site.

Presentation Drawings

Depending on the type of project and type of client, these colored or black and white categories of drawings can include: **a.** schematic plans of the building or parts of it (e.g., residential unit in a multi-family project, general floor plan in an office building. See Figure 4.17); **b.** perspective or axonometry of the building or buildings (see Figures 4.18 and 4.19); **c.** plan perspective or axonometric plans (see Figures 4.20 and 4.21); **d.** interior elevations (see Figures 4.22 and 4.23); **e.** colored and rendered elevations (see Figures 4.24 and 4.25); **f.** schematic sections (if required by the complexity of the project, or by the purpose of the presentation. See Figure 4.26); **g.** section perspective or axonometric perspective; **h.** rendering(s) of the building (see Figures 4.27 through 4.31).

An efficient and accurate parking layout that maximizes the number of parking stalls and minimizes the area required to develop them is important because the parking area can be considered as:

a) An economical asset. Ample parking increases the value of the space provided in the building

b) A legal asset. Zoning by-laws require a minimum number of buildable area set by the authorities. In many cases it is the number of parking stalls that can be accommodated on site that determines the maximum allowable area that can be built, which can be lower than the maximum allowed

Although it is not necessary to show at this stage all the dimensions, the information included in the drawings must permit an accurate calculation of the gross and net area of the building and of the facilities.

The solutions adopted to provide vertical and horizontal circulation are a major component of the interior layout that determines the efficiency of the building. Functionally speaking, spaces dedicated to circulation do not contain any particular activity. In a commercial building this represents a loss in revenue, while in a residential building, a loss in comfort and useful space. Code requirements affect the amount of space dedicated to circulation.

It is important to show elements that need to be demolished, removed or simply avoided because of the financial and technical implications that these acts might have on the project (i.e. Geotechnical or environmental considerations in the case of removal or demolition of large structures).

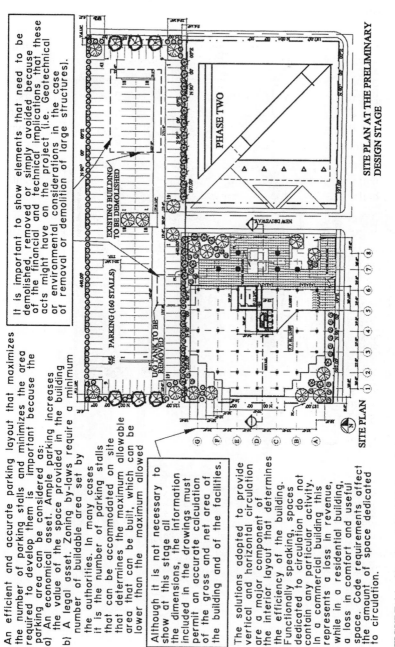

EXISTING BUILDING TO BE DEMOLISHED

PHASE TWO

PARKING (160 STALLS)

U/G TANK TO BE REMOVED

NEW DRIVEWAY

SITE PLAN

SITE PLAN AT THE PRELIMINARY DESIGN STAGE

FIGURE 4.1 Site plan at the preliminary design stage.

4.5

SITE PLAN WITH RENDERED SHADOWS

When the presentation has the purpose of illustrating the massing of the building in the context of the surrounding environment (may be supplemented by photographs of the site and taken from it), an effective drawing is the site plan rendered with the shadows projected by buildings and by natural elements. This technique adds a three-dimensional effect that is very familiar to the observer. Although developed through a presentation type of graphic technique, this is a drawing that can be completed by introducing more specific information such as set-backs or description of materials. The site plan can also provide a very valid reference for technical considerations.

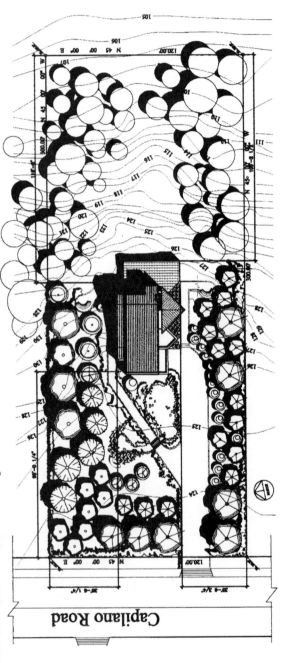

FIGURE 4.2 Site plan with rendered shadows.

4.6

SITE PLAN WITH GROUND FLOOR LAYOUT

This is an extremely useful type of presentation since it indicates the relationship between the interior spaces and the exterior environment. All the elements can be analyzed at once in a dynamic process that can recreate daily movements through the space. The contemplative aspects of the project can be considered as well as all the practical advantages and disadvantages of a particular solution. If this type of site plan is combined with the one depicting shadows, many aspects of the projects can be discussed clearly and with the constructive participation of the client.

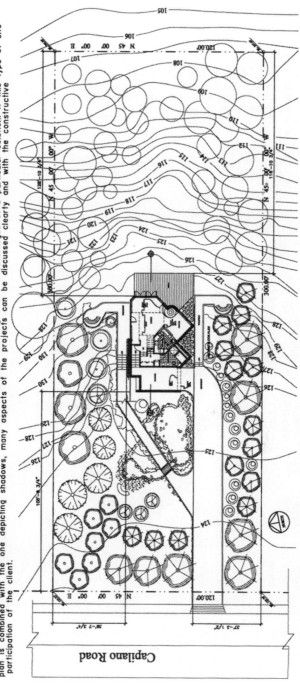

FIGURE 4.3 Site plan with ground floor layout.

4.7

Site plans can be very elaborate, almost like photos.
In this case the observer is in the position to
immediately relate to the image. However in all the
cases in which multiple functions are represented, an
additional layer of information is necessary in order
to indicate the various uses. In this illustration a legend
and numbers provide the necessary explanation. In this
case image and wording has been overlaid. In other
cases they can be kept separate using diagrams.

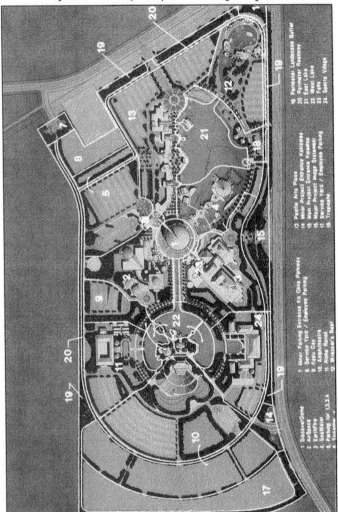

FIGURE 4.4 Site plan with shadow and description of project components.
(Image courtesy McIlhargey/Brown Associates)

In projects where the landscaping is a very important component of the design, by emphasizing the outdoors and only schematically outlining the building, we can achieve a very balanced level of communication.

The Building is still seen as a mass while the detail of the landscape gives the site a character of realism.

In addition this type of presentation offers the opportunity to highlight any landscape feature that might be included in the design.

The building could be shown by using a schematic ground floor plan. However unlike an architectural typology that is developed within two self-contained floors (i.e. single family residences or townhouses), in a multistory building the relationship with the exterior is less direct. In other words, from the interior spaces at the second floor and above the outdoors are enjoyed on a more contemplative basis than from the ground floor. Direct access from the latter offers the possibility of using the outside space on a functional basis as well. These considerations should guide the Architect's decision in showing the roof or the ground floor plan on site plan.

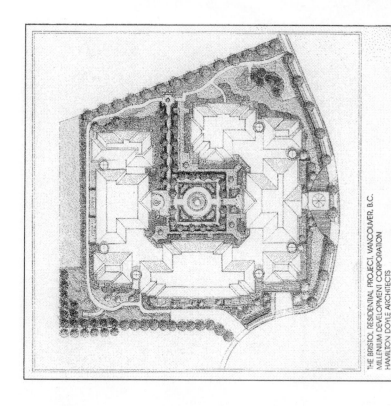

THE BRISTOL RESIDENTIAL PROJECT, VANCOUVER, B.C.
MILLENIUM DEVELOPMENT CORPORATION
HAMILTON DOYLE ARCHITECTS

FIGURE 4.5 Site plan with conceptual landscape layout. *(Image courtesy McIlhargey/Brown Associates)*

Computer images
can be very useful
to analyze and
represent site plans.
Their advantages over
handmade rendering
reside in their greater
flexibility in terms of
changes that might be
required. However,
because of the
precision of
computer drawings,
where only an
impression of the
character of the
project needs to be
conveyed, the
handmade drawings
are preferable.

FIGURE 4.6 Site plan computer generated with shadows. (*Image courtesy E.V. Radvenis Inc.*)

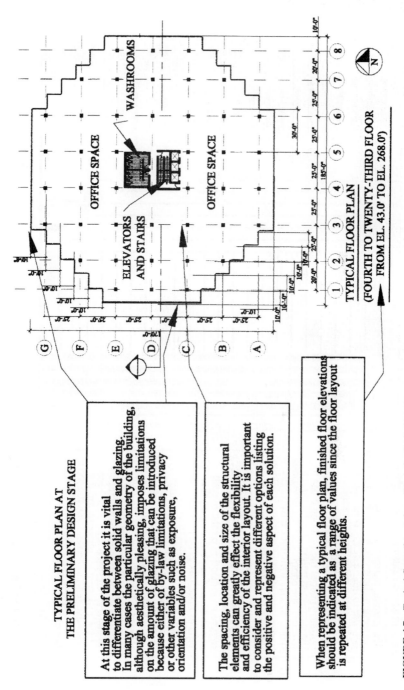

**TYPICAL FLOOR PLAN AT
THE PRELIMINARY DESIGN STAGE**

At this stage of the project it is vital
to differentiate between solid walls and glazing.
In many cases the particular geometry of the building,
although aesthetically pleasing, imposes limitations
on the amount of glazing that can be introduced
because either of by-law limitations, privacy
or other variables such as exposure,
orientation and/or noise.

The spacing, location and size of the structural
elements can greatly effect the flexibility
and efficiency of the interior layout. It is important
to consider and represent different options listing
the positive and negative aspect of each solution.

When representing a typical floor plan, finished floor elevations
should be indicated as a range of values since the floor layout
is repeated at different heights.

Within the plan:
WASHROOMS
OFFICE SPACE
ELEVATORS
AND STAIRS
OFFICE SPACE

TYPICAL FLOOR PLAN

**(FOURTH TO TWENTY-THIRD FLOOR
FROM EL. 43.0′ TO EL. 268.0′)**

N

FIGURE 4.7   Typical floor plan at the preliminary design stage.

4.11

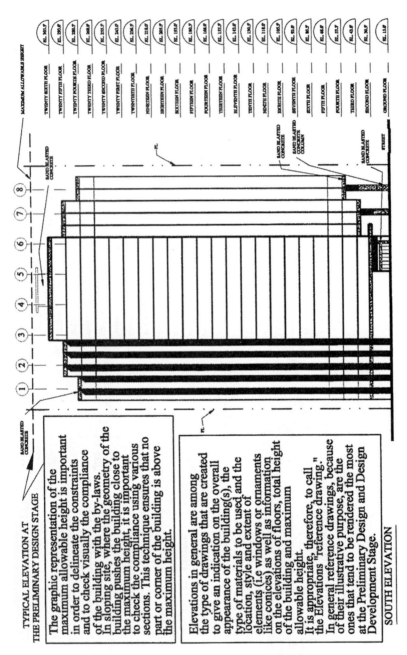

TYPICAL ELEVATION AT THE PRELIMINARY DESIGN STAGE

The graphic representation of the maximum allowable height is important in order to delineate the constraints and to check visually the compliance of the building with the by-laws. In sloping site, where the geometry of the building pushes the building close to the maximum height, it is important to check the compliance using various sections. This technique ensures that no part or corner of the building is above the maximum height.

Elevations in general are among the type of drawings that are created to give an indication on the overall appearance of the building(s), the type of materials to be used and the location, style and extent of elements (i.e windows or ornaments like cornices) as well as information on the elevations of floors, total height of the building and maximum allowable height.

It is appropriate, therefore, to call the Elevations "reference drawing." In general reference drawings, because of their illustrative purpose, are the ones that tend to be rendered the most at the Preliminary Design and Design Development Stage.

SOUTH ELEVATION

Labels on drawing:

SAND BLASTED CONCRETE

MAXIMUM ALLOWABLE HEIGHT

TWENTY SIXTH FLOOR	EL. 265.5'
TWENTY FIFTH FLOOR	EL. 290.5'
TWENTY FOURTH FLOOR	EL. 280.5'
TWENTY THIRD FLOOR	EL. 268.5'
TWENTY SECOND FLOOR	EL. 255.5'
TWENTY FIRST FLOOR	EL. 243.5'
TWENTIETH FLOOR	EL. 230.5'
NINETEEN FLOOR	EL. 218.5'
EIGHTEEN FLOOR	EL. 205.5'
SIXTEEN FLOOR	EL. 193.5'
FIFTEEN FLOOR	EL. 180.5'
FOURTEEN FLOOR	EL. 166.5'
THIRTEEN FLOOR	EL. 155.5'
ELEVENTH FLOOR	EL. 143.5'
TENTH FLOOR	EL. 130.5'
NINTH FLOOR	EL. 118.5'
EIGHTH FLOOR	EL. 106.5'
SEVENTH FLOOR	EL. 93.5'
SIXTH FLOOR	EL. 80.5'
FIFTH FLOOR	EL. 68.5'
FOURTH FLOOR	EL. 55.5'
THIRD FLOOR	EL. 43.5'
SECOND FLOOR	EL. 30.5'
GROUND FLOOR	EL. 15.5'

SAND BLASTED CONCRETE

SAND BLASTED CONCRETE COLUMN

SAND BLASTED CONCRETE

STREET

FIGURE 4.8   Typical elevation at the preliminary design stage.

4.12

CONTEXTUAL ELEVATION

When a structure is built, it is never experienced as an isolated object. It is always surrounded by other buildings and/or natural elements and landscape. It is, therefore, important to place the proposed building in the context in which it will be seen. The influence of the surrounding on the building and vice versa are factors that will have a real effects on how the future construction will be perceived. This global approach is important at every stage of the project. Although in general felt as more important at the early stages, expanding one vision is not an excercise that is limited to the design. At different times different primary focuses are chosen (i.e technical and legal aspects at the Contractual Document stage), but this is only a hiearchical consideration which should not lead to an elimination of factors from our mind in our constant development of the project. One of the most important rule throughout the development of a project is to think laterally, considering the interaction of all of the elements and variables.

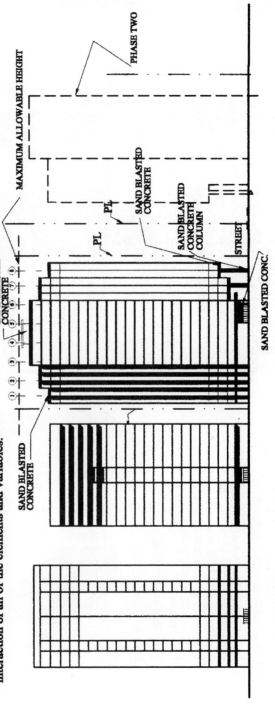

FIGURE 4.9   Contextual elevations.

4.13

SHADOW ANALYSIS OF THE SITE
EFFECTS OF SURROUNDING BUILDINGS
(42° Latitude - June 21st at 10 AM and 2 PM)

In order to establish the characteristics of the various areas of the site and to properly plan built and open spaces an analysis of the shadows cast by the surrounding buildings is fundamental.

- ▓ Shadow at 10 AM
- ▓ Shadow at 2 PM

SHADOW ANALYSIS OF THE SITE
EFFECTS OF PROPOSED BUILDINGS
(42° Latitude - June 21st 10 AM)

The analysis of the shadows cast by the proposed building completes, integrated and verifies the chosen form of development. this allows the identification of the areas where the design can be improved.

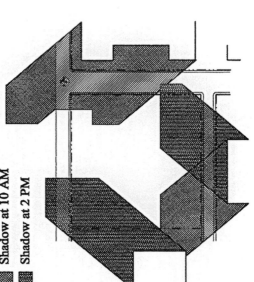

FIGURE 4.10 Shadow analysis.

If the renderings for the project are computer generated from the beginning, at the massing stage, there might be an advantage in using this type of medium. In this case, in fact, details are added at different stages as they are been developed and verified tri-dimensionally.

FIGURE 4.11 Computerized image of the massing of the building. *(Image courtesy E.V. Radvenis Inc.)*

An effective application of computer generated images is to show the massing of the building. if complete models of the building are created, points of view can be changed very easily, since the images are easily manipulated, In addition, variables such as colours, shape or shadows can be quickly modified as well.

FIGURE 4.12 Computerized image of the massing of the building. *(Image courtesy E.V. Radvenis Inc.)*

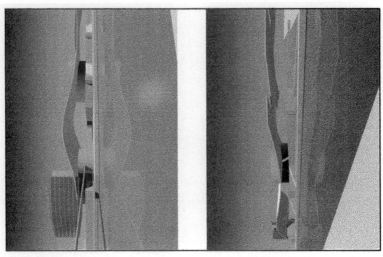

In projects that are
characterized by shapes
with strong tri-dimensional
elements and complex
spacial movements,
computerized images
are very helpful.
Through their use the
Architect is able to
describe accurately and
cost effectively the
complete project by using
a few different points of
view.

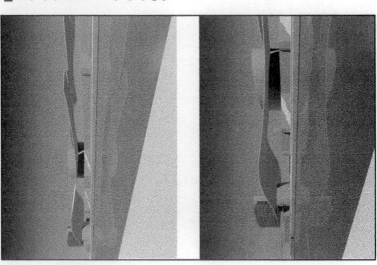

FIGURE 4.13 Computerized image of the massing of the building. *(Image courtesy E.V. Radvenis Inc.)*

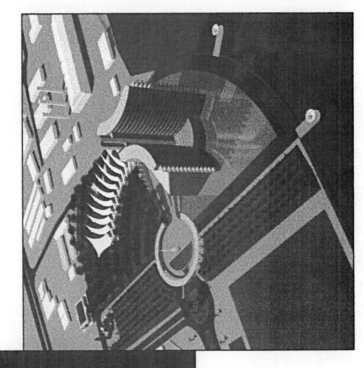

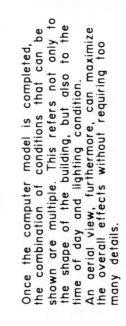

Once the computer model is completed, the combination of conditions that can be shown are multiple. This refers not only to the shape of the building, but also to the time of day and lighting condition. An aerial view, furthermore, can maximize the overall effects without requiring too many details.

FIGURE 4.14 Computerized image of the massing of the building. (*Image courtesy E.V. Radvenis Inc.*)

Schematic aerial views of the Project, showing the surrounding environment and views from the Project and concentrating on the scenery, are part of graphic presentations that can illustrate a major feature which, in some cases, can consist primarily of the natural setting. This is especially true in the case of resorts or summer houses.

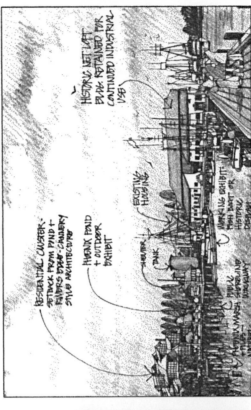

FIGURE 4.15 Graphic representation of the relationship between project and surroundings. *(Image courtesy McIlhargey/Brown Associates)*

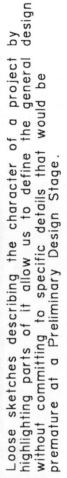

Loose sketches describing the character of a project by highlighting parts of it allow us to define the general design without committing to specific details that would be premature at a Preliminary Design Stage.

FIGURE 4.16 Examples of preliminary sketches. *(Illustrations courtesy McIlhargey/Brown Associates)*

Presentation Floor Plans showing furniture layout and floor textures are commonly used in commercial and residential projects. These plans in office buildings are either prepared for a particular interior space to be occupied by a specific client, or are used as a general real-estate tool to market the property.

In residential projects the purpose of a rendered plan can be diverse as well. These plans can be used in multifamily projects to show display suite arrangements. In design for houses, to show how the interior responds to the client's needs.

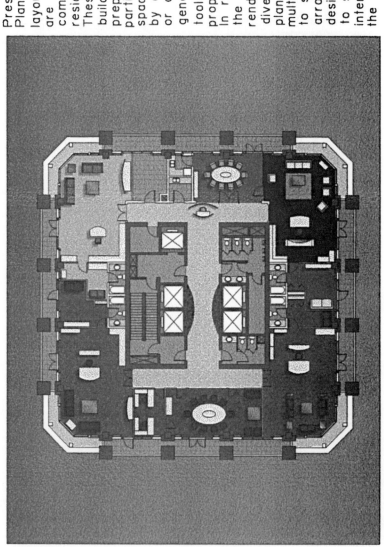

FIGURE 4.17 Example of office schematic plans with furniture layout. (*Image courtesy E.V. Radvenis Inc.*)

Depending on the size and type of project, it is possible that a rendering should be included in the Presentation Drawings at the Preliminary Design Stage. Very often at this stage, however, preliminary sketches are produced first to analyze the design solutions.

These sketches can be used to illustrate the project as well as "preliminary renderings" through which the final rendering is planned.

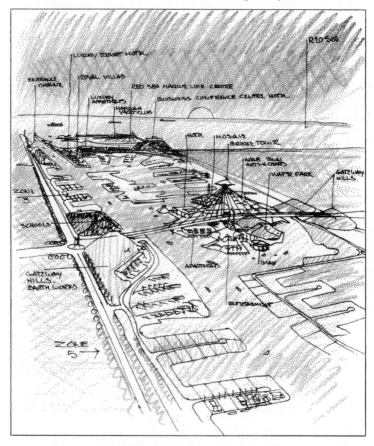

FIGURE 4.18 Preliminary rendering. *(Image courtesy McIlhargey/Brown Associates.*

When a coloured rendering is required at the
Preliminary Design Stage, the pastel technique is
very effective. Relatively quick, it allows us
to explore various formal solutions before
finalizing the aesthetical character of the project.

FIGURE 4.19   Perspective rendered in pastel technique. *(Image courtesy McIl-hargey/Brown Associates)*

For complex layouts or articulated floor levels, a very
useful and illustrative way of representing a Floor Plan
is to create an axonometric view of it.
Especially when the plan shows spaces that are used
for display (i.e. in an exhibition), this type of drawing
provides a representation that shows conditions close to
what can be expected once the facility is built.

FIGURE 4.20 Example of axonometric floor plan. *(Image courtesy McIl-
hargey/Brown Associates)*

FIGURE 4.21 Example of axonometric floor plan. (*Image courtesy McIlhargey/Brown Associates*)

Interior spaces are as important as exterior ones. Very often renderings concentrate on the exterior aspects of a building, representing the interior through sections and plans. The most successful architectural accomplishments recognize the unity of interior and exterior environment.

FIGURE 4.22 Interior elevations. *(Image courtesy E.V. Radvenis Inc. Illustration courtesy McIlhargey/Brown Associates)*

4.25

A rendering offers the opportunity not only to represent the physical space, but also to show the type of vitality and activities that will characterized the environment. In many cases the symbolic element that is associated with the building is also introduced in the image in order to inspire the observer to an appreciation of the meaning associated with the building.

FIGURE 4.23 Renderings of interiors. *(Illustration courtesy McIlhargey/Brown Associates)*

4.26

Colored elevations of the single building can be a good substitution for renderings when the surroundings are not particularly important either because of a transitional phase or because the character of the proposed building is particularly strong setting the standards for the whole area.

FIGURE 4.24 Example of colored rendered elevation. *(Illustration courtesy McIlhargey/ Brown Associates)*

FIGURE 4.25   Example of colored rendered elevation. *(Illustration courtesy McIlhargey/Brown Associates)*

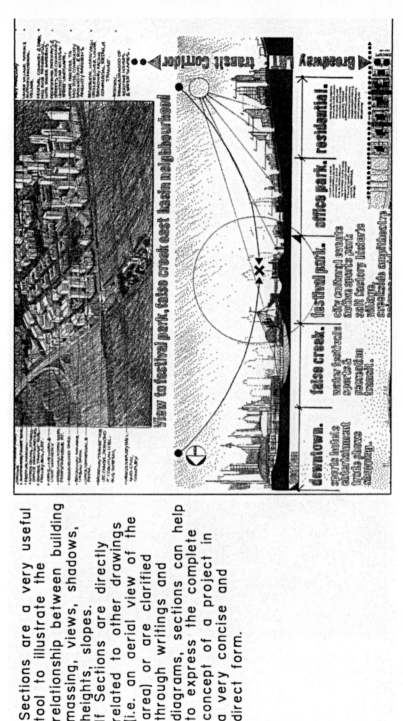

Sections are a very useful tool to illustrate the relationship between building massing, views, shadows, heights, slopes.
If Sections are directly related to other drawings (i.e. an aerial view of the area) or are clarified through writings and diagrams, sections can help to express the complete concept of a project in a very concise and direct form.

FIGURE 4.26 Example of schematic section. *(Illustration courtesy McIlhargey/Brown Associates)*

4.29

When the form and the aesthetical characteristics of
a project are defined, computer generated images are
very helpful in placing the building into the surroundings
by using photographs shot from the same points of view
used to create the computerized image.

FIGURE 4.27   Computer generated rendering superimposed on a photograph
of the surroundings. *(Courtesy E.V. Radvenis Inc.)*

FIGURE 4.28   Hand-made rendering inserted in the surroundings. *(Illustration courtesy McIlhargey/Brown Associates)*

The above illustration exploits the beauty of the
surroundings to a point that they become the focus
of the image. This is very appropriate when a project
is built in function of these surroundings and they are
the specific reason for the development of the complex

FIGURE 4.29 Rendered project settings. *(Illustration courtesy McIlhargey/
Brown Associates)*

Representing the most important parts of a Project is often sufficient to illustrate the fundamental aesthetical and functional solutions.

Handmade renderings are a very appropriate form of representation because they are less exact than computerized images. These qualities allow handmade renderings to suggest textures without too much definition.

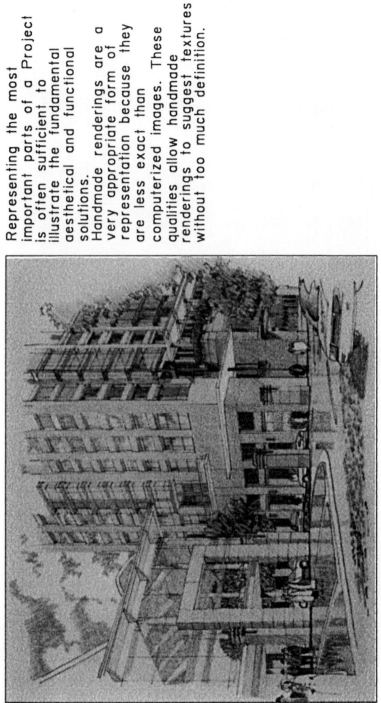

FIGURE 4.30 Partial rendering. *(Illustration courtesy McIlhargey/Brown Associates)*

Sometimes the character of a project is best expressed
by showing a mixture of environment and activities.
This is the case when there is a very strong direction
in the surrounding habitat or when the characteristics of
the target market and the goals of the project are
very well-defined.

FIGURE 4.31   Rendering showing activities and project urban environment. *(Illustration courtesy McIlhargey/Brown Associates)*

DESIGN DEVELOPMENT

Apart from being important as a stage in the development of the project, these drawings are also usually associated with the approval process wherever required by the authorities. They are used to apply for what is usually called a *development permit*. The approval, if required, is related to matters such as:

1. Zoning, which includes: **a.** type of zoning; **b.** the uses allowed under such zoning; **c.** uses that are allowed with special permit and special characteristics; **d.** minimum lot sizes; **e.** maximum lot coverage; **f.** maximum buildable area or floor area ratio (bonuses in the form of increased coefficient or percentage might be granted for particular features or design solutions); **g.** building setbacks; **h.** minimum open space requirement; **i.** maximum allowable height; **j.** restriction due to adjacent zone(s); **k.** required parking and loading zone; **l.** landscaping requirements.

2. Planning, especially concerned with the following: **a.** environmental impact statements; **b.** signage; **c.** site plan review; **d.** design review: this usually requires the following documentation to be submitted (depending on the size, type and complexity of the project, not all the items are applicable): drawings, color presentation, material sample boards, perspective and/or rendering, model, photographic survey, report or design rationale, applications and fees; **e.** environmental issues and other possible departments and/or levels of government; **f.** legal aspects and agreements.

Beginning the development design stage means that the issues included in the above lists that have an impact on the previous stages of the project (programming, schematic design and preliminary design), have been explored and incorporated in the design. Furthermore, the approval process has been investigated at the beginning of the project in order to assess the constraints, the opportunities, the design schedule and the professional fee. Before starting the design stage it is advisable to assess the status of the project and verify that the above assumption is correct by reviewing the complete documentation accumulated during the previous stages. This will allow the architect to assess the status of the project at the preliminary design stage and to verify if: **a.** this stage has been completed; **b.** additional consultants or professionals are needed (including renderers and model makers); **c.** additional information from the client, authorities or consultants are required; **d.** any other initiative has to be undertaken in order to complete the development design stage.

The documentation to be reviewed includes: **a.** the program (to verify the compliance of the design with the requirement of the former); **b.** minutes of meetings and additional requirements added during the development of the project and, therefore, not included in the original program; **c.** by-law requirements to determine design compliance; **d.** approval process to verify the design program, project design schedule and the documentation required versus the documentation already produced; **e.** memos, faxes and correspondence received from the client, authorities or consultants to verify if the pertinent information has been considered in producing the design; **f.** initial construction budget and subsequent revisions.

To complete the design development stage and obtain final approval from the client (which should be the result of the previous approval obtained at each stage and during this phase), the architect must: **a.** complete the design development documentation (which includes the drawings, the outline specifications and a report); **b.** obtain approvals from the authorities having jurisdiction (if required).

Maintaining the scheduling of this stage is dependent on the efficient organization of the project. It is at this stage that the relationship and level of performance of other individuals independent of the architect's office might have a major impact on the design process and completion of documentation. Because these factors are in some measure beyond of the complete control of the architect, a margin in terms of time contingency should be factored in when the design schedule is reviewed at the beginning of this stage. In order to minimize delays, a set of priorities should be established where more lengthy activities are initiated immediately. The following is a general guideline to establish such priorities and begin activities critical in term of scheduling without delay, thus generating the following: **a.** client response/approval having an impact on issues for which a critical activity or initiative must be commenced; **b.** information that requires complex and/or time consuming research on materials, technical procedures or has an impact on cost; **c.** approval for non standard code related issues or by-law variances; **d.** data or approval/response from authorities having jurisdiction (including utility companies in relation to services, type and preferred location of equipment, interpretation of by-laws); **e.** collaboration of special consultants; **f.** any other activity that might require a lengthy process on the part of the architect or other individuals and organization.

In order for the consultants to respond efficiently to the project requirements, the architect has to provide them with the proper information and request from them the necessary input:

1. The architect should provide the consultants with the new information gathered or created in this phase which itself will be totally new or will integrate the information given in the previous stages of the project with respect to:

   a. To all the consultants: the program (this document should include the information indicated in the *Defining a Program* section of this book); site analysis (if different from the one included in the program or distributed during the previous stages of the project); the latest approved design (approval from the client and, if applicable, preliminarily reviewed by the authorities; the code analysis (including type of occupancies, building classification, fire separations and firewalls, exiting system and path, occupant loads, unprotected opening analysis); size, type of glazing system (including type of frames, finishes and type of glass); construction materials and finishes; method of construction and project delivery; construction schematic schedule; the latest survey (if changed from the one included in the program or distributed at the schematic design stage—see Chapter 1 for a comprehensive list of elements to be shown on surveys); the latest geotechnical report (if different from the one included in the program or distributed at the schematic design stage).

b. To the structural consultant: parameters and restrictions for the structural members (i.e., location of columns, maximum sizes of beams and joists); in the program of particular interest for the structural consultant are references to the required flexibility of the spaces and provision for future expansion; size and location of openings (including mechanical and electrical shafts).

c. To the mechanical consultant the following programmatic requirements are particularly important: space flexibility, future expansion, hours of use of the building, temperature and humidity tolerance for the various spaces within the building, particular treatments of special spaces related to air conditioning, fire protection, plumbing installation and noise reduction, special controls and energy management, waste removal.

d. To the electrical consultants the following project information is of particular interest: flexibility of the spaces, expansion requirements, lighting levels for the various uses within and outside the structures, type of equipment to be used, special requirements for particular equipment.

e. For the landscape architect, if the project program gives indications on the type of outside activities to be considered in the design or interior courtyard to be part of the planning of spaces, this information is of primary importance. If no specific indication is given, then the overall image of the project, either described or implied in the program, becomes the reference point for the planning of landscaping. This is a component of the project where the budget will play an important role because it is one of first items that are reviewed in case of predicted cost overrun.

2. From the collaboration with the consultant the architect must obtain the following information:

a. From the structural consultant: finalization of column spacing and structural member sizes; coordination and approval from the structural point of view of all the openings required by the other disciplines; openings to be shown on structural drawings; support for mechanical, electrical and special equipment as required; structural requirements for fire rating and fire separation; miscellaneous items to be embedded in the structure.

b. From the mechanical consultant: decision on centralized or individualized heating and cooling system; location, type and size of air conditioning and all mechanical equipment, including sizes of space(s) required within and outside the building(s); heating system; size and location of major ducts and pipes; provision for expansion.

   c. From the electrical consultant: total load and provision for expansion; requirement for main electrical service and space for any vault or sub-station to be included in the design; distribution schemes; location and size of electrical closets, main risers, special rooms; requirements for conduits; light fixture selection; fire alarm system, intercom and security.

   d. From the landscape consultant: hard landscaping, including material and layout of walkways, sidewalk, driveways, plazas, planters, platforms and decks, stairs and any other landscape structure; soft landscaping including type, number and size of planting, change in levels and mounds; features like fountains or artificial ponds; landscape furniture.

THE DRAWINGS

A blending of technical and artistic quality is the main characteristic of the drawings at the design development stage. The purpose of these drawings is to communicate the aesthetical architectural expression (which includes intrinsic parameters of the building like functions, distribution, orientation, and extrinsic quality like form, material, and colors) in conjunction with regulatory aspects (like zoning and environmental by-laws requirements and restrictions, planning guidelines) and more technical elements (like provision for waste collection, mechanical and electrical equipment). In addition, the exterior areas of the site have to be defined in detail through a landscape plan. The following is a typical set of drawings at the design development stage.

1. Data sheet (see Figure 4.32). The following information should be included: **a.** name of the project; **b.** legal description and address; **c.** project data: information shown should include zoning, zoning requirements, lot area, maximum allowable area (if applicable), maximum site coverage (if applicable), proposed total area of the building, proposed site coverage (if applicable), area of the building by floor, area of the typical units (if multi-family), area of amenities (if included in the project), area of common spaces, other outside areas regulated by local zoning by-laws, parking requirements, parking provided as well as loading (if applicable); **d.** architectural and consultants' drawing list; **e.** name of consultants, contact person, address and telephone number (i.e., architect, landscape architect, environmental consultant, civil engineer); **f.** an illustration of the project.

2. Site plan (see Figure 4.33). The drawing should include: **a.** accurate representation of the site with indicated structures to be demolished and main existing features; **b.** immediate surroundings; **c.** finished proposed grade elevations and finished paving elevations. Data to be related to finished grade and paving elevations beyond and adjacent to the property lines; **d.** parking layout on surface and underground (if required). The underground parking should take into account the width of the structural columns; **e.** dimensioned

interior roads and curbs (if applicable); **f.** location of the building or buildings; **g.** vertical and horizontal vehicular and pedestrian circulation; **h.** accurate representation of the buildings (depending on the type, size and complexity of the building, either the roof plan or the floor plan); **i.** grid line system; **j.** detailed overall dimensions and setbacks; **k.** dimensioned access or accesses to the site; **l.** access or accesses to the building or buildings; **m.** detailed plans of hard and soft landscaping (provided in medium and large projects by a landscape architect).

3. A shadow diagram should be developed as part of the project analysis. For medium and major projects it might be included in the type of documentation that the authorities require as part of the development permit application package.

4. Floor Plans (see Figure 4.34). At this stage the floor plans should indicate the following main elements: **a.** the accurate layout of the perimeter of the building; **b.** floor elevations; **c.** interior layout with walls drawn at correct size; **d.** glazing drawn at the correct size; **e.** door drawn at the correct size; **f.** exits accurately planned and drawn; **g.** detailed exterior and critical interior dimensions; **h.** projection of floor above; **i.** grid line system; **j.** property lines at ground floor and on floors where changes introduce critical dimensions.

5. Elevations (see Figure 4.35). At this stage these drawings should specify: **a.** an accurate shape of the building; **b.** a complete representation of all the architectural elements; **c.** a clear indication of all the main material and texture; **d.** the relationship with the immediate surrounding buildings (usually for major projects); **e.** property lines; **f.** floor elevations; **g.** grid lines system; **h.** maximum allowable height.

6. Sections (see Figure 4.36). Although schematic, the sections should indicate clearly: **a.** an accurate representation of the building at the point of the section; **b.** existing and finished proposed grade; **c.** floor elevations; **d.** roof and roof parapet elevations; **e.** maximum allowable height; **f.** sidewalks and partial streets beyond the property lines (if applicable); **g.** in urban areas and for medium and major projects the immediate surrounding buildings should be included.

7. Rendering (see Figure 4.37).

8. Landscape plans.

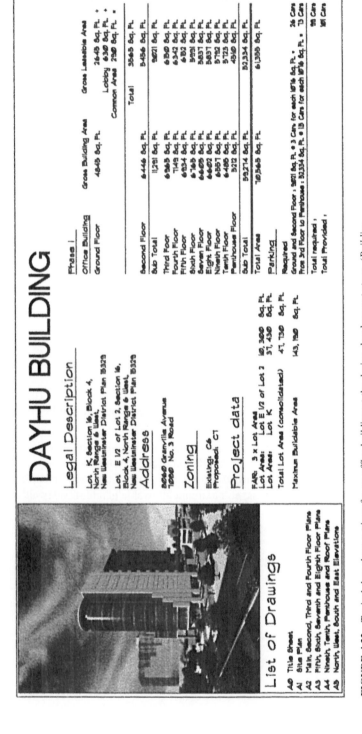

FIGURE 4.32 Typical data sheet settings for an office building at the design development stage. (*Building design by Marco Ciriello while with Chandler Associates Architecture Inc. Image courtesy Chandler Associates Architecture Inc.*)

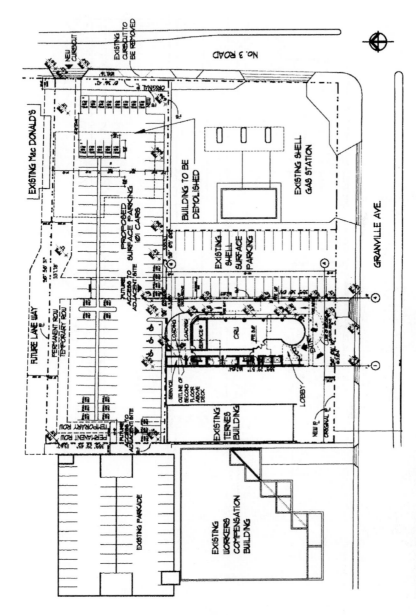

FIGURE 4.33 Typical site plan setting at the design development stage. (*Building design by Marco Ciriello while with Chandler Associates Architecture Inc. Image courtesy Chandler Associates Architecture Inc.*)

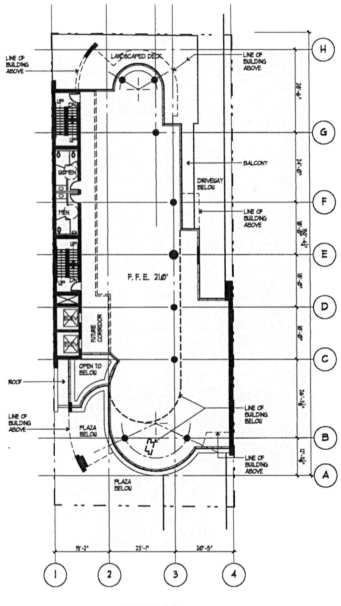

GRANVILLE AVE.

SECOND FLOOR PLAN
ELEV. = 116'-0"

FIGURE 4.34 Typical floor plan at the design development stage. *(Building design by Marco Ciriello while with Chandler Associates Architecture Inc. Image courtesy Chandler Associates Architecture Inc.)*

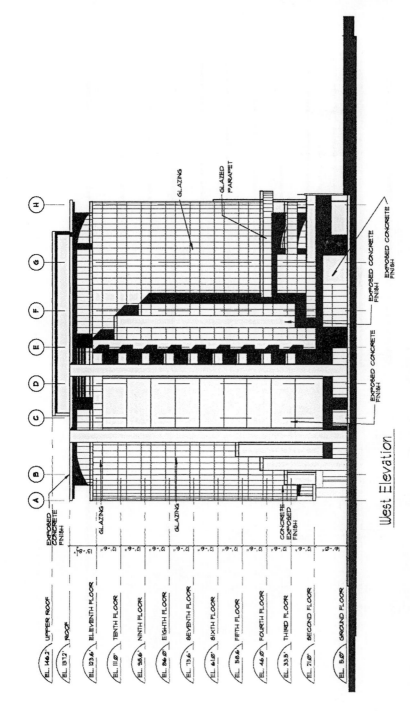

FIGURE 4.35 Typical elevation at the design development stage. (*Building design by Marco Ciriello while with Chandler Associates Architecture Inc. Image courtesy Chandler Associates Architecture Inc.*)

4.43

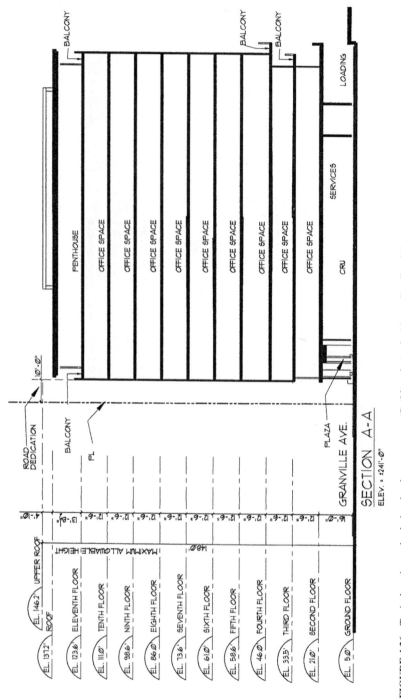

FIGURE 4.36 Typical section at the design development stage. *(Building design by Marco Ciriello while with Chandler Associates Architecture Inc. Image courtesy Chandler Associates Architecture Inc.)*

FIGURE 4.37 Computerized rendering. *(Building design by Marco Ciriello while with Chandler Associates Architecture Inc. Image courtesy Chandler Associates Architecture Inc.)*

OUTLINE SPECIFICATIONS

In the choice of materials it is fundamental to operate within the project budget. Once the selection is restricted or guided by this parameter, other factors can affect the choice made by the architect:

1. Technical characteristics like the suitability of the material for the application proposed with clear technical data and samples, durability and maintenance requirements, clear installation procedures.

2. Aesthetic qualities based on availability of colors, different types, models, textures, and finishes.

3. Reliability dependent on established consistent performance, reputation of the supplier and manufacturer, time for delivery, warranty.

The above factors should be considered as absolute characteristics as well as in comparative terms related to the characteristics of other products. For a more in-depth analysis of the type and structure of the specifications see Chapter 1, *Specifications and Project Manual.*

REPORTS

At this stage there could be a need for various types of reports. The following two are the most common and are part of the scope of work of a design development phase:

1. Design Rationale Report: this is a type of report that is associated with the approval process. It describes the functional as well as the aesthetical characteristics of the project including aspects like project data (i.e., zoning type, areas, number of stories, height, types of occupancy; official design guidelines, general project design philosophy expressed through an urban analysis and/or an environmental analysis and the relationship of the building with its immediate surroundings, the site layout, parking and service facilities required and provided, accessibility, vertical and horizontal circulation, functional distribution, finishes, exterior characteristics and materials used, landscaping and exterior spaces, contribution of the project as part of the urban structure and/or the project impact on the natural environment.

2. Design Report: this is an important part of the design development documentation. It allows individuals other than the design architect to familiarize themselves with the project. Furthermore, it minimizes misunderstanding between the architect and the client by complementing the drawings and expressing concepts and requirements that should not and/or cannot be included in the drawings. Prepared and updated during the design development stage as a working document, it is finalized after final approval by the client and authorities. In preparing the design report, the continuity of the project in the different stages has to be constantly considered. This is important from many points of view: **a.** a greater consistency in the findings and solutions; **b.** clarity in the presentations; **c.** in terms of liability, a constant connection with the premises, client instructions and approval obtained at the various stages; **d.** in terms of client/architect contract, a continuous reference to the scope of work and the terms of the contract.

The following is a guideline for the design report table of contents that integrates the various components of the project, maintaining the conceptual continuity which has been mentioned above. (Depending on the type, size, and complexity of the project, some of the items included in the list do not apply):

1. Index.
2. List of drawings.

3. Executive summary.
4. Key aspects of the program (in an executive summary form).
5. Summary of zoning, codes and environmental requirements.

6. Project objectives:
   a. Financial and administrative.
   b. Functional.
   c. Formal.
   d. Social.

7. Status of the project at the preliminary design stage:
   a. Summary of issues.
   b. Resolutions and approvals.
   c. Course of action for next and future stages of the project.

8. Design development stage.

9. Summary of programmatic issues at the design development stage:
   a. Financial and administrative.
   b. Functional.
   c. Formal.
   d. Social.

10. Summary of design solution to design development programmatic issues:
    a. Architectural:
       (1) Functional aspects: site layout, orientation, parking, circulation, activities and spaces, special features.
       (2) Formal aspects: interior features, interior material and finishes, exterior design, exterior material and finishes.
    b. Geotechnical investigation and parameters:
       (1) Site conditions.
       (2) Site preparation.
    c. Structural design.
       (1) Foundations.
       (2) Structural system design, material and framing.
    d. Mechanical design.
       (1) Type of HVAC system and distribution.
       (2) Sprinkler system.
       (3) Equipment room.
       (4) Controls.
       (5) Operating cost, maintenance program and energy consumption.
    e. Electrical design.
       (1) Description of electrical systems and schematics.
       (2) Lighting and light fixtures.
       (3) Fire alarm system.
       (4) Communication and security systems.
       (5) Controls and other features.

    f. Landscaping design.
       (1) Site planning.
       (2) Hard landscaping.
       (3) Soft landscaping.
       (4) Special features and site furniture.
       (5) Maintenance program and cost.

11. Outline specifications.
12. Building code analysis.
13. Summary of building areas.
14. Construction cost estimate.

There are other types of reports that are less frequently part of the architect's work and are usually beyond the basic scope of work of an architect. One of them is the Marketing Report. For commercial projects, the architect might be asked to collaborate with other agencies in producing brochures and other marketing tools. Usually the architect's input refers to a short version of a Design Rationale Report where the philosophical aesthetical aspects are minimized, although included, and emphasis is given in highlighting selling features and data like areas, parking, amount of glazing, natural lighting and views, interior and exterior features, amount of storage, amenities within and outside the project, facilities and services easily accessible in the neighborhood, social milieu, and potential for future expansion. Graphic material is usually associated with these types of reports. The approval of the client and of the authorities concludes this first stage of the design.

BUILDING PERMIT DRAWINGS

In order to be built, a project needs to be approved by the authorities. Depending on the type, size and complexity of the project, its location, the characteristics of the site, the regulations, bylaws and requirements of the authorities as well as those of the project program, this process can be complex and can involve various levels of government.

The fundamental difference between building permit drawings and construction drawings resides, as in any act of communication, in their purpose. In the case of building permit drawings, the reason for producing a set of drawings is to demonstrate to the authorities that the building complies with the requirements, regulations, by-laws and standards included in the various codes and policies, especially for those requirements that can affect the safety of the future users. In the case of the construction drawings, the purpose is to build the project. These two different reasons dictate the kind and extent of information to be included in the drawings. As a general consideration, it is possible to define the building permit drawings as a stage of the construction drawings. In this sense, the building permit drawings do not need to show all the details that are essential to construct the project. However, some of the documentation that has to be included in the building permit package (i.e., diagrams for the code analysis or indicating the spaces and elements included or excluded from calculations of areas) will not be part of the construction drawing set.

As an average, the percentage of completion of a construction drawing set at the building permit stage can be considered between 70 percent (in exceptional cases 65 percent) and 90 percent. This is dependent on the complete scope of work that is the basis for the architectural contract. If, for example, interior details constitute a substantial part of the scope of work, many of them are not pertinent to the building permit and they do not have any substantial code implication from the safety point of view. This means that once the project is filed for building permit, substantial work still remains to be done before the project documentation can be completed.

Having the purpose of the graphic and written material clearly in mind is fundamental. It provides the architect with a general guideline applicable to any situation. In other words, the fundamental question "what is this information for?" should constantly be related to the type of information included and the type of graphic representation chosen. An example of this would be the fire rating of walls, floors, and roofs. The requirements of building codes provide information on: **a.** location of fire separation(s); **b.** type of material; **c.** value of fire rating; **d.** standards.

As stated, if the purpose of the building permit drawings is to demonstrate the compliance of the project with these requirements, the information to be shown should indicate how the project satisfies the above parameters. Building permit drawing information is illustrated in Figure 4.38.

BUILDING PERMIT DRAWING INFORMATION

The typical information to be included in building permit drawings for each requirement generally can be grouped in four different categories: Location, Type of Material or Equipment, Values (i.e. hours, numbers of items or equipment, distances, areas, height, dimesions) and Standards (i.e UL or ULC #, ASTM, CSA, parameters of performance, technical requirements).

In the case of a fire separation assembly, the compliance with the building code requirements can be graphically shown by indicating on the plans the locations, type and values of the fire separation. On the Wall Schedule, Materials and Standards (which includes type of assemblies) can be indicated.The clear reference to Standards is particularly important because, in such short form, Standards convey very broad information that, in order to be clearly shown, would require very lengthy description. An additional advantage is that the time required by the authorities to process the application is shortened because of the clarity and completeness of the information.

In order to show the type of wall assembly, the most common method is to use "wall tags". In certain parts of the building the assembly requires special corner details of drywall arrangements (i.e. in shaft walls). In such cases wall type references are not sufficient and full details need to be developed.

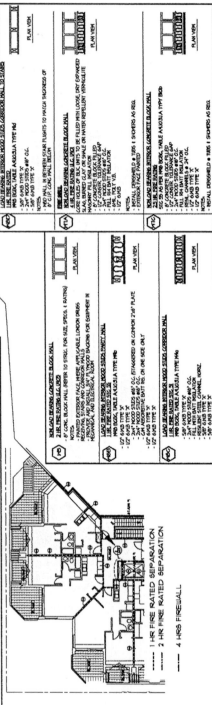

FIGURE 4.38 Building permit drawing information.

4.50

CHAPTER 5
TYPES OF CODES

FUNCTION AND SOCIO-ECONOMICAL EFFECTS OF CODES

There are a number of codes and each code has various functions. These functions are dependent on the purpose of the particular code.

Codes are necessary because the perceived importance of certain aspects that they regulate, as well as the extent to which rules should be applied, are in many cases dependent on individual values that may emphasize certain factors rather than others. The order of priorities and the degree of importance attributed to a particular item are often very subjective.

All codes have a direct influence on the matters which they regulate. Given the increased regional and national scope of their influence, they have a direct effect at economic and social levels.

These considerations are also valid for codes related to the construction industry. In terms of standards of safety, for example, the social ramifications are very obvious. In economic terms, the unification of dimensions, characteristics, materials, and quantities, produce the following repercussions on the market: **a.** a general minimum standard of performance to be applied, resulting in fewer disasters. This, in turn, reduces the social cost in terms of insurance company instability, health related aspects, reduction in the requirements of administrative levels and complexity of infrastructure **b.** the possibility of a direct comparison of products in terms of quality, price and performance; **c.** a free exchange of products manufactured in different regions; **d.** an increase in expertise throughout the industry as well as among the professionals and operators.

BACKGROUND

At the beginning of the 20th century, the realization by groups such as the insurance industry of the concepts expressed in item **a** triggered the idea of developing a model law. Concerns about the regulation of building construction in the United States date back 350 years to the time of the early settlements. However, the early part of the 20th century saw the first concerted effort to establish norms. The new technology allowed the construction of bigger and taller buildings and offered a tangible stimulus that increased the awareness on the part of the public and the above mentioned groups of the potential danger caused by a non-regulated construction industry.

The *National Building Code*, as the model code became known, was promulgated by the National Board of Fire Underwriters (later known as the American Insurance Association). It was updated every ten years. The model code provided a set of rules for local authorities that could be adopted in their entirety or could be used as guidelines for regulations more specifically designed to satisfy local conditions. Because of these advantages, the model code became very popular at the local government level.

In 1915 code enforcement officials began to meet regularly. Three non-profit organizations were formed: **a.** The Building Officials Conference of America (later known as Building Officials and Code Administrators (BOCA) International Inc. was created in 1915. This organization represented code officials from the eastern and mid-western states; **b.** The Pacific Coast Building Officials became the International Conference of Building Officials (ICBO), created in 1922. It represented the western regions; **c.** The Southern Building Code Congress International (SBCCI), representing the southern United States, was formed in 1941. Still active today, these organizations are owned by their voting members, who are representatives of city, county, state and U.S. federal government officials.

Each of these organizations developed its own codes to reflect more closely than the National Building Code its specific concerns. In 1984 the National Building Code was withdrawn in recognition of the effectiveness of these separate codes. Most U.S. cities (97%) have adopted one or more of the three model codes or have designed codes derived from the model codes (see Figures 5.1 through 5.18). The latter case applies particularly in larger urban areas where the number of professionals is sufficient to allow their organizations to provide assistance to the authorities in designing a code that reflects more closely local conditions. The following are the publications released by each organization:

BOCA. BOCA National Building Code, BOCA National Prevention Code, BOCA National Property Maintenance Code, BOCA National Energy Conservation Code, BOCA National Mechanical Code, BOCA National Plumbing Code, BOCA National Private Sewage Disposal Code.

ICBO. Uniform Building Code, Uniform Mechanical Code, Uniform Fire Code, Uniform Housing Code, Uniform Code for the Abatement of Dangerous Buildings, Uniform Sign Code, Uniform Administrative Code, Uniform

ABECC: Alabama Building Energy Conservation Code

ABEES: Alaska Building Energy Efficiency Standards

ABC: Alabama Building Commission

ADAGG: Regulation included in the American with Disabilities Act

ASBC: Alabama State Building Code

ASGC: Arkansas State Gas Code

ASPC: Arkansas State Plumbing Code

CA-DHCD: Codes Administration, Department of Housing and Community Development

CBC: California Building Code

CEC: California Electrical Code

CENC: California Energy Code

CFC: California Fire Code

CMC: California Mechanical Code

CPC: California Plumbing Code

CESCC: California Elevator Safety Construction Code

COLP: Commission on Official Legal Publications

DAAS: Delaware Architectural Accessibility Standards

DBETET: Department of Business, Economic, Turism, Energy, Resources and Technology Division

DSA: Division of the State Architect

DSAAC: Division State Architect Compliance

FSAC: Florida State Accessibility Code

FPDC: Fire prevention Division Chief

GFP: Government Funded Projects

HOT: Hotels

KDHBC: Kentucky Department of Housing, Building and Construction

IMC: International Mechanical Code

IPC: International Plumbing Code

MEC: Model Energy Code

MMC: Minnesota Mechanical Code

NBC: National Building Code

NEC: National Electrical Code

NFPA: National Fire Protection Association

OPLAED: Office of Policy and Legislative Affairs, Energy Division

SPC: Standard Building Code

SMC: Standard Mechanical Code

SFPC: Standard Fire Prevention Code

SBC: Standard Building Code

SOB: State Owned Buildings

SC: Schools

SFBC: South Florida Building Code

SMCD: State of Minnesota Codes Division

TH: Theaters

UBC: Uniform Building Code

UFC: Uniform Fire Code

UMC: Uniform Mechanical Code

UPC: Uniform Plumbing Code

FIGURE 5.1   Abbreviations.

Building Security Code, Uniform Code for Building Conservation, Uniform Zoning Code.

SBCCI.   Standard Amusement Device Code, Standard Building Code, Standard Existing Buildings Code, Standard Fire Prevention Code, Standard Gas Code, Standard Housing Code, Standard Mechanical Code, Standard Plumbing Code, Standard Swimming Pool Code, Standard Unsafe Building Abatement Code.

The activity of the three code organizations is not restricted to the development of the three model codes. All of them offer different types of membership thus allowing the general members to use the same services that are available to the voting members. Among the primary benefits is the technical assistance provided by the permanent staff on matters concerning or related to the model codes. This includes plan reviews, training and education, product evaluation. The verification of product compliance is an important advantage of membership.

TYPE OF CODES BY STATE

State	Type of Code											General Notes
	Building Dwelling	Structural	Plumbing	Mechanical	Electrical	Fire/Life Safety	Accessibility	Energy	Elevator	Gas	Boiler	
AL	SBC 1994 (Reg. of the State FM) no AM All Bd except FP RG of FM	SBC 1994 (Reg. of the State FM) no AM All Bd except FP RG of FM	SPC 1994 (AL State Building Code) no AM SC, HOT, TH-ASBC	SMC 1994 (AL State Building Code) no AM SC, HOT, TH-ASBC	NEC 1996 (AL State Building Code) no AM All SOB SC, HOT, TH-ASBC	SFPC 1994 NFPA 101, '97 NFPA 1 '97 (Reg. of State Fire Marshal) All BD except FP RG of FM no AM	ADAAG All GFP no AM	ASHRAE 90.1 (AL Building Energy Conserv. Code) All SOB over 2000 sf - ABC Ph. (334) 242-4082		SGC 1994 (AL State Building Code) All SOB SC, HOT, TH-ASBC no AM		Alabama Building Commission (ABC) has Authority over the Alabama State Building Code. The Code applies to SOB, SC, HOT and TH. PH (334) 242-4082 Fax (334) 242-4182 Authority Having Jurisdiction: Fire Marshall: Ph. (334) 241-4166 Fax (334) 241-4158
AK	UBC 1997 For AM contact FM Ph.(907) 269-5604	UBC 1997 For AM contact FM Ph.(907) 269-5604	UPC 1997 no AM	UMC 1997 For AM contact FM Ph.(907) 269-5604	NEC 1996 no AM	UFC 1997 For AM contact FM Ph.(907) 269-5604	ADAAG no AM	ABEFS For AM contact FM Ph.(907) 269-5604		UMC 1997 UPC 1997 For AM see note		Codes are mandatory minimum for all buildings except 1, 2 or 3 Family Dwellings, unless otherwise indicated. Plans, except for 1, 2 or 3 Family Dwellings are reviewed at sate level. Anchorage, Juneau, Fairbanks, Kenai Sitka and Soldotna have their departments. Plans should be submitted directly to these cities
AR	SBC 1997 For AM contact SBCCI Ph.(888) 447-2224	SBC 1997 For AM contact SBCCI Ph.(888) 447-2224	ASPC 1995 For AM contact Dept. of Health Ph.(501) 661-2642	SMC 1997 no AM	NEC 1999 no AM	SFPC 1997 For AM contact SBCCI Ph.(888) 447-2224		ASHRAE no AM	ASME A17.1 1992	ASGC For AM contact Dept. of Health Ph.(501) 661-2642	ASME Boiler Pressure Vessel Code 1995 no AM	Codes are mandatory minimum for all buildings. Local Jurisdiction can amend the codes only by applying more stringent rules.

FIGURE 5.2 Types of codes by state.

5.4

TYPE OF CODES BY STATE

State	Type of Code											General Notes
	Building Dwelling	Structural	Plumbing	Mechanical	Electrical	Fire/Life Safety	Accessibility	Energy	Elevator	Gas	Boiler	
AZ	NONE	NONE	NONE	NONE	NONE	UPC 1997 For AM contact Dept. of Building and Fire Safety Ph. (602) 255-4072	ADAAG no AM	ASHRAE 90.1 no AM	ASME A17.1 1993 For AM contact NAESA Ph.(602) 266-8006	NONE	ASME Boiler Pressure Vessel Code 1995	
CA	UBC 1997 (CBC 1998) Jurisdict. DSA Ph.(916) 324-7180	UBC 1997 (CBC 1998)	UPC 1997 (CPC 1998)	UMC 1997 (CMC 1998)	NEC 1996 (CBC 1998)	UPC 1997 (CFC 1998) Jurisdiction FM Ph.(916) 445-8421	CFC 1998 (Title 24 Part 2) Jurisdiction DSAAC Ph.(916) 327-9698	CENC 1998 (Title 24 Part2) Energy Hot Line Ph.(800) 772-3300	CESCC 1998 (Title 24 Part7) Elev. Insp. Ph.(916) 322-3640			California Codes are based on ICBO's Uniform Codes. They are mandatory and local authorities can amend any code by applying more stringent rules. All local amendments must be filed with the California Standards Commission.
CO	UBC 1997 no AM	UBC 1997 no AM	UPC 1997 no AM contact Dept. of Health Ph.(501) 661-2642	UMC 1997 no AM	NEC 1996 no AM	NONE	ANSI A117.1 1992 no AM	MEC 1993 no AM			ASME Boiler Pressure Vessel Code 1995 no AM	State codes apply only to Hotels, Motels and Multifamily Dwellings where not local codes are enforced. Schools are regulated by the UBC, UMC and UPC. These standards have been adopted since 1991 by the Colorado Department of Labor and Employment Public Safety Office. Jurisdiction: FM Ph. (303) 239-4463

FIGURE 5.3 Types of codes by state.

TYPE OF CODES BY STATE

State	Type of Code											General Notes
	Building Dwelling	Structural	Plumbing	Mechanical	Electrical	Fire/Life Safety	Accessibility	Energy	Elevator	Gas	Boiler	
CT	NBC 1996 (State Building Code 2000 CT Suppl.) For AM contact COLP Ph. (860) 741-3027	NBC 1996 (State Building Code 2000 CT Suppl.) For AM contact COLP Ph. (860) 741-3027	IPC 1996 (State Building Code 2000 CT Suppl.) For AM contact COLP Ph. (860) 741-3027	IMC 1996 (State Building Code 2000 CT Suppl.) For AM contact COLP Ph. (860) 741-3027	NEC 1996 (State Building Code 2000 CT Suppl.) For AM contact COLP Ph. (860) 741-3027	NFPA 101, 1997 (State Building Code 2000 CT Suppl.) For AM contact COLP Ph. (860) 741-3027	ICC/ANSI A117.1 1998 (Connecticut Supplement Chapter 11) For AM contact COLP Ph. (860) 741-3027	95 MEC ASHRAE/IES 90.1 (2000 CT Suppl.) For AM contact COLP Ph. (860) 741-3027	ASME A17.1 1996 c/w 1997/98 Addenda For AM contact COLP Ph. (860) 741-3027		ASME Boiler Pressure Vessel Code NBIC	Statewide codes are mandatory. They cannot be amended locally. Copies of the codes are provided by the Commission on Official Legal Publications: Ph. (860) 741-3027, Fax (860) 745-2178.
DE	NONE	NONE	NONE	NONE	NEC 1999 (State Fire Prevention Regulat.) no AM	State Fire Prevention Regulations NFPA 101, 1997, For AM contact FM Ph. (320) 739-5665	State Fire Prevention Regulations ANSI A117.1 1992 (DAAS) For AM contact FM Ph. (320) 739-5665	MEC 1993 ASHRAE 90.1 1989 (Delaware Code, Title 16, Part 7 Chapter 76		NFPA 54 1996 (State Fire Prevent. Regulat.) For AM contact FM Ph. (302) 739-5665		Codes are mandatory minimum standards for all buildings. Local authorities can amend regulations applying more stringent rules.
FL	SBC 1997 no AM	SBC 1997 no AM	SPC 1994 no AM	SMC 1997 no AM	NEC 1996 no AM	SFPC 1991 no AM	ADAAG (FSAC) For AM contact Dpt. of Commun. Affair Ph. (850) 487-1824	FEEBCC 1993 For AM contact Dpt. of Commun. Affair Ph. (850) 487-1824	ASME A17.1 1993 c/w ASME A17.1a 1994 Add. ASME A17.1b 1995 Add	SGC 1997 no AM	ASME Boiler Pressure Vessel Code	State codes are mandatory as minimum Standards. Dade and Broward Counties follow SFBC. Local jurisdiction can amend the codes and adopt more stringent regulations. Dade and Broward County edition of the SFBC cannot be amended locally.

FIGURE 5.4 Types of codes by state.

5.6

TYPE OF CODES BY STATE

State	Type of Code											General Notes
	Building Dwelling	Structural	Plumbing	Mechanical	Electrical	Fire/Life Safety	Accessibility	Energy	Elevator	Gas	Boiler	
GA	SBC 1994 (Georgia State Minimum Strandard Building Code)	SBC 1994 (Georgia State Minimum Strandard Building Code)	SPC 1994 (Georgia State Minimum Strandard Plumbing Code)	SMC 1994 (Georgia State Minimum Strandard Mechanical Code)	NEC 1996 (Georgia State Minimum Strandard Electrical Code)	SFPC 1994 (Georgia State Minimum Strandard Fire Prevention Code)	ADAAG (Georgia Access Law Chapter 120-3-20)	MEC 1995 ASHRAE 90.1 (Georgia State Energy Code for Buildings)		SGC 1994		Statewide minimum Standards Building Codes. These codes incorporates Model Codes and amendment.
HI	NONE	NONE	NONE	Administr. Rules Title 11, Chapter 39 Air Cond. and Vent. for AM contact Ph. (808) 586-4701	NONE	UFC 1988 with 1989 and 1990 supplements (State Model Fire Code)	ADAAG no AM	ASHRAE 90.1 (Hawaii Model Energy Code) for AM contact DBETET Ph. (808) 587-3811		NFPA 54 1998 (State Model Fire Code)		Very minimal statewide Building Codes. All codes must be adopted by a specific County before they can be enforced. Hawaii includes also Administrative Rules (Title 11) issued by the Hawaii Department of Health.
ID	NONE	NONE	UPC 1997 Admin. Law Title 2 Chapter 6 for AM contact PB Ph.(208) 334-3442	NONE	NEC 1999 no AM	UFC 1997 for AM contact State FM Ph. (208) 334-4370	ANSI A117.1 1992 no AM	No Commerc. Code	ASME A17.1 1996 ASME A17.3 1996	NONE	ASME Boiler Pressure Vessel Code	Codes are mandatory minimum for all buildings. Local Jurisdiction can amend the codes only by applying more stringent rules.

FIGURE 5.5 Types of codes by state.

TYPE OF CODES BY STATE

State	Type of Code											General Notes
	Building Dwelling	Structural	Plumbing	Mechanical	Electrical	Fire/Life Safety	Accessibility	Energy	Elevator	Gas	Boiler	
IL	NONE	NONE	Illinois Plumbing Code applies to all BD	NONE	NONE	NFPA 101 1991 Edition with all standards referenced in Chapter 12 for AM State FM Ph. (217) 524-0791	ADAAG (Illinois Accessibility Code)		NONE	NONE	ASME Boiler Pressure Vessel Code 1995 c/w 95, 96, 97 Adden.	Capital Development Board, School Construction Program regulates school construction. Contact (217) 782-8708 - NFPA 101 applies as mandatory minimum to all building except 1 an 2 Family Dwelling and Public Schools, ADAAG (Illinois Accessibility Code applies as mandatory minimum to all buildings except residential
IN	UBC 1997 Indiana Building Code 1998 Ph.(317) 232-6173	UBC 1997 Indiana Building Code 1998 Ph.(317) 232-6173	UPC 1997 Indiana Plumbing Code 1998 Ph.(317) 232-6173	UMC 1997 Indiana Mechanical Code 1998 Ph.(317) 232-6173	NEC 1999 Ph.(317) 232-6173	UFC 1997 Indiana Fire Code 1998 Ph.(916) 445-8421	ADAAG ANSI A117.1 1992 Ph.(916) 445-8421	MEC 1992 (Indiana Energy Conservat. Code) Ph.(916) 445-8421	ASME A17.1 1987 (Indiana Elevator Safety Code) Ph.(916) 445-8421		ASME Boiler Pressure Vessel Code 1992 NBIC 1992	Mandatory statewide Building Codes. More stringent rules can be adopted by local jurisdictions only with the approval of the Fire Prevention and Building Safety Commission.
IA	UBC 1994 Iowa State Building Code 1994 For AM contact State FM Ph.(515) 281-5821	UBC 1994 Iowa State Building Code 1994 For AM contact State FM Ph.(515) 281-5821	UPC 1994 Iowa State Building Code 1994 For AM contact State FM Ph.(515) 281-5821	UMC 1994 Iowa State Building Code 1994 For AM contact State FM Ph.(515) 281-5821	NEC 1996 Iowa State Building Code 1994 For AM contact State FM Ph.(515) 281-5821	NFPA State Fire Marshal Rules	Iowa Administrat. Code Accessibility Requirements (Chapter 16) For AM contact	MEC 1992 ASHRAE 90.1 1989 Iowa State Building Code State FM Ph.(515) 281-5821	ASME A17.1 1990 no AM			Statewide Codes apply only to state-owned buildings and where State Building Codes have been adopted.

FIGURE 5.6 Types of codes by state.

TYPE OF CODES BY STATE

State	Type of Code											General Notes
	Building Dwelling	Structural	Plumbing	Mechanical	Electrical	Fire/Life Safety	Accessibility	Energy	Elevator	Gas	Boiler	
KS	UBC 1997 no AM	UBC 1997 no AM	UPC 1997 no AM	UMC 1997 no AM	NEC 1996 no AM	NFPA 101, 1997 NFPA 1997 (Kansas Fire Prevention Code) For AM FPDC Ph. (785) 296-3401	ADAAG no AM	ASHRAE/ 90.1 1989 (Kansas Corporat. Comm. Order) no AM	ASME A17.1 1996 no AM		Kansas State Boiler Code ASME Boiler Pressure Vessel Code 1995	Statewide codes apply only to state-oned buildings except the Kansas Fire Prevention Code (mandatory statewide) and the ASHRAE Standards (mandatory for all commercial buildings) Local authorities can amend the fire code by introducing more stringent rules. Disposal of hazardous materials is regulated by the Hazardous Waste Management Standards And Regulations
KY	NBC 1996 (Kentucky Building Code 1997) for AM contact KDHBC Ph. (502) 564-8048	NBC 1996 (Kentucky Building Code 1997) for AM contact KDHBC Ph. (502) 564-8048	Kentucky Plumbing Code 2000 for AM contact KDHBC Ph. (502) 564-8048	NMC 1993 (Kentucky Building Code 1997) for AM contact KDHBC Ph. (502) 564-8048	NEC 1999 (Kentucky Building Code 1997) for AM contact KDHBC Ph. (502) 564-8048	NFPA 1 1997 NFPA 101 1997 (1999 Kentucky Fire Prevention Code) KDHBC Ph. (502) 564-8048	ADAAG (Kentucky Building Code 1997) for AM contact KDHBC Ph. (502) 564-8048	MEC 1992 ASHRAE 90.A 1980 and 90B 1975 contact KDHBC Ph. (502) 564-8048	ASME A17.1 ASME A17.3 (Kentucky Building Code) Ph. (502) 564-3626			Codes are mandatory statewide. Local authorities may not amend regulations. The state adopts BOCA's National Codes one year after the Codes are published. Kentucky updates its Building Codes every three years.
LA	SBC 1994 (State Uniform Construct. Code) no AM	SBC 1994 (State Uniform Construct. Code) no AM	SPC 1991 c/w 1992 LA Amend. for AM contact SS-DHH Ph. (225) 763-5553	NONE	NEC 1996 no AM	NFPA 101 1997 no AM		ASHRAE/ 90.1 1996 no AM	ASME A17.1 1996 no AM	NFPA 54 1996 no AM	ASME Boiler Pressure Vessel Code 1995, 1998 Adden.	State codes are mandatory as minimum Standards except for one or two Family Dwelling.

FIGURE 5.7 Types of codes by state.

5.9

TYPE OF CODES BY STATE

State	Type of Code											General Notes
	Building Dwelling	Structural	Plumbing	Mechanical	Electrical	Fire/Life Safety	Accessibility	Energy	Elevator	Gas	Boiler	
ME	NONE	NONE	Main State Plumbing Code (Code of Maine Rules 10 Chapter 238 Ph. (207) 624-8639	NONE	NEC 1999 no AM Ph. (207) 624-8640	NFPA 101, 1997 no AM State FM Ph. (207) 287-3473	ADAAG no AM Ph. (207) 624-8767		ANSI A17.1 1996 ANSI A17.3 1996 Ph. (207) 624-8605	NFPA 54 1996 (Code of Maine Rules 02-582		Codes are statewise minimum Standards. Local Authorities can adopt more stringent rules.
MD	NBC 1996 (Maryland Building Performan Standards For AM Contact CA-DHCD Ph. (410) 514-7212	NBC 1996 (Maryland Building Performance Standards) Contact For AM CA-DHCD Ph. (410) 514-7212	NSPC 1993 and 1994 Suppl. and Chapter 3 of 1995 Suppl. contact CA-DHCD Ph. (410) 514-7212	IMC 1996 (Model Performance Code) no AM	NEC 1996 (State Fire Prevention Code) no AM	NFPA 101, 1997 NFPA 1 1997 (State Fire Prevention Code) contact State FM	Maryland Accessibility Code for AM contact CA-DHCD Ph. (410) 514-7212	MEC 1995 NEC 1996 (Building Energy Standards) contact CA-DHCD Ph.(410) 514-7212	ASME A17.1 for AM contact Div. of industry D.L.R Ph.(410) 333-4153	NFPA 54 1996 (State Fire Prevention Code) no AM		Codes are statewise minimum Standards for all buildings.
MA	NBC 1993 (Mass. State Building Code, CMR 780) Ph.(617) 727-2834	NBC 1993 (Mass. State Building Code, CMR 780) Ph.(617) 727-2834	Mass. State Plumbing Code CMR 248 Ph.(617) 727-2834	Mass. State Plumbing Code CMR 248 Ph.(617) 727-2834	NEC 1999 Mass. State Electrical Code CMR 527 Ph.(617) 727-2834	Mass. Fire Prevention Regulations CMR 527 Ph.(617) 727-2834	Architectural Access Regulations CMR 521 Ph.(617) 727-2834	ASHRAE 90.1 (Mass. State Building Code, Article 13 CMR 780 Ph.(617) 727-2834		661-2642		Codes are mandatory minimum for all buildings statewide. Local authorities may introduce changes only with state approval

FIGURE 5.8 Types of codes by state.

5.10

TYPE OF CODES BY STATE

State	Type of Code											General Notes
	Building Dwelling	Structural	Plumbing	Mechanical	Electrical	Fire/Life Safety	Accessibility	Energy	Elevator	Gas	Boiler	
MI	NBC 1996 (Building Code Rules Parts 1-4) for AM contact Bureau of Construct. Rules Ph.(517) 241-9313	NBC 1996 (Building Code Rules Parts 1-4) for AM contact Construct. Construct. Rules Ph.(517) 241-9313	IPC 1997 (Plumbing Code Rules Part 7) for AM contact Bureau of Construct. Rules Ph.(517) 241-9313	IMC 1996 (Mechanical Code Rules Part 9a) for AM contact Bureau of Construct. Rules Ph.(517) 241-9313	NEC 1996 (Electrical Code Rules Part 8) for AM contact Bureau of Construct. Rules Ph.(517) 241-9313	NFPA 101 1985 For AM contact Office of Fire Safety Ph. (517) 322-1123	NBC 1996 (Building Rules Part 4) for AM contact Bureau of Construct. Codes Ph.(517) 241-9313	Michigan Energy Code for AM contact Dept. of Consumer Industry OPLAED Ph.(517) 241-9313	ASME A17.1 1993 ASME A17.1a 1994	NONE	ASME Boiler Pressure Vessel Code 1992 with Addem.	Codes are mandatory and not amendable if adopted by local authorities. The latter are required to adopt either the state code or one of the nationally-recognized model codes. Where no local code is enforced the state code applies. The Fire/Life Safety Code applies to Schools and Health Care facilities. Different amendments apply
MN	UBC 1997 (MN State Building Code, Chapter 1300-1370) contact MSCD SMCD Ph.(651) 296-4639	UBC 1997 (MN State Building Code, Chapter 1300-1370) contact SMCD Ph.(651) 296-4639	MN Dept. of Health Plumbing Code Chapter 4715 contact SMCD Ph.(651) 296-4639	UMC 1991 c/w 1994 Amendmen. (MMC MN rules Chapter 4715) for AM contact SMCD Ph.(651) 296-4639	NEC 1999 (MN State Building Code MN rules Chapter 1325) for AM contact SMCD Ph.(651) 296-4639	UFC 1997 MN rules Chapter 7510 for AM contact SMCD Ph.(651) 296-4639	ADAAG (MN State Building Code MN rules Chapter 1341) for AM contact SMCD Ph.(651) 296-4639	MN Energy Code MN rules Chapter 7670-7678 for AM contact SMCD Ph.(651) 296-4639	ASME A17.1 1996 ASME A17.1a 1990 a (MN State Building MN rules Chapter 1307) Ph.(651) 296-4639			Statewide mandatory Building Code. Local authorities may only adopt the state code. Fire Code can be amended locally by applying more stringent rules.
MS	SBC 1988 no AM	SBC 1988 no AM	SPC 1988 no AM contact Dept. of Health Ph.(501) 661-2642	SMC 1988 no AM	NONE	NONE						State codes are guidelines. Local autorities have the responsibility for code adoption and enforcement. Contact: Chief Deputy Fire Marshal: Ph. (601) 359-1061 Fax: (601) 359-1076

FIGURE 5.9 Types of codes by state.

TYPE OF CODES BY STATE

State	Type of Code										Boiler	General Notes
	Building Dwelling	Structural	Plumbing	Mechanical	Electrical	Fire/Life Safety	Accessibility	Energy	Elevator	Gas		
MO	NBC 1996 no AM	NBC 1996 no AM contact Division of Design and Construct. Ph. (573) 751-3339	IPC 1995 no AM contact Division of Design and Construct. Ph. (573) 751-3339	IMC 1996 no AM contact Division of Design and Construct. Ph. (573) 751-3339	NBC 1999 no AM contact Division of Design and Construct. Ph. (573) 751-3339	NFPA 101, 1997, NFPA 1 1997 no AM contact State FM Ph. (573) 751-2930	ADAAG no AM contact Division of Design and Construct. Ph. (573) 751-3339	ASHRAE 90.1 1989 no AM contact Division of Design and Construct. Ph. (573) 751-3339		IMC 1996	MO Boiler Pressure Vessel Safety Act and Regul.	Local authorities enforce and adopt Codes. State Codes apply to state facilities. For Amendments to Boiler Code contact Division of Fire Safety Ph. (800) 877-5688
MT	UBC 1997 (Admin.) rules of Montana Division Chapter 70 Building Codes Bureau)	UBC 1997 (Admin.) rules of Montana Division Chapter 70 Building Codes Bureau)	UPC 1997 (Admin.) rules of Montana Division Chapter 70 Building Codes Bureau)	UMC 1997 (Admin.) rules of Montana Division Chapter 70 Building Codes Bureau)	NEC 1999 (Admin. Rules of Montana Division Chapter 70 Building Codes Bureau)	UFC 1994 (Admin. rules of Montana Division Chapter 70 Building Codes Bureau) Ph. (406) 444-2050	UBC 1997	MEC 1993 ASHRAE 90.1 (Admin. rules of Montana Division Chapter 70	ASME A17.1 1996 with 1998-1999 Addend. no AM		ASME 1998 Boiler Pressure Vessel Code	Codes are mandatory minimum Standards for all public and State-owned Buildings. Plumbing Codes and Fire/Life Safety Code are mandatory for all buildings. Codes are updated every three years shortly after the adoption of a new Uniform Codes.For all Codes amendments ,except Fire/Life Safety Code, contact Building Codes Div. Ph. (406) 444-3933
NE	NONE	NONE	NONE	NONE	NBC 1999 no AM	NFPA 101, 1994, NFPA State Fire Code Regulations Title 156) contact State FM Ph. (402) 471-2027	ADAAG 1991 (Nebraska State Fire Code Regulations Title 156) contact for AM State FM Ph. (402) 471-2027	MEC 1983 IECC 1998 MEC appl. to Comm. and Res. IECC to SOB and State funded BD	ASME A17.1 1993 ASME 1994 Add. Nebraska Admin. Code Title 230 Chapter 1	NFPA 54 1992 no AM	NE Admin. Code Title 229 Chapter 1	The State issues official Building Code Interpretations; contact State Fire Marshal Office (402) 471-2027. Plans for commercial constructions to be submitted to the State Fire Marshal's Office c/w application and fee; contact Plans Division Ph. (402) 471-9475 Electrical, Fire/Life Safety and Gas Codes mandatory minimum for all buildings. Accessible Code applies to all new Public Buildings.

FIGURE 5.10 Types of codes by state.

TYPE OF CODES BY STATE

State	Building Dwelling	Type of Code Structural	Plumbing	Mechanical	Electrical	Fire/Life Safety	Accessibility	Energy	Elevator	Gas	Boiler	General Notes
NV	UBC 1991 for AM contact State FM Ph.(775) 687-4290	UBC 1991 for AM contact State FM Ph.(775) 687-4290	UPC 1994 (Nevada Revised Statutes Title 40 Chapter 444) for AM contact State FM Ph.(775) 687-4290	UMC 1991 for AM contact State FM Ph.(775) 687-4290	NBC 1993 no AM	UFC 1991 NFPA 101 1994 for AM contact State FM Ph.(775) 687-4290	ADAAG (Nevada Revised Statutes Title 28 Chapter 338, 180	MEC 1986	ASME A17.1 1990 ASME A 17.3 1990	NONE		Codes are minimum mandatory for all buildings with few exceptions. Plumbing Code amendments require State review and approval. Accessibility Code applies to Public Buildings and Facilities, SOB and Public Schools. Local authorities can amend codes by applying more stringent rules or by adopting more stringent Codes.
NH	NBC 1999 (State Statute R115A for AM Contact FM Ph.(603) 271-3294	NBC 1999 (State Statute R115A for AM Contact FM Ph.(603) 271-3294	NPC 1993 (State Plumbing Code) for AM Contact State Plumber's Board Ph.(603) 271-3294	NONE	NBC 1999 (Electri. Board Rules and State Fire Code) no AM	NFPA 1 1997 NFPA 101 1997 (State Fire Code) for AM contact FM Ph.(603) 271-3294	ADAAG (Architectural Barrier Free Code of NH)	ASHRAE 90.1 1989 for AM Contact Public Utilities Commiss. Ph.(603) 271-2431	ASME A.17.1 1990 ASME A 17.3	NFPA 54 (State Fire Code)	ASME Boiler Pressure Vessel Code	Codes are minimum mandatory for all buildings with few exceptions. Building/Dwelling and Structural Codes not applied to one or two Family Dwelling. Plumbing Code to become more stringent requires State approval. Accessible Code applies to Government-owned, publicly funded buildings and public accommodations. Energy Code applies to commercial and industrial buildings over 4000 sf.
NJ	NBC 1996 (New Jersey Uniform Constr. Code) For AM Contact DCSPD Ph.(609) 984-0040	NBC 1996 (New Jersey Uniform Constr. Code) For AM Contact DCSPD Ph.(609) 984-0040	NSPC 1996 (NJ Uniform Constr. Code) For AM Contact DCSPD Ph.(609) 984-0040	NMC 1993 (NJ Uniform Constr. Code) For AM Contact DCSPD Ph.(609) 984-0040	NEC 1999 (New Jersey Uniform Constr. Code) For AM Contact DCSPD Ph.(609) 984-0040	NFPC 1996 (New Jersey Uniform Constr. Code) For AM Contact DCSPD Ph.(609) 984-0040	ANSI A117.1 1992 (NJ Uniform Constr. Code Subchapt 7) For AM Contact DCSPD Ph.(609) 984-0040	NECC 93 (NJ Uniform Constr. Code Subchapt. 3) For AM Contact DCSPD Ph.(609) 984-0040	ASME A17.1 1993 (NJ Uniform Constr. Code Subchapt 3) DCSPD Ph.(609) 984-0040			Codes are statewide mandatory and cannot be amended locally.

FIGURE 5.11 Types of codes by state.

TYPE OF CODES BY STATE

State	Type of Code											General Notes
	Building/ Dwelling	Structural	Plumbing	Mechanical	Electrical	Fire/Life Safety	Accessibility	Energy	Elevator	Gas	Boiler	
NM	UBC 1997 (1997 New Mexico Building Code) For AM contact Constr. Industry Division Ph.(505) 827-7030	UBC 1997 (1997 New Mexico Building Code) For AM contact Constr. Industry Division Ph.(505) 827-7030	UPC 1997 (1997 New Mexico Plumbing & Mechan. Code) contact Constr. Industry Division Ph.(505) 827-7030	UMC 1997 (1997 New Mexico Plumbing & Mechan. Code) contact Constr. Industry Division Ph.(505) 827-7030	NEC 1999 (1997 New Mexico Plumbing & Mechan. Code) contact Constr. Industry Division Ph.(505) 827-7030	NFPA 101 1997 NFPA 1 1997 no AM	AMSI A117.1 1998 (New Mexico Building Code) contact Constr. Industry Division Ph.(505) 827-7030	MBC 1986		NFPA 54 1996 (New Mexico Building Code) contact Constr. Industry Division Ph.(505) 827-7030	ASME Boiler Pressure Vessel Code	State Building Codes are minimum standard for all buildings and they are statewide mandatory. The Energy Code applies to Commercial Construction
NY	New York State Uniform Fire Prevention & Building Code, Title-9B West Group Ph.(800) 328-9352	New York State Uniform Fire Prevention & Building Code, Title-9B West Group Ph.(800) 328-9352	New York State Uniform Fire Prevention & Building Code, Title-9B West Group Ph.(800) 328-9352	New York State Uniform Fire Prevention & Building Code, Title-9B West Group Ph.(800) 328-9352	New York State Uniform Fire Prevention & Building Code, Title-9B West Group Ph.(800) 328-9352	New York State Uniform Fire Prevention & Building Code, Title-9B West Group Ph.(800) 328-9352	AMSI A117.1 1992 (New York State Uniform Fire Prevention & Building Code Title-9B) Ph.(800) 328-9352	New York State Energy Conserv. Constr. Code, Title-9C For AM West Group Ph.(800) 328-9352	ASME A17.1 1993 (NY State Uniform Fire Prevention & Building Code Title-9B) Ph.(800) 328-9352	NFPA 54 1996 NFPA 58 1996 (NY State Unif. Fire Preven. & Build. Code Title-9B) Ph.(800) 328-9352	ASME Boiler Pressure Vessel Code NBIC	New York State code are statewide mandatory minimum code standards, except for New York City. In order for local authorities to amend the code by introducing more stringent rules, approval from the NY State Fire prevention and Building Code Council is required.
NC	SBC (NC State Building Code, Vol.1) NC Dept. of Insur., Code, Council Section Ph.(919) 733-3901	SBC (NC State Building Code, Vol.1) NC Dept. of Insur., Code, Council Section Ph.(919) 733-3901	SPC (NC State Building Code, Vol.2) NC Dept. of Insur., Code, Council Section Ph.(919) 733-3901	SMC (NC State Building Code, Vol.3) NC Dept. of Insur., Code, Council Section Ph.(919) 733-3901	NEC (NC State Building Code, Vol.4) NC Dept. of Insur., Code, Council Section Ph.(919) 733-3901	SFPC (NC State Building Code, Vol.5) NC Dept. of Insur., Code, Council Section Ph.(919) 733-3901	NC State Accessibility Code Vol.1-C 1999 NC Dept. of Insur., Code, Council Section Ph.(919) 733-3901	ASHRAE (NC State Building Code, Vol.10) NC Dept. of Insur., Code, Council Section Ph.(919) 733-3901		SGC (NC State Building Code, Vol.CVI) NC Dept. of Insur., Code, Council Section Ph.(919) 733-3901	Uniform Boiler Pressure Vessel Act of NC	Statewide minimum standard mandatory codes except for one or two Family Dwelling. North Carolina adopts a Model Code every three years. State amendments are adopted every year.

FIGURE 5.12 Types of codes by state.

TYPE OF CODES BY STATE

State	Type of Code											General Notes
	Building Dwelling	Structural	Plumbing	Mechanical	Electrical	Fire/Life Safety	Accessibility	Energy	Elevator	Gas	Boiler	
ND	UBC 1997 (ND Century Code, State Bldg Code Chapter 54-21.3) Commun. Service Ph. (701) 328-2308	UBC 1997 (ND Century Code, State Bldg Code Chapter 54-21.3) Commun. Service Ph. (701) 328-2308	UPC 2000 (ND State Plumbing Code for AM State Plumbing Board Ph. (701) 328-9977	UMC 1997 (ND Century Code, State Bldg Code Chapter 54-21.3) Commun. Service Ph. (701) 328-2308	NEC 1999 (ND Wiring Standards) for AM contact State Electrical Board Ph. (701) 328-9522	NFPA 101, 1997 UFC 1997 for AM contact Fire Marshal Office Ph. (701) 328-5555	ADAAG (ND Century Code, State Bldg Code Chapter 54-21.3) no AM	MEC 1993 no AM	NONE	UMC 1997 (ND Century Code, State Bldg Code Chapter 54-21.3) Commun. Service Ph. (701) 328-2308		If State Codes are adopted by local authorities, they apply as mandatory minimum to all buildings, except for the Life-Safety Code that applies to Public Buildings.
OH	NBC 1996 (OH Basic Building Code, 1998 c/w 1999 AM) BOCA Mideast Regional Office Ph. (614) 890–1064	NBC 1996 (OH Basic Building Code, 1998 c/w 1999 AM) BOCA Mideast Regional Office Ph. (614) 890–1064	IPC 1995 (OH Basic Plumbing Code, 1998 c/w 1999 AM) BOCA Mideast Regional Office Ph. (614) 890–1064	IMC 1996 (OH Basic Mechanical Code, 1998 c/w 1999 AM) BOCA Mideast Regional Office Ph. (614) 890–1064	NEC 1999 (OH Basic Building Code, 1998 c/w 1999 AM) BOCA Mideast Regional Office Ph. (614) 890–1064	NFPA 1996 (OH Fire Code, 1998 BOCA Mideast Regional Office Ph. (614) 890–1064	ADAAG (OH Basic Building Code, 1998 Chapter 11) West Group Ph. (800) 362-4500	MEC '92 ASHRAE 90.1 (OH Basic Building Code, 1998 Chapter 11) West Group Ph. (800) 362-4500	ASME A17.1 1996 (OH Basic Building Code 98, OH Admin. WG Ph. (800) 362-4500	IMC 1996 (OH Basic Mechan. Code, 1998 c/w 1999 AM) West Group Ph. (800) 362-4500	OH Admin. Code, 4101.5 (OH Basic Building Code, 1998 West Group Ph. (800) 362-4500	The Ohio Basic Building Code (OBBC) is mandatory statewide. It applies to all buildings except: One, two and three Single Family Dwellings, US government and military structures and agricultural buildings. The OBBC is updated every three years: one year after the publication of the BOCA National Codes.
OK	NBC 1996	NBC 1996	NONE	NONE	NONE	NFPA 101 1997 NFPC 1996		ASHRAE/ 90.1 no AM		NFPA 54 1996 no AM	ASME Boiler Pressure Vessel Code 1995, 1998 Adden.	State codes are mandatory as minimum Standards except for one or two Family Dwellings. The Energy Code applies to State-owned and leased facilities.

FIGURE 5.13   Types of codes by state.

TYPE OF CODES BY STATE

State	Type of Code											General Notes
	Building Dwelling	Structural	Plumbing	Mechanical	Electrical	Fire/Life Safety	Accessibility	Energy	Elevator	Gas	Boiler	
OR	UBC 1997 (Oregon Structural Specialty Code 1Q98) Building Tech. Bookstore (800) 275-2665	UBC 1997 (Oregon Structural Specialty Code 1Q98) Building Tech. Bookstore (800) 275-2665	UPC 1997 (Oregon Plumbing Specialty Code 2000) Building Tech. Bookstore (800) 275-2665	IMC 1998 (Oregon Mechanical Specialty Code 1999) Building Tech. Bookstore (800) 275-2665	NBC 1999 (Oregon Electrical Specialty Code) Building Tech. Bookstore (800) 275-2665	UFC 1997 (Oregon Fire Code) Building Tech. Bookstore (800) 275-2665	(Oregon Structural Specialty Code Chapter 11 Tech. Bookstore (800) 275-2665	Oregon Structural Specialty Code Chapter 13 Tech. Bookstore (800) 275-2665		IMC (Oregon Mechanical Specialty Code 1999) Tech. Building Bookstore (800) 275-2665	ASME Boiler Pressure Vessel Code 1995 NBIC Various AM	Statewide Building Code (Oregon Structural Specialty Code), and applies to all buildings. Local authorities cannot amend the Code without the approval of the State. Inquiries about the code to be directed to Building Codes Division, State of Oregon, (503) 378-4133. The Fire/Life Safety Code can be amended by local jurisdictions by introducing more restrictive rules.
PA	NONE	NONE	NONE	NONE	NONE	Fire and Panic Regulations (Penns. Code Title 34 Chapter 49-59) Bureau of Occupational & Ind. Safety Ph. (717) 787-3323	ADAAG (Universal Accessibility Standards) Bureau of Occupational & Ind. Safety Ph. (717) 787-3323	ASHRAE 90 A 1980 ASHRAE 908 1975 (Building Energy Conserv. Act) no AM	Pennsyl. Elevator Regul. Law and PA Code Title 34 Chapter 7 Elevator Section Ph. (717) 787-3765	NONE	ASME Boiler Pressure Vessel Code (Penn. Boiler Law & Regul.)	Sate Codes, except for the Fire and Panic Regulations, are under local authorities. Fire and Panic Regulations apply to all buildings in which four or more people are housed, assembled or employed. Philadelphia Pittsburgh and Scranton have their own Fire Code. Accessible Code is a mandatory minimum for all buildings. The Energy Code is mandatory minimum for all buildings. The Energy Code applies to Residential Buildings over 3 stories and all Comm. Buildings.
RI	NBC 1996 (Rhode Island State Building Code) State Building Commiss. Ph. (401) 222-3033	NBC 1996 (Rhode Island State Building Code) State Building Commiss. Ph. (401) 222-3033	IPC 1995 (Rhode Island State Building Code) State Building Commiss. Ph. (401) 222-3033	IMC 1996 (Rhode Island State Building Code) State Building Commiss. Ph. (401) 222-3033	NBC 1999 (Rhode Island State Building Code) State Building Commiss. Ph. (401) 222-3033	NFPA 101 1997 NFPA 1 1997 (Rhode Island Fire Safety Code) Fire Marshal Ph. (401) 294-0861	ADAAG (Rhode Island State Building Code Reg. SBC-14, 15, State Building Commiss. Ph. (401) 294-0861	ASHRAE 90.1 (RI State Building Code) State Building Commiss. Ph. (401) 222-3033				Codes are statewide mandatory minimum standards for all buildings. Codes cannot be amended by local authorities. The codes are based on the 1996 edition of the BOCA codes.

FIGURE 5.14 Types of codes by state.

TYPE OF CODES BY STATE

State	Type of Code											General Notes
	Building/Dwelling	Structural	Plumbing	Mechanical	Electrical	Fire/Life Safety	Accessibility	Energy	Elevator	Gas	Boiler	
SC	SBC 1997 no AM	SBC 1997 no AM	SPC 1997 no AM	SMC 1997 no AM	NEC 1999 no AM	SFPC 1997 no AM	ANSI A117.1 1998 no AM	MEC '95 90.1 South Carolina Energy Office Ph. (800) 851-8899	ASME A17.1 1986 ASME A17.3 1986 Supplem.	SGC 1997 no AM	NONE	State codes are statewide mandatory minimum standards. Local authorities can modify the Codes by introducing more stringent rules. However they must obtain the approval of the Building Code Council. The enforcement and interpretation of each of the Codes is the responsibility of the local jurisdictions.
SD	UBC 1997 (Fire Safety Standards) for AM contact State Fire Marshal Ph.(605) 773-3562	UBC 1997 (Fire Safety Standards) for AM contact State Fire Marshal Ph.(605) 773-3562	NSPC '96 (Plumbing Commiss. Rules) for AM contact State Plumbing Commiss. Ph.(605) 773-3429	UMC 1994 (Fire Safety Standards) for AM contact State Fire Marshal Ph.(605) 773-3562	NEC 1999 (Wiring Bulletin of South Dakota) contact State Electrical Commiss. Ph.(605) 773-3573	UFC 1994 (Fire Safety Standards) for AM contact State Fire Marshal Ph.(605) 773-3562	ADAAG no AM	NONE	NONE for AM	UMC '94 for AM contact State Fire Marshal Ph.(605) 773-3562	ASME Boiler Pressure Vessel Code 1980 contact State Fire Marshal Ph.(605) 773-3562	Building/Dwelling, Structural, Mechanical, Fire/Life Safety and Gas Codes apply to Schools, Daycare Centres and State-owned buildings. Mechanical and Electrical Codes Applies as mandatory minimum to all Buildings. Accessibility Code applies to Health-care Facilities that are licensed by the State Dpt. of Health.
TN	SBC 1997 no AM	SBC 1997 no AM	SPC 1997 no AM	SMC 1997 no AM	NEC 1996 no AM Rules of The TN Dept. of Commerce & Insuran. Chapter 0780-2-1	NFPA 1 1997 NFPA 101 1997 no AM	NC Handicapped Code 1991 c/w 1996 Revisions NC Dept. of Insurance, Code Council Section Ph.(919) 733-3901	MEC 1992 no AM	ASME A17.1 1986 no AM	SGC 1997 NFPA 54 1996 NFPA 58 1996 no AM	ASME Boiler Pressure Vessel Code 1998 NBIC Boiler & Elev. DIV. 741-2123	State Codes are mandatory minimum standards to all buildings except one or two Family Dwelling and Licensed Health-care Facilities.. Accessibility Code applies to all Public Buildings. Energy Code Applies to Residential Construction. to Health-care Facilities that are licensed by the State Dpt. of Health.

FIGURE 5.15 Types of codes by state.

TYPE OF CODES BY STATE

State	Type of Code											General Notes
	Building/Dwelling	Structural	Plumbing	Mechanical	Electrical	Fire/Life Safety	Accessibility	Energy	Elevator	Gas	Boiler	
TX	NONE	NONE	NONE	NONE	NONE	NFPA 101, 1994	State of Texas Accessibility Standards (TAS) for AM contact Secretary of State Office Ph. (512) 463-3561	MEC '93 ASHRAE 90.1 no AM	ASME A17.1 current ASME A17.3 1994	NONE	Texas Boiler Law	Fire/Life Safety Code applies to Hospitals. Accessible Code applies to Publically-funded, State-owned and State leased buildings. Furthermore it applies to public and private buildings as defined by ADA. Energy Code applies to State-owned and State-funded buildings. applies to public and private buildings
UT	UBC 1997 Utah Uniform Building Standards Act Rules Rule RJ56-56) UT Dpt. of Comm. Ph. (801) 530-6727	UBC 1997 Utah Uniform Building Standards Act Rules Rule RJ56-56) UT Dpt. of Comm. Ph. (801) 530-6727	UPC 1997 Utah Uniform Building Standards Act Rules Rule RJ56-56) UT Dpt. of Comm. Ph. (801) 530-6727	UMC 1998 Utah Uniform Building Standards Act Rules Rule RJ56-56) UT Dpt. of Comm. Ph. (801) 530-6727	NEC 1996 Utah Uniform Building Act Rules Rule RJ56-56) UT Dpt. of Comm. Ph. (801) 530-6727			MEC 1993 ASHRAE 90.1 1989 UT Dept. of Comm. Div. of Occup. & Prof.Lic. Ph. (801) 530-6727)	ASME A17.1 Safety Code for Elevators and Escal. UT Dept. of Comm. Ph. (801) 530-6727)			Statewide mandatory codes. Local authorities can amend the Codes but only after obtaining a State approval of the rules to be amended or introduced.
VT	NBC 1987 c/w 1988 supplem. ('97 VT Fire Prev. & Building Code) Dpt. Of Labour Industry Ph. (802) 828-2106	NBC 1987 c/w 1988 supplem. ('97 VT Fire Prev. & Building Code) Dpt. Of Labour Industry Ph. (802) 828-2106	NPC 1990 (Set of Vermont Plumbing Rules) Dpt. Of Labour, Fire Prevention Division Ph. (802) 828-2106	NMC 1987 c/w 1988 supplem. ('97 VT Fire Prev. Code) Dpt. Of Labour Industry Ph. (802) 828-2106	NEC 1999 ('99 VT Electrical Safety Rule) Dpt. Of Labour, Fire Prevention Division Ph. (802) 828-2106	NFPA 1 '92 NFPA 101 '94 ('97 VT Fire Prevention & Building Code) Dpt. Of Labour, Fire Prevention Division Ph. (802) 828-2106	ADAAG Dpt. Of Labour, Fire Prevention Division Ph. (802) 828-2106	ASHRAE 90.1 1980 ('97 VT Fire & Prevention Safety Code) Dpt. Of Labour, Ph. (802) 828-2106	NONE	NFPA 58 1992 ('97 VT Fire & Prevention Safety Code) Dpt. Of Labour, Ph. (802) 828-2106	ASME Boiler Pressure Vessel Code NBC ('90 VT Boiler & Pressure Vessel Rule) Ph. (802) 828-2106	State codes are mandatory as minimum for all Public Buildings. Plumbing Code applies to all building connected to a public water supply or sewer line. The Electrical Code applies to all buildings. The Energy code applies to State-funded buildings.

FIGURE 5.16 Types of codes by state.

TYPE OF CODES BY STATE

State	Type of Code											General Notes
	Building Dwelling	Structural	Plumbing	Mechanical	Electrical	Fire/Life Safety	Accessibility	Energy	Elevator	Gas	Boiler	
VA	SBC 2000 (Virginia Uniform Statewide Bilding Code) VA Dept, of Housing Develop. Ph. (804) 371-7170	SBC 2000 (Virginia Uniform Statewide Bilding Code) VA Dept, of Housing Develop. Ph. (804) 371-7170	IPC 1995 c/w 1996 suppl. (Virginia Uniform Statewide Bilding Code) VA Dept. of Housing Ph. (804) 371-7170	IMC 1996 (Virginia Statewide Bilding Code) VA Dept, of Housing & Comm. Develop. Ph. (804) 371-7170	NEC 1996 (Virginia Uniform Statewide Bilding Code) no AM	NFPC 1996 (Virginia Statewide Fire Prevention Code) VA Dept, of Housing & Comm. Develop. Ph. (804) 371-7170	ANSI A117.1 (Virginia Uniform Statewide Bilding Code) VA Dept, of Housing & Comm. Develop. Ph. (804) 371-7170	NEEC 1996 no AM		SGC 1994		The Virginia Statewide Building Code, is statewide mandatory minimum standards. Based on BOCA National Codes, it cannot be amended by Local Authorities. Local jurisdictions can amend the Virginia Statewide Fire prevention Code and make it more stringent.
WA	UBC 1997 (State Building Code WAC Chapter 51-40) for Enq. Contact Ph. (360) 586-5880	UBC 1997 (State Building Code WAC Chapter 51-40) for Enq. Contact Ph. (360) 586-5880	UPC 1997 (State Building Code WAC Chapter 51-40 51-47) Contact Ph. (360) 586-5880	UMC 1997 (State Building Code WAC Chapter 51-42) for Enq. Contact Ph. (360) 586-5880	NEC 1996 (Law & Rules for Inst. Elect. wires & Equip. (WAC) 296-46) Ph. (360) 902-5249	UFC 1988 (State Building Code WAC Chapter 51-44 51-45) Contact Ph. (360) 753-0404	AD/AAG (State Building Code WAC Chapter 51-40) Ph. (360) 586-5880	WA State Energy Code (State Building Code WAC Chapter 51-11) Contact Ph. (360) 586-5880	ASME A17.1 1996 (WAC 296-81) For Enq, Contact Ph. (360) 982-6128	UMC 1997 (State Building Code WAC Chapter 51-40) for Enq. Ph. (360) 586-5880	ASME Boiler Pressure Vessel Code 1998 NBIC 1995 with Adden.	Statewide building code called State Building Code (SBC). Building, Plumbing, Mechanical, Electrical and Fire Codes are mandatory minimum for all local authorities required to adopt and enforce a building code. The SBC is part of the Washington Administrative Code (WAC) referred to in various chapters. State Codes are updated every three years.
WV	NBC 1996 (State Building Code) Secretary of State's Office Admin. Law Div. Ph. (304) 558-6000	NBC 1996 (State Building Code) Secretary of State's Office Admin. Law Div. Ph. (304) 558-6000	IPC 1995 (State Building Code) Secretary of State's Office Admin. Law Div. Ph. (304) 558-6000	IMC 1996 (State Building Code) Secretary of State's Office Admin. Law Div. Ph. (304) 558-6000	NEC 1996 (WV State Fire Code) Secretary of State's Office Admin. Law Div. Ph. (304) 558-6000	NFPA, NFPA 101 1997 (WV State Fire Code (29-3-5) Secr. of State's Office Admin. Law Div. Ph. (304) 558-6000	ANSI A117.1 1992 (State Build. Code) Secretary of State's Office Admin. Law Div. Ph. (304) 558-6000	NEEC '93 (State Building Code) Secretary of State's Office Admin. Law Div. Ph. (304) 558-6000				Statewide mandatory Codes.

FIGURE 5.17   Types of codes by state.

TYPE OF CODES BY STATE

| State | Type of Code | | | | | | | | | | | General Notes |
	Building Dwelling	Structural	Plumbing	Mechanical	Electrical	Fire/Life Safety	Accessibility	Energy	Elevator	Gas	Boiler	
WI	WI Admin Code Chapters 50-64 State Document Sales Ph.(800) 362-7253	WI Admin Code Chapters 50-64 State Document Sales Ph.(800) 362-7253	WI Admin. Code Chapters 81-86 State Document Sales Ph.(800) 362-7253	WI Admin. Code Chapters 45-64 State Document Sales Ph.(800) 362-7253	NBC 1996 WI Admin Code Chapters 50-64 State Document Sales Ph.(800) 362-7253	WI Admin Code Chapter 14 State Document Sales Ph.(800) 362-7253	WI Admin. Code Chapter 69 State Document Sales Ph.(800) 362-7253	WI Admin Code Chapter 63 State Document Sales Ph.(800) 362-7253	WI Admin Code Chapter 18 State Docum. Sales Ph.(800) 362-7253		WI Ad. Code Chapter 41-42 State Docum. Sales	Wisconsin has an independent statewide mandatory building code. Local jurisdictions can adopt more stringent regulation except for the Plumbing Code.
WY	UBC 1997 no AM for Enq. contact Ph.(307) 777-7288	UBC 1997 no AM for Enq. contact Ph.(307) 777-7288	UPC 1997 no AM for Enq. contact Ph.(307) 777-7288	UMC 1997 no AM for Enq. contact Ph.(307) 777-7288	NEC 1999 no AM for Enq. contact Ph.(307) 777-7288	UFC 1997 no AM for Enq. contact Ph.(307) 777-7288	ANSI A117.1 no AM for Enq. contact Ph.(307) 777-3641	NONE	NONE			Mandatory statewide Building Codes. More stringent rules can be adopted by local jurisdictions. Building/ Dwelling, Structural, Mechanical, Fire/ Life Safety, Accessibility Codes, Hazardous Materials (UFC 1997) codes apply to Hotels/Motels, Restaurants, Schools, State-owned and publicly funded buildings. In addition Public Health Code (NFPA 101 '94) applies to Medical Facilities.

FIGURE 5.18 Types of codes by state.

In the code development process, anyone can submit a proposal for change, which will be discussed and voted on in a public meeting of the membership. Modality and deadlines for the submission vary among the different organizations. For more detailed information, a member should contact the specific organization in which the change will be proposed.

The advantage of proposing a code change at the national level is that many professional, trade, and supplier organizations hold status within one of the code organizations. This participation is reflected in the number of issues and the broadening of the aspects discussed before the change is finalized. On the other hand, specific conditions are more evident at the local level. These two considerations, in addition to the ones already expressed previously, can put in perspective the relationship between a model code and local code as well as help to clarify their respective roles.

The three code organizations required a body able to provide coordination at the national level. In 1972 the Council of American Building Officials (CABO) was formed. Representatives from the boards of directors of each organization constitute its members. Its main focus is to operate as liaison between public and private organizations on national matters. Its corporate mission statement is as follows:

"The Council of American Building Officials is dedicated to the public health, safety and related societal needs in the built environment through the development and the use of consensus-based regulatory documents, enhancement of professionalism in code administration and facilitating acceptance of innovative building products and systems."

The CABO *One and Two Family Dwelling Code* was developed by BOCA, ICBO and SBCCI in response to the homebuilding industry request for a simple complete code describing the most commonly accepted building practices. This code is referenced in all three Model Building Codes.

In addition to the *One and Two Family Dwelling Code*, the *Model Energy Code* is another CABO document that is published jointly by BOCA, ICBO and SBCCI. A Code Development Committee is responsible for the development of this code and for the incorporation of emerging issues related to thermal performance. The information included is intended to reflect the latest conceptual and technological trends in building energy performance.

In 1975 CABO established the National Coordinating Council (NCC), which soon became the Board for the Coordination of the Model Codes (BCMC). This organization was created in recognition of the need to provide assistance on a daily basis in coordinating the efforts of the three main organizations.

Their mandate can be summarized as follows: **a.** to identify conflicts among the model codes with particular attention to means of egress and type of construction requirements as well as allowable height increase, minimum building heights, sanitation, light, ventilation and general design requirements; **b.** to propose changes to the three model codes; **c.** to process all code change proposals through the code change procedures of each participating organization.

With the growing trend toward a global economy and the accelerated exchange of products between countries, the need for a more effective unification of rules and standards became paramount. In order for American producers to be competitive, they needed to direct their efforts and resources to developing innovative products rather than trying to comply with multiple codes.

In 1994 the International Code Council (ICC) was created and in 1995 the Board for the Development of Model Codes (BDMC) was formed. The ICC mandate has been to develop a single set of codes called *International Codes* replacing the ones currently published by BOCA, ICBO and SBCCI. The BDMC mandate is addressing the emerging technologies and concepts by relating them to existing or new code requirements and standards. The functions of the BDMC are designed to allow the American manufacturers to be on the cutting edge of new technologies, products and materials without being hindered by a bureaucratic process unable to respond quickly to rapid changes in trends.

> **ICC International Codes.** *2000 International Building Code, 2000 International Residential Code* (It replaces the *International One- and Two-Family Dwelling Code* and its predecessor: the *CABO One- and Two-Family Dwelling Code), 2000 International Fire Code, 2000 International Plumbing Code, 2000 International Private Sewage Disposal Code, 2000 International Mechanical Code, 2000 International Fuel Gas Code, 2000 International Property Maintenance Code, 2000 Energy Conservation Code, 2000 International Zoning Code, 2000 International ICC Electrical Code.*

APPROVAL AND ENFORCEMENT PROCESS

In order to have legal status, a model code must be adopted as law by a legislative body. The code is then enforced throughout the geographical area under the jurisdiction of that authority. However, even when model codes do not have an official legal status, they provide a good guideline for design professionals who often apply their standards in the areas for which a particular model code has been conceived.

A state may adopt a code having a considerable range of influence on all aspects of public safety and standards. In this case, very little freedom is left to the local authority to legislate autonomously on these matters. However, the responsibility for enforcing rules established by the state rests in all cases with the local authorities. The latter, therefore, set up an organizational structure capable of handling the duties over which they have jurisdiction. This structure varies in size and complexity depending on the volume and type of building permit applications that those authorities usually process. In some cases local legislative bodies must rely on other jurisdictional structures (such as the county administration) because the number, type and frequency of applications received do not justify the support of permanent staff.

The process starts with a building permit application (see Figure 5.19). Then the plans are reviewed in due time by the building department for code compliance.

TYPICAL BUILDING PERMIT PROCESS
AND CODE ENFORCEMENT DURING
CONSTRUCTION

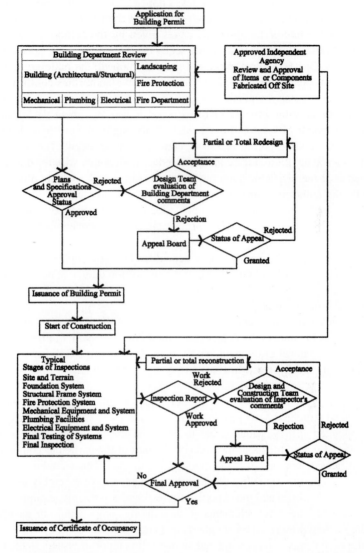

FIGURE 5.19 Typical building permit process and code enforcement during construction.

In smaller projects only a few departments are involved in the review. In larger projects the building inspector acts as coordinator and distributes one set of documents to the departments that need to review them. Where the planning department has already issued an approval, ultimately the building permit set of drawings is circulated to this department as well for compliance with the development permit drawings approved by them.

If the documents are found in compliance with the codes, the building permit is issued and construction can begin. If the authorities find the project, or aspects thereof, not in compliance with the codes, a notice is sent to the applicant identifying the items and the reasons for the rejection. In the latter case the applicants either accept the interpretation of the codes given by the authorities or file an appeal in accordance with the procedure set by the authorities. If the appeal board finds that the objections have merit and grant the appeal, the building permit is issued. If the appeal is denied and the findings of the authorities confirmed, the applicants must revise the plans in accordance with the comments made by the authorities. Usually the process involves a public hearing where the applicants present their points of view and any evidence that might support their claim.

When the building permit is issued, construction can begin. The permit can be withdrawn at any time if the construction does not comply with the documents approved or if the inspector observes violations to the codes which, after notification by the authorities, are not rectified. In case of a repeated violation, or a refusal to comply, the authorities can prescribe monetary sanctions. Further violations or persistence of the non-conforming situation may even result in imprisonment for several months.

The frequency of the inspection is dependent on the complexity of the construction. It is important to consider that the inspection authority needs to verify all the components of the construction. No item may be concealed, closed in or buried until it has been inspected and approved.

The stages and components that are the subject of the inspections are: **a.** Site and Terrain; **b.** Foundation System; **c.** Structural Frame System; **d.** Fire Protection System; **e.** Mechanical Equipment and Systems; **f.** Plumbing Facilities; **g.** Electrical Equipment and Systems; **h.** Final Inspection, which includes final testing of equipment and safety components of the project.

When items are built off site or prefabricated in a plant in another state (i.e., prefabricated structural wall panel system), the authority relies on the expertise of an appointed agency, which issues a certificate attesting compliance with the standards and requirements of the code on the part of the particular components. This certificate accompanies the components to the site. The accredited agencies have to combine the capability of inspecting the process of assembly as well as providing the facilities and the expertise for testing the assembly, equipment and, where necessary, the single elements of the building component(s) in accordance with the method prescribed by standards and codes.

After each inspection is completed an inspection report is issued. In the report the inspector records the status of the construction and any element that need to be rectified because of non-compliance with the code requirements or the building permit documents. As in the permit process, the applicant may appeal the decision of the authorities. At the end of the process the applicant must comply with the board's decision regarding the appeal.

When the final inspection reports from all the inspectors confirm that all requirements have been met and the construction has been approved, an occupancy permit is issued stating that the construction is safe to be occupied.

STANDARDS

A standard can be described as a prescribed set of rules, conditions, or requirements concerned with the definition of terms; classifications of components; delineation of procedures; specifications of dimensions, material, performance, design or operations; descriptions of fit and measurement of size, or measurement of quality and quantity in describing materials, products, systems, services or practices. As is the case for codes, standards must be adopted by the authorities that have jurisdiction in order for those standards to attain legal status.

Thousands of standards have been established relating to a multitude of aspects of very diversified topics. Model construction codes deal with standards that are related to the construction industry and construction practices. Standards acquire an official status suitable for model codes only when they are established following specific modalities and established procedures and when they define quality and quantities in accordance with the requirements of the model codes.

Standards define the minimum level of performance, the quantity and the quality of an item regulated by the model codes. Nothing prevents an owner from specifying items that exceed minimum standards.

The objective of a construction code is to regulate the thousands of standards related to the construction industry. A code becomes effective when it creates a well-ordered system capable of acting as a definite point of reference for any situation that might occur during the design, construction and operation of a project.

The following are the three basic categories of standards used in building codes: **a.** *design standards:* specifying methods of design, fabrication and accepted design procedures; **b.** *material standards:* defining quality requirements and properties of material and products; **c.** *test standards:* defining modality and conditions of testing and including structural unit and system tests, durability and fire test.

Once the code has identified the requirements, the standards are called upon to define the characteristics of the material or the product, how it is designed and how it must be tested in order to satisfy such requirements.

The International Code Council has the following policy to which standards have to comply: **a.** it is important to establish the need to reference a certain standard; **b.** the standards must be expressed in mandatory language; **c.** the standard must be appropriate to the subject that is at hand; **d.** terms need to be defined when they deviate from an accepted and recognized meaning; **e.** clear application and scope of the standard must be identified; **f.** the standards should not be defined referring to or using proprietary material; **g.** a proprietary agency must not be used to prescribe the quality control of the testing; **h.** test standards must indicate in detail the procedures to be used in testing, the type of sample and its preparation; **i.** reporting format of the test results, identifying the key elements of the performance, must be clearly defined in the standard; **j.** the measure of performance must be clearly mentioned either in the standard or in the text of the code; **k.** standards must be readily available; **l.** standards must be developed and maintained through a consensus process such as ASTM (American Society for Testing and Materials) or ANSI (American National Standard Institute).

Standards are referenced in the code as well as the code being referenced in many standards. The last chapter of each model code published by BOCA, ICBO, SBCCI, and ICC includes all the standards that are referenced in these codes as well as listing the organizations that promulgate the standard, the reference number, the edition year and the title.

A tiered system of standards is often the result of a standard referenced in another standard that, in turn, is referenced in the model code. The sequence can be very articulated and very effective as well, the result being that the complete text of each of these referenced standards is now part of the code just as if all of them were included in their entirety in the text of the model code. Using this tiered system the model code can be fairly concise, instead of requiring thousands of pages in order to include all the standards and their complete text.

ANSI is the organization that encourages the development of standards by developing procedures to determine criteria, requirements and guidelines to reach a consensus for American National Standards. ANSI was founded in 1918 by five professional and technical societies and three agencies of the federal government.

The function of ANSI is not precisely to develop standards. The latter are written by organization such as the American Society of Civil Engineers (ASCE), the American Society for Testing and Materials (ASTM) or the Underwriters Laboratories Inc. (UL). Through its Board of Standards Review (BSR), ANSI approves standards and ensures that results are achieved by following the general principles underlying the procedures for establishing a standard. ANSI is the United States representative of the International Organization for Standardization (ISO) and the International Electro-technical Commission (IEC).

METHOD FOR DETERMINING THE ADHERENCE OF MATERIAL TO STANDARDS

In order to accept a material, assembly. or product as adequate for a certain application, the adherence of its characteristics to certain standards has to be established. There are three methods that can be used:

1. The most common method is to conduct actual tests in accordance with nationally or internationally recognized standards. The limits of this method are: **a.** the results are valid for the conditions set in the test. The elements might react differently in an actual condition simply because the circumstances to which the structural member is exposed in a real fire situation could be different; **b.** the used assembly, material or product must adhere strictly to the description made of the tested sample; **c.** since the system has to be identical and testing is rather costly, this approach tends to slow down the introduction of innovations.

2. Use of empirical equations. If enough data on the behavior and characteristics of material, assembly or products are collected through tests to a degree that it is possible to establish a predictable consistency in their behavior and

to create mathematical equations describing the dynamic of the results, then it is possible to extend these results to situations not directly tested. The critical aspects of this approach are: **a.** the correlation between the database and the function of the material, assembly or product to be analyzed; **b.** the extent and number of the tested results; **c.** the correlation between the characteristics of the tested specimens and the material, assembly or product essential to the function for which they have been designed; **d.** the reliability of the calculated results; **e.** the realistic possibility of applying the material, assembly or product in the construction industry.

3. Rational Design Approach. This method has been most recently developed particularly in the field of fire testing. It should lead to models that rely on the knowledge of fields such as mechanics of materials, mechanics and characteristics of phenomena, and dynamics of systems and that will allow the prediction of behavior for categories of materials, assemblies and products exposed to different situations. For the correct development of this approach, a good database is fundamental and should be analyzed with the purpose of establishing laws of behavior under different conditions.

APPROACH TO CODE ANALYSIS

The aspects of the code that will be analyzed are the specific elements that affect the design at the beginning of a project. When these requirements are correctly related to the design and vice versa, the other aspects usually follow of themselves.

A code analysis is one of the first tasks that should be completed at the beginning of a project. This is important not only from the design point of view, but also because code requirements can be very restrictive and costly. For example, in exploring different design alternates for an identical project program, the architect might realize that different configurations vary in degree of complexity. This is reflected, then, in the number and type of requirements to be applied and/or in the materials with which the building can be built (less expensive in certain solutions than in others). These considerations are often applicable either to the whole building or to part of it. In some instances the project is so large and complex that, for example, there is really no choice between using combustible or non-combustible construction, the latter being a requirement in these types of construction (although even in these cases the fundamental question is, "Does the project need to be built as a single building?"). In other projects, which can be successfully resolved in various ways, the approach to the design can be very creative and provide not only a successful solution from an aesthetical and functional point of view, but with the result that the code classification of the building might be less restrictive.

It is very important that the architect have a general mastery of all the code requirements that might affect the design. The specific data cited in a specific article then it can be consulted and confirmed later (unless the specific data are critical) in order to refine the approach to the project and comply with the code. All three U.S. Model Codes and the Canadian National Building Code (CNBC) share a common basic structure that is founded on basic elements from which the requirements are developed:

1. Characteristics of the building.
   a. Type of occupancy: this defines the category of use of the building. From the building program it is expedient to identify the type of uses that will be included in the design. At the diagrammatic stage it is possible to establish a very preliminary distribution of these uses either per floor, in a multi-story building, or on a single floor, in a one-story building. In a multi-occupancy situation, where different occupancies are grouped in a single structure, this analysis might reveal configurations that are more advantageous than others in terms of degree of requirements.
   b. Occupant load: this is calculated per type of occupancy as a function of the floor area (related to a specific occupancy and use) divided by a standard established for different uses (i.e., area per person). The program should indicate the number and type of users. Health-based requirements or labor laws might dictate other outcomes. Once this information is compiled, the most restrictive data should apply (namely the highest number of persons prescribed by any of the documents). It should be taken into account that a considerable discrepancy between the occupant load on different floors—especially if the higher load is located on upper floors—might result in the application of more restrictive rules to the entire structure.
   c. Area of the building: this is the maximum footprint of the building. It corresponds to the maximum perimeter derived by projecting on the ground the outermost wall at any given floor. Three of the building codes calculate the area per floor in order to derive requirements and assign rules, while the Uniform Building Code tabulates the total area of all floors of the building. In order to reduce the number of code requirements, or to build the building more economically, it is useful in some cases to subdivide the building with area separation walls or, as identified in the CNBC and Provincial Codes, with firewalls. These are walls with certain characteristics that allow the areas defined by these separations to be considered as individual buildings. Thus the code requirements can be applied separately to each of these structures. Increasing the side yard can further increase the area of the building in certain model codes (i.e., UBC).
   d. Height of the building: this is usually expressed in number of floors. In certain cases (i.e., the requirements for high buildings in the CNBC and Provincial Codes) this parameter is expressed as an actual dimension.
   e. Sprinklering: in some codes (i.e., CNBC), a building that is sprinklered is exempted from some rules or may benefit from bonuses introduced to encourage the use of sprinkler systems as life/safety devices. These are

the elements that must be established at the beginning of a code analysis because these are data that will affect, either directly or indirectly, the applicable regulations over and over again. Once these parameters are identified, the next step is to determine all the requirements related to the above characteristics. At this point it will become evident that the requirements of the code can affect the cost of construction in ways related to the geometry of the building, its physical characteristics and the internal distribution:

2. Code Requirements
   a. Type of construction: depending on the characteristics of the building, codes prescribe what type of construction materials can be used. This means that the building will generally fall into one of two very broad categories: either a combustible or non-combustible construction. Within these general definitions, codes then refine the requirements by identifying the characteristics of any single components that can be used in each of these general categories. For instance, certain qualities of combustible elements are allowed in a non-combustible construction. Usually the parameters affecting the allowable use of these components are: location, dimensions and characteristics (the latter also expressed in standards).
   b. Fire Rating: once the type of construction is identified, the characteristics of the building dictate a specific fire rating for different components: floor, ceiling, mezzanine, walls and structural components (i.e., columns and beams). The required fire rating of other elements of the building could be a function of the rating of the elements listed above (i.e., exits), or their fire rating could be specified as a fixed value that is not affected by the change in building characteristics (i.e., service rooms). Codes use various methods to catalogue types of buildings in order to assign fire rating. The CNBC lists buildings in terms of type of occupancy called Groups, identified by letters from A to F (i.e., C for residential). Within these general categories CNBC subdivides the construction in terms of maximum number of story. Apart from the category defined as "any height, any area," a further differentiation is created by relating a specific number of stories to the maximum area allowed for a building, subject to specific requirements. The UBC subdivides the buildings in categories identified by Roman numerals from I to V.
   c. Exit System and Requirements: the exiting system is a fundamental aspect of the design of a building. It is usually based on three fundamental components:
      (1) Exit Access: this component is the part of the exit system that leads to the enclosed space of the exit. Types are: corridor, ramp or passage (see Figures 5.20, 5.21 and 5.22).
      (2) Exit: this part of the exit system is the enclosed and protected section that leads to the exit discharge. Examples are the enclosed fire rated exit stairs, ramp or passage (see Figures 5.23, 5.24, and 5.25).

(3) Exit Discharge: this is the end-point of the exit system. It opens onto a public open space or leads to a different building separated by a firewall. A common example of this component is an exterior door (see Figure 5.26).

The exit system is comprised of all three elements in every part of the building. At the ground floor, for example, the exit access and the exit discharge might provide the necessary components to comply with the code requirements. In other cases the exit discharge is the only means of egress that is needed.

CALCULATING THE SIZE OF THE EGRESS SYSTEM

The methods used by the BOCA National Building Code, the Standard Building Code, the Uniform Building Code and the National Building Code of Canada to size the Egress System serving a particular floor are similar. They are based on the following steps: **a.** determine the floor area; **b.** divide floor area by area prescribed for each occupant = *occupant load*; **c.** multiply occupant load by prescribed width of door, ramp or stair for each occupant.; **d.** divide total width of doors for the dimension of the chosen door units (3' 0") to determine the number of doors required; **e.** divide total width of ramp or stairs required by the minimum width of ramp or stairs prescribed by the code. The result is the number of stairs or ramps required for the occupant load; **f.** check if the number of stairs or ramps obtained in item **e** is less than the minimum prescribed; **g.** verify that the doors, stairs and ramps located on the plan satisfy the maximum travel distance prescribed. Since travel distance is dependent on the geometry of the floor plan, the maximum number of doors or exit stairs and ramps prescribed might not be sufficient.

Stair width and exit discharge width are based on the occupant load of the largest single floor. Occupant load does not accumulate from one floor to the next except at the floor of the exit discharge if people are exiting from both upper floor and basement floors and converging at the exit discharge.

ADDITIONAL REQUIREMENTS

BOCA National Building Code

Buildings that require one exit only are identified by the following: specific user groups, maximum occupant loads, travel distance, height of building and/or number of suites. All types of buildings and parking as well as washroom facilities must be accessible to persons with disabilities. Buildings more than one story high must be provided with a fire protected and smoke free elevator.

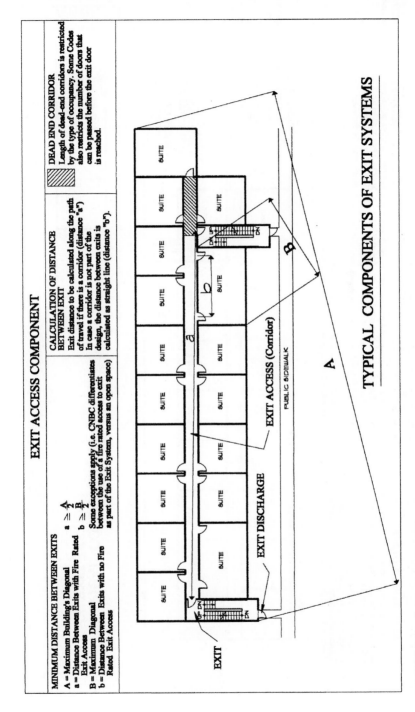

EXIT ACCESS COMPONENT

MINIMUM DISTANCE BETWEEN EXITS

A = Maximum Building's Diagonal
a = Distance Between Exits with Fire Rated Exit Access
B = Maximum Diagonal
b = Distance Between Exits with no Fire Rated Exit Access

$$a \geq \frac{A}{2}$$
$$b \geq \frac{B}{2}$$

Some exceptions apply (i.e. CNBC differentiates between the use of a fire rated access to exit as part of the Exit System, versus an open space)

CALCULATION OF DISTANCE BETWEEN EXIT

Exit distance to be calculated along the path of travel if there is a corridor (distance "a")

In case a corridor is not part of the design, the distance between exits is calculated as straight line (distance "b").

DEAD END CORRIDOR
Length of dead-end corridors is restricted by the type of occupancy. Some Codes also restricts the number of doors that can be passed before the exit door is reached.

TYPICAL COMPONENTS OF EXIT SYSTEMS

FIGURE 5.20   Exit access component.

5.31

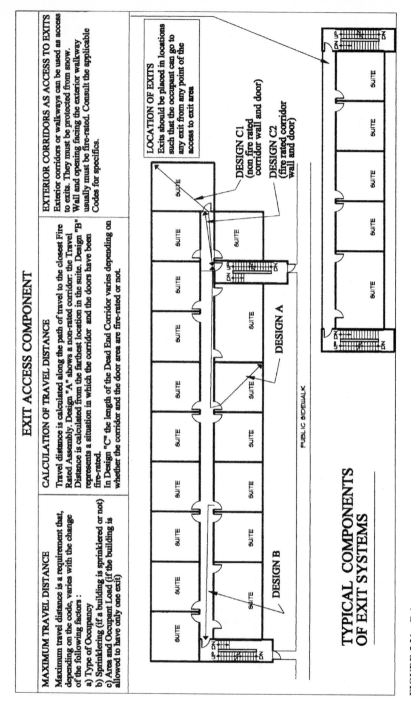

EXIT ACCESS COMPONENT

MAXIMUM TRAVEL DISTANCE

Maximum travel distance is a requirement that, depending on the code, varies with the change of the following factors :

a) Type of Occupancy
b) Sprinklering (if a building is sprinklered or not)
c) Area and Occupant Load (if the building is allowed to have only one exit)

CALCULATION OF TRAVEL DISTANCE

Travel distance is calculated along the path of travel to the closest Fire Rated Assembly. Design "A" shows a non-rated corridor: the Travel Distance is calculated from the farthest location in the suite. Design "B" represents a situation in which the corridor and the doors have been fire-rated.

In Design "C" the length of the Dead End Corridor varies depending on whether the corridor and the door area are fire-rated or not.

EXTERIOR CORRIDORS AS ACCESS TO EXITS

Exterior corridors or walkways can be used as access to exits. They must be protected from snow. Wall and opening facing the exterior walkway usually must be fire-rated. Consult the applicable Codes for specifics.

LOCATION OF EXITS

Exits should be placed in locations such that the occupant can go to any exit from any point of the access to exit area

DESIGN C1
(non fire rated corridor wall and door)

DESIGN C2
(fire rated corridor wall and door)

DESIGN A

DESIGN B

PUBLIC SIDEWALK

SUITE

TYPICAL COMPONENTS OF EXIT SYSTEMS

FIGURE 5.21 Exit access component.

5.32

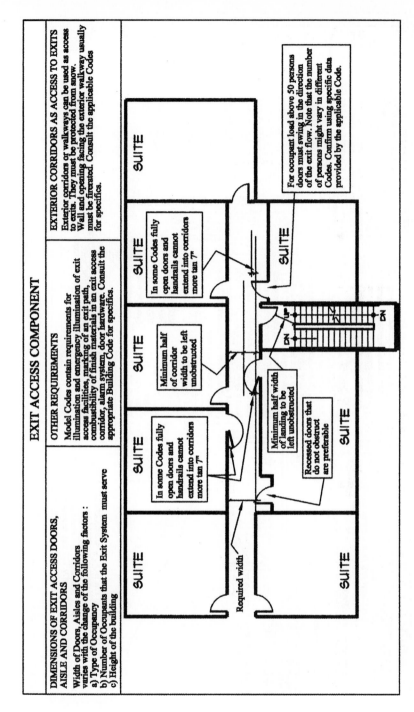

FIGURE 5.22 Exit access component.

EXIT COMPONENT

TYPE OF EXITS

Exits are that component of the Exit System, called Means of Egress, that are enclosed by continuous Fire Rated separations. The Exit leads though a continuous path to an open Public Space that allows exit from the area in case of necessity. In multiple floor buildings stairs are part of the Exit. Elevators are not considered Exits.

FIRE RATING

Specific requirements for Fire Rating vary between different Model Codes. They are all based on:

a) Height of The Building
b) Area of the Building
c) Type of Occupancy

EXTERIOR EXIT STAIRS

Outside exit stairs might be used if they are built to the same standards and fire rating that apply to Interior Exit Stairs (the exterior wall of the Building and the openings must be fire-rated). Model Codes increase the height of the parapet after a certain height of the stairs. Specific requirements varies for different Model Codes. Traditional metal Fire Escape are no longer allowed.

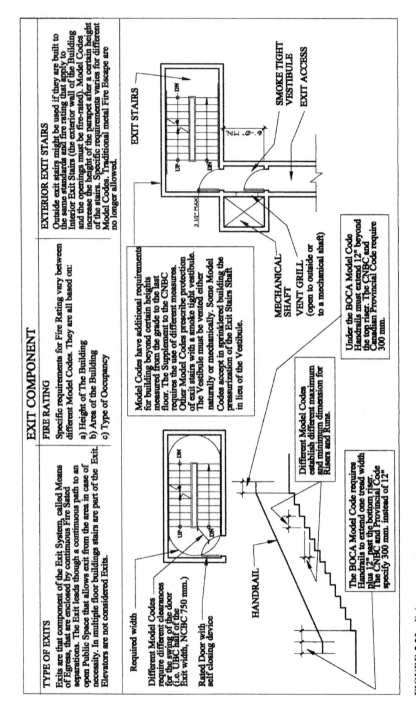

Required width

Different Model Codes require different clearances for the swing of the door (i.e. UBC half of the Exit width, NCBC 750 mm.)

Rated Door with self closing device

Model Codes have additional requirements for building beyond certain heights measured from the grade to the last floor. The Supplement to the CNBC requires the use of different measures. Other Model Codes prescribe protection of exit stairs with a smoke tight vestibule. The Vestibule must be vented either naturally or mechanically. Some Model Codes accept in sprinklered building the pressurization of the Exit Stairs Shaft in lieu of the Vestibule.

Different Model Codes establish different maximum and minimum dimension for Risers and Runs.

The BOCA Model Code requires Handrails to extend one tread width plus 12" past the bottom riser. The CNBC and Provincial Code specify 300 mm. instead of 12"

HANDRAIL

SMOKE TIGHT VESTIBULE

EXIT ACCESS

EXIT STAIRS

MECHANICAL SHAFT

VENT GRILL (open to outside or to a mechanical shaft)

Under the BOCA Model Code Handrails must extend 12" beyond the top riser. The CNBC and Canadian Provincial Code require 300 mm.

6'-0" MIN.

3 1/2" MAX.

FIGURE 5.23 Exit component.

5.34

ACCESSIBLE MEANS OF EGRESS

TYPE OF EXITS

The American with Disability Act (ADA) requires a building to be designed for full access to people with disabilities. Means of Egress for disabled people are required in the same number as Means of Egress for non-disabled people.

An area of refuge must be provided:

a) In unsprinklered buildings in an Exit Stair.

b) In a sprinklered building the area can be adjacent to the Exit Stairs.

For the appropriate size of the Area of Refuge consult the appropriate Code. The Area must be clearly indicated with visual and tactile signage, protected from smoke and fire, provided with instructions for the use, and a two way communication system should be installed so that the primary entry point to the building can be contacted. Different design and configurations can be used to comply with the Code requirements

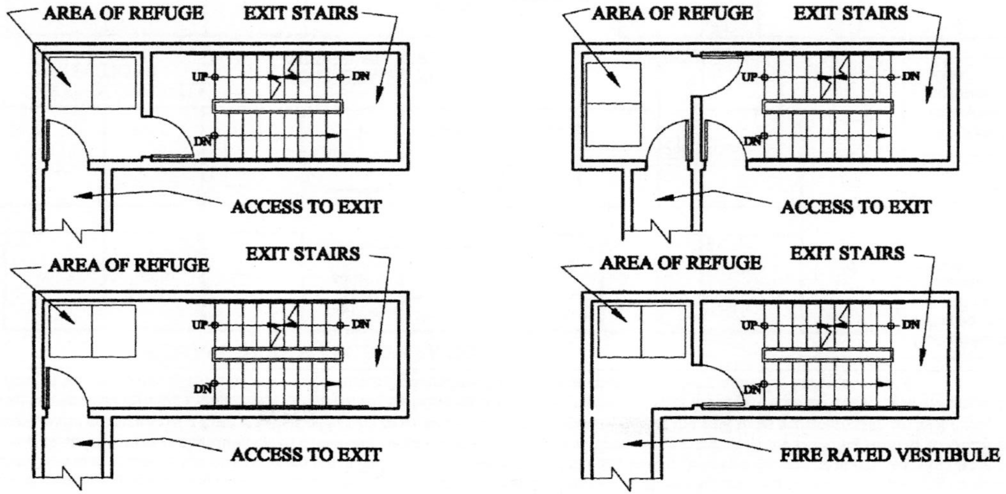

FIGURE 5.24   Accessible means of egress.

HORIZONTAL EXITS

HORIZONTAL EXIT REQUIREMENT

To be considered an horizontal exit the building has to be subdivided by Firewalls or Area Separation Walls, as they are variously called. This type of walls must be built out of non combustible materials with a minimum fire rating of two hours and must run continuously from the lowest floor to a dimension above the roof that varies with the type of Occupancy and Fire Rating. The areas of the Building so divided are considered as separate Buildings. Such portions of the Building have to accommodate the Occupant Load served by the Horizontal Exit (in the case of a floor subdivided in two areas, each area on the opposite side of the wall must accommodate the total occupant load of that floor. The horizontal exit can be provided through a single door if one part of the building is adequately provided with the required exits. In that case the single door will swing in the direction of the exit flow of the occupants of the area in which, without the Horizontal Exit, that portion of the floor would be deficient.

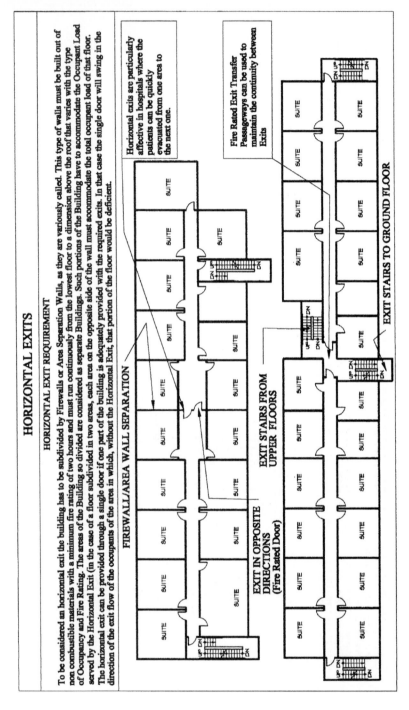

FIGURE 5.25 Horizontal exits.

5.36

EXIT DISCHARGE

COMMON TYPES OF EXIT DISCHARGE

Although the Exit Discharge is ultimately an opening that allows access to a public throughfare, it can be resolved in many ways. The most common types are:

A) An exterior door opening directly from the Exit to a Public Open Path

B) A Foyer outside door with the Exit opening into the Foyer. Model Codes impose restrictions and requirements on this type of Exit Discharge. Consult the applicable Code for specifics.

C) An exterior door from a Passageway or a Vestibule opening onto an Open Public Space. In this case the Exit opens onto the Passageway or Vestibule. This solution is adopted especially because Model Codes apply restrictions on the type of opening that are allowed in an Exit (like doors from any type of space with any type of Occupancy or any type of Service Rooms).

D) Exterior doors opening from the Space for which they serve as exits directly onto a Public Open Space. Specific requirements are associated with this system of Exit Discharge. Consult the applicable Code for specifics

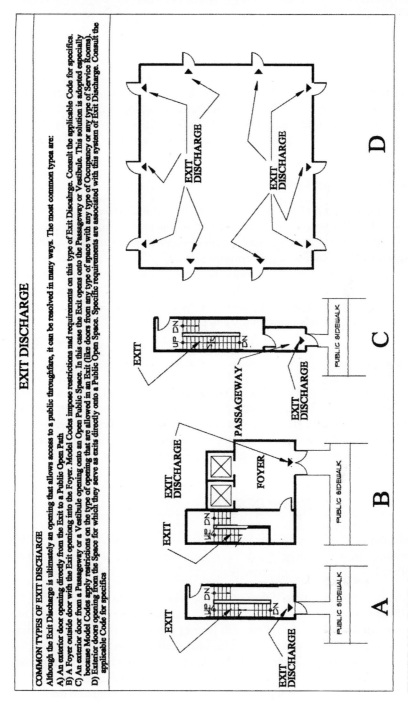

FIGURE 5.26 Exit discharge.

National Building Code of Canada

Egress capacity is calculated on mm. per person. Buildings that require one exit only are identified by specific user groups, maximum occupant loads, travel distance, height of building and/or number of suites. Except for single family dwelling or townhouses, all type of buildings and parking must be accessible to persons with disabilities, including washroom facilities. For multi-family construction accessibility is required only up to the main entrance of the building(s).

Standard Building Code

A reduction of stair width is allowed for specific tread and riser dimensions. For safety and emergency accessibility sleeping rooms on first and second story of multiple dwellings and each sleeping room in single dwelling must have either an outside door or a window of a determined size and sill height. All types of buildings, including single and two-family dwellings, as well as parking and washroom facilities, must be accessible to the disabled except in work places where work cannot reasonably be performed by a disabled person. See special requirements for motels, hotels, multifamily and parking.

Uniform Code

Requirements for only one exit: **a.** second story or a basement within an individual dwelling unit; **b.** second story or basement with two or more dwelling units and a total occupant load of 10 or less; **c.** second story of other types of buildings with low occupant load as per appropriate tables. Windows of specific size must be provided for different occupancy groups and type of rooms below the fourth story.

STAIRWAY AND RAMP DESIGN

Model codes have prescriptions for the design of stairs and ramps. They differ depending on the applicable code. The following are the parameters that are regulated:

1. Stair Design Parameters: user group and function of stairs, height from floor to floor, minimum width of stairs, minimum width and length of landings, minimum number of risers in interior exit stairs, maximum and minimum riser and run dimension, range of the ratio between riser and run dimension, number of handrails, height of railings and handrails, minimum extension of handrail at top and bottom of stairs, protection from snow and ice. Additional requirements for curved stairs include minimum depth of tread and minimum smaller radius. Winding stairs cannot be used for exit under the National Building Code of Canada.

2. Ramp Design Parameters: maximum gradient, maximum length between
   landings, minimum landing dimension, height of railings, minimum extension of railings at top and bottom of ramp, minimum and maximum height
   of railings, requirement for curb and curb height.

TYPES OF FIRE SEPARATIONS AND FIRE RATING

NFPA has developed a diagram (Fire Safety System Tree) that identifies the main
factors to be considered in managing a fire. The management of the fire can be
achieved through three alternate methods: **a.** control of the combustion processes;
b. suppression of the fire; **c.** control of the fire by construction.

Method **c** requires two components to be implemented: **a.** control of the
movement of the fire; **b.** provision for structural stability. The ultimate goal of
fire protection is: **a.** provision of sufficient time for the occupants to reach a safe
place; **b.** minimization of damage to adjacent properties.

The strategy for achieving these goals is dependent on the characteristics of
the materials, the area of the building, the type of occupancy, the number of stories, and the occupant load. In smaller and lower buildings the time needed to
evacuate the building is relatively short and therefore the protection of the structural component is less important than in taller buildings. In the latter the strategy
for evacuation is designed so that the occupant may reach a safe place within the
building, from where the occupants can evacuate via a protected route. Furthermore, in taller buildings fire fighters are expected to enter the building in order to
fight the fire from within the structure and to rescue occupants in distress. Therefore, the code requirements range from no protection, in the case of a single family dwelling, to four hours fire rating protection for structures near high hazard
occupancies. In both cases the avoidance of further damage to the structure and
the provision of protection beyond the requirements dictated by safety and codes
become an economic decision.

There are fundamentally two types of fire rated components: **a.** fire rated separations: these are assemblies that define fire compartments and are used to control
the movement (spread) of fire; **b.** firewalls or area separation walls: these are structures that separate either different buildings or different areas of the same building
which, from the code point of view, are then considered separate buildings.

Fire Resistance of Building Systems

From the points of view of the model codes there are two types of materials:
a. combustible; **b.** non-combustible. Combustible materials (i.e., wood) facilitate
combustion (which causes the development of a flame) and are such that, because
of the standard size or because it would be impractical to use the sizes required
to achieve a specific fire rating, need to be protected by other components (i.e.,
drywall or sprayed fireproofing).

In some cases, even a combustible material can achieve a limited fire rating simply by increasing the dimension of the members. An example of the above case is a timber structure that, although made out of wood, is accredited with specific fire ratings for specified thicknesses that are still found practical.

Non-combustible materials are those that do not facilitate combustion and, therefore, do not burn. They are divided in two categories: **a.** materials which, because of their low thermal conductivity and by using an accepted and practical thickness, can achieve the specified fire rating while maintaining their properties for a specified time (i.e., concrete); **b.** materials which, because of their high thermal conductivity, would require a very high and dense mass as well as considerable dimensions in order to achieve the specified fire rating (i.e., steel and metals in general).

In the first case the material by definition does not need any protection. The second case requires protection for different reasons, depending on the function of the element built out of that particular material. Referencing the NFPA tree regarding the management of a fire and, specifically, the use of the construction as a medium to control fire, the elements of the building can be subdivided for the purpose of the analysis at hand into two groups: **a.** structural; **b.** non-structural.

STRUCTURAL BUILDING COMPONENTS

There are three methods that allow us to fire rate a structural component: **a.** increasing the member size; **b.** encasing the structural member in fire proof material; **c.** protecting the entire assembly rather than a single element with a membrane. Examples of type **a** design are as follows.

Concrete Construction

Concrete is a good insulator, but it loses its compressive strength when subject to higher temperatures. Thus, the structure that might be exposed to fire needs to be over-designed. In the 500°Celsius range, for different ratios between aggregate and cement, the concrete retains between only 25 percent and 35 percent of its original strength. The steel component at elevated temperature loses its tensile strength. The critical temperature is defined as the value at which steel loses 40 percent of its original strength. For regular reinforcing steel this is 538°Celsius. For pre-stressing steel bars the temperature is 427°Celsius. If exposed for two hours to a fire of approximately 1000°Celsius, the temperature at the depth of 2 inches (50 mm) of a concrete slab 6 inches thick is 340°Celsius. Concrete, like many other materials, expands if exposed to rising temperatures. Restraining and continuity of the structure are two elements that improve resistance during fire (see Figure 5.27). Restraining produces an increase in the compression forces that reduces the stress on the bottom reinforcing. Continuity allows the redistribution of the stresses before the critical state of the structure is reached by delaying collapse due to rotation.

Design Data: note that design data are for preliminary design purpose only and do not take into account the structural requirements. For more specific values consult the local code and the project structural engineer.

1 Hour Fire Rating:

- Poured-in-place reinforced concrete: columns min 8" (203 mm), load-bearing walls min. 3.5" (89 mm), floor slabs min. 3.5" (89 mm), concrete one-way or two-way joists min. slab dimension between joists. 3.5" (89 mm).
- Post tensioned: concrete slab min. 3.5" (89 mm).
- Pre-cast concrete: columns min. 6" (152 mm), beams min. 4" (102 mm.), load-bearing wall panels min. 3.5" (89 mm), solid slabs min. 3.5" (89 mm), hollow core slabs min. 8" (203 mm).
- Concrete one-way or two-way joists: slab dimension between joists min. 3.5" (89 mm).
- Concrete masonry: load-bearing walls min. 4" (102 mm) thick. Additional protection might be required.

1.5 Hour Fire Rating:

- Poured-in-place reinforced concrete: columns min. 10" (254 mm), load-bearing walls min. 5" (127 mm), floor slabs min. 4.3" (109 mm), concrete one-way or two-way joists min. slab dimension between joists. 4.3" (109 mm).
- Post tensioned: concrete slab min. 4.25" (108 mm).
- Pre-cast concrete: columns min 8" (203 mm), beams min. 7" (178 mm), load-bearing wall panels min. 5" (127 mm), solid slabs min. 4.3" (109 mm), hollow core slabs min. 8" (203 mm) and used without topping. double and single T require min. 2.75" (70 mm) topping.
- Concrete one-way or two-way joists: slab dimension between joists min. 4.3 (109 mm).
- Concrete masonry: load-bearing walls min. 6" (152 mm) thick. Additional protection might be required.

2 Hour Fire Rating:

- Poured-in-place reinforced concrete: columns min. 12" (305 mm), load-bearing walls min. 6" (152 mm), floor slabs min. 5" (127 mm), concrete one-way or two-way joists min. slab dimension between joists. 5" (127 mm).
- Post tensioned: concrete slab min. 5" (127 mm).
- Pre-cast concrete: columns min. 10" (203 mm), beams min. 7" (178 mm.), load-bearing wall panels min. 6" (152 mm), solid slabs min. 5" (127 mm), hollow core slabs min. 8" (203 mm) and used without topping. Double and single T require min. 3.25" (83 mm) topping.
- Concrete one-way or two-way joists: slab dimension between joists min. 5" (127 mm).

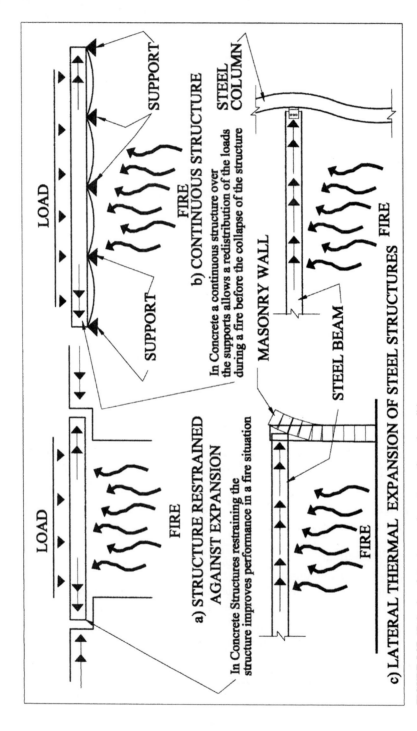

FIGURE 5.27 Behavior of structures under extreme thermal conditions.

- Concrete Masonry: load bearing walls min 8" (203 mm) thick. Additional protection might be required.

3 Hour Fire Rating:

- Poured-in-place reinforced concrete: columns min. 14" (356 mm), load-bearing walls min. 6.5" (165 mm), floor slabs min. 6.2" (157 mm), concrete one-way or two-way joists min. slab dimension between joists. 6.2" (157 mm).
- Post tensioned: concrete slab min. 6.2" (157 mm)
- Pre-cast concrete: columns min 12" (305 mm), beams min. 9.5" (241 mm.), load-bearing wall panels min. 6.5" (165 mm), solid slabs min. 6.2" (157 mm), hollow core slabs min. 8" (203 mm) and used with min. 2" (50 mm) topping. double and single T require appropriate fire-rated ceiling.
- Concrete one-way or two-way joists: slab dimension between joists min. 6.2" (157 mm).
- Brick Masonry: load-bearing walls min. 8" (203 mm) thick, vaults and domes min. 8" (203 mm) thick with rise min. 1/12 the span.
- Concrete Masonry: load bearing walls min. 8" (203 mm) thick. Additional protection might be required.

The following are examples and general discussions of **b** and **c** design.

Steel Construction

Steel is a non-combustible material with a high thermal conductivity. If this characteristic is related to the relative small mass of standard structural members, it becomes clear why the temperature rises fast in these steel members. At a temperature of 593°Celsius, the strength capacity of steel falls at least 40 percent of the original strength at room temperature. This means that the structure is close to the strength that is only just sufficient to resist the applied loads. The relationship between mass and heated perimeter is therefore critical. For example, heavy steel members like a column can function properly for 30 minutes before deforming. However, an open web joist will collapse after 5 to 10 minutes because of its light-weight characteristics. Steel expands considerably if exposed to increasing temperatures. If not restrained, a member could apply pressure on another structural component and introduce an eccentric load for which that component was not been designed. Either the temperature to which the structure is exposed must be controlled and maintained within certain limits (see Figure 5.28), or the design of the structure must take into account the expansion (see Figure 5.27).

Fire Rating Design Type "b"

Material: Sprayed fire proofing

Design Data: note that design data are for preliminary design purpose only and do not take into account the structural requirements. For more specific values consult the local code, the project structural engineer and manufacturers.

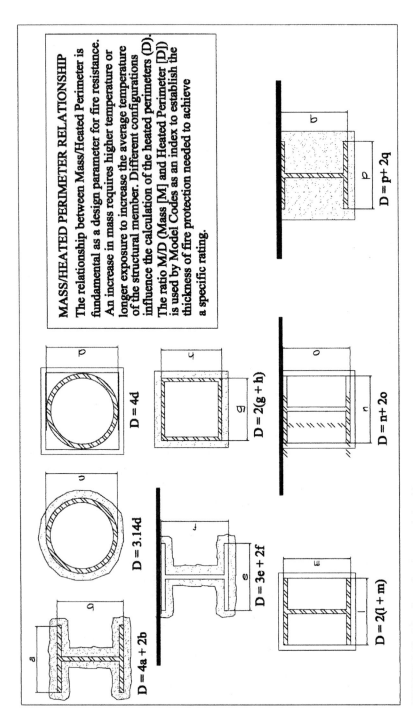

MASS/HEATED PERIMETER RELATIONSHIP

The relationship between Mass/Heated Perimeter is fundamental as a design parameter for fire resistance. An increase in mass requires higher temperature or longer exposure to increase the average temperature of the structural member. Different configurations influence the calculation of the heated perimeters (D). The ratio M/D (Mass [M] and Heated Perimeter [D]) is used by Model Codes as an index to establish the thickness of fire protection needed to achieve a specific rating.

$D = 4a + 2b$

$D = 3.14d$

$D = 4d$

$D = 3e + 2f$

$D = 2(g + h)$

$D = 2(l + m)$

$D = n + 2o$

$D = p + 2q$

FIGURE 5.28 Mass/heated perimeter relationship.

5.44

Spray fireproofing design thickness can be considered approximately:

1 Hr Fire Rating   1" to 2"

1.5 Hr Fire Rating   2" to 3"

2 Hrs Fire Rating   3" to 4"

3 Hrs Fire Rating   4" to 6"

Fire Rating Design Type "c"

Material: T-Bar ceiling or drywall on either suspended ceiling structure or vertical support for columns.

Design Data: a fire rated membrane contributes between 85 to 90 percent of the fire rating. Important elements are type, thickness and fastening. Most common materials are: lath and plaster, gypsum wallboard panels and inorganic acoustical tiles supported on a metallic grid system. Opening to the membrane must be fire stopped and during maintenance the characteristics of the system must not be altered. Acoustical tiles need to be held down with clips to prevent uplifting by positive pressure created by the fire.

Wood Construction

Although wood is a combustible material, this does not mean that wood is less safe than other construction materials such as steel or concrete. When tested, wood can withstand fire conditions set in common standards for 15 minutes, a considerable period if compared with ten minutes, which is the time associated with the structural collapse of open web joists.

This endurance is attributed to the charring process to which the surface of the wood is subjected during fire conditions. The substance produced on the surface has an insulating effect that slows down the rate of charring, which is relatively constant. This rate is approximately 0.6 mm/min for thick members. The uncharred wood loses only between 10 and 15 percent of its original strength.

Design Data: note that design data are for preliminary design purpose only and do not take into account the structural requirements. For more specific values consult the local code, the project structural engineer, and manufacturers.

Material: Protective coating, gypsum board or mineral fiber boards.

For specific thickness and fire ratings, consult the appropriate code and designs determined and tested through certification agencies such as Underwriters Laboratories, Underwriters Laboratories of Canada, Warnock Hershey Professional Services Ltd. or Mutual Research Corporation. Note that fire retardant only delays ignition of the wood but does not affect the rate of charring under a fully developed fire. This means that fire retardant does not increase the fire resistance of a wood member.

CHAPTER 6
NON-ARCHITECTURAL SYSTEMS

A building is comprised of many systems that perform in a pre-determined manner in order to satisfy the many functions of an artificial environment. A building is identified through what can be called its primary reason for being, or main function. A house or an apartment is a place where people reside; an office building is a place of work; a school is a center for learning and teaching. In order to conduct these activities properly, efficiently, and comfortably, the building must be seen as a provider of a whole series of elements that will allow people to perform at their best. These elements range from symbolic to hygienic or climatic. An environment, for example, responds to cultural values that are considered important at the time and place in which that environment was being built. The transition between exterior and interior interconnects the uses of the building with the surrounding environment, which needs to be carefully considered and either emphasized or minimized. The construction must guarantee the safety of the occupants in case of a disaster: therefore, among other things, the building must be structurally sound; vibrations must be minimized and deflection absorbed by containment within pre-established values. To create a comfortable environment, the building must maintain the relative humidity and temperature within ideal ranges related to the type of activity performed. Adequate lighting must be provided. Acoustically the structure has to perform in accordance with the requirements of the main activity to be conducted in it. Rain must be prevented from infiltrating and the building must be sealed against wind or drafts.

These are only a few of the many requirements that buildings will satisfy. Solutions to some of the requirements that have been mentioned are reached through non-architectural systems. The structural, plumbing, mechanical, fire protection, electrical, and landscaping components of a building constitute common examples of these systems.

In projects where the architectural component is the primary discipline and the architect is engaged as prime consultant, the sequence in which these systems have been listed is not casual. It follows a logical determination of priority that indicates in principle how elements are sequentially analyzed (although some part of the different systems can be designed at the same time). In some projects (for example industrial plants) the sequence might be changed because disciplines other than the architectural acquire a primary role. However, it is important in all cases that the analytical sequence be seen as a continuous and comprehensive process in which elements are established through a preliminary discussion among all the disciplines involved in creating the project. The outcome of this discussion, which takes place at the preliminary project meeting among all the consultants (usually arranged at the beginning of every project), might not be conclusive.

When the schematic drawings of the preliminary options for the structure are available, they should be circulated among the consultants for comments and to confirm the assumptions reached at the preliminary meeting. The solution then is narrowed down to the one considered most efficient from every point of view. This process should occur with the schematic design of every discipline. Each consultant will then have the opportunity to provide his or her input and indicate critical aspects between the other disciplines and his or her scope of work. It happens too often that the conclusions reached at the preliminary meeting are accepted at face value and each consultant begins to lay out his or her portion of the work without questioning the findings based on the original assumptions.

The role of the architect in relation to the consultants includes the following tasks: **a.** providing all available information on the project; **b.** circulation of all the documents received from all the consultants in order to facilitate cross coordination; **c.** stimulation and facilitation of an in-depth analysis of all the aspects of a project with an understanding of the roles and responsibility of each consultant; **d.** analysis of the non-architectural systems and coordination of aspects of those systems having an impact on the architectural component of the project; **e.** review of the consultant's invoices against the percentage of work completed.

Identification of the most appropriate systems and materials to be used starts with the code analysis. Once the analysis is completed, the architect has established the basic parameters, which will clarify the spectrum of possible choices. In addition to the above, the following are major factors that will influence the decision on the type of systems to be used: **a.** functional—type of use, interior distribution of uses, type of individual spaces; **b.** formal—geometrical characteristics of the building (i.e., individual dimensions, overall dimensions, massing, symmetry, asymmetry, shape, height); **c.** degree of *openness* of the plan; **d.** interior layout; **e.** construction budget.

In the next three chapters we will analyze how these major factors apply to the different non-architectural systems.

STRUCTURAL SYSTEM

It is often appropriate to describe a structural system as the *skeleton* of the building. However, depending on the style adopted and the era considered, this can be a misleading description. In ancient Greece the structural elements and the exterior aspect of the building were linked very closely since the structural elements themselves were ornate. In many cases elements like columns, (see the Caryatids of the Eretteo in the Acropolis), the bases of columns, capitals, and walls actually were the structure. In other cases, the architectural and structural elements differed so little from each other that they could be considered virtually the same. In time, with the introduction of new materials and techniques, beginning with the Roman Empire and developing in more variety and articulated form in recent times, the difference between structural and architectural elements became more distinct. This evolution is not a small matter and has a substantial effect on the aesthetical aspects of the building, as well as structural aspects. It has presented the architect with the need to consider the different characteristics and behavior of single and discrete elements not only within each system but also relative to the other system (the ultimate goal being for both systems to act as one with the various elements behaving in a coordinate way relative to each other). This latter requirement imposed a study of the necessary compensation within differentials. Furthermore, the coordination between the structural and the architectural system became more complex, due to the number of additional components and the possible conflicts arising during the planning and design of the project.

Some of the architectural styles of the twentieth century (especially those that use concrete and expose the general structure as an architectural statement) have, in many cases, tended to unify the structure with the architectural elements. However, due to other factors (i.e., the increased differential between interior and exterior temperature and, therefore, the increase in positive or negative pressures applied on the surfaces of the building) the relationship between the structural and the architectural component remains intricate in these cases too. If we consider, for example, these increased stresses (suction or pressure) on joints between different exterior materials (see Chapter 9), the study of the deformation of the structure acquires an increasingly important role in the analysis of the building performance. It is therefore fundamental for the architect to understand how the structure tends to behave even if he or she is not the structural designer of the project (see Figure 6.1).

The second aspect mentioned above is the coordination between the physical characteristics of the structural elements and the architectural ones. The obvious reference is the consideration of the size of major items like columns, beams and steel joists. However, secondary elements (i.e., bolts, brackets and bracing) require even more attention. Their size, location, and shape have to be identified very clearly in order, for example, to place and use the right size of stud and avoid any conflict with the application of the finish materials (see Figure 6.2). Incorporating

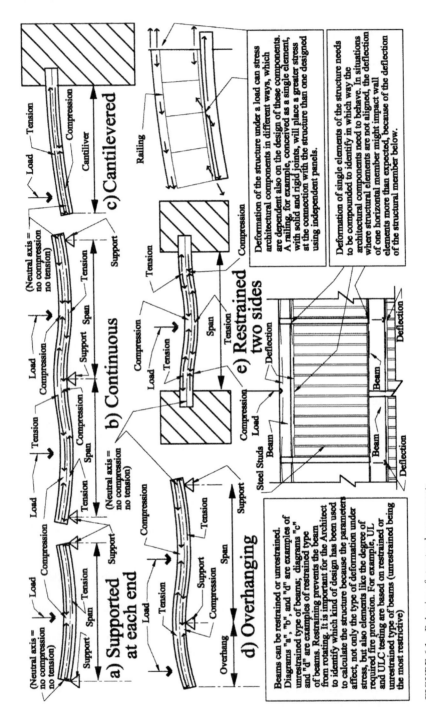

(Neutral axis = no compression no tension)

Load — Tension — Compression — Cantilever — Load

c) Cantilevered

Railing

Deformation of the structure under a load can stress architectural components in different ways, which are dependent also on the design of these components. A railing, for example, conceived as a single element, with solid and rigid joints, will place a greater stress at the connection with the structure than one designed using independent panels.

Deformation of single elements of the structure needs to be compounded to identify in which way the architectural components need to behave. In situations where structural elements are not aligned, the deflection of one horizontal member might impact wall elements more than expected, because of the deflection of the structural member below.

(Neutral axis = no compression no tension)

Load — Compression — Tension — Support — Span — Support — Span

Compression — Tension — Load

Tension — Compression

(Neutral axis = no compression no tension)

b) Continuous

Support

Tension — Compression — Span — Tension

Compression — Load — Span — Tension

Compression

e) Restrained two sides

Deflection

Steel Studs — Beam — Beam — Deflection — Deflection

Compression — Load — Beam

Load — Support — Span — Support — Compression — Tension

Load — Tension — Compression — Support — Span — Overhang

d) Overhanging

(Neutral axis = no compression no tension)

Load — Support — Span — Tension — Support — Compression

a) Supported at each end

Beams can be restrained or unrestrained. Diagrams "a", "b", and "d" are examples of unrestrained type of beams; diagrams "c" and "d" are examples of restrained type of beams. Restraining prevents the beam from rotating. It is important for the Architect to identify which kind of design has been used to calculate the structure because the parameters affect, not only the type of deformation under stress, but also elements like the degree of required fire protection. For example, UL and ULC testing are based on restrained or unrestrained type of beams (unrestrained being the most restrictive)

FIGURE 6.1 Behavior of structural components.

6.4

these elements successfully into the architectural component is dependent not only on the ability of the architect and his or her knowledge of structural systems, but also on the capability of the structural designer to clearly represent graphically all the elements of the system (which might mean drawing one more elevation of the structure, a section or even an axonometric view of a particular detail). If there is a sense of uncertainty in the mind of the architect, the latter should ask the engineer to draw the most appropriate view of the part of the structure that needs clarification. Elevations and axonometric views are types of representations that should not be thought of as used exclusively by architects.

Types of Structural Systems

There are basically four types of material used to create a structure: **a.** wood; **b.** steel; **c.** concrete; **d.** masonry. Each of these materials is used in systems having characteristics and cost implications that make them more suitable than others for certain types of construction (see Figures 6.3 through 6.7).

Structural elements are subject to three main types of stress: shear, which induces members or part of members to slide relative to each other; tension, which tends to stretch a member; compression, which tends to shorten a member and ultimately to crush it (Figure 6.8). The combination of tension and compression forces acting at the same time parallel to the axis of a horizontal member flexes it, inducing deflection. For these reasons these combinations are called flexural stresses (Figure 6.8). The same phenomenon happens on a column where the ratio between the height of the column and the type and amount of stress exceeds its capacity to remain rigid. These columns fail under sudden buckling before they are crushed. The slenderness of columns must therefore be considered in the design of the structural system (Figure 6.8).

CHOOSING THE STRUCTURAL SYSTEM

At the beginning of this chapter we indicated that elements belonging to the regulatory, functional, formal, and economical categories act as critical factors in the choice of the non-architectural system to be used. In structural terms, apart from the fire safety and economical aspects, the functional and formal factors are the principal determinants of the forces to which the building must react, the most important being: **a.** dead and live loads (usually assumed to act vertically); **b.** wind and earthquake loads (assumed to be mainly horizontal); **c.** other loads: i.e., earth and water pressure, temperature change, impact, and vibration.

This is translated into the following parameters: **a.** order of magnitude and type of loads; **b.** span; **c.** height (overall and floor to floor); **d.** lateral and uplift forces.

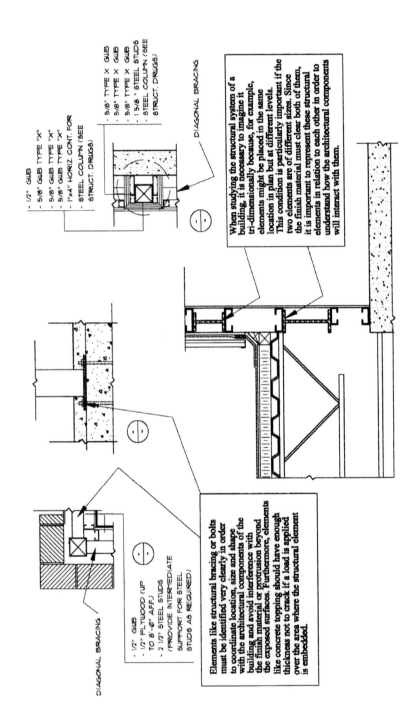

Text labels (rotated) within figure:

- 1/2" GWB
- 5/8" GWB TYPE "X"
- 5/8" GWB TYPE "X"
- 5/8" GWB TYPE "X"
- 1"x4" HORIZ. CONT. FOR
  STEEL COLUMN (SEE
  STRUCT. DRWGS)

- 5/8" TYPE X GWB
- 5/8" TYPE X GWB
- 5/8" TYPE X GWB
- 1 5/8" STEEL STUDS
- STEEL COLUMN (SEE
  STRUCT. DRWGS)

DIAGONAL BRACING

When studying the structural system of a building, it is necessary to imagine it tri-dimensionally because, for example, elements might be placed in the same location in plan but at different levels. This condition is particularly important if the two elements are of different sizes. Since the finish material must clear both of them, it is important to represent these structural elements in relation to each other in order to understand how the architectural components will interact with them.

DIAGONAL BRACING

- 1/2" GWB
- 1/2" PLYWOOD (UP
  TO 8'-0" AFF.)
- 2 1/2" STEEL STUDS
  (PROVIDE INTERMEDIATE
  SUPPORT FOR STEEL
  STUDS AS REQUIRED)

Elements like structural bracing or bolts must be identified very clearly in order to coordinate location, size and shape with the architectural components of the building and avoid interference with the finish material or protrusion beyond the exposed surfaces. Furthermore, elements like concrete topping should have enough thickness not to crack if a load is applied over the area where the structural element is embedded.

FIGURE 6.2 Impact of structural components on architectural elements.

#	Type of Floor Structure	Dead Load of Structure (psf)	Live Load (psf)	Standard Maximum Span (ft)
1	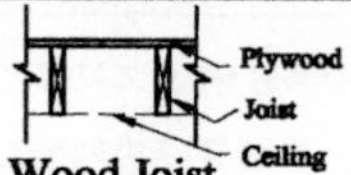 Wood Joist System	Up to 8	Up to 40	Up to 18 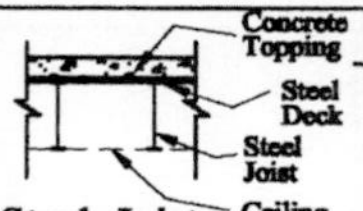
2	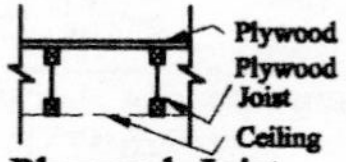 Plywood Joist	Up to 12	Up to 40	Up to 30 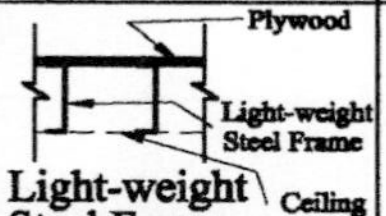
3	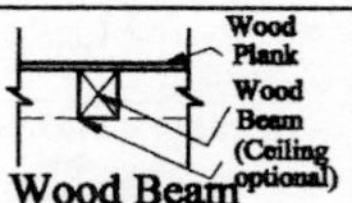 Wood Beam Wood Plank	Up to 16	Up to 40	Planks Up to 6 Beams up to 22 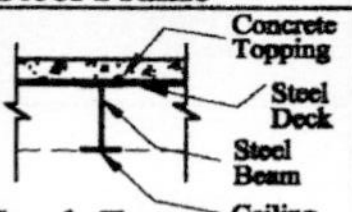
4	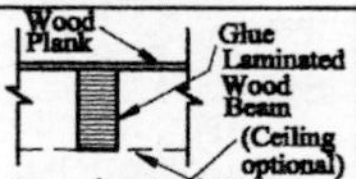 Laminated Beam Wood Plank	Up to 20	Up to 40	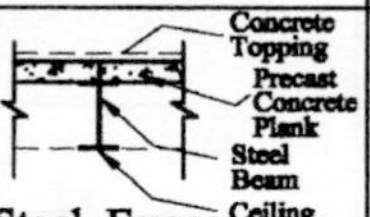 Planks Up to 6' Beams up to 35'
5	Steel Joist	Up to 20	Up to 40	Up to 40 Joice spacing Light Joists 16" to 32" o.c. Heavy Joists 4' to 12" o.c.

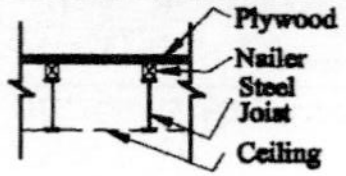

#	Type of Structure	Dead Load of Structure (psf)	Live Load (psf)	Standard Maximum Span (ft)
6	Steel Joist	Up to 110	Up to 100	Up to 60 Same as 5
7	Light-weight Steel Frame	Up to 20	Up to 60	Up to 22
8	Steel Frame	Up to 60	Up to 100	Up to 35
9	Steel Frame	Up to 75	Up to 150	Up to 35
10	Precast Concrete	Up to 75	Up to 150	Up to 35

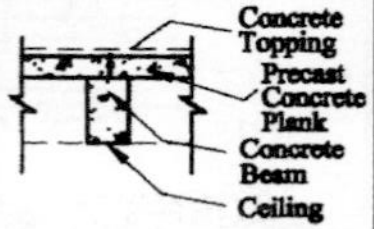

FIGURE 6.3 Types of structural systems.

#	Type of Floor Structure	Dead Load of Structure (psf)	Live Load (psf)	Standard Maximum Span (ft)
12	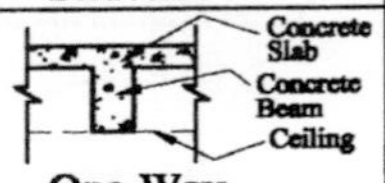 One-Way Concrete Slab	Up to 120	Up to 250	Up to 30 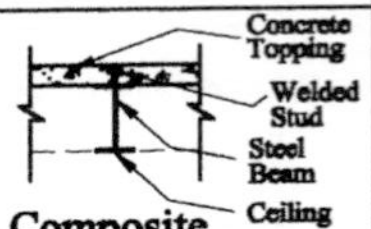
13	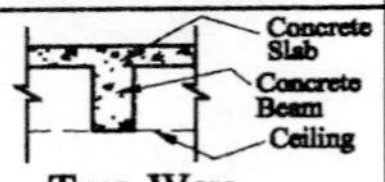 Two-Way Concrete Slab	Up to 120	Up to 250	Up to 30 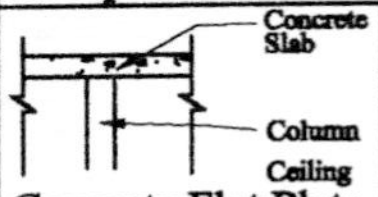
14	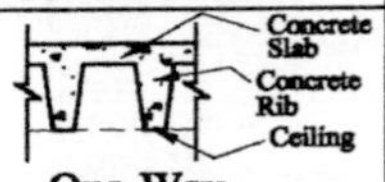 One-Way Concrete Ribbed Slab	Up to 90	Up to 150	Up to 50
15	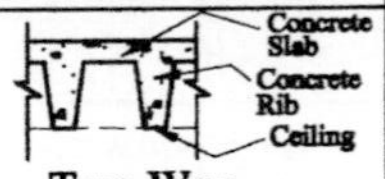 Two-Way Concrete Ribbed Slab	Up to 105	Up to 200	Up to 60
16	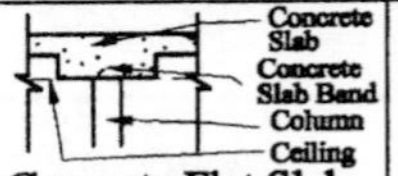 Concrete Flat Slab with Concrete Slab Band	Up to 170	Up to 250	Up to 40

#	Type of Structure	Dead Load of Structure (psf)	Live Load (psf)	Standard Maximum Span (ft)
17	Composite	Up to 70	Up to 200	Up to 35
18	Concrete Flat Plate	Up to 175	Up to 200	Up to 35

FIGURE 6.4 Types of structural systems.

	Type of Roof Structure	Dead Load of Structure (psf)	Live Load (psf)	Standard Maximum Span ft		Type of Structure	Dead Load of Structure (psf)	Live Load (psf)	Standard Maximum Span ft
1	Wood Joist System (Plywood, Joist, Ceiling)	Up to 8	Up to 50	Up to 22	6	Steel Joist (Insulation or Conc. Topping, Steel Deck, Steel Joist, Ceiling)	Up to 24 (with Insul.) Up to 28 (with Conc.)	Up to 50	Up to 96 Same as 5
2	Wood Truss (Sheathing, Wood Truss, Ceiling)	Up to 15	Up to 50	Up to 50	7	Steel Truss (Purling, Steel Deck, Steel Truss)	Up to 25	Up to 60	Up to 200
3	Wood Beam Wood Plank (Wood Plank, Wood Beam, (Ceiling optional))	Up to 22	Up to 50	Planks Up to 6 Beams up to 34	8	Steel Frame (Concrete Topping, Steel Deck, Steel Beam, Ceiling)	Up to 60	Up to 100	Up to 35
4	Laminated Beam Wood Plank (Plywood Panels)	Up to 6	Up to 50	Up to 32	9	Steel Frame (Precast Concrete Plank, Steel Beam, Ceiling)	Up to 75	Up to 70	Up to 35
5	Steel Joist (Plywood, Nailer, Steel Joist, Ceiling)	Up to 20	Up to 50	Up to 96 Joist spacing Light Joists 16" to 32" o.c. Heavy Joists 4' to 12" o.c.	10	Precast Concrete (Precast Concrete Plank, Concrete Beam, Ceiling)	Up to 75	Up to 70	Up to 35

FIGURE 6.5 Types of structural systems.

No.	Type of Roof Structure	Dead Load of Structure (psf)	Live Load (psf)	Standard Maximum Span (ft)	No.	Type of Structure	Dead Load of Structure (psf)	Live Load (psf)	Standard Maximum Span (ft)
12	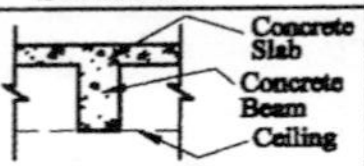 One-Way Concrete Slab	Up to 120	Up to 100	Up to 30	17	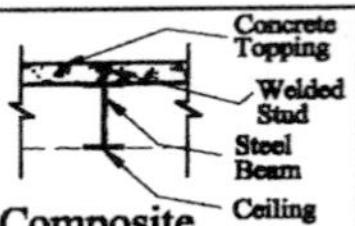 Composite	Up to 70	Up to 100	Up to 35
13	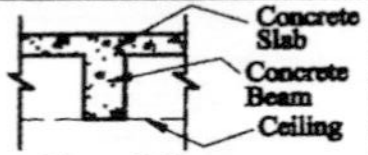 Two-Way Concrete Slab	Up to 120	Up to 100	Up to 30	18	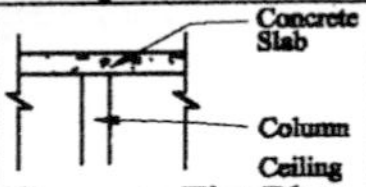 Concrete Flat Plate	Up to 160	Up to 100	Up to 35
14	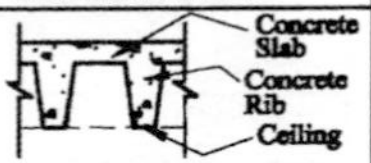 One-Way Concrete Ribbed Slab	Up to 90	Up to 100	Up to 50					
15	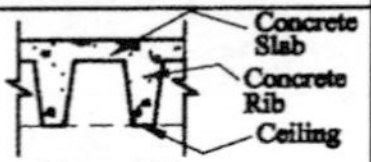 Two-Way Concrete Ribbed Slab	Up to 105	Up to 100	Up to 60					
16	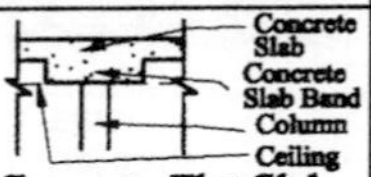 Concrete Flat Slab with Concrete Slab Band	Up to 200	Up to 100	Up to 40					

FIGURE 6.6 Types of structural systems.

	Type of Bearing Wall Structure	Dead Load of Structure (psf)	Standard Max. Vertical Span ft	Compatibility with Type of Floor Structure
1	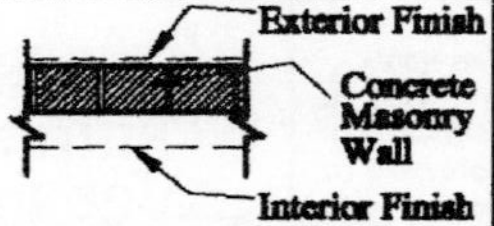 Exterior Finish / Concrete Masonry Wall / Interior Finish — **Concrete Block Wall**	8" Wall Up to 60 12" Wall Up to 90 8" Wall with Brick Veneer up to 100	8" Wall Up to 13 12" Wall Up to 20	1, 2, 3, 4, 5, 6, 7, 8, 9, 10, 11 12, 13, 14, 15, 16, 17, 18
2	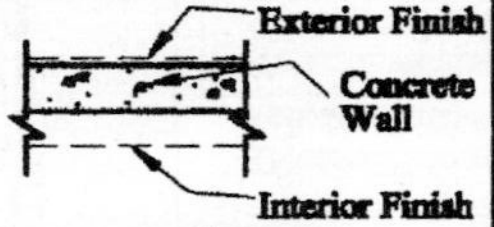 Exterior Finish / Concrete Wall / Interior Finish — **Concrete Wall**	8" Wall Up to 97 12" Wall Up to 145 8" Wall with Brick Veneer up to 112	8" Wall Up to 13 - 17 12" Wall Up to 20 - 25	1, 2, 3, 4, 5, 6, 7, 8, 9, 10, 11 12, 13, 14, 15, 16, 17, 18
3	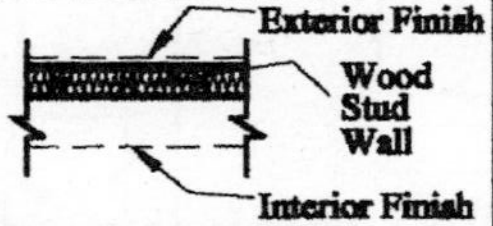 Exterior Finish / Wood Stud Wall / Interior Finish — **Wood Stud Wall**	4" Wall Up to 12 6" Wall Up to 18 4" Stud Wall with Brick Veneer up to 52	4" Stud Wall Up to 14 6" Stud Wall Up to 20	1, 2, 3, 4, 5, 6, 7
4	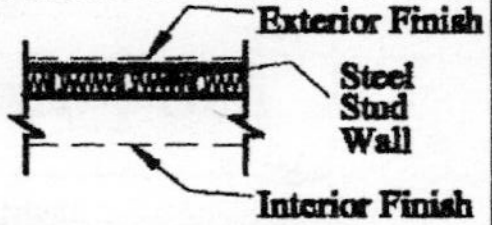 Exterior Finish / Steel Stud Wall / Interior Finish — **Steel Stud Wall**	4" Wall Up to 14 6" Wall Up to 18 4" Stud Wall with Brick Veneer up to 54	4" Stud Wall Up to 13 6" Stud Wall Up to 17	1, 2, 3, 4, 5, 6, 7, 8, 9, 17

FIGURE 6.7 Types of structural systems.

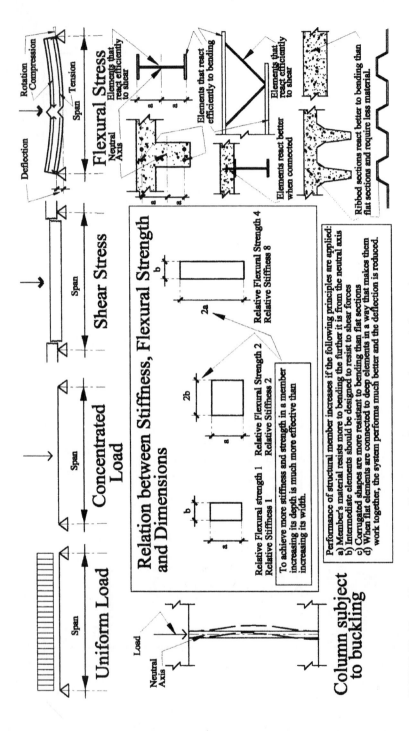

FIGURE 6.8 Type of forces and loads applied on structural members and geometrical properties.

6.12

Order of Magnitude and Type of Loads

The type of occupancy determines the type of load and its values (see Figure 6.9). There are various types of loads: **a.** *Live Load* is the greatest expected load created by the occupants. In any case it is not less than the minimum uniformly distributed load established by the applicable various model and local codes. Live load does not include wind, snow, earthquake or dead load; **b.** *Dead Load* is the weight of all the permanent elements of the building. It can be computed by adding the weight of each single component of a system; **c.** *Impact Load* is the load of an object increased by the kinetic force determined by its movement or by any change in its status (i.e., from a state of uniform movement to a static state or vice versa). This is calculated on a percentage of the dead load to be used designing the structure that would support a particular item or system (i.e., elevators or machinery). The resulting value is added to the prescribed dead load; **d.** *Hydrostatic Load* is the load applied by fluids (i.e., water). The standard unit is 62.4 pounds per cubic feet. Total pressure is the standard unit x depth acting perpendicular to the surfaces; **e.** *Earth Load* is the load applied by the soil. Standard unit equivalent to the pressure created by a fluid that weights 30 pounds per cubic foot, to be considered together with any additional stress.

In addition to the above, the structure can be subject to the following stresses: **a.** *vibration*, which is the stress on the structural elements imposed by objects that are not in a static state (i.e., machinery or people). This movement is transferred onto the structure according to the principle: the less rigid it is, the more it responds to the stress by vibrating. Structures designed for open spaces with long spans tend to vibrate more than structures designed for smaller spaces (the presence of damping [decreasing] interior elements, like partitions, helps in reduce vibrations); **b.** *thermal stresses*, which are stresses that a restrained structural element undergoes when subjected to thermal variations. Because of changes in its geometry, the member transfers such stresses onto other members when it expands and contracts).

The structural calculations are influenced by factors that indicate how and where these types of loads are applied and how they can affect the performance of the building. Examples are: **a.** *Uniformly Distributed Load:* is the load derived by considering the specified load unit uniformly bearing on every part of the structure (see Figure 6.8); **b.** *Concentrated Load:* this is the maximum concentrated load applied on a 2.5 sq. ft. (unless differently specified) that applies to the maximum stress on the structure (see Figure 6.8); **c.** *Partial Loading:* is the total live load applied only to a portion of the structure. This type of load is applicable if it is expected that the total uniform load will be concentrated in only a portion of the building; **d.** *Roof Loads:* need to be designed for live load or snow load (dead load) whichever is greater; accumulation of water, if sufficient drainage is not provided or in anticipation of a temporary drainage system failure (scuppers are placed higher than the low point and the elevations of drains in order not to override the regular drainage system); deflection of the structure, which can cause ponding and additional dead load as well as introducing negative effects on the waterproofing system; heavier loads at drift locations (i.e., snow accumulation near parapets or abating walls) or on the perimeters to avoid uplift of system components (i.e., insulation in an inverted roof).

It is necessary to note that the pitch of the roof affects the considerations expressed in each of the above item (i.e., effect of deflection on the runoff of water).

Span

A structural system can be subdivided in three major components: **a.** horizontal members; **b.** vertical members; **c.** foundations.

Span is a variable that is applied to horizontal and vertical members of all three major components (vertical members tend to deform under eccentric loads or because of their slenderness ratio and undergo stresses that in nature are identical to the one created in horizontal members—see Figure 6.8). Span can be defined as *the unsupported length of a member between two supports.* Long spans, as a single parameter, are very indicative of the type of structures to be used (see Figures 6.3 through 6.7).

Horizontal members, like beams or slabs (slabs are often referred to as *wide beams*), react mainly to two types of stresses: shear and flexural (see Figures 6.1 and 6.9). In addition, torsion can happen when an applied load creates a moment that tends to rotate the structural member around its longitudinal axis.

Shear is important in short rigid heavy-loaded structures, while it is less important in elastic elements like steel. The behavior of a member under shear is to break approximately where the stress created by the vertical component of the force applied by the load and the vertical and opposite reaction of the support is at its maximum (at the support). The behavior of the member under flexural stress is to bend and rotate at the supports (see Figures 6.1 and 6.8). In addition, by bending, the member is stressed by compression and tension.

The depth of the member and the material of which it is made plays a primary role in flexural strength and stiffness (see Figure 6.8). Walls behave like wide columns and are subject to the same type of deformation. For long spans (beyond 100 feet) members need to be engineered using either elements shaped in the form of arches or systems like Space Frame (see Figures 6.10 and 6.11). To cover large areas like a stadium the following structures are more appropriate:

Thin Shells: structures that are used as a curved surface supporting the load by tension, compression and shear. They perform poorly in bending because they are very thin. This type of structure can acquire any shape, although some shapes are more efficient than others. Square buildings are covered efficiently with a dome while for long buildings a barrel vault might be more suitable. Among all the material that can be used to erect a thin shell structure, concrete is the most logical solution because of its ductility.

Folded Plates: two planes that are folded at the ridge, which is called the *fold line,* constitute this structure. At the ridge the two plates, leaning on each other, become stable, requiring no other member. Each plate, acting as

Type of Occupancy	Live Load (psf)	Type of Occupancy	Live Load (psf)	Type of Occupancy	Live Load (psf)
Assembly		**Grandstands**	100	**Penal Institutions**	
Fixed seats	50	**Gymnasiums**	100	Cell Block	40
Movable seats	100	**Hospitals**		Corridors	100
Attics		Operating Rooms and Labs	60	**Residential**	
Non-storage	10	Private Rooms	40	Multifamily	
Storage	30	Wards	40	Private Apartments	40
Balconies		Corridors above first floor	80	Public Rooms	100
Exterior	60	**Hotels**		Corridors	40
Interior	50	Guest Rooms	40	Dwellings	
Interior (movable seats)	100	Public Rooms	100	First Floor and other floors	40
Bowling Alleys, Poolrooms	75	Corridors serving Public Rooms	100	Inhabitable attics	20
Broadcasting Studios	100	**Kitchens (commercial)**	150	**Schools**	
Catwalks	25	**Laboratories**	100	Classrooms	40
Corridors		**Libraries**		Corridors	80
First Floor	100	Reading Rooms	60	**Skating Rinks**	100
Other Floors	As per Occupancy	Stack Rooms	150	**Stairs and Exits**	100
Dance Halls	100	Corridors above first floor	80	**Storage Warehouses**	
Dining and Restaurants	100	**Manufacturing**		Light	125
Dormitories		Light	75	Heavy	250
Non-partitioned	80	Heavy	125	Grain	300
Partitioned	40	Ice	300	**Retail**	
File rooms	125	**Office Buildings**		Stores	75
High Density Storage	150	Office	50	Wholesale	100
		Business with Machines	100	**Theaters**	
		Lobbies	100	Aisle, corridors, lobbies	100
Garage (cars only)	50	Corridors above first floor	80	Orchestra floors	50
				Balconies	50
				Stage floors	150
				Dressing rooms	40
				Projection rooms	100

FIGURE 6.9 Examples of minimum live loads for different types of occupancies.

6.15

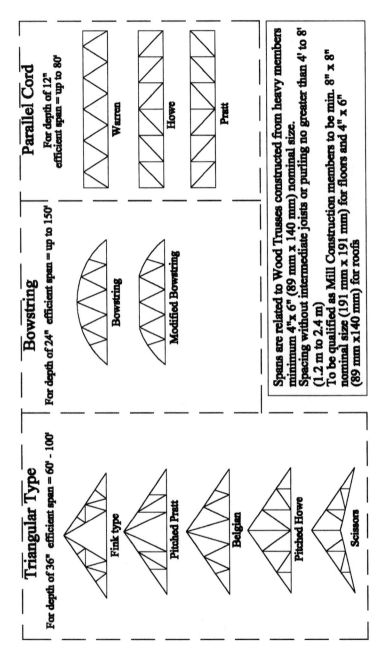

Triangular Type
For depth of 36" efficient span = 60' - 100'

Fink type

Pitched Pratt

Belgian

Pitched Howe

Scissors

Bowstring
For depth of 24" efficient span = up to 150'

Bowstring

Modified Bowstring

Parallel Cord
For depth of 12" efficient span = up to 80'

Warren

Howe

Pratt

Spans are related to Wood Trusses constructed from heavy members minimum 4"x 6" (89 mm x 140 mm) nominal size.
Spacing without intermediate joists or purling no greater than 4' to 8' (1.2 m to 2.4 m)
To be qualified as Mill Construction members to be min. 8" x 8" nominal size (191 mm x 191 mm) for floors and 4" x 6" (89 mm x140 mm) for roofs

FIGURE 6.10   Types of trusses.

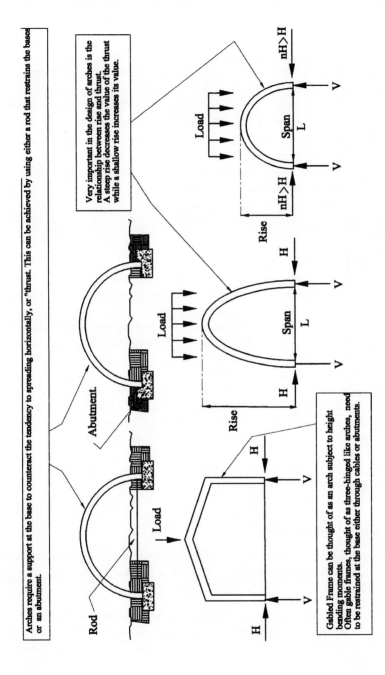

Arches require a support at the base to counteract the tendency to spreading horizontally, or "thrust. This can be achieved by using either a rod that restrains the base or an abutment.

Rod

Abutment.

Load

Very important in the design of arches is the relationship between rise and thrust. A steep rise decreases the value of the thrust while a shallow rise increases its value.

Load

nH>H   Span   nH>H
           L

Rise

V   V

Load

H   Span   H
           L

Rise

V   V

Gabled Frame can be thought of as an arch subject to height bending moments.
Often gable frames, thought of as three-hinged like arches, need to be restrained at the base either through cables or abutments.

H

V   V

H

FIGURE 6.11   Structural characteristics or arches.

6.17

a beam, spans on its own plane between supports at each end. Along the eave, either a wall or a beam stiffens the edge of the plate.

Stressed Skin: applied to one or both sides, it is constituted by members spaced at a certain intervals and connected continuously to sheathing. The system acts like a series of "I" beams with the sheathing being the flange and the internal members reacting to shear. An example of this type of structure is panels made of 2" x 4" spaced 12" or 16" with plywood nailed on both sides. This type of panel as a roof can span up to 32'.

Inflatable Structure: a membrane that can oppose only tension stresses constitutes this type of structure. Since it can float like a balloon, or be potentially unstable like a tent, the membrane needs to be stabilized and held down in order to be effective in buildings.

Height

As a variable, height is closely related to the increase in lateral and uplifting forces. A low rise is mainly subject to dead and live loads that are transferred to the foundation through a system of walls beams and/or pilasters. A high rise must respond to stresses applied by lateral forces like wind and earthquake that are many times more powerful than the ones applied to a low rise. Due to these factors, the design strategy for a low rise and a high rise is very different. The latter needs to become more symmetrical the taller it becomes (see Figure 6.12). Furthermore the type of deformation of frames and the type of connections between members grow more important as the building grows taller (Figure 6.12).

Correct planning and geometry of a high building can help reduce the impact of lateral forces. Symmetrical tri-dimensional shapes perform better than shapes that are non-symmetrical or unbalanced. The latter are difficult to control especially in an earthquake situation. In addition configurations that have weak connections (i.e., "T" or "L" shapes) should be designed as independent units with separate structures (see figure 6.14).

Lateral and Uplift Forces

In order to stabilize the structure of a building so that it will react effectively to lateral forces, three types of elements are used: **a.** shear walls; **b.** braced frames; **c.** rigid frames.

Shear walls can be constructed in concrete, masonry, steel and wood. In order to be effective they need to be continuous throughout the building, down to the foundation, and openings through shear walls should be minimized. Shear walls are particularly effective in narrow buildings and often are integrated with the core to increase the resistance. When they are used in perimeter walls they can limit the number, locations and type of openings allowed (see Figure 6.13).

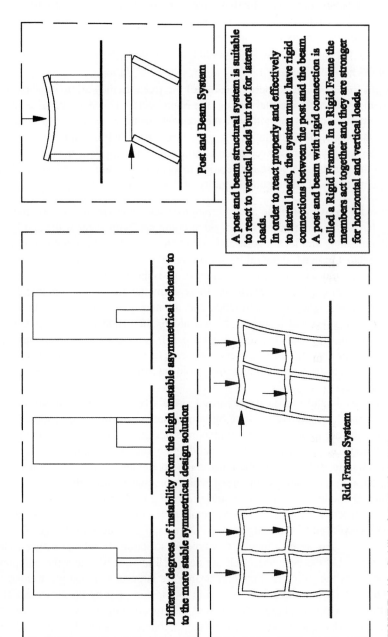

Post and Beam System

A post and beam structural system is suitable to react to vertical loads but not for lateral loads.

In order to react properly and effectively to lateral loads, the system must have rigid connections between the post and the beam. A post and beam with rigid connection is called a Rigid Frame. In a Rigid Frame the members act together and they are stronger for horizontal and vertical loads.

Different degrees of instability from the high unstable asymmetrical scheme to to the more stable symmetrical design solution

Rid Frame System

FIGURE 6.12   Stability of structural systems.

Braced frames are very effective. They can also be integrated into the core design. They allow more design freedom than shear walls, especially if maximum flexibility of the interior space is required and the elements determining the rigidity of the structure are located in the perimeter walls (see Figure 6.13).

Rigid frames are very useful because of the freedom they allow in planning the distribution of internal spaces (see Figure 6.12). However, because of the importance of the rigidity of the connections they are subject to some limitations: **a.** the column spacing is reduced; **b.** variations and irregularities in the pattern columns need to be minimized; **c.** the depth of the columns and the beams is increased in relation to systems that use shear walls and/or bracing to create the required rigidity of the structure.

In order to overcome the above limitations and improve the performance of the systems, rigid frames are in fact often combined with shear walls and bracing. In designing and locating the stabilizing elements it is important to consider that they have to react to lateral forces acting in all the directions. For these reasons they are more effective if the center of resistance is placed at the center of mass (see Figure 6.13). Furthermore, these elements are more economical and more effective if they are continuous and uninterrupted. Major structural elements resisting vertical loads can be technically interrupted and forces can be transferred on other supports (see Figure 6.14). In case of shear elements, the transfer can be very difficult and very expensive (if not prohibitive). In such cases it is better to re-plan the building and avoid interrupting major shear elements (see Figure 6.14).

Shear walls and braced frames (used singularly or in combination) are the solutions used to stabilize low-rise buildings that can be up to 25 stories. Rigid frames alone are impractical due to elaborate design of the rigid connection and the required size of the members. For building beyond that height and up to 35 to 40 stories, core structures are the most common elements used for lateral stability. If the core structure is combined with a bracing system, the height of the building can be increased up to 55 stories (see Figure 6.15).

Tube structures are used for the structure of the tallest buildings. These structures are employed for building from 55 stores and up. The World Trade Center in New York was an example of this type of structure. In tube structures, elements located at the perimeter wall are designed in such way that the complete wall becomes the structure. Spandrel beams are large in size and are welded to the columns. The windows are inserted in the opening left by the structure. The floor functions as a diaphragm that stiffens the construction impeding any torsion of the tubes. The system can be constructed of concrete or steel. Bracing and belt trusses have a particular aesthetical importance since they are exposed. Furthermore, they both enhance the stability of the construction.

The following are guidelines that can be used to consider the characteristics of steel and concrete structures in relation to lateral forces: **a.** steel structures are relatively light and therefore reduce the mass of the building; **b.** steel structure

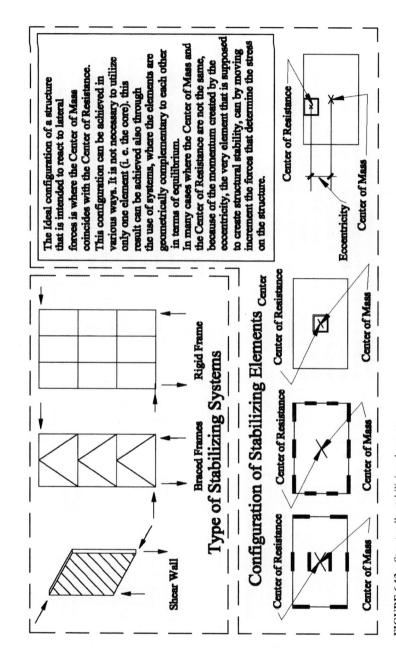

The Ideal configuration of a structure that is intended to react to lateral forces is where the Center of Mass coincides with the Center of Resistance. This configuration can be achieved in various ways. It is not necessary to utilize only one element (i. e. the core). this result can be achieved also through the use of systems, where the elements are geometrically complementary to each other in terms of equilibrium.

In many cases where the Center of Mass and the Center of Resistance are not the same, because of the momentum created by the eccentricity, the very element that is supposed to create structural stability, can by moving increment the forces that determine the stress on the structure.

Center of Resistance

Eccentricity

Center of Mass

Rigid Frame

Braced Frames

Shear Wall

Type of Stabilizing Systems

Configuration of Stabilizing Elements

Center of Resistance

Center of Resistance

Center of Resistance

Center of Mass

Center of Mass

Center of Mass

FIGURE 6.13 Structurally stabilizing elements.

6.21

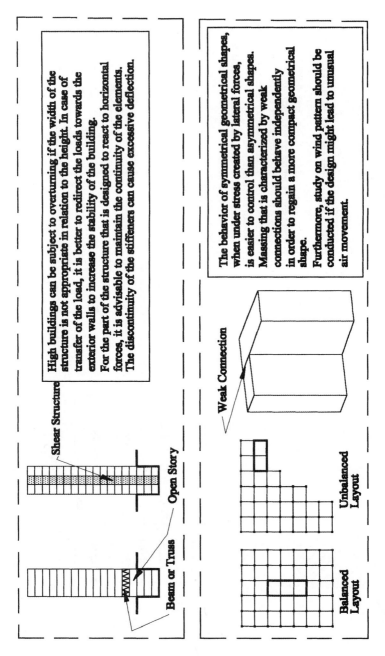

Shear Structure

High buildings can be subject to overturning if the width of the structure is not appropriate in relation to the height. In case of transfer of the load, it is better to redirect the loads towards the exterior walls to increase the stability of the building.

For the part of the structure that is designed to react to horizontal forces, it is advisable to maintain the continuity of the elements. The discontinuity of the stiffeners can cause excessive deflection.

Beam or Truss

Open Story

Weak Connection

The behavior of symmetrical geometrical shapes, when under stress created by lateral forces, is easier to control than asymmetrical shapes. Massing that is characterized by weak connections should behave independently in order to regain a more compact geometrical shape.

Furthermore, study on wind pattern should be conducted if the design might lead to unusual air movement.

Balanced Layout

Unbalanced Layout

FIGURE 6.14 Effect of height on buildings' structural behavior and impact of lateral forces on buildings' geometries.

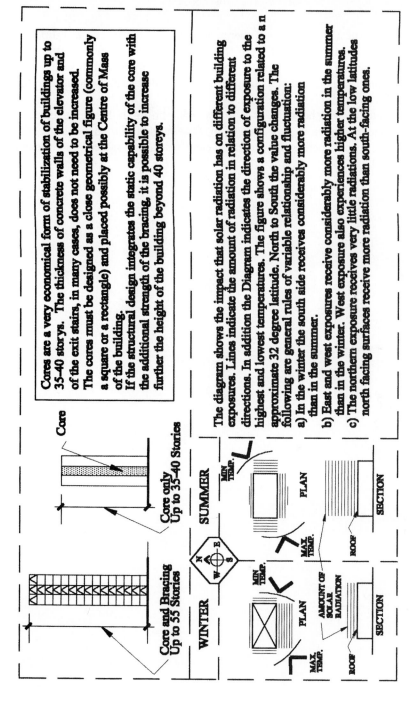

Core

Core only
Up to 35-40 Stories

Core and Bracing
Up to 55 Stories

Cores are a very economical form of stabilization of buildings up to 35-40 storys. The thickness of concrete walls of the elevator and of the exit stairs, in many cases, does not need to be increased.
The cores must be designed as a close geometrical figure (commonly a square or a rectangle) and placed possibly at the Centre of Mass of the building.
If the structural design integrates the static capability of the core with the additional strength of the bracing, it is possible to increase further the height of the building beyond 40 storeys.

The diagram shows the impact that solar radiation has on different building exposures. Lines indicate the amount of radiation in relation to different directions. In addition the Diagram indicates the direction of exposure to the highest and lowest temperatures. The figure shows a configuration related to a n approximate 32 degree latitude. North to South the value changes. The following are general rules of variable relationship and fluctuation:
a) In the winter the south side receives considerably more radiation than in the summer.
b) East and west exposures receive considerably more radiation in the summer than in the winter. West exposure also experiences higher temperatures.
c) The northern exposure receives very little radiations. At the low latitudes north facing surfaces receive more radiation than south-facing ones.

WINTER

SUMMER

MIN. TEMP.

MAX. TEMP.

PLAN

SECTION

ROOF

AMOUNT OF SOLAR RADIATION

FIGURE 6.15   Structural function of the building core and impact of solar radiation on a building.

tends to dissipate a high amount of energy during an earthquake; **c.** steel structure is quite flexible; **d.** because of the high flexibility of the elements of the steel structure, non-structural components need to be securely braced in such a way that movement of nonstructural components is impeded and any damage to the structure is avoided.

Concrete on the other hand is: **a.** massive and brittle; **b.** heavier than steel; **c.** dependent mainly on its own strength to resist lateral forces; **d.** because of the relative rigidity of concrete, non-structural elements are less subject to movement of the building.

CHAPTER 7
ENVIRONMENTAL PRINCIPLES AND MECHANICAL SYSTEMS

As we discussed at the beginning of Chapter 6, one of the main functions of architecture is to provide shelter from extreme outside conditions. The adjective *extreme* is a variable that has some subjective fluctuation depending on individual physical and psychological characteristics. What is uncomfortable for one individual can be perfectly acceptable for another. This statement is valid if considered within one historical period or it can be the starting point to compare tolerances in different historical periods. Because climatic conditions can be susceptible to variations within a short time span, concepts are developed based on a range of data more than on specific and well-defined single numbers (although single numbers, or a defined set of combination of variables grouped into one value, as in the case of effective temperatures, will determine the upper and lower limits of these ranges).

At the heart of the climatic and environmental performance of the building is the philosophical approach through which the design is viewed. Is the building seen as an isolated element, not in relation with the natural environment and its resources, or it is analyzed in relation to its potential impact on the ecosystem?

CLIMATIC AND ENVIRONMENTAL ASPECTS

Traditionally, the combinations of variables that define the impact environmental conditions have on buildings are relative to the human range of comfortable values. The design of architectural and non-architectural systems has therefore been conceived as compensation for the discrepancy between these factors in an effort to create the ideal environment for human beings. This type of approach has led to the development and employment of "active" types of systems (i.e., air conditioning).

With increased awareness of the effects that man-made objects have on the environment, some aspects of the natural habitat (primarily related to the amount of energy used to satisfy these requirements) have been added to the equation. In other words, the reciprocal analysis directed at the impact the building has on the occupants of the natural environment has been only marginally developed. It fundamentally lacks a global view of the natural dynamic of phenomena and a continuous monitoring of their state. In addition, the tendency of our culture to consider only very macroscopic processes without being continuously aware that this is the result of continuous microscopic phenomena, has justified the limitations of its variables as premises of the design. Although the quality and sophistication of thinking must still be developed in regard to the correct relationship between human beings and the natural environment, hints of what that relationship should become are starting to surface. This is especially true in the development of *passive* types of systems. It is in this type of design that man is forced to consider nature as a participant rather than an object.

BASIC THERMAL PRINCIPLES

It is necessary to make a distinction between heat and temperature. Heat is the energy transferred between two elements; temperature is the measure of this stored energy. Temperature is never transferred; energy is. Heat energy is sometimes transferred without a change in temperature: when this happens, the heat is called *latent*. If a change in temperature accompanies the energy transfer, the heat is called *sensible*. There are three types of processes through which heat energy is transferred:

1. *Radiation:* the process through which heat energy is transferred from one object to another without their touching or being necessarily one above the other. Different materials have different capacity for storing energy; stored energy is called *specific heat*. This process happens at different wavelengths, which are dependent on the temperature of the object. The temperature of the surface of the object determines the rate at which the energy is exchanged. Commonly the rate of absorption (absorptivity) and the rate of emission (emissivity) of a surface at a given wavelength are the same. A surface that has a different rate of absorption/emission for different wavelengths is called a *selective surface*. A material can also have different behavior in allowing radiation to pass through *(level of transmissivity)*, and certain materials can have different transmissivity for a different spectrum of wavelength. Glass has the highest degree of transmissivity in certain spectrums (the visible ones) and, therefore, is considered transparent. However, in the infrared range glass has a very low transmissivity: this is the cause of the *greenhouse effect*. The objects in a space enclosed with glazing tend to absorb radiation from the sun, which the glass allowed through, and tend to release heat in the infrared wavelength spectrum. It is this heat that is trapped inside the space since the glass is not transparent for infrared waves.

2. *Convection:* heat transfer that happens only in the air or in liquids. Hot air that rises is an example of convection. This type of heat transfer is directional and only upward or sideways. The latter movement occurs only if inducted by blowing or sucking. At the same humidity, cool air is heavier that hot air and dry air is heavier than humid air. A stack effect is the movement of air in a tall space determined by the rising of the hot air above the cold air and by the movement of the latter that tends to occupy the area of low pressure created by the rising of the hot air.

3. *Conduction:* the mechanism through which heat energy is transferred by contact: from the surface that registers the higher temperature to the one that has the lower. This is the phenomenon that, along with radiation and convection, occurs when heat loss is experienced in a building through a roof or a wall. Each component is in contact with another element at a lower temperature. In addition each material has a different conductivity (k) and resistivity (r), the latter being the reciprocal of the former. These characteristics are calculated in conductance (C) and resistances (R). The resistance of a material is calculated using the formula; $x/k = R$, where x is the thickness of the material and k is the conductivity.

An assembly has a *conductance* which is calculated in U-value. The U-value is the reciprocal of the sum of all the resistance (R) of the component constituting the assembly:

$$U = \frac{1}{(R1 + R2 + \ldots\ldots Rn)}$$

An additional form of heat transfer is what is called *phase change*. It happens when, for example, water changes into vapor. In a phase change, energy can be used up (like the melting of an ice cube), or can be stored (like the freezing of water into ice). This type of energy exchange is particularly important because it models how the body cools down when it is overheated: the body perspires and the perspiration evaporates using up energy and, therefore, cooling down the body.

The basic measurement for heat transfer is the British Thermal Unit (Btu), which corresponds to the amount of energy required to raise the temperature of one pound of water by 1°Fahrenheit.

BASIC ENVIRONMENTAL PRINCIPLES

As indicated, the symmetrical relationship between a built and natural environment is fundamental from two different points of view: **a.** the natural environment is affected by the artificial environment; **b.** an artificial habitat is affected by the natural environment.

The first factor of the equation requires an analysis of the impact that a project will have on the environment. The result of this analysis should direct the design and the choice of systems to be used toward solutions that tend to minimize the difference between the status of the environment before and after the project is constructed.

The goal is to affect the naturally occurring processes at the macro and microclimate level as little as possible, as well as to take advantage of the characteristics of the environment and to use as much as possible the renewable resources offered by the location (always complementing, rather than altering, the natural processes). This is why it is fundamental for an architect to understand the dynamic of the natural environment in order to create what can be called *transparent architecture.*

Both the macro- and the microclimate are important. The former defines the general tendency of the meteorology of an area (it can be extended to large geographical regions as in the case of equatorial or temperate climates). The latter characterizes, within the general macroclimate, the specific elements and cycles occurring in a defined, geographically limited location. For example, a relatively large area can be hot and humid, but the presence of certain natural elements (i.e., mountains or rivers) might introduce dynamics in particular locations for which humidity and temperature levels are kept within less extreme values than other places of that region. In general, the following are factors to be considered in site analysis and site design.

Macroclimate

The characteristics of macroclimates are: **a**. *latitude:* the distance from the equator (which determines the amount of solar energy); **b**. *elevation:* temperature decreases 1°F for each 300 feet; **c**. *proximity of body of water:* reduces temperature extremes; **d**. *Winds:* prevailing winds coming from the south during the summer season and northerly winds during the winter season determine temperature and precipitation fluctuation in many large areas; **e**. *ocean currents:* warm currents mitigate conditions that otherwise are very harsh at the same latitude in coastal regions exposed to cold currents; **f**. *mountains:* at contact with mountains, the air rises, cools down, forms clouds, and discharges moisture in the form of rain, generally on the leeward side (opposite side of the wind direction).

The result of these factors shapes the climate based on characteristics of the air: arid or humid. This can lead to primarily cloudy or clear weather. Cloudy weather is less subject to temperature fluctuation between extremes (since clouds act as blankets). Clear weather temperatures change more drastically. Arid regions experience greater changes in temperature if compared to humid zones (humidity retains more heat energy than dry air).

Microclimate

Once the general characteristics of a macroclimate have been determined for the entire region, the specifics of the site need to be analyzed in order to take advantage of its positive aspects. In doing so, the logical step would be the mitigation of those characteristics that seem to hinder the maintenance of variables within the comfort zone for humans. For instance, it would be simple to introduce trees in order to shield the construction from winter winds or to channel summer breezes towards particular locations. However, as indicated before, the principles of transparent architecture require that, before these steps are taken and design implemented, a thorough analysis of the effects that these changes have on the environment (mineral, flora and fauna components) must be conducted. It is fundamental to remember the *butterfly effect*. Phenomena in the natural world are so closely connected that the flap of butterfly wings in China can cause a hurricane in Florida.

The following are aspects of a microclimate that should be considered: **a.** *solar radiation:* since this is a primary source of energy, the exposure of the site to the amount of solar radiations in very important. This is not only related to temperature, but especially to transfer and absorption of energy by all the elements constituting the local natural and man-made environment (see Figure 6.15). A site on a slope facing south will receive more energy than a site on a flat plane. In turn a flat site will receive more energy than a site on a north-facing slope (see Figure 7.1); **b.** *duration of daylight:* this is another factor that affects considerably the amount of energy absorbed by the elements; **c.** *winds:* the direction and intensity of seasonal winds are both important in order to take advantage of their effect on the construction and the site in general. Exposure to cold winter winds is not desirable because it can affect the amount of energy required to heat the construction (a relatively small increase of the wind speed at freezing temperature can double the amount of energy required to heat a building). In summer, however, the construction should take advantage of the cooling effect of seasonal breezes. In addition, the wind pattern can affect the climate since turbulent air disperses heat more effectively than steady air that tends to maintain the same temperature (see Figures 7.2, 7.3, and 7.4). **d.** *topography:* as indicated for the macroclimate, natural features affect the microclimate as well. Mountains or hills act as barriers directing or impeding the flow of air. Winds at the top of hills or mountains are faster than on the flatter parts. Wind speed increases with altitude because, among other things, the friction with the ground affects it considerably. Wind speed on the slopes is a function of the gradient. Mountains and hills can also determine movement of air by changing the air temperature. In these cases the ground acts as a heat sink, cooling down the air at night. Heavier than the warm air, cooled air slides along the inclined surface of the hills and rests on the flat surface in a valley or a plain. These areas are also damper and foggier because of the difference in earth temperature between the earth and the air. In the middle of the slope the air remains warmer while the top of the hill tends to be cold and windy. By acting as a barrier, the windward side experiences the full impact of the wind, while the leeward side shields the area immediately beneath the hill from the wind (at the bottom of the hill winds are minimal). The leeward side, however, is generally characterized by more precipitation and snow; **e.** *bodies of water:* water stores and releases heat at a different rate than the ground. This difference creates two phenomena: first the change in temperature between day and night is mitigated and also temperatures tends to be less extreme (unless the body of water is affected by cold currents); secondly, the difference in the rate of absorption/emission of the heat determines the flow of a breeze that can be very beneficial during the summer months. **f.** *vegetation:* these components of the natural environment have two effects on the microclimate: one with their physical presence and the other through the chemical and biological processes that they produce. In addition, they provide shelter and food for the local fauna. For example, considering its mass, a tree can be seen as a windbreak: its effect on the air movement can be felt at a horizontal distance between five and ten times the height of the tree (depending on the type and arrangement of the trees). Trees modify temperature by providing shaded areas during the summer and allowing the winter sun to penetrate (deciduous trees). Vegetation in general also affects the environment through photosynthesis. This is a process in which the plant absorbs carbon dioxide and releases oxygen. This determines not only objective quality in terms of breathable air, but also the subjective sense of well being produced by cool, fresh air; **g.** *surface characteristics:* this refers especially to the degree of conductivity and the degree of reflectivity (albedo) that the surface has in relation to radiant energy. Albedo is a variable indicated by fluctuations ranging from 0 to 1 (the latter being the highest level of reflectivity as in a mirror). Grass and ground have a low level of albedo and high conductivity (which helps to moderate the climate). Pavements have a high degree of albedo; **h.** *man-made structures:* these represent the artificial habitat already in existence. The dynamic of interaction between the elements and the natural features (like mountains, body of water, trees) that has been described can be used in large part to analyze the effect that pre-existing structures have on the environment. From the wind to the reflection of energy, these artificial elements can act as a hill or as any surface that radiates a certain amount of heat. Man-made structures, therefore, must be included in the analysis of the microclimate.

DESIGN FOR DIFFERENT CLIMATIC AREAS

Climatic conditions vary widely. The following are basic principles that should be applied in designing for different climate zones.

Cold Climates

In cold environmental conditions, the primary focus is on producing and conserving heat efficiently. This means: **a.** the surface/volume ratio should be minimized by adopting geometries that result in a compact building (cubic or dome-like). The architectural typology should be such that interior units can isolate each other from the outside (like apartments or multi-dwelling); **b.** insulation is one of the primary elements that contribute to conserving heat within the building. High R value should

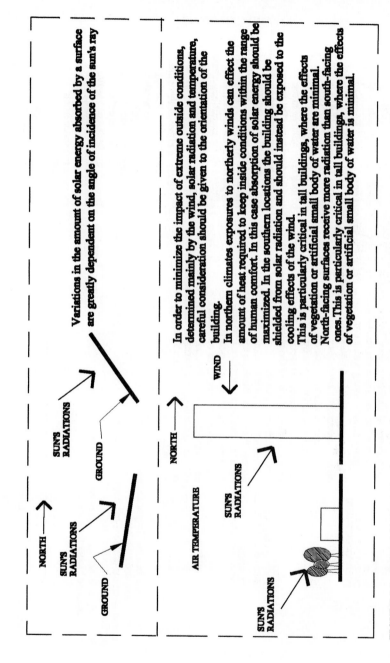

FIGURE 7.1 Relationship between orientations, angle of incidence of solar rays and amount of solar radiation.

7.7

Air movement patterns created by the impact of the wind on an object are dependent on many factors among which are: the geometry and orientation of the object, surrounding elements, wind velocity. The wind pattern then applies a series of positive (pressure) and negative (suction) forces on the surfaces of the object that further influence the movement of the air inside and outside the object. Because the variables can be predicted only when the outside conditions are established and the latter are dependent on factors only partially controllable, the constant performance of a particular design in terms of ventilation must be considered as a range of possible behavior of the elements.

Air movement in a building is dependent on the location, size and ratio between the openings as well as on the presence of obstructions to the air flow within the building.

In principle, to achieve higher air speed, the outlet must be bigger than the inlet.

Wind speed and angle of incidence relative to the surface determines the amount of positive and negative pressure that is applied on a surface. Furthermore it effects the distance that is covered by the air before the pattern of air movement is affected by the conditions created by the presence of an element (i.e. window)

The cooling effect of the wind can be enhanced by creating a shaded area on the windward side of the construction.

In addition by channeling the wind with a funnel effect through the layout of the site features and vegetation, it is possible, in some cases, to increase the speed of air movement.

NEGATIVE PRESSURE

HIGH SPEED WIND PATTERN

LOW SPEED WIND PATTERN

LOW SPEED WIND (NEGATIVE AND POSITIVE PRESSURE)

SUCTION (NEGATIVE PRESSURE HIGHER ON SIDE WALLS)

AIR CUSHION (POSITIVE PRESSURE)

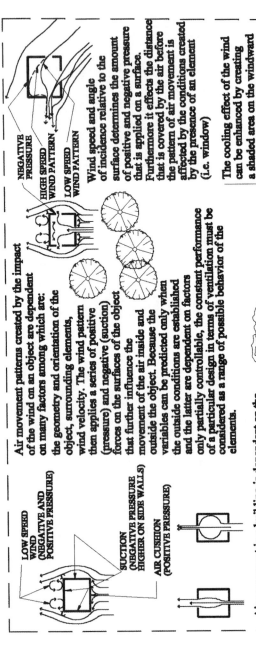

FIGURE 7.2   Air movement patterns.

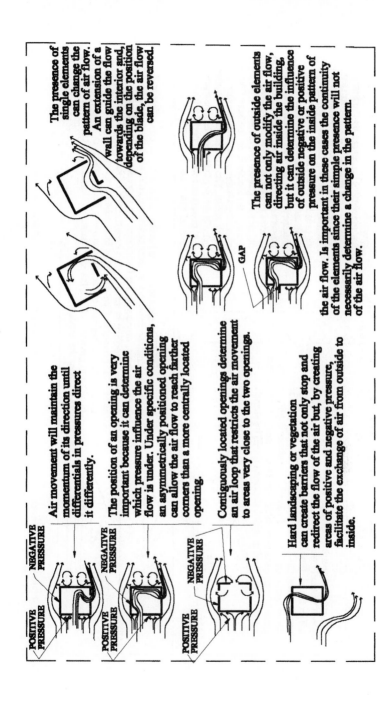

FIGURE 7.3 Air movement patterns.

7.9

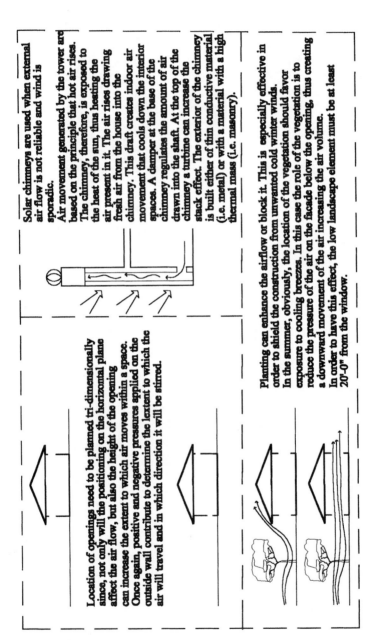

Location of openings need to be planned tri-dimensionally since, not only will the positioning on the horizontal plane affect the air flow, but also the height of the opening can increase the extent to which air moves within a space. Once again, positive and negative pressures applied on the outside wall contribute to determine the extent to which the air will travel and in which direction it will be stirred.

Solar chimneys are used when external air flow is not reliable and wind is sporadic.

Air movement generated by the tower are based on the principle that hot air rises. The chimney, therefore, is exposed to the heat of the sun, thus heating the air present in it. The air rises drawing fresh air from the house into the chimney. This draft creates indoor air movement that cools down the interior spaces. A damper at the base of the chimney regulates the amount of air drawn into the shaft. At the top of the chimney a turbine can increase the stack effect. The exterior of the chimney is built either of thin conductive material (i.e. metal) or with a material with a high thermal mass (i.e. masonry).

Planting can enhance the airflow or block it. This is especially effective in order to shield the construction from unwanted cold winter winds.

In the summer, obviously, the location of the vegetation should favor exposure to cooling breezes. In this case the role of the vegetation is to reduce the pressure of the air on the facade below the opening, thus creating a downward movement of the air increasing the air volume.

In order to have this effect, the low landscape element must be at least 20'-0" from the window.

FIGURE 7.4 Relationship between location of openings and air movement patterns. Principle of solar chimneys.

be used; **c.** glazing should be small and, where the winter sun is often available, windows should face the equator. Multiple layers of glass should constitute the glazing; **d.** the thermal mass of the building becomes a factor only if the building is not continuously occupied. This means that in a building with low thermal mass, it is not required to heat the thermal mass first in order to achieve the required indoor temperature. If the heat is not constantly maintained, this represents a substantial saving; **e.** in order to reduce heat loss in the building, particular attention should be given to airtight construction techniques; **f.** double entrances should used for air-locks.

Temperate Climates

The requirements for this type of climate generally fall under those indicated for cold climates. However, the milder conditions in every season allow us to benefit in the winter from an increase in thermal mass (since the benefits of passive solar design begin to be effective). In the summer the use of natural environmental factors and elements (like shades or winds) creates conditions within the range of suitability for human comfort. For these reasons: **a.** since solar heating in the winter is advantageous, shade or deciduous vegetation can mitigate the solar gain during the summer; **b.** thermal mass is beneficial during the night when, even during the summer, external temperature might fall under certain values; **c.** natural ventilation can reduce the need for mechanical ventilation during the summer.

Hot Dry Climates

High temperature, high solar radiation and a large diurnal range of temperature variations characterize this climate. The following principles are beneficial in designing for this climate: **a.** delaying the transfer of heat from outside to inside by using a large thermal mass is very important in these conditions; **b.** a filter, perhaps an interior courtyard, helps in screening the indoors from dust, heat, or glare. This space can also be used to cool the air through evaporation. A fountain or a pond can provide the humidity necessary to generate the processes of evaporation. Vegetation can shade this area and the combination of cooler air and additional refrigeration provided by evaporation maximizes the benefits; **c.** typical colors should be reflective (like white) and buildings should be grouped in order to cast shade on each other; **d.** small windows and openings in general should be used.

Warm Humid Climates

High temperatures during the night and low variation of diurnal temperature (very often around 5° Celsius), with high humidity that does not allow evaporation from the skin are the fundamental characteristics of this climate. The following strategies can help in re-conducting outside conditions to less extreme indoor conditions: **a.** the use of shades to minimize solar gain; **b.** low thermal mass to rapidly cool the building at night; **c.** good insulation for east and west windows with virtually no opening; **d.** in contrast, north and south walls should have large openings for cross ventilation. Internal obstructions to air flow should be avoided; **e.** access to breezes should be encouraged by spacing the buildings adequately and orienting them to facilitate wind circulation; **f.** in case of conflicts of orientation between the sun and the breeze, the former should be controlled (either through architectural elements or vegetation); **g.** large volumetric ventilation should be provided in order to remove internal heat; **h.** use of the following should be considered: reflective roof, separate ceiling, ventilated attic, reflective foil above the ceiling, insulated ceiling.

NATURAL VENTILATION

Natural ventilation is based on air movement induced by differential pressure that the air, by moving and occupying different areas, tends to equalize. Major factors that will influence the natural ventilation are: the type and orientation of the building, the orientation of the openings, the total area of the openings, the ratio between the size of the openings used as air inlet and those used as air outlet, the horizontal and vertical location of the openings, the type of window and screen system, interior obstructions and elements that convey the air.

Air movement can be determined by changed indoor and outdoor conditions. For example, the positive pressure created by the wind on the windward side of an object and the negative pressure created on the leeward side determine the constant flowing of indoor air towards the outside and the constant flow of fresh air toward the inside (see Figures 7.2, 7.3, and 7.4). Another example is the indoor stack effect. It can be caused by many factors: **a.** the humidity released by equipment and occupants. Since humid air is lighter than dry air, indoor air, once humidified, tends to rise. If released through high windows, it can be replaced by fresh air drawn from a lower opening or from indoor areas with cooler temperatures; **b.** thermo-siphon effect, a phenomenon based on the rising of hot air replaced by cold air, triggered by the greenhouse effect or any other kind of technique that allows the entrapment of heat and the triggering of a stack effect (see Figure 7.4). For the greenhouse effect, the air either is allowed to escape through openings at the ceiling or roof level (for cooling during the summer) or it is conveyed through ducts and re-circulated through the building (for heating purposes during the winter). Atriums can be designed to fulfill the function of space where the thermo-siphon effect is triggered.

MECHANICAL SYSTEMS

In modern times mechanical systems have been used for heating and cooling buildings and artificial environments in general. There are various types of systems, but all of them have three basic components: the source of heating or cooling (called the plant), a distribution system and a discharge. The discharge is intended as indoor discharge, where heating or cooling is introduced in the areas where it is required, and as exhaust, where the residual of the process is eliminated through outside emission. Each of these components is more or less articulated depending on the system used.

Central and Local Systems

Systems can be central or local. Central systems have a centralized source of heat or cooling and an articulated distribution; local systems are self-contained and, since the source is at the desired location, their distribution system is reduced. Comparatively central systems are more energy efficient than local systems and they can achieve better control of the indoor air quality. Furthermore they last longer and they are easier to serve. On the other hand, local systems utilize less space since the distribution is not extended. They are also more economical to buy and install. Furthermore local systems are more flexible since space for different cooling or heating requirements can be easily satisfied.

Central Equipment for Large Buildings

Major equipment that is part of systems requiring space in large buildings includes: **a.** *boilers*, which produce hot water or steam to heat buildings and hot water. A large building requires two boilers (one for back-up). Technically the room can be located anywhere in the building. However it is advisable to plan it along an outside wall since the space requires an intake air supply and an access to replace the boilers. The equipment is a source of noise. Furthermore the equipment and the boilers are very heavy. The boilers can be fueled by gas, oil or electricity. Gas and oil require air inlets for combustion and chimneys and oil requires a tank; **b.** *chilled water plant*, which produces cold water for cooling the building. The chillers are fueled by electricity, gas or steam. They are a source of vibration and noise. Chilled water plants should be located ideally near the boiler room (in large buildings), or in the same room (in smaller buildings). The ceiling height varies from 12', for a medium size building, to 16' for a large building; **c.** *cooling towers* are the mechanisms used to dissipate into the atmosphere the heat removed from the building by the air conditioning system. The mechanism is based on evaporation and convection. The hot water from the condenser splashes down through the tower giving heat to air forced through the tower by fans. The cooled water is collected at the bottom of the tower in pans. This water is then recycled into the chillers. If the towers are not located on the roof, they have to be distanced from the building by a minimum of 100' (30 m) because of the splash, the fog and the microorganisms that are present in such a humid environment. Attention must be given to avoid placing them in the vicinity of windows or fresh air louvers. When the towers are located on the roof, particular attention must be given to the noise and vibration that the operation creates. The height varies from 13' to 40' (4 m to 12 m). Allow airflow between towers by locating them a minimum of one full width apart and design a 4' (1.2 m) crawl space.

Zoning

A building can accommodate uses that require different heating and cooling requirements. Furthermore the geometry of the building, the specific materials and the exposures might compound the reasons for providing an articulated and flexible system. In addition, the zoning requirements do not necessarily correspond to environmental conditions. Another factor that might require a flexible system is the use of separate billing for administrative reasons.

This means that a single source that is not capable of providing various outputs will not perform properly. In order to satisfy different requirements, the building must be subdivided into zones that are homogeneous in their heating and cooling requirements. These zones can be as small as a single room or as large as the capacity of a single unit. It is important to define the zoning at the early stage of the project since it may determine the type of system to be used.

Distribution Systems

There are several types of distribution systems. They are characterized by the circulation of air or water or a combination of both of them, in order to distribute heat or cooling throughout the building.

The following are the common types used in the construction of large buildings: **a.** *all-air systems:* conditioned air is circulated to and from the spaces by using fans that push the conditioned air along long ducts (see Figures 7.5, 7.6, and 7.7); **b.** *air and water systems:* with this system air is ducted to each space. Hot and chilled water is also piped simultaneously to the spaces to modify the temperature. This system circulates less air and requires less ducting (see Figure 7.8); **c.** *all-water systems:* in this case the system provides air directly where it is needed and not from a central location: the ductwork is therefore eliminated. Chilled and heated water is circulated to each space. It is the most compact of all systems (see Figures 7.9, 7.10, and 7.11). If these systems are analyzed comparatively the following observations can be drawn:

All-air systems: **a.** air handling equipment can be designed to control very precisely fresh air, filtration, humidification and dehumidification, heating and cooling; **b.** when the outside air is cool enough, the system can switch to an economizer cycle that maximize the circulation of outside air; **c.** maintenance can be concentrated in areas with no activities since the equipment that requires such maintenance is confined in service rooms.

Air and water and all-water systems: **a.** provide individual control of temperature in the individual spaces that is better than in all air systems.

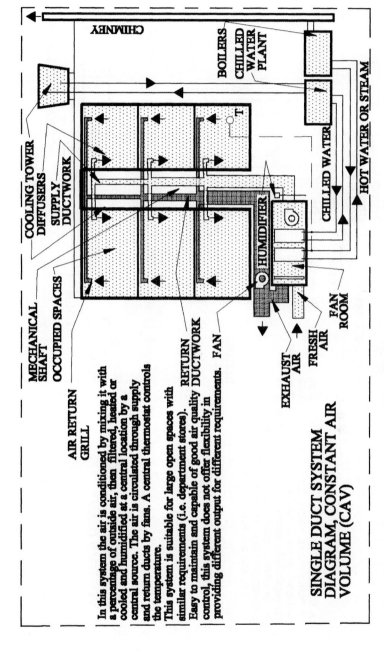

FIGURE 7.5   Single duct system diagram, constant air volume.

7.15

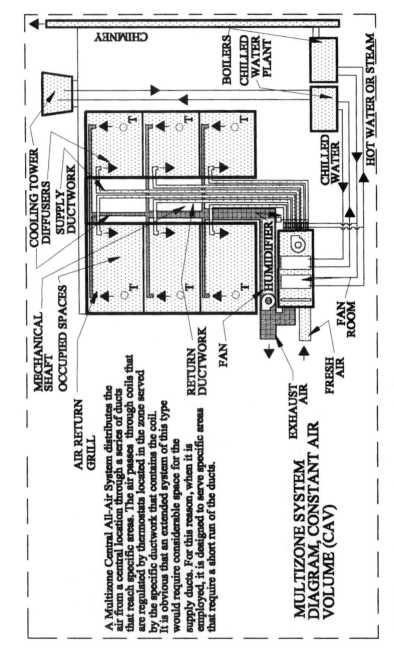

A Multizone Central All-Air System distributes the air from a central location through a series of ducts that reach specific areas. The air passes through coils that are regulated by thermostats located in the zone served by the specific ductwork that contains the coil. It is obvious that an extended system of this type would require considerable space for the supply ducts. For this reason, when it is employed, it is designed to serve specific areas that require a short run of the ducts.

MULTIZONE SYSTEM DIAGRAM, CONSTANT AIR VOLUME (CAV)

FIGURE 7.6   Multizone system diagram, constant air volume.

7.16

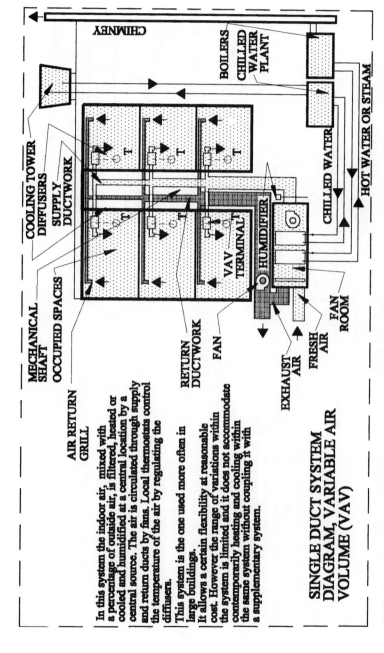

CHIMNEY

BOILERS

CHILLED WATER PLANT

COOLING TOWER

DIFFUSERS

SUPPLY DUCTWORK

CHILLED WATER

HOT WATER OR STEAM

MECHANICAL SHAFT

OCCUPIED SPACES

RETURN DUCTWORK

FAN

VAV TERMINAL

HUMIDIFIER

AIR RETURN GRILL

EXHAUST AIR

FRESH AIR

FAN ROOM

In this system the indoor air, mixed with a percentage of outside air, is filtered, heated or cooled and humidified at a central location by a central source. The air is circulated through supply and return ducts by fans. Local thermostats control the temperature of the air by regulating the diffusers.

This system is the one used more often in large buildings.

It allows a certain flexibility at reasonable cost. However the range of variations within the system is limited and it does not accommodate contemporarily heating and cooling within the same system without coupling it with a supplementary system.

SINGLE DUCT SYSTEM DIAGRAM, VARIABLE AIR VOLUME (VAV)

FIGURE 7.7   Single duct system diagram, variable air volume.

7.17

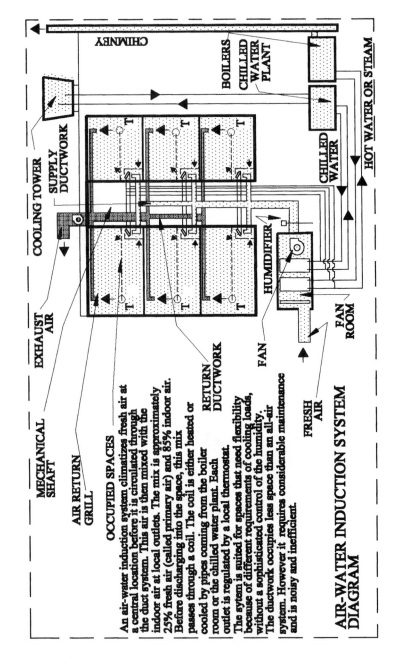

FIGURE 7.8 Air-water induction system diagram.

CHIMNEY

BOILERS

CHILLED WATER PLANT

COOLING TOWER

SUPPLY DUCTWORK

CHILLED WATER

HOT WATER OR STEAM

EXHAUST AIR

MECHANICAL SHAFT

AIR RETURN GRILL

OCCUPIED SPACES

An air-water induction system climatizes fresh air at a central location before it is circulated through the duct system. This air is then mixed with the indoor air at local outlets. The mix is approximately 25% fresh air (called primary air) and 85% indoor air. Before discharging into the space, this mix passes through a coil. The coil is either heated or cooled by pipes coming from the boiler room or the chilled water plant. Each outlet is regulated by a local thermostat.

The system is suited for spaces that need flexibility because of different requirements of cooling loads, without a sophisticated control of the humidity. The ductwork occupies less space than an all-air system. However it requires considerable maintenance and is noisy and inefficient.

RETURN DUCTWORK

HUMIDIFIER

FAN

FAN ROOM

FRESH AIR

AIR-WATER INDUCTION SYSTEM DIAGRAM

7.18

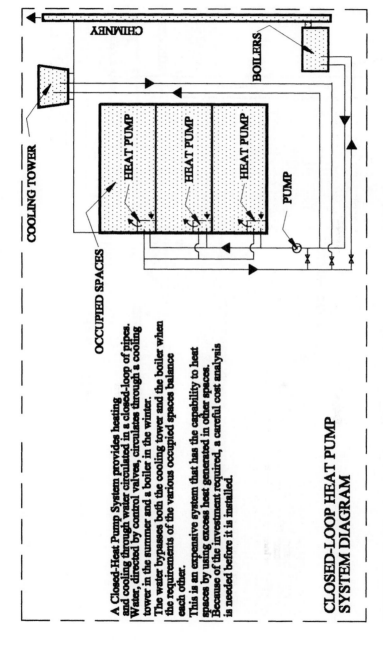

A Closed-Heat Pump System provides heating and cooling through water circulated in a closed-loop of pipes. Water, directed by control valves, circulates through a cooling tower in the summer and a boiler in the winter.

The water bypasses both the cooling tower and the boiler when the requirements of the various occupied spaces balance each other.

This is an expensive system that has the capability to heat spaces by using excess heat generated in other spaces. Because of the investment required, a careful cost analysis is needed before it is installed.

CLOSED-LOOP HEAT PUMP SYSTEM DIAGRAM

FIGURE 7.9   Close-loop heat pump system diagram.

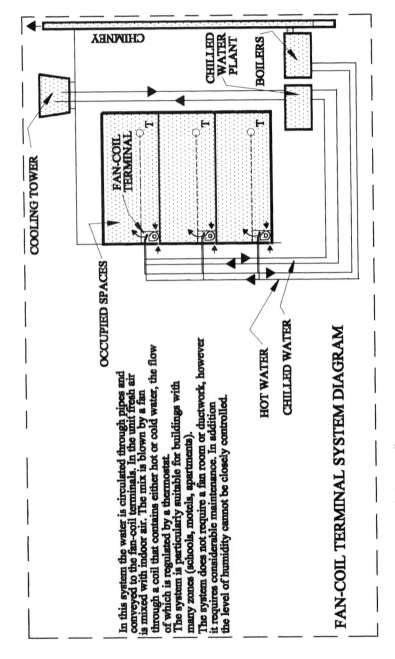

FAN-COIL TERMINAL SYSTEM DIAGRAM

In this system the water is circulated through pipes and conveyed to the fan-coil terminals. In the unit fresh air is mixed with indoor air. The mix is blown by a fan through a coil that contains either hot or cold water, the flow of which is regulated by a thermostat.

The system is particularly suitable for buildings with many zones (schools, motels, apartments).

The system does not require a fan room or ductwork, however it requires considerable maintenance. In addition the level of humidity cannot be closely controlled.

HOT WATER

CHILLED WATER

FIGURE 7.10 Fan-coil terminal system diagram.

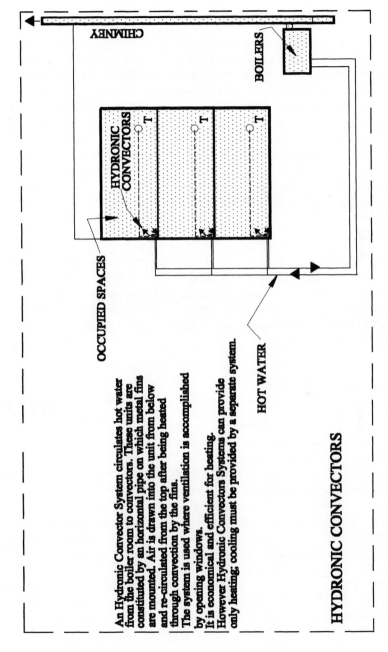

An Hydronic Convector System circulates hot water from the boiler room to convectors. These units are constituted by an horizontal pipe on which metal fins are mounted. Air is drawn into the unit from below and re-circulated from the top after being heated through convection by the fins.
The system is used where ventilation is accomplished by opening windows.
It is economical and efficient for heating.
However Hydronic Convectors Systems can provide only heating, cooling must be provided by a separate system.

HYDRONIC CONVECTORS

FIGURE 7.11   Hydronic convectors.

The most popular system for medium size construction, usually up to five stories, is the packaged central heating and cooling unit.

The units are of two types: **a.** *single-packaged* unit functions as boiler room and chimney, chilled water plant and fan room. It is very compact. It can be mounted on the roof or outside the building on a concrete pad (see Figure 7.12); **b.** *split-packaged* system has two units (or they can be considered one unit with two components)—the compressor and condensing coil that are mounted outside, and the internal unit that contains the circulating fan and the cooling as well as the heating coils. Split-packaged units, like single-packaged units, can also be installed on the roof or on a concrete pad outside the building. If they are installed on the roof, the inside component can be hung from the roof structure. If the outside component is installed on a concrete pad (for example at the ground floor), then the inside component can be placed on the floor (see Figure 7.12).

If the units are installed on the floor, the ductwork is connected to the side of the units. In the roof application, the ductwork is installed at the bottom of the units (see Figures 7.12 and 7.13). Both types of units can accommodate a single or multi-zone design and they come as a constant air volume or variable air volume unit. Comparatively, split-packaged units are more expensive but more efficient since the ductwork is totally contained within the heated envelope of the building. These units operate through electrical supply or a combination of electricity and gas.

PLUMBING SYSTEMS

The purpose of a plumbing system is to distribute an element like water or gas to fixtures, equipment, or valves, and if residuals or by-products are created during the use of the structure, to dispose of such residuals or by-product. The system can be subdivided in three components: supply, fixtures (including outlets), and waste (sanitary and storm drainage). The supply provides the element (i.e., clean water): the second allows the use of the element for the intended purpose; the third removes contaminated water and solid waste (sanitary); or collects, removes and disposes of the run off mainly produced by rain (storm). Except for older systems, the supply, the sanitary waste and the storm drainage must be kept separate because the latter two can contaminate the supply.

Building and plumbing codes regulate plumbing installations. The main areas that these codes tend to consider are: The size of drain, the size of vent pipes, material allowed, size of supply lines, distance of traps, distance between supports, number and type of fixtures required, number and type of fixtures connected to a vent or a drain pipe, placements of cleanouts, height and slope of drains, and use of connections.

In order to be efficient and economical, the run in a plumbing system (especially horizontal) should be minimized (see Figure 7.14). This means that spaces

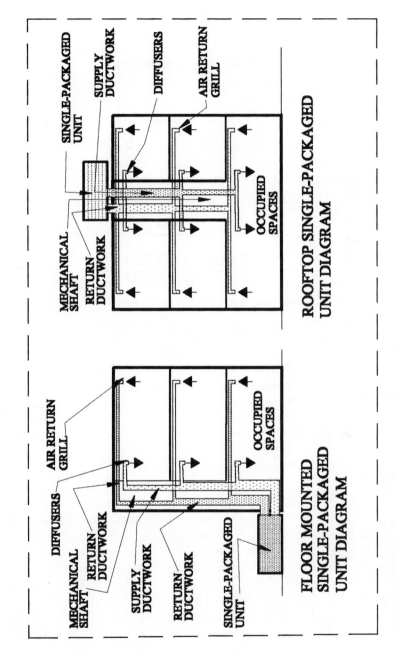

FIGURE 7.12   Floor mounted and roof top single packaged unit diagram.

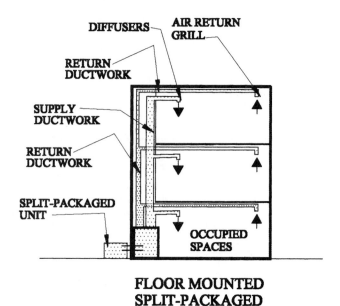

FLOOR MOUNTED
SPLIT-PACKAGED

FIGURE 7.13   Floor mounted split-packaged unit diagram.

requiring plumbing installations ideally should be grouped. On the same floor, bathrooms for example, should be located along common walls with the toilets back to back. On different floors they should be stacked. All the lines should run as much as possible vertically, thus minimizing any offset. This is especially important for the sewer and storm lines.

Supply

A closed system distributes clean water for various uses such as drinking water. the supply is divided into two systems: cold and hot water. Sources of water in nature are of three types: rain water, surface water, and underground water. The cycle occurs in the following way: water evaporates from the surface and creates clouds; at the right temperature this moisture falls in the form of rain; part of the water flows along the surface, collecting in some form of natural water reservoir (from small bodies to the oceans). Water from melting glaciers is added to the surface collections. Some rain is also absorbed into the ground. Water is filtered through rocks and other soil layers and deposited in underground reservoirs. Many surface springs originate from these underground reservoirs: this is the purest water in nature.

Rainwater may have some acidity (called pH) because in the vapor state and during its descent, it can combine with acidic substances that alter its composition. Pollution of air caused by the industrial era has increased this problem

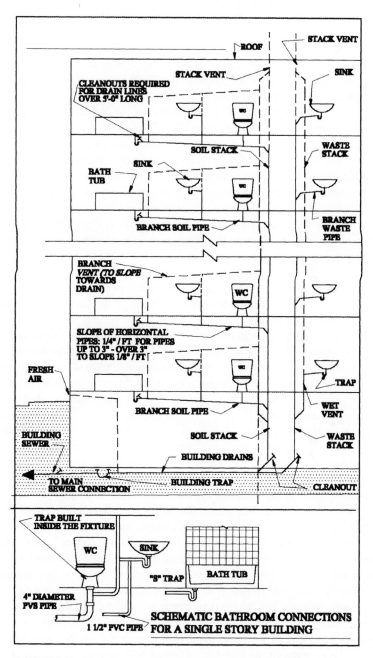

FIGURE 7.14 Typical waste system diagram for multistory building.

through the introduction of substances that raise the pH level of rainwater. The pH scale ranges from 0 to 14: the lower the number, the greater the acidity of the water. A pH of 7.0 indicates water that is neutral, neither acid nor alkaline. Above 7.0, water is alkaline while from 6.9 to 6.0 it is slightly acidic. At 5.0, water is very acidic. Acidic water is not only harmful for humans but corrodes pipes.

Another characteristic of water is its hardness. This refers to the amount of minerals the water contains (like limestone or calcium). Minerals are deposited in the water either as it percolates through the soil layers or as it flows or lies on the surface. Hard water, although not harmful for humans, creates deposits that tend to disrupt the water flow in pipes or cause problems in the functioning of appliances such as hot water tanks or in fixtures such as bathroom faucets. Hard water can be softened by using an ion exchange process. This process uses two tanks. One tank contains zeolite, a substance that collects the mineral carried by the water. The second container has salt that is used to clean the zeolite from the minerals removed from the water. The cleaning of the zeolite takes place periodically, depending on the concentration of minerals that the water usually carries in a particular region.

Substances and bacteria that can cause a variety of diseases may contaminate water. An example of harmful substances is the range of chemicals used in agriculture to protect crops from parasites. Apart from banning and forbidding their use, the next best solution is to filter water in order to reduce the deleterious effect of these chemicals. To eliminate the risk of diseases deriving from bacterial contamination, chlorine is added to the water in a concentration of 0.5 ppm (parts per million). In order to makes the water more digestible, oxygen is added as well. This process has a negative effect on some types of pipes because oxygen accelerates the process of rusting.

In nature, the water supply is subject to natural pressure that is regulated by the law of gravity. Utility companies increase this natural pressure during distribution to the location where the supply will be used. When the supply reaches the building, therefore, this pressure sometimes is sufficient to reach the upper floors and at other times needs to be further increased. One psi of pressure lifts a column of water 2.3 ft high. This means that to lift water 100 feet we need 43.5 psi (100 ft/2.3 ft psi = 43.5 psi), plus a certain residual needed for fixtures like faucets (7 to 8 psi), hose bibs (30 psi) or toilets (15 psi). An additional consideration in identifying the required pressure is the friction between the water and the inside walls of the pipe. The loss of pressure due to friction, therefore, is a function of the size of the pipe and the rate of the flow of the water. At a given rate of flow, the bigger the pipe the less the friction. The utility company or the authorities provide information on the pressure of the water available in a particular area. From this information and by applying the principles exposed above, it is possible to verify if the pressure of the water is sufficient or if pumps are necessary and to size the latter.

If pumps are required, one of three methods are commonly used to provide water at the level of the last floor: **a.** *downfeed system* is constituted by a tank (or tanks), mounted on the roof, filled with water raised by pumps (one back-up) located in the basement. This reservoir provides water by gravity. Usually the tank is subdivided into two sections. For repairs or cleaning, one section can be closed and emptied, while the other continues to function. A float switch allows monitoring of the water level and regulates the functioning of the pump. Because the weight of tank is considerable the negative aspect of this system is that structural members need to be increased in order to support the extra load; **b.** *pneumatic tank system* is based on the fact that air can be compressed while water cannot. A tank is located in the basement. It is not filled completely with water and some air is left inside. This air is compressed to push the water higher than the level allowed by the pressure of the main supply. The system requires space in the basement; **c.** *tankless system* utilizes pumps that keep the water at the required pressure. No tank is required. The negative aspect is that the pumps are continuously turned on and off and run at various speeds, increasing maintenance cost and shortening the lifespan of the equipment.

Whatever system might be used, the water velocity should generally be maintained at 8 ft./s or less. Main pipes might be allowed to carry water at a velocity of 10 ft./s. Building codes determine the minimum pressure required at each type of fixture. High velocity creates two potential problems: it increases the rate of corrosion of the pipes (especially provoked by water with a low pH) and the noise when any valve, including a faucet, shuts off the flow. To eliminate the second problem (called water hammer) a surge arrestor should be installed. This apparatus consists mainly of a vertical short section of a pipe that extends beyond the water level creating an air chamber. It is this chamber that absorbs the fluctuation in the water pressure (see Figure 7.15).

To calculate the flow of the water required in a system, a reference called a fixture unit is used (see Figure 7.15). The unit is calculated on the assumption that not all the fixtures will be functioning at the same time. In order to determine the unit, an arbitrary fixture is chosen as basic reference. Then all the other fixtures are rated in comparison to the requirement of the basic unit. Fixture unit calculations are used only to size the main supply pipes and not the branches. The latter are calculated based on the maximum total flow required for the total number of fixtures served by that branch and the minimum water pressure required at each fixture. The fixture unit assigned to each fixture takes into account: **a.** the water flow from the fixture outlet (gal/min); **b.** average duration of flow during the use of the fixture; **c.** frequency of use.

The total fixture units can be obtained by adding each unit associated to the fixture. Once this value is known, it is possible to introduce it into tabulations, which are available and thus will automatically give the required pipe size per type of function of the pipe.

The supply system, for various reasons (i.e., repairs) might need to be shut off. For this purpose, shut-off valves are provided in several locations. In addition, valves might need to be installed to regulate the water flow without shutting it off completely. On each side of the water meter, for example, two shut-off valves are installed. These allow isolation of the entire interior distribution system (the water meter in warm climate can be outside, while in cold climates it

FIXTURE TYPE	FIXTURE UNIT VALUE		MIN. CONNECTION (ins.)		DRAINAGE	
	PRIVATE	PUBLIC	COLD WATER	HOT WATER	FIXTURE UNIT VALUE	MINIMUM TRAP SIZE
BIDET	2	4	1/2"	1/2"	2	1 1/2"
BATHTUB	2	4	1/2"	1/2"	2	1 1/2"
KITCHEN SINK	2		1/2"	1/2"	2 or 3	1 1/2"
DISHWASHER	2				2	1 1/2"
FLOOR DRAINS	1				2	2"
LAVATORY	1		3/8"	3/8"	2	1 1/2"
SHOWER PER HEAD	2	4	1/2"	1/2"	2	2"
URINAL (PEDESTAL)			1"		6	3"
URINAL WALL, LIP			1/2"		2	2"
WATER CLOSET, TANK-OPERATED	3	5	3/8"		4	3"
WATER CLOSET, VALVE-OPERATED	6	10	1"		6	3"

TYPE OF WATER CLOSETS

WASHDOWN

SIPHON-VORTEX

BLOWOUT

SIPHON-JET

REVERSE-TRAP

AIR CHAMBER

TYPICAL COPPER PIPE CONNECTION

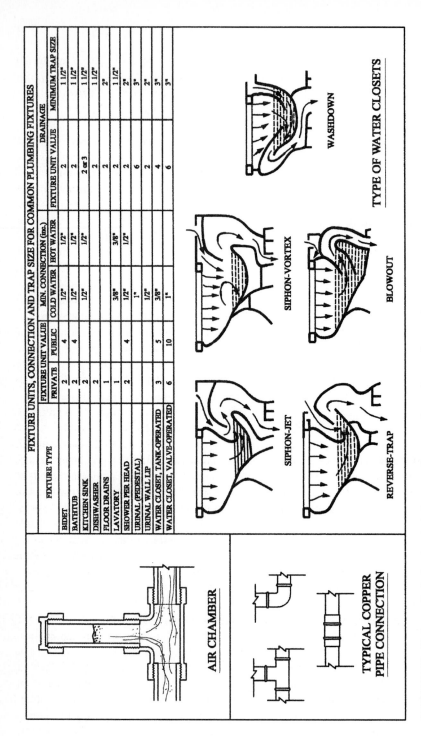

FIGURE 7.15 Fixture unit, air chamber, typical copper pipe connection and types of water closets.

7.28

must be inside). Valves are also placed near the plumbing fixture (i.e., under the sink or near the toilet), at the entrance of an apartment to shut off the entire branch serving that apartment or in the basement to shut off an entire floor (this is a less costly solution often adopted in multifamily development instead of installing an individual shut off for each apartment).

Valves are usually made of cast iron, brass or bronze. In bathrooms and kitchens, for example, faucets are made of nickel-plated brass. There are various types of valves: **a.** *globe valves* allow regulation of the flow of the water as well as complete shut off; **b.** *gate valve*, as the name suggests, is a type of valve that either shuts off the system or it leaves it open, without any intermediate reduction; **c.** *pressure release valve* is used to release pressure in a device or a section of the system that might be subjected to an amount of pressure exceeding that which can be withstood by its components or the material with which the system is constructed; **d.** *check valves* are devices that allow the flow of water in only one direction. If the flow is reversed, a component of the valve obstructs the opening for the flow of water within the valve and shuts off the system; **e.** *angle valves* can regulate the flow of water or shut off the flow. Faucets constitute one example. This type of valve works with a screw that, as it is tightened, brings a washer closer and closer to the opening for the water flow. In doing so it regulates the flow until it is tightly pressed against the opening, thus shutting off the flow completely; **f.** *ball valve* is a very rapid mechanism for shutting off the water (quarter turn).

To carry water supply two type of pipes are used: **a.** *copper*: this material is used to construct pipes of smaller diameter (common sizes range from ½ inch to 1½ inches). Copper pipes have thinner walls than pipes built with other materials and are subdivided in three major categories: K, L and M (with M being the one with the thinnest walls). Copper is corrosion resistant since oxidation tends to build a thin protective film inside the pipe walls. However, acid water with a low pH tends to corrode the copper and contaminate it with this metal. In such areas copper should not be used. There are two types of connectors for copper pipes: compression connections and solder connections (see Figure 7.15); **b.** *plastic:* a relatively modern technological development allowing a greater choice of the materials with which pipes can be constructed. Plastic pipes for water supply are of the PVC type. They are white with light blue lettering (versus the ABS type that are used mainly in drainage work and are of larger size, black with white lettering). Plastic pipes do not corrode but deteriorate when exposed to the ultraviolet rays of the sun. The connection is similar to that used for copper pipes.

Apart from the minimum requirements established by the code, the factors that will determine the size of the pipes are: **a.** the pressure at the main public water supply; **b.** the pressure to be provided at each fixture; **c.** the pressure loss due to height; **d.** recommended velocity of the water to prevent corrosion and noise; **e.** additional 10 percent minimum capacity for future expansion.

The suggested steps to be followed to determine pipe sizes are as follow: **a.** *create a preliminary diagram* with risers, horizontal mains, branch lines indicating the number and type of fixtures for the required flow; **b.** *determine the total* *fixture unit* adding each value associated to each fixture. This will allow determination of the total required water flow in gal/min (charts are available that readily compare fixture units with required water flow); **c.** *determine the length of pipe* for each stack calculated from the street main; **d.** *investigate the available minimum pressure* in the street main; **e** *determine the minimum pressure needed* for the fixture with highest demand; **f.** *determine the pressure loss* in pipes due to height of stacks. Consult one of the many charts available that compare water flow rate and pressure loss with pipe sizes). In addition to this loss, a value must be added for friction created by fittings, valves and other components. This loss is compared with the pressure reduction experienced in certain lengths of pipe. This value then is used and added to the length of the risers. Charts rate all the components of the distribution system and assign to them the appropriate length of pipe that corresponds to the same pressure loss cause by the component. The formula that allows calculation of pressure loss is $p= 0.433h$ where p is the pressure in psi and h is the height or pressure head; **g.** Determine the pipe size from either a chart provided in the applicable plumbing code or other comparable charts.

The formula that determines the rate of flow is $Q = AV$ where A is the pipe cross sectional area in square feet and V is the water velocity in ft/s (as stated above water velocity should not exceed 8 ft./sec for branches and 10 ft./s for main supply pipes).

In any water distribution system, pipes should be located in walls or spaces that will not be subject to temperatures causing the water to freeze. Either pipes are insulated or they are placed in insulated spaces. Furthermore, pipes should be sloped min ¼ inch per foot towards valves that would allow the water to be drained. Sufficient valves should be installed to allow the entire system to be emptied. Before being installed, any water supply pipe must be disinfected following a procedure indicated by the authority having jurisdiction.

In the hot water system, water is delivered to an appliance. The performance of that appliance is a function of its capacity and the recharge rate (the time needed for the hot water tank to re-heat cold water). There are various hot water systems in which either the appliance heats the water and stores it until hot water is needed or the appliance heats the water when it is needed: **a.** *continuous loop system:* the water from the main supply comes to the hot water tank, which heats it and then stores it. From there the water is delivered to the faucets. One negative characteristic of this system is that the hot water in the pipes between the hot water heater and the faucets loses heat. This water is wasted when very hot water is needed because the pipes need to be emptied of this water before the hot water from the tank reaches the faucet; **b.** *closed loop system:* a hot water re-circulating system constituted by a hot water return pipe, a pump and a water temperature sensor that regulates the operation of the pump. In this system hot water is continuously circulated in the system with a minimal heat loss in the pipes; **c.** *heat tracing:* it is installed around the hot water supply pipe under the insulation. This system requires low maintenance and is very efficient in terms of heat loss; **d.** *in-flow heater:* in this system the water is heated only when the faucet is turned on. Generally the cost of the system is higher and the performance in terms of flow is less than common systems. However from an energy consumption point of view it is very efficient.

One of the temperature maintenance systems indicated above should be used whenever a fixture is more than 25 feet away from the source of hot water. In the construction of the hot water system, one important aspect is the expansion of the materials and especially of the pipes when such material is heated. Expansion of pipes can be calculated using the following formula:

$\Delta L = L \times k \times (T2 - T1)$ where ΔL is the change in length, L is the length, k is the coefficient of expansion, $T1$ is the original temperature and $T2$ is the final temperature.

Pipe support should be placed maximum at 4 feet for plastic and minimum at 6 feet for copper.

Plumbing Fixtures

These are components placed at the terminals of the water distribution system and at the beginning of the waste distribution system (such as kitchen sinks, showers, water closets, bathtubs, lavatories, urinals, drinking fountains). Plumbing and building codes regulate many aspects of these fixtures (i.e., minimum number of fixture per type of occupancy, materials, type of connections, overflows, backflow and others). Since the fixture is the point at which the water supply system can enter into contact with the waste distribution system, attention is given to prevent contamination of the water supply. One technique is to use a trap. Traps can be incorporated in the fixture (see Figure 7.15) or be part of the piping system (see Figure 7.14).

Various types of water closets are available. These can differ in size and the type of flushing system, as well as in the amount of water used for flushing (see Figure 7.15). Pressure balancing or temperature-limiting valves are recommended in showers to avoid fluctuation of flow and temperature that might be very uncomfortable for the user.

To maintain the quality of the water, the supply system needs to be separated from the other plumbing systems. Codes require a minimum distance that should be always maintained between the fixture outlet and the flood level rim of the receptacle in order to avoid the possibility of backflow or back siphonage. Usually this gap ranges between 2 to 3 inches. The measure depends on whether or not the outlet could be affected by an adjacent wall. At the flood level rim an outlet is provided in addition to the drain being placed at the lowest level of the fixture. This outlet should be connected in the section of the pipe between the drain and the beginning of the trap.

Water can overflow because of malfunctioning of a fixture or because of human error. In places like mechanical rooms, kitchens, lockers and shower rooms, laundry rooms, and any other interior space that can be subject to floods, it is advisable to install a floor drain.

WASTE SYSTEM

This part of the plumbing system conveys various types of waste to the point of discharge. As in the water supply, there are two sections of the waste system: one public and the other private. The property line between public and private domains defines the two systems. At the property line (or near it) a connection in the form of a manhole is provided. From this connection, another section of the pipe is then hooked up to the main pipe (either sewer or storm). In small project construction, the mechanical engineer or the architect can design the system up to the connection with the public system (which is regulated by the authorities having jurisdiction). In medium and larger projects the plumbing system designed by the mechanical engineer ends at three feet outside the building. The civil engineer then continues the design to the main public distribution system. Fundamentally there are three type of waste: domestic, storm, and industrial.

Domestic

Domestic waste comes from dwellings that combine water discharge from fixtures like water closets, sinks or showers. Usually a treatment for solid wastes is recommended. This treatment separates the solid from the liquid portion of the waste. Then the liquid is run through a process in which bacteria eliminate impurities from it. The resulting by-product is chlorinated and discharged into a water body. The solid waste is delivered to anaerobic chambers (containing a different kind of bacteria that process the material). Once the cycle is completed, the material is dried and used either as fertilizer or as landfill.

Unfortunately, not all locations where a sewer system is provided are equipped with an efficient common facility. In the long run, this can produce a very dangerous situation. Solid treatment is required in accordance with the capability of the area where waste is to be discharged, resulting in a safe discharge. Requirements may change when the number of people in the settlement increases. If the quality of the environment is not monitored, an increase in population can cause problems very rapidly.

Where a main treatment plant is not available and a sewer system is not in place, local systems can be constructed. One type of treatment is the cesspool. It is a chamber made of porous material that allows the waste to soak into the surrounding ground. Eventually the ground becomes saturated and a new chamber needs to be installed. Pipes then are re-routed into it. A septic tank and a leach field constitute another type of treatment system. The tank is made out of steel. The solid waste is deposited at the bottom of the tank while the liquid part of the waste passes through the pipes installed in the leach field. The sections of the pipes are not connected head to head. A space is left to allow the liquid to seep into the gravel bed created under the pipes. The gravel filters the liquid before it is soaked into the ground.

The components of the sewer system within the building are (see Figure 7.14): **a.** *soil stack (or waste stack)*, pipes which collect the solid and liquid waste from the fixture to the sloped house drain (or building drain); **b.** *vent (or vent stack)* provides ventilation to the pipes preventing the build-up of gasses and equalizing the pressure in the various branches. The size of the pipe should not be reduced and should be designed to provide ventilation throughout the system (i.e., a loop type of design); **c.** *stack vent* is the upper portion of the soil stack above the highest branch drain that extends above the roof and to which the vent is connected. A VTR (vent through the roof) is any vent that extends above the roof. A stack vent can be used instead of carrying a vent stack above the roof, as long as the connection between the vent stack and the stack vent is made 6 inches above the flood rim of the highest fixture; **d.** *branch vents* are ramifications of the vents that reach close to the fixtures. Parts of the branch vents are the individual vents that are installed to vent the individual fixture traps. In general all the trapped fixtures are required to have individual traps (although there are exceptions). Individual vents can be: a wet vent, a circuit vent and a loop vent (see Figure 7.16); **e.** *traps* are a section of the pipe providing a water seal that prevents gasses from the sewer system from entering the interior space. Some codes require the installation of a building trap that seals the entire building; **f.** *building sewer* is that section of the pipe outside the building that connects the building sewer system to the public main sewer system.

Pipe material varies. Cast iron is the most common material used (see Figure 7.16 for types of fittings). However PVC, because is inexpensive and light, is also very popular. Copper, galvanized steel, and ABS are also used.

A sanitary sewer system should be designed to utilize the smallest section of the pipe that allows the waste material to flow without creating noise and fluctuation of pressure. The latter characteristic is particularly important because an excessive negative pressure created at the trap might siphon the water seals permitting the gasses to enter the interior space through the fixture. Waste pipes can be sized using the fixture unit method.

Horizontal pipes should be sloped (including all type of vents in order to drain possible condensation to the soil or waste pipes). Codes indicate the requirements of minimum slopes for pipes. Often they are ½ inch per foot for pipe 3½ inches or less and ⅛ inch or ¼ inch for larger pipes (see Figure 7.14).

Pipe supports should be spaced to eliminate sagging of the pipes. Different materials require different spacing: cast iron soil pipe maximum every 5 feet and behind every hub; threaded pipes maximum every 12 feet; copper tubing maximum every 10 feet. Supports must be provided also at the base of every stack.

From the point of view of the flow, the critical sections of the system are: long horizontal runs (more than 100 feet in length); change of direction that are more than 45°; where the building sewer starts as well as the base of all stacks. It is necessary to install a cleanout at each of these locations. A cleanout is a pipe connected to the system that provides access to it (see Figure 7.16). It has a plug screwed to its end that can be removed to flush out any obstruction that may have been created in the system. For pipes up to 4 inches, cleanouts are of the same size as the pipe they serve. For larger pipes they can be 4 inches or optionally larger. In commercial kitchens located in restaurants or cafeterias, or places

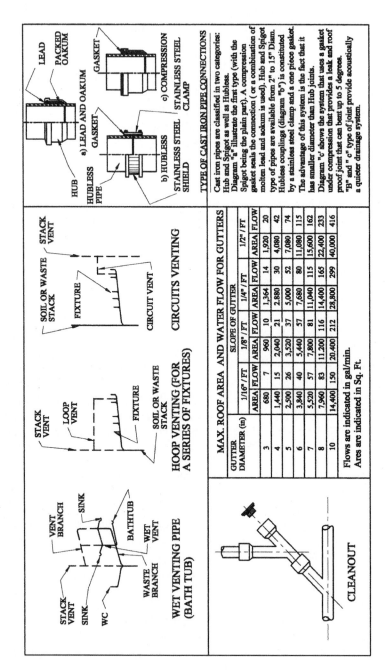

STACK VENT · LOOP VENT · FIXTURE · SOIL OR WASTE STACK

HOOP VENTING (FOR A SERIES OF FIXTURES)

SOIL OR WASTE STACK · FIXTURE · STACK VENT · CIRCUIT VENT

CIRCUITS VENTING

VENT BRANCH · SINK · BATHTUB · WET VENT · WASTE BRANCH · WC · SINK · STACK VENT

WET VENTING PIPE (BATH TUB)

CLEANOUT

LEAD · PACKED OAKUM · HUB · GASKET · HUBLESS PIPE · STAINLESS STEEL SHIELD · GASKET · STAINLESS STEEL CLAMP

a) LEAD AND OAKUM b) HUBLESS c) COMPRESSION

TYPE OF CAST IRON PIPE CONNECTIONS

Cast iron pipes are classified in two categories: Hub and Spigot as well as Hubless.
Diagram "a" illustrate the first type (with the Spigot being the plain part). A compression gasket seals the connection (or a combination of molten lead and oakum is used). Hub and Spigot type of pipes are available from 2" to 15" Diam. Hubless couplings (diagram "b") is constituted by a stainless steel clamp and a one piece gasket.

The advantage of this system is the fact that it has smaller diameter than Hub joints.

Diagram "c" shows the system that uses a gasket under compression that provides a leak and roof proof joint that can bent up to 5 degrees.

"B" and " c" type of joint provide acoustically a quieter drainage system.

MAX. ROOF AREA AND WATER FLOW FOR GUTTERS

GUTTER DIAMETER (in)	1/16"/FT		1/8"/FT		1/4"/FT		1/2"/FT	
	AREA	FLOW	AREA	FLOW	AREA	FLOW	AREA	FLOW
3	680	7	960	10	1,364	14	1,920	20
4	1,440	15	2,040	21	2,880	30	4,080	42
5	2,500	26	3,520	37	5,000	52	7,080	74
6	3,840	40	5,440	57	7,680	80	11,080	115
7	5,520	57	7,800	81	11,040	115	15,600	162
8	7,960	83	11,200	116	14,400	165	22,400	233
10	14,400	150	20,400	212	28,800	299	40,000	416

Flows are indicated in gal/min.
Ares are indicated in Sq. Ft.

FIGURE 7.16 Venting pipe layouts, cleanout, cast iron pipe connections and maximum roof area and water flow for gutters.

where oil or flammable materials might be discharged into the sewer, interceptors must be installed. These devices separate the undesirable element from the remaining waste.

Storm

Storm waste is primarily from roofs, the side of buildings, and the site. In the natural environment the water table (the level of the underground water) is reconstituted by the percolating of ground water into the ground. With the spread of the built environment, this process has been altered. Water is diverted and discharged into another area that has capacities and tolerances set by the characteristics of the environmental components of the surroundings. In many cases, if the flow represents an environmental problem at the discharge (i.e., the water body is too small or there are problems with potential erosion) retention ponds are created to equalize the flow. These ponds need to be properly drained in order to avoid water stagnation. In other cases, if the problem is localized at the point of final discharge some work to consolidate the stability of the immediate surrounding can be undertaken. To determine the storm-sewer requirements the following formula can be used: $Q = CIA$ where: Q is the maximum rate of run off (ft^3/s), C is the run off coefficient of the run off area, I is rainfall intensity (in/hr), A is the watershed area (acres). The coefficient of the watershed area is based on the characteristics of the surface and the rate of absorption. It ranges from 6.0 to 9.0 for built environment and 0.3 to 0.5 for surfaces that are not paved.

In order to convey the ground water into the storm system, two methods can be used: **a.** *swales* are sloping channels that are created to lead the water to specific points. The water is then either is collected or disposed; **b.** *catch basins* are small chambers covered with a grate that collects the water of a specific area. The catch basin is then connected to the storm water system that conveys the water to the discharge point.

The rainwater drainage from buildings must be added to the value obtained above. Rainwater can be collected either by gutters (in sloped roofs) or by roof drains (in flat roofs) (see Figures 7.16 and 7.17). In order to avoid puddles while conveying water properly to the drain, the recommended slope of flat roof is 2 percent. The best location of roof drains is either near exterior walls (although interior walls if relatively close to the perimeter can be suitable if their location does not change at any floor) or near a column. It is not recommended that drains be placed at the mid-span of the structure. In steel construction, for example, slopes are directly provided by the layout of the structural members. Usually this means that in order to slope the roof, low and high points run along the lines of the beams (then back slopes can be achieved using sloped insulation).

The calculation of the size of the pipes is dependent on the rate of water flow and the area of the roof that is served by the drain (see Figures 7.16 and 7.17). In addition, local codes require provisions for roof scuppers in case roof drains become clogged.

Pipes for the storm system are made of different material: **a.** *buried outside the building:* vitrified clay, concrete, ductile iron, PVC (polyvinyl chloride), ABS (acrylonitrile butylene styrene), composite pipe or steel. The pipe material is chosen according to the size required (concrete and steel for the larger size and ABS or PVC for the smaller sizes). In addition, required strength, corrosion resistance, smoothness and costs are all factors that influence the choice; **b.** *in the building:* cast iron, plastic, wrought iron, or steel. Cast iron is especially used for non-exposed runs of pipes (as in walls).

Industrial

Industrial waste is created by industrial facilities. This type of waste almost always undergoes some kind of treatment to remove harmful substances. Because of this nature, in many cases the treatment cannot be conducted in public treatment plants. At the connection, the storm and the sewer systems require chambers known as manholes. These can be defined as cleanouts for larger lines. They can be found in parking lots or streets as well as in plazas and any other open space with underground lines.

WASHROOM LAYOUTS AND REQUIREMENTS FOR HANDICAPPED ACCESS

Washrooms are among the most important facilities to be made accessible to persons with disabilities. These requirements are generally established by the ANSI Standard A117.1 (although local authorities may introduce rules that modify these standards. For washroom requirements see Figures 7.17 and 7.18).

A fundamental toilet stall dimension is the 5 foot radius that is required for a person in a wheel chair to turn around. The toilet seat should be mounted 1 foot 7 inches from the floor. Grab bars should be mounted to the wall at a height 2 feet, 9 inches.

There should be enough space under the sink for a person to position the wheel chair comfortably. The mirror above the sink should be tilted to allow the reflection to be seen by the person in the wheel chair. Faucets should be of the lever type and placed on the side of the sink.

Although in many cases this is not required by building codes, additional consideration should be given to: **a.** bath tubs: they should be elevated and provided with grab bars and seats at the height of the wheel chair; **b.** showers: they should be 5 feet wide with a seat at the height of the wheel chair and provided with a flexible hose.

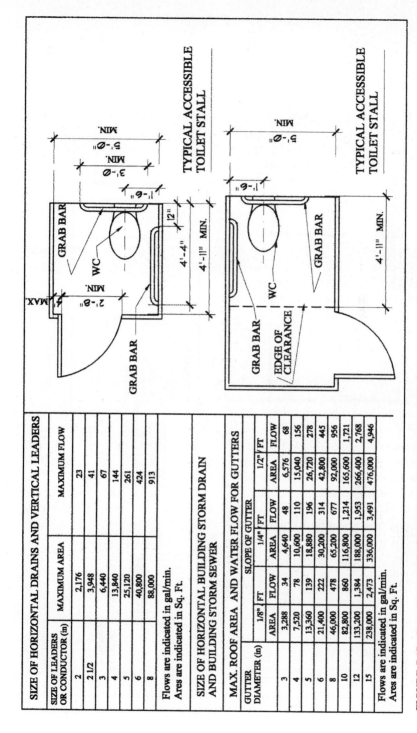

SIZE OF HORIZONTAL DRAINS AND VERTICAL LEADERS

SIZE OF LEADERS OR CONDUCTOR (in)	MAXIMUM AREA	MAXIMUM FLOW
2	2,176	23
2 1/2	3,948	41
3	6,440	67
4	13,840	144
5	25,120	261
6	40,800	424
8	88,000	913

Flows are indicated in gal/min.
Ares are indicated in Sq. Ft.

SIZE OF HORIZONTAL BUILDING STORM DRAIN AND BUILDING STORM SEWER

MAX. ROOF AREA AND WATER FLOW FOR GUTTERS

GUTTER DIAMETER (in)	SLOPE OF GUTTER					
	1/8" FT		1/4" FT		1/2" FT	
	AREA	FLOW	AREA	FLOW	AREA	FLOW
3	3,288	34	4,640	48	6,576	68
4	7,520	78	10,600	110	15,040	156
5	13,360	139	18,880	196	26,720	278
6	21,400	222	30,200	314	42,800	445
8	46,000	478	65,200	677	92,000	956
10	82,800	860	116,800	1,214	165,600	1,721
12	133,200	1,384	188,000	1,953	266,400	2,768
15	238,000	2,473	336,000	3,491	476,000	4,946

Flows are indicated in gal/min.
Ares are indicated in Sq. Ft.

GRAB BAR

WC

GRAB BAR

5'-0" MIN.

3'-0" MIN.

1'-6"

12"

4'-4"

4'-11" MIN.

2'-8" MIN.

4" MAX.

TYPICAL ACCESSIBLE TOILET STALL

GRAB BAR

WC

EDGE OF CLEARANCE

GRAB BAR

3'-0" MIN.

1'-6"

4'-11" MIN.

TYPICAL ACCESSIBLE TOILET STALL

FIGURE 7.17 Size of horizontal drains and vertical leaders; size of horizontal building storm drain and building storm sewer and typical accessible toilet stalls.

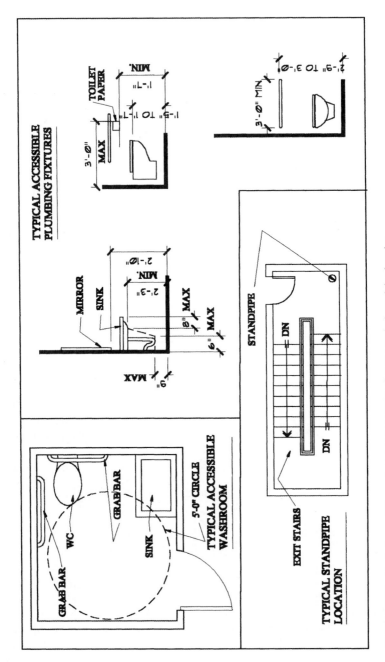

FIGURE 7.18 Typical accessible washroom and plumbing fixtures; typical standpipe location.

CHAPTER 8
FIRE PROTECTION, LIGHTING, AND ELECTRICAL SYSTEMS

We continue the analysis of non-architectural systems by introducing three components of the building that are closely related: the fire protection system, the electrical system and the lighting system.

FIRE PROTECTION SYSTEM

The strategy against fire has been illustrated in Chapter 5. The advantages of a combination of measures are evident. Containment and suppression can work very well together in limiting the spread of fire (accomplished mainly through the containment strategy) and suppressing it (achieved through suppression techniques).

Equipment that can contribute to the suppression of fire includes fire department personnel and equipment, portable fire extinguishers and automatic sprinkler systems. Automatic sprinkler systems are especially effective because of the size and the distribution of the system throughout the building, as well as the capacity for early detection and quick intervention. Other components of the fire protection system include: stand pipes, siamese connections, fire pumps, and optional water storage tanks.

Fires are classified as A, B, C, or D (denoting an increasing potential severity of the fire). The contents of the building determine the classification, A being a fire caused by the burning of common material like paper or wood while D is a fire created by certain elements such as magnesium or potassium. Each of these types of fire determines the strategy and the technology to be employed in the suppression. Where water is not recommended, either because it cannot mix with the burning substance (i.e., oil, which floats on water) or because the water itself can contribute to the combustion (i.e., magnesium or potassium, which can ignite in contact with water at room temperature), then a gas such as CO_2 is used.

Fire Alarm Systems

A fire alarm system is installed for the purpose of detecting signs of fire. It alerts the occupant to the problem; it alerts the fire fighting department to the situation (this is done through a monitoring agency, the police department, or directly); it activates fire suppressing systems; it indicates (with various degrees of specificity depending on the type of system) where in the building the trouble is occurring; it shuts down different type of systems that might increase the rate at which the fire is spreading, represent an additional hazard, or impede the rapid evacuation of the building (i.e., a fan that might migrate the smoke); it operates systems that can help in the containment of the fire or expedite the evacuation of the building (i.e., fire dampers that close non-rated openings, the release of doors locked magnetically for security). The main components of the system are:

1. The control panel: this component can be of two types: **a.** conventional or *point wired*. A system of this type is the simplest and most common for small and medium size buildings. A series of circuits are run from the panel. At various intervals detecting devices are installed. The various circuits create a zone that is represented on the panel for easy identification. A graphic representing the plan of the building schematically can complement the actual panel with the arrangement of the zones. On the panel, the zones are indicated with lights that go on when there is trouble in that particular zone. In order to monitor the status of the entire system, the panel continuously sends small electrical charges along the circuits. If the circuit is somehow interrupted, the panel registers that interruption as trouble and signals it as malfunction requiring service. The limitation of this system is that various detection devices can be connected to a circuit that creates the zones. Because the panel monitors the condition of the circuits and not the status of the single devices, the panel is not set up to identify which devices detected the fire, in which specific place of the zone it is located or which device needs service in case of malfunctioning. This can cause loss of time in attacking the origin of the fire as well as intensive maintenance. The advantage from the point of view of maintenance is that highly trained personnel are not required; **b.** addressable or *intelligent* system: this is a more sophisticated system capable of very accurate monitoring and reporting of the exact condition, location and status of the trouble. Fundamentally, it is a computer that operates and regulates a series of devices. The major difference from conventional systems is that addressable systems can identify exactly which devices have initiated the signal since every device has an *address*. Furthermore addressable systems monitor the entire system to identify malfunctioning, in which case they can pin point the exact location

of the section of the system that is malfunctioning. Another advantage of these systems is the fact that they can be modified with relative ease. However, maintenance requires highly specialized technicians since each system has specific requirements.

2. Detectors: these devices tend to replicate the human capability to detect fire through touch, smell and sight. There are four types of detectors: **a.** manual, also called *pull stations*, are usually installed near exit doors (so they are activated when a person leaves the building in an emergency). Although very effective when the building is occupied, they are ineffective when the building is empty; **b.** smoke detectors can be based on several different principles: ionization, photoelectric and air aspiration. The first detects ionization as part of the combustion process. The second is based on a photoelectric process where one component emits light and another detects it. If smoke travels through the path of the light, it interrupts the beam and the alarm is activated. A detection chamber, a fan (that draws air in the device) and a series of tubes that convey the air into the detection chamber constitute the third type. This type of smoke detector can be better concealed than the other two. The advantages of smoke detectors are that they can identify fire at its initial stage; **c.** thermal detectors are oldest form of automatic detection. There are two types most commonly used. One is activated at a set temperature; the second, called rate-to-rise detectors, responds to rapidly rising temperature. These units are *spot type* detectors. This means that they are installed in series and each of them covers a specific area. The positive aspects of these devices are that they are reliable and inexpensive. The negative side is that, by operating on temperature, they detect the fire when it is in an advanced stage. This renders them unsuitable in life-threatening situations. They are therefore not permitted in such many cases; **d.** flame detectors work on a specific spectrum of ultraviolet and/or infrared radiation. This type of device is used especially in situations where a smoke detector cannot be used because smoke might be a by-product of the operation (i.e., motor vehicle industries, refineries or mines).

3. Alarm output devices: once the fire is detected, the system needs to respond. Bells, horns, speakers, chimes and visual alert devices (i.e., strobe or flashing lights) are used to alert occupants. In addition to alerting the occupants, the system sends a signal directly or indirectly (through a monitoring station) to the fire department. The third aspect of output devices is the control of other systems (mechanical and electrical).

Standpipe and Siamese Connection

Domestic water systems rarely deliver water at a pressure and in a quantity sufficient to fight fire. Standpipes are vertical pipes where water under pressure is provided or can be introduced. They are installed for the purpose of fighting the fire from within the building. For this reason, standpipes are installed in rated accessible enclosures (usually exit stairs). They allow the fire fighters (and occupants in the case of wet standpipes) to use fire hoses connected to the standpipe(s). Building codes determine when and where standpipes should be used and their characteristics (see Figure 7.18).

There are three classes of standpipes that are defined in the "Installation of Standpipe and Hose System NPA 14, National Fire Protection Association" (for systems specific requirements consult local authorities and codes): **a.** Class I: this class of standpipe is designed to provide sufficient supply for the simultaneous use of two hoses (2½ inch hose valve connection) with a volume of water for each hose of 250 gal/min at a pressure of 65 psi. It is provided for the use of fire fighters or people trained in the use of heavy hose streams. As initial design approach, the size of the pipe for building up to 100 feet high (measured from to the highest hose outlet) should be a minimum 4 inches. In higher buildings a minimum 6 inch pipe should be considered; **b.** Class II: this system provides hose cabinets with a 1½ inch hose valve connection and a 100 foot hose stored in it. Both fire fighters and occupants have access to this equipment. Water is supplied at a rate of 100 gal/min and a pressure of 65 psi; **c.** Class III: the requirements for this system are a combination of Class I and Class II with both 2½ inch and 1½ inch hose valve connections and 100 foot hoses. Volume of water at the connection and the requirements for pipe diameter are the same as in Class I. This type of system is required for buildings more than 150 feet high.

The maximum height of standpipes cannot exceed 275 feet. Beyond such height the pipes need to be split into zones that contain their height within these limits. If pressure reduction valves at hose connections are installed (they contain pressure not exceeding 100 psi), then the height can be extended to 400 feet. The hose connection valve should be placed between 4 and 6 feet. The supply may be municipal water as it is available directly from the main, if this supply can be delivered for Class I and III at a rate of 500 gal/min for a period of 30 minutes for one riser (with an additional 250 gal/min for each additional riser to a maximum of 2500 gal/min) at a minimum pressure of 65 psi (measured at the highest outlet). If the municipal main is not capable of supplying water at these levels, either the fire fighter is equipped to increase the volume and the pressure of the water (a solution not always accepted by the authorities) or a fire pump can be installed in the building. The source of energy for the pump must be able to supply energy even in case of failure of the main distribution system.

Standpipes can be of two types: **a.** dry: this type is used when below freezing temperatures are reached in the space where the pipe is installed (i.e., parkades). In this case, the standpipe becomes an extension of the fire fighters' equipment. At the lowest level the pipe is connected to fittings that are called siamese connection. The fire department connects the fire truck to the siamese connection. In this way water at the required pressure is pumped into the standpipe. Fire fighters then carry hoses into the building and hook them to the 2½ inch hose valve connections at the various floors; **b.** wet: in places where temperatures below freezing are not a factor, this type of standpipe is used. Since water is available, this system is provided

with fire hose for the use of the occupants and the fire fighters. A siamese connection (or more than one) is provided in wet standpipe systems as well in order
to increase pressure or overcome the failure of the main supply.

Siamese connections allow two fire hoses to be connected if the standpipe is
a 4 inch pipe, or four hoses to be hooked up if the pipe has a diameter of six
inches. All standpipe risers should be connected at or below the street entrance
and in multi-zoned systems all standpipes should be connected at the floor or
below the lowest hose outlet. Depending on how many risers are required, more
than one siamese connection might be required. Some jurisdictions require one
siamese connection for every 300 feet of exterior wall that faces one street or a
public space.

Sprinkler System

A sprinkler system is basically a grid of pipes that carry an agent (water or other
substances) to sprinkler heads that ultimately spray the agent in the interior space
to eliminate the conditions for combustion. The basic layout is one or more main
pipes that branch out to the local sections on which sprinkler heads are installed
(see Figure 8.1).

In larger buildings the grid of pipe is subdivided in multiple zones that guarantee the functioning of different sprinkler sections in case of failure of one or
more of the other sections. In addition, zones can reduce the water pressure loss
due to long sections of the main pipes running from the point of main supply of
the agent to the branches. Control valves are installed in strategic locations in
order to shut down the all systems or the various zones. This is required for testing and repairs. Drains and test connections are also part of the system. Drains,
installed away from the main supply of water, allow removing the water from the
system when it needs to be serviced while test connections simulate the water
flow to test the system. This operation should be conducted every six months.
Headroom in buildings, therefore, not only should take into account the space for
the pipes and sprinkler heads, but also the added space required by the sloping of
the pipes. In dry and pre-action systems, special valves control the flow of the
water, keeping it out of the pipes until a signal from a detection device is emitted
(see description below about different types of sprinkler systems).

In order to alert the occupants, and in many cases the fire department personnel, that the sprinkler system has been activated, the flow of water is monitored
by water flow switches that detect the flow of the water and send a signal to the
central station.

Sprinkler heads are valves opened by the melting of a fuse rated for a specific
temperature. Not all the sprinkler heads are opened at once (except in the deluge
system). Water is sprayed only by those sprinkler heads that are exposed to a temperature rising above the value for which the heads are rated. Normally two heads
are sufficient to suppress the fire, with up to 12 heads necessary in case of highly
inflammable building contents. Each sprinkler head covers approximately between

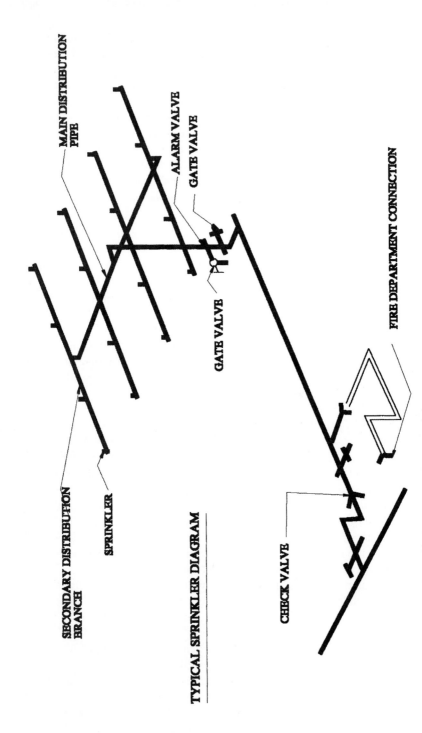

MAIN DISTRIBUTION PIPE

ALARM VALVE

GATE VALVE

SECONDARY DISTRIBUTION BRANCH

SPRINKLER

GATE VALVE

TYPICAL SPRINKLER DIAGRAM

FIRE DEPARTMENT CONNECTION

CHECK VALVE

FIGURE 8.1   Typical sprinkler diagram.

8.6

150 to 225 square feet. The range of temperature that triggers the opening of the head is between 57°F and 107°F. At this point regular heads respond in 3 to 4 minutes, while quick response heads (QR) have a shorter lag time of 30 seconds. Typical sprinkler mountings are: upright (above the pipe), pendent (below the pipe) and sidewall sprinkler (they discharge the water horizontally).

The materials commonly used for the piping system are: steel, copper and plastic (the use of the latter might not be permissible for certain occupancies or for dry and pre-action systems).

There are three basic sprinkler types: **a.** wet system: the main characteristic of this system is that the water is always present in the pipes. It is a very simple system and this simplicity is one of the qualities of the wet system. Other positive aspects are that the installation and maintenance are relatively inexpensive, and the system can be easily modified and quickly rest after a fire. Negative aspects are that the system is not suitable for sub-freezing environments and the concern for piping leakage is a factor in some cases; **b.** dry system: in this system the pipes are filled with pressurized air or nitrogen, which keeps a valve in a closed position. This valve, called a dry pipe valve, prevents water from entering the system. In case of fire, the sprinklers open and the air escapes, relieving the pressure. The valve then opens and the water flows into the system. The advantages in using this system are: suitability in environments where the temperature can reach sub-zero values (the dry sprinkler valve is then located in a heated space to prevent the water from freezing) and the absence of water in the pipes eliminates the risk of leakage. The negative aspects are: an increased complexity of the system; a higher cost of installation and maintenance; lower flexibility; more time required to activate the system.

In addition the system must be drained completely after usage; **c.** pre-action system: the difference between this system and the dry system is that a pre-action valve (electrically operated) activates the former. This valve is in turn activated by heat, smoke or flame detection devices. The system works in two stages: at a signal from the detection device the valve opens and water is released into the system. Virtually this now becomes a wet system where, for water to be released into the space, the sprinklers must open. There are several variations on the basic type of pre-action systems: adding pressurized air or nitrogen into the pipes creates a variation of this process. In this case, the pre-action valve further holds the water in the event that the detection devices malfunction and trigger the release of the valve in the absence of fire. This system is used in spaces where the temperature is below freezing; A second variation of the pre-action system is the *deluge system*. The latter uses open sprinkler heads. At a signal from an independent detection system the deluge valve opens releasing water immediately from all the sprinkler heads. This type of sprinkler is used in places where fire can spread very quickly throughout the entire construction (i.e., airport hangars). A third variation is the *on-off system*. This system operates on a cycle. The basic principle of its operation is based on a deluge system with the addition of a thermal detector.

When the fire is extinguished, the thermal detector allows the control panel to shut off the water. If the fire starts again, the cycle restarts. The disadvantages of this type of systems are the higher cost of installation and maintenance; difficulties in modifying the system and the decrease in reliability with time. On the positive side, these systems are very suitable in water sensitive environments.

An additional sprinkler system is under review: the mist system. Water is highly pressurized (1000 psi) and released in the form of microscopic droplets that are sprayed into the space. This system uses very little water and tests show it to be very efficient in cooling the space and suppressing fire. Piping for this system is ½ inch stainless steel while the nozzle has a diameter of approximately ¼ inch. Very sophisticated detectors regulate the discharge of the water. The mist system might replace the Halon system which, due to environmental concerns, has been prohibited.

ELECTRICAL SYSTEMS

Physics indicates that matter is electrical in structure. Natural phenomena such as lightning are one of the many expressions of this force. Electricity, however, except when it manifests itself through light, has a characteristic that eludes our senses— contrary to matter, electricity has no mass. For this reason, for more than two millennia the nature of electricity was not known. In recent times it has become possible to understand its behavior, to use it to produce desired results under the cause/effect principle, but it has still not been fully explained. Even today, when we need to explain the basic principles of the characteristics of electricity, we use comparisons with the flow of a visible medium (i.e., water). In order to understand this entity and its effect, it is therefore important to know not so much its very essence but rather the dynamics and the conditions in which it occurs.

Atomic Theory and Electrostatic Principles

Although physicists have discovered particles smaller than the atom, the latter is still considered the basic component of matter. Certain type of atoms can combine with each other creating molecules, which, by associating, create compounds.

The parts of an atom are: the nucleus (made up of protons and neutrons) and electrons. Protons have a positive electrical charge, neutrons no charge and electrons a negative charge. Electrons rotate in orbits around the nucleus (much like planets around the sun). The normal electrical state of an atom is to be neutral. This means that the number of protons and electrons are the same. Under certain conditions, electrons are induced to leave the atoms and become free, or else an atom can become receptive to acquiring more electrons than its normal neutral state would allow. In this case the atom becomes electrically charged and is called an *ion*. An ion, therefore, can have a positive or negative charge depending on whether it acquired or released electrons. These charges are referred to as *static electricity*. The behavior of static electricity is the basis of an understanding of electricity in motion, or *dynamic electricity*. The latter is the type of electricity that runs through electrical systems and produces the desired effects of energy.

An ion is in a very unstable condition and, in the shortest time allowed by the external conditions, it will tend to become neutrally charged again. This is a very fundamental aspect because one of the mechanisms used in creating and maintaining a flow of *current* is to prevent this from happening in order to use the flow of electrons (which is the definition of *current*) to create dynamic energy.

The Law of Charges states that similar charges repel while opposites attract each other. The first case occurs when a negative charge encounters another negative charge as well as when a positive charge meets another positive charge. On the other hand, when a positive charge is exposed to a negative charge or vice versa, they are attracted to each other.

Since atoms comprise matter, the behavior of each atom can extend certain properties to the entire object. Therefore it is possible to cause an object to become electro-statically charged, either positively or negatively. A common way to produce this result is to rub certain material with a piece of cloth (i.e., glass with silk, thus charging the glass with positive electrostatic energy). The newly created forces extend beyond the physical limit of the charged object, creating a field around it called an *electrostatic field*. This can be defined as the area in which the force can be felt. The forces extend in every direction with an intensity that decreases at the rate of the square of the distance. Conventionally a positive charge moves outward and a negative inward.

When two objects that are equally oppositely charged enter in contact, there is a rapid exchange of energy after which the objects become neutral again. The same exchange in energy occurs if a path is created for the electrons to move from one object to another. This path can be created by bridging between the two objects using any type of material with high electrical conductivity (i.e., metal—see Figure 8.2). Then we can use their characteristics in order to create a current of energy. In principle, if we can prevent the charges from being equalized and achieve an adequate flow of electrons, we will be on the path to creating dynamic energy that can do work over a prolonged period of time.

Dynamic Electricity

As we have described, in order to create dynamic electricity, which is practical electricity utilized to produce work, we need a source of electron flow and a path that will direct this flow towards a specific location where the work is to be performed. The source type of energy determines the type of current obtained. There are two types: **a.** DC (or *direct current*): this type is generated by sources that do not create energy through cycles (i.e., a battery); **b.** AC (or *alternate current*): this electrical current is created through devices that run through cycles (i.e., alternators).

These systems can be explained using an analogy borrowed from the principles of hydrodynamics (see Figures 8.2 and 8.3). The electrical example used for the comparison will utilize a DC type of energy source.

The fundamental components of this hydraulic system are: the water, the containers, the pipes, and the pump. The water flows because of the pressure applied by the amount of water in the first container. This pressure forces the water through the horizontal section of the pipe and, ultimately, drops into the second container by gravity. From this second container, the water is forced by pressure to the pump, which pushes the water again to the first container.

In electrical terms, the above system can be described as follows: **a.** water = electrons; **b.** containers = plates of the battery (see Figure 8.3); **c.** pipes = path for electrons (wires) (see Figures 8.2 and 8.3); **d.** pump = the acid/water solution that charges the two plates by transferring, through chemical reactions, electrons from one plate to the other. This process creates the positive and the negative poles. The poles of the battery force the electrons to enter the circuit from the negative side and leave from the positive (see Figure 8.3).

In this electrical system the electrons are contained in the two plates made of different materials (containers). The solution of acid-water contained in the battery transfers some electrons by chemical reaction from one plate to the other, polarizing them (the pump). The wire (pipe) connects the negative and the positive poles. This is one of the ways that we have seen in which an electron path can be created. The negative charge, therefore, travels to the positive charge. The solution has also the function of not allowing the charges to be equalized ensuring, in this way, that the pressure and a continuous flow is maintained. In this case the pressure is determined by the different electrical potential between two different points, which is called *voltage*. The *volt* (named after Alessandro Volta, an Italian scientist) is the unit of measure and is commonly symbolized with a capital V or E. The amount of energy that flows through the system is called *current flow* measured in *amperes* (after Andre Ampere, a French scientist) and symbolized with a capital I. Every electron path will oppose a *resistance*, as small as it might be. This resistance is measured in *ohms* (named after the German scientist Georg Simon Ohm).

The concept of resistance is actually more important than just a measure of the conductivity of the medium. It is the very essence of the work created by electric current. In fact, if we add an element to the previously illustrated hydraulic system that would produce work (which fundamentally is resistance), we can complete the analogy between this system and the electrical system (see Figure 8.3).

The relationship between the current pressure, current flow, and resistance is part of the basic principles of electrical theory. Ohm's law is the equation expressing this relationship:

$$\text{Current (I) (in amperes)} = \frac{\text{Voltage (E) (in volts)}}{\text{Resistance (R) (in ohms)}}$$

Using abbreviations, the above formula and its derivatives can be expressed as follows:

$$I = \frac{E}{R} \qquad E = IR \qquad R = \frac{E}{I}$$

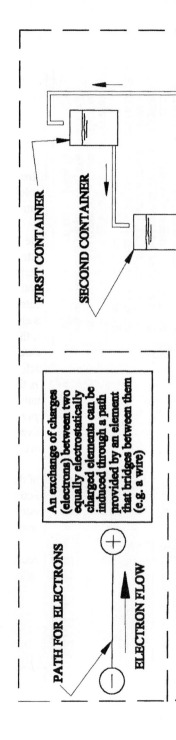

FIRST CONTAINER

SECOND CONTAINER

PUMP

A model that describes water flow from one container to another can be used to exemplify the elements that constitute an electrical system capable of channeling the energy towards a specific location. In the model illustrated, water flows from one container to the other pushed by the pressure of the water in the first container. In order to complete the cycle and return the water from the second container to the first one, a flow must to be created with the use of a pump (since the pressure of the water contained in the second container would not be sufficient to push the water through the vertical rise of the second section of the pipe).

PATH FOR ELECTRONS

An exchange of charges (electrons) between two equally electrostatically charged elements can be induced through a path provided by an element that bridges between them (e.g. a wire)

ELECTRON FLOW

The diagram below translates into electrical components the hydraulic model illustrated on this page. The battery is the pump, which produces a flow of electrons that leaves from the negative pole and, through the path provided by the wire, is directed towards the positive pole.

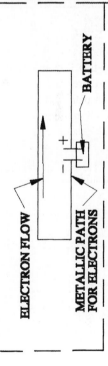

ELECTRON FLOW

METALLIC PATH FOR ELECTRONS

BATTERY

FIGURE 8.2   Path of electrons, water flow model and basic electrical circuit.

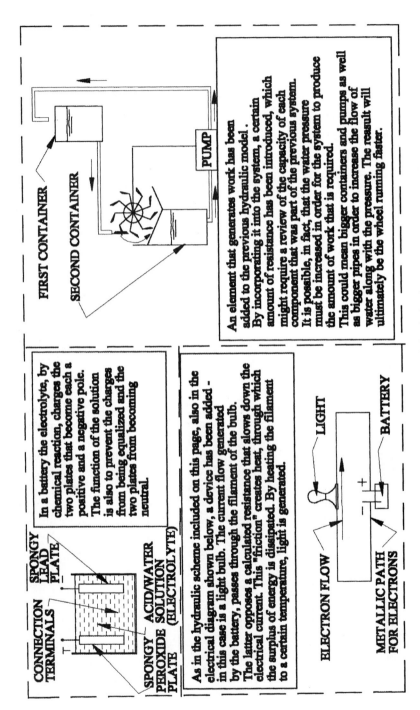

FIRST CONTAINER

SECOND CONTAINER

PUMP

An element that generates work has been added to the previous hydraulic model.

By incorporating it into the system, a certain amount of resistance has been introduced, which might require a review of the capacity of each component that was part of the previous system. It is possible, in fact, that the water pressure must be increased in order for the system to produce the amount of work that is required.

This could mean bigger containers and pumps as well as bigger pipes in order to increase the flow of water along with the pressure. The reasult will ultimately be the wheel running faster.

CONNECTION TERMINALS

SPONGY LEAD PLATE

SPONGY PEROXIDE PLATE

ACID/WATER SOLUTION (ELECTROLYTE)

In a battery the electrolyte, by chemical reaction, charges the two plates that become each a positive and a negative pole.

The function of the solution is also to prevent the charges from being equalized and the two plates from becoming neutral.

As in the hydraulic scheme included on this page, also in the electrical diagram shown below, a device has been added - in this case is a light bulb. The current flow generated by the battery, passes through the filament of the bulb.

The latter opposes a calculated resistance that slows down the electrical current. This "friction" creates heat, through which the surplus of energy is dissipated. By heating the filament to a certain temperature, light is generated.

LIGHT

BATTERY

ELECTRON FLOW

METALLIC PATH FOR ELECTRONS

FIGURE 8.3 Electrical battery diagram. Hydraulic model and the principle of electrical resistance.

Electromagnetism

The fundamental principle on which AC electrical current is based is the relationship between electricity and electromagnetism. The latter is a property of some materials and creates an invisible force field that surrounds the object. This force is similar to the electrostatic fields already discussed and has an intensity that is measurable as well as a direction.

Magnetism can be a natural part of the characteristics of a certain object or it can be artificially created. The first type of *magnet* (a term that defines the objects that have this property) is characterized by a relatively weak magnetic field. The second type can be very strong and powerful and its characteristic is to attract certain kinds of metal. Artificial magnets, called *temporary magnets,* can be made of materials that are easily magnetized, but they lose this characteristic in a short period of time. Other materials (i.e., steel, cobalt or nickel) are harder to magnetize but retain this property for a long time; they are called *permanent magnets.*

In 2600 BC, the Chinese observed that a suspended magnet always orientated itself towards north, with the other end pointing south. It is logical that the two ends of the magnet have been called: the north pole (the one pointing north) and the south pole (the pole that points to the south).

A magnet is characterized by a continuous flux of imaginary lines of forces which are concentrated mainly at the ends of the magnets from which they radiate. These forces conventionally are represented as always leaving from the north pole and entering again from the south pole (see Figure 8.4). The behavior between poles of different magnets is similar to the behavior of electrostatic charges: north and south poles attract opposite poles (i.e., a north pole attracts a south poles) and repel other north or south poles (i.e., a south pole repels another south pole. See Figure 8.4).

There are two major theories that try to explain the nature of magnetism: **a.** Weber's theory, based on the fact that stroking certain materials with a magnet can create another magnet. This could suggest that this action tends to align in one direction all the elements of the material that is in the process of being magnetized (which presupposes that these elements have a polarity of their own). Once the elements are aligned, the material is magnetized. The previous neutral state is determined by the fact that the elements are disposed at random with no particular uniform direction so a strong directional field is not created; **b.** the Domain theory, based on the hypothesis that an atom becomes electro-magnetically charged when more than half of its electrons spin around their axis all in the same direction. A non-magnetic atom has half of the atoms that spin in one direction and half in the opposite direction. When the atoms reach a concentration of 10^{14} a domain is created. It has been calculated that there are approximately 10 million domains in one cubic millimeter. In a non-electromagnetic object the domains are arranged at random. An external magnet can force the domains to be aligned all in one direction creating a new magnet.

The capability of a material to become a magnet is called *magnetic suscepti-bility*. Materials are subdivided in categories defined by their magnetic suscepti-bility: **a.** diamagnetic materials have strong negative susceptibility. They do not react to magnetic forces and are generally called *non-magnetic*; **b.** paramagnetic materials are materials with a positive susceptibility. However this characteristic is very weak; **c.** ferromagnetic materials are the materials with the highest level of susceptibility.

A magnetic circuit is different from a circuit created with an electric current. In the former, the only element is the magnet and the main task is to concentrate the magnetic flux in limited areas: reducing the gap between the two poles will increase the flux intensity (see Figure 8.4).

A magnetic field is also created around a conductor (an element carrying an electric current, i.e., a wire). The direction of the current traveling along the con-ductor determines the direction of the forces around the conductor. The same relationship is observed in a conductor traveling through an electromagnetic field (see Figure 8.5). An *electromagnet (or solenoid)* is a magnet created by wrapping around an element a conductor in the shape of a coil. Both electromagnets and magnets, by interacting with a loop of wire, can create a surge of voltage though a process known as electromagnetic *induction* (see Figure 8.6).

AC Current

Less than 10 percent of the power in United States is direct current (DC). The remaining 90 percent is alternating current (AC). That is why it is very important to understand the difference between the two types of sources as well as the fun-damental principles of AC.

One of the primary characteristics of alternating current is that it changes direction periodically. It flows out of a terminal along the conductor and flows back along the same conductor to the same terminal. This is caused by what is called an *alternating voltage*. In other words, the voltage changes periodically. The terminal will be negatively charged for a period of time emitting electrons that travel through the conductor. Then cyclically the same terminal will become positively charged attracting back the same electrons.

This is a periodic function, since it repeats a full set of events in sequences that occur at specific intervals of time. This type of function can be represented by a vector that rotates within a circle (see Figure 8.7). The radius of the circle represents the maximum *amplitude* of the electric current (amplitude is the max-imum value of the current expressed in volts). We can conventionally divide the circle into upper and lower quadrants defining the first as positive and the second as negative.

The vector will occupy different positions through its 360° revolutions, which will correspond to certain states of the system occurring at specific times. This motion projected onto a linear representation of the time lapsed between defined points provides a graphic image of the behavior of the current (see Figure 8.7).

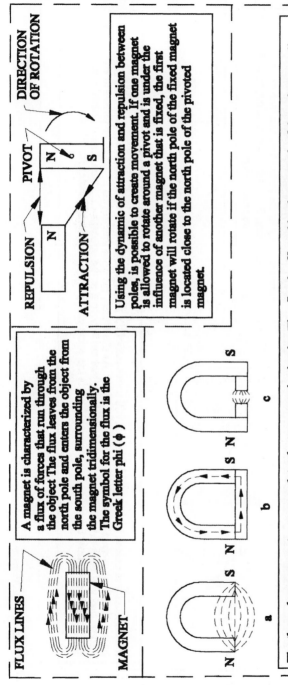

FLUX LINES

MAGNET

A magnet is characterized by a flux of forces that run through the object The flux leaves from the north pole and enters the object from the south pole, surrounding the magnet tridimensionally. The symbol for the flux is the Greek letter phi (ϕ)

DIRECTION OF ROTATION

PIVOT

REPULSION

ATTRACTION

Using the dynamic of attraction and repulsion between poles, is possible to create movement. If one magnet is allowed to rotate around a pivot and is under the influence of another magnet that is fixed, the first magnet will rotate if the north pole of the fixed magnet is located close to the north pole of the pivoted magnet.

The three above magnets are complete electromagnetic circuits. The flux is affected by the strength of the poles as well as by their distance. The latter, when reduced, increases the concentration of the flux at a determined point. Another element that can change the concentration of the flux is the type of element that is placed between the two poles. This can be a metal bar (in scheme b) or a gas (in scheme c). This phenomenon occurs because the flux tends to take the path created by the element with less reluctance (aterm that indicates the amount of resistivity that a material is going to oppose to the electromagnetic flux.

FIGURE 8.4 Principle of magnet behavior and flow of electromagnetic energy.

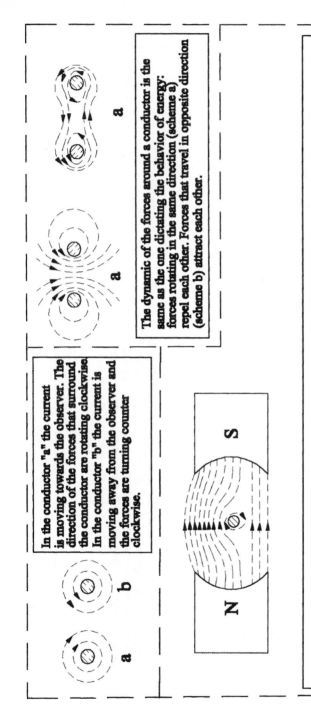

In the conductor "a" the current is moving towards the observer. The direction of the forces that surround the conductor are rotating clockwise. In the conductor "b" the current is moving away from the observer and the forces are turning counter clockwise.

The dynamic of the forces around a conductor is the same as the one dictating the behavior of energy: forces rotating in the same direction (scheme a) repel each other. Forces that travel in opposite direction (scheme b) attract each other.

If a conductor is placed in a magnetic field, it will move out of the field. The direction of the motion will be determined by the direction towards which the forces are traveling. As illustrated, the lines that travels in the same direction will apply a force that will push the conductor towards the lines that are traveling in the opposite direction. These lines do not apply any pressure and allow the conductor to move. This is the principle by which an electric motor functions.

FIGURE 8.5   Electromagnetic forces surrounding a conductor.

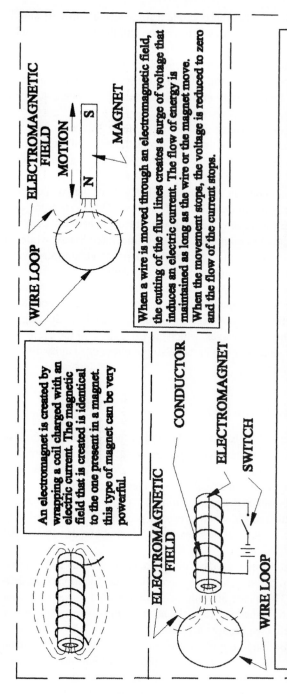

ELECTROMAGNETIC FIELD

MOTION

N S

MAGNET

WIRE LOOP

When a wire is moved through an electromagnetic field, the cutting of the flux lines creates a surge of voltage that induces an electric current. The flow of energy is maintained as long as the wire or the magnet move. When the movement stops, the voltage is reduced to zero and the flow of the current stops.

An electromagnet is created by wrapping a coil charged with an electric current. The magnetic field that is created is identical to the one present in a magnet. this type of magnet can be very powerful.

ELECTROMAGNETIC FIELD

CONDUCTOR

ELECTROMAGNET

SWITCH

WIRE LOOP

In the case of an electromagnet the motion required to create current in the wire loop is provoked by the activation of the electrical current running through the coil. When the switch is closed, the magnetic field expands crossing the loop. This movement creates an electrical current that runs through the loop. This current dies quickly. It reappears only when the switch is opened again. This action causes the current in the coil of the electromagnet to be cut off. in turn the electromagnetic field contracts towards the electromagnet. The flux lines then cut again through the loop of wire, creating again an electrical current. The interaction between electromagnetic fields and a circuit is the principle applied in an electrical generator.

FIGURE 8.6 Electromagnets.

8.17

The curve created by plotting the current is called a *sine wave* because its amplitude at any point is equal to the r sine q, where r is the length of the vector and q is the angle between its position and the horizontal axis.

Two observations can be drawn: **a.** the voltage changes amplitude constantly and changes polarity periodically; **b.** the current changes amplitude constantly and direction periodically. Two alternations (one positive and one negative) form a period (see Figure 8.7).

A magnet and a conductor U-shape constitute the basic AC generator. The conductor that rotates within the magnetic field creates the cycle of AC current. When only one conductor is used, the current generated is called single phase current (see Figure 8.8).

This is a basic way to generate an AC current. The cycle of the AC power is dependent on the revolutions per minute (rpm) of the wire. One *hertz* is the unit of revolution (one complete revolution) that measures the cycle between peaks of the sine wave. 60 hertz is the most common AC power in United States, while 50 hertz is the most common in Europe. The common peak of the voltage sine wave is 110 or 120 volts in United States. In Europe it is 220 volts.

More complex is the process that generates the three-phase current produced by an alternator with three wires shaped in three separate loops (see Figure 8.8). The loops are rotated relative to each other and equally spaced at 120° angles. This arrangement creates three sine waves, which are offset by ⅓ of the cycle (see Figure 8.8). A three-phase generator can create a single phase current by discontinuing two of the three loops.

From the Power Source to the User

In a building, the source of power is not usually within the construction (unless the building is equipped with an emergency power system). A utility company that reaches the consumer through an overhead or underground distribution system provides the main supply of electrical current (see Figures 8.9 and 8.10). Through this system, the power is distributed at high voltage to minimize losses over long distances. For this reason, when overhead primary lines are used they must be at least 10 feet above ground or sidewalk, 15 feet above driveways and 18 feet above streets.

In order to be used safely in everyday life, primary power has to be transformed to an electrical current with a lower voltage; this is the function of a *transformer* (see Figure 8.11). This piece of equipment is connected to each building distribution system and is furnished either by the utility company or by the owner of the building/development (see Figures 8.12 and 8.13).

A transformer is simply made out of an iron core, which is surrounded on each side by two separate coils of wire, one called primary which carries the current supply and the second called secondary, carrying the transformed energy (see Figure 8.9). The ratio between the numbers of turns of each coil (number of primary/number of secondary = (Np)/(Ns)) determines how much the supply

A vector that rotates around its end can describe a periodic function. A time value can be assigned to the period . This value allows the identification of the graphic representation of the position of the vector, not only in terms of its angle, but also in chronological terms. This permits to graphically represent the behavior of the element that is periodically functioning in a specific manner. In the case of the alternating current, the two variables, amplitude and time, define the sine wave, a name given to the resulting curve.

Plotting the amplitude of the current along an axis that allow to represent the intervals of time that lapses between one value of the amplitude, permits the graphic representation of the periodic function. In the example used the time is indicated by eight equal intervals that correspond to the moment in which the vector reaches the eighth position in the circle. In turn that corresponds to the values of amplitudes that the electrical current reaches at that specific time. The interval between H and D is the positive alternation. The interval between D and H is the negative alternation. The interval between H and H is called a period.

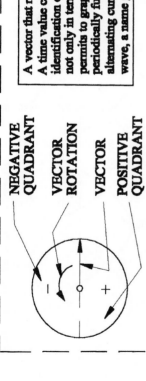

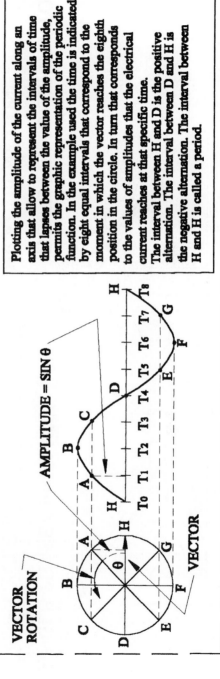

NEGATIVE QUADRANT

VECTOR ROTATION

VECTOR

POSITIVE QUADRANT

AMPLITUDE = SIN θ

VECTOR ROTATION

VECTOR

FIGURE 8.7 Periodic function in alternating current.

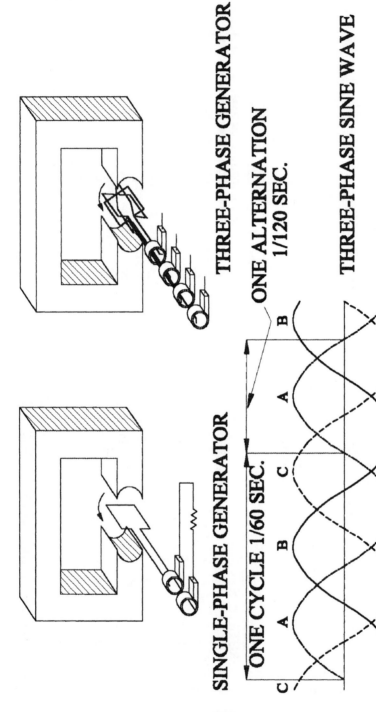

FIGURE 8.8 Single-phase and three-phase generator. Three-phase sine wave.

8.20

electrical current will be transformed. If there are 100 turns used in the primary and 300 are used in the secondary, the ratio is 1:3. This means that the current carried in the secondary has three times the voltage of the current in the primary. This means that the voltage ratio (Vp/Vs) is the same as the turn ratio. The example provided is of a step-up transformer. The same relationship can be applied for a step-down transformer.

Different types of voltage are needed for different applications, uses and type of buildings. Residences use 120/240 volts single-phase system. Some appliances use the 240 volts current while lighting uses the 120 volts. 120/240 is the supply for small commercial buildings up to 25,000 sq. ft. or for residential developments up to 50,000 sq. ft. Larger commercial and industrial developments require three-phase services of 277/480 volts to 2400/4160 volts. This flexibility is achieved by using different wiring configurations called *wye* and *delta* (see Figure 8.12). By connecting different wires that carry electrical current at different voltage, it is possible to create the combinations that have been listed above (see Figure 8.5).

In the case of very small buildings, the transformers are mounted on poles (oil cooled, 18 inches diameter x 36 inches height). In medium buildings, they can be mounted either on poles or on the ground. If transformers are mounted on the ground, they can be placed either outside or inside the building.

In larger constructions, for economical reasons, power might be brought to the building at higher voltage (i.e., 13,800 volts). In this case the owner often provides a larger transformer that steps down the power to the 480/277 volts. This transformer could be located on a concrete pad outside (see Figures 8.9 and 8.13). Alternatively it could be placed either in a room within or separate from the building (see Figure 8.9). The 272 volt current can be used directly while the 480 volt current is connected to smaller electrical transformers located in closets. These transformers reduce the current to the required voltage and distribute it to the single panels in the various parts of the building (see Figure 8.9). In this type of arrangement there could be more than one closet, depending on the size and articulation of the building.

A meter, or a series of meters that record the consumption in large and medium size buildings are placed in front of the transformer, while in small buildings they are located behind it (see Figure 8.9).

Dry type transformers insulate internal wires using rubber or vinyl, while oil filled transformers use a fluid resistant to heat. This fluid separates the wires, insulating them from a transfer of energy and heat. If an oiled filled transformer is used, it must be located in a fire rated vault (some codes require 3 hrs fire separation). This type of transformer is a large piece of equipment provided by the utility company. Large dry transformers provided by the owner can be placed either directly in the electrical room or mounted outside on a concrete pad.

When dry transformers are placed inside, switchgears constituted by disconnect switches, secondary switches, fuses and circuit breakers can be accommodated in the same room. When oil filled transformers are used, the switchgear needs to be placed in a separate room. In all cases, these rooms need to be accessible from the outside for maintenance and to replace broken equipment. An inside door can provide a secondary means of access and exit. Switchgear panels vary considerably in dimensions depending on the size of the building.

As they transform energy, transformers generate heat. Switchgears have the same effect. Heat then is dissipated into the surrounding environment through the cooling fins of the transformers. The heat rating of the transformer is the product of the voltage and the amperage (VA) handled by the transformer. This product is expressed in one thousand times (x) VA (KVA). When transformers are placed inside, therefore, it is important to provide the rooms with adequate natural or mechanical adequate ventilation.

When emergency power is needed, generators running on fuel can supply it. A fuel tank must be included in the design. In the preliminary design a room for an emergency power generator can be considered 12 feet wide with a length of 18 feet, for a commercial building up to 150,000 square feet, or 22 feet for a building up to 400,000 square feet.

Since the power will switch from the primary supply provided by the utility company to the one provided by the generator, the latter should be placed near the switchgear. A generator is very noisy and creates vibrations. Both should be placed outside the building in a separate construction or, if placed inside, away from any occupied space. The change in the power source will require up to ten seconds, during which period the power will be interrupted. If UPS (Uninterrupted Power Supply) is required (i.e., for computer applications) a room for batteries must be provided. A typical room for batteries serving approximately 10,000 square feet. needs to be 500 square feet with an additional 200 square feet required for electronic equipment. A generator needs cooling air and combustion air.

Distribution System

In summary, when the primary current reaches the site where it will be consumed, it will be transformed by the electrical system into a form that is suitable for the operation of equipment requiring transformed power. The electrical system, therefore, should consist of all the components needed to make the electrical current available to the equipment. These components can be categorized as follows: **a.** equipment that transforms the electrical current (already described); **b.** equipment that distributes the electrical current; **c.** equipment and elements that regulate the electrical current flow and guarantee the operational safety of the operation of the system; **d.** fixtures

Equipment that Distributes Electrical Current

The following elements can be included in the category of distribution equipment for electrical current:

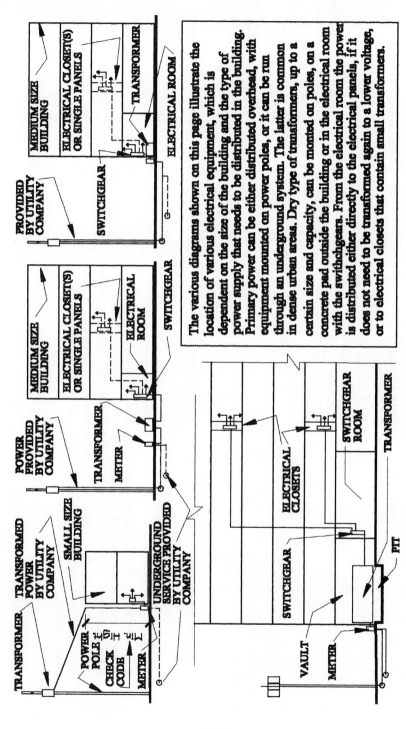

The various diagrams shown on this page illustrate the location of various electrical equipment, which is dependent on the size of the building and the type of power supply that needs to be distributed in the building. Primary power can be either distributed overhead, with equipment mounted on power poles, or it can be run through an underground system. The latter is common in dense urban areas. Dry type of transformers, up to a certain size and capacity, can be mounted on poles, on a concrete pad outside the building or in the electrical room with the switchgears. From the electrical room the power is distributed either directly to the electrical panels, if it does not need to be transformed again to a lower voltage, or to electrical closets that contain small transformers.

FIGURE 8.9   Relation between the size of the building and the location of electrical equipment.

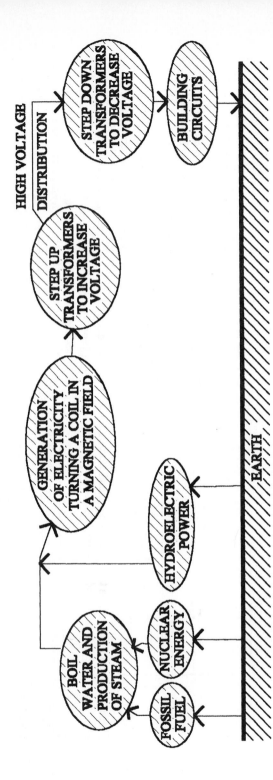

HIGH VOLTAGE

DISTRIBUTION

STEP DOWN TRANSFORMERS TO DECREASE VOLTAGE

BUILDING CIRCUITS

STEP UP TRANSFORMERS TO INCREASE VOLTAGE

GENERATION OF ELECTRICITY TURNING A COIL IN A MAGNETIC FIELD

HYDROELECTRIC POWER

BOIL WATER AND PRODUCTION OF STEAM

NUCLEAR ENERGY

FOSSIL FUEL

EARTH

In the production, distribution and consumption of the electrical current the earth has a double role: at the beginning of the cycle it provides the raw material used to generate heat or motion that allows the coil to rotate within the magnetic field. This movement produces the electrical current. At the other end earth acts as a safety element allowing to discharge excess current.

DIAGRAM OF THE CURRENT CYCLE

FIGURE 8.10   Diagram of electrical power generation and distribution process.

8.24

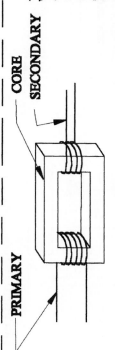

PRIMARY

CORE

SECONDARY

A transformer is simply made out of an iron core, which is surrounded on each side by two separate coils of wire. One is called primary and the other secondary. The primary coil carries the power supply, while the secondary carries the modified current.

The coils have a different number of turns. The coil with the most number will carry the higher voltage, while the one with fewer turns will carry the electrical current with a lower voltage. A step up transformer increases the voltage and a step down transformer decreases it. Since DC voltage does not change in values, transformers operates only with AC current. The two coils are not connected and the transfer in energy occurs through magnetic coupling or mutual inductance (the first one been the voltage generated by the interaction between magnetism and a conductor and the second refers to the transfer of energy between circuits not connected to each other by virtue of the field of forces that surround the conductor while it is carrying the electrical current).

The fundamental principles though which the transformer works is the expanding and contracting of the magnetic field related to the cycle of the AC current. As in the primary coil the voltage increases at the beginning of the cycle, the magnetic field expands cutting across the secondary coil. this phenomenon creates a surge of voltage which in turn produces electrical current. After the peak of the sine wave is reached, the voltage in the primary coil decreases, determining a contraction of the electromagnetic field. A second surge of voltage is created in the secondary coil, therefore, a second flow of electrical current is created.

There are three types of transformers.: air-core, iron-core and powered-metal-core. The type of function of the transformer determines the type of core metal used to construct it. Powered-metal and air-core transformers are used to build radios and televisions, while iron-core transformers are used in substations that distribute electrical power.

FIGURE 8.11 Transformer.

The scheme for a transformer consists of a primary wiring and a secondary wiring. The flexibility of providing more than one voltage of current output is determined by the combination in which the segments of the secondary wiring are grouped.

In a single-phase two wire arrangement (scheme a) the output is only an 120 volt current, since there are no combinations that allow a change of voltage.

Scheme b and c offer a variety of output because the wiring can be grouped in different ways.

Scheme b is a delta-wye system 120/208 or 120/208 3 phase four wires.

Scheme c is a delta-delta system 120/240 volts three phase four wires, or 240 volts three phase three wire or 480 volts three phases three wires.

A neutral connection can be taken from the centre point, in the wye type of connection, while in the delta this can be provided by one of the midpoints of the secondary system.

For primaries usually a delta connection is used.

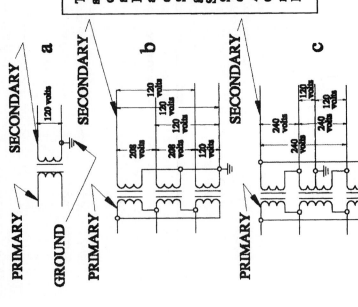

FIGURE 8.12   Different transformer diagrams.

8.26

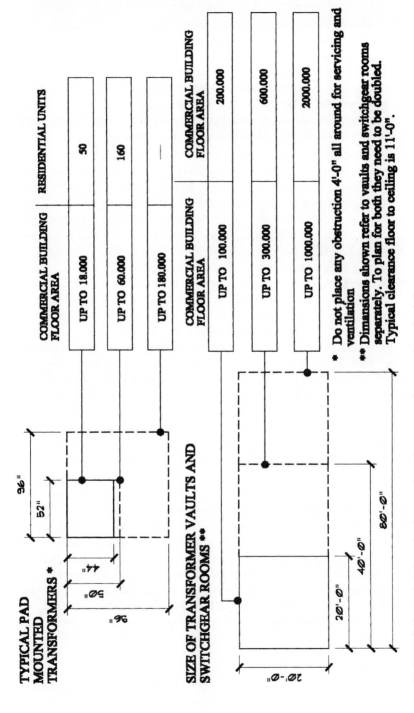

FIGURE 8.13 Typical sizes of pad mounted transformers, transformer vaults and switchgear rooms.

1. *Panel boards*: the current ready to be distributed arrives at individual panel boards (see Figure 8.14). They provide connection for different circuits which will create the local electrical system (i.e., an apartment). Furthermore, the *breakers* have the function of disconnecting the flow of electrical currents in case the system experiences some kind of malfunction. Since panel boards are often recessed in the wall (which is sometimes also a fire rated wall), the measurements should be considered carefully in order to establish the depth of the wall that is required to accommodate that equipment.

2. *Wires* constitute the path for the electrons to travel from point A to point B. Wires are of different sizes according the type of electrical current that they carry. These are sized under the names: American Wire Gage (AWG) or the Thousand Circular Mill system (KCMIL). Minimum AWG gauge for building use is 14 (see Figure 5.48). Maximum AWG size is 0000 (called also four ought, one ought being 0). Beyond this size, the system changes using the KCMIL system (known until recently as MCM). In the AWG system the smaller the number the higher the capacity of the wire; in the KCMIL system it is the reverse. Wires can be *solid* or *stranded* (see Figure 8.15). The flexibility required in working with the wires determines the choice between the two types. Stranded wire has the same cross section area of conductive material as the solid. The former, being an assembly with residual air spaces between each wire, is larger in overall diameter (see Figure 8.15). Wires are grouped in circuits connected to the panel board. The capacity of a circuit is a function of the type of wire used and the number of appliances or fixtures connected to that circuit. Sufficient 15A and 20A circuits to provide 3W of power for every 3 sq. ft. of floor space are required by code. These circuits should serve not more that 500 to 600 sq. ft. If a circuit carries a motor or is in function for more than three hours, its capacity should be multiplied by a safety factor of 1.25.

3. *Conduits* function as protection to the wires, which is required in many medium and all large size buildings (see Figure 8.15 for conduit sizes). Conduits can run, for example, into walls or be cast into a concrete slab. They provide a raceway for the wiring, which, apart from being protected, can also be replaced easily. Different kinds of conduits exist depending on the type of application: **a.** rigid conduit is rigid pipe with threaded connections (when used for exterior they must be galvanized; for interior use they can be enamel coated); **b.** intermediate metallic conduit (IMC) has thinner walls than rigid conduits and is generally accepted in lieu of rigid conduits; **c.** electrical metallic tubing (EMT), known as thin wall, is made of thin galvanized metal (connections are not threaded, but use a clamping system); **d.** flexible metal conduit, commonly called *flex*, is available with or without a waterproof jacket. Generally it is allowed in every application except underground; **e.** interlocked armored cable, commonly called "BX" cable, comes directly from the factory and wires cannot be added to the assembly. For this reason, it is not a proper conduit. However, it functions as protection for the wires. It cannot be used underground and cannot be embedded in concrete.

4. *Receptacles* are the devices that allow energy to be consumed (see Figure 8.16). Known also as outlets, receptacles should, as a rule of thumb, be placed in such a way that any point along the floor line is within 12 feet from a receptacle on a wall, including walls that are 2 feet or more in length (consult the local code for specifics). Usually the maximum height from the finish floor is 12 inches, 4 feet if above counters, or 3 feet 6 inches in laundry rooms. In a room of considerable size, all the receptacles should not be placed on the same circuit to avoid remaining in the dark should a breaker disconnect the power. GFI outlets (see shutoff devices) should be used in washrooms (minimum of one when within 6 feet from a water source, check the local code for specifics), garages, basements and outside. For requirements related to people with disabilities check the local code.

Equipment and Elements that Regulate the Electrical Current Flow

This category comprises: **a.** shut off devices including the following: *fuses*, constituted by a soft metal link in a glass plug or fiber cartridge, are rated according to the maximum load allowed in a particular circuit. The largest glass plug is rated at 30 ampere while fiber cartridges have much higher ratings. Fuses are used only once and after burnout must be replaced); *circuit breakers,* which are switches that, once they detect a malfunctioning in a circuit, interrupt the current flow in a particular circuit by disconnecting it from the source (see Figures 8.14 and 8.17). Although more expensive than fuses, the main advantage over the latter is that breakers can be reset. Where maintenance or replacement supply is an issue, breakers should be preferred to fuses; **b.** *ground fault (circuit) interrupter* (GFI or GFCI) is a particular device that detects any power losses to the ground (even with no consumption), and breaks the circuit. Any 15 or 20 amp circuit that services a bathroom, garage or outdoor space, as well as temporary circuits on construction sites or high voltage circuits require this device;

c. switches are used to interrupt the power in a portion of the circuit, thus cutting off an appliance or a fixture. Switches can be two-way, three-way or four-way (see Figure 8.15). In every room a minimum of one wall switch controlling lighting outlets is required. Height of switches from finish floor is four feet to the center of the switch and they should not be placed behind doors. For requirements related to people with disabilities check the local code; **d.** grounding is a part of the electrical system that ensures a great margin of safety. This function is provided by a wire that is connected to a pole, in turn connected to the ground. Through this connection any excess of energy is dissipated into the ground instead of harming an individual who comes into contact with the electrical current. Three pronged outlets have the third prong connected to the ground wire. Appliances might have a wire connected to the metal case to dissipate any current that might be transferred to them.

RESIDENTIAL PANEL BOARD

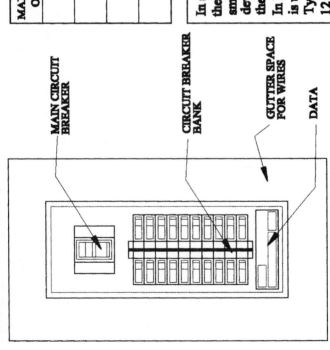

MAXIMUM NUMBER OF CIRCUITS	BOX DIMENSIONS		
	WIDTH	HEIGHT	DEPTH
12	9" TO 15"	16" TO 20"	3 3/4" TO 4 5/8"
20	9" TO 15"	20 1/4" TO 24"	3 3/4" TO 4 5/8"
30	12" TO 15"	30" TO 33"	3 3/4" TO 4 5/8"
40	14" TO 15"	34" TO 39"	4" TO 4 5/8"

In small residential and commercial buildings panel boards are the main connection of the transformed power. They are the smallest of the switchgear equipment that is installed in larger developments. In addition, in larger constructions they provide the last main distribution equipment for local areas.

In Large industrial buildings a three-phase circuit breaker panel is used. The panel height depends on the number of poles. Typical width is 20" and depth is 5 3/4". Typical height is: 12 poles 21 1/2", 20 poles 27 1/2", 30 poles 33 1/2" 42 poles 36 1/2".

MAIN CIRCUIT BREAKER

CIRCUIT BREAKER BANK

GUTTER SPACE FOR WIRES

DATA

FIGURE 8.14   Typical residential panel board.

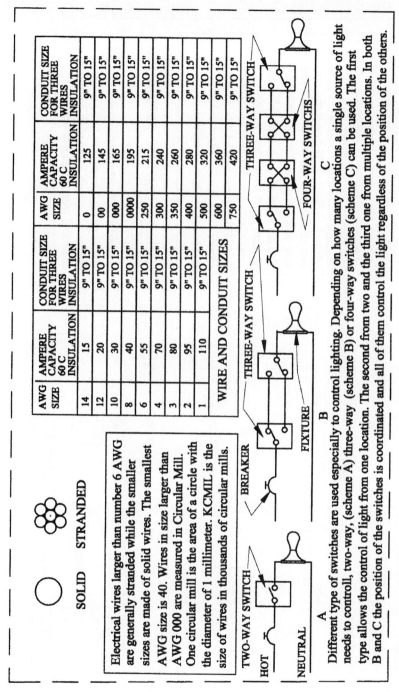

AWG SIZE	AMPERE CAPACITY 60 C INSULATION	CONDUIT SIZE FOR THREE WIRES INSULATION	AWG SIZE	AMPERE CAPACITY 60 C INSULATION	CONDUIT SIZE FOR THREE WIRES INSULATION
14	15	9" TO 15"	0	125	9" TO 15"
12	20	9" TO 15"	00	145	9" TO 15"
10	30	9" TO 15"	000	165	9" TO 15"
8	40	9" TO 15"	0000	195	9" TO 15"
6	55	9" TO 15"	250	215	9" TO 15"
4	70	9" TO 15"	300	240	9" TO 15"
3	80	9" TO 15"	350	260	9" TO 15"
2	95	9" TO 15"	400	280	9" TO 15"
1	110	9" TO 15"	500	320	9" TO 15"
			600	360	9" TO 15"
			750	420	9" TO 15"

WIRE AND CONDUIT SIZES

SOLID   STRANDED

Electrical wires larger than number 6 AWG are generally stranded while the smaller sizes are made of solid wires. The smallest AWG size is 40. Wires in size larger than AWG 000 are measured in Circular Mill. One circular mill is the area of a circle with the diameter of 1 millimeter. KCMIL is the size of wires in thousands of circular mills.

TWO-WAY SWITCH
HOT
NEUTRAL
A

THREE-WAY SWITCH
BREAKER
FIXTURE
B

THREE-WAY SWITCH
FOUR-WAY SWITCHS
C

Different type of switches are used especially to control lighting. Depending on how many locations a single source of light needs to control, two-way, (scheme A) three-way (scheme B) or four-ways switches (scheme C) can be used. The first type allows the control of light from one location. The second from two and the third one from multiple locations. In both B and C the position of the switches is coordinated and all of them control the light regardless of the position of the others.

FIGURE 8.15   Electrical wire and conduct sizes. Typical types of light switches.

8.31

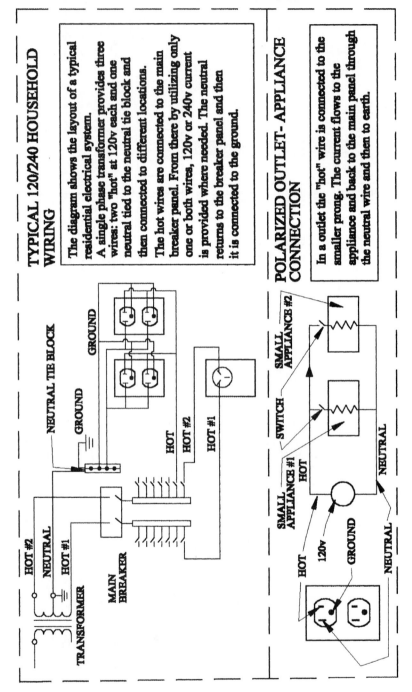

TYPICAL 120/240 HOUSEHOLD WIRING

The diagram shows the layout of a typical residential electrical system.

A single phase transformer provides three wires: two "hot" at 120v each and one neutral tied to the neutral tie block and then connected to different locations.

The hot wires are connected to the main breaker panel. From there by utilizing only one or both wires, 120v or 240v current is provided where needed. The neutral returns to the breaker panel and then it is connected to the ground.

POLARIZED OUTLET- APPLIANCE CONNECTION

In a outlet the "hot" wire is connected to the smaller prong. The current flows to the appliance and back to the main panel through the neutral wire and then to earth.

FIGURE 8.16 Typical 120/240 household wiring. Polarized outlets for appliance connection.

APPLIANCE REQUIRED CIRCUIT		REQUIRED CIRCUIT PROTECTION		LOADS FOR PRELIMINARY ESTIMATE			
TYPE	VOLTS	TYPE	AMPERE	LOAD	LOW	AVERAGE	HIGH
RANGE	240	LIGHTING	15	LIGHTING	2	3	5
WATER HEATER	240	SMALL APPLIANCE	20	CONVENIENCE OUTLETS	1	2	3
AUTOMATIC WASHER	240	INDIVIDUAL APPLIANCES	20	HVAC*	4	5.5	7
CLOTHES DRYER	240			MISCELLANEOUS	0.2	0.5	0.7
DISHWASHER	120				WATT PER SQ. FT.		
FREEZER	120						
GARBAGE DISPOSAL	240			* FUEL-FIRE HEATING, ELECTRICAL REFRIGERATION			
FURNACE MOTOR	120						

In order to calculate the total load, to the wattage indicated in the table shown on this page, miscellaneous items must be added. They include devices like: electric blankets (200W), fryers (1600W), portable fans (200W), razors, frying pans and others. In the case of residential use, therefore, more so than specific functions associated with industrial or commercial activities, life styles play an important role in providing to the correct estimated consumption.

WATTAGES OF RESIDENTIAL DEVICES

TYPE	WATTS	TYPE	WATTS
CLOTHES DRYER	4000 TO 6000	RANGE	8000 TO 14000
DISHWASHER	1000 TO 1500	REFRIGERATOR	400 TO 600
AUTOMATIC WASHER	500 TO 800	BROILER	1200 TO 1700
HAND IRON	600 TO 1200	SEWING MACHINE	60 TO 90
MICROWAVE OVEN	1000 TO 1500	STEREO	30 TO 100
FREEZER	300 TO 500	TELEVISION	500 TO 1200
GARBAGE DISPOSAL	600 TO 900	VACUUM CLEANER	300 TO 1200
FURNACE MOTOR	400 TO 700	WATER HEATER	2000 TO 5000
INCANDESCENT LAMP	FROM 10 UP	PROJECTOR	300 TO 500
FLUORESCENT LAMP	15 TO 60	AIR CONDITIONER	800 TO 2500
MIXER	120 TO 150	AIR CONDITIONER (CENTRAL)	2500 TO 6000
POWER TOOLS	UP TO 1000		
RADIO	40 TO 150		

FIGURE 8.17 Required voltage and protection for appliance circuits. Preliminary estimate load unit values for electrical circuits and wattage of residential devices.

FIXTURES AND EQUIPMENT

Wiring is gauged using a system similar to the one used to gauge metal. The gauging is associated with the capacity of the wire to carry a maximum electrical load without overheating. Since excess energy is converted into heat, the risk of overloading wires is, of course, fire. It is important, therefore, to consider the consumption of each electrical apparatus connected to a particular circuit and define the total electrical load applied to that circuit (see Figure 8.17).

One of the primary fixtures connected to an electrical circuit is lighting. This is a special and complex component that requires a particular attention because of its importance in contributing to the perception of the space.

LIGHTING

Lighting is one of the fundamental aspects of an environment. Its effect on the human psyche is very profound. In a project, therefore, careful attention should be given to lighting design.

There are basically two types of sources: natural and artificial. The source of natural light is the sun; the source of artificial light is some type of electrical fixture. In each category it is possible to identify different types of light with distinct characteristics.

These characteristics can be referenced to parameters that define the quality of the lighting design related to activities and artistic expression of the space: **a.** *illumination level:* lighting should be designed so that the level of illumination is appropriate to the tasks that are performed in the space (see Figure 8.18); **b.** *uniformity of illumination:* lighting on the *workplane* should be uniform. The workplane is an imaginary plane that coincides with the surface where the tasks are performed. It can be horizontal (i.e., a desk) or vertical (i.e., a wall). Difference in lighting levels on the work plane can result in distractions, errors or visual inaccuracy (see Figure 8.18). On the other hand, uniformly distributed light throughout the environment can have an adverse effect on the occupants by creating a dull space (see the following section, *Design Approach*); **c.** *visual comfort:* visual comfort is determined by avoiding lighting stimuli that overpower or reduce the definition of the environment or of an object. Glare is one example that can produce discomfort in an environment. Comfort is therefore achieved mainly by balancing the other variables (see Figure 8.19); **d.** *color rendering:* this characteristic refers to the capability of the light not to alter colors (see Figure 5.52); **e.** *color temperature:* it indicates the warmth or coolness of the light (see Figure 8.19); **f.** *energy efficiency:* this is the amount of energy that is used by the system related to the type and amount of output (see Figure 8.20). Efficiency in energy consumption can be achieved through the contribution of different aspects of the design: improved design practices, efficient lighting hardware, improved operation and maintenance, integration with daylight. The latter is particularly important. The percentage of daylight and electric light that constitute the lighting system can affect the performance of multiple factors contributing to the consumption of energy. Since the lighting system is responsible for 50 percent of the consumption generated in a building, a relative saving related to lighting can be still considerable in absolute terms. Related savings can be experienced in other building systems requirements such as the mechanical system. The following are examples of units of heat produced by different light sources compared to their light output: Incandescent 12 units of heat per each unit of light; Fluorescent lamp 3 units of heat for each unit of light; Sunlight 2 units of heat for each unit of light.

Furthermore, if the component of the building can become more efficient by emphasizing the advantages and attenuating the adverse aspects of a source, then the efficiency of the system increases dramatically. For example, 50 percent of the direct light from the sun is in the infrared part of the spectrum. This type of radiation does not contribute to the amount of light in the building. If reflective glass (heat mirror type) is used, then the amount of infrared rays can be intercepted while allowing the daylight to pass through the glass. The result would be less heat build-up in an area where excess heat has to be subsequently removed by the mechanical system.

Design Approach

The design of a lighting system goes beyond the choice of a particular fixture: it requires tri-dimensional thinking that integrates all the variables. To consider, for example, only the lighting level on the workplane means ignoring the importance of the surrounding environment in the total perception of the space. For this reason the approach to lighting design starts with general consideration and ends with the choosing of the specific luminaire.

Fundamentally there are three types of lighting: **a.** *ambient* is the type of lighting that is diffused, with no specific focus. It creates the general level of illuminance; **b.** *task* is a very direct type of lighting, normally mounted close to the task to be performed.; **c.** *accent* is directed to specific areas that the designer wants to highlight (i.e., a wall, a painting, a plant or other object of interest.)

The balanced combination of these three types of lighting is what creates a good design. In certain cases, one or two types are so reduced that they appear almost non-existent. Sometimes task lighting, for example, could provide the majority of the illuminance. In other cases, accent lighting creates the dramatic, non-distractive look that is needed for the function of the building (i.e., a museum). The following are the suggested steps to be followed in designing a lighting system:

1. Determine the overall impression of the space that is most appropriate: lighting can affect moods, induce a sense of privacy, an impression of spaciousness, a sense of intimacy, a level of energy, a feeling of relaxation.
2. Establish elements that need to be lit: they can be predominantly horizontal planes (workplane), or more architecturally driven elements (i.e., walls, objects, specific small areas, display cases).

ILLUMINATING ENGINEERING SOCIETY OF NORTH AMERICA - ILLUMINATING RECOMMENDATIONS

ILLUMINANCE CATEGORY		RANGE OF ILLUMINANCE		
		2	3	5
A	PUBLIC SPACES WITH DARK SURROUNDINGS	2	3	5
B	SIMPLE ORIENTATION FOR SHORT TEMPORARY VISITS	3	7.5	10
C	WORKING SPACES WHER VISUAL TASKS ARE ONLY OCCASIONALLY PERFORMED	10	15	20
	VISUAL TASK			
D	HIGH CONTRAST OR LARGE SIZE	20	30	50
E	MEDIUM CONTRAST OR SMALL SIZE	50	75	100
F	LOW CONTRAST OR VERY SMALL SIZE	100	150	200
G	LOW CONTRAST OR VERY SMALL SIZE OVER A PROLONGED PERIOD	200	300	500
H	PERFORMANCE OF VERY PROLONGED AND EXACTING VISUAL TASK	500	750	1000
I	PERFORMANCE OF VERY SPECIAL VISUAL TASKS OF EXTREMELY LOW CONTRAST AND SMALL SIZE	1000	1500	2000

IESNA suggest a method for determining the appropriate Illuminance (Lighting Level) that the Society has developed.

The approach is based on the following parameters:

1. The task (i.e. contrast, size)
2. The age of the occupants
3. The importance of speed and accuracy
4. The reflectance (brightness) of surrounding surfaces.

Illuminance category are associated with a letter from "A" to "I". Within these general description about 600 specific tasks are listed in the IESNA Lighting handbook.

The category are associated with three lighting levels. In order to determine which level is appropriate, reference must be made to the factors determining the illuminance. A number is assigned to each factor. The value is either -1, 0 or +1. The total of the sum of the applicable values for each factor determines which lighting level to be used within a category of tasks.

If the sum totals -1, 0 or +1 the middle Illuminance level must be used. In case the sum totals -2 or lower, the lower Illuminance level is used. If the total value of the factors is + 2 or more, then the highest Illuminance is used.

In choosing the age factor most of the time the highest value is used in order to include occupants over 55. In these cases dimmers are installed to decrease lighting level when the maximum lighting level is not necessary.

FACTORS TO DETERMINE ILLUMINANCE VALUE

FOR ILLUMINANCE CATEGORY "A" THROUGH "C"

FACTOR	-1	0	+1
OCCUPANT AGE	UNDER 40	40-55	+1
ROOM SURFACE REFLECTANCE	>70%	30-70%	<30%

FOR ILLUMINANCE CATEGORY "D" THROUGH "I"

FACTOR	-1	0	+1
WORKER AGE	UNDER 40	40-55	+1
SPEED AND/OR ACCURACY	NOT IMPORT.	IMPORT.	CRITICAL
REFLECTANCE OF TASK BACKGROUND	>70%	30-70%	<30%

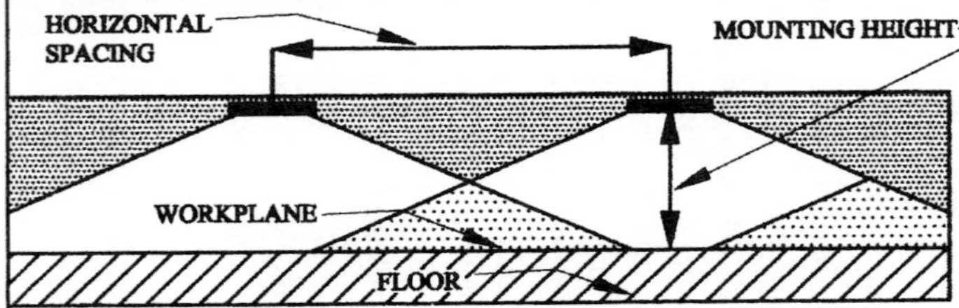

In laying out the light fixtures it is important to follow the spacing suggested by the manufacturer in order to achieve a uniform illumination on the workplane. Luminaries protometric reports provide a value called Spacing Criterion. This number, generally between 0.5 and 2.0, is multiplied by the distance between the luminare and the work plane. The resulting number is the maximum recommended spacing of the luminaries.

The effect of non-uniform Luminance is:

1. Non sufficient light levels in some areas
2. Discomfort and distraction
3. Poor appearance of the environment

FIGURE 8.18 Recommended illuminance values and light fixture horizontal spacing.

TYPICAL CRI VALUES FOR LAMP TYPES

SOURCE	LAMP TYPE	TYP. CRI VALUE	LAMP TYPE	LAMP TYPE	TYP. CRI VALUE
INCANDESCENT/HALOGEN	INCANDESCENT/HALOGEN	100	METAL HALIDE	CLEAR LAMPS	65
FLUORESCENT	COLOUR WHITE T12	62		COATED LAMPS	70
	WARM WHITE T12	53		CERAMIC ARC TUBE	83
	TRIPHOSPHOR	73-90+	HIGH-PRESSURE SODIUM	STANDARD	22
	T8	73-90+		DELUX	60-66
	T1D	82-90+		WHITE HPS	70-85
	COMPACT FLUORESCENT	82-86	LOW-PRESSURE SODIUM	LOW PRESS. SODIUM	0
MERCURY VAPOR	CLEAR LAMPS	15			
	COATED LAMPS	50			

COLOUR TEMPERATURE VALUES OF LIGHT SOURCES (IN DEG. KELVIN)

TYPE OF SOURCE	DEG. K.		
NORTHLIGT/BLUE SKY	8600	HIGH PRESSERE SODIUM LAMP	2000
OVERCAST SKY	7500-6500	HIGH PRESSERE SODIUM LAMP	2000
DAYLIGHT FLUORESCENT	6400	CANDLE	1900
MERCURY VAPOR	5900	40 WATT INCANDESCENT LAMP	2500
SUMMER SUNLIGHT	5700		
TRIPHOSPHOR FLUORESCENT	4100	COLOUR TEMPERATURE CATEGORY	
METAL HALIDE	4000	WARM (YELLOW-WHITE)	LESS THEN 3500K
TRIPHOSPHOR FLUORESCENT	3500	NATURAL (WHITE)	3500K- 4000K
TRIPHOSPHOR FLUORESCENT	3000	COOL (BLUE-WHITE)	MORETHEN 4000K
HALOGEN INCANDESCENT	3000		

Perception of true colours in a space can increase the perception of the lighting level. The Colour Rendering Index is the unit of measure used to rate how accurately colours are perceived under a specific type of lamp. Its values range between 0 and 100, with 100 being associated with the best colour rendering. CRI between 75 and 100 are "excellent. Between 65 and 75 are "good, while between 55 and 65 are "fair" and between 0 and 55 are considered "poor". Very specialized lamps with an extraordinary CRI are available commercially.

The colour temperature of a lamp is not associated with the heat emitted by the lamp. It refers to the spectrum of its light (i.e. if the light is "warm" or "cool"). The colour is expressed in degree Kelvin (K). The reference is the colour that a blackbody radiator acquires when it is heated at different high temperature. First it becomes red, then orange, yellow and finally bluish. Color temperature is associated with aesthetics. The choice of which colour temperature to use is based on architectural considerations. Typically lower temperatures are used with a lower level of lighting. In "high energy" places the lighting design is based on type of lamps with higher colour temperatures. Neutral white ranges between 3500 and 4000 K. If different types of lamps are used, the difference in colour temperature should be minimized. In fact different lamps should preferably have the same colour temperatures.

Glare is a problem that increases with the widening of the luminaries angle. Methods to control glare include louvers and, in fluorescent lamps, low glare flat lenses. Indirect lighting can be very effective. However spacing and distance from the ceiling are important factors to be considered in order to achieve a uniform level of Illuminance.

This is especially important in work environments. Visual Comfort Probability (VCP) is the unit measure used to rate the glare control of a luminaries. It ranges from 0 to 100: the higher is the value, the more effective is the glare control. A VCP of 70 is adequate for a commercial interior. In large areas with computers a VCP of 90 is often used. Since louvers can control glare effectively but also reduce the efficiency of the fixture by reducing the level of output, a balance between the reduced glare and the level of output of the lamp needs to be considered. Low-glare clear lens is an alternate to the louver that reduces the high angle glare allowing high percentage of light to pass.

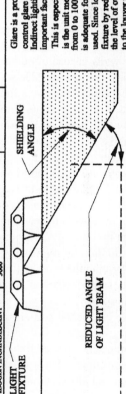

SHIELDING ANGLE

LIGHT FIXTURE

REDUCED ANGLE OF LIGHT BEAM

FIGURE 8.19 Typical CRI values for lamp types. Color temperature values of light sources and glare con-

3. Identify the direction and distribution of the light; this aspect requires an understanding of the output of different fixtures (i.e., narrow beams, diffused light, upwards and downwards lighting) as well as the type of reflectance of surfaces in relation to color, finishes and materials (see Figures 8.20 and 8.21).

   This part of the process can be complex since light bounces off surfaces affecting indirectly adjacent planes. An environment where lighting illuminates mainly horizontal surfaces, without emphasizing the space around them, induces awareness movement of other people and encourages interaction. On the other hand, in a space where lighting illuminates vertical surfaces (i.e., walls) or overhead surfaces and reduces light on horizontal surfaces, people and objects become secondary and the atmosphere becomes more intimate.

   The pattern, color and brightness of the light related to the overall appearance of the environment depends upon the intensity of the light as well as the reflectance and transmittance properties of the surface on which the light shines. When secondary sources (light transmitted mainly through reflectance and/or transmittance) are the major elements in a light system, a sense of intimacy is created.

   The distribution of light can alter the proportions of a space by lighting certain walls instead of others. In a corridor, for example, the space will appear wider if the side walls are illuminated more. Direction, furthermore, can accentuate textures (light washing over a stone wall can be very dramatic), or can minimize imperfections (as in the case of drywall) by being diffused. Computer programs can be very effective in providing an accurate analysis of a specific design.

   Another aspect associated with the distribution and direction of light is represented by the response that people have to uniformly distributed lights or highly contrasted lighting design. Although a well-lit space tends to be perceived as larger than a poorly lit space, environments that are evenly lit tend to provide fewer stimuli and decrease the attention of the occupants, as in the case of cloudy days. On the contrary, a more contrasted lighting distribution (as on a sunny day) has the opposite effect.

4. Determine the level of lighting required: this is not only driven by the type of tasks performed in the space, but should take into account the type of atmosphere the designer wants to introduce. Different tasks are related to different mental attitudes. A general low level of lighting stimulates intimacy, while a well-lit environment tends to be perceived as energetic. Parameters such as: fixture efficiency, lamp lumen output, the reflectance of surrounding surfaces, the effect of light losses from lamp lumen depreciation and dirt accumulation, room size and shape as well as the availability of natural light are all fundamental factors that contribute to define the required lighting level. However, perception of illuminance can be increased not only by introducing more or more powerful luminaries, but also through stimuli that are perceived as contributing to the general level

of lighting. Experiments have shown that elements that sparkle or small lights, too small to actually increase the luminance level, if strategically distributed, can stimulate the brain to interpret these signs as an increase in lighting level.

In determining the level of lighting two methods can be applied: the Point Grid Method and the Zonal Cavity Method. The first one is based on both Lambert's Law and the Inverse Square Laws (see Figures 8.21 and 8.22).

5. Determine color temperature and color rendition (see Figure 8.19): usually this parameter is established as a general consideration at the beginning of the design of the lighting concept. It is then specifically identified in concurrence with the choice of fixture and lighting levels. The color of the light is associated with psychological responses. A warmer light is normally used when a sense of intimacy is desired. Cooler lights are associated with dynamism and high energy. Color rendition is also important especially in places where the appreciation of items on display is determined greatly by appearance (i.e., food, art, fashion).

6. Verify assumption: the data at this stage can be acquired in different ways. These methods are presented in order of practicality, not necessarily in order of effectiveness:

   a. Computer Modeling: there are many computer programs that can analyze the lighting layout. Some give specific reading of the intensity of the light throughout the space. Others include providing an image that takes into consideration the effect of the light reflected from the various surfaces. The limits of this approach are related to the fact that the perception of the observer is reduced to a bi-dimensional image, which is very different from the tri-dimensional effect that is experienced in a real environment. In this case, the sensitivity and professional expertise of the designer plays an important role in interpreting the image. However, in spite of these limitations, a computer simulation is a very good tool to evaluate the design.

   b. Scale Models: This is a relatively easy instrument to construct because designers often create scale models to illustrate the project or to study its form. A scale model for lighting purpose does not need to be refined: a massing model is sufficient. It should reproduce on the interior the color and type of finish that will be used for the construction of the project and needs to be sealed in order to avoid infiltration of light that might alter the observations. Because the amount of light that will enter the model is also in proportion with the scale, if the model has been constructed accurately in terms of proportions and size of the exterior opening, the observations are also very accurate. The advantage of a scale model is that changes to the interior space size or to the exterior openings can be easily made. The results can be photographed by creating an opening for the camera lens and sealing the gap around the lens in order to avoid light infiltration. For accurate observations the model can be tested with a sun machine that recreates different lighting exterior conditions. This type of instrument can be found as part of the standard equipment of utility companies or university research labs or large corporations.

A mathematical tool that is rather useful is the daylight factor. It represents the ratio between indoor and outdoor illumination. The higher the value, the more illumination will be available in the indoor space. The solution with the highest number, therefore, is the one that will provide the most lighting inside. The findings are particularly important because, under diffuse lighting, the ratio between indoor and outdoor illumination does not vary, regardless of what type of light intensity is outside. The results of specific testing done under specific outdoor light conditions can therefore be generalized.

c. Post-Occupancy Evaluation: this is the ultimate test, when the occupants who have been using the facilities for a while evaluate the actual environment. A questionnaire can be designed to solicit a response from the occupants on the quality of the lighting design. The questions asked in the questionnaire should be directed to finding out how well the parameters used to produce the lighting layout and system have been satisfied with answers sought about glare (i.e., if the space is glare free), how easy it is to read printed words or the computer screen, if colors in the environment seem natural, if the color of the light is appropriate, and if the environment is well lit and comfortable. In addition, it is possible to list a series of adjectives to qualify the environment from the point of view of the lighting quality, like pleasant, ugly, interesting, chaotic, gloomy, distracting, comfortable, or ordinary.

It is important, therefore, that the fixtures, equipment, layout and controls be designed allowing for adjustments of variables the levels of which may not be completely balanced. Unless an error in the fundamental principles of the design has been made, these adjustments should be reduced to minor aspects.

d. Mock-ups: where it is possible, full size models of the typical areas should be constructed. These spaces should duplicate accurately the spaces that will be built. This includes: size, finish, details, furniture and colors. The building of full-scale mock-ups is especially important in designs that experiment with new concepts and ground-breaking ideas in lighting design.

Of the three methods, **a** and **b** are very common and always recommended. The construction of a full size model is rarely used because of the cost and time required to build it. In fact, since the model must duplicate part of the actual environment, it must be built when the design and most of the working drawings are completed. This can impact considerably on the project schedule by delaying the start of the construction. Especially in the private sector, these associated costs are not seen favorably.

There are three primary factors involved in our perception of light: the nature of light, the human eye and the type of light source. In addition the characteristics of the surrounding environment have a further effect on how we perceive light and vice versa.

THE NATURE OF LIGHT

Modern theories explain light as an electromagnetic radiation constituting a small part of the electromagnetic spectrum. As quantum theory developed, it became apparent that many forms of electromagnetic radiation, including light, are emitted or absorbed by a substance in conjunction with transitional energetic states of the particles constituting these substances. When these changes occur very small bundles of energy called light quanta, or photons, are emitted or absorbed. Each photon has an energy that is directly proportional to its frequency.

The Human Eye

The human eye has often been compared to a photographic camera. In reality the process that occurs in this visual organ is only part of the whole. In fact, the reconstruction of the images into a coherent projection happens in the brain. Let us follow this path.

Light enters the eye through the *cornea* where most refraction takes place. From the cornea the light passes into the *aqueous humor*, where it is refracted even further. (see Figure 8.22). The light then passes through the *crystalline lens*. About 9 mm in diameter and 4 mm thick, the lens is constituted of approximately 22,000 layers and is pliable, changing shape to adjust its focus. The crystalline lens provides approximately 20 percent of the refraction power of the eye. In front of the crystalline lens, the *iris* expands and contracts in order to regulate the amount of light that enters further into the eye. The iris is capable of contracting to a diameter of 2 mm. and expanding to 8 mm. under the action of the *ciliary muscle*. Light passes through the crystalline lens and enters the inner eye which is filled with *vitreous humor*. This gelatinous substance completes the process of refraction of light. The re-directed, converging rays stimulate the *retina* in a way that allows the individual to experience various types of information.

The retina, which covers 65 percent of the interior surface of the eye, represents the first step in the neurological interaction between the eye and the brain. Defined as the embryonic outgrowth of the brain, it is a very complex tissue made of many light-sensitive nerve cells, the *rods* and the *cones*. They convert light energy into signals that are carried to the brain by the *optic nerve*. The rods are more numerous—about 120 million—while there are only 6 million cones. These two types of cells have different functions in the perceptive process. The cones are most effective in bright light and provide color vision. This type of vision is called *photopic*. The cones are not effective in dim light. In such conditions, the

EFFICACIES OF COMMON LIGHT SOURCES

SOURCE	POWER (WATTS)	LAMP EFFICACY	LAMP TYPE	POWER (WATTS)	LAMP EFFICACY
INCANDESCENT	100	17	XENON SHORT ARC LAMP	1000	30
HALOGEN	300	20	HIGH-PRESSURE SODIUM-LOW WATTAGE	300	90
FLUORESCENT T5, 4'	28	100	HIGH-PRESSURE SODIUM-HIGH WATTAGE (DIFFUSE)	250	100
FLUORESCENT T8, 4'	32	90	LOW-PRESSURE SODIUM, U TYPE	180	160
CFL	26	70			
MERCURY VAPOUR	175	45			
METAL-HALIDE, LOW WATTAGE	100	80			
METAL-HALIDE, HIGH WATTAGE	400	90			
HIGH-PRESSURE MERCURY LAMP	1000	50			

The Illuminating Engineering Society of North America (IESNA) defines lamp efficacy as "the quotient of the total luminous flux emitted divided by the total lamp power imput". The values are expressed in lumens per watt (lm/W).

It is important that for fluorescent and HID lamps the wattage of the ballast as well as any reduction in lumen output due to the lamp combination must be taken into account to determine the system efficacy.

TYPE OF REFLECTIONS

There are three basic type of reflections:

A. Specular: it originates when the light strikes the surface of a mirror or of a polished surface. The light is reflected at an angle that is the same as the angle of incidence.

B. Spread: it occurs when the light is reflected on a rough surface and the reflected angle is similar to the incident angle.

C. Diffuse: in this case the light strikes a mat surface and is reflected in many directions.

SPECULAR (POLISHED SURFACE) SPREAD (ROUGH SURFACE) DIFFUSE (SMOOTH MATTE SURFACE)

REFRACTION

If the light travels through two mediums and its speed increases or decreases in going from one to the other, the light is refracted and bends.

The ratio between the speed of light in a vacuum and the speed in a particular medium is called the Index of refraction of that medium ($n = c/v$). Light that travels through a medium with a low index and passes through a medium with a high index ($n1 > n2$) bends towards the normal. Vice versa, light that passes from a medium with a high index to one with a lower index bends away from the normal. If the light, for example, travels through air (which has an index of virtually 1) at 45 degrees and passes through a glass with a coefficient of 1.52 the refracting angle will be 28 degrees: $n_1 \sin\theta_1 = n_2 \sin\theta_2$; $1 \sin 45° = 1.52 \sin\theta_2$

$$\theta_2 = 28°$$

SNELL'S LAW

$$n_1 \sin\theta_i = n_2 \sin\theta_t$$

n_1 = the refractive index of medium 1
n_2 = the refractive index of medium 2
θ_i = the incident angle of the light ray
θ_r = the reflected angle
θ_t = the refracted angle

INCIDENT RAY NORMAL REFLECTED RAY REFRACTED RAY AIR GLASS

TOTAL INTERNAL REFLECTION

Given two mediums in which the light travels from the medium with the higher index of refraction to the one of the lower index, the Critical Angle is called the incident angle that is equal to the angle of refraction created by the second medium. In this case the light will travel along the border between the two materials. If the incident angle decreases further, the light is reflected into the first medium.

FIGURE 8.20 Efficacies of common light sources. Types of light reflections and principles of light refrac-

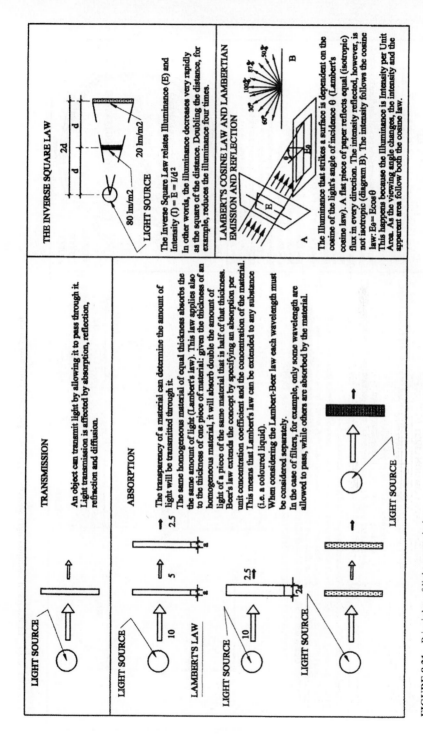

TRANSMISSION

An object can transmit light by allowing it to pass through it. Light transmission is affected by absorption, reflection, reflection and diffusion.

ABSORPTION

The transparency of a material can determine the amount of light will be transmitted through it.

The same homogeneous material of equal thickness absorbs the same amount of light (Lambert's law). This law applies also to the thickness of one piece of material: given the thickness of an homogeneous material, it will absorb double the amount of light of a piece of the same material that is half of that thickness. Beer's law extends the concept by specifying an absorption per unit concentration coefficient and the concentration of the material. This means that Lambert's law can be extended to any substance (i.e. a coloured liquid).

When considering the Lambert-Beer law each wavelength must be considered separately.

In the case of filters, for example, only some wavelength are allowed to pass, while others are absorbed by the material

LAMBERT'S LAW

THE INVERSE SQUARE LAW

The Inverse Square Law relates Illuminance (E) and Intensity (I) = E = I/d^2

In other words, the illuminance decreases very rapidly as the square of the distance. Doubling the distance, for example, reduces the illuminance four times.

LAMBERT'S COSINE LAW AND LAMBERTIAN EMISSION AND REFLECTION

The illuminance that strikes a surface is dependent on the cosine of the light's angle of incidence θ (Lambert's cosine law). A flat piece of paper reflects equal (isotropic) flux in every direction. The intensity reflected, however, is not isotropic (diagram B). The intensity follows the cosine law: Eθ = Ecosθ

This happens because the illuminance is Intensity per Unit Area. As the viewing angle changes, the intensity and the apparent area follow both the cosine law.

FIGURE 8.21 Principles of light transmission.

8.43

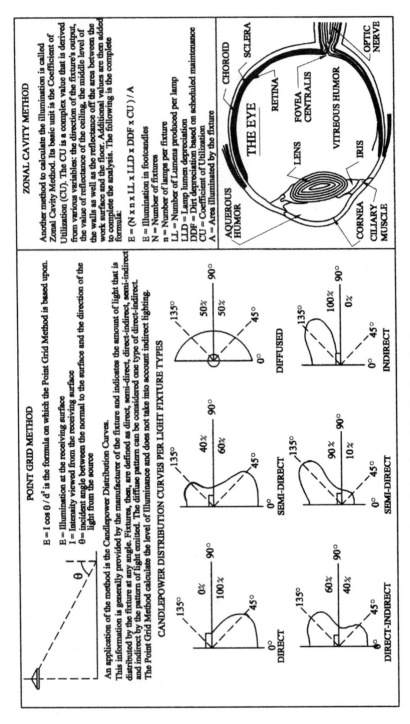

POINT GRID METHOD

$E = I \cos \theta / d^2$ is the formula on which the Point Grid Method is based upon.

E = Illumination at the receiving surface
I = Intensity viewed from the receiving surface
θ = incident angle between the normal to the surface and the direction of the light from the source

An application of the method is the Candlepower Distribution Curves.
This information is generally provided by the manufacturer of the fixture and indicates the amount of light that is distributed by the fixture at any angle. Fixtures, then, are defined as direct, semi-direct, direct-indirect, semi-indirect and indirect by the pattern of light emitted. The diffuse pattern can be considered one type of direct-indirect. The Point Grid Method calculate the level of Illuminance and does not take into account indirect lighting.

CANDLEPOWER DISTRIBUTION CURVES PER LIGHT FIXTURE TYPES

DIRECT

DIRECT-INDIRECT

SEMI-DIRECT

SEMI-DIRECT

DIFFUSED

INDIRECT

ZONAL CAVITY METHOD

Another method to calculate the illumination is called Zonal Cavity Method. Its basic unit is the Coefficient of Utilization (CU). The CU is a complex value that is derived from various variables: the direction of the fixture's output, the value of reflectance of the ceiling, the middle level of the walls as well as the reflectance off the area between the work surface and the floor. Additional values are then added to complete the analysis. The following is the complete formula:

$E = (N \times n \times LL \times LLD \times DDF \times CU) / A$

B = Illumination in footcandles
N = Number of fixtures
n = Number of lamps per fixture
LL = Number of Lumens produced per lamp
LLD = Lamp lumen depreciation
DDF = Dirt depreciation based on scheduled maintenance
CU = Coefficient of Utilization
A = Area illuminated by the fixture

THE EYE

SCLERA
CHOROID
RETINA
FOVEA CENTRALIS
OPTIC NERVE
LENS
VITREOUS HUMOR
IRIS
AQUEOUS HUMOR
CORNEA
CILIARY MUSCLE

FIGURE 8.22 Point grid and zonal cavity methods of determining illuminance level.

rods respond very well. However rods cannot detect colors. In dim light, therefore, reality appears to be mainly black and white. This is called *scotopic* vision. There are three types of cones: red, green and blue cones. This means that each type is specialized to detect that particular color wavelength. While several rods share a nerve fiber, cones are largely connected individually.

Most of the cones, except for the blue cones, are placed in a very small region (only 0.3 mm) of the retina called *fovea centralis*. This is where vision reaches the most accurate definition. The vision of an eye spans approximately 200 degrees. Of this visual information only the data that fall under the 15 degrees controlled by the fovea are very defined. The rest become the more summary the farther from the fovea they strike the retina. For this reason the eye moves continuously in order to convey the focus of attention within the range of the area where the maximum definition is achieved. This is an important aspect of vision because the brain, which acts as coordinator, then composes the different and very detailed images.

The connection of the eye to the brain is performed by the *optic nerve*. This is where all the nerve fibers converge to reach the brain. The nerve leaves the eye near the fovea. This is called the blind spot (because of the absence of rods and cones); the optic nerve connects with the brain at the *chiasma*. From this area connections radiate to the different parts of the visual centers residing in the left and right side of the *cortex* (outer part of the brain). When the image strikes the retina, it is upside down. The brain inverts that image providing the consciously perceived orientation. The relationship eye-brain is particularly important because an object is defined or recognized by focalizing different parts of it through a sequence of eye movements that direct the fovea to concentrate on these parts.

Type of Light Source

Before this subject is introduced, the meaning of some specific terms must be clarified. These terms are commonly used in lighting design and their understanding on the part of the architect is fundamental in order to consider products, design a lighting system, or communicate properly with an electrical consultant: **a.** intensity (I): the amount of light emitted by a source. Its unit of measure is the *candlepower* (cp), which is the amount of light emitted by a candle; **b.** flux (F): the amount of light flowing through an area in mid-air measuring one square foot one foot away from a source emitting one candlepower. Its unit of measure is one *lumen* (l). It has a reference wavelength of 555 nm (nanometers), which is the peak response of photopic vision (generated by the cones). Almost every light measurement uses the photopic luminous efficiency function. This is important because the photopic as well as the scotopic measurements reveal different amount of lumens at the same wave length; **c.** illumination (E): the amount of light arriving on a surface one foot away from the source. Fundamentally it is the ratio between the flux and the area of the surface:

$$E = F/A$$

In other words, the number of lumen/area = E. Its unit is one footcandle (fc); **d.** luminance (L): it is the amount of light reflected by a surface. A perfect luminance is indicated as 100 percent or 1.0. One footcandle reflected by such surface produces one footlambert, which is the basic unit used to measure the luminance. An opaque surface will reflect light: its luminance is called reflectance (r). A translucent surface will allow the light to pass: its luminance is called transmittance (t).

Natural Light

There are two basics types of natural light: sunlight and daylight. The first is the direct light from the sun. The second is the diffuse light created especially by the higher light frequencies scattered by the small dust particles and gas molecules present in the atmosphere. The amount of daylight and sunlight is dependent on the atmospheric conditions. Clouds, for example, increase the daylight level and decrease the sunlight level. An additional source of daylight is the reflection of natural light on elements that surround the building or a specific interior space.

An overcast sky can produce between 500 and 3000 foot candles (which is between 10 and 50 times more than the amount of light needed indoors). The sky under such conditions is three times brighter at the zenith than it is at the horizon. The following are values that can be used to calculate the values of illumination in a space: winter 1000 FC, spring, and fall 1800 FC, summer 3000 FC. A clear sky produces between 6,000 and 10,000 foot candles and around the sun is ten times brighter than the darkest area of the sky.

In order to design an effective daylight system, it is necessary to take into account both conditions. There are geographical areas that represent an exception where the overcast sky is the predominant source of light (parts of the Northwest and Pacific Northwest in the U.S.) and vice versa in other areas where a clear sky is the main condition to be considered (parts of the Southwest of the U.S.). In these areas the predominant condition should determine the design. As general rule, in overcast conditions the main factor to be considered is the quantity of the light, while in the case of natural light produced by a clear sky, the quality of the light is the fundamental consideration.

There are very important positive psychological influences and practical advantages to indicate that, where possible, daylight should be considered as the main source of lighting. Research has shown that where daylight is a major component of the lighting system in educational facilities the results of tests improve up to 20 percent; in work places considerable improvement in absenteeism, quality and amount of work output is experienced. The private sector, where certain environmental considerations are measured mainly against return, becomes sensitive if improvement in terms of savings in energy cost, maintenance and higher return in workforce investment can be demonstrated. Even a small increase in efficiency is the factor that produces the highest economical benefits. Improving lighting conditions is not only a good practice in terms of comfort but also a good investment.

The following are basic goals which need to be achieved in designing for daylight use (most of them can be applied also in designing the artificial lighting system): **a.** carry the natural light as far as possible into the building; **b.** prevent glare; **c.** prevent high brightness-shadow ratio. More than absolute illumination, it is the relative contrast between illuminated areas and less illuminated areas that determines how clearly we see in a specific environment (more so than absolute illumination); **d.** prevent veiling reflections; **e.** diffuse the light; emphasize the artistic possibility that can be achieved with the creative use of daylight (where it is not distracting or disrupting).

The use of natural light must take into account two fundamental characteristics: it is a variable source and the source itself is beyond human control. As a system, it is less flexible than artificial lighting since distribution of natural light starts mainly at the perimeter of the building. For example, in an environment that has a ceiling at 10 feet and windows between 7 feet and 8 feet high, in order to extend daylight influence, elements along the perimeter must be introduced that reflect the light beyond 20 to 25 feet into the interior space of the building. In such an environment, in fact, 25 feet is the maximum distance at which the intensity of natural light is effective. As a rule of thumb, light penetration falls to a lower than useful level at a distance between two to three times the measurements of the height of the opening through which the light passes. This means that, in considering the use of daylight as a main component of the illumination system, the entire building should be seen as a source of lighting (see Figure 8.23).

It is important that light considerations are introduced at the very beginning of the design since the shape and orientation of the building can facilitate or impede the access of natural light.

PASSIVE AND ACTIVE SYSTEMS

Elements that create a system that uses daylight as a source of illumination can be classified through four main functions: **a.** components that allow daylight to enter the building; **b.** components that re-distribute sunlight by diffusion and reflection (technique known as reflected daylight); **c.** components that eliminate excessive illumination on interior surfaces: these elements include vertical walls, louvers, screens, trellises or shrubbery; **d.** components that eliminate glare and direct radiation: blinds, curtains or special glazing are all part of these components of a passive daylight distribution system.

Two types of systems (or their combination) can be used to fulfill the first two functions: passive systems (which are constituted mainly by elements of the building) and active systems (which continuously track the sun in its movement).

Passive Systems

To perform function **a** and allow light into the building in passive systems, a designer can choose from: **a.** side lighting: windows and glazing in general (see Figure 8.24); **b.** top lighting: skylights, clerestory windows and roof monitors (see Figure 8.24).

LIGHT PENETRATION AND BUILDING DESIGN

Planning of the lighting system should start at the initial stages of a project. This is very important especially when the designer intends to maximize the use of daylight.

Direct natural light enters the building at an angle that varies with the seasons, the sun being higher during the summer and lower during the winter. This poses the problem of the penetration of light into the building. In fact the light propagates mainly by being reflected two or three times by surfaces like walls, floors, ceilings, furniture and other elements. Each time that the light is reflected the surface absorbs part of it, releasing only a percentage. After several reflections the intensity of the light is not sufficient anymore and the space becomes dark.

This applies not only to buildings but in general to the mechanism through which light is perceived. Even outdoor lighting is perceived only after light is reflected by particles in the atmosphere.

There are various techniques that can be used in order to increase light penetration into interior spaces. One is the use of an atrium. How effective this design tool can be depends on many factors: the size of the atrium, the height of the building, the size and inclination of the opening at the top of the atrium, the level of light transmitted by the transparent surfaces, the finish on the reflective surfaces, the height floor to floor and the opening at each floor to the atrium.

LIGHT PENETRATION AND FLOOR PLAN LAYOUT

The layout of the plan has an enormous influence on the quality and amount of daylight that penetrates the building.

Since the average penetration beyond the point of entry is between 20' a 25' for a building with 10' high ceiling and openings 8' high, a deep building will rely mainly on the electrical lighting system, more than the natural light, to fulfill the occupancy requirement.

Scheme "A" illustrates this case. In order to improve the performance of the natural lighting system, one important approach is to reduce the depth of the building and explore different configurations. After this process is completed, it is possible to introduce techniques that increase even further the penetration and the quality of the daylight system.

Scheme B and C are two example of alternative layouts. It must be observed that, in many cases, because in these alternate the configuration is less compact, the area of the building increases or the size of the lot needs to be larger. If this is not possible, in order to maximize the penetration of the daylight the designer might need to use technological solutions, such as light shelves or light pipes (more suitable than layout solutions.)

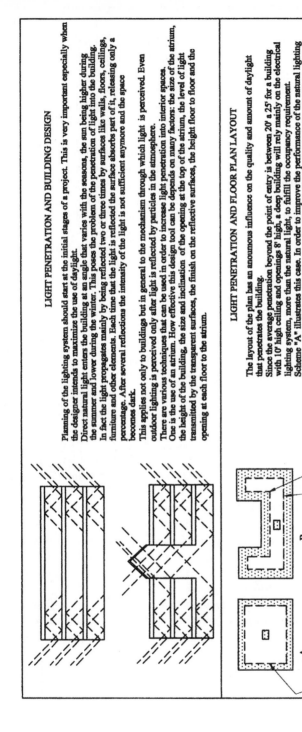

FIGURE 8.23 Light penetration and floor plan layout.

8.48

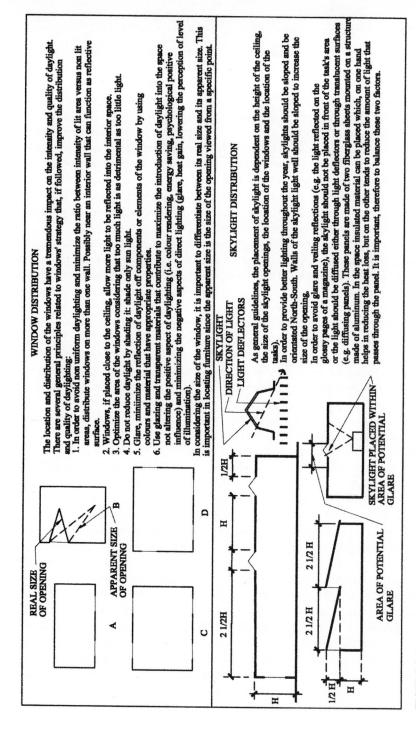

WINDOW DISTRIBUTION

The location and distribution of the windows have a tremendous impact on the intensity and quality of daylight. There are several general principles related to windows' strategy that, if followed, improve the distribution and quality of daylighting:

1. In order to avoid non uniform daylighting and minimize the ratio between intensity of lit area versus non lit areas, distribute windows on more than one wall. Possibly near an interior wall that can function as reflective surface.

2. Windows, if placed close to the ceiling, allow more light to be reflected into the interior space.

3. Optimize the area of the windows considering that too much light is as detrimental as too little light.

4. Do not reduce daylight by shading it: shade only sun light.

5. Glare, minimize the reflection of daylight off components or elements of the window by using colours and material that have appropriate properties.

6. Use glazing and transparent materials that contribute to maximize the introduction of daylight into the space not altering the positive aspect of daylighting (i.e. colour rendering, energy saving, psychological positive influence) and minimizing the negative aspects of direct lighting (glare, heat gain, lowering the perception of level of illumination).

In considering the size of the window, it is important to differentiate between its real size and its apparent size. This is important in locating furniture since the apparent size is the size of the opening viewed from a specific point.

REAL SIZE OF OPENING

APPARENT SIZE OF OPENING

A   B

C   D

SKYLIGHT DISTRIBUTION

SKYLIGHT

DIRECTION OF LIGHT

LIGHT DEFLECTORS

As general guidelines, the placement of skylight is dependent on the height of the ceiling, the size of the skylight openings, the location of the windows and the location of the tasks).

In order to provide better lighting throughout the year, skylights should be sloped and be orientated North-South. Walls of the skylight light well should be sloped to increase the size of the opening.

In order to avoid glare and veiling reflections (e.g. the light reflected on the glossy pages of a magazine), the skylight should not be placed in front of the task's area or the light should be diffused either through light deflectors or through translucent surfaces (e.g. diffusing panels). These panels are made of two fiberglass sheets mounted on a structure made of aluminum. In the space insulated material can be placed which, on one hand helps in reducing the heat loss, but on the other tends to reduce the amount of light that passes through the panel. It is important, therefore to balance these two factors.

1/2H   H   2 1/2 H

H

2 1/2 H

2 1/2 H

1/2 H   H

AREA OF POTENTIAL GLARE

SKYLIGHT PLACED WITHIN AREA OF POTENTIAL GLARE

AREA OF POTENTIAL GLARE

FIGURE 8.24 Level of light, window, and skylight distribution.

In both cases, glass represents an important element of the assembly. There are a variety of types of glass on the market : clear, tinted, heat absorbing, reflective, and selectively reflective. Except clear glazing, most of the glazing designed to reduce heat or glare also reduces the amount of light passing through. This is the case for reflective and tinted glass. In the case of glare, they are effective only if, in order to minimize the difference between outside and inside illuminance levels, the interior space is lit by artificial light. In most of the cases where daylight is intended to be used as a major component of the lighting system, clear glazing with complementary elements that mitigate the negative effects of direct sun lighting or that reduce the amount of light introduced in the space (i.e., reducing the size of the exterior opening and, if appropriate, increasing the number of openings) often remains the best solution.

Recent research in the sector of glazing materials has developed a technology called *dynamic envelopes*. Small individual units that behave like sunglasses constitute the exterior glazing. These units, controlled by a computer, can change their properties (i.e., color, reflectance, transmittance, thermal conductivity) in accordance with the exterior conditions.

Another technology that is progressing is one related to glass blocks. There are two basic types of glass blocks: transparent or translucent. Their U value is equal to 12 inches of concrete. Various patterns diffuse or redirect light in various ways to provide transmission of light without glare. Their use can provide solutions for spaces that require fire separation, sound attenuation, insulating values and reduced condensation.

As alternates to the above, translucent membrane roofs and structural composite panels can be used. The first is made of coated fiber glass fabric: it has poor insulating values which makes it suitable for buildings that are not air conditioned or for buildings constructed in mild climates. A typical use is in stadiums and other sport facilities where a double membrane is used to increase the insulating value. Structural composite panels are two layers of fiberglass attached to an aluminum I beam that separates them. This system is suitable for smaller structures.

To perform function **b** (i.e., redirect, redistribute and diffuse the daylight), three fundamental components form systems that are commonly used: **a.** a collection component consists of reflectors or surfaces that direct the light towards the optical path. Among these types of systems are blinds with a reflective upper surface (placed on the upper portion of the window). Another example is the use of overhangs as reflective surfaces (see Figure 8.25). By re-directing light to the ceiling (through which the light is then reflected into the interior space), neither of these examples produce glare. These systems can project daylight to ceilings up to 30 or 40 feet into the interior space. A mirror on a roof can also be very effective in re-directing the light into the building (reflecting light onto surfaces, atriums or light pipes; **b.** An optical path is the component that reflects the light or carries it through a series of reflections, to the place where light is needed. This includes any surface that diffuses light (i.e., walls, ceilings or other diaphragms). Among these we can consider a hierarchy of descending importance in reflecting light: ceilings, back walls, side walls, floors and/or small pieces of furniture.

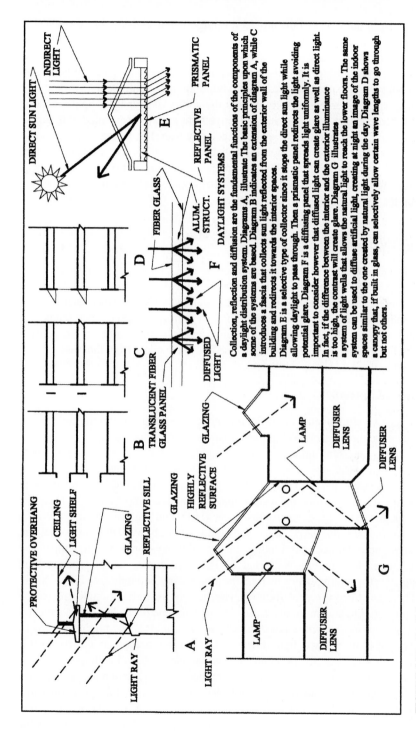

FIGURE 8.25 Daylight systems.

Thus, at the initial stages of the project it is important to consider in a general way types of finishes for the most important elements, while small pieces of furniture, which contribute the least to the reflection of light, can be specified later. In addition to the above, lenses, prisms, hollows, internally reflective light guides, and fiber optics are also used. Lenses tend to build up heat. With the improvement of coatings with 95 percent reflectivity and the ability to propagate light with less than 50 percent loss, the internally reflective light guides (also called light pipes) are becoming very popular. They are especially useful in laboratories or museums or any other space with lighting specific requirements; **c.** a diffuse system consists of components that allow the spreading of light at the place where it is required. They include diffuser lenses or fiber optic with holes in their walls permitting the light to spread around the space.

Active Systems

The main element that differentiates an active from a passive system is the collection component. A common sun tracking system is called *Heliostat*, a tracking mirror that directs the light beam to a secondary stationary mirror, which then conveys the light into either pipes or an atrium. The first mirror, through motors, is adjusted continuously to follow the path of the sun. These systems can be very expensive and require maintenance, which might discourage the client from their use.

Artificial Lighting

There are two components in artificial lighting: the lamp and the fixture.

There are three general categories of lamps: **a.** incandescent: light is produced by heating a tungsten filament located in a glass enclosure filled with gas. There two types that differ according to the type of gas used in the glass enclosure: common incandescent and halogen (see Figure 8.26); **b.** discharge: light is produced by electric discharges ionizing a gas trapped within the lamp enclosure. There are two general types: high-intensity-discharge (HID) and fluorescent lamps. Within the high-intensity-discharge, four types are commonly available: high-pressure mercury vapor lamps, metal-halide lamps, high-pressure sodium lamps, and xenon lamps (see Figures 8.26 and 8.27); **c.** solid-state lamps produce light through electro-luminescence by transforming energy into light (see Figure 8.28).

There are three types of fixtures classified by the vertical angle created by their projected light (see Figure 8.22). The *distribution* of the luminaire indicates whether it has a *concentrated* or *diffused* output of light: **a.** downlighting (direct): this type of fixture directs light downward. It tends to accentuate horizontal surfaces by diminishing the importance of vertical elements and ceilings. This type of fixture will diffuse light only if it is provided with an internal spread reflector or a diffusing cover made of plastic or glass. However, in spite of its diffusing properties, it must be taken into account that the ceiling just above the fixture does not receive light; **b.** multidirectional (semi-direct): these are very flexible but complex fixtures. Since they spread light in many directions, the percentage of light spread in each direction is important. Contrasts created by the downward beam can be equalized by the reflection on the ceiling and walls; **c.** uplighting (indirect): used mainly to create a uniform light throughout the space. This form of indirect lighting can be mounted on walls, suspended fixtures or furniture. When the ceiling is used as reflective surface, it becomes the predominant feature. Uplighting usually is not sufficient to perform tasks that require specific and detail performance. The distance between the source and the reflecting surfaces determines the uniformity of the light reaching the surface: the closer the source, the less the uniformity.

There is really no difference in approach to design between natural and artificial lighting except for the characteristics of flexibility and variability that have been mentioned. In an optimum design (in other than decorative lighting), artificial lighting should be complementary to natural lighting and supplement it when the latter becomes insufficient. In order to do this, lighting controls became very important. Manual controls are cheaper but create the problem of being unreliable due to the fact that their function is left to the judgment of the individual and his or her perception and training. Automatic controls are more expensive but more reliable and consistent in their performance.

In layering the lighting system (ambient, task and accent lighting), if the design can optimize natural ambient and accent lighting, task lighting is the type of application that up to now has been dominated by artificial lighting. In many cases, if sunlight is available, natural light wells can accomplish the same function, but they require vision on the part of the designer—in order to be creative with the design—and on the part of the client who must not be discouraged by the relative initial cost.

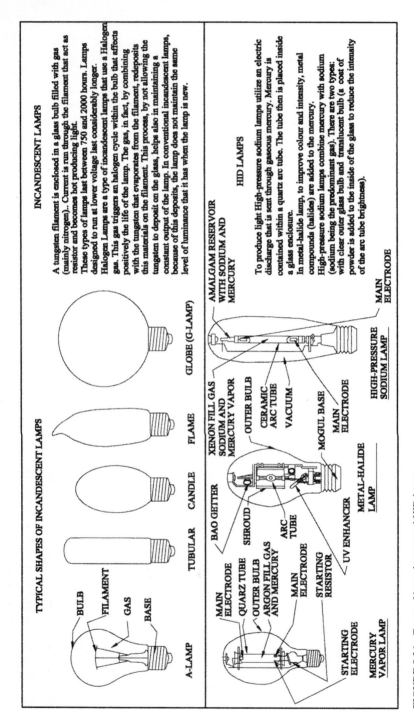

INCANDESCENT LAMPS

A tungsten filament is enclosed in a glass bulb filled with gas (mainly nitrogen). Current is run through the filament that act as resistor and becomes hot producing light.

These types of lamps last between 750 and 2000 hours. Lamps designed to run at lower voltage last considerably longer.

Halogen Lamps are a type of incandescent lamps that use a Halogen gas. This gas triggers an halogen cycle within the bulb that affects positively the life of the lamp. The gas, in fact, by combining with the tungsten that evaporates from the filament, redeposits this materials on the filament. This process, by not allowing the tungsten to deposit on the glass, helps also in maintaining a constant output of the lamp. In conventional incandescent lamps, because of this deposits, the lamp does not maintain the same level of luminance that it has when the lamp is new.

HID LAMPS

To produce light High-pressure sodium lamps utilize an electric discharge that is sent through gaseous mercury. Mercury is contained within a quartz arc tube. The tube then is placed inside a glass enclosure.

In metal-halide lamp, to improve colour and intensity, metal compounds (halides) are added to the mercury.

High-pressure sodium lamps combine mercury with sodium (sodium being the predominant gas). There are two types: with clear outer glass bulb and translucent bulb (a coat of powder is added to the inside of the glass to reduce the intensity of the arc tube brightness).

TYPICAL SHAPES OF INCANDESCENT LAMPS

A-LAMP TUBULAR CANDLE FLAME GLOBE (G-LAMP)

BULB
FILAMENT
GAS
BASE

AMALGAM RESERVOIR
WITH SODIUM AND
MERCURY

MAIN
ELECTRODE

HIGH-PRESSURE
SODIUM LAMP

XENON FILL GAS
SODIUM AND
MERCURY VAPOR

OUTER BULB

CERAMIC
ARC TUBE

VACUUM

MAIN
ELECTRODE

MOGUL BASE

UV ENHANCER

METAL-HALIDE
LAMP

BAO GETTER

SHROUD

ARC
TUBE

MAIN
ELECTRODE

QUARZ TUBE

OUTER BULB

ARGON FILL GAS
AND MERCURY

MAIN
ELECTRODE

STARTING
RESISTOR

STARTING
ELECTRODE

MERCURY
VAPOR LAMP

FIGURE 8.26 Types of incandescent and HID lamps.

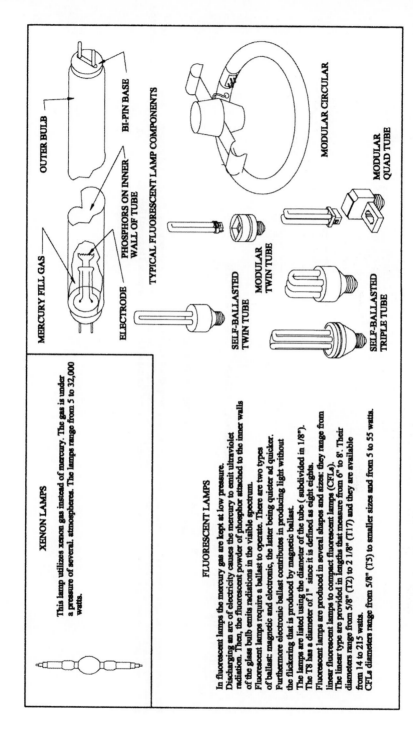

FIGURE 8.27 Types of xenon and fluorescent lamps.

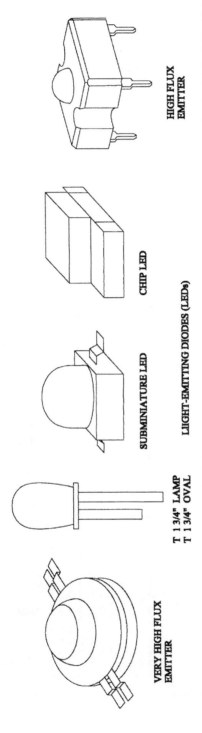

VERY HIGH FLUX EMITTER

T 1 3/4" LAMP
T 1 3/4" OVAL

SUBMINIATURE LED

CHIP LED

HIGH FLUX EMITTER

LIGHT-EMITTING DIODES (LEDs)

LEDs convert energy into light. Their size and durability makes them suitable for applications like traffic signals or decorations. The fixture is constituted mainly by the plastic bulb and the chip, where the light is generated. The electric current is passed through different materials. Their composition establishes the colour of the light. They are considerably durable. Recent developments in the industry are very promising and indicates that the use of LEDs can be expanded to general lighting.

FIGURE 8.28   Types of solid-state lamps.

8.56

CHAPTER 9
ARCHITECTURAL ELEMENTS

A building can be subdivided into different components. The categories created depend on the purpose of the subdivision and what is achieved by categorizing the parts of the building in a certain way. For construction and contractual reasons, for example, the systems used are the ones indicated in the specifications (see Chapter 1). For design reasons the differentiation is of another sort, although easily related to the categories to be used for construction. At the analysis stage, this differentiation should take into consideration the purpose of the elements and mechanics of systems, more than sequences (although, as indicated, sequences and mechanics of construction need to be considered at the detail stage). Function, program (see Chapter 3), site analysis (see Chapter 3), urban and environmental analysis, technical performance and cost are all factors that must be part of the considerations that lead to a specific subdivision of the parts of a project. In the following pages, the elements of a building will be seen from the point of view of their behavior as a system and their technical function. Some considerations on the appearance will be also introduced but these aesthetic aspects will be secondary to the technical ones. With this intent the building elements can be subdivided into the following categories:

1. *The Structural System* is subdivided into the substructure (below grade) and superstructure (above grade), which is a common denominator throughout the building and, therefore, will be part of every category that follows (see Chapter 6).
2. *The Envelope System* includes, and is affected by major elements such as:
   a. the roof, which in turn relates to components such as glazing in general and skylights specifically; dormers, chimneys and other architectural pene-

trations; sheathing or other roof decks, waterproofing, insulation, air barriers and vapor barriers; flashing and other protective components; cornices or other type of fascias; soffits; plumbing systems, with specific reference to components used for drainage or penetrations for stacks as well as fixtures like hose bibs (see Chapter 7); mechanical elements such as roof top units and other elements part of the heating and ventilating system (see Chapter 7); electrical installation like lighting (see Chapter 8); landscape (i.e., roof gardens); special installations (i.e., window-washing equipment); **b.** exterior walls, which include components such as wall assemblies (structural and non-structural) which can be constructed on site (i.e., a stud wall), prefabricated (i.e., panels) or a combination of systems; interior finish, structural members of walls or buildings (which can be common to both the wall and the building), waterproofing or water resistant elements, insulation and air and vapor barriers (within the cavity or applied outside the cavity) as well as exterior finish; windows and general glazing; doors; cornices (which in many cases are shared with the roof system) and other ornaments, miscellaneous supporting elements (i.e., shelf angles, brackets and ties for masonry or slabs); flashing and other protective components; mechanical installations (i.e., venting and exhausting); electrical installation (i.e., outlets, wall mounted lighting); landscaping (i.e., planters); **c.** balconies, terraces and decks which are comprised of and affected by components such as: sheathing or other types of decks, waterproofing and flashing; paving or finish floor material; railing, parapet or other types of guards; cornices or other types of fascias; soffits, mechanical installation for exhaust and venting. (In certain cases, these elements can be considered part of the roof system).

3. *The interior system* includes: **a.** floors and ceilings; **b.** interior walls and partitions including doors and interior glazing; **c.** plumbing; **d.** electrical fixtures (see Chapter 8); **e.** ventilation and exhaust components (see Chapter 7); **f.** electrical and communication components, which include: power distribution, safety systems, emergency supply, telephone, wireless systems and interior communication; **g.** vertical circulating systems such as ramps and stairways as well as mechanical devices like elevators and escalators.

The following pages provide the basic principles that will permit the location of each element listed above in the context of the fundamental technical behavior of the system in which it has been placed (exterior and interior as general categories and then roof, exterior walls, and interior walls). After this differentiation, selected elements that have been placed in each of these systems are analyzed and their main characteristics are discussed. This should provide the basis for selecting the most appropriate main components of the system.

ENVELOPE SYSTEM

This system refers to all the components that are applied, installed, or constructed to reach the *lock-up* stage, when the building is sealed and the interior can be finished. In wood construction, because the walls are often part of the structure, the skeleton of the interior walls is built in conjunction with the exterior walls. In steel and concrete construction, where the interior partitions are not load bearing and usually made of metal studs, the walls are framed after the lock-up stage is completed. In fact, in commercial buildings like offices or mercantile construction, apart from common facilities such as washrooms or exit stairs, the interior cannot be pre-determined until a tenant is found.

The envelope system responds to specific requirements which are not only aesthetical but also environmental. Since it is the diaphragm between the interior and the exterior, from the technical point of view its primary function is to provide a shelter from the natural elements and, in doing so, it has to respond properly to continuous changes and differential conditions. These differences require very flexible performances from the systems. Therefore, before any decision is made, an analysis of the conditions under which these systems must work is fundamental. From the environmental point of view the envelope must satisfy thermal and waterproofing requirements that are part of the definition of comfort. The optimum performance of the envelope is reached when the characteristics of the assembly respond to specific phenomena and the solutions to potential problems created by these phenomena are incorporated in the design.

THERMAL ASPECTS AND PROPERTIES OF MATERIALS

Through the centuries, considerations on the required thermal performance of a building have gone full cycle due to realization of the importance of the amount of energy that is expended in maintaining the range of inside space temperature within particular values. Long ago, elements like location, orientation, wind, vegetation, natural features (i.e., water bodies), mass, volume, and type of materials were all factors that were directly responsible for interior comfort. With advances in science and technological development, heating systems acquired more importance than environmental conditions. In other words, once these systems became commonly available, it became possible to heat up or cool down an artificial environment with very little consideration for the environmental characteristics. During the energy crisis of the early seventies it became clear that the high cost of energy required a review of the approach to the climatization of buildings. In addition, changes in the natural environment which are becoming increasingly evident and the keen awareness that most energy resources are finite have placed even more pressure on design considerations related to energy consumption and a renewed awareness of environmental factors.

If the principles of physics have always been very important in predicting the performance of a system, those principles become even more important now that the performance needs to be maintained within specific values. In order to make sure that those specific values can be guaranteed, the analysis of the design must be very detailed. We discussed the principle of heat transfer in Chapter 7. It is now necessary to expand the concepts by applying them to the exterior elements of a building.

Normally, walls consist of layers of materials or elements that not only have a specific performance but are also separated by voids that contain air. In most assemblies, therefore, heat transfer occurs through the three basic mechanisms discussed in Chapter 7: convection, radiation and conduction (see Figure 9.1).

It is necessary to differentiate between two types of heat transfer: **a.** steady state; **b.** dynamic state.

Steady State

This is the condition in which the temperature of the various elements remains constant. This means that the outside temperature as well as the inside temperatures does not change (although, because of the difference in temperature, heat transfer still occurs). It is evidently a situation that in reality is not maintained for a long period of time or, if it is, requires conditions that minimize the differentials between the external temperature during the day and that registered during the night (i.e., a state that occurs during cloudy conditions). In most cases, exterior conditions change and often do so very suddenly. Nevertheless the steady state is a very useful analysis in establishing the characteristics and performance of the envelope of a building. The basic unit for the steady condition is the Btu (see Chapter 7).

A specific thermal conductivity (k) characterizes every material and is constant for that specific material. A thermal conductor is a material with a high thermal conductivity, while a thermal insulator is a material with a low thermal conductivity. More commonly, to compare the thermal performance of different materials, the reciprocal of k is used, which is called thermal resistivity (r). When 1/r is substituted for the equation of heat transfer by conduction, the denominator of the ratio becomes r L. This is finally resolved as R = r L, where R is defined as the thermal resistance of the material (see Figure 9.1). Therefore, where r is the unit of thermal resistivity per 1" of thickness of the material, R is the thermal resistance of the actual component of the assembly (since the basic units has been multiplied by the thickness of the component).

The mass and the density of a material greatly affect the thermal performance. Very dense materials do not perform well as insulators. Ideally a material should contain small pockets of air, since still air is a very good insulator. However if the space occupied by air allows the air to circulate, this creates convection and heat loss. There is, therefore, an ideal balance between mass and air

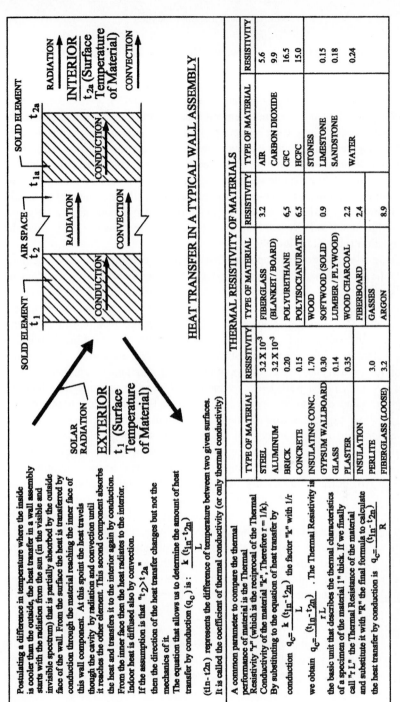

Postulating a difference in temperature where the inside is cooler than the outside, the heat transfer in a wall assembly starts with the radiation from the sun (in the visible and invisible spectrum) that is partially absorbed by the outside face of the wall. From the surface the heat is transferred by conduction through the material reaching the inner face of this wall component. At this point the heat travels though the cavity by radiation and convection until it reaches the other element. This second component absorbs the heat and transfers it to the interior again by conduction. From the inner face then the heat radiates to the interior. Indoor heat is diffused also by convection.

If the assumption is that "$t_2 > t_{2a}$"

then the direction of the heat transfer changes but not the mechanics of it.

The equation that allows us to determine the amount of heat transfer by conduction (q_c) is : $\dfrac{k\,(t_{1n}-t_{2n})}{L}$

($t_{1n}-t_{2n}$) represents the difference of temperature between two given surfaces.
It is called the coefficient of thermal conductivity (or only thermal conductivity)

A common parameter to compare the thermal performance of material is the Thermal Resistivity "r" (which is the reciprocal of the Thermal Conductivity of the material "k". Therefore $r = 1/k$).
By substituting to the equation of heat transfer by conduction $q_c = \dfrac{k\,(t_{1n}-t_{2n})}{L}$ the factor "k" with $1/r$

we obtain $q_c = \dfrac{(t_{1n}-t_{2n})}{rL}$. The Thermal Resistivity is the basic unit that describes the thermal characteristics of a specimen of the material 1" thick. If we finally call "r L" the Thermal Resistance of the material and substitute it with "R" the final formula to calculate the heat transfer by conduction is $q_c = \dfrac{(t_{1n}-t_{2n})}{R}$

HEAT TRANSFER IN A TYPICAL WALL ASSEMBLY

THERMAL RESISTIVITY OF MATERIALS

TYPE OF MATERIAL	RESISTIVITY	TYPE OF MATERIAL	RESISTIVITY	TYPE OF MATERIAL	RESISTIVITY
STEEL	3.2×10^{-3}	FIBERGLASS (BLANKET / BOARD)	3.2	AIR	5.6
ALUMINUM	3.2×10^{-3}	POLYURETHANE	6.5	CARBON DIOXIDE	9.9
BRICK	0.20	POLYISOCIANURATE	6.5	CFC	16.5
CONCRETE	0.15			HCFC	15.0
INSULATING CONC.	1.70	WOOD		STONES	
GYPSUM WALLBOARD	0.30	SOFTWOOD (SOLID)	0.9	LIMESTONE	0.15
GLASS	0.14	LUMBER / PLYWOOD		SANDSTONE	0.18
PLASTER	0.35	WOOD CHARCOAL	2.2	WATER	0.24
INSULATION		FIBERBOARD	2.4		
PERLITE	3.0	GASSES			
FIBERGLASS (LOOSE)	3.2	ARGON	8.9		

Diagram labels: SOLID ELEMENT t_1 — AIR SPACE t_2 — SOLID ELEMENT t_{2a}; CONDUCTION, RADIATION, CONVECTION; SOLAR RADIATION; EXTERIOR t_1 (Surface Temperature of Material); INTERIOR t_{2a} (Surface Temperature of Material).

FIGURE 9.1   Heat transfer in a typical wall assembly. Thermal resistivity of materials.

content of a material below and above which the heat loss increases. Even higher insulating characteristics than air are associated with certain gasses (see Figure 9.1). These elements are used, for example, to improve the thermal performance of insulation material or glass insulated units.

Water and moisture are other elements that affect the capacity of a material to delay heat transfer. Since water is a very poor insulator in relationship to air (see Figure 9.1), if a material becomes wet and water replaces air, the heat loss increases.

The *R-value* of an assembly constituted by different components in sequence (i.e., an assembly like the one shown on figure 9.1) is calculated by adding the R-values of each component that is part of that assembly. If the element (i.e., a wall) is constituted by different sections of assemblies or components (i.e., a single monolithic panel) side by side, the total R-value of the element (R_0) is given by the equation shown on Figure 9.2.

There is an additional component that should be considered in any assembly: this is the air film that is close to the exterior and interior surface of the element. Any surface tends to slow down the movement of air because of the friction that is created between the surface and the air. The rougher the surface, the thicker the film of air created along this surface. Inside air moves less than outside air, therefore, the value of the surface resistance that is given to the two films is substantially different: 0.7 for the internal surface and 0.2 for the external. These values appear to be small and, in fact, do not improve very much the overall performance of an assembly like a wall. However there are cases (i.e., glazing) in which the thermal resistance has to be attributed mainly to the film of air close to the surface.

The above principles indicate the mechanism through which conduction and convection work. The third type of heat transfer is through radiation. The following basic principles can guide in the understanding of the behavior of heat transfer by radiation: **a.** the exchange of radiant energy happens continuously between two objects, but mainly from the object at higher temperature to the object at lower temperature; **b.** the object must be in direct visual contact. If another object is interposed between the two, this third object will mediate the exchange of radiant energy; **c.** although they might receive radiation from the sun (short wave) and long wave radiation from surrounding objects, an object emit only long wave radiations; **d.** each material has three types of responses to radiation: it can reflect it, absorb it or transmit it. The sum of the three responses corresponds to the total amount of incident radiations received from the source. In other words absorptivity + transmissivity + reflectivity = 1 (see Figure 9.2); **e.** each material has a particular capacity to emit radiation that is called emissivity. The emissivity is a property of the surface of the object and not of its entire mass. For long wave radiation the emissivity of a material is equal to its absorptivity (see Figure 9.2). The following is the equation that indicates at what rate radiant energy is emitted:

$q_t = e \, \beta \, T^4$ where e is the emissivity of the object, T is the temperature of the object in Kelvin scale ($T \, °F = (T + 492)K$: for example a temperature of $32°F$ is equal to $524K$) and β is a constant.

ASSEMBLY IN PARALLEL WITH DIFFERENT "R" VALUES

The heat loss of an element that is composed of sections caracterized by different "R" values is calculated through the following formula: $Ro = A_1 + A_2 + A_3 + A_4 \ldots$, where A_1, A_2, A_3, $A_4 \ldots$ are

$$\frac{A_1}{R_1} + \frac{A_2}{R_2} + \frac{A_3}{R_3} + \frac{A_4}{R_4} \ldots$$

the areas of the sections that have different "R" values, and R_1, R_2, R_3, R_4 are these "R" values of each section.

R1	R2	R3

THERMAL CHARACTERISTICS OF SURFACES

TYPE OF MATERIAL	LONGWAVE RADIATION		SHORTWAVE RADIATION	
	EMISSIVITY ABSORPTIVITY	REFLECTIVITY	ASORPTIVITY	REFLECTIVITY
GYPSUM BOARD	0.90	0.10	0.60	0.40
CONCRETE	0.90	0.10	0.60	0.40
MARBLE	0.90	0.10	0.30	0.70
BRICK	0.90	0.10	0.70	0.30
WOOD	0.90	0.10	0.60	0.40
ALUMINUM FOIL	0.05	0.95	0.20	0.80
BRASS (polished)	0.05	0.95	0.30	0.70
STAINLESS STEEL	0.20	0.80	0.30	0.70
CAST IRON	0.45	0.55	0.70	0.30
GLASS	0.90	0.10	0.05	0.07
PAINTS				
BLACK	0.90	0.10	0.90	0.10
WHITE	0.90	0.10	0.10	0.90
GREEN	0.90	0.10	0.70	0.30
ALUMINUM	0.55	0.45	0.50	0.50

THERMAL BRIDGE

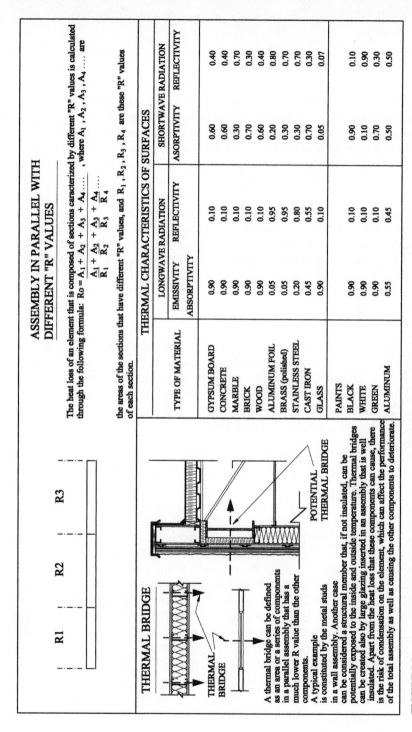

THERMAL BRIDGE

POTENTIAL THERMAL BRIDGE

A thermal bridge can be defined as an area or a series of components in a parallel assembly that has a much lower R value than the other components.

A typical example is constituted by the metal studs in a wall assembly. Another case can be considered a structural member that, if not insulated, can be potentially exposed to the inside and outside temperature. Thermal bridges can be created also by large glazing inserted in an assembly that is well insulated. Apart from the heat loss that these components can cause, there is the risk of condensation on the element, which can affect the performance of the total assembly as well as causing the other components to deteriorate.

FIGURE 9.2   Assembly in parallel with different R values. Thermal characteristics of surfaces.

From the above equation it is clear that temperature is the fundamental factor in radiation. However, in buildings, radiation is fundamental in the mechanism of heat transfer only when conduction and convection do not play an important role, as in the cavities of walls and roofs. In these cases, materials with high reflectivity and low emissivity/absorptivity are very effective in limiting the propagation of radiant heat on the opposite side of the incident radiation. From Figure 9.2, we can see that aluminum foil is among the materials that can provide this function (and since the emittance is a property of the surface, the thickness of the foil is irrelevant and can be minimized). This is in fact a material that is often used to line cavities in order to prevent radiant heat from being transferred (see Figure 9.3). Since shortwave radiation from the sun behaves like light, a white surface is very effective in reflecting radiation. However the color white is not effective against the long wave radiation, because it absorbs 90 percent of them, reflecting only 10 percent (see Figures 9.2 and 9.3). At this point we can reintroduce the concept of *U-value* and apply it to a specific example (see Figure 9.4).

Dynamic State

Under this state, not only the U-value is important, but the mass of the element is another important factor that affects its performance. We have seen that when the heat flow is unidirectional (steady state) only the U-value has an effect on the heat loss. This means that either the interior or the exterior is constantly cooler than the other. When this relationship changes, the thermal mass (or thermal capacity as it is also called) of a component becomes an important factor. In fact the capacity for storing heat and releasing it at a later time, when it is needed, is the basic principle of an effective design capable of responding to the dynamic state of the environment. The time between storing the energy and its release is called time lag. The thermal capacity of a material can be defined as its ability to store heat and represents the amount of energy required to raise the temperature of one square foot of material by 1°F. The basic unit to describe the thermal capacity is $Btu/(ft.^2 \bullet °F)$. The formula that determines the thermal capacity of a component is: $TC = SD \, x \, SH$, where SD is the surface density of the material (i.e., concrete has a density of 145 psf. (See Figure 9.5) and SH is the specific heat (see Figure 9.5). The first is calculated by multiplying the density of a material in psf for the thickness of the actual component; the second is the amount of heat energy that is necessary to raise 1 pound of the material 1°F. The value of the thermal capacity of a material is directly proportional to the amount of heat that the material can store. From the analysis of the variation in fluctuation of the specific heat of different materials it is possible to observe that, except for water, the values are fairly close. This means that the surface density of a material is the predominant factor in determining the thermal capacity. In conclusion, the thermal capacity of a material is not a significant factor in colder climates where the heat flow is mainly from the inside to the outside. Also it is not relevant in tropical climates where the heat transfer is mainly from outside to inside.

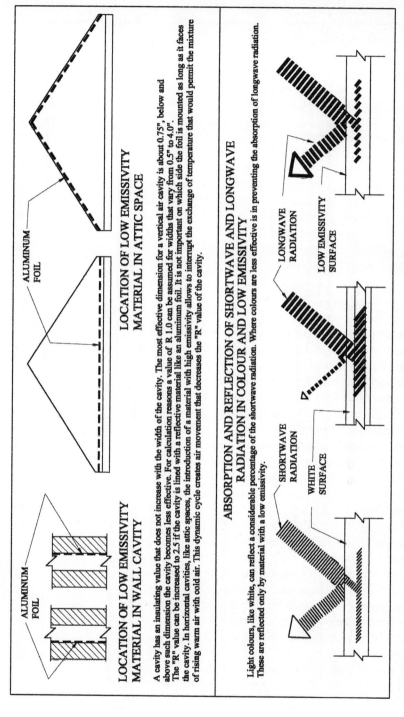

LOCATION OF LOW EMISSIVITY MATERIAL IN ATTIC SPACE

ALUMINUM FOIL

LOCATION OF LOW EMISSIVITY MATERIAL IN WALL CAVITY

ALUMINUM FOIL

A cavity has an insulating value that does not increase with the width of the cavity. The most effective dimension for a vertical air cavity is about 0.75", below and above such dimension the cavity becomes less effective. For calculation reasons a value of R 1.0 can be assumed for widths that vary from 0.5" to 4.0". The "R" value can be increased to 2.5 if the cavity is lined with a reflective material like an aluminum foil. It is not important on which side the foil is mounted as long as it faces the cavity. In horizontal cavities, like attic spaces, the introduction of a material with high emissivity allows to interrupt the exchange of temperature that would permit the mixture of rising warm air with cold air. This dynamic cycle creates air movement that decreases the "R" value of the cavity.

ABSORPTION AND REFLECTION OF SHORTWAVE AND LONGWAVE RADIATION IN COLOUR AND LOW EMISSIVITY

LONGWAVE RADIATION

LOW EMISSIVITY SURFACE

SHORTWAVE RADIATION

WHITE SURFACE

Light colours, like white, can reflect a considerable percentage of the shortwave radiation. Where colours are less effective is in preventing the absorption of longwave radiation. These are reflected only by material with a low emissivity.

FIGURE 9.3 Location of low emissivity materials in wall cavities and attic spaces. Absorption of shortwave and long wave radiation.

9.9

DETERMINATION OF THE "U-VALUE" OF AN ASSEMBLY

The determination of the "U-value" of an assembly starts with the calculation of the "R" values of the single components.
In the case of a stud wall with .5" Gypsum Board on each side, 2" x 4" Studs @ 16" o.c., 3.5" Fiberglass Batt Insulation, a .5" air cavity and 3.5" Brick Veneer, the total "R-value" of the wall is the combination between the "R-Value" of the Elements without the Studs and the "R-Value" of the assembly at the Studs:

Component	Assembly at Cavity R-Value	Assembly at Studs R-Value
Inside Air Film	0.7	0.7
1/2" Gypsum Wall Board	0.5 x 0.60 = 0.30	0.5 x 0.60 = 0.30
3 1/2" Batt Insulation	3.5 x 3.2 = 11.2	
1 1/2" x 3 1/2" Studs @ 16" o.c.		3.5 x 1.0 = 3.5
1/2" Gypsum Sheathing	0.5 x 0.60 = 0.30	0.5 x 0.60 = 0.30
2' Air Cavity		1.0
3 1/2" Brick Veneer	3.5 x 0.20 = 0.70	3.5 x 0.20 = 0.70
Outside Air Film	0.2	0.2
Total "R-Value"	14.40	6.70

Since the Studs are spaced every 16", the ratio between the two "R-Values" is 1/16.
If we convert the two "R-Values" in "U-Values" we obtain
$1/R = 1/14.40 = 0.069$
$1/R = 1/ 6.70 = 0.149$
In order to calculate the "U-Value" of the total wall we can apply the formula used to determine the total "U-Value" of a non uniform assembly:

$$U_o = \frac{A_1U_1 + A_2U_2 + A_3U_3 + \cdots}{A_1 + A_2 + A_3 + \cdots}$$

Since the height of the wall components is the same we can disregard it and substitute for the numerator the ratio the width of the elements instead of their areas.
This width is for the Studs 1.5" and for the cavity 14.5" (derived from 16" minus half of the Stud on each side (3/4"x2).
Instead of the area as denominator we can use the ratio of 1/16, which represent the interval of the elements with different "U-Value".

The formula then becomes: $U_o = \dfrac{14.5\,(0.069) + 1.5\,(0.149)}{16} = 0.076 > 0.069$

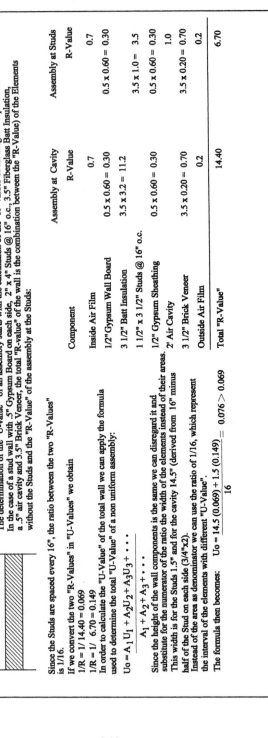

FIGURE 9.4   Determination of the U-value in an assembly.

SPECIFIC HEAT OF MATERIALS

TYPE OF MATERIAL	SPECIFIC HEAT BTU/(lb °F)	TYPE OF MATERIAL	SPECIFIC HEAT BTU/(lb °F)
STEEL	0.12	FIBERGLASS (BLANKET / BOARD)	0.17
ALUMINUM	0.21	EXP. POLYSTYRENE	0.18
BRICK	0.19	POLYISOCIANURATE	0.18
CONCRETE	0.16	VERMICULATE	0.21
GYPSUM BOARD	0.26	PERLITE	0.21
GLASS	0.18	WOOD	0.50
MARBLE	0.21	WOOD CHARCOAL	0.20
LIMESTONE	0.20	FIBERBOARD	2.4
INSULATION LIGHTWEIGHT INSUL. CONCRETE	0.18	AIR	0.25
		WATER	1.0

MATERIALS' VOLUME DENSITY

TYPE OF MATERIAL	WEIGHT LB/FT³	TYPE OF MATERIAL	WEIGHT LB/FT	TYPE OF MATERIAL	WEIGHT LB/FT
STEEL	490	OAK	47	ICE	57
CAST IRON	450	PINE	37	AIR	0.075
CONCRETE	145	DOUGLAS FIR	28	GRANITE	165
REINF. CONCRETE	150	PLYWOOD	36	MARBLE	170
LIGHT CONCRETE	70-105	INSULATION		ASPHALT	81
INSUL. CONCRETE	25-50	FIBERGLASS	1.0-2.5	TAR	75
BRICK	110-130	POLYSTYRENE	2.0		
CONCRETE BLOCK	135	POLYISOCIANURATE	2.0		
MORTAR	130	GYPSUM BOARD	50		
WOOD		GLASS	160		
HEM FIR	28	WATER	63		

WATER VAPOR AND VAPOR PRESSURE IN SATURATED AIR

TEMPERATURE	WATER VAPOR (GR/LB DRY AIR)	VAPOR PRESSURE (PSF)
-20	1.8	0.89
-10	3.2	1.56
0	5.5	2.66
10	9.2	4.45
20	15.0	7.27
30	24.1	11.65
40	36.4	17.52
50	53.4	25.65
60	77.3	36.92
70	110.4	52.31
80	155.7	73.07
90	217.4	100.64
100	301.0	136.84
110	414.2	183.80

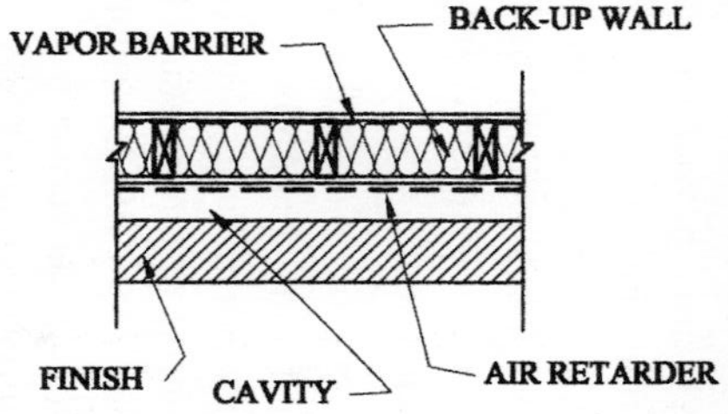

Air retarders have a dual function: on one hand they diminish the flow of air through the assembly, second they minimized the flow of air within the wall between the studs. This is particularly effective if batt insulation, mineral wool or loose fill insulation is used. From this point of view, if insulation boards are used, the reduction of movement of air within the wall cavity between the studs becomes less critical.

BACK-UP WALL

VAPOR BARRIER

AIR RETARDER

FINISH   CAVITY

TYPICAL EXTERIOR
RAINSCREEN ASSEMBLY

FIGURE 9.5   Specific heat of materials, material volume density and water vapor and vapor pressure in saturated air.

TYPES OF INSULATING MATERIAL

From the above analysis it is clear that (both in the steady and dynamic state) insulating materials play a primary role in the process of heat transfer, not only in terms of the amount of energy consumed to maintain the indoor temperature within specific values, but also to control the dew point (point of condensation), as we will see in the following pages.

There are many types of insulating materials (see Figure 9.6). The types of insulating material can be classified in the following categories:

1. *Fibrous materials*: their insulating characteristics are due to the air content between the fibers. Fibrous insulation can be further subdivided into: **a.** *glass fibers (fiberglass)*: the basic material is molten glass converted into fibers. Available in batt or blankets (both unfaced or faced with asphalt-impregnated paper) and boards; **b.** *rock wool*, which is composed of molten rocks reduced to very fine fibers constitute the basic material. Available in batt or blankets (both unfaced or faced with asphalt impregnated paper) and boards; **c.** *cellulose fibers*, derived from newspapers or wood. This type is highly flammable if not treated. Mainly available in loose-fill to be blown in for retrofit applications.

2. *Foam insulation:* plastic foam is the common material for rigid board insulation. All plastic foams are combustible and require the protection of boards (commonly ½ inch of gypsum board) to avoid their exposure to flame and sudden rise of temperature. Four types are commonly available: **a.** *expanded polystyrene (EPS)*: insulating agent is the air inside the beads. The density of the boards varies from 1.0 to 3.0 pcf with the 1.0 commonly used; **b.** *extruded polystyrene (XEPS)*: HCFC gas is used instead of air. A popular brand of this type of insulation is *Styrofoam* made by Dow Chemical Company; **c.** *polyurethane (PUR)*: HCFC gas is used instead of air; **d.** *polyisocyanurate (PIR)*: HCFC gas is used instead of air. Because both PUR and PIR type of insulation use facers (like aluminum foil, glass fiber, wood fibers) they retard the migration of the gas. Also, they have higher insulating values than XEPS.

3. Cellular glass rigid board is a type of insulation that is used where structural strength is needed. It is made by expanding molten glass. The product is then cooled to transform a closed cell structure into beads. It is used on plazas, parkades and around slab on grade.

4. Where the space to be insulated is of an irregular shape, foamed-in-place insulation is very useful. In a few minutes, the components expand and solidify to a volume 30 times their original state.

5. Granular materials derive their insulating value from the air trapped in the beads. This type includes: **a.** *rigid perlite board* is made using perlite mixed with mineral fibers. It is a non-combustible product used very often in flat roof applications; **b.** *loose-fill granular* is commonly available as

perlite granules (the basic material is volcanic perlite rock that expands if exposed to heat) and vermiculite granules (derived from mica.) Both perlite and vermiculite are used especially to fill cavities as in masonry walls. Their weight and ability to fill every void makes them very suitable for this application. Furthermore they are non-combustible; **c.** *insulating concrete*, which consists of concrete mixed with perlite or vermiculite. A common application is insulating steel decks with a high degree of fire resistance.

Studies have shown that insulation is more effective if applied on the outside of the wall, rather than in the cavity.

The Model Energy Code (MEC) is the by-law that regulates the minimum amount of insulation required in the different element of a construction. Apart from providing a prescriptive method, the code allows a more detailed analysis in which it is possible to apply trade offs between the various elements as long as the overall performance of the building complies with the minimum required.

In the case of the slab on grade, the insulation does not need to be extended to the full undersurface of the slab. The critical location is along the perimeter. Analyzing the possible direction of heat transfer (horizontal, vertical and radiating form points of the slab like waves through the soil), it becomes clear that heat loss through the horizontal and radiating movement of heat energy is a function of the distance it travels. As a rule of thumb it is possible to use the following guidelines: no insulation is required if the HDD (annual heating degrees days) are less than 2,500, 2' in width or height if the HDD are less than 6,000 or 4' if they are more than 6,000.

AIR AND VAPOR MOVEMENT

In the dynamic state, another critical aspect is the migration of air through an assembly from the inside to the outside and vice versa. This phenomenon is called air leakage. This movement is one of the major problems not only for heat loss but also for possible water condensation because air always contains a certain amount of vapor. However, water vapor moves through the envelope independently from air movement.

Potential air leakage occurs particularly at the joint of different materials or at the joint of different elements (i.e., a door or a window with a wall). The rate of leakage is dependent on two factors: the size of the opening and the different pressure on the two size of the opening. The pressure, in turn, depends on the relative humidity and the temperature of the air. Hotter air tends to expand. It tends also to hold more moisture/vapor, which increases the pressure of the air (see Figure 9.5). The basic unit to measure and calculate air leakage is cubic feet per hour (ft^3/h). If all the leakages are accounted and added, this total leads to the calculation of air exchange per hour. This value (which is often used to indicate the efficiency of a structure in relation to air movement through the exterior assemblies) is given in terms of percentage of the total air present in an interior space. For example, a 0.5

VAPOR PERMEABILITY OF MATERIAL

TYPE OF MATERIAL	PERMEABILITY PERM.INCH	TYPE OF MATERIAL	PERMEABILITY PERM.INCH
METALS	0.0	INSULATION	
BRICK WALL	3.2	MINERAL WOOL	116.0
GYPSUM BOARD	20.0	EXTR. POLYSTYRENE	1.2
ALUMINUM FOIL.	0.0	FIBERGLASS	116.0
PLYWOOD EXT. TYPE	0.2	EXP. POLYSTYRENE	5.0
PLYWOOD INT. TYPE	0.5	POLYURETHANE	0.5
CONCRETE	3.2	AIR CAVITY	240.0

PERM RATINGS OF COMPONENTS

TYPE OF MATERIAL	PERM RATING PERM	TYPE OF MATERIAL	PERM RATING PERM
BRICK 4" THICK	0.8	4 MIL POLYETHYLENE SHEET	0.08
CONCRETE BLOCKS 8" THICK	2.4	6 MIL POLYETHYLENE SHEET	0.06
PLASTER ON METAL LATH	15.0	8 MIL POLYETHYLENE SHEET	0.03
BUILDING PAPER TYPE A	0.25	PRIMER AND ONE COAT OF OIL PAINT	1.6 - 3.0
BUILDING PAPER TYPE B	0.38	EXTERIOR OIL PAINT THREE COATS	0.3 - 1.0
ALUMINUM FOIL	0.0		
ALUMINUM FOIL ON GYPSUM	0.1		

TYPE OF INSULATION MATERIALS

Insulation Material
- Granular
  - Cellular Glass
  - Perlite Vermiculite
- Plastic Foams
  - Thermoset
    - Polyurethane
    - Polyisochanurate
  - Thermoplastic
    - Rigid
      - Extruded Polystyrene
      - Molded Polystyrene
    - Flexible
- Fibrous
  - Inorganic
    - Glass Fiber
    - Mineral Fiber (Rock Wool)
  - Organic
    - Wood Fiber Board
    - Cloth Felt

The location of the Vapor Retarder is dependent on two factors: the temperature of the outside and inside air and the amount of outside and inside vapor. If the indoor relative humidity is kept at or below 35%, the Vapor Retarder in not needed on the inside face of the insulation.

It is clear that in this cases the migration of the vapor can be from the outside to the inside during the summer even in temperate climates.

In order to function properly a Vapor Retarder should retard the migration of the vapor as well as provide permeability between itself and the cooler side. This is achieved by ensuring that the Vapor Retarder does not trap any vapor within the assembly and enough ventilation is provided in the cavity of a wall or in an actic space.

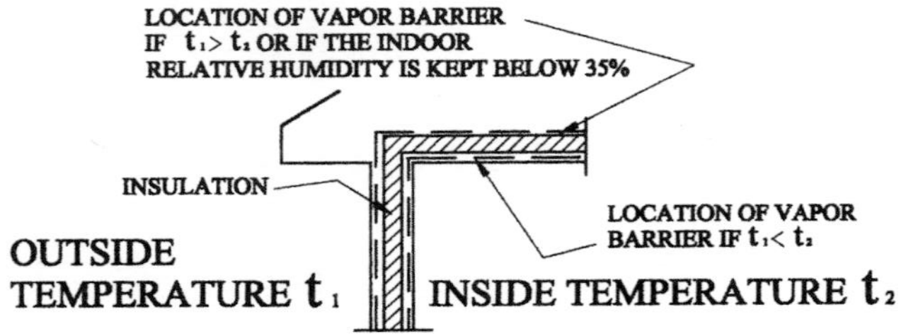

LOCATION OF VAPOR BARRIER IF $t_1 > t_2$ OR IF THE INDOOR RELATIVE HUMIDITY IS KEPT BELOW 35%

LOCATION OF VAPOR BARRIER IF $t_2 < t_1$

INSULATION

OUTSIDE TEMPERATURE t_1

INSIDE TEMPERATURE t_2

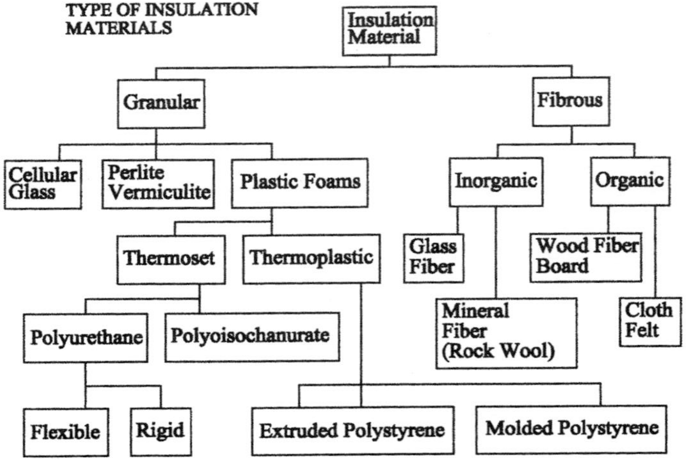

FIGURE 9.6 Vapor permeability of materials, perm ratings of components, and type of insulation materials.

rate of exchange means that in one hour half of the air contained in a house is exchanged. In order to limit this dispersion of air (and consequentially heat), a rate of maximum air leakage is assigned to many elements like windows or doors by associations and codes. For example, the maximum rate of 9.0 ft^3/(h • ft^2) under a pressure of 1.57 psf is assigned to residential or commercial windows by the American Architectural Manufacturers' Association (AAMA). In a window 3' x 2', then, the maximum air leakage allowable becomes 54 ft^3 per hour.

The strategy that has been adopted to reduce air leakages, vapor build-up, and water penetration is to introduce an air barrier and a vapor barrier as well as to control, if necessary, the pressures that are applied on the exterior skin of the exterior wall. These pressures are caused by having two different conditions on the outside and inside face of the wall. Mitigating the effect of these conditions on the building is achieved by employing various techniques as well as by making sure the finish is detached from what can be called the back-up wall.

An air barrier, in reality an air retarder (since it does not stop the air completely), is an element that prevents the flow of air without preventing vapor migration. In addition, since an air retarder is applied on the outside of the structure, it must also stop water from infiltrating the assembly. An air retarder should allow as little air leakage as possible. The standards that rule the performance of the air retarders is ASTM E 1677 *Standards Specifications for an Air Retarder Material or System for Low Rise Frame Building Walls* and require that materials used as air retarders should not exceed 0.06 ft^3/(min • ft^2). For vapor permeability, see Figure 9.6. Often building paper is used for this purpose. One negative aspect of building paper is that, since the various sheets must overlap and the edges and joints must be sealed to be water repellent, it does not allow vapor to pass. As an alternative to building paper 5 to 10 mil plastic sheets having micropores that allow vapor to travel are used. In masonry construction a good air retarder consists of a cold coat of asphalt emulsion applied on the exterior face of the wall.

Before we consider the various materials that can be used as vapor retarders, we need to explore a few concepts related to the mechanics of how vapor travels and its effect on the components of an assembly.

We have previously indicated that vapor exerts a pressure independent of the pressure applied by dry air. We have also indicated that there is a maximum amount of vapor that air can hold at a certain temperature before it becomes saturated. The pressure applied by vapor is called *saturation vapor pressure*. The dew point, which is the point at which vapor condenses into a liquid form, occurs when the concentration of vapor has caused the air to pass the saturation point. The dew point, therefore, is reached not only by adding vapor to the air, but also with a change in water temperature (from warmer to colder) without any of the vapor present in the air being extracted.

An indication of the status of the ratio between the humidity present in the air and the amount of humidity present at the saturation point for a specific temperature is given by what is called the relative humidity. Alternatively, the ratio can be calculated between the weight of the water vapor held in the air and the weight of the water vapor held in the saturated air. It has to be noted that vapor pressure can be considerable. For a difference in temperature in the order of 60 °F and a relative humidity of 40 percent indoor and 60 percent outdoor, the difference of the pressure could reach 20 psf, which is the pressure applied by very high-speed winds.

Vapor can transmigrate, either carried by air or by means of the permeability of the material. The latter characteristic allows vapor to move through an element that does not permit the passage of air. Therefore, even if we are able to stop air from migrating, an assembly is still required in order to prevent this second phenomenon, which is called vapor diffusion. The mechanism through which it happens is very similar to the movement of heat and is from an area of higher vapor pressure to an area of low pressure. The equation that determines vapor diffusion is:

$$w = \frac{m}{l}(P2 - P1)$$

where w is the weight of unit water that passes through a unit of material in a unit of time, expressed in gr/(h • ft2). The reference is 1 lb = 7000 grains (gr). L is the thickness of the component (in inches), $P1$ and $P2$ is the difference in pressure across the component and m is the permeability of the material. The pressure is quantified in inches of mercury (Hg) where 1 in. Hg = 70.72 psf. As with the R-value, where rL = R, the quantity m/L is equal to M, that is called the permeance of the component. The equation to calculate the vapor diffusion then becomes w=M (P2–P1). This means that permeance (M) = permeability of the material (m)/thickness of the component (L). This is also called *perm rating* (see Figure 9.6).

There are two types of condensation: surface (which occurs on the surface of a material or on the outside skin of an assembly (i.e., the interior gypsum wallboard), and interstitial condensation (which forms within an assembly or inside a material). The second type is the most problematic because it is less visible, evaporates with difficulty, and produces the most damage to the components of an assembly.

Vapor retarders are components of an assembly made of materials that have a perm rating of 1.0 or less. The reference for vapor retarders is the ASTM Standard E96 *Standard Test Methods for Vapor Transmission of Materials*. Using this standard, two methods are applied in order to determine the perm rating of materials. When comparing performances it is important to use results from the same methods, since the values obtained by using one or the other are different. A vapor retarder should be placed, for a climate with 4000 heating degree days or more, on the inside face of the insulation. In regions with a warm and humid climate like Florida or the Gulf Coast, the vapor retarder should be placed on the outside. If the winter indoor humidity is kept at or below 35 percent and the climate is mixed, usually a vapor retarder on the inside face is not necessary. Vapor retarders should never be placed on both sides of the insulation.

Vapor retarders can be classified as flexible or coatings. Sheets of material like polyethylene constitute the first category, while the second is comprised of products like paint or asphalt emulsion, polymeric compounds or resins. They can be sprayed or painted.

In choosing a good vapor retarder, not only the perm rating should be considered but also the resistance of the material to tearing, its ability to prevent the passage of water, and its durability. Clear polyethylene in 4, 6, 8, or 10 mil is commonly used. In many cases, the use of this material has been questioned because of the forces applied on it by the migration of air and vapor, which is induced by negative and positive pressure created by wind, temperature and vapor. For higher strength, a cross-laminated polyethylene or fiber-reinforced polyethylene can be used.

The effectiveness of vapor retarders depends also on the level of ventilation that is provided in the cavity or the attic space. In fact, vapor retarders and ventilation (or permeability to vapor migration) can be considered one system. From this point of view, two basic functions should be attributed to vapor retarders: minimizing the migration of vapor and not trapping vapor in the assembly, thereby allowing the materials to breathe. In a wall assembly, therefore, if the vapor retarder is placed on the inside, the air retarder/water repellent membrane needs to allow vapor to go through and be dispersed in the air. Conversely, if the vapor retarder is placed on the outside face of the insulation, then the inside finish should be permeable to vapor (see Figure 9.7).

In attic spaces ventilation is prescribed by codes (1/300 minimum of attic area, although a 1/100 ratio is recommended). This ventilation is normally provided through screens placed along the eaves of the roof. The amount of ventilation is one aspect; the other is the movement of air that must be provided through cross ventilation. In sloping roofs this is accomplished by using gable ventilation, ridge ventilation, turbine ventilators or gable fan (see Figure 9.8). In flat roofs, a space between the insulation and the sheeting must be provided. In this case, cross ventilation is almost always sufficient if the screens installed under the eaves are placed on opposite sides (see Figure 9.8).

Vapor retarders are placed also under slab on grade in order to avoid the migration of moisture through the slab (due to capillary action). This is in the form of 6 to 10 mil polyethylene sheets placed on a bed of gravel or sand. In crawl spaces, to prevent accumulation of vapor in the space, a vapor retarder is usually placed between two layers of sand. In addition, codes require a minimum ventilation of 1 sq. ft. clear for every 1,500 sq. ft. of crawl space area. The importance of installing a vapor retarder is demonstrated by the fact that in its absence the required ventilation increases ten fold.

WATER MOVEMENT

The control of water movement is one of the major functions of the building envelope. There are two primary sources of leakage in a building: rain and subsoil water. Gravitational forces constitute the main factor that drives rainfall. It seems therefore logical to think in vertical terms when defining strategy in the design of elements that functionally are supposed to keep the rain out of the building. In reality, there are as many vertical as there are horizontal (or even

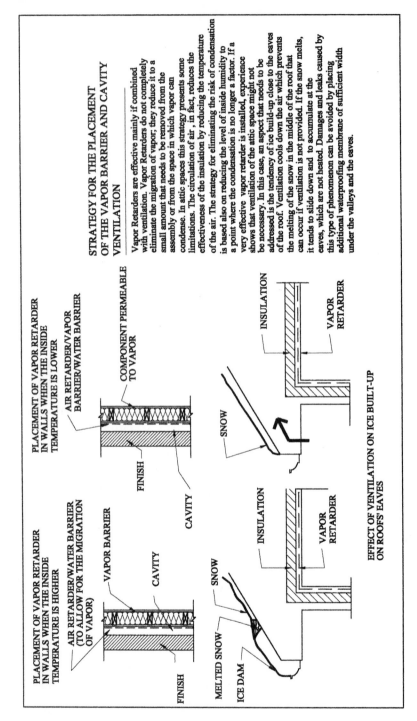

STRATEGY FOR THE PLACEMENT OF THE VAPOR BARRIER AND CAVITY VENTILATION

Vapor Retarders are effective mainly if combined with ventilation. Vapor Retarders do not completely eliminate the migration of vapor; they reduce it to a small amount that needs to be removed from the assembly or from the space in which vapor can condense. In attic spaces this strategy presents some limitations. The circulation of air , in fact, reduces the effectiveness of the insulation by reducing the temperature of the air. The strategy for eliminating the risk of condensation is based also on reducing the level of inside humidity to a point where the condensation is no longer a factor. If a very effective vapor retarder is installed, experience shows that ventilation of the attic space might not be necessary. In this case, an aspect that needs to be addressed is the tendency of ice build-up close to the eaves of the roof. Ventilation cools down the air which prevents the melting of the snow in the middle of the roof that can occur if ventilation is not provided. If the snow melts, it tends to slide down and to accumulate at the eaves, which are not heated. Damages and leaks caused by this type of phenomenon can be avoided by placing additional waterproofing membrane of sufficient width under the valleys and the eaves.

PLACEMENT OF VAPOR RETARDER IN WALLS WHEN THE INSIDE TEMPERATURE IS LOWER

AIR RETARDER/VAPOR BARRIER/WATER BARRIER

COMPONENT PERMEABLE TO VAPOR

FINISH

CAVITY

PLACEMENT OF VAPOR RETARDER IN WALLS WHEN THE INSIDE TEMPERATURE IS HIGHER

AIR RETARDER/WATER BARRIER (TO ALLOW FOR THE MIGRATION OF VAPOR)

VAPOR BARRIER

CAVITY

FINISH

INSULATION

VAPOR RETARDER

SNOW

EFFECT OF VENTILATION ON ICE BUILT-UP ON ROOFS' EAVES

INSULATION

VAPOR RETARDER

SNOW

MELTED SNOW

ICE DAM

FIGURE 9.7   Strategy for the placement of the vapor barrier and cavity ventilation.

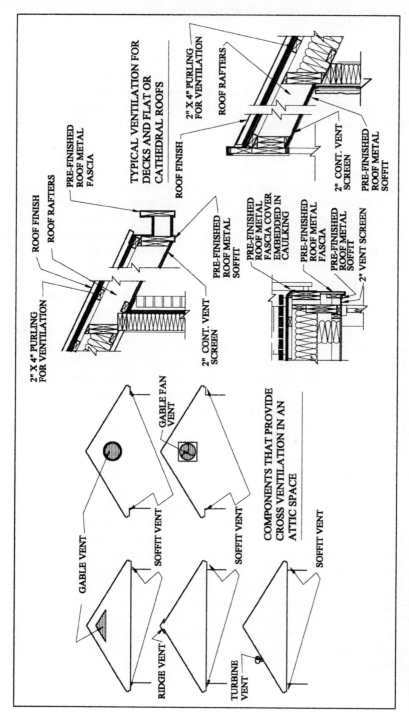

FIGURE 9.8 Type of vents for attic space and ventilation of roofs.

upward) forces that can drive water into materials and assemblies. Like the movement of air and vapor, differential pressure as well as wind and temperature can direct water, thus determining a pattern that is sometimes unpredictable. It is therefore important to make sure that all the variables are factored into the final equation. Basic strategies include: slope of horizontal surfaces, overlapping of elements, inclusion in the design of capillary break, drip edge, caulking of joints (see Figure 9.9).

The above elements, while fundamental in maintaining a water-tight design, also contribute to a system that minimizes the impact of environmental elements. At this point we reintroduce the previously mentioned concept of the back-up wall. If this element is considered in relation to an outer component (such as a brick veneer skin), it becomes a drainage wall. This combination (which is not limited to the use of bricks as outer exterior skin) describes an exterior assembly that is called the rain screen design. The rain screen principles should be applied when the outside assembly or the material used is not thick enough or has a porosity that cannot prevent rain or humidity from reaching the inside face of the wall or those components of the wall that will deteriorate when in contact with water or excess vapor. The required thickness is a function of the permeability of the material. When the thickness of the wall is sufficient or its porosity has been improved with a finish or a product applied to it, the wall becomes the only barrier that is needed against the rain. Common materials used to build these types of walls are stones, concrete blocks, bricks, pre-cast or cast-in-place concrete.

What the rain screen tries to achieve is the equalization of the pressure applied on the outside face and on the inside face of the outer skin. In this way the suction that is created on the windward side of the building is neutralized. If the pressure on the outside face of the skin is greater than the pressure in the cavity, the rain is sucked into the cavity and pushed up the wall, soaking the membrane. It does not take winds of very high speed to produce this effect. In order to equalize the pressure, openings need to be provided in the outer skin (i.e., weep holes in brick veneer skins or screens in other types) that allow enough air in the cavity. If the cavity is sealed, the system will not perform as a rain screen assembly. The Brick Institute of America recommends a 24 inch maximum spacing of the weep holes. In addition, an outlet at the top of the compartment should be provided. In brick veneer walls this can be achieved by installing a metal vent brick (of the same dimensions as a brick) at the top near the shelf angles. One vent brick per cavity is the rule of thumb that can be used. In order for this principle to work the individual cavity compartments must be unobstructed.

The building is subject not only to positive but also to negative pressure on the leeward wind side. This means that the air in the cavity is encouraged to travel from the areas of high to low pressure. This can favor the penetration of rain in the cavity. Compartmentalization, therefore, is also another design principle that should be applied in rain screen design. At the corners of the building as well as at specific intervals that divide the area of the cavity, vertical and horizontal subdivisions should be installed. These subdivisions do not need to be airtight. As rule, for wind loads less than 15 psf a maximum compartment area should be 400 sq. ft. For higher wind speeds the compartments should not exceed 100 sq. ft. Horizontal elements in the compartmentalization are usually created by structural elements like shelf angles in brick construction (see Figure 9.10).

Since the outer skin has a certain porosity, some water is expected to pass through and collect in the cavity. This means that it must be allowed to escape. Weep holes or screens are provided at the bottom of the wall in order to eliminate the water (see Figure 9.10).

For the control of subsoil water the following are elements that should be incorporated in the design (see Figure 9.11): **a.** slope the finish grade away from the building, minimum ½ inch per foot; **b.** collect all the water from the roofs, canopies, balconies, decks, terraces and direct it through a piping or gutter system directly to the storm sewer; **c.** do not compact the soil directly against basement or foundation walls. Apply either a layer of gravel with a filter cloth against the soil or a drainage mat over the waterproofing or dampproofing; **d.** apply a waterproofing membrane or two coats of dampproofing on all the vertical surfaces enclosing living space. A careful analysis should be conducted to verify the water table and employ the most suitable product for the required application; **e.** install a 4" or 6" drain pipe all around the basement or foundation walls with the proper slope (¼ inch per foot), apply a filter cloth over it and surround the pipe with crushed gravel. Do not install below the foundation; **f.** install waterstops at cold joints.

As we have seen, many components and parts constitute a building. Different materials have different characteristics and are suitable for different functions. This aspect poses the problem of differential movement between the different parts. This movement, if not controlled, can contribute to the air, vapor and water leakage in the building.

MOVEMENT IN BUILDINGS

In construction, the approach to the analysis of the movement of different parts is not very different from any design approach: from the general to the detail, without losing the sense of continuity that this process requires (see Chapter 1).Therefore, a building must first be analyzed from the point of view of its overall shape in order to establish where building separation joints are required (see Figure 9.12). Then, when these parts are identified, each of them must be investigated to identify critical aspects and parts (i.e., meeting of different materials) to discover within each assembly where tolerances and movement allowances need to be provided. This is an analysis that should be conducted at one of the initial stages of the design (while the design is still developing) and is particularly critical in cases where definite dimensions of the space must be maintained and constraints do not allow flexibility of expansion of the overall dimensions of the building. These areas of functional non-tolerance need to be identified and the various allowances included in the design.

TYPICAL ELEMENTS USED IN THE CONTROL OF RAINWATER LEAKAGE

One of the fundamental rules that should be used in the control of rainwater leakage is the redundancy of the elements used. This principle guarantees a back-up secondary line of defense in case the primary element fails to perform its function. This can happen either because certain materials (like caulking) have a limited life span beyond which the material should be replaced, or because of exceptional events that might create unpredictable circumstances. It is especially this latter situation that creates the need for the redundancy. For example an overlapped joint, created to prevent water from entering using gravity as the mechanism of prevention, might be exposed to capillary action that will suck the water into the joint, making it ineffective. In many cases, since the thickness of the joint cannot be expanded, a capillary break is introduced to eliminate the effect of the suction. The same happens at the edge of a material. Even if the vertical surface under the overhang is sealed, a drip edge is still provided to prevent water to travel horizontally and reach the joint. Slopes of surfaces are provided in part for the same reason: to prevent water from reaching the most vulnerable parts of the building, usually the joints. In addition slopes allow water to be conveyed to controlled points of collection like drains and prevents water from remaining on the surface and puddling (with the risk of freezing and damaging the material or the assembly).

Overlapping between two different components can be created by introducing a third element that functions as transition between the two. Often this function is provided by the Flashing.
In the prevention of rainwater leaks, flashing is the most commonly used component. Flashing is made of different materials which need to be flexible enough to take the shape of the elements that it connects and be durable, and resistant. Aluminum, stainless steel, PVC, copper covered with asphalt saturated felt or mylar combined with fiberglass scrim and vinyl film bonded together are common materials or assemblies used.

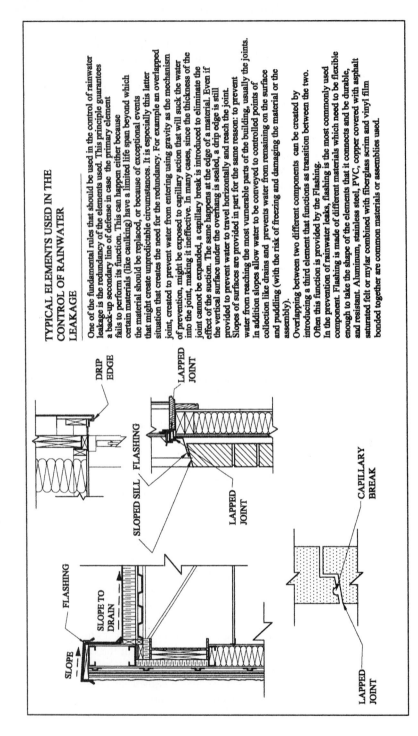

DRIP EDGE

LAPPED JOINT

SLOPED SILL FLASHING

LAPPED JOINT

FLASHING

SLOPE TO DRAIN

SLOPE

CAPILLARY BREAK

LAPPED JOINT

FIGURE 9.9 Typical elements used in the control of rainwater leakage.

RAIN SCREEN PRINCIPLES

A Rain Screen wall is composed of two fundamental elements: the Barrier Wall and the Back-up Wall. The first intercepts most of the rain, the second provides the secondary Water Barrier and the Air Retarder. In the case of tropical climates the surface of the back-up wall facing the cavity also functions as the Vapor Retarder.

The back-up wall provides the structural stability to the system as well. For this reason the Barrier Wall is tied back to the Back-up Wall with anchors. Because the two elements move independently, the design of the anchors must be vertically flexible but horizontally rigid. In addition vertical expansion joints must be provided at specific maximum intervals.

The cavity needs to allow the circulation of air, since its purpose is to equalize the pressure on both sides of the Barrier Wall. Without the equalization of the pressure, the rain water would be sucked towards the cavity and driven up into it.

Since the Barrier Wall might not be built with material the is totally waterproof, it is expected that some water will be collected in the cavity. At the bottom of it provision for draining it out must be introduced in the design. This can take the form of a screen or weep holes.

The above principles apply to every type of Rain Screen Wall and not only to Brick Veneer.

Rain Screen Design has some limitation since the equalization of the pressure does not happen instantaneously. In fact the external conditions change constantly with the wind that can sudden changes in its speed considerably. For this reasons it should not be assumed that the Back-up Wall does not need to perform as a waterproofing element. All the redundancy that should be applied in the design of a Non-Rain Screen Wall should be applied to a Rain Screen Wall.

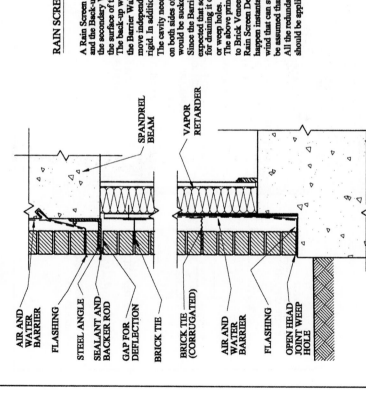

SPANDREL
BEAM

VAPOR
RETARDER

AIR AND
WATER
BARRIER

FLASHING

STEEL ANGLE

SEALANT AND
BACKER ROD

GAP FOR
DEFLECTION

BRICK TIE

BRICK TIE
(CORRUGATED)

AIR AND
WATER
BARRIER

FLASHING

OPEN HEAD
JOINT WEEP
HOLE

FIGURE 9.10 Rain screen principles.

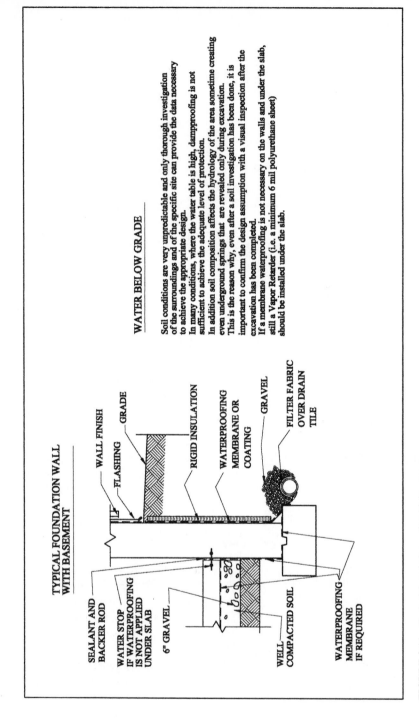

FIGURE 9.11 Typical foundation wall with basement.

9.24

As a guideline: we can reduce the causes of the movement of buildings to general categories: **a.** *thermal*, which is the type of movement induced in material by change in temperature. It is an actual physical change in the geometry of the element that either contracts or expands. The amount of movement is determined by the following formula:

$$\sigma_t = \alpha L \, (t_{max} - t_{min})$$

where σ_t is the amount of thermal movement, L is the length of the component, t_{max} and t_{min} are the respective maximum and minimum temperatures reached by the material, and α is the coefficient of thermal expansion. It is important to consider that the temperature is not the atmospheric temperature, but is the temperature of the material. The difference between the two can be as much as 60°F (33°C) depending on the type of material, wind speed, color or amount of insulation. As a rule of thumb 50°F (28°C) should be added to the difference between the maximum and minimum atmospheric temperature; **b.** *elastic and creep* are the stresses a material undergoes when a load is applied on it. In Chapter 6 we discussed the different loads and deformations. Some of the deformations are non-permanent and others are permanent. This depends on various factors: the magnitude of the load, the characteristics of the material (like the modulus of elasticity, see Figure 9.13), its dimensions and geometry as well as the amount of time the load has been applied on the component. Prolonged loading of a component can cause creep, which is a permanent deformation cause by loading of the component for long time. This deformation does not mean certain failure of the structural element. It does mean, though, that a stress might be transferred on other components, unless tolerances have been included in the design. For example, to absorb the deflection of a slab or a beam, on top of non-load bearing walls a space or a deflection panel must be provided (see Figure 9.12); **c.** *moisture*: in many materials, deformations are provoked by the absorption of moisture (see Figure 9.13).

The formula that calculates this potential deformation is: $\sigma_m = JL$ where σ_m is the expansion or the shrinkage of the component, J is the moisture coefficient, and L is the length of the component. In many cases, the geometrical deformation is reversible. In others (bricks that expands after been exposed to air or water, or concrete that shrinks during the curing period), the deformation is permanent. Moisture coefficient for bricks can be averaged to 0.0005, for concrete to 0.0006. For wood, the shrinkage occurs mainly along the cross section, because the fibers run perpendicular to it. It is in fact the pulp and not the fibers that lose moisture in the process of drying the wood. In the construction industry moisture content of wood is between 8 percent and 15 percent; **d.** *earthquake*: geometrical changes in the form of a building require that the parts structure be separated in order to create tolerances needed to minimize stresses. However, movements provoked by earthquakes can be considerable. For these reasons, the joint needs to be wider than a building joint. A prefabricated cover is inserted in the gap created in the structure; **e.** *foundation settlement* is movement that often happens between an

existing building and an addition. Because the existing building has already set-
tled, the new part will move during its own settlement. It is important, therefore,
to detail the connection between the existing and the new section in order to allow
for this movement and prevent cracking of the structure and of finishes; **f.** *vibration*: equipment, machinery and outside causes (i.e., trains or airplanes) can produce vibrations that can be not only noisy but also dangerous because they can
deform considerably a component if this component is restricted in its movement.
These deformations are different from moisture or heat induced changes. Vibrations are more related to possible impacts of one component on another. On the
other hand, friction might create heat that in turn will cause most of the materials
to expand. For this reason tolerances should be provided.

These deformations, because of their particular characteristics, need different
types of joints that can be listed under the following categories: **a.** *building separation* is a type of joint that runs continuously from the roof to the foundations
(see Figure 9.12). It must be considered that the separation into autonomous elements, from the building code point of view, does not create two buildings: by
law the building is still one structure. The continuity of any prescribed fire separation, therefore, needs to be maintained (vertically and/or horizontally) for the
complete extent of the joint; **b.** *construction*: this is a joint used to control the
location of joints in large areas that cannot be constructed as monolithic element
(also called cold joints). Typical examples are a large slab on grade or the connection between sections of long vertical walls or between a wall and a slab. Construction joints are often combined with expansion or control joints. Where these
types of joints are exposed to the risk of water leakage, they are often sealed with
waterstops (see Figure 9.11); **c.** *expansion*: this is a joint that allows movement
due to the expansion of one or more components. The joint filler in an expansion
joint that must be compressible. An example of expansion joint is the one provided in a masonry wall. Without it, the mortar or the bricks would break due to
the stress caused by the expansion; **d.** *control*: These types of joints are provided
because of the shrinkage of the material. They either provide a gap between the
components that constitute an element (i.e., a brick wall), or the joint determines
the location of the cracking (usually when the element is monolithic). In the latter case a control joint creates a weakness in the element that does not prevent the
deformation or the cracking from appearing, but simply controls where such
deformation or cracking will occur. For example, in a large slab on grade that will
be exposed, control joints are recommended at intervals of 10 feet to 15 feet.
Where a gap is created it is filled with compounds that would prevent water and
air leakage through the element. These materials do not need to be compressible
since the two components eventually will move away from each other. However,
their elastomeric properties are important. In other cases, where the material that
is used needs to be rigid for structural reasons, an element is installed that would
prevent the bonding of the compound to the surfaces of the different components
(often located on each sides of the compound). In concrete block, for example,
where a control joint is provided, the common hole created by the two halves of
two concrete blocks (each on one side of the control joint) is filled with mortar

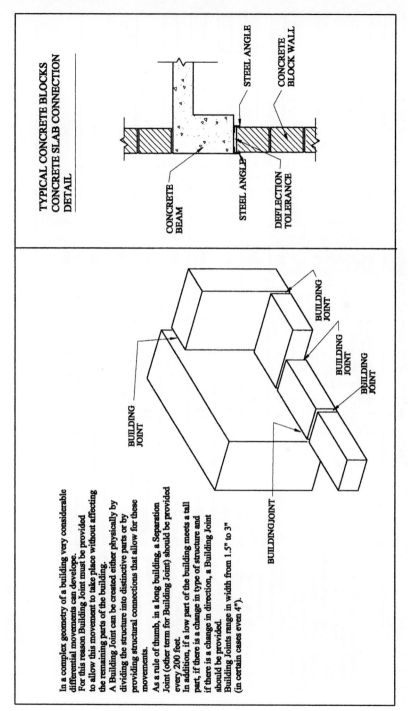

TYPICAL CONCRETE BLOCKS
CONCRETE SLAB CONNECTION
DETAIL

STEEL ANGLE

CONCRETE
BLOCK WALL

CONCRETE
BEAM

STEEL ANGLE

DEFLECTION
TOLERANCE

In a complex geometry of a building very considerable differential movements can develop.
For this reason Building Joint must be provided to allow this movement to take place without affecting the remaining parts of the building.
A Building Joint can be created either physically by dividing the structure into distinctive parts or by providing structural connections that allow for these movements.
As a rule of thumb, in a long building, a Separation Joint (other term for Building Joint) should be provided every 200 feet.
In addition, if a low part of the building meets a tall part, if there is a change in type of structure and if there is a change in direction, a Building Joint should be provided.
Building Joints range in width from 1.5" to 3" (in certain cases even 4").

BUILDING JOINT

BUILDING JOINT

BUILDING JOINT

BUILDING JOINT

BUILDINGJOINT

FIGURE 9.12 Typical location of building joints. Typical concrete blocks–concrete slab connection detail.

DEFORMATION DUE TO MOISTURE AND TEMPERATURE FOR SELECTED MATERIALS

Materials that are exposed to change in temperature, loads, moisture and water penetration, as well as to forces like earthquakes undergo deformations of their geometrical dimensions. These changes, sometimes reversible, others not reversible, can produce considerable stresses if the material is not allowed to move. A restrained component can reach very easily its maximum tolerable stress and stop performing the function for which it has been designed.

When this occurs it means that the material is in a Plastic state, having gone beyond the elastic condition.

The factor that calculates the amount of deformation a material undergoes for a given load is the Modulus of Elasticity. It is constant for every type of material and it represents the ratio between the Strain (deformation per unit dimension) and the Stress (load per unit area):

$$E = \frac{Stress}{Strain}$$

	COEFFICIENT OF THERMAL EXPANSION PER °F	DEFORMATION DUE TO TEMPERATURE CHANGES		MOISTURE DEFORMATION ON WETTING FROM DRY TO SATURATED OR FROM SATURATED TO DRY	MODULE OF ELASTICITY E	FAILING STRESS COMPRESSION AND TENSION	DEFORMATION REQUIRED TO CAUSE FAILURE
		OF 80 °F PER CENT	OF 230 °F PER CENT	PER CENT			PER CENT
CONCRETE	6×10^6	0.05	0.14	0.03	2.5×10^6	2500 C / 250 T	0.10 / 0.01
BRICK	3×10^6	0.024	0.07	0.007	3×10^6	6000 C / 500 C	0.20 / 0.016
MARBLE	3×10^6	0.024	0.07	0.001	10×10^6	25000 C / 600 C	0.25 / 0.006
LIME STONE	3×10^6	0.024	0.07	0.001	10×10^6	25000 C / 600 C	0.25 / 0.006
SANDSTONE	7×10^6	0.056	0.016	0.07	5×10^6	2500 C / 600 C	0.25 / 0.006
REINFORCED POLYESTER	10×10^6	0.08	0.23	0.001	1.5×10^6	15000 T	1.00
STEEL	7×10^6	0.08	0.16	NONE	30×10^6	4000 T	0.13
COPPER	10×10^6	0.056	0.23	NONE	17×10^6	50,000 T	0.29
ALUMINUM	14×10^6	0.08	0.32	NONE	10.3×10^6	4000 T	0.39

FIGURE 9.13 Deformation due to moisture and temperature for selected material.

that provides the stiffening of that part of the wall. To avoid adherence of the mortar to the interior surface of both blocks, felt impregnated with asphalt separates the mortar from one of the surfaces. In this case the exterior part of the gap is filled with an elastic compound to create a watertight and airtight seal; **e.** *isolation*: as the name indicates, these joints are provided to isolate components from other elements that might cause the one or the other to deform or crack. An example could be a slab on grade separated from a steel column. In creating isolation joints, an element that prevents the bonding of the two components is inserted. A common material can be wax paper or a fiber sheet.

The materials with which the joints are filled are various and they need to be applied in specific sequences with specific modalities. They are: **a.** *primer,* used to improve the adherence of the sealing compounds to the substrate; **b.** *backer rod*, constituted by a compressible material that is inserted in the gap. A backer rod has three functions: to provide a backing for the compound that will ultimately fill the gap, to allow the sealant compound to be worked and compacted with tools and to fill the gap temporarily until the final sealant is put in place; **c.** *bond breaker* that prevents the sealant compound from bonding to a third surface that will create stresses on it. These stresses could reach the point of detaching the compound from the surface of the component; **d.** *sealant compound*, which is the material that fills the gap and creates the weather tight seal.

Sealants are rated in terms of their capacity for compression and elongation. If the characteristics of the material allow a compound to stretch and compress 25 percent more or less than its normal volume, it is called a Class 25 sealant. They fall into three categories: low-range sealants (class 5 or less), medium-range sealants (class up to 9.5) and high-range sealants (class above 9.5).

All the above materials must be compatible with each other and with the surfaces on which they will be applied. For this reasons material like concrete or bricks must be scrubbed to remove any chemicals applied to them (instead of washing these surfaces, sometimes agents compatible with the primer, backer rod and sealing compound might be used).

The formula that calculates the required width of a sealed joint is:

$$J = (100/x)\ (W)$$

where J is the width of the sealed joint, x is the class of the compound and W is the unsealed gap determined by the analysis of factors like moisture, heat, construction tolerances.

ROOFS

One of the major elements of the envelope system is the roof. Four main parameters must be taken into account in the design of a roof: wind, rainwater, moisture and thermal performance. A selection of various roofing materials is available and the choice is dependent on performance, aesthetical considerations, technical characteristics and cost.

Among the above aspects, slope is one of the determining factors in narrowing down the range of systems that can be used. From this point of view we can categorize roofs as low slope or high slope.

1. Low slope roofs can be built with one of two systems: **a.** *conventional system*, commonly composed of five major components: roof deck, vapor retarder, thermal insulation, roofing membrane and flashing as well as a top cover (see Figure 9.14). In this system, the membrane is installed above the insulation. The advantages of this system are: it protects the insulation and allows a wide range of choices in the type of insulating materials; the membrane can be serviced and checked easily; certain systems do not require the top cover. However the disadvantages are: the membrane is exposed to thermal environmental variations and moisture can be trapped between the membrane and the vapor retarder; **b.** *protected membrane roof system (PMR)*: this system is composed of four major components: roof deck, roofing membrane, flashing, thermal insulation and top cover (in this system the membrane is also the vapor retarder, see Figure 9.14). The advantages of this system are that it protects the membrane from damage and temperature fluctuations, and it does not trap the insulation between the membrane and the vapor retarder. The disadvantages are that the insulation is exposed to the weather so the system requires the installation of insulating materials only suitable for exterior, and a top cover is required to hold down the insulation.

2. High slope roofs: the fundamental elements of the high slope roofs are: deck, vapor retarder, thermal insulation, covering or membrane and flashing (see Figures 9.14 and 9.15).

Each component of the various systems can be built with different materials. The following is a review of different options for each system and of the characteristics of each option.

The Deck. This is the structural support and the base on which the other elements rest. Common types of decks are structural concrete, steel decks, lightweight insulated concrete, wood planks or panels. The properties of the deck that should be considered before choosing the type of deck or finalizing the roof design are: flexibility (a flexible deck under load will influence the slope of the roof and might redirect water away from the drainage. In addition the flexibility might introduce stresses on the membrane if it is fully bonded to the deck); the material (decks can function as vapor retarder if their perm rate is low and the continuity can be maintained); flammability (fire ratings are a fundamental attribute for certain types of constructions); ability to maintain the surface continuity and support the membrane (cracking in concrete, for example might be too wide for the membrane to bridge over without failing. Inspection of the decks before applying the membrane is fundamental).

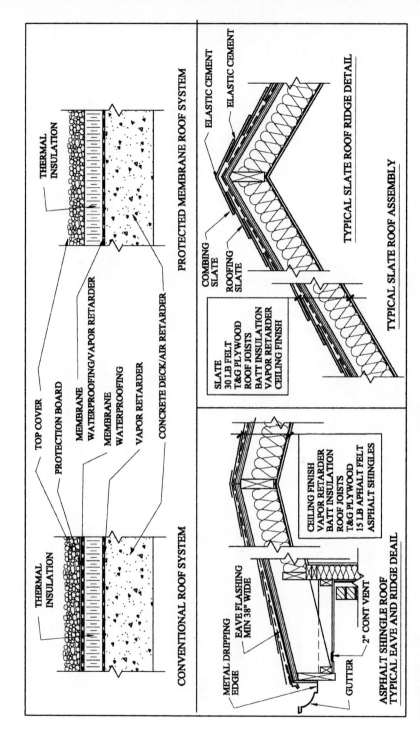

FIGURE 9.14 Conventional roof system, protected membrane roof system, asphalt shingle roof typical eave and edge detail. Typical slate roof assembly.

THERMAL INSULATION

TOP COVER

PROTECTION BOARD

MEMBRANE WATERPROOFING/VAPOR RETARDER

MEMBRANE WATERPROOFING

VAPOR RETARDER

CONCRETE DECK/AIR RETARDER

PROTECTED MEMBRANE ROOF SYSTEM

THERMAL INSULATION

CONVENTIONAL ROOF SYSTEM

ELASTIC CEMENT

ELASTIC CEMENT

COMBING SLATE

ROOFING SLATE

TYPICAL SLATE ROOF RIDGE DETAIL

TYPICAL SLATE ROOF ASSEMBLY

SLATE
30 LB FELT
T&G PLYWOOD
ROOF JOISTS
BATT INSULATION
VAPOR RETARDER
CEILING FINISH

CEILING FINISH
VAPOR RETARDER
BATT INSULATION
ROOF JOISTS
T&G PLYWOOD
15 LB ASPHALT FELT
ASPHALT SHINGLES

METAL DRIPPING EDGE

EAVE FLASHING MIN 38" WIDE

2" CONT VENT

GUTTER

ASPHALT SHINGLE ROOF
TYPICAL EAVE AND RIDGE DEAIL

9.31

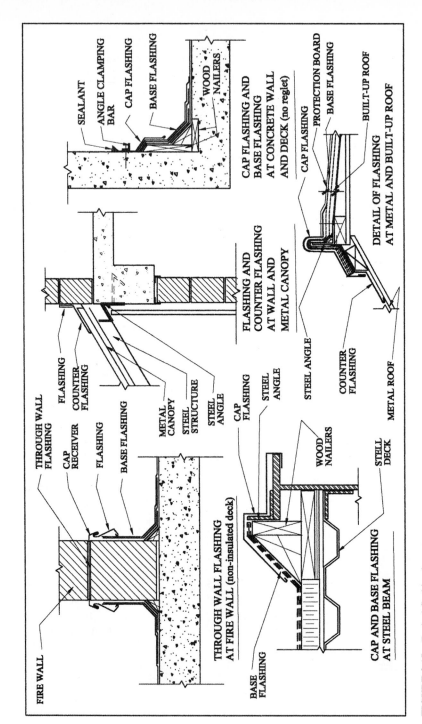

FIGURE 9.15 Typical flashing layouts.

9.32

Vapor Retarder. As we have already seen in this chapter, vapor barriers should be placed on the warm side of the insulation (in order to be below the dew point) and used in cold climates where the temperature may fall below 45°F or where inside humidity is high. In a roof this function can be performed by one element or a series of elements that, when working together, provide the necessary continuity that an effective vapor retarder requires. In addition continuity needs to be provided between roof and wall vapor retarders. (because of the possible leakage of air at the perimeter of the roof). In the conventional roof assembly the vapor retarder is an individual component separate from the membrane; in the PMR the membrane functions also as vapor retarder (see Figure 9.14). Among the typical vapor retarders are: bituminous vapor retarders, polyethylene sheets or aluminum foil. In addition to the vapor retarder, an air retarder is necessary in order to minimize heat loss and reduce the transfer of moisture transported by the air of the building into the assembly. As in the case of the vapor retarders, the function of air retarders can be provided by various elements that work in combination. Usually, in conventional roofs, where the combined approach is necessary because of lack of continuity of a single component, the deck, the airtight membrane and the fasteners might provide the continuity necessary for the air retarder. In this case, the membrane needs to be sealed around the fasteners. In the PMR, when decks do not act as air retarders, commonly the membrane is the air retarder and no additional component needs to be installed. As with the vapor retarder, continuity needs to be provided between the roof and the wall air retarders (see Figure 9.15). Since air retarders, by definition, need to resist airflow, they are subject to wind up-lift (see Figure 9.15). For this reason, they need to be secured to a structurally sound sub-base. As is the case for vapor retarders, air barriers also should be located on the warm side of the insulation.

Insulating Material. This is a component of the roofing system that has various functions. The most obvious is to reduce the heat loss from the building. Other important functions are: to maintain the temperature of the vapor barrier below the dew point; to protect the membrane in a PMR system from UV radiations and to provide structural support to the paving in an accessible roof, deck or plaza. Insulation for the roof can be subdivided into two major categories: porous and non-porous. The first type, which includes open cell plastics and fibrous insulation, is mainly associated with conventional roofing. The second, of which the closed cell type is a major component, is used in PMR roofing. The ratio between heat loss and amount of insulation is not linear. If the amount of insulation in a roof is doubled the heat loss is cut in half, while if it is doubled again, the heat loss becomes one quarter of the original loss. This means that the curve created by the ratio will rise sharply indicating that, if insulation is increased considerably, a minimum decrease in heat loss is experienced.

The performance of the insulation can be diminished by the following factors: **a.** *amount of moisture*: as we have seen in the earlier discussion on thermal performance, water has a low thermal resistance compared to the air trapped in the insulation material. Even a small amount (i.e., 1 percent) of increase in the moisture content of the insulation can create in certain assemblies a double heat loss. In order to remove moisture that might be trapped in the insulation, ventilation needs to be provided. The insulation will absorb most of the water through its horizontal edges. In the case of the upper edge, any cover (like pavers or concrete topping) should not rest directly on the insulation but spacers should be provided. The lower surface of the insulation is more critical. If an air space is provided, the effectiveness of the insulation will diminish. For this reason closed cell insulation provides the best answer to moisture penetration in the roof insulation; **b.** *aging*: insulation material tends to lose its effectiveness with time. Granular insulation enhanced with the use of gasses is particularly sensitive to aging deterioration, with consequential drop in the R-value. In order to minimize aging, foils are applied to the outside face of the insulation. They have also the function of minimizing moisture absorption; **c.** *thermal bridging*: this can be caused by gaps between the insulation sheets, elements of the roof system (i.e., fasteners, curb components or building structural members) that are connected to the outside face of the insulation or roof surface as well as to the elements below the insulation, This potential problem can be resolved by: reducing considerably the gap between the insulation boards, installing multi-layer insulation or through the use of shiplap joints. In the case of components of the roof system or elements of other systems, the introduction of thermal breaks made with material with high thermal resistivity can be a solution. Another solution can be to insulate these elements from the outside temperature (see the *Thermal Aspects and Properties of Materials* section in this chapter); **d.** *airflow*: where air circulates it reduces the ability of the insulation to prevent heat loss.

ROOFING MATERIAL

This component is subdivided into roofing materials for low and high slope roofs. The following are commonly available:

Low Slope Roofs

Roofing materials for this type of roof are essentially membranes. There are many types of membranes that can be generically differentiated: **a.** *built-up roofs (BUR):* made of several layers of felt (from three to five and as few as two if polyester felt is used) impregnated with bitumen (type I, II, III, IV or V characterized by different melting points that makes them suitable for different applications). Felts commonly used are glass fibers although organic felts are also used. In the traditional application, a first layer of felt (heavier than the subsequent ply felt sheets) is applied either on bitumen bed or nailed to the deck. Even if it is nailed, it is important that the felt be laid over a first coat of bitumen since this will guarantee the adhesion of the felt to the substrate. Subsequent layers are applied on top with each felt mopped with hot bitumen to create the required waterproofing and the bonding between the layers. In addition to hot applied bitumen, cold applied emulsions can be used. A variation of a BUR is a PMR built-up roof system where a closed cell type of insulation is placed over the membrane instead of under it. On the insulation a layer of ¾ inch crushed stones or pavers is installed to protect the membrane and against wind up-lift forces. Slopes can vary between ¼ inch to ½ inch per foot. Potential problems are related to the presence of moisture or air during the application, which can lead to blistering. Traffic can squeeze the asphalt out of the felt, creating voids; severe overheating of the asphalt causes it to become too hard when it cools; **b.** *prefabricated sheets*, which can be subdivided into: *thermoplastic* membranes that can be welded together using heat because there is no vulcanization of the molecules. These types of membranes (i.e., PVC) are resistant to very critical weather conditions, bacterial growth and pollutants. They are also easily repaired if minor damages occur. Part of this category are: PVC (polyvinyl chloride), PVC blends, EIP (ethylene interpolymer), CPA (copolymer alloys); *elastomeric sheets* made of synthetic rubber that has been through a curing process in the factory that transforms the material into a thermoset product. They have considerable tensile strength and good resistance to pollutants and UV. Part of this category are: EPDM (Ethylene-Propylene-Diene Monomer) and Neoprene (polychloroprene); *elastomeric non-vulcanized sheets* cure through exposure to the sun once the membrane is applied on the roof. This type of membrane includes: CSPE (chlorosulfonated polyethylene), CPA (chlorinated polyethylene), PIB (polyisobutylene), NBP (butadiene acrylonitrile); *modified bituminous sheets* are made of bitumen and modifying polymers. The result is a superior grade of bitumen. The amount of modifier varies, giving approximately 12 grades of modifiers that enhance certain characteristics more than others. These membranes can be applied made by torching the back, with a self-adhesive backing or mopping the adhesive. The polymer modifiers are SBS (styrene-butadiene-styrene), APP (atactic polypropylene), and IPP (isotactic polypropylene); **c.** *cast in situ:* they can be subdivided into: *hot applied rubberized asphalt* which is a monolithic membrane applied hot on the deck. A modified version is two-ply with a polyester mat in between; *cold applied liquid compound.* These materials cannot be applied below freezing temperature. Generally they are either rolled or sprayed; *polyurethane foam roof* is made of three components: the polyurethane foam, a protective cover and a vapor retarder. The foam is ejected with a gun and solidifies, expanding 20 to 30 times its original volume in a matter of seconds. The foam is sensitive to UV radiation. The coating needs to be highly waterproof to protect the foam that is sensitive to water.

High Slope Roofs

Roofing materials for this type of roof vary considerably. The following is a general selection: **a.** *asphalt shingles* are composed of a reinforcing mat, asphalt coating and granules. Many are self-adhesive and they come in many colors and styles; **b.** *fiber-cement* shingles simulate wood shingles, slate and tiles with the advantages of higher fire rating and, in many cases, less weight. Many styles and colors are available; **c.** *metal roofing*, one of the most versatile, includes panels as well as shingles. Aluminum, steel and copper are the metals used. The panels come in four different types: exposed fasteners, traditional metal roofing, architectural standing seam, and structural standing seam. The exposed fasteners are used in very inexpensive buildings. The difference between architectural and structural standing seam is that the first type does not have the structural capacity to span between secondary structural members and therefore needs a continuous support underneath. The aluminum painted and the aluminum coated steel require a minimum slope as low as ½ inch per foot, while the others should be used in roofs with a slope not less than 3:12. These two types do not require any underlay (although it is always beneficial to provide a certain amount of redundancy). In all the other types of metal roofs (panel and shakes-shingles) an underlay consisting of a 30 lb. felt is required; **d.** *slate* is a fairly heavy, very durable natural material. It is available in a variety of natural colors, although some of the colors can change with the exposure of the slate to the weather and the sun. Slates whose color does not change much are called *permanent* slate; those in which the color changes considerably are called *weathering* slate. There are two grades: standard commercial slate and textural slate. The difference is that the second is delivered in a variety of size and thickness. The first is sorted at the source. The second is less expensive. The thickness is approximately ¼ inch. The minimum slope of the roof is 4:12. Common underlay over plywood is 30 lb (see Figure 9.14); **e.** *tiles*: this is another heavy product made out of clay or concrete, available in a variety of colors and sizes. The minimum slope of the roof should be between 3:12 and 4:12. A common underlay is a 30 lb. felt; **f.** *wood shakes* are a traditional West Coast wood roofing material. Cedar is the most common species that is used (although redwood and southern yellow pine are also common). The wood is split at least on one side to give them a rough look that is very suitable for the West Coast style of architecture among others. Wood shakes can be pressure-treated either for fire and/or weather. The roof should have a 4:12 minimum slope. Common underlay is a 30 lb. felt on open or solid sheathing; **g.** *shingles*: are similar to shakes but sawn and thinner. This process gives them a smooth appearance. The minimum roof slope needs to be a 4:12 ratio with a maximum of 12:12 ratio. Common underlay is 30 lb. asphalt felt on open or solid sheathing.

Top Covering Material. This is installed especially in low-slope roofs to protect the membrane from the UV radiation and, in systems where it is necessary in order to counteract the wind uplift. Covering materials can take various forms: pavers, gravel, liquid-applied materials, mineral and metal surfaces.

Where weight for wind up-lift is required, the pressure applied on the membrane combined with the slope of the roof might cause the membrane to slip along the surface of the deck (and if it does not slip, unnecessary stress is applied anyway). It is therefore important not to exceed the required weight. A roof should be always inspected after a storm to verify if the covering material is still placed properly and did not receive any damage. Hail is especially dangerous for covering materials.

Flashing. Typical applications include three components. They are: **a.** *base flashing*, the component that in low slope roofs connects with the membrane on one side and on the other extends over the parapet and is secured on the outside face of it. It is a part of the membrane system that is usually made either of the same material as the membrane or is compatible with it. This type of layout reduces the risk of leakage in case of failure of the counter flashing or the cap flashing. It also prevents water infiltrating behind the base flashing; **b.** *cap flashing*: This is the part that covers a parapet. Its main function is to protect the base flashing from UV radiation. As per the counter flashing, it should not be used if not required; **c.** *counter flashing*: it is not always used, since its main purpose is to protect the base flashing from UV radiation. In fact, if not required should not be installed since it conceals elements and renders maintenance of the membrane more difficult. In many cases, where the base flashing and the counter flashing are secured to elements that need to move relative to each other, it is important to keep the base flashing and the counter flashing separate by securing one to one element and the other to the other element (see Figure 9.15).

In general, flashing failures can be attributed to the following factors: the incompatibility between membrane and base flashing; failure of the caulking; lack of provision for differential movements between different parts of the system and/or of the building (especially when components are attached at the same time to these different parts); movement of the membrane which is pulled and with its movement drags the base flashing away from the parapet to the point of sometimes detaching it. In the various systems not all of the components listed above are present.

There are two fundamental forces to which the roof system needs to react: wind up-lift and lateral forces. The first is created especially by negative (suction) and positive (pressure) action of the air (see Figure 9.16). The second is produced by the horizontal migration of the components (i.e., the membrane or the deflection of the deck)) relative to each other. This movement is due, especially, to thermal fluctuation (i.e., in the case of expansion of the components) and load induced structural movements (i.e., related especially to deflection of the deck, inducing the membrane to slide along the deck).

In order to counteract these forces there are basically three types of applications: the membrane and the other components are loose-laid on the deck and the structural performance is provided by the weight of the ballast; the membrane fully or partially adheres to the deck and the stability of the remaining components is provided by the weight of the ballast; the system is mechanically fastened to the structural deck.

Exterior Walls

The exterior wall performance related to air, water and heat movement has been in principle already analyzed in this chapter. However, since exterior walls can be built in different materials and they can be structural or non-structural, we will

WIND PRESSURE AND UP-LIFT ON ROOFS

Type and intensity of wind forces on a roof depend on four major factors: wind velocity, the incident angle of the wind and the slope of the roof as well as the height of the parapet.

A positive pressure is potentially applied by the wind either blowing directly on the surface of the roof, or entering the interior space and pushing on the components from below.. If the component of the roof assembly that faces the interior is not adequately sealed, the positive wind pressure applied to it will transfer to the element above it. This cycle will continue until the wind finds a continuous barrier capable of stopping the transfer of air. If it reaches the waterproofing membrane , the wind will apply an uplift force on it. This force could displace the membrane if either the weight of the top cover, or the adherence of the membrane cannot counteract the pressure applied by the wind.

Negative pressure occurs where the air is stagnant. This can happen in different situations: near the leeward side of the parapet or on the leeward side of a sloped roof as well as on the windward side. As the wind is pushed up by the vertical elements of the building, it creates an angle, which is dependent on the speed of the wind and the height of the vertical elements. If the roof at that location slopes more than that angle, that part of the roof is under a positive pressure. As the angle decreases, the pressure diminishes up to a critical slope on which the pressure is minimized. If the slope is lessened further, the area starts to be under a negative pressure, because of vortices created on the layers of air below the edge of the flow of the wind. Lowering the pitch of the roof increases the amount of negative pressure up to a point where it is decreased again if the roof is designed to have a lower slope. As a parameter one can consider that in a building 100' wide and 250' long, the critical angle is 5 degrees for a building height of 20', while for a building 100' high it is 20 degrees and 30 degrees for a building 200' high.

In terms of the effect that the height of the parapet has on negative pressures, a 5' high parapet is required in order to minimize the negative pressure in a building 50' wide, 100' long and 25' high.

In a conventional system, air trapped in the assembly could create bellowing of the membrane if this air can collect in the area of the roof with the lowest negative pressure. Because the edges of the roof are the most critical area, careful consideration should be given to the continuity between the Vapor and Air Retarders of the roof and the wall .

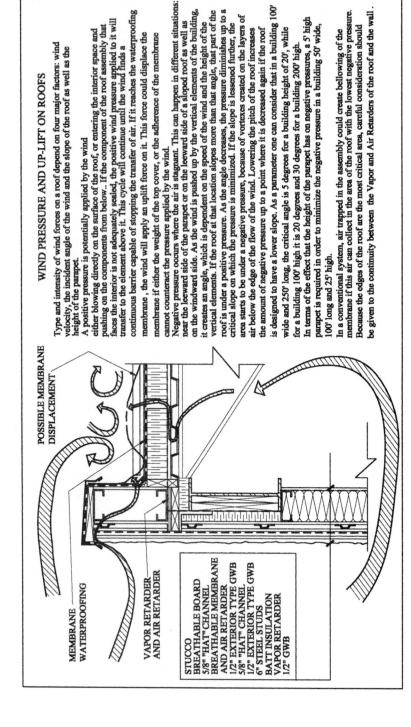

POSSIBLE MEMBRANE
DISPLACEMENT

MEMBRANE
WATERPROOFING

VAPOR RETARDER
AND AIR RETARDER

STUCCO
BREATHABLE BOARD
5/8" "HAT" CHANNEL
BREATHABLE MEMBRANE
AND AIR RETARDER
1/2" EXTERIOR TYPE GWB
5/8" "HAT" CHANNEL
1/2" EXTERIOR TYPE GWB
6" STEEL STUDS
BATT INSULATION
VAPOR RETARDER
1/2" GWB

FIGURE 9.16 Wind pressure and up-lift on roofs.

9.38

continue with an additional analysis of their characteristics. When the walls do not have a structural function, particular care should be taken in detailing the top of the wall. Movement and deflection of the structure should not place any load on these non-load bearing walls.

The choice of the materials with which the exterior walls are built is dependent on aspects like function, aesthetics, cost, weight, transparency, light penetration, structural requirements and/or cost. Although there are many possibilities, these walls are generally built of:

Concrete. This is a very plastic material that is flexible enough to achieve unique technical as well as aesthetical solutions. The system is composed of a concrete aggregate and a steel component. The concrete aggregate is a mix of cement, water and aggregate (sand and crushed rocks or gravel). The steel component is in the form of bars.

There are different types of cement that are used for different purposes: *Type I* is common cement used for general purposes; *Type II* is used for piers and heavy retaining walls with particular resistance to sulfates in draining structures; *Type III* reaches the required strength in approximately a week and is used when forms need to be removed quickly; *Type IV* is used in massive structures like dams; *Type V* is used where ground water contains a high percentage of sulfates.

Concrete needs time to cure. A 3000 psi concrete reaches 50 percent of its strength in three days; in seven days its strength is at 70 percent and at 28 days is 100 percent. For higher ultimate strength, the process may take a longer period. The ideal curing temperature is 73°F (28.3°C). During curing time and in temperatures above the 50°F, the concrete must be kept wet.

Concrete aggregate has a high resistance to compression forces, while steel behaves very well under tensile stress. The combination of the two characteristics provides a balanced behavior of the structural components to complex forces that might act on them (see Chapter 7). Reinforced concrete can be used as the only structural element or in conjunction with other structural systems. As exterior enclosure it is the most common system used for underground structures and foundations (see in this chapter topics regarding temperature, air and water control). Since cast-in-place concrete is not poured all at the same time, it is very important to key the various parts of the walls as well as to use water stops to prevent water penetration through the cold joints (see Figure 9.17). In addition, concrete is a porous material that needs to be treated if water is to be prevented from migrating through the wall. A membrane waterproofing should be installed or coats of dampproofing should be applied. Sealing of concrete walls should not be limited to underground construction but treatment should be applied to every concrete wall that is directly exposed to moisture or water. Control joints should be created every 30 feet (see also *Thermal Aspects and Properties of Materials* in this chapter). In addition to water membranes and dampproofing, there are products (such as crystals) that are added to the concrete mix to create a barrier against water. These products tend to expand in contact with water; therefore they are very effective especially in conditions where they are most required.

Concrete structures can be used in conjunction with a variety of other structural systems (i.e., wood, steel and/or masonry). Special connections must be used and/or pockets in the walls can provide the necessary bearing for some types of members (see Figures 9.17 and 9.18). Finishes on concrete walls can be applied using different techniques and products (compatible with the type of finish or finish element). Components like brick veneer, stone, granite and other hard natural elements are tied back to the wall with special ties (see Figure 9.17). Acrylic stucco can be applied as a thin coat (approximately ⅛ inch) like paint or troweled to achieve different textures. Stucco is not recommended on horizontal surfaces because in such conditions it is not resistant to water. The wall therefore should be protected either with more effective waterproofing or with flashing.

Masonry Walls. Are commonly built with concrete blocks, clay bricks, glass blocks and stonework. *Concrete blocks*, the most commonly used component of this type of wall, are used to construct walls made of single units bonded together with mortar. If the structural requirements demand it, cores within the units are filled with steel bars and structural grout. There are two types of units: Type I, although more expensive, are moisture-controlled units and require less stringent layout of control joints. Type II carries higher moisture content, therefore control joists need to be placed more carefully. In addition, units are graded. The N grade is intended more for veneer use and where moisture control is desired. Grade S is for general purpose where only moderate moisture control is necessary. The units are also identified by width, height and length. Their nominal size is usually ⅜ inch larger than the actual size. This means that the nominal size includes normally the width of the mortar joint. The widths of the concrete block units are 4", 6", 8", 10" and 12". The standard height is 4" and 8". The usual length is 16" and 18". Concrete brick length is 8" and 12" and the typical height is 2⅔ inch.

There are four types of mortar: Type N, S, O and P. The first type is of medium strength, suitable for walls above grade, where high compressive and transverse strength is not required. Type S is of high strength and is recommended where transverse strength is required and where winds reach speeds above 80 mph per hour (135 kph). Type M is a high strength mortar, used below grade where transverse strength is considerable. Type O is a low strength mortar used in non-load bearing walls and where the wall is not exposed to weathering. Mortar joint width ranges from ¼ to ¾ inch. Working the mortar with the appropriate tool and compressing it helps to compact the material, which then becomes more resistant to water. There are different types of joints that can be created by recessing them between the units or extruding the mortar to protrude in relation to the exterior face of the masonry wall.

Masonry walls, like concrete walls, require construction, expansion and control joints. Their width is dependent on the spacing of the joints: maximum distance of control joints should be 60 feet. Regardless of the distance, vertical control joints are needed in the following locations: over an opening (along one side only if the opening is less than 6 feet, otherwise the control joint should be placed on both sides), at pilasters, at change in wall thickness, where walls intersect, at any change in height, where control joints occur in walls on which the masonry wall rests, and where control joints are created in roofs or floors resting on the masonry wall. Expansion joints are needed: every 30 feet, at floor lines, within 10 feet of one side of a corner, at wall offsets, at change in wall height and below shelf angles (if shelf angle is required).

The units come in a variety of colors and textures. The greatest selection of colors is available in the smooth face *integral glazed* units. The texture can be smooth, split face, fluted or customized. This allows exposure of the concrete blocks without any additional finish (although sealers need to be applied to the outside face of the wall.) If a different finish is applied to it, such as brick or synthetic and natural stones, the principles indicated for concrete walls apply to concrete masonry walls as well.

Structural clay bricks, not to be confused with veneer bricks used only as a finish, are also commonly used for masonry walls. As in the case of many concrete block walls, structural clay brick walls combine the structure with the finish. Sealers need to be applied on the outside, since brick is a porous component. Portions of structural brick walls can span between supports without needing any other structural element (i.e., a shelf angle as is used for brick veneer). This can be particularly important in earthquake zones where it could be more expensive to secure veneer bricks than to build a suspended wall in structural bricks. The units come in different shapes and common widths are 3½, 5½ and 7½ inches (versus the 2½ inch and 3½ inch of the veneer units). The common heights are 2 ½ inch and 3½ inch, while the lengths are usually 7½ inch or 11½ inch. Other sizes are available and special orders can be placed (paying a premium). As with any element built with units, the geometry of a wall built with structural clay bricks starts with the basic dimensions of the units. This means not only that the dimensions of the wall should be a multiple of this module, but also that an indication of the starting point should be given on the drawings. This benchmark should correspond to one element of the building (i.e., the concrete floor slab) and it should be coordinated with other possible modular elements that might be incorporated in the design of the project.

Wood Stud Framing. Wherever combustible construction is allowed, wood framing is the most common type of wall built in North America (see Figure 9.19). Light frame construction (as this type of wood framing is called, which is differentiated from timber construction) is allowed in buildings up to three or four stories, if an approved sprinkler system is installed. Light frame construction is also mixed with timber construction where column joists and sub-floors are built with dimensional lumber beyond certain sizes (for the definition of timber construction consult the local building codes). In these cases walls are usually built using the same system as for light frame construction.

The thickness of lumber is categorized as: *board*, for lumber less than 2" nominal thickness; *dimensional*, from nominal 2" to, but not including, the nominal 5"; *timber*, for lumber 5" or more in the least dimension. Lumber can be provided as rough-sawn or surface finish. This becomes an aesthetical choice if part of the structure or members of the wall are to be left exposed.

Lumber is also graded for the features that enhance or reduce the value of the product in terms of its strength, durability or utility. The grades are divided into two major categories: *shop grade* for lumber rated visually for characteristics (like knots) that make it less attractive or more difficult to work. This type of grading applies to finished products (like furniture) or finishing material (like hardwood flooring or paneling); *stress grade*, the category in which lumber is graded for structural uses. This grading is particularly important in wood frame construction because it defines the type of stresses that can be placed on the components. Lumber for stress grading can be either visually or machine graded. When visually graded the lumber is checked for splits, knot density, decay and other characteristics that can lower the structural properties. Typical grades classed through the visual method are (in descending order of strength): *Select, Number 1, Number 2 or Construction.* When the lumber is machine evaluated, it is stressed in a non-destructive way to test its physical characteristics and then is visually inspected. These tests are more accurate than the visual test alone. Types of machine-graded lumber are: *MSR (Machine-Stressed-Rating), ME (Machine-Evaluated) and E-Rated Lumber.*

Walls in light frame construction are composed of vertical elements (called studs) and horizontal components (called plates, which are studs placed horizontally). The studs, because their shorter dimension is nominal 2", are part of the above-mentioned category of product called dimensional lumber. Any element in this category comes pre-cut in certain lengths (with 2 foot variations: 4', 6', 8' 10', 12' etc.). The width and height of the pieces are nominal (taken when the lumber has been only rough-cut and not yet refined). The relationship between the commonly used nominal sizes, the typical sizes, the board feet and the length of the cut lumber per 1,000 board feet is indicated in Figure 9.20 (one board foot is equal to 144 cubic inches. Width in inches x length in inches x height in inches divided by 144 gives the number of board feet).

In addition, wood is graded for moisture content. Wood can be dried in the yard or placed in a kiln to dry. If wood moisture content is very high (above 25 percent) it can cause considerable shrinkage after installation. Wood between 10 percent and 15 percent of moisture content will not undergo considerable movement during the drying process and these movements are controllable with proper detailing. Moisture content is not only important for shrinkage but also for structural characteristics. Moisture can reduce the strength of wood by 50 percent. On the other hand, some properties in wood that has only 8 percent moisture content might decrease with the further decrease of the percentage of moisture (when the wood becomes too brittle because of dryness).

To complete the structure of the wall, panels are nailed to the studs. The most common types of wood panels used are included in one of the following three categories: plywood, composite panels or mat-formed panels. The first type of panel is created by using plies of veneer wood, pressed and bonded together. Composite panels are created by using veneer or any other approved wood-based material. Mat-formed panels (of which a commonly used product is OSB) do not contain veneer. These panels provide lateral stability to the wall by connecting all the studs. There are degrees of stability that can be produced with the proper design. Ultimately, a wall can be made to act as a shear wall. In this case, not only the quality of the panel, but also the nailing pattern is important. In these cases, the wall needs to act as a vertical diaphragm capable of resisting vertical and horizontal forces (see Chapter 6 for shear walls).

There are three standards for structural panels in the U.S.: *U.S. Product Standard PS, 1-83*, which applies only to plywood. Wood species, glue type, moisture content, veneer grading, techniques of construction and workmanship are among the characteristics that are analyzed. Qualified agencies are appointed to certify that the products comply with the standards; *The Voluntary Product Standard PS 2-92* applies to all three types of wood-base panel products. These requirements create a common understanding in the industry on the performance and characteristics of wood-base panels. The products are tested and certified by approved test agencies; *APA (American Plywood Association) Performance Standard and Policies for Standard-Use Panels (PRP 108)* are similar to P2 but also include siding panels. Plywood is graded also according to the characteristics of the veneer used on the front and the back of the panel. The identification is made using two letters (i.e., A-A. B-C or C-C etc.), which indicate the grade of the two sides. The grades are as follow: *grade N*—natural finish with a smooth veneer surface, which is free of open defects. Six repairs made in wood only (parallel to grain) are allowed in a 6' x 8' panel; *grade A*—this plywood must be smooth and suitable for painting. 18 repairs can be made parallel to the grain (wood or synthetic); *grade B*—the surface must be solid. Repairs (wood or synthetic) and knots (up to 1" across) are permitted; *grade C (plugged)*—this is a better grade than C with splits not more than ⅛ inch in width and knot holes not more than ½ inch; *grade C*—in this grade stitching is allowed. Tight knots are allowed up to 1½ inch and knot holes up to 1 inch. Discoloration and defects that do not affect the structural performance of the panel are allowed; *grade D*—stitching is allowed in this grade also, as well as knots 2½ inch in diameter and splits. The use of this grade is limited to interior applications.

Another important classification in wood-base panels is related to the location in which the panels can be installed (dependent mainly on the degree of exposure to moisture): *exterior panels* can be permanently exposed outside; *exposure 1* (called also CDX in the industry) are panels that should not be exposed to the weather but that can resist some exposure due to construction delays, high humidity and some leakage. This is often mistaken for an exterior grade and wrongly used for exterior applications. Its construction is similar to the one used for exterior grades but some of the standards are different; *exposure 2* panels are suitable for interior and required to resist moderate delays in construction; *interior panels* are suitable only for interior and can only be exposed to minor temporary humidity. As indicated, the wall sheathing (the panels attached directly to the studs) is protected with water barriers like building paper or plastic sheets that are vapor permeable (see *Air and Vapor Movement* in this chapter). Once the wall is protected, then any type of finish can be applied to it. Weight of the material used is an important factor in the design of the wall, since the latter needs to be structurally designed in conformity to these stresses. Other than these considerations (to be introduced right at the beginning of the design), there is practically no limit to the finish that can be applied.

Steel Stud Framing. These types of walls are similar to wood framed walls. Vertical elements provide the support for the sheathing. These vertical elements (called metal studs) are U-shaped cold-formed steel units (see Figure 9.21). They are part of a series of units of different sizes and shapes that are used either as main structural and complementary elements (i.e., joist closures and runner channels), or for furring over other structural components (see Figure 9.21). They are also available in various gauges (term used to define the thickness of the material, where each gauge corresponds to a specific thickness. See Figure 9.22). By welding together basic cold-formed shapes, more complex geometries are created (see Figure 9.22). The vertical units are fastened to a top and bottom channel (with the same function that a wood plate has in the walls framed in wood studs). These channels are then secured to the structure (see Figure 9.23). By bending the metal sheet, additional strength is added. Cold-formed components of a system can be joined by using bolts, screws or by welding. These components can include prefabricated panels and curtain walls.

Prefabricated Panels. These types of systems include metal panels, concrete and/or glazing. Metal and glazing are inserted in light frames, which in turn are secured to the structure of the wall and then to the building structure (or directly to the latter). As necessary for any system, expansion and contraction of the various components should be allowed for. If the system has cavities that are not sealed and fire rated, fire-stopping needs to be installed (see local codes for maximum space between the outside finish of the building and outside sheathing of the walls).

When thin sheets of metal are used as exterior finish, some stiffening on the interior face of the sheet should be provided. This reinforcing should curve the panel slightly towards the outside to prevent the panel, with thermal changes, curving towards the inside. Thin panels do not offer great soundproofing: an investigation of the sound absorbing characteristics of the system should be made. Relying mainly on caulking for water tightness is always a questionable choice because of the high standards of workmanship that caulking requires and also because of the limited lifetime that caulking materials have. Because of these reasons it becomes even more questionable if caulking is applied to systems that are not easily accessible. For these systems flashing and proper design of the joints between the panels should be the solutions adopted for water movement control (see the *Water Movement* section in this chapter, and Figure 9.9). In addition, any water or moisture that penetrates the panel needs to be stopped and drained to the outside through weep holes. Other types of panels are usually composed of rigid insulation between an interior and an exterior skin (i.e., plywood or concrete). For these types of products, it is important to provide for heat and moisture build-up that might be created if the panel is completely sealed all around. Like the previously described pre-fabricated wall systems, these types also are secured to the framing and/or to the building structure directly. Normally this is where tolerances for movements and for expansion and contraction are provided. These systems usually allow for an amount of moisture to penetrate (since is very difficult to prevent it). When the moisture builds up and condenses, it is important to remove the water.

Curtain Walls. Schematically they can be defined as lightweight exterior cladding attached to the structure and composed of a metal frame and panel units (see the *Glass* section in this chapter). This is a complex system composed of many subcomponents that create a multitude of joints. There are fundamentally three types of systems within the curtain walls assemblies: *stick system,* composed of separate parts of framing and glazing units that are assembled on site. For this reason it is not used widely since quality control is very difficult. The joints are all created in the field, sometimes under difficult conditions; *mullion-and-panel systems* provide an intermediate system where few parts erected on the field. First vertical supports are secured to the structure and then complete window units (already assembled but commonly without glass) are inserted and secured to the verticals; *panel systems* are complete units built in factories and then transported to the site (usually without glass) and secured to the building structure. Units could be one or two stories high and attached to each floor or every second floor. This is the system with the fewest field joints. The *structural sealant glazed curtain wall system* is a fourth type; in this system, the aluminum mullions are not exposed and the glass is kept in place by structural sealant. This type of curtain wall should be considered very carefully because the detailing and the design are of the utmost importance. Quality control of the construction is another aspect fundamental to erecting a successful system. For these reasons, the most critical steps of the process (like the application of the structural seal) should be performed in a controlled environment (i.e., the factory). In addition, maintenance of the system is a fundamental aspect. For this reason all the parties involved in the project, including the owner, should know their respective responsibility and what this type of curtain wall system requires.

Regardless of the system used, curtain walls must perform all the functions that an exterior wall must perform, which is to control the flow of air, water and snow, moisture, heat, solar radiation, to react to wind load, earthquake forces and to adjust to building movements. The fundamental principles applied are those of the *rain screen* design (see the *Water Movement* section in this chapter). There are two aspects that can affect the performance of the system: one is the behavior of the curtain wall components, which are located mainly within the system (see Figure 9.24); the second is the performance of the elements that interface with components of the building in contact with the curtain wall system (see Figure 9.25).

A large part of the curtain wall system is composed of glass. In many ways, glass is also the most critical component in terms of performance of the system. There are many glass types and many glass unit types with technologically enhanced performance. An analysis of their characteristics is provided in the pages that follow.

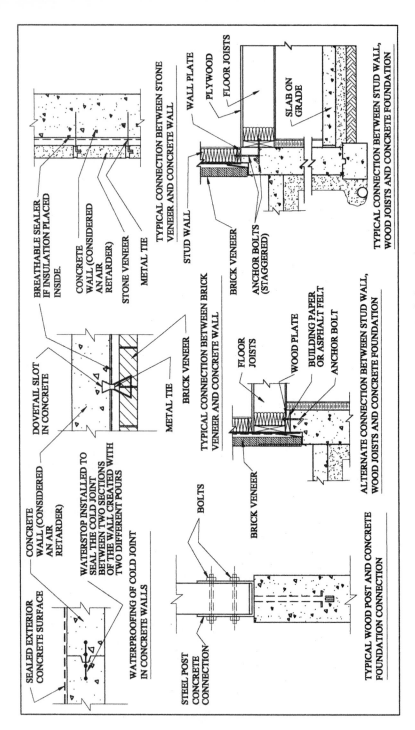

FIGURE 9.17 Typical types of ties. Waterproofing of cold joints in concrete walls. Typical connection between stud walls. Wood joists and concrete foundations.

9.46

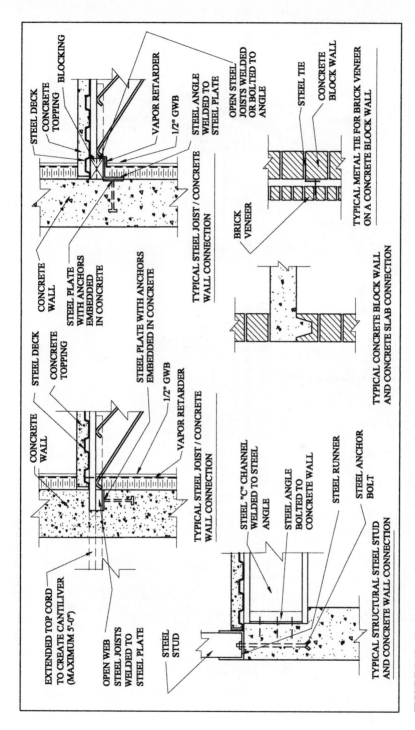

FIGURE 9.18 Typical connections between different types of structures.

9.47

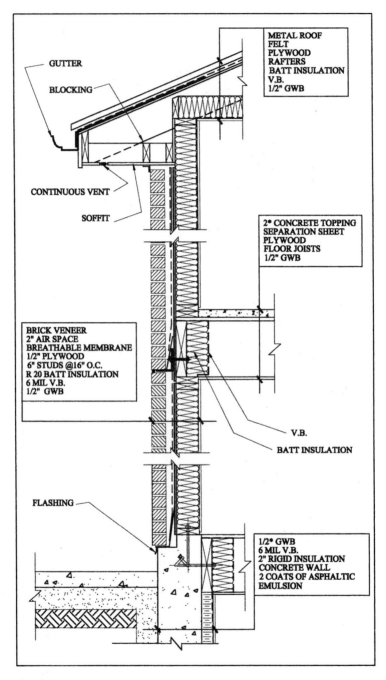

GUTTER

BLOCKING

METAL ROOF
FELT
PLYWOOD
RAFTERS
BATT INSULATION
V.B.
1/2" GWB

CONTINUOUS VENT

SOFFIT

2" CONCRETE TOPPING
SEPARATION SHEET
PLYWOOD
FLOOR JOISTS
1/2" GWB

BRICK VENEER
2" AIR SPACE
BREATHABLE MEMBRANE
1/2" PLYWOOD
6" STUDS @16" O.C.
R 20 BATT INSULATION
6 MIL V.B.
1/2" GWB

V.B.

BATT INSULATION

FLASHING

1/2" GWB
6 MIL V.B.
2" RIGID INSULATION
CONCRETE WALL
2 COATS OF ASPHALTIC
EMULSION

FIGURE 9.19   Typical roof, wall, floor, and foundation elements in a wood framing construction.

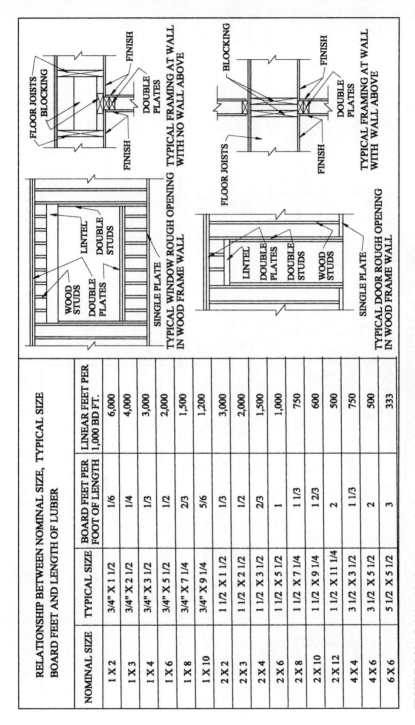

RELATIONSHIP BETWEEN NOMINAL SIZE, TYPICAL SIZE BOARD FEET AND LENGTH OF LUBER

NOMINAL SIZE	TYPICAL SIZE	BOARD FEET PER FOOT OF LENGTH	LINEAR FEET PER 1,000 BD FT.
1 X 2	3/4" X 1 1/2	1/6	6,000
1 X 3	3/4" X 2 1/2	1/4	4,000
1 X 4	3/4" X 3 1/2	1/3	3,000
1 X 6	3/4" X 5 1/2	1/2	2,000
1 X 8	3/4" X 7 1/4	2/3	1,500
1 X 10	3/4" X 9 1/4	5/6	1,200
2 X 2	1 1/2 X 1 1/2	1/3	3,000
2 X 3	1 1/2 X 2 1/2	1/2	2,000
2 X 4	1 1/2 X 3 1/2	2/3	1,500
2 X 6	1 1/2 X 5 1/2	1	1,000
2 X 8	1 1/2 X 7 1/4	1 1/3	750
2 X 10	1 1/2 X 9 1/4	1 2/3	600
2 X 12	1 1/2 X 11 1/4	2	500
4 X 4	3 1/2 X 3 1/2	1 1/3	750
4 X 6	3 1/2 X 5 1/2	2	500
6 X 6	5 1/2 X 5 1/2	3	333

FIGURE 9.20 Relationship between nominal size, typical size, board feet and length of lumber. Various framing layouts.

COLD-FORMED FRAMING PROFILES AND SIZES

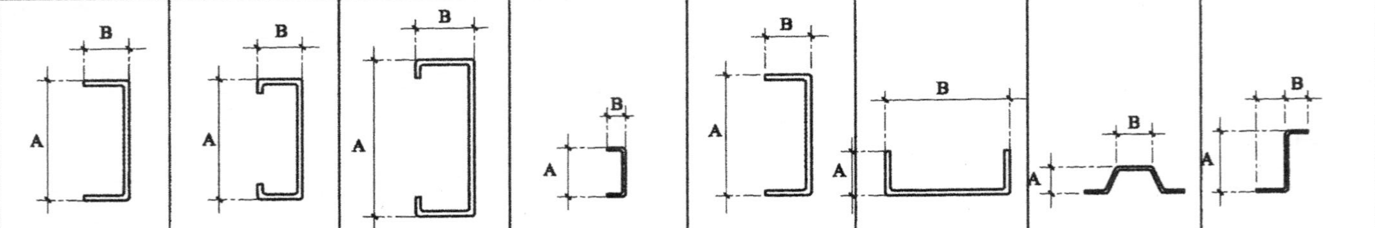

CHANNEL STUDS		"C" STUDS		"C" JOISTS		FURRING CHANNEL		"C" JOISTS CLOSURE		RUNNER CHANNEL		FURRING "HAT" CHANNEL		"Z" FURRING	
A	B	A	B	A	B	A	B	A	B	A	B	A	B	A	B
2 1/2"	1"	2 1/2"	1 1/4"	5 1/2"	1 7/8"	3/4"	1/2"	5 1/2"	1 1/4"	3/4"	2 11/16"	7/8"	1 3/8"	3/4"	1"
3 1/4"	1 3/8"	3"	1 3/8"	6"	1 7/8"	1 1/2"	1/2"	6"		1"	3 13/16"	1 1/2"	1 1/4"		1 1/2"
3 5/8"		3 1/4"	1 1/2"	7 1/4"	1 3/4"			7 1/4"		1 3/8"	3 7/16"				2"
4"		3 1/2"	1 5/8"	8"	2"			8"		1 1/4"	4 3/16"				3"
6"		3 5/8"		9 1/4"	2 1/2"			9 1/4"		1 1/2"	6 3/16"				
		4"		10"				10"		1 3/4"	8 3/16"				
		5 1/2"		12"				12"							
		6"													
		7 1/2"													
		8"													

FIGURE 9.21   Cold-formed framing profiles and sizes.

GAUGE, THICKNESS AND WEIGHT OF METAL SHEETS

STEEL STANDARD GAUGE No	WEIGHT PSF	SHEET THICKNESS IN.	GALVANIZED SHEET GAUGE No	WEIGHT PSF	SHEET THICKNESS IN.
4	9.3750	0.2242	8	7.03125	0.1681
6	8.1250	0.1943	10	5.78125	0.1382
8	6.8750	0.1644	12	4.53125	0.1084
10	5.6250	0.1345	14	3.28125	0.0785
12	4.3750	0.1046	16	2.65625	0.0635
14	3.1250	0.0747	18	2.15625	0.0516
16	2.5000	0.0598	20	1.65625	0.0396
18	2.0000	0.0478	22	1.40625	0.0336
20	1.5000	0.0359	24	1.15625	0.0276
22	1.2500	0.0299	26	0.90625	0.0217
24	1.0000	0.0239	28	0.78125	0.0187
26	0.7500	0.0179	30	0.65625	0.0157
28	0.6250	0.0149	32	0.56250	0.0134
30	0.5000	0.0120			
32	0.40625	0.0097			
34	0.34375	0.0082			
36	0.28125	0.0067			
38	0.25000	0.0060			

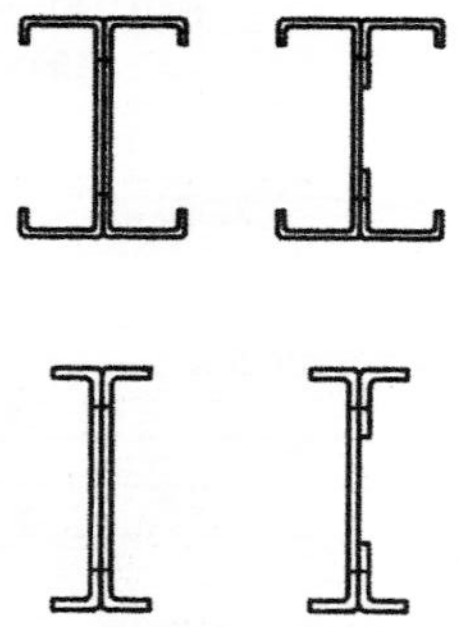

COMPLEX GEOMETRIC SHAPES IN COLD-FORMED STEEL

Basic cold-rolled shapes are very similar to geometries created with the hot-rolled system. Zees, angles and channels can be bent in one simultaneous process. More complex sections can be obtained by welding together the basic geometric shapes. An "I" section, for example, can be created by welding either two "C" sections or one "C" section and an angle.

FIGURE 9.22 Gauge, thickness and weight of metal sheets.

9.51

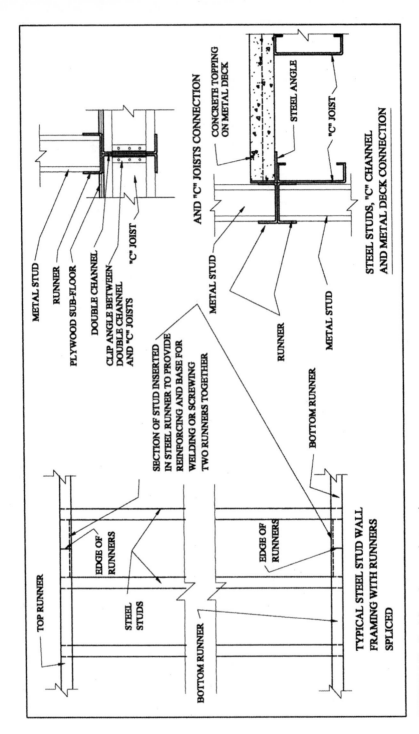

METAL STUD

RUNNER

PLYWOOD SUB-FLOOR

DOUBLE CHANNEL

CLIP ANGLE BETWEEN DOUBLE CHANNEL AND "C" JOISTS

"C" JOIST

AND "C" JOISTS CONNECTION

CONCRETE TOPPING ON METAL DECK

STEEL ANGLE

"C" JOIST

METAL STUD

RUNNER

METAL STUD

STEEL STUDS, "C" CHANNEL AND METAL DECK CONNECTION

SECTION OF STUD INSERTED IN STEEL RUNNER TO PROVIDE REINFORCING AND BASE FOR WELDING OR SCREWING TWO RUNNERS TOGETHER

BOTTOM RUNNER

TOP RUNNER

EDGE OF RUNNERS

STEEL STUDS

EDGE OF RUNNERS

BOTTOM RUNNER

BOTTOM RUNNER

TYPICAL STEEL STUD WALL FRAMING WITH RUNNERS SPLICED

FIGURE 9.23 Steel frame layout and connections.

9.52

AIR, VAPOR CONTROL, RAIN SCREEN DESIGN, SOLAR RADIATION AND MOVEMENT CONTROL IN CURTAIN WALL SYSTEMS

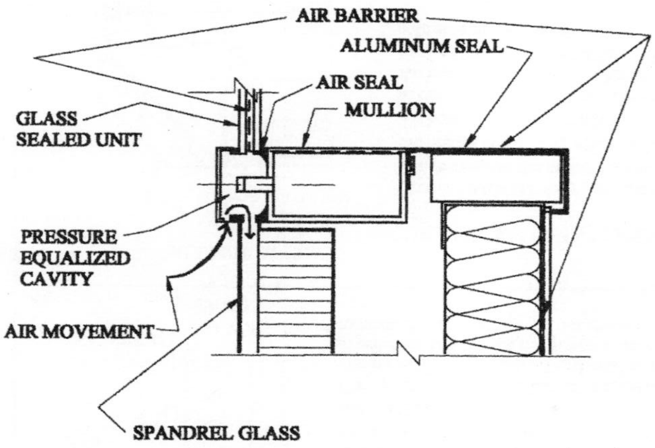

One of the function of a Curtain Wall system is to prevent the movement of air from the indoor to the outdoor and vice versa.

This is accomplished by ensuring that the air retarder is continuous.

Since the elements forming the system are mainly metal and glass, as basic components they offer a very good barrier to air movement. If the connections between the parts of the system are also sealed effectively, the continuity is reached within the curtain wall. The interface with other elements needs to be equally effective, as well as the material used as vapor retarder in the other assemblies. In many cases the common polyethylene sheet is not sufficient because of the negative and positive pressures created, for example, in a wall assembly. A more rigid material should be used (i.e. GWB).

A second function of the curtain wall is to minimize thermal movement and heat loss. This is achieved by using elements of the system that have a low thermal transmission: double glazed units (possibly with gas in the cavity and Low-E with Selective Tinted glass) and thermally broken mullion. Then well insulated panels behind the spandrel glass could be supplemented with additional insulation in a wall behind these panels. Since condensation becomes a factor, a good vapor retarder should be installed in the other assemblies, since again the curtain wall system uses materials that are very effective vapor retarders.

Rain Screen design principles are applied to the curtain wall systems by allowing outside air to infiltrate at the base of the snap-on cap and circulate between the spandrel panel and the infill panel behind it. This minimizes the differential pressure between the outside of the curtain wall system and the spaces within the system.

Solar radiation can be detrimental to people and objects. The transmission of the radiation to the indoor spaces is controlled through the use of special glass units with low UV transmission. Components of the curtain wall system that are made with material that could be sensitive to UV radiations should be protected since they can deteriorate quickly because of exposure to the sun.

Curtain walls need to allow for movement of the building due to: structural deflection, expansion and contraction of materials and movements due to gradual deformation of the structure or foundation settlements.

Relative to movements the most critical component is the glass. A tolerance of a typical Curtain Wall system is in the order of 4 to 5 mm around the glass unit.

AIR BARRIER
ALUMINUM SEAL
AIR SEAL
MULLION
GLASS SEALED UNIT
PRESSURE EQUALIZED CAVITY
AIR MOVEMENT
SPANDREL GLASS

FIGURE 9.24 Air and vapor control, rain screen design, solar radiation and movement control in curtain wall systems.

9.53

CURTAIN WALL DETAIL AT PARAPET

The design of the connection between the parapet and the curtain wall system is particularly important. Parts beyond the thermal break must be always on the warm side. Top of vertical tube should be insulated to avoid heat loss due to stack effect. Condensation and frost might develop in the tubes as well, draining into the inside. The components of the system, if exposed to the outside temperature fluctuations, might move beyond their capability and determine malfunctioning of the parts of the system and the seals. The continuity of the air barrier is important as well. The material of the air barrier should be rigid (i.e. metal). In order to maintain its continuity it should be connected to the roof air barrier system.

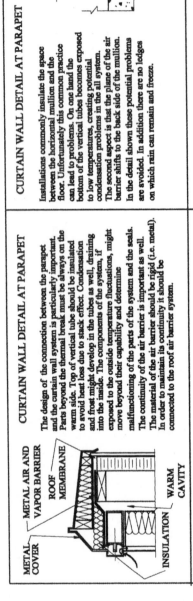

METAL COVER
METAL AIR AND VAPOR BARRIER
ROOF MEMBRANE
INSULATION
WARM CAVITY

CURTAIN WALL DETAIL AT PARAPET

Installations commonly insulate the space between the horizontal mullion and the floor. Unfortunately this common practice can lead to problems. On one hand the bottom of the vertical tubes becomes exposed to low temperatures, creating potential condensation problems in the all system. The second aspect is that the plane of the air barrier shifts to the back side of the mullion. In the detail shown these potential problems are avoided. In addition there are no ledges on which rain can remain and freeze.

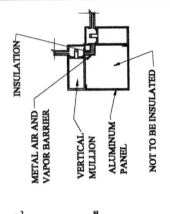

CURTAIN WALL INTERIOR AND EXTERIOR CORNER DETAIL

Corner details can vary considerably depending on the design of the building. For this reason the manufacturer should be involved in the development of the details at the early stage of the working drawings.
Air barrier should be made of a rigid material.
In case of an inside corner, the space inside the interior cladding between the two interior mullions should not be insulated, otherwise the air barrier at the back of the outer layer of insulation will become a vapor barrier placed on the cold side of the insulation.

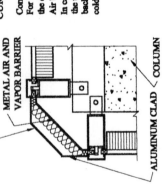

INSULATON
METAL AIR AND VAPOR BARRIER
VERTICAL MULLION
ALUMINUM PANEL
NOT TO BE INSULATED

ALUMINUM CLAD
METAL AIR AND VAPOR BARRIER
ALUMINUM CLAD
COLUMN
ALUMINUM CLAD

FIGURE 9.25 Various curtain wall details.

GLASS

The fundamental basic material of glass is sand (from sandstone) with sodium oxide and calcium oxide as additives. The process of making glass involves: granulating the compound and melting it. Then, carried over a molten bed of tin (which is heavier than the molten compound), the mix is led through a process that cools the glass to specific floating temperature. Flotation of glass is the best method for reducing the stress that has accumulated in it. At this stage of the process, the glass is introduced into a chamber where it is heated to a point where any stress that the glass may have accumulated during the process is released. The glass then is cooled once more very slowly in order not to produce new stresses. After this process the glass is coated and packed. The glass produced through this process is called *float glass*. This is the most common process through which glass is produced anywhere in the world and it is the only type of glass used for modern windows and curtain walls. Float glass thickness ranges from ³⁄₃₂ inch (2.5 mm), called single strength glass (SS) to 1" (25 mm). Double strength glass (GS) is ⅛ inch thick. Using techniques that introduce additional manipulation of the product can further increase performance of float glass. There are two types of glass produced though these processes: tempered and heat strengthened. Both are obtained by heating the glass at high temperatures and cooling it down very rapidly (tempered glass is processed at higher temperatures). This creates tension stresses (within the core of the glass sheet) and compression (on both exterior surfaces) that increase the strength of the glass both to bending and impact. There are a few important differences between the tempered and heat strengthened glass.

Tempered glass is stronger, more expensive and breaks into small blunt parts. For this reason, where openings on the outside wall are required for fire fighting access, panels of glazing are marked very visibly with a capital "T". If a fire fighter needs to access the interior of a building in case of an emergency, he or she can safely break that panel without being injured by the sharp fragments into which a simple non-safety float glass would break. The negative aspect of tempered glass is that even small impurities can spontaneously develop into bigger entities within the glass (requiring sometimes years to reach the critical size) and the glass can suddenly explode. This is its hazardous characteristic.

Heat strengthened glass is less strong than tempered glass but is less expensive and does not present the risk of exploding. For this reason, in curtain walls, heat strengthened glass is used as spandrel glass (which is the portion of glass that in a glazing system is usually installed in front of the structure of the building to conceal it). Since heat can be trapped between the glass and the interior components of the building (very often these being the building structure), the glass need to resists higher temperatures than normal. For this reason heat strengthened glass is used in these locations.

In addition to the above types, chemically strengthened glass is produced by applying chemicals to the surface of float glass and producing the same stresses that are produced in the thermal process. The advantage is that this type of glass can be considerably thinner than heat processed glass, making it more suitable for horizontal applications or where the weight of the structure is a factor. However, chemically strengthened glass is considerably more expensive than glass produced through heat strengthening.

Using various layers of glass with films inserted in between also produces different types of glass: **a.** *safety glass*: this type can be laminated or tempered. We have already indicated the characteristics of tempered glass. However not all tempered glass as well as not all laminated glass qualify as safety glass. They need to meet the requirements of the Consumer Product Safety Commission's (CPSC) *Safety Standards For Architectural Glazing Materials*, 16 CPR 1201. In a laminated glass, the film used, which can be clear or tinted, is of three different standards thicknesses (although higher thicknesses can be used for special orders): 15 mil (0.38 mm), 30 mil (0.75 mm) and 60 mil (1.5mm). When laminated glass breaks, the glass tends to remain in place being still bonded by the plastic sheet. This makes it very suitable for skylights and in locations where earthquake forces can be a factor. Safety glass is divided into *Category I*, which can be used in openings up to 9 sq. ft., and *Category II* which can be used for bigger openings; **b.** *fire-resistant glass:* wired glass is commonly used for openings in fire separations (especially closures). Building codes establish the maximum areas of these openings. The thickness of the glass must be minimum ¼ inch (6 mm). It has to be considered that wired glass is not a safety glass. Since its strength is half of that of the annealed glass, it can break, exposing sharp edges. Also the wire can protrude becoming a potential hazard.

Another type of glass that has recently appeared on the market is a wireless type of glass that is composed of two sheets of glass with gel in between. During fire, the gel absorbs the heat. This system can reach a two-hour fire separation. In normal conditions there is no difference between this system and normal glazing; **c.** *security glazing*: this type is made of one of more layers of glazing fused with plastic sheets. Increasing the thickness of the plastic layer increases the strength of the assembly.

Performance of Glazing

The performance of glazing is rated through parameters that identify its characteristics: **a.** *shading coefficient (SH)* is defined as the ratio between the solar heat gain of glass and the solar heat gain of DS glass (DS glass is a double strength glass ⅛ inch thick). The solar heat gain is the sum of the heat transmitted through the glass and the portion of heat absorbed by the glass and transferred to the interior space. The SH refers to direct sunlight beam. Therefore it is not an important reference for glass that is not exposed to direct sunlight (i.e., north exposure or protected by large overhangs). The smaller the SH, the less light is transmitted; **b.** *visible transmittance:* the values of this parameter measure the ability of glass to transmit light in the visible spectrum. The higher the value, the more light is transmitted through the glass; **c.** *UV transmittance*: ultraviolet radiation can be detrimental to humans and objects. For this reason, it is important to rate the amount of this type of radiation that a particular type of glass transmits to the interior. The lower the number, the less radiation is allowed to pass; **d.** glass behaves as any other material by transmitting, absorbing and reflecting radiations. In addition the high transmissivity of glass for short wave radiation and its opacity for long wave radiation can create considerable problems in maintaining the interior temperature within comfortable values (see also *Thermal Aspects and Properties of Materials* in this chapter). Higher values of emissivity (which correspond to lower values of absorptivity) indicate a higher ability of the material to reflect back short wave radiation from the sun; **e.** *U-value*: this value in glass is very small. As we have seen, most of the U-values are given by the air film on the inside and outside face of the glass. However U-values of glazing have been increased by the creation of a sealed unit, which will be discussed later; **f.** *Relative Heat Gain (RHG):* this is a datum that compares the performance of different glass during the summer period. The reference is the performance of a clear glass assuming that the differential in the temperature between outside and inside is 14°F and the amount of solar radiation is 200 Btu/h • ft^2 . The formula that provides the value is RHG = shading coefficient (200) + U (inside-outside temperature difference). A lower RHG is obviously better than a higher value; **g.** *luminous efficacy* (LE): this parameter is the ratio between the visible transmittance (the ability to transmitting visible light) and the shading coefficient. A higher value, therefore, indicates that a glass, with the same heat gain of another, allows more light to be transmitted to the interior space. A value of 1.5 and above is a high value; **h.** *structural properties*: the most important factor in the structural resistance of a glass is its bending capability. Cracks in glass are determined by various factors—the load applied, the size of the glass, its orientation, the internal defects, the edge conditions. Since the behavior of glass under stress varies considerably between different samples of the same type, the structural performance of glass is expressed in probabilities. The factor that is used is 8/1000, which means that out of 1000 lights it is possible that eight will break. This corresponds to a safety factor of 2.5. In load terms, if 6000 psi is the maximum stress to be imposed on glass, then the calculation has to be made using 6000/2.5 = 2500 psi, which is the new value of the maximum stress. This is for an average use of glass. For high-rises and other special construction, the safety factor is corrected by multiplying the ultimate stress for even more stringent and higher values.

Improving Glass Performance

In a glazing system, glass is where most technological advancement has been achieved. The approaches that are used to enhance glass performance can be divided into three types (which can be combined to further improve the performance of the product): **a.** *changing the chemical composition* and physical properties of the glass. In this category, tinted glass (or heat absorbing glass) is the oldest technology. The function of tinted glass is to absorb solar radiation and heat before it passes through the glass. In doing so, it can reduce heat gain between 25 percent and 55 percent. A tint can be added to both tempered and heat strengthened glass. The thickness of the glass increases the amount of solar radiation and heat absorbed. Unfortunately, much of what is absorbed is also released back to the interior in the form of heat. Tinted glass reaches a higher temperature than clear glass under the same condition. If tinted glass is directly exposed to high temperatures, it should be of the heat strengthened type. However, tints that are spectrally selective can improve the performance by reducing the transmission of the ultraviolet and infrared radiation from the sun, allowing more light to pass. This type of glass is very suitable where daylight is used extensively. Color can affect considerably the performance of tinted glass. In terms of visible and UV transmittance, green tinted glass allows considerably more light to pass through than gray tinted glass; **b.** *apply coatings to glazing material.* This includes: *reflective coating,* which can be applied in two ways: a process called *magnetic sputtering* or another called *pyrolytic.* The first is less resistant and should not be exposed to the outside. The second, being applied when the glass is still hot, penetrates the glass and therefore is stronger. Both heat strengthened and tempered glass can be treated by applying a reflective coating. A coating is most effective when it is applied on the outside of a glass and the glass installed with the coating facing the outside. In this way heat is prevented from entering the glass.

One negative effect of reflective coating is the lowering of the amount of light allowed into the interior space. Reflective glass may have another adverse effect on the surroundings. Light is reflected and may create glare that could be very dangerous for motorists. In addition the multiple reflection of the sunlight among buildings could increase the outside temperature in the street considerably. *Low emissivity coating* is a film which works in the same way as the reflective coating except that it reflects a percentage of the heat migrating from the inside to the outside back to the interior. A coating that has a rating of 0.2 indicates that 20 percent of the heat leaving the interior space is reflected back to it. The techniques used for applying this type of coating are very similar to the one used for applying the reflective coating. From the point of view of the appearance, however, unlike the reflective coating, a low-E coating is virtually invisible.

The benefits of low-E coating are very evident in cold climate. However they can be very beneficial in hot climate as well. A low-E coat can affect the amount of radiation entering the interior space in the same way a reflective coating does. *Multiple layers of glass assembly,* commonly called sealed units, are composed of layers of glass (normally two, which can increase to three), separated by a spacer, with a space generally filled with air between the layers of glass. This allows for various combinations that also employ techniques described above (see Figure 6.17). The basic unit is 1 inch thick where the width of the air space is adjusted in accordance with the thickness of the glass. In other words, if the glass is ½ inch thick (multiplied by two, which is the number of the sheets of glass), the air space becomes ¼ inch wide.

There are many possible combinations that can be installed to form the unit, from the simple double clear glazing unit with the cavity filled with air (with a U-value of .50, to the double glazing filled with argon, with one low-E coat and one reflective glass (an U-value of 0.25). It has to be considered that tinted glass would not add to the U-value (although it would improve the performance of the unit in terms of UV transmission).

The choice of which combination to use and how many panes of glass to use is dependent greatly on the type of climate, size of the glazing, exposure, structural capabilities, tasks to be performed in the indoor space, aesthetics and economic considerations (for values of different types of glass sealed units see *Technical Characteristics and Window Glazing* in this chapter).

Curtain walls are not the only glazing systems that appear on the exterior of a building. In fact, more commonly used glazing is of smaller sizes and smaller proportions in relation to the solid part of the exterior walls. Windows and window systems are the most common products of smaller proportions.

WINDOWS

This is another element of the envelope that has an enormous importance from the aesthetical, functional and technical aspect of a building. The two major components of a window are the frame and the glass.

The performance of the window varies according to the combination between the different material with which the frame is built and the different types and number of sheets of glass that are part of the window assembly. In addition, films and coats applied to the glass can improve or alter the performance as well. This is particularly critical if related to energy consumption.

As we have seen in this chapter, glass by itself does not have high thermal performance. Therefore, windows are potentially a source of heat loss as well as a source of heat gain. This means that, if not carefully analyzed and if the right type of window is not accurately chosen for the type of climate in which the project will be built, it could be very expensive (and sometime prohibitive) to exploit the beauty of panoramic scenery and the possibilities that natural light offers.

Parameters for Window Evaluation

From the technological point of view, there are four evaluating parameters that can help in choosing the right type of window: **a.** *U-factor (AL)* indicates the heat loss experienced through the window. To affect the rate of heat transfer through a window assembly the characteristics of the two major components (the frame and the glass or glass unit) are important. In order to appreciate their performance, however, the characteristics of every subcomponent need to be analyzed and known. This will achieve the best combination within the ranges of possibilities available in the market; **b.** *solar heat gain coefficient (SHGC)* indicates the amount of solar radiation either admitted directly through transmittance, or absorbed and then released by the glass. The second phenomenon varies, since the direction of the transmission of the absorbed heat (towards the exterior or the interior) depends on the outside and inside temperature. If the outside temperature is lower than the inside temperature, most of the heat transfer will happen towards the outside, and vice versa. The SHGC values range between 0 and 1: the lower the value, the less the heat gain (see also the section titled "Glass" in this chapter); **c.** *visible transmittance (VT)* is a parameter that indicates the amount of visible light transmitted by the window. The VT value is calculated including the frame and ranges between 0 and 1. The higher the value, the more light is transmitted. Most of the windows have a VT between 0.2 to 0.8. Obviously in terms of daylighting, the higher the value, the better the window assembly; **d.** *air leakage (AL)* refers to the amount of air escaping through the window (see also *Air and Vapor Movement* in this chapter). A lower AL indicates that less air passes through the window assembly. An efficient window should have an AL value of .30 or less.

The National Fenestration Rating Council (NFRC) is the body that administers and implements the above parameters. It is a non-profit organization that is composed of the public and private sectors in a joint effort to monitor the quality and performance of window industries. Windows that are part of the Energy Star program bear a label indicating the NFRC ratings.

Different Types of Windows. The type of frame, the operating system and their style can be used to differentiate windows. In addition the type of glass and glass assembly adds to the description of the unit.

Types of Window Frames

Typical frame materials are: aluminum, aluminum with thermal break, wood and wood clad, fiberglass, vinyl, insulated vinyl, hybrid and composite, steel, stainless steel, as well as bronze. Although frames represent only between 10 percent and 30 percent of the area of the window, they determine many aspects of the performance of the window and the physical characteristics of the unit (i.e., thickness, durability, color and character). Furthermore, frames affect the U-value since they account for an average of 50 percent of the heat loss experienced through the window (the frame is included in the U-value rating shown on the label from the NFRC). Condensation is also a process that can be affected by the choice of the frame.

Fundamentally there are two techniques that are used to improve the thermal resistance of the frame; the first is to use a thermal break separating the outer part of the frame from the inner part. The material that functions as thermal break has a high thermal resistivity. The second is to utilize materials that have a low thermal conductivity in order to build the entire frame (for example, wood or vinyl). Both of these choices, however, have limited commercial application because of durability, fire rating and maintenance. A more attractive material is fiberglass, stronger than vinyl and requiring less maintenance than wood. If the frame is filled with foam insulation, its thermal performance can be further enhanced.

However, even in the case of fiberglass, the fire rating related to the combustibility of the material limits the use of this type of frame.

Operating Systems for Windows

Typical operating systems are: casement and intermediate casement, awning, hopper and intermediate projected, slider, top hung, double hung, vertically and horizontally pivoted, intermediate combination and jalousie (see Figures 9.26 and 9.27).

Some operating systems are more suitable than others for certain applications. Casement and intermediate casement windows are traditionally used in residential buildings and homes, small hotels and office buildings as well as in some institutional facilities. Hinges in the form of a compass regulate the opening. These windows come in various types of frames. Double-glazing, and where necessary also triple-glazing, is commonly installed.

The awning type of window has a wide variety of applications: from industrial to residential and office. It can offer a combination of settings for the opening, which can be operated individually or simultaneously. Hopper and intermediate projected are used for different applications, which include office, industrial and institutional buildings. In some cases, this type of window has been installed in residential projects.

The slider is probably the most common type of window. It is available in virtually every type of frame and it has been used in every type of building. The quality varies considerably: from very economical to very sophisticated systems. The top hung type of window is used in sawtooth roofs and monitors. They usually have a steel frame and either a manual or motorized operation. Double hung windows are used in various types of projects and they are built using different types of frame materials. Used in conjunction with fixed lights, they also provide a combination of options. Vertically and horizontally pivoted windows are mainly built in metal. Used especially in industrial buildings, they are mechanically operated. In the horizontal application the top unit swings in and the bottom swings out.

An intermediate combination window offers a variety of opening systems for multiple ventilation possibilities. From casement to projected, they are used in a very broad type of projects (i.e., residential, offices, institutional, hospitals and others). Jalousie windows provide good ventilation. However, they do not provide tight weather protection. Tinted or other kind of glass can be installed. If frosted glass is used, privacy and ventilation are optimized.

Technical Characteristics and Window Glazing

The range of possibilities in window glazing is considerable. What follows are some of the available options.

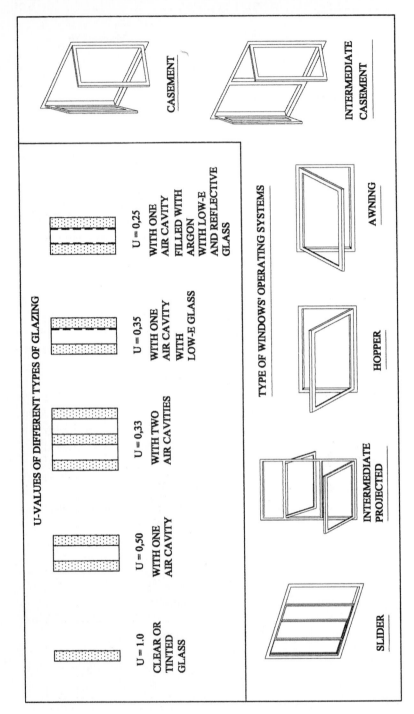

FIGURE 9.26 U-Values of different types of glazing. Types of window operating systems.

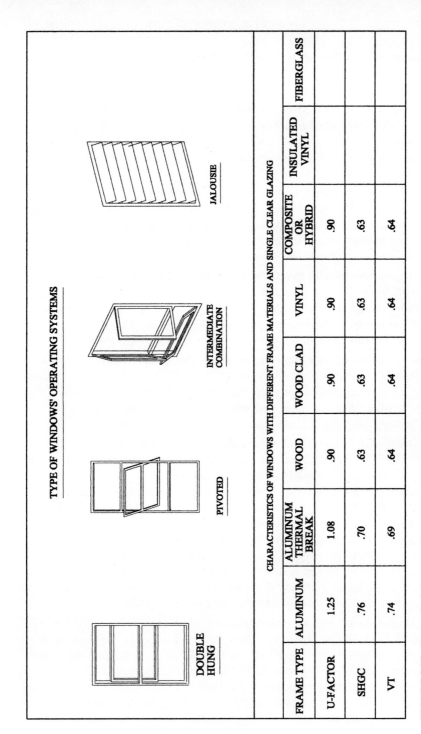

FIGURE 9.27 Types of window operating systems.

Single Clear Glazing: U-value 1.11–SHGC 0.86–VT 0.90 (see Figure 9.27 for U-values of window). This type of glazing provides the highest transfer of energy but it transmits the most daylight.

Single-Glazed with Bronze or Gray Tinted Glass: U-value 1.11–SHGC 0.73–VT 0.68 (see Figure 9.28 for U-values of window). This type of glazing reduces the solar gain; however, it also reduces the visible light, even more than more efficient colors like green or blue. Tinted glass has no effect on the U-value.

Double-Glazed Clear Glass: U-value 0.49–SHGC 0.76–VT 0.81 (see Figure 9.28 for U-values of window). This unit is made of two sheets of clear glass separated by an air space. This unit cuts the heat loss in half, if compared to single clear glazing. Heat gain and transmission of visible light are not affected by the second glass.

Double-Glazed with Bronze or Gray Tinted Glass: U-value .49–SHGC 0.62–VT 0.62 (see Figure 9.28 for U-values of window). The outside layer is tinted glass, while the inside layer is clear. The unit reduces the solar gain, but also reduces the visible light. Tinted glass has no effect on the U-value; therefore this unit has the same U-value as a double clear glazing unit.

Double-Glazed with High Performance Tinted Glass: U-value .49–SHGC 0.48–VT 0.69 (see Figure 9.29 for U-values of window). This combination of glazing, also called spectrally selective tinted glass, reduces the heat gain below the value associated with bronze or gray tinted glass but it has a VT similar to that one of clear glass.

Double-Glazed with high solar gain low-E glass: U-value .30–SHGC 0.71–VT 0.75 (see Figure 9.29 for U-values of window). This combination describes a unit composed of high transmission low-E glass with the cavity filled with argon gas. This unit reduces heat loss but allows solar gain to be transmitted. This combination is particularly indicated for passive solar design. In a climate that requires the same amount of energy for heating as it requires for cooling, low, medium or high solar gain and low-E glass are combinations that within a year produce the same consumption of energy due to heat loss, because the parameters compensate each other in the winter and in the summer. A low solar gain in conjunction with a low-E glass, however, is particularly indicated for cooling design climates.

Triple-Glazed with low solar gain and low-E glass: U-value 0.13–SHGC 0.33–VT 0.56 (see Figure 9.29 for U-values of window). This unit has three layers of glazing and two low-E coating. The air space is filled with ½ inch argon or ¼ inch of krypton gas. The spacers are of the low conductance type. A different technology is used for the middle layer a sheet of plastic instead of glass. In certain products, two layers of plastic are installed in order to create a quadruple unit. These sheets can be low-E as well, adding further performance to the unit. These products do not perform well in extreme heat, due to the possible softening of the plastic.

CHARACTERISTICS OF WINDOWS WITH DIFFERENT FRAME MATERIALS AND BRONZE OR GRAY TINTED GLASS

FRAME TYPE	ALUMINUM	ALUMINUM THERMAL BREAK	WOOD	WOOD CLAD	VINYL	COMPOSITE OR HYBRID	INSULATED VINYL	FIBERGLASS
U-FACTOR	1.25	1.08	.90	.90	.90	.90		
SHGC	.65	.60	.54	.54	.54	.54		
VT	.56	.52	.48	.48	.48	.48		

CHARACTERISTICS OF WINDOWS WITH DIFFERENT FRAME MATERIALS AND DOUBLE CLEAR GLAZING

FRAME TYPE	ALUMINUM	ALUMINUM THERMAL BREAK	WOOD	WOOD CLAD	VINYL	COMPOSITE OR HYBRID	INSULATED VINYL	FIBERGLASS
U-FACTOR	.79	.64	.49	.49	.49	.49	.44	.44
SHGC	.68	.62	.56	.56	.56	.56	.52	.52
VT	.67	.62	.58	.58	.58	.58	.62	.62

CHARACTERISTICS OF WINDOWS WITH DIFFERENT FRAME MATERIALS AND DOUBLE GLAZED WITH BRONZE OR GRAY TINTED GLASS

FRAME TYPE	ALUMINUM	ALUMINUM THERMAL BREAK	WOOD	WOOD CLAD	VINYL	COMPOSITE OR HYBRID	INSULATED VINYL	FIBERGLASS
U-FACTOR	.79	.64	.49	.49	.49	.49	.44	.44
SHGC	.57	.52	.46	.46	.46	.46	.49	.49
VT	.50	.47	.44	.44	.44	.44	.47	.47

FIGURE 9.28 Characteristics of windows with different frame materials and different glazing types.

	CHARACTERISTICS OF WINDOWS WITH DIFFERENT FRAME MATERIALS AND DOUBLE GLAZING HIGH PERFORMANCE TINTED GLASS							
FRAME TYPE	ALUMINUM	ALUMINUM THERMAL BREAK	WOOD	WOOD CLAD	VINYL	COMPOSITE OR HYBRID	INSULATED VINYL	FIBERGLASS
U-FACTOR	.79	.64	.49	.49	.49	.49	.44	.44
SHGC	.46	.41	.36	.36	.36	.36	.38	.38
VT	.57	.53	.49	.49	.49	.49	.53	.53

	CHARACTERISTICS OF WINDOWS WITH DIFFERENT FRAME MATERIALS AND DOUBLE GLAZING WITH HIGH SOLAR GAIN AND LOW-E GLASS							
FRAME TYPE	ALUMINUM	ALUMINUM THERMAL BREAK	WOOD	WOOD CLAD	VINYL	COMPOSITE OR HYBRID	INSULATED VINYL	FIBERGLASS
U-FACTOR	.64	.52	.36	.36	.36	.36	.30	.30
SHGC	.64	.58	.52	.52	.52	.52	.55	.55
VT	.62	.57	.53	.53	.53	.53	.57	.57

	CHARACTERISTICS OF WINDOWS WITH DIFFERENT FRAME MATERIALS AND TRIPLE GLAZED WITH LOW SOLAR GAIN AND LOW-E GLASS							
FRAME TYPE	ALUMINUM	ALUMINUM THERMAL BREAK	WOOD	WOOD CLAD	VINYL	COMPOSITE OR HYBRID	INSULATED VINYL	FIBERGLASS
U-FACTOR			.24	.24	.24	.24	.17	.17
SHGC			.25	.25	.25	.25	.26	.26
VT			.40	.40	.40	.40	.43	.43

FIGURE 9.29 Characteristics of windows with different frame materials and different glazing types.

Guidelines for Selection of Windows for Different Climates

The following guidelines provide orientation in selecting the right window for a particular climate:

1. For climates where the need for cooling is the major factor (70 percent of the energy spent), select windows with U-value of 0.70 minimum. This value is not a determinant factor in hot climates. SHGC should be less than 0.40. This is the most important value in hot climates. A VTglass above 0.70 (this value is only for glass), which corresponds to a VTwindow of 0.50 (including the frame). It is important to maximize the amount of daylight allowed in the interior space. AL should be 0.30 or below. Air leakage in this type of climate can cause a rise in indoor humidity and discomfort.

2. For a mixed climate where the requirements for cooling and heating are the same and represent 30 percent of the energy consumption, the U-value should be less than 0.40. This reduces the energy consumption considerably. The choice of the SHGC value is critical since a low value helps during the summer but limits the heat gain during the winter (which is a positive requirement). If the climate has moderate cooling requirements used a value of 0.55. If the requirements are considerable a SHGC less than 0,40 is recommended. A VTglass above 0.70 (this value is only for glass), which corresponds to a VTwindow of 0.50 (including the frame). It is important to maximize the amount of daylight allowed in the interior space. AL should be .30 or less.

3. For climates where heating is the major requirement and the energy consumed between cooling and heating is more than 70 percent consumed by the second factor, windows should have the following characteristics: U-value should be less than 0.30. In North America climate in the heating regions varies considerably, reaching temperatures that are extreme. In certain cases, triple glazing might be advisable with U-values as low as .015. However, U values can be offset by high SHGC (in the order of 0.55 and above. In this case, a U-value of 0.40 could be acceptable. Required SHGS value can change depending on the extremes that temperatures reach during the summer and the winter. In areas where cooling is not a factor, the highest possible SHGC available should be used. Where cooling is a factor, windows with an SHGC of less than 0.55 should be used. A VTglass above 0.70 (this value is only for glass), which corresponds to a VTwindow of 0.50 (including the frame), should be used. It is important to maximize the amount of daylight allowed in the interior space. AL should be .30 or less.

EXTERIOR DOORS

An exterior door has two basic functions: to provide security and to protect from weather. A door also has an aesthetical aspect and, when it is used as an entry door, it also acquires a semantic value. The second is related to the fact that the entry greets, and in commercial buildings, should attract individuals into the premises. An exterior door tends to give an indication of the positive characteristics of the functions carried on inside the building.

For the aspect of security, there are different classes of doors evaluated through standards issued in the United States by the National Institute of Justice (which are equivalent to the ASTM's grades): **a.** *Class I/Grade 10,* for single family residential buildings located in low crime rate areas; **b.** *Class II/Grade 20,* for residential buildings located in medium crime rate areas or for apartments located in low and medium crime rate areas; **b.** *Class III/Grade 30,* for residential buildings in higher than average crime rates areas or small commercial buildings located in low or medium crime rate areas; **c.** *Class IV/Grade 40,* for commercial buildings located in high crime rate areas.

For metal doors, the Hollow Metal Manufacturers Association indicates the minimum requirements for materials depending on the location and the type of use. These categories are indicated by numbers such HMMA 860, HMMA 861, etc.

In terms of weather protection, the major aspects for doors are water and air movement as well as thermal performance. Because of tolerances applied for the operation of the door, a door cannot be considered a very reliable barrier against water and air (it can perform relatively well in terms of thermal protection). For water protection, it is recommended that the door either be recessed in the building or that a cover be provided above it. For air protection, recessing the door will protect it from indirect exterior movement of air or where the incident angle of the air movement in relation to the door is not too acute. Another reason for recessing the door is that wind can push it open and damage it. Even if the door is recessed, however, movement and infiltrations into the interior space can be substantial. To reduce infiltration, two approaches can be considered (and also used together): **a.** *weather stripping* can be added around the door to seal the gaps. Various materials are used for weather stripping: EPDM rubber, bent metal, felt, foam rubber and plastic. Rubber and foam materials have the advantage of remaining flexible, being cost effective and sealing well (if material with the appropriate thickness is installed). Metal is more durable but transmits heat more than rubber or foam and can be damaged easily by being bent in the wrong direction; **b.** a *vestibule* may be provided to filter the outside air by limiting the infiltration to this specific area.

Infiltration is not the only reason for controlling air movement. Interior space in tall buildings can experience movement of air because of stack effect due to vertical elements (i.e., stairs or elevator shafts). This movement not only can increase the infiltration of air through the door but can also make it more difficult to operate the door. Use of revolving doors is an alternate method for diminishing the impact of differential pressure between inside and outside.

There are a variety of exterior doors made in different styles and materials. In the last two decades new styles and materials have been introduced providing choices other than the traditional:

1. *Wood Doors*: wood is the original material used for exterior doors (see Figure 9.30). There are two types of solid wood or plywood panel doors: *stiles* (where vertical strips of wood keep the layers of solid wood or the plywood panels together) and *rails* where the strips of wood are laid horizontally. In both cases, the finish can be solid or veneer.

   Wood doors are very attractive but, when exposed to water or moisture, can move more than other materials. In recent years manufacturers have improved the products by alternating the direction of the grain of the various layers. However, wood doors still require maintenance that other materials do not require. Glazing can be inserted in wood doors. In this case, penetration of moisture must be prevented at the edge of the channel in which the glass is inserted. This is particularly critical in the case of a door with a veneer finish.

2. *Metal Doors* (see Figure 9.30): in response to the instability of wood doors, the market developed metal doors during the 1960's. Initially these doors did not provide the styles and appearance that present day metal doors have achieved. Metal doors are durable and their thermal capability is enhanced by the introduction of a variety of insulating material installed in the cavity between the metal panels. In addition, in order to improve the appearance of the doors, a vinyl finish is added an element the early models lacked. This finish creates the impression that the door is made out of wood. The difference between this type of door and real wood doors is difficult to detect. Weather stripping is another area where metal doors have improved.

3. *Fiberglass Doors*: the advantage of this type of door is that it is possible to stamp the exterior surface of the door to appear like real wood. In addition, the material can be stained with common products used for wood. Another advantage of fiberglass doors is that they are more resilient than metal (which is more easily dented easier than fiberglass). Fiberglass doors are commonly insulated to improve their thermal characteristics.

4. *Composite Doors*: these are the latest development where the core of the door is made of one material and the finish is made of another. One example are doors with a steel or fiberglass core covered with wood veneer, which is a combination that offers the feel and the look of the real wood without the problems presented by wood arising from thermal and moisture factors.

Door Operating Systems

Exterior doors, like interior doors, can be operated in many ways, depending on their characteristics and functional aspects:

1. *Swinging Doors*: These are doors hinged to rotate along their vertical axis at one of their edges. They can swing in one direction (called single-acting) or in two directions (called double-acting). The swinging direction of a

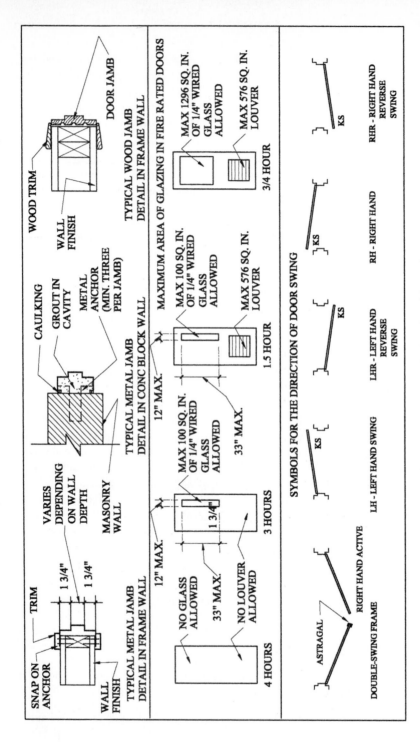

FIGURE 9.30 Wood and metal door details. Glazing in fire rated doors. Symbol for direction of door swing.

door needs to be specified in order to provide the right hardware. The specification follows conventional symbols and diagrams, which are illustrated in Figure 9.30. Double doors can have one or two active sides.

2. *Sliding Doors*: Depending on the operating system, these doors can slide horizontally or vertically. Horizontally sliding doors are very common doors that can be manually or automatically operated. They can be equipped with a top and bottom rack or the rack can be installed only at the top. These types, if rigid, need spaces on the side toward which they slide. They are not affected by wind or air pressure. However, they are not accepted as a means of egress unless they are collapsible or can swing in case of emergency (check the local regulations for specifics). In public spaces where they provide the only means of entrance, the timing of the opening and closing needs to meet ADA requirements. Sliding doors are normally glazed and require tempered safety glass.

For industrial applications there are two types of horizontally sliding doors: telescoping doors and folding doors. Both can be manually or automatically operated. The first type is composed of a series of rigid panels that slide to close normally into a recess in the wall (where the opening needs to be maximized). The motor operates the first panel that, through a series of cables, drags the remaining panels to the closing or opening position. The mechanism is arranged in a way that all the panels reach the final position at the same time. The second type is composed of a series of narrow sections that are pivoted along one edge which one section shares with the following one. The advantage of this type versus the telescoping system is that only two guide channels are required (since all the sections in the folding type are on the same line). The second reason is structural. The sections in the folding mechanism even in the closing position do not form a straight line but are at an angle relative to each other. This provides more resistance to wind load, resulting ultimately in thinner material. Both types need a foundation under the bottom rail.

Vertically sliding doors are typical of garage doors or industrial uses (i.e., loading). They can be manually operated or motorized. Recently, this type of door is becoming more common in residential construction. In this context, they are glazed and offer the possibility during the summer period of opening a large section of the exterior wall. The drawback in this case is that these doors do not have a very high thermal performance. They can be operated by being moved straight up, or they can be pivoted to form a canopy, or again they can be moved up straight up and rolled back. Usually all these types of doors are counterweighted, which requires approximately 15 inches of wall space beyond the jamb. The other side requires only 4 inches. In height, the narrower the horizontal sections of the door, the smaller the space needed between the top of the door and the ceiling. As a rule of thumb the space that should be provided is 1½ times the height of each horizontal section.

3. *Revolving Doors*: These types of doors are used where heavy traffic is not an issue. In locations and uses that might draw a large confluence of people, these doors need to be supplemented with other types that require less time for their operation. The advantages of revolving doors are the minimum rate of air exchange between the interior and the exterior (since the door is able to provide access without losing the seal towards the exterior). These type of doors, when they function as an exit, are strictly regulated by building codes that either disallow them or place a limit on the exit unit to be attributed to the door and also limit the distance of any other exit from the revolving door (check local codes for specifics).

Fire Rating for Doors

In situations where the exterior door can be exposed to fire hazard for example, because it is near an exit, too close to another building (therefore in a fire rated exterior wall assembly), or because it is near an opening in another fire rated compartment, the door needs to be fire rated. Such doors must bear the certification of an accredited testing agency (i.e., UL) that specifies the rating and they must be tested following standards like the ASTM E152. Fire rated doors must have a specific fire rating related to the fire rating of the wall or assembly in which they have been installed. The tolerances around the door are prescribed by the various codes. As a general rule, the following maximum gaps can be used: ⅛ inch for the jamb, ⅜ inch at the non-combustible floor and ⅜ inch at the top. Building codes specify that the door must open when a specific maximum force is applied to it (consult local codes for specifics). Fire doors must be provided with a self-closing mechanism that guarantees the continuous function of the door as fire separation. Exterior exit doors require panic hardware. For reason of security, many secondary doors in buildings do not have hardware on the outside and are operated only from the inside. Since exterior exit doors, whether rated or not, need to be equipped with panic hardware, this security requirement does not interfere with the function of the door.

Some doors are only required to function as smoke separation (in cases where the wall or the assembly in which the door is installed functions as smoke separation). Building codes might specify that these doors must have a minimum fire rating of 20 minutes. This rating can be provided by certified metal doors as well as certified solid core wood doors.

INTERIOR SYSTEMS

Interior space must accommodate a variety of functions that sometimes can be performed in a common open space (since their similar nature allows them not to conflict with each other) or they may need to be conducted in separate spaces (because the characteristics of one activity can be an obstacle to the good performance of another activity). A common denominator that can create the latter situation is noise.

The transmission of noise is studied by the science of acoustics, the principles of which needs to be applied routinely in the design of a building. Apart from being a component of a good design, the requirements of minimum sound separation between various functions are also a matter of code regulation.

Acoustic Principles

Acoustics is the science that studies the generation and propagation of sound. Sound is the reaction of the ear to changes in the atmospheric pressure caused by the vibration of elements.

There are two types of sounds: direct sound (which is airborne sound) and reverberated sound (created by the bouncing of sound waves off an object after they have been generated by a source). In architecture both are important. The principles of the physical nature of direct sound and reverberated sound are the same and are based on the vibration of some element.

Sounds propagate in waves very much like concentric ripples caused by a pebble thrown into a body of water. However, sound can have different wave forms from square to sine wave (see Figure 9.31). If we consider a sequence of pebbles that are thrown, we have a model that resembles the mechanics of a sound. The action of throwing and the pebble reaching a particular spot will have a certain frequency (f). In turn the waves will have a speed (the distance traveled in a unit of time defined by the symbol v) and a wavelength (the distance between the waves identified by the symbol λ). The relationship that relates the three factors is ruled by the following equation: $v = f \lambda$. In addition, the intensity is inversely proportional to the square of the distance.

When the sound reaches an obstacle, it is partially absorbed (and transformed into heat energy), transmitted, and reflected. The principle through which it is propagated or reflected is the same: vibration. When an object vibrates, it compresses the air on one side of it, which, in the same way the pebble in the pond acts upon molecules of water, provokes movement of the air molecules. The vibration of the object is cyclical, which means that the object will come back to its static position before it will bend in the direction opposite to the one originally occupied when it vibrated for the first time. This will cause a depression (called *rarefaction*) in the air on the same side where the first sound wave originated. The molecule of air will respond to this phenomenon by moving in the opposite direction (towards the object). This will create the release of another sound wave, similar to the first one. This movement (cycle) will keep repeating until the object stops vibrating (due to friction or dispersed and absorbed energy created in other ways). Since the human ear is capable of hearing sounds in the range of 20 to 20,000 cycles per second, being very sensitive in the 125 to the 6000 cycles per second range, the lack of perception of sound does not mean that the object is not vibrating anymore, but rather that the vibration cycles have fallen below the audible frequency. In these low frequencies, the sound can be perceived only as vibration.

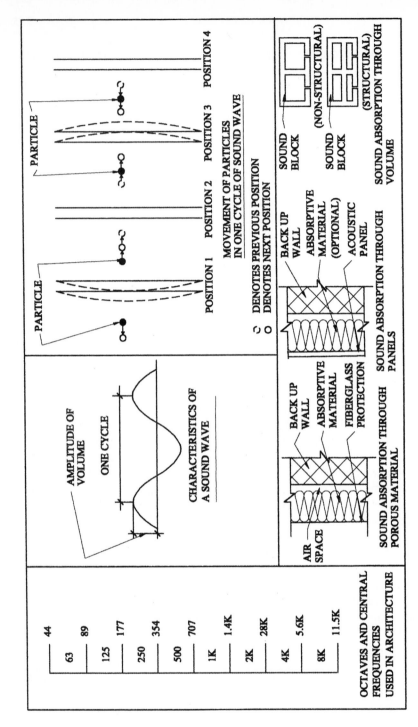

FIGURE 9.31 Principles of acoustics and acoustical characteristics of materials.

9.74

It is therefore the oscillating movements of molecules of air (or other mediums) that create the sound wave (see Figure 9.31). The molecules are pushed from an original position to occupy a different position. When the molecules reach this position they come to rest. Then they come back towards the object because of the above-mentioned rarefaction. This movement covers a particular distance, which determines what is called the frequency of the wave. Throughout this process, the speed of the molecule is maximum in the middle of the cycle and zero at the extremes. The velocity (which is an average of 0.1 mm/sec) is determined by the loudness of the sound (in very loud sounds this distance can be measured as 1 cm/sec) and its frequency. The frequency (identified by the ear as pitch and measured in hertz or one cycle per second) is a fundamental characteristic, since the behavior of the sound and of the materials is greatly dependent on it. The loudness of the sound is also an important parameter in relation to the energy contained in the sound wave (measured in W/m^2). The relationship between energy and frequency of the sound wave is called sound spectrum.

The frequency also determines the wavelength. If we consider that sound travels in air at the speed of 1130 ft/sec (344 m/s), the wavelength of a sound at 40 Hz is 1130 / 40 = 28.25' (8.6 m). Because of the negligible difference, sound is considered in round numbers to travel through the air at 1000 ft/sec. This makes the calculation very easy since the wavelength of a sound at 100 Hz becomes 10' while the wavelength of a sound of 2 kHz is 6 inches. For architectural purposes, in order to group levels of sounds that, if considered individually, would be too numerous, sounds are divided into specific octaves (these are sounds that range between an upper and lower frequency, see Figure 9.31).

The frequency of the sound is also important because it provides indications on where in space the speed of the particles will be at the maximum. Since any sound-absorptive material functions better if it slows down the particles at that location, the frequency and the design of a sound absorbing assembly have a direct relationship. The distance of the vibrating particles relative to each other, then, is another factor that determines the above. Since the distance between the particles varies, when it corresponds to the wavelength, the particles move in synchrony (as if they were connected by a rigid element); when their distance is a fraction of the wavelength, their positions in the cycle vary relative to each other. This means that, at a particular instant in time, their velocity is not the same.

The intensity level of the sound is expressed in decibels (dB) which is the logarithmic relation between the given intensity (I) and the reference intensity (I_{ref}) set at $10^{-12} W/m^2$ (which is the threshold of audible sounds, called *threshold of audibility*): 10 log I/I_{ref}. The minimum change in sound audible to the human ear is 3 dB.

In the analysis of sound, the two aspects that can be identified and which particularly affect architecture are the behavior of sound in the environment where it is generated and the effect of sound on spaces other than the space where the sound is generated. It is important to consider that a material suitable for one aspect does not necessarily perform as well if used in another aspect (see comments below in *porous* with specific reference to acoustic tiles).

1. The behavior of sound in the environment where it is generated: As we indicated, the sound reaching a partition can be reflected (known as *reflection coefficient* ρ); absorbed (referred to as Absorption Coefficient *a*) or transmitted (called Transmission Coefficient τ). Their total sum is equal to 1. The individual values range between 0 and 1. From the point of view of reflection, it is not important to differentiate between the percentage of sound that is absorbed and the amount that is transmitted. Therefore the index of absorption, in this case, groups both values:

$$\rho + a = 1.0$$

The capacity of a material to absorb sound is very important. Reflection of sound creates reverberation, which is the sound that bounces back on surfaces. Depending on the reverberation time, the sound tends to mix with the new sound that is created, sometime enhancing it (as for certain instruments) in other cases overlapping it negatively (i.e., in a conference). The reverberation time (T_r), which is the time that passes before a sound of 60dB has stopped, is the ratio between the volume of the space and the total absorptivity of the materials expressed in sabins:

$$T_r = .049V/A$$

There are different reverberation times recommended for each activity. If the volume is given as the capacity of the space and its design, then the variable that is usually manipulated with the choice of the appropriate absorptive material is A.

It is important to control the amount of sound that is reflected by using material that provides the right percentage of absorption. This characteristic of the material is measured in what is called the Noise Reduction Coefficient (NRC). It is calculated using the absorption coefficient of a material at 250, 500, 1,000, and 2,000 Hz and averaging it (divided by 4). The NRC is particularly important in environment where speech is the primary source of noise (this is why the limitation of the frequencies must be considered, since frequencies above the 2kHz do not occur in speech generated sound). In other cases, where higher frequencies are generated in a given space, the *a* related to these frequencies must be analyzed. In acoustically sensitive spaces a NRC of 0.60 or 0.70 could be used as a guideline.

The coefficient *a* is a characteristic of the material. The sound absorption of an element (A) created with that material is the product of *a* and the area of the surface (S) of the element: A = Sa. This product, known also as *unit of absorption*, is called either a foot sabin (if expressed in feet) or a meter sabin (if expressed in meters). Because of the relationship between feet and meters, one meter sabin = 10.76 foot sabin.

There are different absorption materials with different characteristics and mechanics. Four main categories can be identified:

a. *Panels*: solid sheets of material with an air space between them and the back up wall. The principle of noise reduction is the fact that the panel vibrating will convert some of the sound energy into other forms (a phenomenon called *dumping*). The highest dumping happens at the resonance frequency, which is the natural frequency of a material if it is solicited by a force and left vibrating without any interference. These frequencies depend on the mass of the panel and the cushion of air behind it. The thinner the film of air, the stiffer the cushion. The more mass the panel has, the less it will vibrate. The formula that allows the identification of the resonance frequency in a particular component is the following: $f_{res} = 170/\sqrt{m\ d}$, where m = mass of the panel in lb/ft$_2$ and d is the air space behind the panel. Adding a porous material in the cavity increases the rate of absorption since it affects the vibration of the panel. Usual material utilized for this purpose is fiberglass (see Figure 9.31).

b. *Volume*: the principle on which this type of sound absorption works is based on the friction that air creates against materials. The mechanism is the same as the interaction that is observed in a bottle. The molecules of air in the neck of the bottle, stimulated by the molecules of air outside of the bottle, start vibrating in the narrow space. This creates considerable friction with the walls of the neck, dissipating some of the sound energy. One example of this type of sound absorption is the sound block (see Figure 9.31). This unit is very similar to a normal concrete block. The difference is that the cavities are closed on one side (to create the *bottle effect*), and laid out with the part that is closed on top (since mortar has to be placed between one unit and the next). The advantage of this technique is that the units constitute the wall and no additional back-up wall is required. Common installations are in industrial environments, gymnasiums or swimming pools. Structural units are available, where there are two cavities of which one is filled with reinforcing and concrete: the other cavity functions as an acoustical absorber (see Figure 9.30).

c. *Porous*: in general, these are materials or products that are made of fibers with and air space between them or material that has voids on the surface between which the sound can be trapped (i.e., acoustic tiles, fiberglass insulation; see Figure 9.31). The sound enters the material and puts the molecules of air in motion. Because of the friction between the molecules and the material, the sound energy for the most part is transformed into heat and loses its characteristics. Given the characteristics of a certain material, the flow resistance (i.e., the rate of air flow through the material) is at its maximum at a certain mass. If the material is too dense, the air will not be able to penetrate and set the process in motion. If it is too loose, the air will pass through without creating any friction. It appears that material with fine fibers and high density is the most efficient from the point of view of flow resistance. A density commonly used for fiberglass is between 1 and 9 lb/ft^2.

Increase in the thickness of the material increases the sound absorption of the material for low frequencies, but does not increase considerably its absorption of sound at high frequencies. The reason is that long waves created by low frequencies determine the location where the particles reach the higher speed (therefore where the material is most effective in attenuating the sound). For short waves, the speed is reached closer to the back-up wall; therefore an increase in the thickness of the material does not represent an improvement. In both cases, it is effective to move the material away from the wall creating an air gap, since near the wall the particles have a velocity close to zero. In general, a 4" thick fiberglass blanket can provide an effective sound barrier in both the high and the low frequencies.

It is a good practice to protect fiberglass in order to prevent particles from filling the voids between the fibers, diminishing the sound absorption capacity of the material. Common materials are fabrics (where the finish is exposed and has a decorative function) or any thin membrane that does not interfere with the transmission of sound into the fiberglass (an example is 1 mil plastic sheets).

In the case of fabric-covered porous material, another application is to suspend an acoustically designed geometric element from the ceiling. Like any other sound absorption element in a space (people, seating, floor, walls and ceiling finishing), these elements can be very effective in contributing to the successful acoustical performance of the space and can be even decorative. People also contribute to the absorption of sound.

   d. *Composite*: this category refers either to elements that, because of their characteristics, behave by combining more that one principles of sound absorption, or the element is actually an assembly comprised of components, each of which has different characteristics. One example of this latter case is the previously mentioned panel with fiberglass behind it (Figure 9.31). Another is the commonly used wood slat screen. The components are basically spaced vertical strips of wood with insulation behind them. Among the other type of elements that act as sound absorbers applying more than one characteristic, a common example is the ceiling acoustic tile. The surface of these tiles is scored, to create the effect of a porous material and yet it acts also as panel (because of the air space between the tiles and the floor structure above). It is important to consider that the sound transmission through acoustical ceiling tiles is very high (see Figure 9.32). When considering the performance of materials, therefore, their effect on the acoustics of the space where the sound is generated is only one aspect. The other is their performance in controlling the impact of sound on spaces other than the ones where the sound is generated.

2. The effect of sound on spaces other than the space where the sound is generated (see Figure 9.32). There are two types of sounds that might affect other spaces: structure-borne and airborne sounds. The former is created by the vibrations of the separation caused by an impact upon it. The latter originates from a source and it travels through air to reach the separation.

The attenuation of the first type of sound is dependent on the use of materials that are not high impact (i.e., felts to be installed under the floor finish, resilient flooring, carpet with thick underlay). In the case of airborne sounds, the transmission coefficient (τ) of the material is particularly important. In fact it is the reciprocal of τ ($1/\tau$), defined as its sound insulation, that gives a better definition of the amount of noise transmitted through the separation. The transmission loss (TL) is the basic measurement and is defined by the following formula: TL (in dB) = $10log$ ($1/\tau$). The higher the TL, the greater the sound isolation. The value of TL is dependent on the sound frequencies. The following are important characteristics of the components and assembly:

1. *Mass of the elements*: more mass corresponds to more TL.
2. *Stiffness*: the stiffer the component, the smaller the TL.
3. *Air cavity between the elements*: two or more elements separated by air function better acoustically than one element having the same mass equal to the sum of the individual masses of the multiple elements. Especially in the middle frequencies the sound loss is more than the loss caused by the simple mass of the panels. This is because the air is not rigid and can respond with limits to the bouncing back and forth of the sound wave between the panels. This effect is even more accentuated if a porous material is inserted between the panels. In this case the air, as we have seen in the description above, dumps even more acoustical energy because of the friction.
4. *Continuity of sound isolation material at connections or through various assemblies*: it is important, for example, to make sure that gaps (i.e., top and bottom of wall) or air spaces (i.e., above an acoustical ceiling) are properly treated for airborne sound transmission (see Figure 9.32). The value of TL, as it relates to the octave ranging from 125 Hz to 4kHz, is represented by one index: the Sound Transmission Class (STC). The higher the number, the higher the sound isolation. Codes require a minimum STC dependent on occupancies. For residential, the minimum is an STC of 50 or 55 (depending on the location of the wall and adjacent spaces). The performance of an assembly in laboratory tests can be very different from the performance of the same assembly in the field. Therefore, good practice in these cases suggests exceeding the minimum value. However, since increasing minimum requirements is based on individual judgment, each case must be carefully reviewed within its own particular functional and economic circumstances and characteristics.

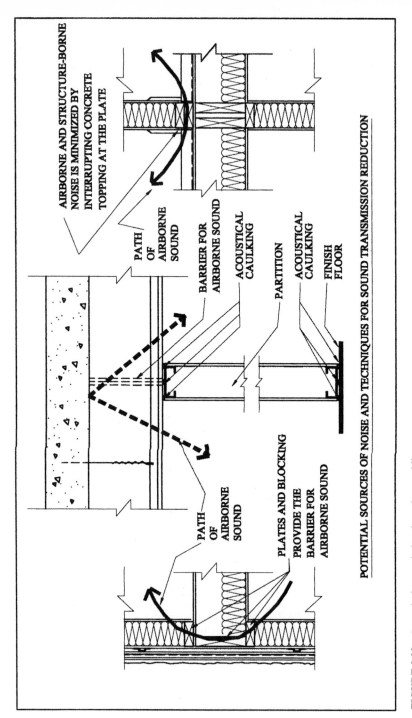

FIGURE 9.32 Acoustical transmission through assemblies.

AIRBORNE AND STRUCTURE-BORNE NOISE IS MINIMIZED BY INTERRUPTING CONCRETE TOPPING AT THE PLATE

PATH OF AIRBORNE SOUND

BARRIER FOR AIRBORNE SOUND

ACOUSTICAL CAULKING

PARTITION

ACOUSTICAL CAULKING

FINISH FLOOR

POTENTIAL SOURCES OF NOISE AND TECHNIQUES FOR SOUND TRANSMISSION REDUCTION

PATH OF AIRBORNE SOUND

PLATES AND BLOCKING PROVIDE THE BARRIER FOR AIRBORNE SOUND

An additional aspect of the transmission of noise is sound diffraction. This parameter defines the ability of sound to go around an obstacle by bending. Sound diffraction is dependent on frequency. High frequency sounds bend less than low frequency sounds. The minimum size of a square panel to provide some absorption at different frequencies, height and width should be five times the wave frequency expected.

INTERIOR PARTITIONS

Interior space is usually subdivided by partitions that range in height (extending from floor to ceiling or various intermediate heights that allow a degree of visual privacy or only a demarcation of the space). Interior walls can be structural or non-structural. In the latter case, particular care should be placed in detailing the top of the wall if it runs from the floor to the ceiling. Movement and deflection of the structure should not place any load on these non-load bearing walls. The materials with which the elements are built can vary considerably and are dependent on aspects like function, aesthetics, cost, weight, transparency, light penetration, structural requirements and/or cost. Among the many possibilities, partitions are generally built of concrete, concrete masonry, or brick masonry.

Concrete

One of the reasons why this material is chosen for building interior partitions is the shear strength that it offers. Shear walls provide lateral stability to the construction (see Chapter 6). When this is their function, these types of walls run from foundation to roof without any interruption or offset. Another reason for choosing this material is for its vertical and horizontal structural capacity combined with a certain aesthetical boldness that in various environments could add to the quality of the space.

These walls could be left exposed or painted as well as furred and covered with any finish. When left exposed, an architectural finish must be specified. Finishes vary and many of them are dependent on the quality of the surface of the forms as well as the type of form liner. There are basically three methods through which the finish of the concrete is altered: changing the color of the concrete; controlling the quality of the form and introducing a form liner; treating the concrete when it is not completely dry. The first method should not be used on multiple panel walls because it is difficult to match the exact color when the additive is not placed in different pours. The second method can offer interesting textures and geometrical shapes sculptured into the concrete using molds. The third method alters the surface of the concrete by scoring, scratching, chiseling, hammering, or sandblasting. When using this third method it is important to specify the degree of roughness of the finish. In all three cases, it is better to create a mock-up on site before applying a particular finish to all the surfaces.

Furring can take the form of "z" bars, hat channels, metal or wood studs as well as strips of plywood, if moisture is not a factor (see Figure 9.25). If metal or wood studs are used, they are not usually placed directly on the wall for various reasons: the concrete wall usually has vertical and horizontal tolerances that might affect the alignment of the studs; there might be the presence of moisture that could affect the wood and the steel of the studs; electrical wiring may be laid out more efficiently if it runs in the space between the studs and the concrete wall; sound transmission could be improved.

Concrete Masonry

This material is usually chosen for the following wall characteristics:

1. The interior wall must have a structural capacity. In this case masonry walls can be connected to various other structural systems like: concrete, steel or wood (see Figures 9.12, and 9.23). As indicated earlier in this chapter, allowance must be provided for differential movement and expansion at the point of connection. In addition, the expansion of the masonry wall needs to be taken into account. As a general rule, the value of the wall expansion for water and thermal absorption is 0.0007. This means that a wall 50 feet long will expand 2 x 50 x 12 x 0.0007 = .89 of an inch. These vertical expansion joints should be placed between 50 and 100 feet apart with the joint not closer than 30 feet from a wall intersection with another wall.

   In spacing the joints, it is important to consider the type of sealant that will be used. The sealant specification regarding its elastomeric or compressibility characteristics can dictate the maximum spacing of the joints.

2. The wall must have a particular fire rating and needs to be built in non-combustible material (fire wall or area separation wall). In this case the characteristics of the masonry partition is defined by the code and by tests conducted by accredited laboratories (i.e., the UL). Usually the dimension may change between 1 hr and 1.5 hr (going from 6" in the first case, to 8" in the second) For some types of products, in order to increase the fire rating beyond the 2 hrs, the basic masonry unit does not change and maintains the same dimensions. Filling the cores with a special material might be required in order to satisfy increased fire rating.

3. The wall surrounds a utility space or an area where the structure of the wall will be exposed (i.e., in parkades or factories). Since aesthetics is not a factor in these areas, either no finish is required or paint will be applied (which helps to create more light in the space, seal the concrete wall and improve the hygiene by keeping the wall cleaner). In utility spaces (i.e., mechanical, electrical, telephone or cable rooms) on some of the walls where equipment will be hung, ¾ inch plywood is usually installed. In this case, electrical drawings are fundamental in order to specify where the plywood should be located and its dimensions.

4. The wall needs lateral strength for possible impacts (i.e., in warehouses). Where machinery is used, it is not advisable to build walls in frame construction (because of the possibility of the wall being damaged by heavy equipment). For these reasons, either the entire walls are built of masonry (concrete can be more expensive) or, if they do not provide structural support as well, they are built only partially of masonry and the remaining part of a cheaper material (this second solution is not common). If additional strength to impact is required when the complete wall is built of masonry, the cores of the concrete blocks can be filled and reinforced with structural grout up to a certain height.

If the wall is not structural, tolerances need to be left at the top of the wall in order to avoid any stress transferred onto the wall due to structural movement/deflection or wall expansion (see Figure 9.12 for the typical connection between non-load bearing concrete block wall and concrete slab). Under non-load bearing concrete block walls, slab on grade needs to be thickened to avoid cracking under the weight (see Figure 9.33).

Brick Masonry

These types of walls are not used as much as other types. However, they are very rich in texture and character. There is also a sense of heritage and solidity associated with their appearance that tends to create a sense of security and warmth in the interior space. From the point of view of fire rating, brick masonry is one of the better materials (since it has been exposed to fire already). A 4 inch wall can provide 1¼ hour. However, if plaster is applied to the wall, the rating can be increased to 2½ hours. This is because one of the important aspects of these products that affects their fire resistance is their wall thickness. Hollow bricks have a

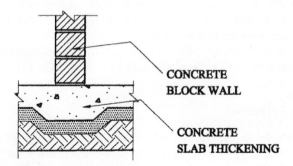

CONCRETE
BLOCK WALL

CONCRETE
SLAB THICKENING

**TYPICAL CONCRETE SLAB DETAIL
UNDER NON-LOAD BEARING
CONCRETE BLOCK WALL**

FIGURE 9.33 Typical concrete slab detail under non-load bearing concrete block wall.

wall thickness that varies and the surfaces of the units can be exposed to different temperatures during fire. For these reasons, they do not behave uniformly, resulting in spalling and shattering of the units. The *equivalent thickness* is the measure of fire endurance of hollow bricks and it is the value obtained by multiplying the overall dimension of the unit by the percentage of the solid material in the unit.

If combustible material is incorporated into the structure of the wall, in order to maintain the 2.5 hour fire rating, then the masonry portion needs to be 8 inches thick with plaster applied on the exposed side. Without the plaster, the rating of the same wall drops to 2 hours.

Wood Framing

As described previously, this is the most common wall used if combustible construction is an option. What has been described in the exterior walls is also valid for interior walls. Although the studs and plates have a fire rating assigned to them (approximately 20 minutes), most of the fire rating of these walls is achieved by adding layers of materials (usually gypsum wallboard). Rating can be increased up to 4 hours (rarely used since beyond a certain rating, codes require the partition to be built in non-combustible materials)

Codes assign fire rating to generic assemblies (for these reasons they usually are more stringent than UL ratings). UL testing assigns rating to proprietary systems. When using the systems rated by UL agencies, it is important not to change materials, products, or method of assembly because the test and their rating is valid only for that particular assembly. In the case of code-rated assemblies, there is more flexibility, although all the specifications and characteristics indicated in the appropriate sections need to be incorporated as reference in the contract documents. In terms of acoustics, an STC is assigned to the assemblies as well.

The function of the space and an idea of the type of installations that will be placed inside the space are very important in order to decide on the components of the wall. Suspended cabinets, interior handrails, heavy wall units, shelves or even heavy paintings, require blocking to avoid having to coordinate the location of the fasteners with the location of studs or to limit the choices of possible locations of these elements. In order to cope with these aspects related to existing walls, special fasteners can be used that can work for limited applications.

Steel Stud Framing

In non-combustible construction these walls are the equivalent of wood stud walls. The basic characteristics have been described in discussing the steel stud exterior walls. The process of identifying the fire rating is the same as the one presented for the interior wood framed walls. Blocking is even more important for metals stud walls. If a stud is used to secure elements to the wall, then screws rather than nails should be used.

CHAPTER 10
GRAPHIC SYMBOLS

In Chapter 1 we explored the dynamic of communication, placing particular emphasis on graphics. In Chapter 3 we analyzed graphic representations in relation to concepts and conceptual organizations. In this chapter we will review a particular graphic representation related to technical drawings. Technical drawings are usually part of a series of contract documents. Each of these documents has a particular role in the agreement between the parties (as indicated in Chapter 1). Further information that is necessary but is not intended to be part of the types of symbols included in the drawings will be assumed to appear in one of the other contract documents.

STANDARDS

The approach to graphic representations is not completely standardized. This does not mean that there are no standards available; it means that these standards are not used by all professionals. They become mandatory if the project is under the control of the institution that issued them. In the main body of graphic communication, however, it appears that certain symbols are commonly used (i.e., symbols for building and detail sections, details, doors, floor elevations) and certain conventions for dimensioning are also commonly accepted. Other symbols are created as different standards for different offices. For these reasons a legend indicating all the symbols used and their meaning should be included in all graphic material. The following is a list of sources and documents containing recognized standards.

Military handbooks:

MIL-STD-12D	Abbreviations for use on drawings and in technical publications.
MIL-STD-14A	Architectural symbols.
MIL-STD-18	Structural symbols.
MIL-STD-17B	Mechanical symbols.
MTL-STD-100E	Engineering drawing practices.
DOD-STD-100C	Engineering drawing practices.

National Standards:

ANSI Y14.1	Drawing sheet size and format.
ANSI Y14.2	Line conventions and lettering.
ANSI Y14.3	Multi and sectional views.
ANSI Y14.5M	Dimensioning and tolerancing.
ANSI Y32.4	Graphic symbols for plumbing fixtures for diagrams used in architecture and building construction.
ANSI Y32.9	Graphic symbols for electrical wiring and layout diagrams used in architecture and building construction.
ANSI/AWS A3.0	Standard welding terms and definitions.
ANSI/AWS 2.4	Symbols for welding and non-destructive testing.
ASTM E3	Standards for metric use.

Whether standard symbols are used or not, it is important to consider the basic principles that determine their characteristics and how they are used. This under-standing can help in reducing errors and omissions as well as improving com-munication among the participants in the project.

PRINCIPLES OF COMMUNICATION FOR TECHNICAL DRAWINGS

Although in principle the basic components that create a communication system do not change, other than for the conceptual graphic expression illustrated in Chapter 3, technical drawings need a very minute flexibility in manipulating the components. Although concepts may be expressed within a broad view, details need to be very specific and they must respond to a greater variety of elements with specific arrangements. For these reasons, the interrelationship between words and graphic is very articulated in technical drawings. Where technical drawings are more illus-trative (almost becoming a hybrid between technical and conceptual), then the type of organization shown in Chapter 3 can apply also to them. An example of this case is represented by a sequence of drawings that illustrate steps in assembling a particular object (see Figure 10.1a). The sequence requires a structuring of the symbols that diversifies the grammatical roles of each of them (the nouns, verbs, adverbs or adjectives in language systems). For example, the arrow in the case shown on Figure 10.1 has the same function as a verb. It is like saying: *insert* (the object) here. In technical drawings (such as the traditional *working drawings* or *construction drawings* used in architecture and related disciplines) where, instead of symbols, words describe the action, an arrow has a completely different meaning (see item 4 below).

Because of the above disparities between drawings that express concepts and technical drawings, we will identify the elements that create the communication system for technical drawings differently from the ones listed in Figure 3.11. The relationship is very direct and can be identified clearly. These elements can be grouped as it follows:

1. Discrete components (comparable to consonants and vowels in language) are elements that require other components to create a meaning. They range from arcs to composite shapes, from geometrical regular figures to single lines (see Figure 10.1b).

2. A series of conventions to indicate whether or not the discrete elements are in relationship and the type of rhythm that links them (i.e., no space, single space, double space in the written language). These conventions can correspond to the law of geometry as well as to the law of perception (i.e., proximity versus distance). On this subject see also Figure 3.9.

3. A corollary of subsystems (or *units*), related to elements of the tangible world and/or to abstract items of the conceptual world, are created by combining the discrete elements using the conventions, spacers and rules of the graphic system. (They can be compared to words in the language system). Through this process, these units have acquired a direct and unambiguous relationship with the objective of the communication and therefore a meaning is associated with them. An example is a generic geometrical figure labeled within its boundaries as a particular object (see Figure 10.1c). Another example is a specific geometric figure that does not need labeling because its shape resembles very closely the object to which it is related and its location reinforces the meaning: i.e., a toilet placed in a bathroom (see Figure 10.1d). However, this case is an example of what was mentioned at the beginning of this chapter. The additional necessary information not provided on the drawings appears in the specifications where characteristics, models, or types are defined (as indicated in Chapter 1 and Figure 1.11).

4. A series of spacers that indicate the relationship between units, in this case an arrow between a sentence and a geometric figure, can provide a link similar to the period placed at the end of a sentence. Between the two components, the arrow creates a direct relationship that excludes all the other elements that are part of the drawings (see Figure 10.1e).

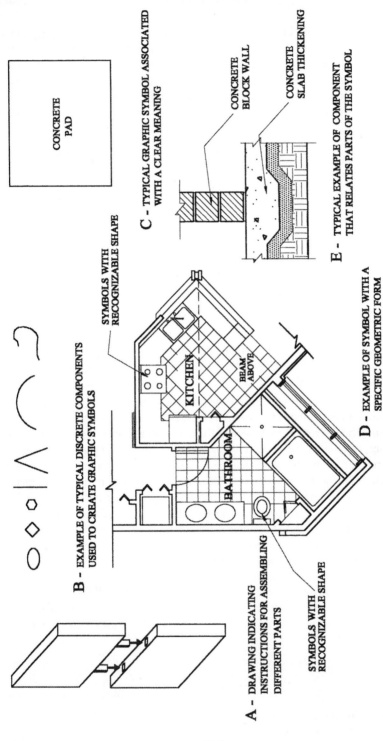

FIGURE 10.1 Characteristics and functions of graphic symbols.

CONCRETE
PAD

SYMBOLS WITH
RECOGNIZABLE SHAPE

B – EXAMPLE OF TYPICAL DISCRETE COMPONENTS
USED TO CREATE GRAPHIC SYMBOLS

KITCHEN

BEAM
ABOVE

BATHROOM

SYMBOLS WITH
RECOGNIZABLE SHAPE

A – DRAWING INDICATING
INSTRUCTIONS FOR ASSEMBLING
DIFFERENT PARTS

D – EXAMPLE OF SYMBOL WITH A
SPECIFIC GEOMETRIC FORM

CONCRETE
BLOCK WALL

CONCRETE
SLAB THICKENING

C – TYPICAL GRAPHIC SYMBOL ASSOCIATED
WITH A CLEAR MEANING

E – TYPICAL EXAMPLE OF COMPONENT
THAT RELATES PARTS OF THE SYMBOL

10.4

5. A legend can function as a codifier. In the legend, the relationship between the meaning and the symbol is specified once and for all. Symbols of wall, floor or roof types constitute a similar case. For the correct use of these symbols it is necessary to know that the direction in which the symbols are oriented must follow the sequence of the material listed in the legend (see Figure 10.2a).

In addition to the above, *qualifiers* are used for both conceptual drawings and for technical drawings (see Figure 3.11). This is similar to the role that facial and vocal expression, tone of voice, and gestures have in verbal expression. There is no difference of intent, for example, between raising the tone of the voice in a verbal communication in order to attract someone's attention, and in graphic communication drawing a thicker line to emphasize an element. Likewise, a gesture that points to an item can be compared with an arrow that starts from a word and ends near a series of lines representing the object described by the words (see also item 4 above).

Types of Symbols and Relation to Meaning

From the point of view of achieving clear and unmistakable meaning, we have to consider the symbol as the complete set of information. This is fundamental because one of the causes of failure in communication resides in considering the separate components of the message (i.e., the graphic symbol and the explanatory wording) as autonomous entities rather than a system. The risk is to feel that the act of communication has been accomplished as soon as one of these elements is represented (usually the graphics). This is very natural since the information in our thoughts can be complete and this can result in seeing the partial information transferred to the drawings as complete as well. One of the tendencies of our brain is to fill the gaps and assign meanings even though a portion of the message is missing. This is why spell-checking requires particular attention: a word where a letter is missing could be seen as a complete entity. In the case of the symbol the relationship of the parts is even more complex than a word.

From this point of view there are three possible cases that allow the association of the symbol with the meaning (the message):

1. The graphics are sufficient to convey the meaning that a drawing needs to communicate (see Chapter 3 for the role of drawings). The message is so complete that a displacement of the graphic symbols would immediately raise questions because of the ambiguity of the communication (i.e., a toilet in the middle of a bedroom or a door in a wall at the second floor that does not lead to stairs). In other words the relationship between the form of the symbol and the meaning is contextually sensitive. This means that the form also relates to the meaning depending on context in which the form is placed. An oval on a rectangle drawn in a bathroom is very likely to be a sink on a bathroom counter. If the same oval is placed in another room in a corner it becomes very ambiguous and its meaning requires further information.

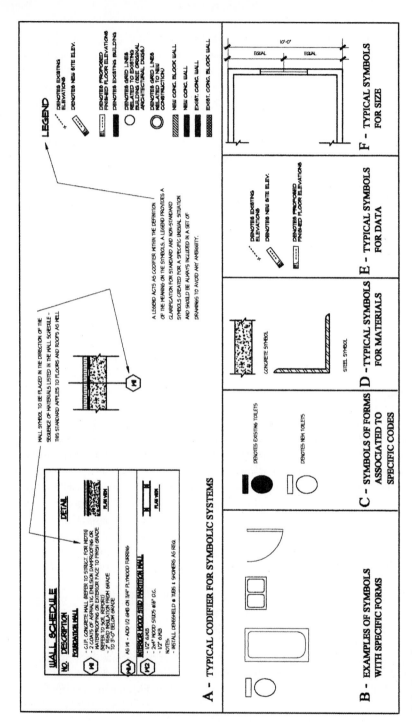

FIGURE 10.2 Different types of symbols.

Examples of these types of symbols are provided in Figure 10.2b. These symbols still identify only the object. The type, material, and characteristics are indicated somewhere else (either in a schedule or in the specifications).

2. The information is contained within the relationship among the components of the symbol: the graphics and the words, for example, are very closely related spatially (see Figures 10.1c and 10.1e).

3. In order to understand the meaning, one needs to refer to additional information not appearing on the graphics. In this case, either a legend or a schedule is created that gives meaning to the graphics and to the numeric or alphabetic characters. The information may also be found in another drawing (such as a similar detail) where there may be some repetition as well as additional information (see Figure 10.2a).

Following is a list and description of the elements that are identified by graphic symbols:

1. Shapes (the geometric form of the object): this is a very immediate type of communication and, in this case, the symbols are part of the first category listed above (see Figure 10.2b). A second case is when the graphic part of the symbol is spatially closely associated with the written explanation. In this instance, the symbol belongs to the second category (see Figure 10.1e). The third case is when the shape is actually used very often in the drawings. Then usually a legend is set up to avoid repetitions in specifying each individual case (see Figure 10.2c. For additional examples of this type of symbols see also Figures 10.4 and 10.5).

2. Materials: if the graphic is part of accepted standards, then for an experienced observer this set of symbols can belong to the first category since the meaning is known and no reference to a legend is necessary. In another case the symbols indicating the material need to be accompanied by a legend and this places them in the third category (see Figure 10.2d and Figure 10.6, which shows some additional samples of this type of symbols).

3. Types of systems (such as an assembly): these symbols are used in order to avoid repetitions. By definition, therefore, they belong to the third category since they require a constant reference to another or more sets of symbols (see Figure 10.2a). An example of a case where more than one set of symbol is necessary to complete the information is a door and window schedule (see Chapter 11 for a more complete discussion on schedules). Examples of this type of symbols are shown in Figure 10.7.

4. Data (i.e., floor elevations): these symbols usually consist of a graphic component and an alphabetic and numeral component, which are visually closely related. However the comments on symbols illustrating materials can apply to symbols used for data. It is the familiarity of the observer that determines the category to which these symbols belong (see Figure 10.2e. For additional examples of this type of symbols see also Figure 10.3.

5. Sizes (i.e., dimensions): dimensions are the most common types of symbols used to identify the exact size of a component or an object. Since the graphics and the wording are always close together without requiring any additional information, these symbols are part of the second category (see Figure 10.2f). In addition, sizes for particular components of the project (i.e., equipment, structural columns, joists or special material) are provided in schedules (see Chapter 11 for a review of schedules).

6. Reference: these symbols indicate the type of drawing (i.e., section, detail) and their location (i.e., the number of the sheet). For examples of this type of symbols see Figure 10.7.

7. Entities: these are symbols that refer to items such as property lines, project components that are above or below another project component or brake lines. In addition they can highlight characteristics of certain parts of the project such as existing components or components that need to be demolished. For examples of this type of symbols see Figure 10.7.

Refer to Figure 10.8 for additional architectural miscellaneous symbols.

Engineering Symbols

In principle, the symbols of structural components of the project are used in the same way architectural elements are represented, except for the concrete structure. In the latter case, the parts of the structure that are represented in the plan drawings are the ones at or below the horizontal cut line. Slab bands and beams shown are the ones under the slab. This symbolic system is the opposite of the technique used to show members in a steel or wooden structure. In the latter case beams, joists, and lintels are above the cut line. Figure 10.9 provides some general examples of symbols used by structural engineers.

Structural symbols (this also applies to mechanical, plumbing and electrical drawings, as seen in Figures 10.10 through 10.15) are not always consistent, and different offices use variations. A legend should be always provided and if it is not on the drawings, the architect should require it to be included.

Use of Symbols

Symbols can be also identified as reference for the items to which they apply and reference for items directly related to these items. An example of this is a product like a fiberglass shower stall that does not need to be dimensioned because its size and type will be indicated in the specifications. However, the walls surrounding the stall must be dimensioned. In this case, the specific tolerance and method of installation of the product would require that the elements around it be of a specific size. In another case, it might be that by converting the space into a planter, for

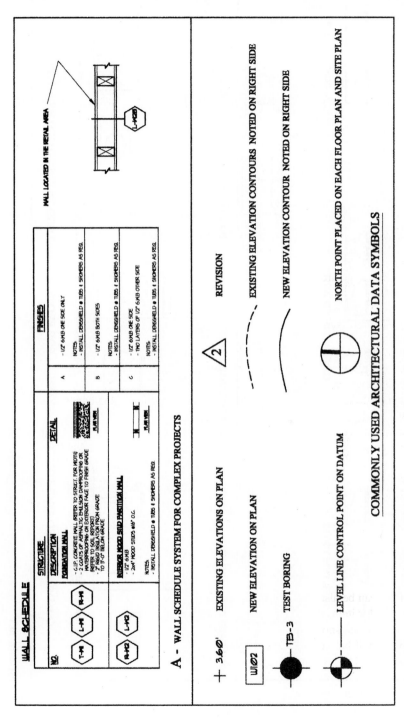

FIGURE 10.3 Wall schedule system for complex projects and data types of graphic systems.

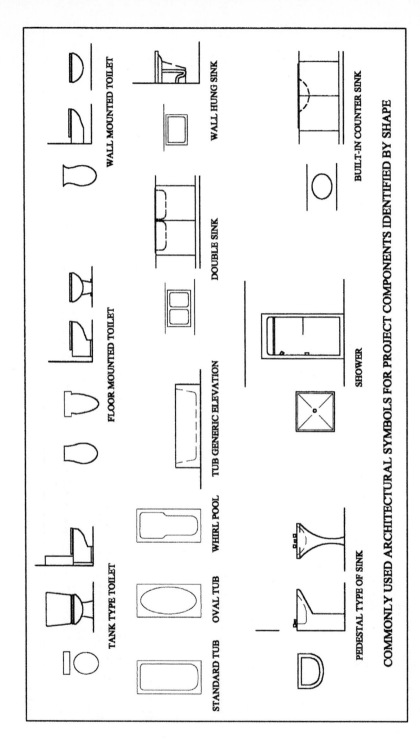

TANK TYPE TOILET

FLOOR MOUNTED TOILET

WALL MOUNTED TOILET

STANDARD TUB   OVAL TUB   WHIRL POOL   TUB GENERIC ELEVATION   DOUBLE SINK   WALL HUNG SINK

PEDESTAL TYPE OF SINK   SHOWER   BUILT-IN COUNTER SINK

COMMONLY USED ARCHITECTURAL SYMBOLS FOR PROJECT COMPONENTS IDENTIFIED BY SHAPE

FIGURE 10.4   Symbols for project components identified by shape.

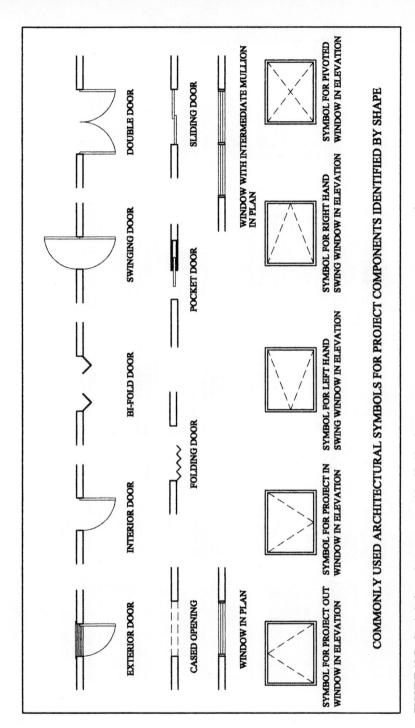

EXTERIOR DOOR INTERIOR DOOR BI-FOLD DOOR SWINGING DOOR DOUBLE DOOR

CASED OPENING FOLDING DOOR POCKET DOOR SLIDING DOOR

WINDOW IN PLAN WINDOW WITH INTERMEDIATE MULLION IN PLAN

SYMBOL FOR PROJECT OUT WINDOW IN ELEVATION SYMBOL FOR PROJECT IN WINDOW IN ELEVATION SYMBOL FOR LEFT HAND SWING WINDOW IN ELEVATION SYMBOL FOR RIGHT HAND SWING WINDOW IN ELEVATION SYMBOL FOR PIVOTED WINDOW IN ELEVATION

COMMONLY USED ARCHITECTURAL SYMBOLS FOR PROJECT COMPONENTS IDENTIFIED BY SHAPE

FIGURE 10.5   Symbols for project components identified by shape.

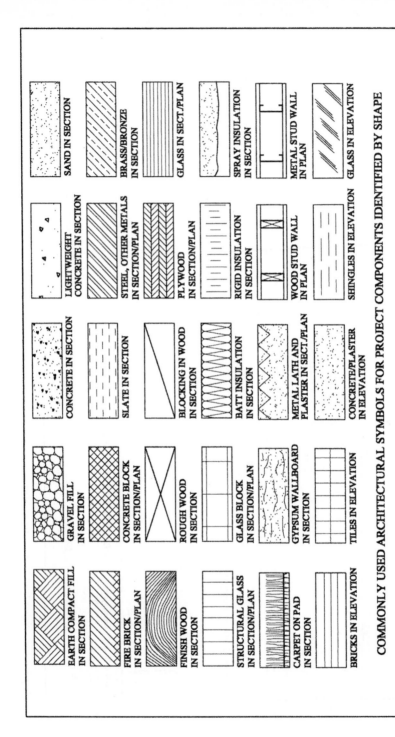

FIGURE 10.6 Symbols for materials.

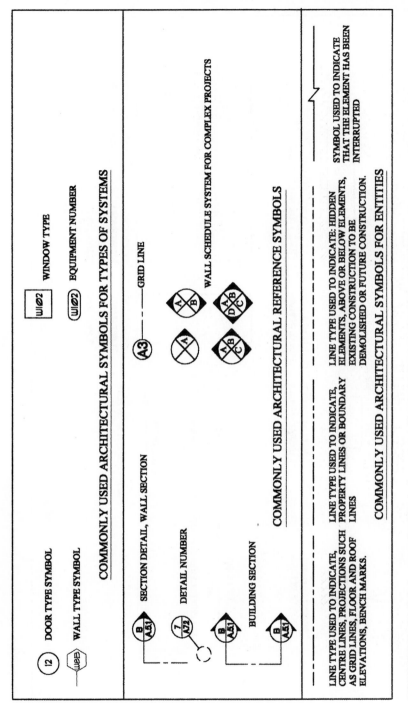

FIGURE 10.7 Symbols for types of architectural systems, architectural reference and architectural entities.

10.13

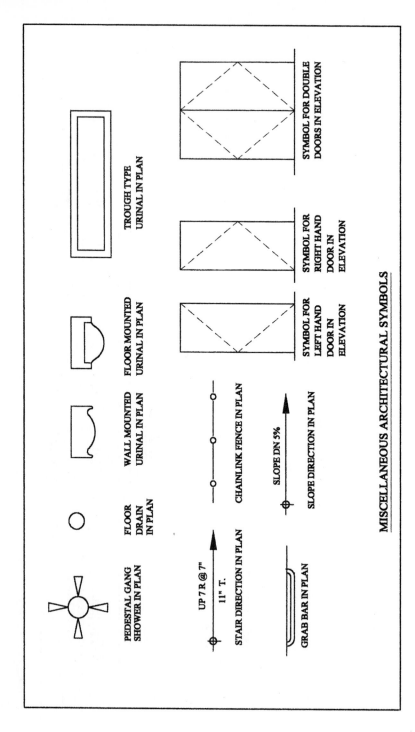

FIGURE 10.8 Miscellaneous architectural symbols.

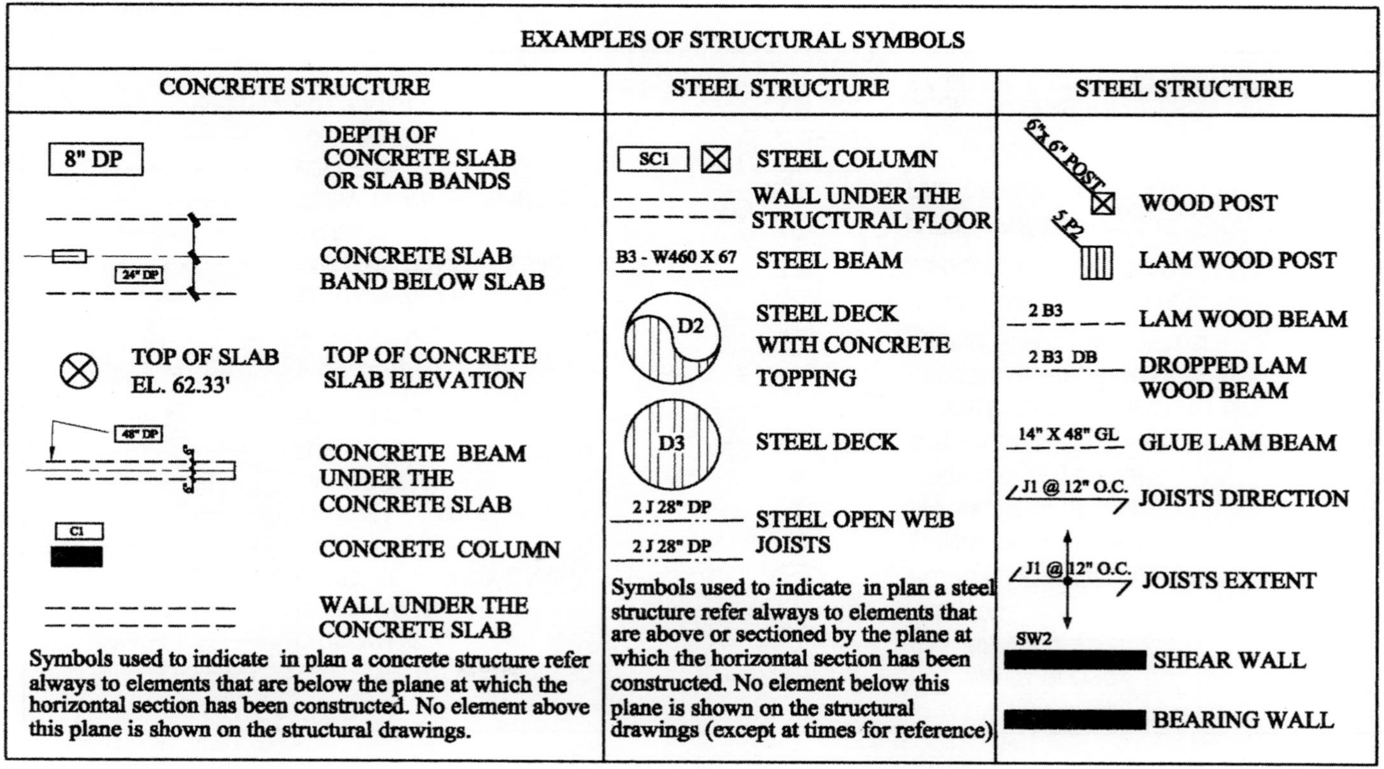

EXAMPLES OF STRUCTURAL SYMBOLS

CONCRETE STRUCTURE	STEEL STRUCTURE	STEEL STRUCTURE
8" DP — DEPTH OF CONCRETE SLAB OR SLAB BANDS	**SC1** ⊠ — STEEL COLUMN	6"x 6" POST ⊠ — WOOD POST
24" DP — CONCRETE SLAB BAND BELOW SLAB	— — WALL UNDER THE STRUCTURAL FLOOR	LP2 — LAM WOOD POST
⊗ TOP OF SLAB EL. 62.33' — TOP OF CONCRETE SLAB ELEVATION	B3 - W460 X 67 — STEEL BEAM	2 B3 — LAM WOOD BEAM
48" DP — CONCRETE BEAM UNDER THE CONCRETE SLAB	D2 — STEEL DECK WITH CONCRETE TOPPING	2 B3 DB — DROPPED LAM WOOD BEAM
C1 — CONCRETE COLUMN	D3 — STEEL DECK	14" X 48" GL — GLUE LAM BEAM
— — WALL UNDER THE CONCRETE SLAB	2 J 28" DP — STEEL OPEN WEB JOISTS	J1 @ 12" O.C. — JOISTS DIRECTION
		J1 @ 12" O.C. — JOISTS EXTENT
		SW2 ▬ — SHEAR WALL
		▬ — BEARING WALL

Symbols used to indicate in plan a concrete structure refer always to elements that are below the plane at which the horizontal section has been constructed. No element above this plane is shown on the structural drawings.

Symbols used to indicate in plan a steel structure refer always to elements that are above or sectioned by the plane at which the horizontal section has been constructed. No element below this plane is shown on the structural drawings (except at times for reference)

FIGURE 10.9   Examples of structural symbols.

10.15

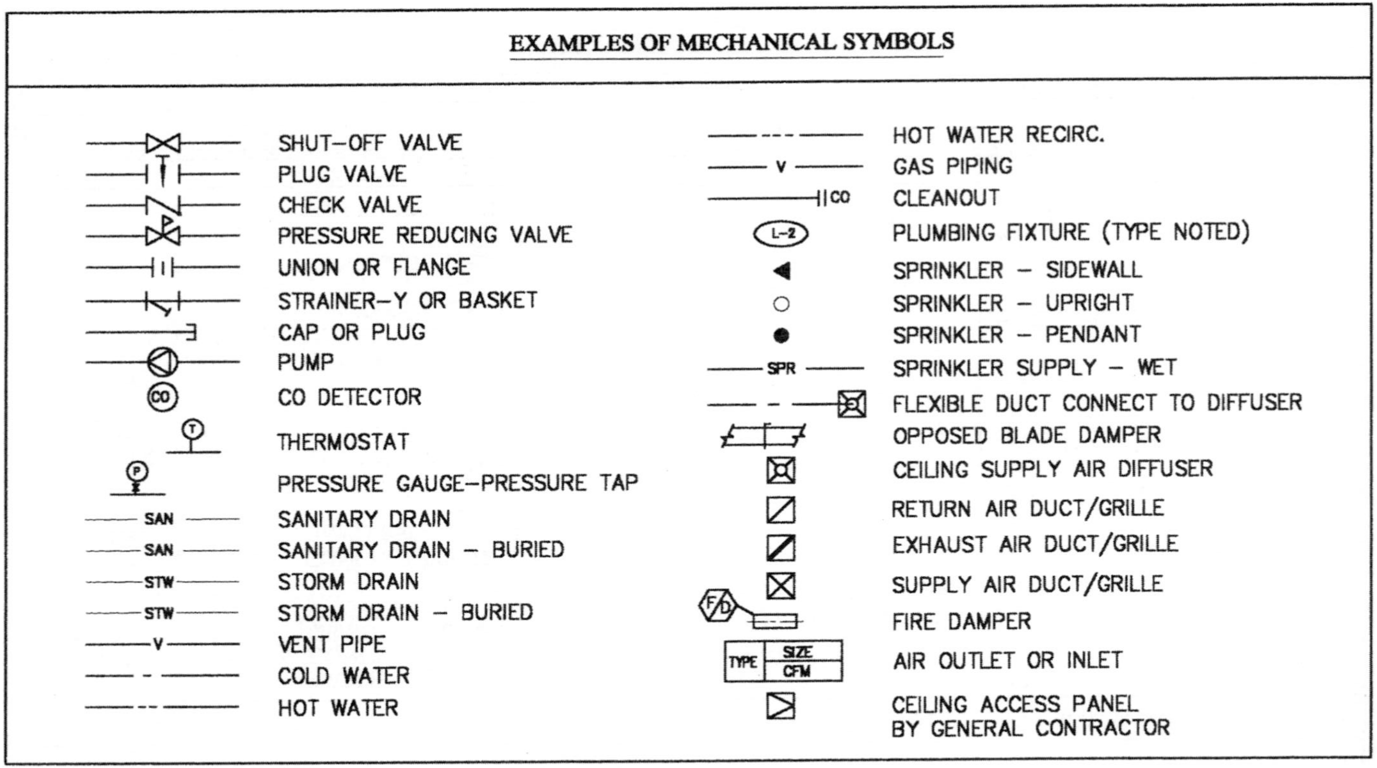

EXAMPLES OF MECHANICAL SYMBOLS

Symbol	Description
	SHUT-OFF VALVE
	PLUG VALVE
	CHECK VALVE
	PRESSURE REDUCING VALVE
	UNION OR FLANGE
	STRAINER—Y OR BASKET
	CAP OR PLUG
	PUMP
(CO)	CO DETECTOR
(T)	THERMOSTAT
(P)	PRESSURE GAUGE—PRESSURE TAP
—— SAN	SANITARY DRAIN
—— SAN	SANITARY DRAIN – BURIED
—— STW	STORM DRAIN
—— STW	STORM DRAIN – BURIED
—— V ——	VENT PIPE
	COLD WATER
	HOT WATER

Symbol	Description
	HOT WATER RECIRC.
—— V ——	GAS PIPING
‖CO	CLEANOUT
(L-2)	PLUMBING FIXTURE (TYPE NOTED)
▼	SPRINKLER – SIDEWALL
○	SPRINKLER – UPRIGHT
●	SPRINKLER – PENDANT
—— SPR	SPRINKLER SUPPLY – WET
	FLEXIBLE DUCT CONNECT TO DIFFUSER
⊠	OPPOSED BLADE DAMPER
	CEILING SUPPLY AIR DIFFUSER
⊠	RETURN AIR DUCT/GRILLE
⊠	EXHAUST AIR DUCT/GRILLE
⊠	SUPPLY AIR DUCT/GRILLE
(FD)	FIRE DAMPER
TYPE / SIZE / CFM	AIR OUTLET OR INLET
◇	CEILING ACCESS PANEL BY GENERAL CONTRACTOR

FIGURE 10.10   Example of mechanical symbols.

10.16

ELECTRICAL SYMBOLS

SYMBOL	DESCRIPTION	MOUNTING
	SURFACE MOUNTED LUMINAIRE	CEILING
	SURFACE MOUNTED LUMINAIRE	WALL
	RECESSED LUMINAIRE	CEILING
	RECESSED LUMINAIRE	WALL
	RECESSED WALL WASHER LUMINAIRE	CEILING
	ROADWAY/AREA LUMINAIRE	POLE
	LOW LEVEL AREA LUMINAIRE	POST
	TRACK LIGHT	AS SHOWN
	SURFACE MOUNTED FLUORESCENT LUMINAIRE	CEILING
	RECESSED MOUNTED FLUORESCENT LUMINAIRE	CEILING
	LUMINAIRE CONNECTED TO EMERGENCY POWER OR NIGHT LIGHT	
	FLOODLIGHT	AS SHOWN
	EXIT LIGHT	CEILING
	EXIT LIGHT	WALL
Ⓑ	INDICATES LUMINAIRE TYPE 'B' – SEE LUMINAIRE SCHEDULE	
②	INDICATES NOTE REFERENCE NO. 2	
C2	INDICATES CIRCUIT NO.2 FROM PANEL 'C'	
WP	INDICATES WEATHERPROOF DEVICE	
EX	INDICATES EXPLOSION–PROOF DEVICE	
	SINGLE POLE TOGGLE SWITCH (3=3 WAY, 4=4 WAY, D=DIMMER)	+48"(1200)
P	TOGGLE SW. (P=PILOT LT., P.C.=PULL CHAIN, K=KEY OPERATED)	+48"(1200)
a	LOW VOLTAGE LIGHT SWITCH (LETTER INDICATES CCT CONTROLLED)	+48"(1200)

FIGURE 10.11 Example of electrical symbols.

ELECTRICAL SYMBOLS

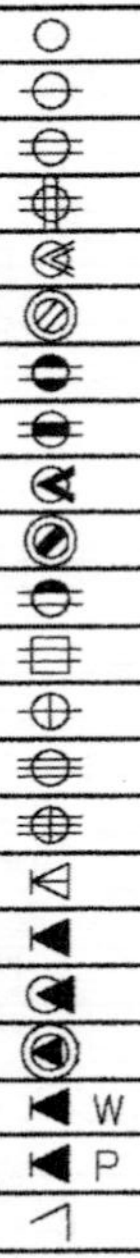

SYMBOL	DESCRIPTION	MOUNTING
	OUTLET/JUNCTION BOX	
	SINGLE CONVENIENCE RECEPTACLE	
	DUPLEX CONVENIENCE RECEPTACLE	
	FOURPLEX CONVENIENCE RECEPTACLE	
	DUPLEX CONVENIENCE RECEPTACLE PEDESTAL MOUNTED	
	DUPLEX CONVENIENCE RECEPTACLE FLUSH MOUNTED	
	DUPLEX CONVENIENCE RECEPTACLE SPLIT WIRED	
	DUPLEX CONVENIENCE RECEPTACLE ISOLATED GROUND (I.G.)	
	DUPLEX CONVENIENCE RECEPTACLE I.G. PEDESTAL	
	DUPLEX CONVENIENCE RECEPTACLE I.G. FLUSH MOUNTED	
	DUPLEX CONVENIENCE RECEPTACLE SWITCH ONE SIDE	
	DUPLEX CONVENIENCE RECEPTACLE GROUND FAULT INTERRUPTING	
	TWISTLOCK RECEPTACLE–RATING TO MATCH PROTECTIVE DEVICE	
	SINGLE RECEPTACLE 208/240V–1Ø (AMPERAGE AS NOTED)	
	SINGLE RECEPTACLE 208/240V–3Ø (AMPERAGE AS NOTED)	
	CABLE TELEVISION OUTLET	
	TELEPHONE OUTLET	
	TELEPHONE OUTLET PEDESTAL MOUNTED	
	TELEPHONE OUTLET FLUSH MOUNTED	
W	TELEPHONE OUTLET – WALL MOUNTED	
P	PAY TELEPHONE OUTLET	
	DATA OUTLET	

FIGURE 10.12 Example of electrical symbols.

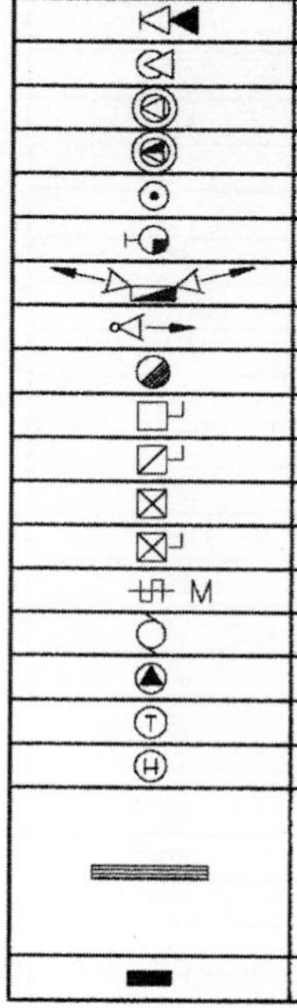

ELECTRICAL SYMBOLS

SYMBOL	DESCRIPTION	MOUNTING
▼	COMBINATION TELEPHONE/DATA OUTLET	
▽	DATA OUTLET PEDESTAL MOUNTED	
◉	DATA OUTLET FLUSH MOUNTED	
◉	COMBINATION TELEPHONE/DATA OUTLET FLUSH MOUNTED	
⊙	ALARM PUSHBUTTON OUTLET	
🕓	CLOCK – 'D' DENOTES DOUBLE FACE	
	EMERGENCY LIGHTING BATTERY UNIT – WITH OR WITHOUT HEADS	AS SHOWN
	EMERGENCY LIGHTING FLOOD LIGHT – SINGLE OR DOUBLE	
◐	RECESSED EMERGENCY LIGHT	
⬓	UNFUSED DISCONNECT SWITCH	AS SHOWN
⬓	FUSED DISCONNECT SWITCH	AS SHOWN
⊠	MAGNETIC MOTOR STARTER	+60"(1500)
⊠	COMBINATION DISCONNECT/MAGNETIC MOTOR STARTER	+60"(1500)
M	MANUAL MOTOR STARTER	AS SHOWN
○	ELECTRIC MOTOR CONNECTION	
◑	FIXED WIRE EQUIPMENT CONNECTION	
T	THERMOSTAT	+60"(1500)
H	DEHUMIDISTAT	+60"(1500)
	ELECTRIC BASEBOARD HEATER UNLESS NOTED AS FOLLOWS: FF = FORCE FLOW, UH = UNIT HEATER, CH = CONVECTION HEATER KS = KICKSPACE HEATER, PD = PATIO DOOR HEATER (B.I. INDICATES BUILT–IN THERMOSTAT)	
▬	ELECTRICAL DISTRIBUTION PANELBOARD	SURFACE

FIGURE 10.13 Example of electrical symbols.

ELECTRICAL SYMBOLS

SYMBOL	DESCRIPTION	MOUNTING
	ELECTRICAL DISTRIBUTION PANELBOARD	FLUSH
	SPEAKER	CEILING
	SPEAKER	WALL
	MICROPHONE OUTLET	+12"(300)
	INTERCOM COMMUNICATION HANDSET	+60"(1500)
	AUTOMATIC HEAT DETECTOR 135° R.O.R.	CEILING
	AUTOMATIC HEAT DETECTOR 190° FIXED TEMP.	CEILING
	IONIZATION SMOKE DETECTOR	CEILING
	SMOKE ALARM	CEILING
	FIRE ALARM PULL STATION	+54"(1370)
	FIRE ALARM BELL & PULL STATION	
	FIRE ALARM BELL	DN.12"(300)
	FIRE ALARM BUZZER	+7'0"(2100)
	MAGNETIC DOOR HOLDER	FLOOR/WALL
	SMOKE ALARM LED INDICATOR	DN.12"(300)
	FIRE ALARM STROBE LIGHT	DN.12"(300)
	SMOKE ALARM STROBE LIGHT	DN.12"(300)
	END OF LINE RESISTOR	+66"(1675)
FS	FLOW SWITCH	
PS	PRESSURE SWITCH	
TS	TAMPER SWITCH	

FIGURE 10.14 Example of electrical symbols.

ELECTRICAL SYMBOLS		
SYMBOL	DESCRIPTION	MOUNTING
⊖⊏◁◀	COLUMNAR SERVICE POLE WITH DEVICES AS NOTED	
⊖⊞⊖	MULTI SERVICE RECESSED FLOOR BOX WITH DEVICES AS NOTED	FLOOR
◯	FIXED WIRE CONNECTION TO PRE—WIRED FURNITURE SCREENS	
◁▷	INTRUDER ALARM MAGNETIC DOOR SWITCH	
◁▶	INTRUDER ALARM PASSIVE INFRARED DETECTOR	CEILING
E	INDICATES EXISTING DEVICE TO REMAIN	
R	INDICATES EXISTING DEVICE TO BE REMOVED OR RELOCATED	

FIGURE 10.15   Example of electrical symbols.

instance, the dimensions should not be given because that space, no longer critical, could actually function as a variable and absorb any shift in the exact location of the elements built during construction.

The use of the symbol and the type of information that it carries, therefore, in most cases is not standard. In these cases, the symbol is inserted in a unique general system such as the project, which is generated by a design that has its own characteristics and its own idiosyncrasies.

As in any system, in order to identify what symbols to include and the type of information the symbol needs to carry, the following questions should be answered:

1. Within the system of the project, what is the role of the element(s) that need to be identified by the symbols?

2. Is the element a finished product that simply needs to be installed or must it be assembled or custom-built on site?

3. What information is needed in order to install the product, assemble it, or to custom build the element?

4. What are the characteristics of the element that will influence other elements?

From the above analysis, it is possible to identify critical types of symbols that require particular attention because the relation between them and the meaning requires multiple types of information that are not grouped all in one place. These types of representations are the ones that can potentially produce ambiguity, conflicts and incompleteness of information. In these cases, strategies should be developed in order to minimize this miscommunication. The more complex the project, the more these risks increase.

One strategy that is effective in complex projects is to reduce the number of specific items and allow more flexibility in the system by organizing symbols in such way that the variables can be combined. For example, in the wall schedule it is advantageous to differentiate between the type of structures of the walls and the type of finishes (see Figure 10.3a). This method permits minimization of the number of wall types and eliminates possible repetitions (due to long lists of walls). Less critical are floor and roof schedules. However, it is better to use the same system for all the assembly schedules.

In projects that consist of more than one type of building or structure, multiple symbols can be used, for example, for the same element or assembly (i.e., a wall type). Suppose that the project has a tower, a series of low rises and a retail component. If the same wall type is used for the three structures, this wall can be called T-W1A, the wall for the low rise L-W1A and the wall for the retail R-W1A (see Figure 10.3a). The advantage of using this system is that it is possible to identify immediately that the same wall is present in all the structures. This not only simplifies preliminary pricing and the coordination of the contractor, but if changes need to be implemented, this differentiation becomes a reminder for the designer that the changes will affect various types of building (which often have different characteristics and requirements).

CHAPTER 11

CONSTRUCTION DRAWINGS, CONTRACTS, AND DOCUMENTS

GENERAL APPROACH

General aspects of the construction drawings were discussed in Chapter 2 and Chapter 3. The topic of this chapter is the technical development of construction drawings and their relationship with different types of construction contracts, other construction documents, and various types of project delivery models. The latter are models of project organization that apply to cases in which the project is directly or indirectly carried on by the owner. These models, as we will see, greatly affect the relationship between the architect and the owner/client.

The type of information forming an integral part of any graphic and written communication is dependent on the scope of that communication and the circumstances in which this scope of work will be implemented. In the case of architecture, fundamental aspects of these circumstances are described in the construction contract and in the project manual. Because there are different types of contracts (and potentially different requirements and amendments included in the project manual), the graphic portion of the contract documents (i.e., the construction drawings) must be adequately approached to reflect the different types of project delivery models and contractual construction contracts.

TYPES OF PROJECT DELIVERY MODELS

A project delivery model is the conceptual representation of the organization of a project. It indicates the participants in the project, their role, their scope of work and their relationship to one another. The model is defined by two components:

the general organization of the project and the type of construction contract. In terms of the general organization, an owner who wishes to initiate a project can do it in two ways:

1. Directly: the owner engages the architect. The consultants may be hired either by the owner or by the architect. Once the design and the contract documents are completed, the owner hires either a contractor or a construction manager to build the project. In this case, the owner and the architect's client are the same person.

2. Indirectly: the owner engages an individual or a company to develop the project on the owner's behalf. It is this individual or company that engages all the consultants, including the architect. The architect's client and the owner, therefore, are two separate entities. The common models of project organization under this indirect format are:

   a. Project management: in this situation, at the beginning of the project, the owner hires a project manager who will represent the owner for all aspects of the project, from its conception to the project closing. Among other tasks, the scope of work of a project manager includes the development of a detailed project program, assistance in the project financing, overview of the design stage, budget control, control of the design schedule, verification of adherence of the design objective to the project program objective, assistance in the management of the approval process, tendering, construction monitoring, marketing, leasing and sales, coordination of project closing.

   b. Developer proposal: in this case, the owner first develops a preliminary project program and a budget. (Sometimes, the owner finds or owns the land as well.). Then he or she approaches a developer who hires the project team and proceeds with the project after having agreed with the owner on the terms of the contract. In this type of indirect delivery model, the developer at the completion of the project either leases or sells the project back to the owner at the amount and/or at conditions stipulated at the beginning of the project.

   c. Design-built: in this format, the owner hires a designer-builder who in turn hires the project team (including the architect). During the design stage the work of the consultants is monitored by the design-builder who makes every effort not to exceed the budget established at the beginning of the project. After the design is completed, the cost of construction is established and the project goes into the construction phase.

From the construction point of view, either in the architect-owner direct relationship or the architect-client-owner indirect structure, the same optional types of construction contracts can be used.

The main differences between these different construction contracts reside in the duties and relationship of the parties as well as in the types and modalities of the compensation. These are general categories including many aspects that need to be very well defined in the documents. The effect of the terms specified in these different contractual agreements are far reaching into every aspect of the project. For example, they can affect the professional fees, the required level of details, the cost of construction, the scheduling as well as the climate of collaboration that is created during construction. For these reasons the type of construction contract most suitable for the project must considered very seriously. If possible, this should happen at the very early stage of the project. If a consensus on the type of construction contract is not reached at the beginning of the project, it should be obtained no later than the beginning of the contract documents.

TYPES OF CONSTRUCTION CONTRACTS

A contract can be drawn in any form as long as the parties named in the contract agree to the terms. However, one of the difficulties in wording a contract is that it must be general enough to include all the most common circumstances and situations as well as being specific enough to avoid possible misunderstandings. The degree of clarity expressed in the construction contract is an aspect that also affects the degree of ambiguity of the construction drawings. For instance, whether an item is or is not to be included in the scope of work is determined to a large degree by the terms of the construction contract as well as by the drawings. The two need to be coordinated in order not to generate confusion, extra costs, lawsuits and omissions which potentially could lead to disaster. For these reasons it is better to use standard forms of construction contracts commonly used in the industry. Professional associations, such as the American Institute of Architects (AIA), can provide these standard forms. The following are the most common types of standard construction contracts:

1. *Stipulated price*: this is a contract that defines rights and obligations between the owner and the general contractor. The latter performs the scope of work according to the contract documents for a sum of money specified in the contract. In the majority of cases, the general contractor's responsibility for the construction extends to the total completion of the project and, under specific circumstances, beyond the completion.

   During construction, the performance of the contractor is periodically reviewed by the construction coordinating consultant (often the architect) who is also the impartial arbiter of the construction contract, advising the owner and the contractor as to their respective obligations. In this respect it has to be clarified that although the role of the coordinating consultant is specified in the stipulated sum type of construction contract, there is no contractual relationship between the coordinating professional and the general contractor. The former, however, has a separate contract with the owner. It is this contract that defines the rights and obligations of these two parties (which must be coordinated with the terms of the stipulated price type of construction contract).

The general contractor is usually compensated for his work on a monthly basis (in projects that move more rapidly, he may receive compensation biweekly) upon presentation of a progress claim. The latter shows the declared percentage of completion of the scope of work, the corresponding amount due at that time, the total contract value, the amount of the contract paid up to that stage, any change orders (changes to the contract documents authorized by the owner), and the new contract value.

During construction, if items cannot be reasonably deemed necessary and part of the scope of work through the contract documents, the general contractor is entitled to extra payment over and above the contract amount. The value of this extra scope of work is reviewed by the coordinating professional, who advises the owner on the equity of the claim. Furthermore, the construction contract usually defines that, in addition to the extra construction cost, a percentage of the latter must be paid to the general contractor and the sub-trades for the added coordination and increased activities involved in a change implemented during construction. Because the price is stipulated before construction starts and is guaranteed by the general contractor, as long as there are no legitimate changes in the contract documents, any loss or savings experienced by the general contractor are not passed on to the owner.

The contractor is in complete charge of the construction coordination, including coordination of the sub-trades and allocation and subdivision of the scope of work among them. There is no contractual relation between the coordinating professional and the sub-trades and there should not be any dealing between the former and the latter. Any aspect of the scope of work is filtered through the general contractor, who is responsible for the overall construction activities. In the past, this type of construction contract was the most commonly used. With the changes occurring in the industry, other types of contract are becoming popular.

2. *Cost-plus*: The fundamental difference between this type of construction contract and the stipulated price resides in the general contractor compensation, which is based on a pre-determined percentage of the actual cost of construction. The competitive bids of the sub-trades are made known to the owner and, once accepted, the percentage agreed upon in the contract is added to these bids to form the cost of construction. Any justifiable additional cost or saving experienced during the contract is usually passed on to the owner, unless the loss is caused directly by a negligent act of the general contractor. This type of financial relationship in turn allows a flexibility of project scheduling and implementation of changes during construction that is not so easily accomplished with the stipulated price type of contract.

In the cost-plus contract, the general contractor remains in complete charge of the construction and is still the individual having a contractual relationship with the owner. The role of the coordinating professional in relation to reviewing of the construction and arbitrating the construction contract does not change either.

There are many variations in the basic form of the cost-plus type of contract. For example, unlike the stipulated price, the cost-plus tendering of the project to the sub-trades can happen in stages without substantially affecting the final construction cost. In addition, bonuses for achieving savings (based sometimes on percentage of their value) are paid to the general contractor as incentives.

The cost-plus construction contract is used especially when possible cost overruns are very likely to happen (i.e., where certain conditions cannot be foreseen, which can happen in renovations, or where the original project program can change during construction). This type of construction contract is usually used for smaller types of projects.

3. *Construction management*: this contract is quite different from the above two and is agreed upon between a construction manager and the owner. Usually this is only one of the construction contracts signed by the owner since the latter also signs contracts directly with the sub-trades. This is because the owner in the construction management contract assumes the role of a general contractor and the construction manager is his or her representative during the construction stage.

In an advisory capacity, the scope of work of the construction manager extends beyond the specific construction-related coordination (since the construction manager is involved in the project from its preliminary stage). In this capacity, he or she advises the owner and the design team on matters related to construction budget and scheduling, characteristics and types of alternate materials, detailing and/or impact of the design on future maintenance of the construction.

One of the major duties of the construction manager is tendering the scope of work to the sub-trades. In this case, the construction manager performs the same activities that are performed by a general contractor in the cost-plus type of construction contract. In fact, the construction manager is often hired because of the staging of the tendering. During tendering and during the construction contract negotiation, the construction manager tries to obtain from the sub-trades the best prices on labor and materials, passing all the saving on to the owner (unless the construction management contract has a provision for bonuses or for a percentage of these savings to be paid to the construction manager).

The construction manager, unlike the coordinating consultant, maintains personnel stationed on site (at least a superintendent), who constantly monitor the work of the sub-trades and coordinate construction activities. The construction manager is compensated either with a sum based on a percentage of the cost of construction or a fixed fee. Bonuses are often included in the contract and paid usually for two reasons: if the construction manager completes the project before the date set in the contract (or on an updated official construction schedule) and/or if she or he achieves savings.

Because the owner is the general contractor, he pays any overrun of the budget, the construction manager being accountable only in case of negligence and/or misrepresentation of his or her qualifications and expertise. Therefore, as in the case of the general contractor in the cost-plus type of contract, it is important that a construction manager has a very reputable track record, is backed up by an organization employing individuals that personally or collectively are very experienced in every aspect of the project for which the construction manager is hired (from conception to project closing), has a good relationship with the sub-trades (which means also that the construction manager can provide future repeat business), is experienced in budgeting from a general contractor point of view, is not overloaded and extended in his activities and is financially accountable in case of failure of performance. Because the role of construction manager is to act as general contractor on behalf of the owner, many construction companies offer the option of being hired as construction managers.

4. *Design-built stipulated price*: this contract reflects what has been described in the owner indirect project delivery models.

5. *Unit price*: this is a particular type of contract that is used in situations in which the tasks are repetitive and/or the activities are not too articulated so that the quantity becomes the major reference factor. An example is a prototype building that is repeated: once the initial price of the construction of the basic unit has been established, it is used as base for the rest of the units. A unit price type of agreement can very often refer to only one portion of a larger scope of work and be part of other types of construction contracts (in architecture this is the most common way in which the unit price type of contract is used).

RELATION BETWEEN CONSTRUCTION DRAWINGS AND TYPE OF CONSTRUCTION CONTRACT

By combining a number of project organization models with different types of construction contracts, it is possible to obtain a variety of project delivery models. This provides an opportunity to choose the most appropriate model for a range of projects. First it is necessary to analyze the effect these different models has on the production of contract documents.

From this point of view, there is no great difference between the direct and indirect owner's involvement in the project. However, for this statement to be accurate, the communication between the owner and his or her representatives (i.e., the project manager, developer or builder/designer) must be effective and the project program as well as its objectives must be clear to all members of the project team. This is very important because in the owner's indirect involvement paradigm, it is the owner's representative who provides the project directive to the architect and the rest of the design team.

On the other hand, the impact of the different types of construction contracts on the contract documents is considerable. There are also other variables that impact the documentation (i.e., the reputability of the general contractor or construction manager, the complexity of the project, the project schedule). For clarity we will assume these factors are equal in our comparison of the different possible scenarios.

As we have seen, in the stipulated price construction contract the total sum of money owed to the general contractor is established and agreed upon before the construction starts. To identify his or her scope of work, the contractor uses the contract documents as reference. This means that the documents need to be comprehensive in their description and representation of the scope of work. In addition the process usually leads to the choosing of the general contractor is based on competitive bids, with a tendering period of between two and three weeks. During this time the general contractor distributes the drawings to the sub-trades for prices. Each sub-contractor gives the general contractor his or her price to which the general contractor adds his or her portion of the work.

In this scenario, where many participants are involved in a competitive process and where there are time constraints, the need for clarity becomes paramount. In fact, aspects of the contract documents that are not completely clear could, legitimately and in good faith, be interpreted by the general contractor, or one of the sub-trades, in a way that allows them to be competitive. If a possible discrepancy of intents between the interpretation on the part of the general contractor and the scope of work intended by the consultant is discovered during construction, the financial consequences can be disastrous. In fact, in the stipulated price construction contract, changes that happen during construction can entail a very high cost and in many cases could impact other aspects as well. Extra costs can be due to objective aspects (such as extra work caused by modifications of portions of the construction already built). However, extra cost can be due to the fact that hiring another contractor always represents a problem and an expense. If the price for the extra scope of work given by the original general contractor is not accepted, the situation described above becomes a reality. Another contractor will increase his or her price since the scope of work might be small and set-up charges might be very high in relation to the value of the work. Other repercussions associated with having another contractor do only part of the work is that his or her involvement might later give rise to a problem with the warranties.

For the above reasons, unless it is absolutely necessary, a change during construction in a stipulated price type of construction contract should be avoided. In the construction industry, a change caused by incomplete construction documentation is certainly not deemed to be a necessary change, but rather an error or an omission.

In the case of cost-plus construction contract, the drawings still need to be complete but the general contractor is actually working more in collaboration with the owner and the design team. This is possible because in the cost-plus construction contract the general contractor is not held responsible for cost overrun in the same degree that applies in the case of the stipulated price construction contract. This means that as long as the scope of the extra work is the same as if the work had been included in the contract documents at the time of the bid, there will not be any loss to be absorbed by any of the parties involved in the project. This is the reason why it is possible with the cost-plus construction contract to tender the work in stages.

In the cost-plus contract, coordination of the contract documents is fundamental. It is important to know which aspects of one stage of the construction might affect the next stage and how this might occur. From this point of view, in order to minimize conflicts, it is recommended to subdivide the tendering and the construction of the project in the following contract document packages:

1. Demolition, Site Clearing, and Site Preparation
2. Mechanical, Fire Protection, and Electrical Systems
3. Structural Components (i.e., Framing, Concrete and/or Steel Structure)
4. Building Envelope Components
5. Interior Systems and Finish

Although still allowing the staging of the tender, a cost-plus with guaranteed maximum upset price (which is often used as a variation of the cost-plus) is less flexible than the pure cost-plus construction contract because the closer the price approaches the maximum upset cost of construction, the more the general contractor will start thinking in terms of stipulated price construction contract. For this reason, with the guaranteed maximum upset price contract documents must not leave aspects of the project poorly documented.

The contract documents prepared for a construction management type of contract maintain the structure common to the ones prepared for the stipulated price and, especially, the cost-plus construction contracts. However, because of the involvement of the construction manager from the early stage of the project, these documents might need less information (especially if details are typical). This is because a project manager can supplement the basic information shown on the drawings by describing products and detail solutions in writing with specific references (he or she can also use photos of elements with characteristics similar to those characterizing the items that are expected to be built). In addition because of the construction manager's direct relationship with the sub-trades, verbal explanations can be very accurate (the verbal consensus is later registered in written documents). This methodology is especially effective for interior elements and finishes (while the description of the scope of work related to the building envelope can still be very dependent on the accuracy and completeness of the working drawings).

CONSTRUCTION DRAWINGS

In Chapter 2, we analyzed the general organization of the drawing set (see Figures 2.15, 2.16 and 2.17). Now we can expand by exploring additional general characteristics and by subdividing some of the general categories of the type of drawings that we have listed (see Figures 11.1 and 11.2). Each of them will be described in detail in relation to the type of information that they should carry.

GENERAL APPROACH

There are general factors common to all categories of construction drawings (from the site plan to the details) and decisions that have to be made in order to show the building in the most effective and concise form:

1. Choosing the size of the paper (see Chapter 1).

2. Appropriate scale: One of the main variables that can allow the achievement of good communication in a graphic representation is the scale at which the elements are shown. If the scale is too small the data are not clearly indicated; if it is too big, the drawing will look out of proportion and/or it might need to be split into two sections in order to show the complete drawing, which is very inefficient.

   The scale, therefore, must be large enough to allow easy reading of the information, but not too big to cause inefficient solutions (refer to the description of each drawing for the type of information to be included). A good way to think of a scale is like a zoom lens which, through a succession of enlargements, can provide a detailed image of the object. These enlargements are recorded on each type of drawing.

   As an example, the scale for a site plan, depending on the size of the property and the type of project, can range from ¹⁄₁₆ inch = 1 foot to an engineering scale up to 1:60 (sometimes 1:80). If the scale needs to be smaller, than the site plan becomes more a key plan, where only schematic information is provided (see the detail description of the key plan below). In this case, the image of the complete site plan needs to be split and shown at larger scale on separate sheets.

   Among the horizontal sections from the site plan, the next enlarged type of drawings is the general floor plans. A scale of ¹⁄₁₆ inch = 1 foot can be useful for large open interior spaces where a few dimensions and symbols do not clutter the drawings. If the interior is divided into smaller areas, this scale presents some limitations. However, it can still be used to provide an overview of the project showing the interior distribution. Some judgment must be exercised in introducing these intermediate scales in the drawing set. In order to comply with the rule of synthesis (in other words, to avoid redundancy) one must always question the necessity of a particular drawing. Does it carry unique information that cannot be shown as effectively on other drawings? Especially for intermediate scale the answer is usually "no." The next scale for general floor plans is ⅛ inch = 1 foot. This is a scale which, in some less articulated layouts, allows the representation of some secondary elements and symbols, especially for areas that will not be

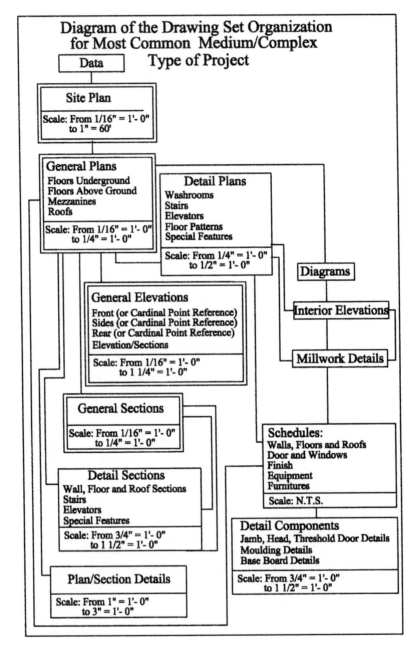

FIGURE 11.1 Diagram of the drawing set organization for the most common medium/complex type of projects.

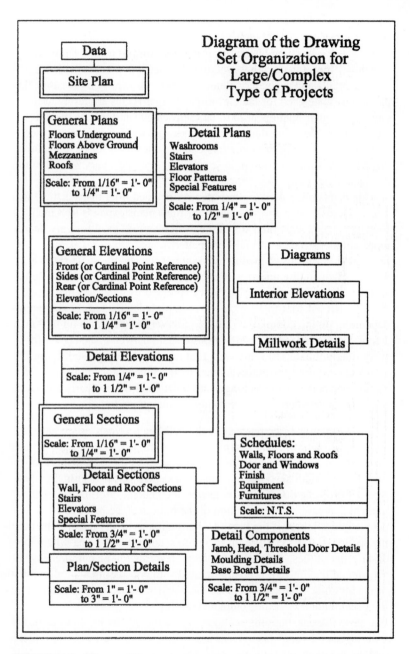

FIGURE 11.2 Diagram of the drawing set organization for large/complex type of projects.

enlarged using bigger scales (i.e., common areas in a residential complex, such as corridors, or lobbies).

The scales for building elevations can range from $\frac{1}{16}$ inch = 1 foot to $\frac{1}{4}$ inch = 1 foot. On drawings where $\frac{1}{4}$ inch scale is used, some more refined details and secondary elements can be shown. In most cases, this is the largest scale used for the elevations. Larger scales are rarely used unless particular features need to be represented (in this case the drawing is more a detail elevation than a building elevation). For the building sections the scales used are of the same range as the ones used for the elevations. If the $\frac{1}{4}$ inch = 1 foot is chosen, in small/simple projects very few additional details are required.

A scale that is often used to illustrate very detailed floor plans is the $\frac{1}{4}$ inch = 1 foot. Occasionally, the scale used for floor plans expands to $\frac{1}{2}$ inch = 1 foot. This latter scale (and sometime even larger) is used for very detailed representations (i.e., a special floor pattern).

For detail elevations of medium and large projects, the scale starts at $\frac{1}{4}$ inch = 1 foot and increases with the articulation of the elements. Detail sections (i.e., wall sections) are best expressed using scales that range from $\frac{3}{4}$ inch = 1 foot to $1\frac{1}{2}$ inch = 1 foot. plan details and section details, depending on the complexity, can require very large scales up to 3 inch = 1 foot. For general interior elevations a scale between $\frac{1}{16}$ inch = 1 foot (very diagrammatic) to $\frac{1}{4}$ inch = 1 foot can be generally used. Larger scales are required for more detailed work. Schedules and diagrams do not require a specific scale, as long as all the elements are clearly shown and proportions between the components are maintained.

3. Choosing sections: The purpose of the building sections, as we have seen, changes with the size and complexity of the project. As already indicated, in small and simple projects the building sections function also as substitutes for the detail sections and sometimes even for the details. In other types of projects, building sections provide general information on the internal and external organization of the building (see below for the detailed description of the type of information to be included in the building sections). It is therefore important to section the building where the description of these interior and exterior features can be comprehensively shown and maximized. It is important also to consider that another function of the building sections is to place the detail sections and the details into the general context of the complete building.

For these reasons, building sections should include major features of the building such as changes in floor and ceiling elevations; exterior typical and unique elements (i.e., canopies, balconies, type of roofs, terraces, decks, roof gardens, glazing and the like); changes in materials; interior significant elements (i.e., special partitions); stairs, elevator shafts and other type of shafts (i.e., mechanical chases); fire walls and typical fire separation as well as smoke separations; special structural elements (i.e., building joints). For examples of building sections, see Chapters 2, 3, and 4.

4. Dimensioning: In dimensioning the building it is important to follow standards that are commonly recognized in the industry (see Figures 11.3, 11.4, and 11.5). The dimensions should:

   a. Provide the authorities with easy reference in order to check the drawings for compliance with the bylaws (planning and building). This refers to overall dimensions for gross area take offs and to specific dimensions for distances, clearances, heights, set-backs, easements, road dedications, accesses and similar information. In some cases, instead of using the construction drawings, the authorities might require overlays for area calculations and special drawings for code compliance where some of this information should be shown or repeated (see also Chapter 5).

   b. Allow an accurate layout of the building on the site. It is important to include references to grid lines, angles of the geometrical elements of the building perimeter, general dimensions and set-backs, angles and dimensions of the property lines (this can be provided by a survey plan), starting dimensions and critical dimensions if the property lines are not at 90° to each other. This last aspect is very important since sometimes the angle is so close to the right angle that the difference in setbacks along a property line between the two extreme sides of the building might be only 1 inch. However, if the starting point of the layout is the closer side and the building is set right on the setback line, the other side will be over this line by 1 inch.

   c. Facilitate the construction process by referring to clear and unmistakable benchmarks. It is important to choose elements of the building that are quite constant in their geometrical shape (i.e., in an exterior wall the exterior sheathing versus the exterior stucco). In addition, grid lines, used as reference, can provide the continuity between different scales of drawings.

   d. Allow the easy checking of the shop drawings. Dimensions, especially of details, should provide the distances and clearances that, for example, an element or components of an exterior assembly have from a steel structure. This methodology will be beneficial when the shop drawings arrive and a review of the dimensions and of the geometrical characteristics of each element is required.

   e. Provide the proper information to compare the plans with the various surveys provided during different stages of the construction. This is a reference that is very important in order to verify with absolute accuracy critical aspects of the project, such as, among others, setbacks, floor and roof elevations as well as overall dimensions of the building. This is done with surveys taken at different stages of the project. These stages change in accordance with the characteristics of the project and depending on the elements present in the design. The most common are: foundation forming stage, stages of the construction of the structure, roof construction and completion of the construction. The architect then reviews these plans for compliance with the construction drawings.

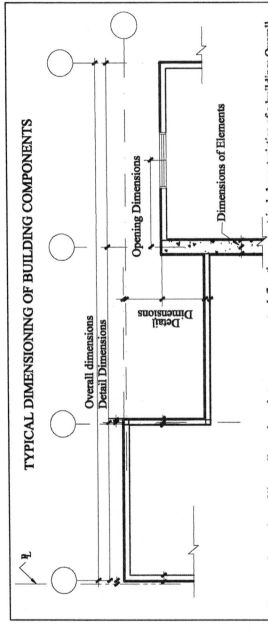

TYPICAL DIMENSIONING OF BUILDING COMPONENTS

There are four orders of linear dimensions that are necessary to define the geometrical characteristics of a building: Overall Dimensions, Detail Dimensions (to locate Major Parts or to locate Opening of the Building) and Elemental Dimensions. In addition angular dimensioning could substitute some of the linear dimensions.

In order to develop these four types of dimensioning, there are two fundamental sets of points of reference: the Boundaries of the Property and the Grid Lines. The first set is important because of the legal and regulatory aspects associated with it. On the other hand, Grid Lines are an important common reference during the Design Stage and the Construction Process. Grid Lines allow us to identify the location of components drawn at different floor level; to locate elements drawn on different sheets and/or at different scale; to communicate effectively with the consultants; to layout the Construction on site and carry on the construction activities to reflect the geometries shown on the Drawings.

FIGURE 11.3   Typical dimensioning of building components.

11.14

TYPICAL DIMENSIONING OF BUILDING COMPONENTS

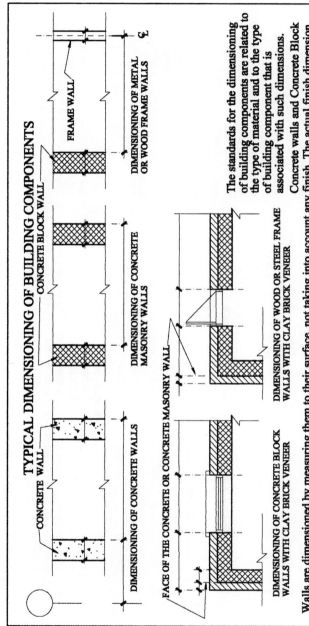

DIMENSIONING OF CONCRETE WALLS

DIMENSIONING OF CONCRETE MASONRY WALLS

DIMENSIONING OF METAL OR WOOD FRAME WALLS

CONCRETE WALL

CONCRETE BLOCK WALL

FRAME WALL

FACE OF THE CONCRETE OR CONCRETE MASONRY WALL

DIMENSIONING OF CONCRETE BLOCK WALLS WITH CLAY BRICK VENEER

DIMENSIONING OF WOOD OR STEEL FRAME WALLS WITH CLAY BRICK VENEER

The standards for the dimensioning of building components are related to the type of material and to the type of building component that is associated with such dimensions.

Concrete walls and Concrete Block

Walls are dimensioned by measuring them to their surface, not taking into account any finish. The actual finish dimension of the wall is indicated in the Wall Schedule. From a Concrete or a Concrete Block Wall to a Metal and Wood Framing Walls the measurement is indicated from the face of the Concrete or Concrete Block Wall to the centre of the Framing Wall. For Windows or Doors opening in Concrete or Concrete Block Walls the dimension is provided by giving the size of the opening. The general notes mentioned above will clarify where the opening has been considered (e.g. to the face of the Concrete / Concrete Block Wall or the finish opening of the Window or Door.

FIGURES 11.4   Typical dimensioning of building components.

11.15

TYPICAL DIMENSIONING OF BUILDING COMPONENTS

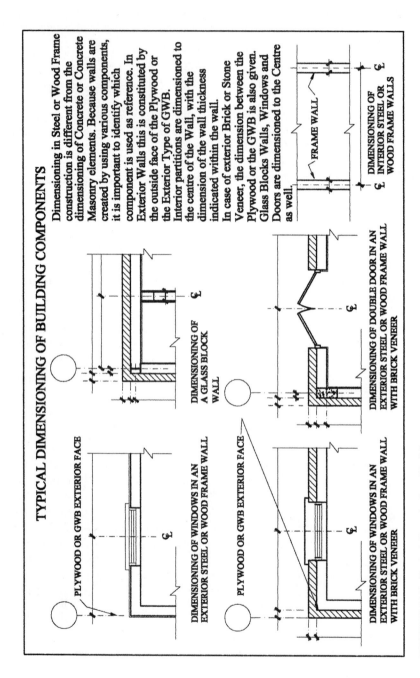

Dimensioning in Steel or Wood Frame construction is different from the dimensioning of Concrete or Concrete Masonry elements. Because walls are created by using various components, it is important to identify which component is used as reference. In Exterior Walls this is constituted by the outside face of the Plywood or the Exterior Type of GWB.

Interior partitions are dimensioned to the centre of the Wall, with the dimension of the wall thickness indicated within the wall.

In case of exterior Brick or Stone Veneer, the dimension between the Plywood or the GWB is also given. Glass Blocks Walls, Windows and Doors are dimensioned to the Centre as well.

DIMENSIONING OF INTERIOR STEEL OR WOOD FRAME WALLS

FRAME WALL

PLYWOOD OR GWB EXTERIOR FACE

DIMENSIONING OF WINDOWS IN AN EXTERIOR STEEL OR WOOD FRAME WALL WITH BRICK VENEER

DIMENSIONING OF A GLASS BLOCK WALL

PLYWOOD OR GWB EXTERIOR FACE

DIMENSIONING OF WINDOWS IN AN EXTERIOR STEEL OR WOOD FRAME WALL WITH BRICK VENEER

DIMENSIONING OF DOUBLE DOOR IN AN EXTERIOR STEEL OR WOOD FRAME WALL WITH BRICK VENEER

FIGURES 11.5 Typical dimensioning of building components.

11.16

TYPES OF CONSTRUCTION DRAWINGS

Each drawing has a particular purpose and should not carry more information than what is required by its function. The organization of a drawing set indicated in Figures 2.15, 2.16 and 2.17 becomes the more detailed diagrams shown on Figures 11.1 and 11.2.

It has to be pointed out that, unless absolutely clear because of the type of symbols used or because the information is contained in the specification, all the elements appearing in the construction set must be fully described in terms of materials and dimensions at least once. If repetitions are not absolutely necessary, they should be avoided and only referenced in the other places where these elements appear. Let us analyze each drawing.

Data

The function of this drawing is to provide information about the address and legal description of the property, the list of the drawings (including the consultant's sets), the information of the project team (name of firms, addresses, phone, fax and e-mail addresses), list of abbreviations, materials and symbol schedule as well as the key plan. This last drawing locates the property in relation to the surrounding properties and streets. It can be a schematic drawing that delineates only the grid of the streets with the geometry of the parcels, or a detail drawing that indicates in addition the geometry of the surrounding construction and features to the streets and the parcels.

Site Plan

A site plan provides the necessary information on the property, the immediate surroundings, the location of the construction, existing and proposed site features and existing and proposed utilities (if not shown of a separate civil drawing(s)). It is used to lay out the building on site and to bring all the services close to the building where building connections will be created (which point usually defines the demarcation between the scope of work of the civil sub-contractor and the plumbing sub-contractor). Furthermore, the site plan is important for the hard and soft landscaping (if they are not shown on separate landscape drawing(s)), driveways, fences, gates, lighting and all the features that need to be built on site. In order to describe these items, the following data should be included in the drawing:

1. Property line dimensions and angles.
2. Road dedications, easements, rights-of-way and any other servitudes.
3. Existing and proposed ground elevations.
4. Geometry of the building with dimension from the property lines and overall dimensions of the major components of the exterior as well as the total dimension of the building (see sections and dimensions in this chapter).

See also Chapter 4 and Figures 4.2 and 4.3 for a discussion on building representation on site plans.

5. Grid lines.

6. Driveways, surface parking and curb crossing.

7. Streets flanking the site.

8. Site furnishing, street lighting, electrical poles, transformers and electrical boxes as well as other electrical equipment.

9. Utilities, fire hydrants and siamese connection (if not indicated on the civil engineering and mechanical drawings).

10. Direction of traffic.

11. Landscaping (if not indicated on a separate landscape drawings).

General Floor Plans

On the horizontal plane, the next level of information is shown on the building floor plans. The function of these drawings is to provide a closer overview of the building and its interior distribution. In addition, in cases where this does not create confusion, detail dimensioning, wall, door and glazing types, and changes in floor materials can be shown for common areas to avoid creating additional detail floor plans. When larger scale plans can show the all building (i.e., at a ¼ inch scale), for a small/simple project these are usually the only plans that are needed. If this is the case, the information listed below should be integrated with the one listed in the detail floor plans.

Changes in level that are less than half a story and/or do not overlap can be accommodated shown on the same plan. Difference in floor elevations that exceed that height and/or overlap require different plans (or partial floor plans). A classic case is a mezzanine that needs a separate floor plan because, in most cases, it is built over part of the floor below. The following information should be included in the drawings:

1. The structural system.

2. Exterior walls (including wall type symbols, fire rating and veneer finish, such as bricks or stones), glazing (including glazing symbols), doors (with symbols on common doors), entrances (with symbols on common entrances), lines of elements projecting above (see Chapter 10 for symbols and Figure 10.7 for symbols of sections), symbols of plan and section details, symbol of wall or detail sections, siamese connection and hose bibs (if not included in the mechanical drawings), dimensions (see section on dimensions in this chapter).

3. Interior distribution with room names (if names do not fit, use numbers and a legend), symbols of wall assembly type for demising, fire walls, fire rating of walls, symbols of wall materials (especially concrete and masonry), opening

in floors and floor edges (with indication of part of the building open to below) doors, schematic built-in cabinets (if scale permits), floor elevations, stairs and ramps (with arrow and up or down indication), elevator(s) and elevator shaft(s), symbols of plan details, lines of floor or major elements above (i.e., roofs, skylights), plumbing fixtures (if scale permits), dimensions.

4. Mechanical and/or electrical shafts, outline of major mechanical and electrical equipment and service space (i.e., electrical closets, transformers).

5. Balconies, decks, terraces with railings and/or parapets showing floor elevations, slopes and location of drains, planters with location of drains, dimensions.

6. Exterior adjacent spaces with finish paving and grading elevations, slopes, hard and soft surfaces, curbs (describing height and width), catch basins or drains as well as trench drains, stairs and ramps (with arrow and *up* or *down* indication), railings, retaining walls (with elevation of top of wall), planters with location of drains (with elevation of top of wall), site furniture, existing and new lamps, transformers, line of major part of the building below (i.e., perimeter wall of underground parking), dimensions.

7. General references such as grid lines, section lines, and part of the floor plan or elements shown at larger scale.

Building Elevations

Although elevations are fundamental to complete a set of construction drawings, their function is more representational than technical. Elevation drawings are not dimensioned. However, they do carry important graphic information related to the geometrical form of the building, height, floor and roof levels, type and location of materials, form of glazing and doors, as well as features of the building. Because of this function, all the elements should be labeled in order to associate the graphic with the meaning. The following are elements and data that should be shown on building elevations:

1. The complete geometric form of the building (sometimes a partial section is required to show parts of the construction that otherwise are concealed. Examples are interior courtyards or a U-shaped building).

2. All materials (graphically and with labels either directly using words and arrows or using numbers referred to a legend).

3. Glazing, doors, louvers (exhaust and intake), balconies, terraces, decks (also at the ground floor), railings, roofs and roof features, flashing, gutters and rain water leaders, structures above the roof (i.e., A/C units, elevator mechanical room and overrun, chill tower, stairs), screens above the roof, expansion and control joints, building joints, line of building curbs (dotted if concealed behind finish) and benchmarks for material layout (i.e., bricks), scuppers, canopies, stairs and ramps (dotted if they lead below the basic grade shown),

siamese connections planters, outline of the building below grade, wall-mounted lighting fixtures, structural supports. elevations of fences and other elements that might conceal the building can be shown separately.

4. References such as floor and roof levels (including the roof parapet), maximum permissible height, grid lines, property lines, section lines and part of the elevation shown at larger scale.

Building Sections

The function of this type of drawings has been already discussed earlier in this chapter. They can be developed showing only the sectioned interior elements or also the non-sectioned elements in elevation. If the second case is chosen, the building sections can substitute the interior elevations (or part of the required views). Apart from the interior elevation, the drawings should contain:

1. The complete view of the building showing floor(s) and roof(s) as well as roof parapet(s) (with elevations indicated and symbols of roof as well as floor types. If feasible, types of materials should be included), structures or elements above the roof (i.e., A/C units, elevator machinery room, chill tower, screens), interior sectioned walls (with fire rating, type of materials and symbols of the type of wall assembly), ceilings and ceiling levels (with dimensions from finish floor or structural floor), labeling of the type of space use, sectioned interior and exterior glazing (with sill and head either dimensioned from finish floor or with their elevation indicated), exterior grading adjacent to the exterior wall (with grade elevation indicated), exterior surface type adjacent to the exterior wall.

2. The upper structural and foundation system.

3. General reference such as grid lines, symbols of details and/or wall sections, property lines (if close to the building).

Detail Plan

This type of plan is provided when the size of the general building plan does not allow a clear presentation of all the information. Ultimately all the elements that are to be built and can clearly be shown on the plans (such as walls, glazing, doors, floor finishes, built-in cabinets, washrooms fixtures and accessories, stairs and ramps, planters or railings, to mention a few) need to be fully identified. What could not be included in the general floor plans must be shown on the detail plans.

Apart from specific areas that are particular to each project, in multi-story buildings the detail plans always include stair and ramp plan(s) as well as elevator plans (all of them supplemented by detail sections and details as described below). The information shown on detail plans include:

1. The complete area highlighted in the general floor plan(s) including all the elements shown and the structural system.

2. Detail dimensioning of all the elements not sized in the general floor plan(s), all walls and doors as well as interior and/or exterior glazing not labeled in the general floor plans with their symbols indicating the type, wall materials (especially concrete and masonry), exterior door thresholds, edges of the different types of floor finishes, floor elevations, furring on walls (especially concrete and masonry walls), exterior wall veneer finish (i.e., brick or stones), built-in cabinets and other mill work, washroom accessories (i.e., toilet paper holder, towel holder, soap holder, shower curtain rod or shower door), floor drains.

3. General references such as symbols of details and/or detail sections, grid lines.

Detail Sections

The scope of these types of drawings is to indicate all the elements of a system that, for clarity, is better shown within the context of the system (i.e., a stair, an exterior wall). In a multi-story building, apart from other particular detail sections that might be required, the typical detail sections represent stair(s) and ramp(s) as well as elevator shafts. In addition, detail sections often show complete exterior walls systems (in this case these drawings are also called *wall sections*). In medium/complex and large/complex types of projects, detail sections frequently include interior systems.

Where the elements sectioned require shop drawings (i.e., a steel stair or a steel structure in an exterior wall system), it is important to dimension the elements using references that will facilitate the review of the documents provided by the manufacturer (see also section on dimensioning in this chapter). Detail sections should show:

1. Complete graphic representation and dimensions of all the components of the system(s) including symbols of type of materials. Dimensioning can be substituted by description (i.e., 3 inch x 3 inch steel angle) for some of the components, where appropriate. In addition, hidden components of the sectioned system or of the building (i.e., within a wall system or behind a wall) should be indicated for clarity or continuity of the information (i.e., a flight of stairs behind a central wall).

2. General references such as floor elevation(s), grid lines and symbol of details and symbols of assembly(ies) or system(s).

Details

Details are developed to show specific limited parts of the building. It is important to remember that it is through details and the reference symbols shown on the other drawings (i.e., different types of plans and sections) that a general contractor and/or a construction manager, as well as the sub-trades, can understand the extent to which a particular detail is used throughout the project (and derive from this information the quantity of materials and product to be ordered and/or fabricated). In developing details, the following should be considered:

1. Their purpose: There are three major reasons for developing details:
   a. Allow the architect to verify in a very specific form the feasibility of the design intentions.
   b. Describe to third parties, through graphics and words, the units that are part of the building component(s), assembly(ies) or system(s). These third parties are: the owner, the consultants, the general contractor or the construction manager, the sub-trades, the suppliers. In terms of construction, a general contractor or construction manager should be able to understand from the details the type of sub-trades involved in building that detail and, along with the sub-trades, define clearly the sequence of operations.
   c. Administer the construction contract (including the shop drawings).

2. The general approach: details should be complete and self-explanatory. This means that the detail either contains the information required or it includes the reference that indicates where this information can be retrieved. Details should be chosen in a manner that illustrates every part of the building that is best shown graphically and/or cannot be described or communicated in any other way. Apart from showing all the elements of the building (i.e., walls, floors, roofs, glazing, doors, connections between the assemblies and the structure, railings, parapets, planters and others), details describe the specifics of how the building performs in relation to fundamental aspects such as:
   a. *Structural Integrity*: this includes vertical and lateral forces (see Chapter 6). This aspect is not restricted to structural elements, but is extended to non-structural components such as architectural, mechanical and electrical. In the case of seismic forces, for example, all the components need to be restrained. As we have seen, not only earthquakes should be considered but wind as well (pressure and suction).
   b. *Water and moisture control*: as indicated in Chapter 7, all the sources of water and moisture must be considered including flood, rain, sub-surface sources, condensation provoked by temperature and humidity levels influenced by weather, people, and equipment.
   c. *Thermal control:* this can be accomplished not only by detailing the building properly and using the appropriate components (i.e., appropriate amount of insulation and type of glazing), but also by introducing elements that can control the influence of the environment on the building (i.e., shading devices, and/or landscaping). See Chapter 7 for an in depth analysis of thermal control.
   d. *Acoustical Control*: this aspect starts with the identification of the source of noise outside and within the building. Secondly, it is important to define the characteristics of the noise. The next step is to review the effect that this noise has on the activities outside and inside the building. This

will allow us to identify the level of attenuation that is required. At this point the options can be evaluated with regards to the type of material(s), assembly(ies) and/or systems to be used within the following possibilities:

(1) Change the sound source.

(2) Change the receiver.

(3) Affect the path of the sound by:

    (a) Using the appropriate STC (Sound Transmission Class) or IIC (Impact Isolation Class) associated with component(s), assembly(ies) and/or systems.

    (b) Sealing the joints and connections between component(s), assembly(ies) and/or systems. For specifics about acoustics, see Chapter 9.

e. *Building and component movement:* this refers to expansion and contraction due to thermal fluctuation; movements due to vibration; structural deformations; moisture. Tolerances must be built into the system(s) and assembly(ies). In order to develop the appropriate tolerances, first the nature of the movement must be identified, then the characteristics of the materials can provide the extent of the movement. Ultimately the type of joints can be chosen as well as the materials that fill the joint. It is important to keep in mind that all the factors listed above can affect the design of the joint. A review of these factors, therefore, should be conducted.

f. *Code compliance:* a major topic developed in codes is safety. This includes all the aspects listed in this section since any of them could, for example, affect the structural integrity of the parts of the building. Fire safety, obviously, is another aspect that strongly affects details (i.e., fire stops, combustible and non-combustible materials, permissible cavities). A major area of interest for code compliance is the accessibility for persons with disabilities. Although the major impact in this particular field is experienced in the general and detail plans and the sections, detail plans require particular attention because components such as curbs or railings need to be designed with particular dimensions in mind. For code related aspects see Chapter 5.

g. *The type of detail:* details are sub-divided into two categories—plan details and section details. In some cases, because of its complexity, the same details of components, assembly(ies) and/or systems need to be shown using both views. In other cases, just one type of detail is sufficient. However, in the case of one type of detail, sometimes plan details or section details at different levels of the same assembly are necessary in order to represent all the conditions and the relationship among the components (see Figure 11.6). The choice of which to use is dependent on the geometrical characteristics of the elements and how they are assembled. When a plan detail and a section detail (or two detail plans at different levels and detail sections at different locations) are necessary, they should be shown on the same page, aligned side by side or one above of the other. This increases the clarity of the details.

4. *The information to be included:* All the elements that are part of the assembly(ies) or system(s) are to be described as well as represented through geometrical shapes, reference symbols of type of assembly(ies) or system(s). In addition, all materials must be symbolically and descriptively indicated.

Schedules

This type of information is a combination of matrixes and drawings. The matrixes describe the characteristics of the elements, while the drawings show the geometrical properties. Sometimes general notes are added in the matrix to indicate items that apply to all the individual elements. There are different types of schedules for the different disciplines:

1. Architectural schedules: the most common are:
   a. Wall, floor, and roof: in this type of schedule the components of the assemblies are described, a symbol for each type of assembly is assigned (see Chapter 11) and, in most cases, a schematic drawing of the assembly is included (see Figure 11.7). It is very important to document characteristics like fire rating or acoustical performance by stating the value and the source (i.e., UL test number or the applicable building code indicating the year of the current edition, and the related table(s) and article(s)).
   b. Door: the fundamental structure does not change. Information such as number and symbol of the door, type of door, dimensions of the door, material of the door and the frame, type and size of any glazing, any fire rating and general remarks are shown in the matrix. This is indicated for every door that is shown on the drawings. The graphic component of the door schedule illustrates mainly the elevation of the door that defines the type (usually indicated with a capital letter). Conventionally the door takes the same number of the room into which the door opens. As with the walls, roofs and floors, characteristics such as the fire rating and the acoustical performance need to be listed. However, the doors, being a finish product, do not carry a specific UL assembly number that can be quoted. Each unit will bear a number (UL) that will relate to a certain standard for testing, which is indicated in the specifications of the project. On the schedule, therefore, only the required fire rating and, if necessary, the acoustical performance is indicated (see Figure 11.8).
   c. Windows: this is very similar to the door schedule. The obvious changes are the categories of information shown in the matrix and the fact that the elevations show the type of windows.
   d. Finish: in this schedule all the spaces (on the plans identified by numbers) are listed and walls, floors and ceiling finishes are identified. Furthermore, notes can indicate colors, type of treatment and any other information that is necessary in order to describe in general terms the

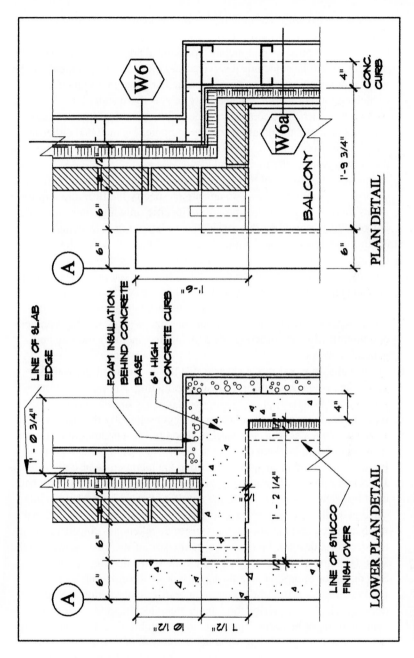

FIGURE 11.6 Examples of detail plans.

finishes. Accessories like moldings and baseboards are included in the finish schedule (See Figure 11.9).

e. Equipment: in projects that include specialized and large spaces (i.e., kitchens, photo labs, technical services and industries) equipment can be very complex and need to occupy a particular place in a sequence (which could require the dimensioning of specific installations). Although the schedule consists of a descriptive and a graphic component, the data and the diagrams of the equipment is included either in the specification or a separate booklet, while the list of the equipment on the drawings takes the form of a legend.

f. Furniture: an example of this type of schedule can be found in projects of large corporations. These organizations specify the furniture requirements directly in the project program. Specific drawings then show the layout, which is used by the consultants to lay out their systems.

2. Structural schedules: items commonly specified through schedules are:

a. Columns: schedules are created for concrete, steel columns and wood posts. They refer to the graphics of the column or the post shown on the drawings through a symbol included in the matrix. For concrete columns, the matrix includes the size, the vertical bar ties and, sometime, the tie layout; for steel columns, the size is shown along with general remarks. In case of wood posts, the matrix includes the size and general remarks.

b. Shear walls: in wood frame shear walls, the assembly of the wall is given (i.e., stud sizes, spacing, sheathing, nailing, end posts, holdowns and through bolts).

c. Beams: the materials for the beams vary, consequently the type of schedules varies as well. For steel or wood beam schedules, the size and the type of beam is given (i.e., sawn lumber or parallel strand lumber). For built-up wood beams, the number of the members is also provided.

d. Joists and rafters: different types of joists can be described in the schedules. For steel joists, the depth, the specified live and dead load is indicated as well as general remarks (such as the mentioning of additional mechanical equipment shown on plans to be taken into consideration in the structural design). For wood joists the size of the joists as well as the spacing is given. (If the spacing varies, the schedule refers to the plans). Schedules for rafters include the same type of information.

e. Decks: different types of decking require different schedules. Steel decking schedules describe the type of steel decking and other components that might be part of the structural assembly (i.e., the concrete topping and steel mesh). For a wood deck, the type of material with the thickness as well as the nailing pattern is provided. Examples of these schedules are shown on Figure 11.10.

3. Mechanical: depending on the type of project there are many types of mechanical schedules (see Figure 11.11). The following are two common examples:

    a. Equipment: these types of schedules describe the characteristics of the equipment (i.e., A/C units). These schedules are similar in principle to the furniture or equipment schedules described in the architectural section of the schedules: they have a matrix and a graphic representation of the items (included usually in the specifications or provided to the architect for reference). The matrix provides all the necessary technical information that is not only directed to the contractor, but also to the consultants. For example, data like weight are important for the structural engineer, while electrical information (i.e., volts, phase and amperage) is fundamental for the electrical consultant.

    b. Grills and diffusers: since these items are exposed, technical information is also supplemented by data on the appearance (i.e., type of finish, color).

4. Electrical: a general example of the two most commonly used schedules are illustrated in Figure 11.12. They are:

  a. Equipment.

  b. Lighting or luminaire.

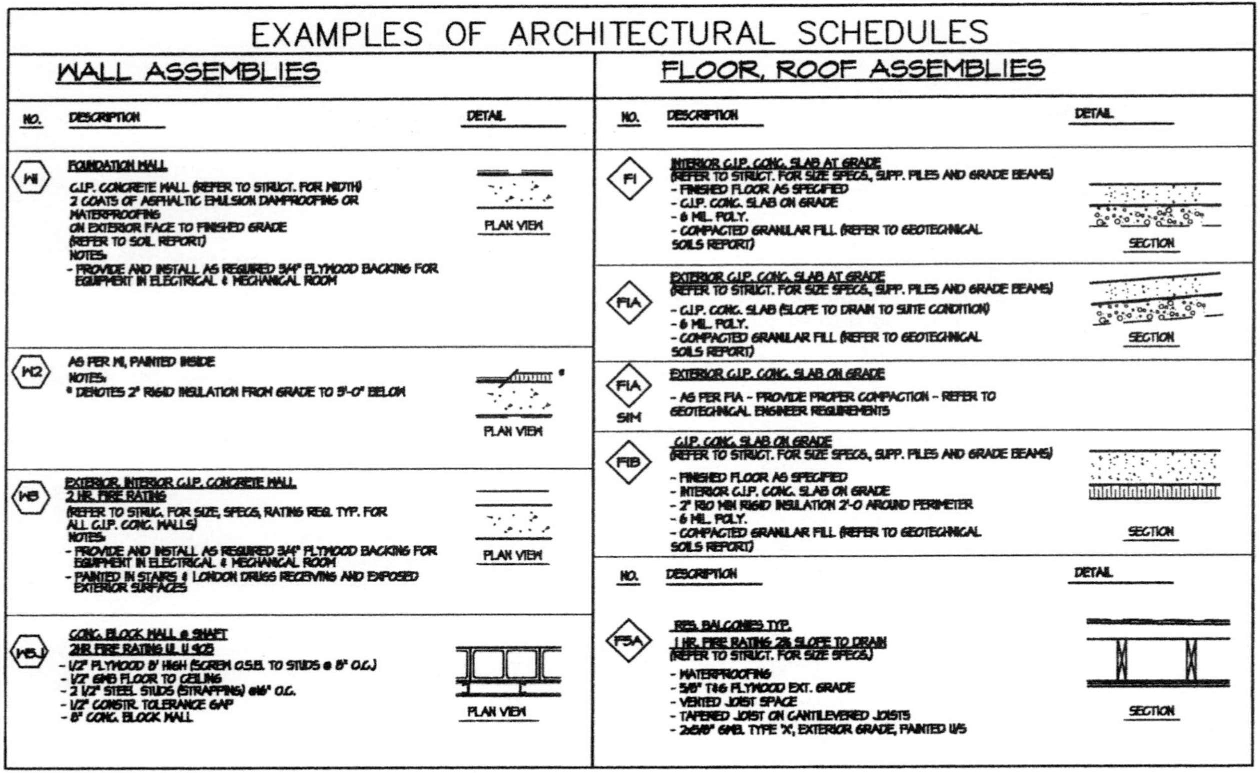

EXAMPLES OF ARCHITECTURAL SCHEDULES

WALL ASSEMBLIES

NO.	DESCRIPTION	DETAIL
W1	**FOUNDATION WALL** C.I.P. CONCRETE WALL (REFER TO STRUCT. FOR WIDTH) 2 COATS OF ASPHALTIC EMULSION DAMPPROOFING OR WATERPROOFING ON EXTERIOR FACE TO FINISHED GRADE (REFER TO SOIL REPORT) NOTES: - PROVIDE AND INSTALL AS REQUIRED 3/4" PLYWOOD BACKING FOR EQUIPMENT IN ELECTRICAL & MECHANICAL ROOM	PLAN VIEW
W2	AS PER H.M. PAINTED INSIDE NOTES: • DENOTES 2" RIGID INSULATION FROM GRADE TO 5'-0" BELOW	PLAN VIEW
W3	**EXTERIOR INTERIOR C.I.P. CONCRETE WALL** 2 HR. FIRE RATING REFER TO STRUCT. FOR SIZE. SPECS. RATING REQ. TYP. FOR ALL C.I.P. CONC. WALLS NOTES: - PROVIDE AND INSTALL AS REQUIRED 3/4" PLYWOOD BACKING FOR EQUIPMENT IN ELECTRICAL & MECHANICAL ROOM - PAINTED IN STAIRS & LANDING DRUMS RECEIVING AND EXPOSED EXTERIOR SURFACES	PLAN VIEW
W5	**CONC. BLOCK WALL @ SHAFT** 2HR. FIRE RATING @ U.L. 905 - 1/2" PLYWOOD 8' HIGH (SCREW C.S.A. TO STUDS @ 8" O.C.) - 1/2" GWB FLOOR TO CEILING - 1 1/2" STEEL STUDS (STRAPPING) @16" O.C. - 1/2" ACOUSTIC TOLERANCE GAP - 8" CONC. BLOCK WALL	PLAN VIEW

FLOOR, ROOF ASSEMBLIES

NO.	DESCRIPTION	DETAIL
F1	**INTERIOR C.I.P. CONC. SLAB AT GRADE** (REFER TO STRUCT. FOR SIZE SPECS., SUPP., PILES AND GRADE BEAMS) - FINISHED FLOOR AS SPECIFIED - C.I.P. CONC. SLAB ON GRADE - 6 MIL. POLY. - COMPACTED GRANULAR FILL (REFER TO GEOTECHNICAL SOILS REPORT)	SECTION
F1A F1A SIM.	**EXTERIOR C.I.P. CONC. SLAB AT GRADE** (REFER TO STRUCT. FOR SIZE SPECS., SUPP., PILES AND GRADE BEAMS) - C.I.P. CONC. SLAB SLOPE TO DRAIN TO SITE CONDITION) - 6 MIL. POLY. - COMPACTED GRANULAR FILL (REFER TO GEOTECHNICAL SOILS REPORT) **EXTERIOR C.I.P. CONC. SLAB ON GRADE** - AS PER F1A - PROVIDE PROPER COMPACTION - REFER TO GEOTECHNICAL ENGINEER REQUIREMENTS	SECTION
F1B	**C.I.P. CONC. SLAB ON GRADE** (REFER TO STRUCT. FOR SIZE SPECS., SUPP., PILES AND GRADE BEAMS) - FINISHED FLOOR AS SPECIFIED - INTERIOR C.I.P. CONC. SLAB ON GRADE - 2" RIG MIN RIGID INSULATION 2'-0 AROUND PERIMETER - 6 MIL. POLY. - COMPACTED GRANULAR FILL (REFER TO GEOTECHNICAL SOILS REPORT)	SECTION
F5A	**@ BALCONIES TYP.** 1 HR. FIRE RATING 2% SLOPE TO DRAIN (REFER TO STRUCT. FOR SIZE SPECS) - WATERPROOFING - 5/8" T&G PLYWOOD EXT. GRADE - VENTED JOIST SPACE - TAPERED JOIST ON CANTILEVERED JOISTS - 2xGYP GWB. TYPE 'X', EXTERIOR GRADE, PAINTED U/S	SECTION

FIGURE 11.7 Examples of architectural schedules.

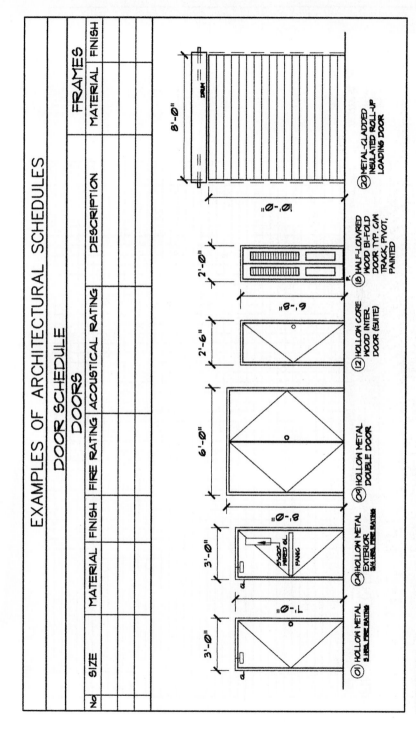

FIGURE 11.8 Examples of architectural schedules.

11.29

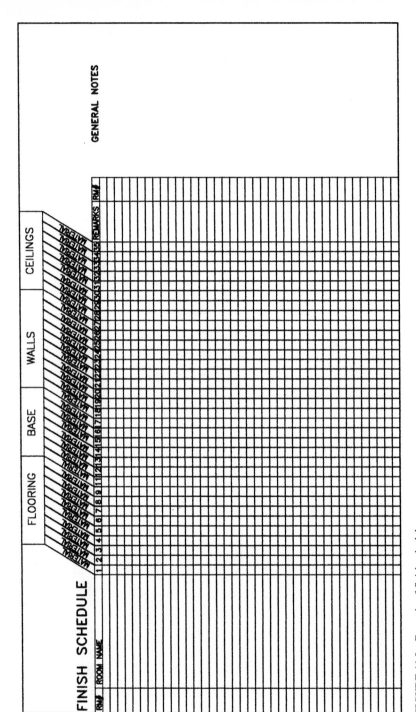

FIGURE 11.9 Example of finish schedule.

EXAMPLES OF STRUCTURAL SCHEDULES

FLOOR / ROOF DECKING SCHEDULE

MARK	DESCRIPTION
D1	1 1/2" DP. 20 ga STEEL ROOF DECK
D2	2 1/2" DP. CONCRETE TOPPING R / W 6X6 10/10 W.W.M. AT CENTRE ON 3" DP. 20 ga. COMPOSITE STEEL FLOOR DECK
D3	2 1/2" DP. CONCRETE TOPPING R / W 6X6 8/8 W.W.M. AT CENTRE ON 1 1/2" DP. 22 ga. COMPOSITE STEEL FLOOR DECK

OPEN WEB STEEL JOIST SCHEDULE

MARK	DEPTH	SPECIFIED DEAD LOAD	SPECIFIED LIVE LOAD	REMARKS

HANGER SCHEDULE

NO.	DESCRIPTION

STEEL COLUMN SCHEDULE

NO.	SIZE	REMARKS

WOOD POST SCHEDULE

NO.	POST SIZE	NO. OF LAMS

WOOD BEAM SCHEDULE

NO.	BEAM SIZE	TYPE

STEEL BEAM SCHEDULE

MARK - SIZE	FACTORED END REACTION

WOOD JOIST SCHEDULE

NO.	SIZE	SPACING

WOOD RAFTER SCHEDULE

NO.	RAFTER SIZE	SPACING

FIGURE 11.10 Examples of structural schedules.

EXAMPLES OF MECHANICAL SCHEDULES

HVAC EQUIPMENT

Mark	Service	Manufacturer	Model	CFM	Fan Motor			Heat.(BTUH)	Cool.(BTUH)	Gas Input (BTUH)	Unit Wt. (lbs.)	Electrical		Accessories	Remarks
					S.P.	RPM	HP					Volt/Ph.	AMP		

DIFFUSERS/GRILLES

Mark	Service	Manufacturer	Model	Size	Mounting	Finish	Accessories	Remarks

FIGURE 11.11 Examples of mechanical schedules.

EXAMPLES OF ELECTRICAL SCHEDULES

LUMINAIRE SCHEDULE

TYPE	LUMINAIRE		VOLT	LAMP		SEE NOTE
	MANUFACTURER	CATALOGUE NO.		QTY.	TYPE	
A						
B						
C						
D						
E						

NOTE:

EQUIPMENT SCHEDULE

NO.	MECH. REF.	DESCRIPTION	LOAD	VOLT	∅	CCT. NO.	BKR. SIZE	FEEDER	NOTE
1									
2									
3									
4									
5									
6								2#12	

NOTE:

PANEL SCHEDULE

PANEL	CCTS	BUS	VOLTAGE	∅	W	MAIN BKR.	I.G. PAD	1P 15	2P 15	3P 15	1P 20	2P 20	3P 20	2P 30	3P 30	2P 40	3P 40	3P 50	3P 60	3P 100	SEE NOTE
A	84	400	120/208	3	4			59													
C	168	600	120/208	3	4			25				4		60							
IG	126	225	120/208	3	4		✓	94									1		1		

NOTE:

FIGURE 11.12 Examples of electrical schedules.

INDEX